The Statutory Rules of Northern Ireland

1994

PART I

Published by Authority

BELFAST: HMSO

Printed in the United Kingdom for HMSO
Dd. 8074241. C3. 11/94. Gp. 121

ISBN 0 337 90194 5

CONTENTS

PART I

PREFACE

Scope and arrangement of Volume

1.   This volume gives the full text of all Northern Ireland statutory rules (within the meaning of paragraph 5 below) made during the year 1994 except local rules, revoked rules, temporary rules or rules exempted by that Order or regulations made thereunder. Where a rule is not printed at length in the volume a note explaining its omission is inserted in its place.

2.   The statutory rules are arranged in numerical sequence with the subject-matter and numbers shown in the headline to each page. The volume is published in two parts, Part I published in advance of Part II, containing the rules numbered 1 to 255.

3.   Where, during the interim period specified by or under section 1(4) of the Northern Ireland Act 1974, a statutory rule is, by paragraph 3(3) of Schedule 1 to that Act, subject to annulment in pursuance of a resolution of either House of the Parliament of the United Kingdom, the fact that that rule is to be laid before that Parliament is recited in italics at the beginning of the rule.

Contents of the Volume

PART I

4.   Part I contains—
   (*a*)   a list showing the registered numbers and titles of the statutory rules included in Part I;
   (*b*)   the text of statutory rules of a general character as distinct from rules of a local character (No. 1 to No. 255).

Meaning of Statutory Rules

5.   The term "statutory rule" covers the various forms of subordinate legislation included in the definition of that expression contained in art. 4 of the Statutory Rules (N.I.) Order 1979 (S.I. 1979/1573 (N.I. 12)). Statutory instruments made under the Medicines Acts 1968 (c. 67) and 1971 (c. 69) are, as provided by paragraph 11 of Schedule 4 to the 1968 Act, registered as Northern Ireland statutory rules but as they are included in the United Kingdom volumes they are not printed at length in Northern Ireland volumes.

Citation

6.   For the purposes of citation statutory rules are given titles. In addition they may be identified by the year and number, e.g. "S.R. 1976 No. 2".

Production in Court

7.   Under section 2 of the Documentary Evidence Act 1868 (c. 37) read with section 2 of the Documentary Evidence Act 1882 (c. 9) *prima facie* evidence of any proclamation, order or regulation made by certain rule-making authorities may be given in courts of justice by production of a copy purporting to be printed by the Government Printer or under the superintendence or authority of Her Majesty's Stationery Office. The Act of 1868 has since been extended by numerous Acts (see

entry relating to it in Chronological Table of the Statutes Northern Ireland) to rules, etc., made by other rule-making authorities including Northern Ireland rule-making authorities. The copies of orders, regulations, rules, etc., made by the authorities referred to above as printed in these volumes may therefore be produced as *prima facie* evidence.

Information as to Statutory Rules in Force

8.   The Index to the Statutory Rules and Orders of Northern Ireland contains, under subject headings, summaries of all powers to make statutory rules conferred by statute. Below each summary appear particulars of any general rules made in exercise of it which were in force at the date of publication of the Index. The Index is published every three years by Her Majesty's Stationery Office.

Authority for publication

9.   The annual volumes of Statutory Rules are published in pursuance of the Statutory Rules (N.I.) Order 1979 (S.I. 1979/1573 (N.I. 12)) and are prepared under the direction of the Statute Law Committee for Northern Ireland by the Statutory Publications Office, Department of Finance and Personnel, Stormont, Belfast BT4 3SW. Any communication regarding them should be sent to that Office.

NUMERICAL LIST OF THE
NORTHERN IRELAND STATUTORY RULES
REGISTERED DURING 1994 AND INCLUDED IN
PART I OF THIS VOLUME

Orders printed in *italics* are Local Orders and where marked § these Orders will be summarised in Part II.

Orders marked * are of temporary effect and, if Local, the titles are printed in *italics*. These Orders are not printed at length in this volume.

Orders marked † have been revoked.

Orders marked Ø are made as Statutory Instruments under the Medicines Act 1968 (c. 67) and the Medicines Act 1971 (c. 69) and are also registered as Northern Ireland Statutory Rules. As they are included in the Annual Volume of Statutory Instruments they are not printed at length in this volume.

Numerical List

Numerical List

STATUTORY RULES OF A GENERAL CHARACTER
ISSUED IN 1994

1994 No. 1

HEALTH AND SAFETY

Health and Safety (Training for Employment) Regulations (Northern Ireland) 1994

Made	*10th January 1994*
Coming into operation . .	*7th March 1994*

The Department of Economic Development, being the Department concerned(**a**), in exercise of the powers conferred on it by Article 2(5) of the Health and Safety at Work (Northern Ireland) Order 1978(**b**) and of every other power enabling it in that behalf, after consultation with the Health and Safety Agency for Northern Ireland and such other bodies as appeared to it to be appropriate, hereby makes the following Regulations:

Citation and commencement

1. These Regulations may be cited as the Health and Safety (Training for Employment) Regulations (Northern Ireland) 1994 and shall come into operation on 7th March 1994.

Interpretation

2. In these Regulations—

"the 1978 Order" means the Health and Safety at Work (Northern Ireland) Order 1978;

"educational establishment" means a university, college, school or similar educational or technical institute;

"relevant training" means work experience provided pursuant to a training course or programme, or training for employment, or both, except if—

(*a*) the immediate provider of the work experience or training for employment is an educational establishment and it is provided on a course run by the establishment; or

(*b*) it is received under a contract of employment.

Meaning of "work" and "at work"

3. For the purposes of the 1978 Order—

(*a*) the meaning of the word "work" shall be extended to include relevant training;

(**a**) *See* Article 2(2) of S.I. 1978/1039 (N.I. 9)
(**b**) S.I. 1978/1039 (N.I. 9)

(*b*) a person provided with relevant training is at work throughout the time when he would be in the course of his employment if he were receiving such training under a contract of employment, but not otherwise, and the meaning of "at work" shall be so extended;

and in that connection, in the other relevant statutory provisions, "work" and "at work" shall be construed accordingly.

Meaning of "employee", "employer" etc

4. For the purposes of the relevant statutory provisions a person provided with relevant training shall be treated as being the employee of the person whose undertaking (whether carried on by him for profit or not) is for the time being the immediate provider to that person of the training; and "employee", "worker", "employer" and related expressions in those provisions shall be construed accordingly.

Revocation

5. The Health and Safety (Youth Training Programme) Regulations (Northern Ireland) 1985(**a**) are hereby revoked.

Sealed with the Official Seal of the Department of Economic Development on 10th January 1994.

(L.S.)
 Philip B. Strong
 Assistant Secretary

(**a**) S.R. 1985 No. 121

EXPLANATORY NOTE
(This note is not part of the Regulations.)

These Regulations give the protection for and duties of employees under the Health and Safety at Work (Northern Ireland) Order 1978 ("the 1978 Order") and the other relevant statutory provisions to those who are provided with "relevant training" as defined in regulation 2. "Relevant statutory provisions" is defined in Article 2(2) of the 1978 Order.

For the purposes of the 1978 Order and the other relevant statutory provisions regulation 3 extends the meaning of "work" and "at work" to include relevant training as defined in regulation 2; and regulation 4 provides that the trainee shall be treated as if he were the employee of the person whose undertaking is the immediate provider of the training.

The Regulations do not apply if the immediate provider of the relevant training is an educational establishment and it is provided on a course run by the establishment nor if the training is received under a contract of employment.

Regulation 5 revokes the Health and Safety (Youth Training Programme) Regulations (Northern Ireland) 1985.

1994 No. 2

COMPANIES

Disclosure of Interests in Shares (Amendment) Regulations (Northern Ireland) 1994

Made	*10th January 1994*
Coming into operation . .	*11th March 1994*

The Department of Economic Development, in exercise of the powers conferred on it by Article 218A of the Companies (Northern Ireland) Order 1986(**a**) and of every other power enabling it in that behalf, hereby makes the following Regulations:

Citation and commencement

1. These Regulations may be cited as the Disclosure of Interests in Shares (Amendment) Regulations (Northern Ireland) 1994 and shall come into operation on 11th March 1994.

Amendments of Part VII of the Companies (Northern Ireland) Order 1986

2. Part VII of the Companies (Northern Ireland) Order 1986 shall be amended in accordance with regulations 3 to 9.

Article 206

3. In Article 206(1) (obligation of disclosure) for the words "of the interests which he has, or had" there shall be substituted "with respect to his interests (if any)".

Article 207

4.—(1) In Article 207(**b**) (interests to be disclosed) for paragraph (2) there shall be substituted the following paragraphs—

"(2) Where a person is interested in shares comprised in relevant share capital, then—

(*a*) if in some or all of those shares he has interests which are material interests, he has a notifiable interest at any time when the aggregate nominal value of the shares in which those material interests subsist is equal to or more than 3 per cent. of the nominal value of that share capital; and

---

(**a**) S.I. 1986/1032 (N.I. 6); Article 218A was inserted by Article 69(5) of the Companies (No. 2) (Northern Ireland) Order 1990 (S.I. 1990/1504 (N.I. 10)).

(**b**) Article 207(2) was amended by Article 69(2) of the Companies (No. 2) (Northern Ireland) Order 1990.

(*b*) he has a notifiable interest at any time when, not having such an interest by virtue of sub-paragraph (*a*), the aggregate nominal value of the shares in which he has interests (whether or not including material interests) is equal to or more than 10 per cent. of the nominal value of the relevant share capital.

(2A) For the purposes of this Part, a material interest is any interest other than—

(*a*) an interest which a person authorised to manage investments belonging to another has by virtue of having the management of such investments under an agreement in or evidenced in writing;

(*b*) an interest which a person has by virtue of being the operator of—

(i) an authorised unit trust scheme;

(ii) a recognised scheme; or

(iii) a UCITS (as defined in paragraph (8)); or

(*c*) an interest in shares in a listed company which, if that company were not listed, would fall to be disregarded by virtue of Article 217(10);

(*d*) an interest of another which a person is taken to have by virtue of the application of Article 211 (notification of family and corporate interests) or 213 (obligation of disclosure arising under Article 212) where the interest of that other person falls within sub-paragraph (*a*), (*b*) or (*c*).''.

(2) In paragraph (5) of that Article, after the words ''Article 206(1)'' there shall be inserted ''or (3)''.

(3) After paragraph (5) of that Article there shall be inserted the following paragraphs—

''(6) For the purposes of paragraph 2A, a person is authorised to manage investments belonging to another if—

(*a*) he is an authorised person under Chapter III of Part I of the Financial Services Act 1986(**a**) and may manage that other's investments without contravening any prohibition mentioned in paragraph (7); or

(*b*) he is an authorised credit institution which may manage that other's investments without being in breach of its authorisation.

(7) The prohibitions referred to in paragraph (6)(*a*) are—

(*a*) any prohibition contained in rules—

(i) which make provision of a description mentioned in section 48(2)(*a*) and (*b*) of the Financial Services Act 1986; and

(ii) which are made by the Secretary of State, the Treasury, a designated agency, a recognised professional body or a recognised self-regulating organisation, and

(*b*) any prohibition imposed under section 65 of that Act.

(**a**) 1986 c. 60

(8) In this Part "UCITS" means a collective investment scheme which—

(*a*) is constituted in a member State other than the United Kingdom; and

(*b*) complies with the conditions necessary for it to enjoy the rights conferred by Council Directive 85/611/EEC(**a**) co-ordinating the laws, regulations and administrative provisions relating to undertakings for collective investment in transferable securities;

and sub-section (8) of section 86 of the Financial Services Act 1986 (meaning of "constituted in a Member State") applies for the purposes of sub-paragraph (*a*) as it applies for the purposes of that section.".

Article 208

5. For Article 208 ("percentage level" in relation to notifiable interests) there shall be substituted the following Article—

" *"Percentage level" in relation to notifiable interests*

208.—(1) Subject to the qualifications mentioned in paragraphs (2) and (3), "percentage level", in Article 207(5)(*b*), means the percentage figure found by expressing the aggregate nominal value of all the shares comprised in the share capital concerned in which the person has material interests immediately before or (as the case may be) immediately after the relevant time as a percentage of the nominal value of that share capital and rounding that figure down, if it is not a whole number, to the next whole number.

(2) In relation to a notifiable interest which a person has when the aggregate nominal value of the shares in which he is interested is equal to or more than 10 per cent. of the nominal value of that relevant share capital, paragraph (1) shall have effect as if for the words "has material interests" there were substituted "is interested".

(3) Where the nominal value of the share capital is greater immediately after the relevant time than it was immediately before, the percentage level of the person's interest immediately before (as well as immediately after) that time is determined by reference to the larger amount.".

Article 210

6.—(1) In Article 210 (particulars to be contained in notification), in paragraph (2), for sub-paragraph (*a*) there shall be substituted the following sub-paragraph—

"(*a*) subject to paragraphs (2A) and (2B), state the number of shares comprised in that share capital in which the person making the notification knows he had material interests immediately after the time when the obligation arose, or".

(**a**) OJ No. L375 31.12.85 p. 3

(2) After that paragraph there shall be inserted the following paragraphs—

"(2A) Where, immediately after the relevant time, the aggregate nominal value of the shares in which the person making the notification is interested is equal to or more than 10 per cent. of the nominal value of that relevant share capital, paragraph (2)(*a*) shall have effect as if for the words "had material interests" there were substituted the words "was interested.".

(2B) Nothing in paragraph (2) or (2A) requires a notification to state, in relation to any shares, whether the interest of the person making the notification is (or is not) a material interest.".

Article 214

7.—(1) In Article 214 (obligation of persons acting together to keep each other informed) in paragraph (3)(*a*), for the words "if he were under the obligation of disclosure with respect to that interest" there shall be substituted "if he were under the wide obligation of disclosure with respect to that interest" and after sub-paragraph (*b*) there shall be inserted—

"and

(*c*) except in the circumstance mentioned in paragraph (3A), the number of shares (if any) out of the number given under sub-paragraph (*a*) in which he knows that, immediately after the time when the obligation to give the notice arose, he had interests (apart from the agreement) which were not material interests.".

(2) After Article 214(3) there shall be inserted the following paragraphs—

"(3A) The circumstance referred to in paragraph (3)(*c*) is that the aggregate nominal value of the shares comprised in relevant share capital in which the person is interested (apart from the agreement) is equal to or more than 10 per cent. of the nominal value of the relevant share capital.

(3B) For the purposes of paragraph (3)(*a*) "the wide obligation of disclosure" means the obligation to disclose the number of shares in which the person concerned has any interest (material or otherwise).".

Article 217

8. For Article 217 (interests to be disregarded) there shall be substituted the following Article—

"*Interests to be disregarded*

217.—(1) Subject to paragraphs (5) and (6), the following interests in shares are disregarded for the purposes of Articles 206 to 210—

(*a*) where property is held on trust and an interest in shares is comprised in that property, an interest of a person, being a discretionary interest or an interest in reversion or remainder or an interest of a bare trustee;

(*b*) an interest which a person has by virtue of holding units in—

(i) an authorised unit trust scheme;

(ii) a recognised scheme; or

(iii) a UCITS;

(*c*) an interest of a person which is an exempt security interest within the meaning of paragraph (2);

(*d*) an interest which a person has by virtue of his being a beneficiary under a retirement benefits scheme as defined in section 611 of the Income and Corporation Taxes Act 1988(**a**);

(*e*) an interest which a person has in shares as a result of the acceptance of a takeover offer made by him (either alone or jointly with one or more other persons) for shares where—

(i) the offer is subject to a threshold acceptance condition; and

(ii) the threshold acceptance condition is not fulfilled;

(*f*) an interest of a person which is an exempt custodian interest within the meaning of paragraph (4);

(*g*) an interest which a person has by virtue of his being a personal representative of any estate;

(*h*) an interest which a person has—

(i) by virtue of his being a trustee of an authorised unit trust scheme, or

(ii) in relation to a recognised scheme or a UCITS, by virtue of his being entrusted with the custody of the property in question (whether or not under a trust).

(2) An interest in shares is an exempt security interest for the purposes of paragraph (1)(*c*)—

(*a*) if it is held by a person who is—

(i) a person authorised under Part I of the Banking Act 1987(**b**), an authorised credit institution, a person authorised under the law of a member State other than the United Kingdom to accept deposits who would, if he were to accept such deposits in the United Kingdom require authorisation under Part I of that Act, or an authorised insurance undertaking; or

(ii) a person authorised under the law of a member State to deal in securities or derivatives, who deals in securities or derivatives on a relevant stock exchange or on a relevant investment exchange, whether as a member or otherwise; or

(iii) a relevant stock exchange, a relevant investment exchange or a recognised clearing house; or

(*b*) if it is held by the Bank of England or by the central bank of a member State other than the United Kingdom;

(**a**) 1988 c. 1
(**b**) 1987 c. 22

and it is held by way of security only for the purposes of a transaction entered into in the ordinary course of his or its business as such a person.

(3) For the purposes of paragraph (1)(*e*)—

(*a*) "takeover offer" has the same meaning as in Part XIVA(**a**); and

(*b*) "a threshold acceptance condition" means a condition that acceptances are received in respect of such proportion of the shares for which the takeover offer is made as is specified in or determined in accordance with the terms of the takeover offer.

(4) For the purposes of paragraph (1)(*f*) an interest of a person is an exempt custodian interest if it is held by him—

(*a*) as a custodian (whether under a trust or by a contract); or

(*b*) under an arrangement pursuant to which he has issued, or is to issue, depositary receipts in respect of the shares concerned.

(5) An interest referred to in any sub-paragraph of paragraph (1) (except for sub-paragraph (*c*)) is disregarded only if the person referred to in the relevant sub-paragraph or in paragraph (4) is not entitled to exercise or control the exercise of voting rights in respect of the shares concerned; and for this purpose he is not so entitled if he is bound (whether by contract or otherwise) not to exercise the voting rights, or not to exercise them otherwise than in accordance with the instructions of another.

(6) In the case of an interest referred to in paragraph (1)(*c*), an interest of a person referred to in paragraph (2) is disregarded only if that person—

(*a*) is not entitled (within the meaning of paragraph (5)) to exercise or control the exercise of voting rights in respect of the shares concerned; or,

(*b*) is so entitled, but has not evidenced any intention to exercise them or control their exercise nor taken any step to do so.

(7) For the purposes of paragraphs (5) and (6), voting rights which a person is entitled to exercise or of which he is entitled to control the exercise only in certain circumstances shall be taken into account only when the circumstances have arisen and for so long as they continue to obtain.

(8) An interest in shares of a company is also disregarded for the purposes of Articles 206 to 210—

(*a*) if it is held by a market maker in securities or derivatives for the purposes of his business; but

(*b*) only in so far as it is not used by him for the purpose of intervening in the management of the company.

(9) For the purposes of paragraph (8) a person is a market maker in securities or derivatives if—

(**a**) Part XIVA was substituted for Articles 421, 422 and 423 of the Companies (Northern Ireland) Order 1986 by Article 26 of the Companies (Northern Ireland) Order 1989 (S.I. 1989/2404 (N.I. 18)) (*a*) he is authorised under the law of a member State to deal in securities or derivatives and so deals on a relevant stock exchange or on a relevant investment exchange (whether as a member or otherwise); and

(*b*) he holds himself out at all normal times as willing to acquire and dispose of securities or derivatives at prices specified by him and in so doing is subject to the rules of that exchange;

and he holds an interest for the purposes of his business if he holds it for the purposes of a business carried on by him as a market maker in a member State.

(10) The following interests in shares in a public company which is not listed are also disregarded for the purposes of Articles 206 to 210—

(*a*) an interest which subsists by virtue of a scheme made under section 25 of the Charities Act (Northern Ireland) 1964(**a**), section 24 or 25 of the Charities Act 1993(**b**), section 11 of the Trustee Investments Act 1961(**c**) or section 42 of the Administration of Justice Act 1982(**d**);

(*b*) an interest for the life of himself or another of a person under a settlement in the case of which the property comprised in the settlement consists of or includes shares, and the conditions mentioned in paragraph (11) are satisfied;

(*c*) an interest of the Accountant General of the Supreme Court in shares held by him;

(*d*) an interest of the Probate Judge subsisting by virtue of section 3 of the Administration of Estates Act (Northern Ireland) 1955(**e**);

(*e*) an interest of the President of the Family Division of Her Majesty's High Court of Justice in England subsisting by virtue of section 9 of the Administration of Estates Act 1925(**f**).

(11) The conditions referred to in paragraph (10)(*b*) are, in relation to a settlement—

(*a*) that it is irrevocable; and

(*b*) that the settler (within the meaning of section 670 of the Income and Corporation Taxes Act 1988) has no interest in any income arising under, or property comprised in, the settlement.

(12) A person is not by virtue of Article 216(4)(*b*) taken to be interested in shares by reason only that he has been appointed a proxy to vote at a specified meeting of a company or of any class of its members and at any adjournment of that meeting, or has been appointed by a corporation to act as its representative at any meeting of a company or of any class of its members.

(**a**) 1964 c. 33 (N.I.)
(**b**) 1993 c. 10
(**c**) 1961 c. 62
(**d**) 1982 c. 53
(**e**) 1955 c. 24 (N.I.)
(**f**) 1925 c. 23 as amended by 1970 c. 31 section 1(6) and Schedule 2, paragraph 5

(13) In the application of paragraph (1)(*a*) to property held on trust according to the law of Scotland, for the words "or remainder or an interest of a bare trustee" there shall be substituted "or in fee or an interest of a simple trustee".".

Article 228

9. In Article 228 (interpretation for Part VII), for paragraph (1) there shall be substituted the following paragraph—

"(1) In this Part—

"associated index", in relation to a register, means the index kept in relation to that register in pursuance of Article 219(6);

"authorised credit institution" means a credit institution as defined in Article 1 of Council Directive 77/780/EEC(**a**) which is authorised to carry on the business of a credit institution by a competent authority of a member State other than the United Kingdom;

"authorised insurance undertaking" means an insurance undertaking which has been authorised in accordance with Article 6 or 23 of Council Directive 73/239/EEC(**b**) or Article 6 or 27 of Council Directive 79/267/EEC(**c**), or is authorised under the law of a member State to carry on insurance business restricted to re-insurance;

"authorised unit trust scheme" has the same meaning as in Chapter VIII of Part I of the Financial Services Act 1986;

"depositary receipt" means a certificate or other record (whether or not in the form of a document)—

(*a*) which is issued by or on behalf of a person who holds shares or who holds evidence of the right to receive shares, or has an interest in shares, in a particular company; and

(*b*) which evidences or acknowledges that another person is entitled to rights in relation to those shares or shares of the same kind, which shall include the right to receive such shares (or evidence of the right to receive such shares) from the person mentioned in paragraph (*a*);

"derivatives" means—

(*a*) options to acquire or dispose of shares; and

(*b*) rights under a contract falling within paragraph 8 of Schedule 1 to the Financial Services Act 1986 (futures), where the property in question is shares;

"designated agency" has the same meaning as in the Financial Services Act 1986;

(**a**) OJ No. L322, 17.12.77, p. 30, as amended by Council Directive 86/524/EEC (OJ No. L309, 4.11.86, p. 15) and Council Directive 89/646/EEC (OJ No. L386, 30.12.89, p. 1)
(**b**) OJ No. L228, 16.8.73, p. 3
(**c**) OJ No. L63, 13.3.79, p. 1

"listed company" means a company any of the shares in which are officially listed on a relevant stock exchange and "listed" shall be construed accordingly;

"material interest" shall be construed in accordance with Article 207(2A);

"operator", in relation to a collective investment scheme, shall be construed in accordance with section 75(8) of the Financial Services Act 1986;

"recognised clearing house", "recognised professional body", "recognised scheme", and "recognised self-regulating organisation" have the same meaning as in the Financial Services Act 1986;

"register of interests in shares" means the register kept in pursuance of Article 219 including that part of the register kept in pursuance of Article 221;

"relevant investment exchange" means an exchange situated or operating in a member State on which derivatives are traded;

"relevant share capital" has the meaning given by Article 206(2);

"relevant stock exchange" means a stock exchange situated or operating in a member State;

"UCITS" has the meaning given by Article 207(8);

"units" has the same meaning as in section 75 of the Financial Services Act.".

Revocation

10. The Listed Companies (Disclosure of Share Interests) (Exclusions) Regulations (Northern Ireland) 1979(**a**) are hereby revoked.

Transitional provisions

11.—(1) In this regulation "commencement" means the commencement of these Regulations.

(2) Where a person—

(*a*) has a notifiable interest immediately after commencement, but did not have such an interest immediately before commencement; or

(*b*) had a notifiable interest immediately before commencement, but does not have such an interest immediately after commencement; or

(*c*) had a notifiable interest immediately before commencement and has such an interest immediately after commencement but the percentage levels of his interest immediately before and immediately after commencement are not the same;

(**a**)   S.R. 1979 No. 229. By virtue of Article 69(6) of the Companies (No. 2) (Northern Ireland) Order 1990, these Regulations have effect as if made under Article 218A(1)(*d*) of the Companies (Northern Ireland) Order 1986.

then he comes under an obligation to notify the company with respect to the interest which he has or had in its shares; and the provisions of Part VII of the Companies (Northern Ireland) Order 1986 shall apply as if that obligation arose under Article 206 of that Order.

Sealed with the Official Seal of the Department of Economic Development on 10th January 1994.

(L.S.)   *A. L. Brown*
                                              Assistant Secretary

EXPLANATORY NOTE
(This note is not part of the Regulations.)

These Regulations amend Part VII of the Companies (Northern Ireland) Order 1986 ("the 1986 Order") which imposes an obligation to disclose certain interests in shares comprised in certain issued share capital of public companies. Exemptions from that obligation, contained in that Part and in the Listed Companies (Disclosure of Share Interests) (Exclusions) Regulations (Northern Ireland) 1979 (S.R. 1979 No. 229) are amended or superseded. In some cases the changes made are because continuance of certain exemptions in their present form would be incompatible with Council Directive 88/627/EEC on the information to be published when a major holding in a listed company is acquired or disposed of (OJ No. L348, 17.12.88, p. 62).

Regulation 4 amends Article 207 of the 1986 Order to make special provision for certain interests in relation to the percentage level of interest constituting a notifiable interest within the meaning of that Part. Amendments to Article 206 (regulation 3), Article 210 (regulation 6) and Article 214 (regulation 7) and the substitution of Article 208 (regulation 5) are amendments consequential upon the amendment to Article 207 of the 1986 Order.

Regulation 8 supersedes Article 217 of the 1986 Order (interests in shares to be disregarded for the purposes of Articles 206 to 210) and the above-mentioned Regulations by substituting a new Article 217. Exemptions provided under new paragraph (1) are subject to certain conditions as to the control of voting rights attaching to the shares concerned (see paragraphs (5), (6) and (7)). The exemption provided under paragraph (8) is subject to a condition as to intervention in the management of the company. Paragraph (10) provides for additional classes of interest to be exempted where the company concerned is not a listed company. Paragraph (12) continues the exemption for proxy holders formerly contained in paragraph (2) of Article 217.

Regulation 9 substitutes a new paragraph for Article 228(1) of the 1986 Order (definitions to be applied for Part VII).

Regulation 10 revokes the Listed Companies (Disclosure of Share Interests) (Exclusions) Regulations (Northern Ireland) 1979 (S.R. 1979 No. 229).

Regulation 11 makes transitional provisions to ensure that interests becoming disclosable as a result of the Regulations should be subject to an obligation to notify and that disclosure takes place where as a result of the Regulations a person no longer has a notifiable interest or the percentage of his interest changes.

1994 No. 3

INDUSTRIAL RELATIONS

Industrial Relations (Continuity of Employment) Regulations (Northern Ireland) 1994

Made	*11th January 1994*
Coming into operation . .	*7th February 1994*

The Department of Economic Development(**a**), in exercise of the powers conferred on it by Article 68(4) of the Industrial Relations (Northern Ireland) Order 1976(**b**) and of every other power enabling it in that behalf, hereby makes the following Regulations:

Citation, commencement and revocation

1.—(1) These Regulations may be cited as the Industrial Relations (Continuity of Employment) Regulations (Northern Ireland) 1994 and shall come into operation on 7th February 1994.

(2) The Industrial Relations (Continuity of Employment) Regulations (Northern Ireland) 1976(**c**) are hereby revoked.

Interpretation

2. In these Regulations—

"the No. 1 Order" means the Industrial Relations (Northern Ireland) Order 1976;

"relevant compromise contract" means—

(*a*) any agreement authorised by Article 78(2)(*f*) of the No. 1 Order(**d**) to refrain from instituting or continuing any proceedings arising out of a contravention, or alleged contravention, of Article 20 of that Order before an industrial tribunal; or

(*b*) any contract authorised by Article 77(4)(*aa*) of the Sex Discrimination (Northern Ireland) Order 1976(**e**) settling a complaint arising out of a dismissal.

(**a**) Formerly the Department of Manpower Services; *see* S.I. 1982/846 (N.I. 11) Article 3
(**b**) S.I. 1976/1043 (N.I. 16); Article 68 was amended by S.I. 1993/2668 (N.I. 11) Article 18(1) and Schedule 5 paragraph 5
(**c**) S.R. 1976 No. 261
(**d**) As inserted by S.I. 1993/2668 (N.I. 11) Article 16(2)
(**e**) As inserted by S.I. 1993/2668 (N.I. 11) Article 16(4) and Schedule 4 paragraph 1(*a*)

Application

3. These Regulations apply to any action taken in relation to the dismissal of an employee which consists of—

(*a*) the presentation by him of a relevant complaint of dismissal; or

(*b*) his making a claim in accordance with a dismissal procedures agreement designated under Article 26 of the No. 1 Order(**a**); or

(*c*) any action taken by the Agency under relevant conciliation powers; or

(*d*) the making of a relevant compromise contract.

Continuity of employment where employee re-engaged

4.—(1) The provisions of this regulation shall have effect to preserve the continuity of a person's period of employment for the purposes of Schedule 1 to the Act of 1965 and for the purposes of that Schedule as applied by Article 68(1) of the No. 1 Order(**b**).

(2) If in consequence of any action to which these Regulations apply a dismissed employee is reinstated or re-engaged by his employer or by a successor or associated employer of the employer the continuity of that employee's period of employment shall be preserved and, accordingly, the period beginning with the date on which the dismissal to which the action relates takes effect and ending with the date of reinstatement or re-engagement, as the case may be, shall count in the computation of the employee's period of continuous employment.

Exclusion of operation of sections 34 and 34A of the Act of 1965 where redundancy or equivalent payment repaid

5.—(1) Where—

(*a*) in consequence of any action to which these Regulations apply a dismissed employee is reinstated or re-engaged by his employer or by a successor or associated employer of the employer; and

(*b*) the terms upon which he is so reinstated or re-engaged include provision for him to repay the amount of a redundancy payment or an equivalent payment paid in respect of the relevant dismissal,

sections 34 and 34A of the Act of 1965(**c**) (which require the continuity of the period of employment to be treated as broken where a redundancy payment or an equivalent payment is paid and he is subsequently re-engaged) shall not apply if that provision is complied with.

(2) For the purposes of this regulation the cases in which a redundancy payment shall be treated as having been paid are cases mentioned in paragraphs (*a*) and (*b*) of section 34(3) of the Act of 1965.

(**a**) As amended by S.I. 1993/2668 (N.I. 11) Article 18(2) and Schedule 6
(**b**) As amended by S.I. 1987/936 (N.I. 9) Article 25(1) and Schedule 3 paragraph 4(14)
(**c**) Section 34A was inserted by S.I. 1976/1043 (N.I. 16) Article 82(1) and Schedule 5 Part II paragraph 24

Sealed with the Official Seal of the Department of Economic Development on 11th January 1994.

(L.S.)   *D. Gibson*

Under Secretary

EXPLANATORY NOTE

(This note is not part of the Regulations.)

These Regulations revoke and replace with additional provisions the Industrial Relations (Continuity of Employment) Regulations (Northern Ireland) 1976 ("the 1976 Regulations"). The 1976 Regulations provided for the preservation of continuity of employment for the purposes of the individual employment rights contained in the Industrial Relations (Northern Ireland) Order 1976 ("the No. 1 Order") where a dismissed employee was reinstated or re-engaged in consequence of—

(*a*) the presentation of a complaint of unfair dismissal;

(*b*) the making of a claim in accordance with a dismissal procedures agreement designated under Article 26 of the No. 1 Order; or

(*c*) action taken by the Labour Relations Agency under Article 62 of that Order in a dispute relating to an unfair dismissal claim.

The 1976 Regulations also provided that continuity of employment was not broken in redundancy cases where any such employee repaid a redundancy payment or an equivalent payment.

The additional provisions in these Regulations provide for the preservation of continuity of employment for the purposes of the individual employment rights contained in the No. 1 Order where a dismissed employee is reinstated or re-engaged in consequence of the following—

(*a*) the presentation of a complaint under Article 63 of the Sex Discrimination (Northern Ireland) Order 1976 ("the Sex Discrimination Order") arising out of a dismissal;

(*b*) action taken by the Labour Relations Agency under Article 64(2) of the Sex Discrimination Order; or

(*c*) the making of a compromise contract authorised by—

    (i) Article 78(2)(*f*) of the No. 1 Order and relating to a complaint of unfair dismissal; or

    (ii) Article 77(4)(*aa*) of the Sex Discrimination Order and relating to a complaint arising out of a dismissal.

1994 No. 4

ROAD TRAFFIC AND VEHICLES

One-Way Traffic (Bangor) (Amendment) Order (Northern Ireland) 1994

Made	*10th January 1994*
Coming into operation . .	*26th February 1994*

WHEREAS the Department of the Environment has published a notice in compliance with Article 23(1) and (2) of the Road Traffic (Northern Ireland) Order 1981(**a**);

AND WHEREAS no objections or representations have been received;

NOW THEREFORE the Department, in exercise of the powers conferred on it by Article 21(1) of the Road Traffic (Northern Ireland) Order 1981 and of every other power enabling it in that behalf, makes the following Order:

Citation and commencement

1. This Order may be cited as the One-Way Traffic (Bangor) (Amendment) Order (Northern Ireland) 1994 and shall come into operation on 26th February 1994.

Amendment

2. The Schedule to the One-Way Traffic (Bangor) Order (Northern Ireland) 1992(**b**) shall be amended by the addition thereto of the following item—
"

Column 1	*Column 2*
Castle Street, from a point approximateley 44 metres north-west of its junction with Market Lane to its junction with Main Street	North-westerly towards Main Street

"

Sealed with the Official Seal of the Department of the Environment on 10th January 1994.

(L.S.)   *E. J. Galway*
                                                      Assistant Secretary

---

(**a**) S.I. 1981/154 (N.I. 1); *see* Article 2(2) for the definition of "Department"
(**b**) S.R. 1992 No. 188

EXPLANATORY NOTE

(This note is not part of the Order.)

This Order amends the provisions of the One-Way Traffic (Bangor) Order (Northern Ireland) 1992.

The amendment provides for the introduction of a one-way traffic system in part of Castle Street, Bangor.

Any person who acts in contravention of the Order shall be guilty of an offence and shall be liable on summary conviction to a fine not exceeding level 3 on the standard scale (£400).

Traffic signs indicating the effect of the Order have been erected on the road.

1994   No. 5

This Order has been exempted from printing by the Statutory Rules (Northern Ireland) Order 1979. A summary is given in the List of Statutory Rules of a Local Character under the heading ROADS.

1994 No. 6

HEALTH AND SAFETY

Notification of New Substances Regulations (Northern Ireland) 1994

Made	*12th January 1994*
Coming into operation . .	*28th February 1994*

ARRANGEMENT OF REGULATIONS

PART I

INTERPRETATION AND GENERAL

PART III

RIGHTS AND DUTIES OF THE COMPETENT AUTHORITY

16. Risk assessments.
17. Information to be sent by the competent authority to the European Commission.

PART IV

DISCLOSURE OF INFORMATION

18. Disclosure of information provided under Part II.
19. Treatment of confidential information.
20. Entry of substances in the European List of Notified Chemical Substances.

PART V

MISCELLANEOUS AND GENERAL

21. Enforcement and civil liability.
22. Prohibition of placing on the market of unnotified substances.
23. Exemption certificates.
24. Fees for notifications etc.
25. Revocations, amendments and transitional provisions.

Schedule 1. Characteristic Properties of Dangerous Substances.

Schedule 2. Information Required in the Technical Dossiers (which sets out the provisions of Annex VII to the Directive).

Schedule 3. Additional Information and Tests Required Under Regulation 5 (which sets out the provisions of Annex VIII to the Directive).

Schedule 4. Fees for Notifications etc.

The Department of Economic Development, being a Department designated by the European Communities (Designation) (No. 3) Order 1981(a) for the purposes of section 2(2) of the European Communities Act 1972(b) in relation to measures relating to the notification and control of substances, in exercise of the power conferred on it by the said section 2(2) and being the Department concerned(c) in exercise of the powers conferred by

---

(a) S.I. 1981/1536
(b) 1972 c. 68
(c) *See* Article 2(2) of S.I. 1978/1039 (N.I. 9)

Articles 17(1), (2), (3), (4) and (5), 40(2) and (4) and 55(2) of, and paragraphs 1(1), (4) and (5), 14(1) and 15 of Schedule 3 to, the Health and Safety at Work (Northern Ireland) Order 1978(a) and of every other power enabling it in that behalf, after consultation in accordance with Article 46(1) of that Order with the Health and Safety Agency for Northern Ireland and such other bodies as appeared to it to be appropriate, hereby makes the following Regulations:—

PART I

INTERPRETATION AND GENERAL

Citation and commencement

1. These Regulations may be cited as the Notification of New Substances Regulations (Northern Ireland) 1994 and shall come into operation on 28th February 1994.

Interpretation

2.—(1) In these Regulations—

"the 1978 Order" means the Health and Safety at Work (Northern Ireland) Order 1978;

"the approved supply list" means the list described in regulation 4(1) of the Chemicals (Hazard Information and Packaging) Regulations (Northern Ireland) 1993(**b**);

"the competent authority" means—

(*a*) for Northern Ireland, the Department of the Environment and the Department acting jointly; or

(*b*) for Great Britain or another member State, the authority appointed in accordance with Article 16.1 of the Directive, and

unless the contrary intention appears, a reference to "the competent authority" shall be taken as a reference to the competent authority for Northern Ireland;

"controlled conditions" in relation to the use of a substance in "process-orientated research and development" or "scientific research and development" means the use of that substance under conditions which are under the control of the person undertaking that process-orientated research and development or scientific research and development, as the case may be;

"dangerous substance" means a substance which is in one of the categories of danger referred to in Column 1 of Part I of Schedule 1, having characteristic properties described in the corresponding entry in Column 2 of that Schedule and further described in Part II of that Schedule;

"the Department" means the Department of Economic Development;

(a) S.I. 1978/1039 (N.I. 9)
(b) S.R. 1993 No. 412

"the Directive" means Council Directive No. 67/548/EEC, relating to the classification, packaging and labelling of dangerous substances(**a**) as amended in particular for the seventh time by Council Directive No. 92/32/EEC(**b**);

"EINECS" means the European Inventory of Existing Commercial Chemical Substances(**c**);

"ELINCS" means the European List of Notified Chemical Substances(**d**);

"the Executive" means the Health and Safety Executive established under section 10 of the Health and Safety at Work etc. Act 1974(**e**);

"importer" means a person who imports a new substance into the European Communities' customs territory;

"IUPAC" means the International Union of Pure and Applied Chemistry;

"member State" means a member State of the European Communities;

"monomer unit" means the reacted form of a monomer in a polymer;

"new substance" means any substance except a substance listed in EINECS;

"notification" means the documents with the requisite information sent to the competent authority in pursuance of regulation 4 or 6—

(*a*) in the case of a new substance manufactured within the European Communities, by the manufacturer who places the substance either alone or in a preparation on the market; or

(*b*) in the case of a new substance manufactured outside the European Communities—

(i) by any person established in the European Communities who is responsible for placing that substance either alone or in a preparation on the market, or

(ii) by the sole representative of its manufacturer;

"placing on the market" in relation to a substance or preparation means supplying that substance or preparation, or making it available to another person within the European Communities and includes importation of the substance;

"polymer" means a substance consisting of molecules characterised by the sequence of one or more types of monomer units and comprising a simple weight majority of molecules containing at least 3 monomer units which are covalently bound to at least one other monomer unit or other reactant and consisting of less than a simple weight majority of molecules of the same molecular weight; such molecules being distributed over a range of molecular weights wherein differences in the molecular weight are primarily attributable to differences in the number of monomer units;

(**a**)   O.J. No. L196, 16.8.67, p. 1 (O.J./S.E. 1967 p. 234)
(**b**)   O.J. No. L154, 5.6.92, p. 1
(**c**)   O.J. No. C146A, 15.6.90, p. 1
(**d**)   O.J. No. C130, 10.5.93, p. 1
(**e**)   1974 c. 37

"preparation" means any mixture or solution of two or more substances;

"process-orientated research and development" means the further development of a substance in the course of which pilot plant or production trials are used to test the fields of application of the substance;

"scientific research and development" means scientific experimentation, analysis or chemical research carried out under controlled conditions including the determination of intrinsic properties, performance and efficacy as well as scientific investigation relating to product development;

"sole representative", in relation to a substance manufactured outside the European Communities, means a person established in the European Communities who has been appointed by the manufacturer of the substance for the purpose of notifying the substance;

"substance no longer polymer" means—

(a) a substance which had been placed on the market before 31st October 1993; and

(b) had not been notified under the Notification of New Substances Regulations (Northern Ireland) 1985(**a**) as then in operation by reason that it was reasonably considered by the person placing the substance on the market to be a polymer;

"substance" means a chemical element or compound in the natural state or obtained by any production process, including any additive necessary to preserve the stability of the product and any impurity deriving from the process used, but excluding any solvent which may be separated without affecting the stability of the substance or changing its composition.

(2) The Interpretation Act (Northern Ireland) 1954(**b**) shall apply to these Regulations as it applies to a Measure of the Northern Ireland Assembly.

Application

3.—(1) Subject to paragraphs (2) and (3), these Regulations shall apply in relation to all new substances that are placed on the market either alone or in a preparation.

(2) These Regulations shall not apply in relation to—

(a) a new substance which is placed on the market exclusively as, or exclusively for use as an active ingredient in—

(i) a medicinal product as defined in section 130 of the Medicines Act 1968(**c**), or

---

(**a**) S.R. 1985 No. 63, as amended by S.R. 1986 No. 188 and S.R. 1991 No. 472
(**b**) 1954 c. 33 (N.I.)
(**c**) 1968 c. 67

(ii) a product specified in an order made under section 104 or 105 of that Act which is for the time being in force and which directs that specified provisions of that Act shall apply in relation to that substance or preparation as such provisions have effect in relation to medicinal products within the meaning of the Act;

(*b*) a new substance which is placed on the market exclusively as, or exclusively for use in, food within the meaning of Article 2(2) of the Food Safety (Northern Ireland) Order 1991(**a**) including any additives and flavourings;

(*c*) a new substance which is placed on the market exclusively as, or exclusively for use in, an animal feeding stuff within the meaning of the Feeding Stuffs Regulations (Northern Ireland) 1992(**b**) including any additives;

(*d*) a new substance which is placed on the market exclusively as or in, or exclusively for use as an active ingredient in, a plant protection product covered by Council Directive No. 91/414/EEC(**c**) concerning the placing of Plant Protection Products on the market;

(*e*) a radioactive substance within the meaning of regulation 2(1) of the Ionising Radiations Regulations (Northern Ireland) 1985(**d**);

(*f*) a substance in the form of waste which is covered by Council Directive No. 91/156/EEC(**e**) or Council Directive No. 91/689/EEC(**f**);

(*g*) a new substance which is placed on the market exclusively as or in a cosmetic product within the meaning of the Cosmetic Products (Safety) Regulations 1989(**g**);

(*h*) subject to Council Regulation EC 2455/92(**h**) on the export notification and information exchange of dangerous substances, a new substance intended exclusively for export to a country which is not a member State;

(*i*) a new substance which is a substance no longer polymer; or

(*j*) a substance to which the Explosive Acts (Northern Ireland) 1875 to 1970(**i**) or the Explosives (Northern Ireland) Order 1972(**j**) applies.

(3) Regulations 4 and 6 shall not apply to a new substance which has been duly notified by its manufacturer or other person responsible for placing it on the market in accordance with Article 7 or 8 of the Directive in Great Britain or another member State.

(**a**) S.I. 1991/762 (N.I. 7)
(**b**) S.R. 1992 No. 270, as amended by S.R. 1993 No. 349
(**c**) O.J. No. L230, 19.8.91, p. 1
(**d**) S.R. 1985 No. 273
(**e**) O.J. No. L75, 26.3.91, p. 32
(**f**) O.J. No. L377, 31.12.91 p. 20
(**g**) S.I. 1989/2233
(**h**) O.J. No. L251, 29.8.92, p. 13
(**i**) 1875 c. 17; 1924 c. 5 (N.I.) 1970 c. 10 (N.I.)
(**j**) S.I. 1972/730 (N.I. 3)

PART II

NOTIFICATIONS

Full notifications

4. Subject to regulations 6 and 7, a notifier shall not place a new substance on the market in a total quantity of one tonne or more per year unless he has sent to the competent authority a notification including—

(*a*) a technical dossier supplying the information necessary for evaluating the foreseeable risk, whether immediate or delayed, which the substance may create for human health and the environment and containing all available relevant data for this purpose and including at least the information and results of the tests referred to in Part A of Schedule 2 together with a detailed and full description of the studies conducted or bibliographic references to them;

(*b*) a certificate in writing from the body which carried out the tests for the purpose of the technical dossier stating that those tests were carried out in accordance with the principles of good laboratory practice referred to in regulation 14(1);

(*c*) a declaration concerning the unfavourable effects of the substance in terms of the various foreseeable uses of the substance;

(*d*) if the substance is a dangerous substance, proposals for the purposes of the Chemicals (Hazard Information and Packaging) Regulations (Northern Ireland) 1993 for—

  (i) the classification and labelling of the substance for supply, and

  (ii) the safety data sheet referred to in regulation 6 of those Regulations;

(*e*) in the case of a substance manufactured outside the European Communities, where appropriate, a statement by the manufacturer that the notifier has been appointed, for the purpose of sending to the competent authority a notification of the substance in question, as his sole representative and that he has informed all the importers of the same substance manufactured by him of the name of the sole representative; and

(*f*) if so desired, a statement that the notifier requests, on reasoned grounds, that the notification be exempted from the provisions of regulation 13 for a period which shall not exceed one year from the date of the notification.

Requirements for further testing for substances notified under regulation 4

5.—(1) Any notifier of a substance already notified under regulation 4 shall inform the competent authority—

(*a*) when the quantity of the substance placed on the market reaches 10 tonnes per year from a single manufacturer or when the total quantity of substance reaches 50 tonnes per manufacturer; the competent authority may then require some or all of the additional tests, studies or both as appropriate laid down in Schedule 3 at level 1, to be carried out within the time limit that the competent authority shall determine;

(*b*) when the quantity of the substance placed on the market reaches 100 tonnes per year from a single manufacturer or when the total quantity of the substance reaches 500 tonnes per manufacturer; the competent authority shall then require the additional tests, studies or both as appropriate laid down in Schedule 3 at level 1, to be carried out within the time limit that the competent authority shall determine, unless the notifier can give good reason why a given test or study is not appropriate or that an alternative test or study would be preferable;

(*c*) when the quantity of the substance placed on the market reaches 1,000 tonnes per year from a single manufacturer or when the total quantity of the substance reaches 5,000 tonnes per manufacturer; the competent authority shall then draw up a programme of tests, studies or both as appropriate according to Schedule 3 at level 2 to be carried out by the notifier within the time limit determined by the competent authority.

(2) Where additional testing has been carried out, either in accordance with paragraph (1) or voluntarily, the notifier shall forthwith provide the competent authority with the results of those tests together with a certificate in writing from the person who carried out the tests stating that those tests were carried out in accordance with the principles of good laboratory practice referred to in regulation 14(1).

Reduced notification requirements for substances placed on the market in quantities of less than one tonne per year by a single manufacturer

6.—(1) Subject to the following paragraphs and regulation 7, a person responsible for placing a new substance on the market in a total quantity of less than one tonne per year from a single manufacturer shall not place that substance on the market unless he has sent to the competent authority a notification including a summary of—

(*a*) a technical dossier supplying the information necessary for evaluating the foreseeable risks, whether immediate or delayed, which the substance may create for human health and the environment and containing all available relevant data for this purpose and including at least the information and results of the tests referred to in Part B of Schedule 2; and

(*b*) all the other information referred to in sub-paragraphs (*b*) to (*f*) of regulation 4.

(2) Subject to paragraph (4), where the quantities to be placed on the market are below 100 kg per year from a single manufacturer, the person responsible for placing the substance on the market may restrict the information in the technical dossier referred to in paragraph (1)(*a*) to that provided for in Part C of Schedule 2, he shall also provide all the other information referred to in paragraph (1)(*b*) and this information shall be notified to the competent authority in summary form.

(3) At the request of the competent authority, the person responsible for placing the substance on the market shall provide it with the full information referred to in paragraph (1) or (2) as appropriate, together with a detailed and full description of the studies conducted or bibliographic references to them.

(4) Subject to paragraph (5) and the conditions set out in this paragraph, the following new substances shall be treated as having been notified under these Regulations—

(*a*) polymers except those containing in combined form 2 per cent or more of a new substance;

(*b*) subject to paragraph (6), substances placed on the market in quantities of less than 10 kg per year per manufacturer;

(*c*) substances placed on the market in quantities of less than 100 kg per year per manufacturer and intended solely for the purposes of scientific research and development on condition that the person placing the substance on the market maintains a record of the identity of the substance, labelling data and a list of customers in member States;

(*d*) substances placed on the market for the purposes of process-orientated research and development with a limited number of customers in quantities that are limited to those purposes, subject to the following conditions—

(i) the substance is duly notified within one year of its first having been placed on the market unless on reasoned grounds provided by the person responsible for placing the substance on the market the competent authority approves an extension for up to a further year,

(ii) the person responsible for placing the substance on the market has notified to the competent authority the following information about the substance, namely, identity, labelling data, and a justification for the quantity placed on the market,

(iii) the person responsible for placing the substance on the market has provided a list of the customers,

(iv) the person responsible for placing the substance on the market has provided an assurance that the substance or a preparation in which it is incorporated will only be handled by or on behalf of a customer listed pursuant to head (iii) in controlled conditions and will not be made available to the general public at any time, and

(v) the person responsible for placing the substance on the market satisfies any condition imposed by the competent authority, which shall be limited to requiring the information provided for in paragraph (1).

(5) In the case of any substance to which paragraph (4) applies and which on the basis of the information available might reasonably be expected to be very toxic, toxic, carcinogenic, toxic for reproduction or mutagenic, the person responsible for placing the substance on the market shall forthwith notify to the competent authority any appropriate information relating to paragraphs 2.3, 2.4 and 2.5 of Part A of Schedule 2, and, where available, any acute toxicity data.

(6) In the case of a substance to which paragraph (4)(*b*) applies, which on the basis of the information available might reasonably be expected to be dangerous for the environment and which is intended to be used outside physical containment, the person responsible for placing the substance on the market shall forthwith notify to the competent authority any appropriate information relating to paragraph 2.3 of Part C of Schedule 2.

(7) Substances to which paragraphs (1), (2) and (4) apply shall be packaged and labelled in accordance with the requirements of the Chemicals (Hazard Information and Packaging) Regulations (Northern Ireland) 1993 insofar as the notifier may reasonably be expected to be aware of their dangerous properties, and if it is not reasonably practicable to label the substances completely on the basis of tests carried out in accordance with Part A of Schedule 2, the label shall in addition to the label deriving from such tests carry the warning "Caution — substance not yet fully tested".

(8) A notifier who has sent to the competent authority a notification dossier in conformity with paragraph (2), shall before the quantity of the substance reaches 100 kg per year from a single manufacturer or a total quantity of 500 kg per manufacturer, provide the competent authority with the information necessary to complete the dossier to the level of Part B of Schedule 2.

(9) A notifier who has sent to the competent authority a notification dossier in conformity with paragraph (1), shall before the quantity of the substance reaches 1 tonne per year from a single manufacturer or a total quantity of 5 tonnes per manufacturer, send to the competent authority a full notification in conformity with regulation 4.

Notifications relating to polymers

7. Subject to regulation 6(4)(*a*), in relation to polymers the specific provisions relating to the information supplied in a technical dossier contained in a notification sent to the competent authority under regulation 4 or 6(1) or (2) shall be those set out in Part D of Schedule 2.

Placing of notified substances on the market

8.—(1) A substance notified in accordance with regulation 4 may, in the absence of any objection by the competent authority, be placed on the market no sooner than 60 days after receipt of a notification which is in conformity with the requirements of that regulation.

(2) If, within 60 days from receipt of the notification, the competent authority decides the notification is not in conformity with regulation 4, it shall inform the notifier in writing forthwith, and the substance shall only be placed on the market 60 days after receipt by the competent authority of the information necessary to bring the notification into conformity with that regulation.

(3) A substance notified in accordance with regulation 6(1) or (2) may, in the absence of any objection by the competent authority, be placed on the market no sooner than 30 days after receipt of a notification which is in conformity with the requirements of the relevant paragraph of regulation 6.

(4) If, within 30 days from receipt of the notification referred to in paragraph (3), the competent authority decides the notification is not in conformity with the relevant paragraph of regulation 6, it shall inform the notifier in writing forthwith, and the substance shall only be placed on the market 30 days after receipt by the competent authority of the information necessary to bring the notification into conformity with that paragraph.

(5) In the case of a notification made under regulation 6, if the competent authority has informed the notifier in writing that the notification has been accepted as in conformity with that regulation, the substance may be placed on the market no sooner than 15 days after receipt of the summary of the dossier by the competent authority.

(6) If a notification under regulation 4 or 6 has been accepted as conforming to the requirements of these Regulations, the competent authority shall forthwith advise the notifier of the official notification number which has been allocated to the notification.

Requirements for further information

9.—(1) Subject to paragraph (2), in relation to a substance already notified, the competent authority may in writing require further information, verification or confirmation tests concerning the substance or its transformation products within the time limit which it may specify.

(2) The competent authority may only require further information in accordance with paragraph (1) if—

(*a*) it is satisfied that the further information is reasonably required to evaluate the risks created by the substance to human health or the environment; or

(*b*) it is acting in accordance with a decision of the European Commission under Article 18(2) of the Directive.

(3) When further information has been obtained by the notifier in pursuance of paragraph (1), the notifier shall forthwith provide the competent authority with that information in writing.

(4) The information required under paragraph (1) may include requiring the information referred to in Schedule 3 earlier than required under regulation 5.

Follow-up information

10.—(1) The notifier of a substance already notified in accordance with regulation 4 or 6 shall inform the competent authority of—

(*a*) any change in the annual or total quantity of the substance placed on the European Communities' market, by him or in the case of a substance manufactured outside the European Communities for which the notifier has been designated as the sole representative of the manufacturer, by him and other importers whom he represents;

(*b*) new knowledge of which he may be aware of the effects of the substance on human health or the environment or both;

(*c*) new uses for the substance of which he may be aware;

(*d*) any change in the composition of the substance as given in paragraph 1.3 of Part A, B or C of Schedule 2 as appropriate; and

(*e*) any change in his status as manufacturer, importer or sole representative.

(2) Any importer of a new substance manufactured outside the European Communities who imports that substance under a notification made by a sole representative shall ensure that the sole representative is provided with up-to-date information on the quantity of the substance placed on the European Communities' market by that importer.

Notification of substances previously notified

11. In the case of a new substance which had originally been notified at least ten years previously, a subsequent notifier need not provide the information included in Part A, B or C of Schedule 2 with the exception of that specified in paragraphs 1 and 2 of the relevant Part.

Substances manufactured outside the European Communities

12.—(1) Subject to paragraph (2), where for a substance manufactured outside the European Communities—

(*a*) more that one notification exists for the same substance manufactured by the same manufacturer (whether to one or more competent authorities of member States); and

(*b*) the cumulative annual tonnage or the cumulative total tonnage determined by the European Commission and the competent authorities of the member States, on the basis of information notified under Articles 7(1), 8(1) and 14 of the Directive, exceeds for the first time any of the limits specified in regulation 5,

each notifier established in Northern Ireland shall carry out the additional testing required under paragraph (1) of regulation 5 and shall provide the competent authority with the results of those tests in accordance with paragraph (2) of that regulation.

(2) Where the manufacturer has appointed a sole representative, the obligation to comply with paragraph (1) shall not apply to previous notifiers other than the sole representative, and only to the sole representative if he is established in Northern Ireland.

(3) Where in accordance with paragraph (1), the obligation to carry out further testing falls upon one or more notifiers established in Northern Ireland, the competent authority shall inform each such notifier of the identities of other notifiers within the European Communities and draw attention to the collective responsibilities of notifiers under Article 11 of the Directive.

Further notification of the same substance and avoidance of duplication of testing on vertebrate animals

13.—(1) In the case of a substance that has already been notified under regulation 4, 6(1) or 6(2), the competent authority may agree that a subsequent notifier of that substance may, for the purposes of paragraphs 3, 4 and 5 of Part A or B of Schedule 2 or paragraphs 3 and 4 of Part C of Schedule 2, refer to the results of tests, studies or both as appropriate included in the technical dossier sent by the previous notifier if—

(a) the subsequent notifier can provide evidence that the substance intended to be notified is the same as the one previously notified, including the degree of purity and the nature of the impurities; and

(b) the previous notifier has given his consent in writing that such reference may be made.

(2) Without prejudice to paragraph (1), where a prospective notifier intends to notify a new substance to the competent authority under regulation 4, 6(1) or (2), he shall enquire of the competent authority as to—

(a) whether or not the substance that he intends to notify has already been notified to a competent authority of a member State; and

(b) the name and address of the previous notifier.

(3) Any enquiry made in accordance with paragraph (2) shall be supported by evidence that the prospective notifier has the intention to place the substance on the market and a statement of the quantities involved.

(4) Where—

(a) the competent authority is satisfied that the prospective notifier intends to place the substance on the market in the quantities stated;

(b) the substance had been notified previously; and

(c) the previous notifier had not requested an exemption from the provisions of this regulation in accordance with regulation 4(f), to which the competent authority has agreed,

after informing the previous notifier of its intention, the competent authority shall provide the prospective notifier with the name and address of the previous notifier.

(5) Where the competent authority has given the prospective notifier the name and address of the previous notifier in accordance with paragraph (4), those notifiers shall take all reasonable steps to reach an agreement to share information in accordance with paragraph (1) so as to avoid the duplication of testing on vertebrate animals.

(6) Where, notwithstanding the requirements of paragraph (5), the prospective notifier has failed to reach an agreement with the previous notifier, he shall forthwith inform the competent authority in writing and shall not commence testing on vertebrate animals within 30 days of the receipt of that information by the competent authority.

(7) Where, in accordance with paragraph (5), notifiers have agreed to share information to avoid the duplication of testing on vertebrate animals, and additional testing is required under regulation 5, they shall take all reasonable steps to reach agreement to share the information required by that regulation.

Tests under these Regulations to conform to the principles of good laboratory practice

14.—(1) Where a notifier requires tests to be carried out for the purposes of making a notification under regulation 4, 5 or 6, he shall take all reasonable steps to ensure that those tests are carried out in accordance with the principles of good laboratory practice referred to in Article 1 of Council Directive No. 87/18/EEC(**a**) on the application of the principles of good laboratory practice and the verification of their application for tests on chemical substances.

(2) Where the tests are carried out at a laboratory not under the control of the notifier, the notifier shall, before the tests are commenced, inform the person having control of that laboratory that the tests are required for the purposes of these Regulations.

(3) A person having control of a laboratory in which tests are carried out for the purposes of these Regulations shall, if it be the case, provide the notifier at his request with a certificate in writing that the tests were conducted in accordance with the principles of good laboratory practice.

(4) The principles of good laboratory practice referred to in paragraph (1) are specified in Annex B of Commission Directive 90/18/EEC(**b**) adapting to technical progress the Annex to Council Directive 88/320/EEC(**c**) on the inspection and verification of Good Laboratory Practice.

Notifications and reports to be in English

15. Notifications and reports required under these Regulations shall be in English.

PART III

RIGHTS AND DUTIES OF THE COMPETENT AUTHORITY

Risk assessments

16.—(1) In the case of a substance notified under regulation 4 or 6(1) or (2), the competent authority shall carry out an assessment of the real and potential risks created by the substance to human health and the environment in accordance with the general principles referred to in Article 3(2) of the Directive and that assessment shall include recommendations—

(*a*) on the most appropriate method for testing the substance; and

(*b*) where appropriate, on measures which will enable the risks to human health and the environment in relation to the placing on the market of the substance to be lessened.

(2) The assessment carried out in accordance with paragraph (1) shall be reviewed in the light of any additional information becoming available to the competent authority, in particular any information provided in accordance with regulation 5, 6(8) or (9), 9 or 10.

(**a**) O.J. No. L15, 17.1.87, p. 29
(**b**) O.J. No. L11, 13.1.90, p. 37
(**c**) O.J. No. L145, 11.6.88, p. 35

Information to be sent by the competent authority to the European Commission

17.—(1) When the competent authority has received a notification under regulation 4 or 6(1), information on additional testing under regulation 5 or 6(8) or (9) or additional information under regulation 9 or 10, it shall forthwith send to the European Commission a copy of that information or, in each case, a summary thereof.

(2) Where the competent authority has required additional tests, studies or both as appropriate in accordance with regulation 5 or further information from the notifier in accordance with regulation 9(1), the competent authority shall notify the European Commission of the tests chosen in pursuance of the regulation concerned, the reasons for the choice, the results and where appropriate an assessment of those results.

(3) In the case of information received in pursuance of regulation 6(4), the competent authority shall send to the European Commission such elements of that information as would, in its opinion, be of common interest to the Commission and other competent authorities.

(4) The competent authority shall send to the European Commission a copy of any risk assessment carried out in pursuance of regulation 16 or a summary thereof as soon as it becomes available.

(5) The competent authority shall—

(*a*) give effect to any decision of the European Commission under Article 18.2 of the Directive addressed to it;

(*b*) in a case where the competent authority has furnished a summary of the dossier or further information in accordance with paragraphs (1) to (4), allow the European Commission or another competent authority access to the full dossier and information; and

(*c*) have regard to suggestions made by other competent authorities for further testing or information made in accordance with Article 18.2 of the Directive.

PART IV

DISCLOSURE OF INFORMATION

Disclosure of information provided under Part II

18.—(1) Subject to paragraphs (2) to (4), insofar as any provision in Part II is made under section 2(2) of the European Communities Act 1972, information notified under that provision shall be treated as relevant information for the purposes of Article 30 of the 1978 Order.

(2) Where a person sending a notification in pursuance of Part II indicates that it contains certain information the disclosure of which might harm his competitive position and should be kept confidential, full justification for that indication shall be given and the competent authority shall decide which information shall be kept confidential and shall inform the notifier of the decision.

(3) Nothing in paragraph (2) shall apply to the following information which, where applicable, cannot be kept confidential—

(*a*) the trade name of the substance;

(*b*) the name of the manufacturer and notifier;

(*c*) the physico-chemical data concerning the substance provided in paragraph 3 of Part A, B or C (as appropriate) of Schedule 2;

(*d*) the possible ways of rendering the substances harmless;

(*e*) the summary results of toxicological and ecotoxicological tests;

(*f*) if essential to the classification and labelling for the purpose of introducing the substance into Annex I to the Directive, the degree of purity of the substance and the identity of any impurity or additive which is known to be a dangerous substance;

(*g*) the recommended methods and precautions referred to in paragraph 2.3 and the emergency measures referred to in paragraph 2.4 or 2.5 of Part A, B or C (as appropriate) of Schedule 2;

(*h*) in the case of a substance which is a dangerous substance, the information to be contained in the safety data sheet provided for the purposes of regulation 6 of the Chemicals (Hazard Information and Packaging) Regulations (Northern Ireland) 1993; and

(*i*) in the case of a substance listed in the approved supply list, analytical methods that make it possible to detect the substance when discharged into the environment and to determine the direct exposure of humans.

(4) If the manufacturer, an importer or the notifier himself subsequently discloses previously confidential information he shall inform the competent authority accordingly and such information shall no longer be treated as being confidential for the purposes of these Regulations.

Treatment of confidential information

19.—(1) Information which the competent authority has agreed shall be kept confidential shall not be disclosed except—

(*a*) with the consent of the notifier;

(*b*) to another competent authority or to the European Commission;

(*c*) to the extent necessary to evaluate the notification and carry out the risk assessment pursuant to regulation 16(2); or

(*d*) for the purpose of legal proceedings.

(2) The competent authority shall inform the other competent authorities and the European Commission of what information it has agreed shall be kept confidential.

(3) Where the competent authority receives information which another competent authority has agreed shall be kept confidental, it shall also treat that information as confidential and shall not disclose it except in accordance with paragraph (1).

Entry of substances in the European List of Notified Chemical Substances

20.—(1) A person who makes a notification under regulation 4 or 6(1) or (2) may at the time of making the notification—

(a) in the case of a substance that is not a dangerous substance, request the competent authority to require the European Commission to enter it in ELINCS in the form of its trade name for the maximum of 3 years from the date of the entry; or

(b) in the case of a substance which is a dangerous substance, request the competent authority to require the European Commission to enter it in ELINCS in the form of its trade name until such time as that substance has been introduced into Annex I of the Directive;

and in either case the competent authority shall accede to that request.

(2) In a case in which—

(a) a request had been made in accordance with sub-paragraph (a) of paragraph (1); and

(b) the notifier considers that the publication of the chemical name in the IUPAC nomenclature itself could reveal information concerning the commercial exploitation or manufacture of the substance,

the notifier may request the competent authority to require the European Commission to enter it in ELINCS in the form of its trade name for so long as the competent authority sees fit, and in such a case the competent authority shall accede to that request unless it considers that the publication of the chemical name in the IUPAC nomenclature itself could not reveal information concerning the commercial exploitation or manufacture of the substance.

PART V

MISCELLANEOUS AND GENERAL

Enforcement and civil liability

21.—(1) Insofar as any provision of regulations 4 to 20 is made under section 2(2) of the European Communities Act 1972(**a**)—

(a) subject to paragraph (2), the provisions of the 1978 Order which relate to the approval of codes of practice and their use in criminal proceedings, enforcement and offences shall apply to that provision as if that provision had been made under Article 17 of that Order; and

(b) breach of any duty imposed by any provision of those regulations shall confer a right of action in civil proceedings, if that breach of duty causes damage.

(2) Notwithstanding regulation 4 of the Health and Safety (Enforcing Authority) Regulations (Northern Ireland) 1993(**b**), the enforcing authority for these Regulations shall be the Department.

(**a**) 1972 c. 68
(**b**) S.R. 1993 No. 147

Prohibition of placing on the market of unnotified substances

22. Where the Department has reasonable cause to believe that a person has or is likely to have in his possession a new substance to which these Regulations apply and which has not been duly notified in accordance with regulation 4 or 6 or Article 7.1 of the Directive it may, by notice in writing prohibit that person from placing that substance on the market or disposing of it until 60 days, or in the case of a substance that is required to be notified under regulation 6 30 days, after in either case it has been duly notified.

Exemption certificates

23.—(1) Subject to paragraph (2) and to any provision imposed by the European Communities in respect of the notification, control and regulation of substances, the Department may, by a certificate in writing, exempt any person or class of persons, substance or class of substances from all or any of the requirements or prohibitions imposed by these Regulations and any such exemption may be granted subject to conditions and to a limit of time and may be revoked by a certificate in writing at any time.

(2) The Department shall not grant any such exemption unless, having regard to the circumstances of the case and in particular to—

(*a*) the conditions, if any, that it proposes to attach to the exemption; and

(*b*) any requirements imposed by or under any statutory provision which applies to the case,

it is satisfied that the health and safety of persons who are likely to be affected by the exemption or the protection of the environment will not be prejudiced in consequence of it.

Fees for notifications etc.

24. The fee fixed by Column 2 of Schedule 4 shall be payable in advance by a notifier to the Department in relation to any matter referred to in the corresponding entry in Column 1 of that Schedule.

Revocations, amendments and transitional provisions

25.—(1) The following Regulations are hereby revoked—

(*a*) the Notification of New Substances Regulations (Northern Ireland) 1985(**a**);

(*b*) the Notification of New Substances (Amendment) Regulations (Northern Ireland) 1986(**b**); and

(*c*) the Notification of New Substances (Amendment) Regulations (Northern Ireland) 1991(**c**).

(2) The Chemicals (Hazard Information and Packaging) Regulations (Northern Ireland) 1993 shall be amended as follows—

(*a*) in regulation 5(3)—

(**a**) S.R. 1985 No. 63
(**b**) S.R. 1986 No. 188
(**c**) S.R. 1991 No. 472

(i) for "the Notification of New Substances Regulations (Northern Ireland) 1985" there shall be substituted "the Notification of New Substances Regulations (Northern Ireland) 1994 (S.R. 1994 No. 6)", and

(ii) for "regulation 4(1)", there shall be substituted "regulation 4 or 6(1) or (2)"; and

(b) in regulation 19(3) at the end (but before the full stop) there shall be added the words "and as if the maximum period of imprisonment on summary conviction specified in subsection (5) thereof were 3 months instead of 6 months"; and

(c) regulation 20(1) shall be revoked.

(3) After 28th February 1994, any notification made under the Notification of New Substances Regulations (Northern Ireland) 1985 as in operation immediately before that date shall be treated as a notification made under these Regulations, and the requirements of these Regulations shall apply to any such notification as they apply to a notification made after that date.

(4) Between 28th February 1994 and 31st August 1994, it shall be a sufficient compliance with these Regulations, if a notifier provides such information (if any) about a new substance as was required by the Notification of New Substances Regulations (Northern Ireland) 1985 as in operation immediately before the coming into operation of these Regulations, and other additional information as required under these Regulations by 31st August 1994.

(5) In the case of a new substance which was not required to be notified under the Notification of New Substances Regulations (Northern Ireland) 1985 as for the time being in operation by virtue of a certificate of exemption granted under regulation 12 of those Regulations, it shall be a sufficient compliance with these Regulations if the notifier notifies the substance in accordance with these Regulations before 31st August 1994.

Sealed with the Official Seal of the Department of Economic Development on 12th January 1994.

(L.S.)   *Philip B. Strong*
                                               Assistant Secretary

SCHEDULE 1   Regulation 2(1)

Characteristic Properties of Dangerous Substances

PART I

CATEGORIES OF DANGER AND CHARACTERISTIC PROPERTIES

Column 1	Column 2
Category of danger	*Property*

Physico-Chemical Properties

Explosive	Solid, liquid, pasty or gelatinous substances which may also react exothermically without atmospheric oxygen thereby quickly evolving gases, and which under defined test conditions detonate, quickly deflagrate or upon heating explode when partially confined.
Oxidizing	Substances which give rise to a highly exothermic reaction in contact with other substances, particularly flammable substances.
Extremely flammable	Liquid substances having an extremely low flash point and a low boiling point and gaseous substances and preparations which are flammable in contact with air at ambient temperature and pressure.
Highly flammable	The following substances—

    (*a*) substances which may become hot and finally catch fire in contact with air at ambient temperature without any application of energy,

    (*b*) solid substances which may readily catch fire after brief contact with a source of ignition and which continue to burn or to be consumed after removal of the source of ignition,

    (*c*) liquid substances having a very low flash point, or

    (*d*) substances which, in contact with water or damp air, evolve highly flammable gases in dangerous quantities.

Flammable	Liquid substances having a low flash point.

Health Effects

Very toxic	Substances which in very low quantities cause death or acute or chronic damage to health when inhaled, swallowed or absorbed via the skin.
Toxic	Substances which in low quantities cause death or acute or chronic damage to health when inhaled, swallowed or absorbed via the skin.

Column 1 *Category of danger*	Column 2 *Property*
Harmful	Substances which may cause death or acute or chronic damage to health when inhaled, swallowed or absorbed via the skin.
Corrosive	Substances which, on contact with living tissues, may destroy them.
Irritant	Non-corrosive substances which, through immediate, prolonged or repeated contact with the skin or mucous membrane, may cause inflammation.
Sensitizing	Substances which, if they are inhaled or if they penetrate the skin, are capable of eliciting a reaction of hypersensitization such that on further exposure to the substance, characteristic effects are produced.
Carcinogenic	Substances which, if they are inhaled or ingested or if they penetrate the skin, may induce cancer or increase its incidence.
Mutagenic	Substances which, if they are inhaled or ingested or if they penetrate the skin, may induce heritable genetic defects or increase their incidence.
Toxic for reproduction	Substances which, if they are inhaled or ingested or if they penetrate the skin, may produce or increase the incidence of non-heritable adverse effects in the progeny or the impairment of male or female reproductive functions or capacity.
Environment	
Dangerous for the environment	Substances which, were they to enter into the environment, would present or may present an immediate or delayed danger for one or more compartments of the environment.

PART II

CRITERIA FOR THE CATEGORIES OF DANGER "VERY TOXIC", "TOXIC" AND "HARMFUL"

Substances shall be classified as "very toxic", "toxic" or "harmful" in accordance with the following criteria:—

(*a*) Where the acute toxicity in animals of the commercial substance has been determined by a method which permits estimation of the LD_{50} or LC_{50}, classification as very toxic, toxic or harmful shall be effected using the following parameters as reference values:

Category of danger	LD_{50} Oral in rat mg/kg body weight	LD_{50} Dermal in rat or rabbit mg/kg body weight	LD_{50} Inhalation in rat mg/litre/4 hours	
			gases and vapours	aerosols and particulars
Very toxic	≤ 25	≤ 50	≤ 0.5	≤ 0.25
Toxic	> 25 to 200	> 50 to 400	> 0.5 to 2	> 0.25 to 1
Harmful	> 200 to 2,000	> 400 to 2,000	> 2 to 10	> 1 to 5

(*b*) Where the acute oral toxicity in animals of the commercial substance has been determined using the fixed dose procedure, classification as very toxic, toxic or harmful shall be effected on the basis of the discriminating dose. This is the dose level which produces evident toxicity, but no mortality, and is one of four fixed dose levels (5, 50, 500 or 2,000 mg/kg body weight). "Evident toxicity" is a term used to describe signs of toxicity following administration of a test substance, which are of a severity such that administration of the next higher fixed dose level would be expected to result in mortality. As this test method is based on the selection of doses from a series of fixed doses, it is inappropriate to give values for classification. The following parameters are used as reference values:

Category	Discriminating dose (mg/kg body weight)
Very toxic	< 5
Toxic	5 to < 50
Harmful	50 to < 500

The 2,000 mg/kg dose level is used primarily to obtain information on signs of toxicity that may occur with substances which are of low acute toxicity and are not classified on the basis of acute toxicity;

(*c*) If facts show that for the purposes of classification it is inadvisable to use the reference values given in paragraphs (*a*) and (*b*) because the substances produce other effects, the substances shall be classified according to the magnitude of these effects.

(This Schedule sets out the provisions of Annex VII to the Directive)

Information Required in the Technical Dossiers

PART A

INFORMATION REQUIRED FOR THE TECHNICAL DOSSIER FOR A FULL NOTIFICATION UNDER REGULATION 4

Tests under this Part shall be according to methods recognised and recommended by the competent international bodies where such recommendations exist.   .

If it is not technically possible or if it does not appear scientifically necessary to give information, the reasons shall be clearly stated and subject to acceptance by the competent authority.

The name of the body or bodies responsible for carrying out the studies shall be mentioned.

0.   **IDENTITY OF MANUFACTURER AND THE IDENTITY OF THE NOTIFIER: LOCATION OF THE PRODUCTION SITE**

For substances manufactured outside the European Communities and for which, for the purpose of notification, the notifier has been designated as the manufacturer's sole representative, the identities and addresses of the importers who will be bringing the substance into the European Communities.

1.   **IDENTITY OF THE SUBSTANCE**
1.1   **Name**
1.1.1   Names in the IUPAC nomenclature
1.1.2   Other names (usual name, trade name, abbreviation)
1.1.3   CAS number and CAS name (if available)
1.2   **Molecular and structural formula**
1.3   **Composition of the substance**
1.3.1   Degree of purity (%)
1.3.2   Nature of impurities, including isomers and by-products
1.3.3   Percentage of (significant) main impurities
1.3.4   If the substance contains a stabilizing agent or an inhibitor or other additives, specify: nature, order of magnitude:... ppm; ...%
1.3.5   Spectral data (UV, IR, NMR or mass spectrum)
1.3.6   Chromatographic data (HPLC, GC)
1.4   **Methods of detection and determination**

A full description of the methods used or the appropriate bibliographical references.

Apart from methods of detection and determination, information shall be given on analytical methods which are known to the notifier and allow detection of a substance and its transformation products after discharge into the environment as well as determination of the direct exposure of humans.

2.   INFORMATION ON THE SUBSTANCE

2.0   Production

Information given in this section should be sufficient to allow an approximate but realistic estimation of human and environmental exposure, associated with the production process. Precise details of the production process, particularly those of a commercially sensitive nature, are not required.

2.0.1   Technological process used in production

2.0.2   Exposure estimate related to production:

      — working environment,
      — environment

2.1   Proposed uses

Information given in this section should be sufficient to allow an approximate but realistic estimation of human and environmental exposure to the substances as associated with the proposed/expected uses.

2.1.1   Types of use: description of the function and the desired effects

2.1.1.1   Technological process(es) related to the use of the substance (where known)

2.1.1.2   Exposure estimate(s) related to use (where known):

      — working environment,
      — environment

2.1.1.3   Form under which the substance is marketed: substance, preparation, product

2.1.1.4   Concentration of the substance in marketed preparations and products (where known)

2.1.2   Fields of application with approximate breakdown:

      — industries,
      — farmers and skilled trades,
      — use by the public at large

2.1.3   Where known and where appropriate, the identity of the recipients of the substance

2.1.4   Waste quantities and composition of waste resulting from the proposed uses (where known)

2.2   Estimated production and/or imports for each of the anticipated uses or fields of application

2.2.1   Overall production and/or imports in tonnes per year:

      — the first calendar year,
      — the following calendar years

For the substances manufactured outside the European Communities and for which, for the purpose of notification, the notifier has been designated as the manufacturer's sole representative, this information must be given for each of the importers identified under section 0 above.

2.2.2   Production and/or imports, broken down in accordance with 2.1.1. and 2.1.2 expressed as a percentage:
— the first calendar year,
— the following calendar years

2.3   **Recommended methods and precautions concerning:**

2.3.1   Handling

2.3.2   Storage

2.3.3   Transport

2.3.4   Fire (nature of combustion gases or pyrolysis, where proposed uses justify this)

2.3.5   Other dangers, particularly chemical reaction with water

2.3.6   If relevant, information concerning the susceptibility of the substance to explode when presented in the form of a dust

2.4   **Emergency measures in the case of accidental spillage**

2.5   **Emergency measures in the case of injury to persons (e.g. poisoning)**

2.6   **Packaging**

3.   **PHYSICO-CHEMICAL PROPERTIES OF THE SUBSTANCE**

3.0   **State of the substance at 20°C and 101.3 kPa**

3.1   **Melting point**

3.2   **Boiling point**

3.3   **Relative density**

3.4   **Vapour pressure**

3.5   **Surface tension**

3.6   **Water solubility**

3.8   **Partition coefficient n-octanol/water**

3.9   **Flash point**

3.10   **Flammability**

3.11   **Explosive properties**

3.12   **Self-ignition temperature**

3.13   **Oxidizing properties**

3.15   **Granulometry**

For those substances which may be marketed in a form which gives rise to the danger of exposure by the inhalatory route, a test should be conducted to determine the particle size distribution of the substance as it will be marketed.

4.   **TOXICOLOGICAL STUDIES**

4.1   **Acute toxicity**

For tests 4.1.1 to 4.1.3, substances other than gases shall be administered via at least two routes, one of which should be the oral route. The choice of the second route will depend on the nature of the substance and the likely route of human exposure. Gases and volatile liquids should be administered by the inhalative route.

4.1.1   Administered orally

4.1.2   Administered by inhalation

4.1.3   Administered cutaneously

4.1.5   Skin irritation

4.1.6   Eye irritation

4.1.7   Skin sensitization

4.2   **Repeated dose**

The route of administration should be the most appropriate having regard to the likely route of human exposure, the acute toxicity and the nature of the substance. In the absence of contra-indications the oral route is usually the preferred one.

4.2.1   Repeated dose toxicity (28 days)

4.3   **Other effects**

4.3.1   Mutagenicity

The substance shall be examined in two tests. One shall be a bacteriological (reverse mutation) test, with and without metabolic activation. The second shall be a non-bacteriological test to detect chromosome aberrations or damage. In the absence of contra-indications, this test should normally be conducted *in vitro*, both with and without metabolic activation. In the event of a positive result in either test, further testing according to the strategy described in Annex V to the Directive should be carried out.

4.3.2   Screening for toxicity related to reproduction

4.3.3.   Assessment of the toxicokinetic behaviour of a substance to the extent that can be derived from base set data and other relevant information.

5.   **ECOTOXICOLOGICAL STUDIES**

5.1   **Effects on organisms**

5.1.1   Acute toxicity for fish

5.1.2   Acute toxicity for daphnia

5.1.3   Growth inhibition test on algae

5.1.6   Bacteriological inhibition

In those cases where biodegradation may be affected by the inhibitory effect of a substance on the bacteria, a test for bacterial inhibition should be carried out prior to undertaking the biodegradation.

5.2   **Degradation**

           — biotic,

           — abiotic: If the substance is not readily biodegradable then consideration should be given to the need to carry out the following tests: hydrolysis as a function of pH.

5.3   **Absorption/desorption screening test**

6.   **POSSIBILITY OF RENDERING THE SUBSTANCE HARMLESS**

6.1   **For industry/skilled trades**

6.1.1   Possibility of recycling

6.1.2   Possibility of neutralization of unfavourable effects

6.1.3   Possibility of destruction:

           — controlled discharge,

           — incineration,

           — water purification station,

           — others

6.2   **For the public at large**

6.2.1   Possibility of recycling

6.2.2   Possibility of neutralization of unfavourable effects

6.2.3   Possibility of destruction:

           — controlled discharge,

           — incineration,

           — water purification station,

           — others.

PART B

INFORMATION REQUIRED FOR THE TECHNICAL DOSSIER FOR A NOTIFICATION UNDER REGULATION 6(1)

Tests under this Part shall be according to methods recognised and recommended by the competent international bodies where such recommendations exist.

If it is not technically possible or if it does not appear scientifically necessary to give information, the reasons shall be clearly stated and subject to acceptance by the competent authority.

The name of the body or bodies responsible for carrying out the studies shall be mentioned.

In addition to the information requested below, member States may, if they consider it necessary for the risk assessment, require that the notifier provides the following additional information:

           — vapour pressure,

           — daphnia acute toxicity test.

0.   **IDENTITY OF MANUFACTURER AND THE IDENTITY OF THE NOTIFIER: LOCATION OF THE PRODUCTION SITE**

For substances manufactured outside the European Communities and for which, for the purpose of notification, the notifier has been designated as the manufacturer's sole representative, the identities and addresses of the importers who will be bringing the substance into the European Communities.

1.   **IDENTITY OF THE SUBSTANCE**

1.1   **Name**

1.1.1   Names in the IUPAC nomenclature

1.1.2   Other names (usual name, trade name, abbreviation)

1.1.3   CAS number and CAS name (if available)

1.2   **Molecular and structural formula**

1.3   **Composition of the substance**

1.3.1   Degree of purity (%)

1.3.2   Nature of impurities, including isomers and by-products

1.3.3   Percentage of (significant) main impurities

1.3.4   If the substance contains a stabilizing agent or an inhibitor or other additives, specify: nature, order of magnitude: ... ppm; ...%

1.3.5   Spectral data (UV, IR, NMR or mass spectrum)

1.3.6   Chromatographic data (HPLC, GC)

1.4   **Methods of detection and determination**

A full description of the methods used or the appropriate bibliographical references.

Apart from methods of detection and determination, information shall be given on analytical methods which are known to the notifier and allow detection of a substance and its transformation products after discharge into the environment as well as determination of the direct exposure of humans.

2.   **INFORMATION ON THE SUBSTANCE**

2.0   **Production**

Information given in this section should be sufficient to allow an approximate but realistic estimation of human and environmental exposure, associated with the production process. Precise details of the production process, particularly those of a commercially sensitive nature, are not required.

2.0.1   Technological process(es) used in production

2.0.2   Exposure estimate related to production:

— working environment,
— environment

2.1	**Proposed uses**

Information given in this section should be sufficient to allow an approximate but realistic estimation of human and environmental exposure to the substances as associated with the proposed/expected uses.

2.1.1	Types of use: description of the function and the desired effects
2.1.1.1	Technological process(es) related to the use of the substance (where known)
2.1.1.2	Exposure estimate(s) related to use (where known):

— working environment,
— environment

2.1.1.3	Form under which the substance is marketed: substance, preparation, product
2.1.1.4	Concentration of the substance in marketed preparations and products (where known)
2.1.2	Fields of application with approximate breakdown:

— industries,
— farmers and skilled trades,
— use by the public at large

2.1.3	Where known and where appropriate, the identity of the recipients of the substance

2.2	**Estimated production and/or imports for each of the anticipated uses or fields of application**
2.2.1	Overall production and/or imports in tonnes per year:

— the first calendar year,
— the following calendar years

For substances manufactured outside the European Communities and for which, for the purpose of notification, the notifier has been designated as the manufacturer's sole representative, this information must be given for each of the importers identified under section 0 above.

2.2.2	Production and/or imports, broken down in accordance with 2.1.1. and 2.1.2 expressed as a percentage:

— the first calendar year,
— the following calendar years

2.3	**Recommended methods and precautions concerning:**
2.3.1	Handling
2.3.2	Storage
2.3.3	Transport
2.3.4	Fire (nature of combustion gases or pyrolysis, where proposed uses justify this)
2.3.5	Other dangers, particularly chemical reaction with water

2.4	**Emergency measures in the case of accidental spillage**

2.5	**Emergency measures in the case of injury to persons (e.g. poisoning)**
2.6	**Packaging**

3.   **PHYSICO-CHEMICAL PROPERTIES OF THE SUBSTANCE**

3.0   **State of the substance at 20°C and 101.3 kPa**

3.1   **Melting point**

3.2   **Boiling point**

3.6   **Water solubility**

3.8   **Partition coefficient n-octanol/water**

3.9   **Flash point**

3.10   **Flammability**

4.   **TOXICOLOGICAL STUDIES**

4.1   **Acute toxicity**
For tests 4.1.1 to 4.1.2, one route of administration is sufficient. Substances other than gases should be treated by oral administration. Gases should be tested by inhalation.
4.1.1   Administered orally
4.1.2   Administered by inhalation
4.1.5   Skin irritation
4.1.6   Eye irritation
4.1.7   Skin sensitization

4.3   **Other effects**
4.3.1   Mutagenicity
The substance should be examined in a bacteriological (reverse mutation) test with and without metabolic activation.

5.   **ECOTOXICOLOGICAL STUDIES**

5.2   **Degradation: biotic.**

PART C

INFORMATION REQUIRED FOR THE TECHNICAL DOSSIER FOR A NOTIFICATION
UNDER REGULATION 6(2)

Tests under this Part shall be according to methods recognised and recommended by the competent international bodies where such recommendations exist.

If it is not technically possible or if it does not appear scientifically necessary to give information, the reasons shall be clearly stated and subject to acceptance by the competent authority.

The name of the body or bodies responsible for carrying out the studies shall be mentioned.

0.   **IDENTITY OF MANUFACTURER AND THE NOTIFIER IF THESE ARE NOT THE SAME: LOCATION OF THE PRODUCTION SITE**

For substances manufactured outside the European Communities and for which, for the purpose of notification, the notifier has been designated as the manufacturer's sole representative, the identities and addresses of the importers who will be bringing the substance into the European Communities.

1.   **IDENTITY OF THE SUBSTANCE**
1.1   **Name**
1.1.1   Names in the IUPAC nomenclature
1.1.2   Other names (usual name, trade name, abbreviation)
1.1.3   CAS number and CAS name (if available)

1.2   **Molecular and structural formula**

1.3   **Composition of the substance**
1.3.1   Degree of purity (%)
1.3.2   Nature of impurities, including isomers and by-products
1.3.3   Percentage of (significant) main impurities
1.3.4   If the substance contains a stabilizing agent or an inhibitor or other additives, specify: nature, order of magnitude: … ppm; …%
1.3.5   Spectral data (UV, IR, NMR or mass spectrum)
1.3.6   Chromatographic data (HPLC, GC)

1.4   **Methods of detection and determination**

A full description of the methods used or the appropriate bibliographical references.

Apart from methods of detection and determination, information shall be given on analytical methods which are known to the notifier and allow detection of a substance and its transformation products after discharge into the environment as well as determination of the direct exposure of humans.

2.   **INFORMATION ON THE SUBSTANCE**

2.0   **Production**

Information given in this section should be sufficient to allow an approximate but realistic estimation of human and environmental exposure, associated with the production process. Precise details of the production process, particularly those of a commercially sensitive nature, are not required.

2.0.1   Technological process(es) used in production
2.0.2   Exposure estimate related to production:

— working environment,
— environment

2.1   **Proposed uses**

Information given in this section should be sufficient to allow an approximate but realistic estimation of human and environmental exposure to the substances as associated with the proposed/expected uses.

2.1.1   Types of use: description of the function and the desired effects

2.1.1.1   Technological process(es) related to the use of the substance (where known)

2.1.1.2   Exposure estimate(s) related to the use of the substance (where known):
— working environment,
— environment

2.1.1.3   Form under which the substance is marketed: substance, preparation, product

2.1.1.4   Concentration of the substance in marketed preparations and products (where known)

2.1.2   Fields of application with approximate breakdown:
— industries,
— farmers and skilled trades,
— use by the public at large

2.1.3   Where known and where appropriate, the identity of the recipients of the substance

2.2   **Estimated production and/or imports for each of the anticipated uses or fields of application**

2.2.1   Overall production and/or imports in tonnes per year:
— the first calendar year,
— the following calendar years

For substances manufactured outside the European Communities and for which, for the purpose of notification, the notifier has been designated as the manufacturer's sole representative, this information must be given for each of the importers identified under section 0 above.

2.2.2   Production and/or imports, broken down in accordance with 2.1.1. and 2.1.2 expressed as a percentage:
— the first calendar year,
— the following calendar years

2.3   **Recommended methods and precautions concerning:**

2.3.1   Handling

2.3.2   Storage

2.3.3   Transport

2.3.4   Fire (nature of combustion gases or pyrolysis, where proposed uses justify this)

2.3.5   Other dangers, particularly chemical reaction with water

2.4   **Emergency measures in the case of accidental spillage**

2.5   **Emergency measures in the case of injury to persons (e.g. poisoning)**

2.6   **Packaging**

3.   **PHYSICO-CHEMICAL PROPERTIES OF THE SUBSTANCE**

3.0   **State of the substance at 20°C and 101.3 kPa**

3.9   **Flash point**

3.10   **Flammability**

4.   **TOXICOLOGICAL STUDIES**

4.1   **Acute toxicity**

One route of administration is sufficient.
Substances other than gases should be tested by oral administration.
Gases should be tested by inhalation.

4.1.1   Administered orally

4.1.2   Administered by inhalation.

PART D

(The provisions set out in this Part were introduced into Annex VII of the Directive by Commission Directive 1993/105/EEC)(**a**)

INFORMATION REQUIRED FOR THE TECHNICAL DOSSIER FOR A NOTIFICATION UNDER REGULATION 7

Without prejudice to the provisions of Article 3(1) of the Directive tests under this Part shall be according to methods recognised and recommended by the competent international bodies where such recommendations exist.

If it is not technically possible or if it does not appear scientifically necessary to give information, the reasons shall be clearly stated and be subject to acceptance by the competent authority.

The name of the body or bodies responsible for carrying out the studies shall be mentioned.

A.   For the purpose of this Part

— "homopolymer" is a polymer consisting of only one kind of monomer unit.

— "copolymer" is a polymer consisting of more than one kind of monomer unit.

— "polymer for which a reduced test package is acceptable", "RTP polymer", is a polymer that satisfies the criteria laid down in section C.2 of this Part.

— "family of polymers" is a group of polymers (either homopolymers or copolymers) with different number-average molecular weights or different compositions resulting from different ratios of monomer units. The difference in the number-average molecular weight or in the composition is determined not by unintentional process-related fluctuations but by deliberate alterations to the process conditions, the process itself remaining the same.

— "M_n" is the number-average molecular weight.

— "MW" is the molecular weight (of any particular molecule).

(**a**)   O.J.No. L294, 30.11.93, p. 21

B.   Family approach

To avoid unnecessary testing, grouping of polymers into families shall be allowed.

The concept consists of testing representative members of a family with:

— M_n variable for homopolymers or

— composition variable with M_n approximately constant for copolymers or

— for $M_n > 1000$, M_n variable with composition approximately constant for copolymers

In certain cases where there are dissimilarities in the effects seen in the representative members, depending on the M_n- or composition-range, additional testing of other representative members shall be required.

C.   Information required for the technical dossier referred to in regulation 7

Appropriate available information on the properties of the monomer(s) may be taken into account for the assessment of the properties of the polymer.

C.1   POLYMERS WITH STANDARD TEST PACKAGE

C.1.1   POLYMERS PLACED ON THE EUROPEAN COMMUNITIES' MARKET IN QUANTITIES OF ≥1 TONNE PER ANNUM (OR TOTAL QUANTITIES OF ≥5 TONNES)

In addition to the information and tests referred to in regulation 4, laid down in Part A of Schedule 2, the following polymer-specific information is required:

1.   IDENTITY OF THE SUBSTANCE

1.2.1   Number-average molecular weight

1.2.2   Molecular weight distribution (MWD)

1.2.3   Identity and concentration of starting monomers and starting substances which will be bound in the polymer

1.2.4   Indication of end groups and identity and frequency of reactive functional groups

1.3.2.1   Identity of non-reacted monomers

1.3.3.1   Percentage of non-reacted monomers.

2.   INFORMATION ON THE SUBSTANCE

2.1.1.5   Statement, with relevant information, if the polymer has been developed to be environmentally degradable.

3.   PHYSICO-CHEMICAL PROPERTIES OF THE SUBSTANCE

3.6.1   Water extractivity

Without prejudice to regulation 16, further tests may be required additionally in certain cases, e.g.:

— Light-stability if the polymer is not specifically light stabilized

— Long-term extractivity (leachate test); depending on the results of this test, appropriate tests on the leachate may be requested on a case by case basis.

C.1.2 **POLYMERS PLACED ON THE EUROPEAN COMMUNITIES' MARKET IN QUANTITIES OF < 1 TONNE PER ANNUM (OR TOTAL QUANTITIES OF < 5 TONNES) BUT ≥ 100 KGS PER ANNUM (OR TOTAL QUANTITIES OF ≥ 500 KGS)**

In addition to the information and tests referred to in regulation 6(1), laid down in Part B of Schedule 2, the following polymer-specific information is required:

1. **IDENTITY OF THE SUBSTANCE**

1.2.1 Number-average molecular weight

1.2.2 Molecular weight distribution (MWD)

1.2.3 Identity and concentration of starting monomers and starting substances which will be bound in the polymer

1.2.4 Indication of end groups and identity and frequency of reactive functional groups

1.3.2.1 Identity of non-reacted monomers

1.3.3.1 Percentage of non-reacted monomers.

2. **INFORMATION ON THE SUBSTANCE**

2.1.1.5 Statement, with relevant information, if the polymer has been developed to be environmentally degradable.

3. **PHYSICO-CHEMICAL PROPERTIES OF THE SUBSTANCE**

3.6.1. Water extractivity.

C.1.3 **POLYMERS PLACED ON THE EUROPEAN COMMUNITIES' MARKET IN QUANTITIES OF < 100 KGS PER ANNUM (OR TOTAL QUANTITIES OF < 500 KGS)**

In addition to the information and tests referred to in regulation 6(2), laid down in Part C of Schedule 2, the following polymer-specific information is required:

1. **IDENTITY OF THE SUBSTANCE**

1.2.1 Number-average molecular weight

1.2.2 Molecular weight distribution (MWD)

1.2.3 Identity and concentration of starting monomers and starting substances which will be bound in the polymer

1.2.4 Indication of end groups and identity and frequency of reactive functional groups

1.3.2.1 Identity of non-reacted monomers

1.3.3.1 Percentage of non-reacted monomers.

2. **INFORMATION ON THE SUBSTANCE**

2.1.1.5 Statement, with relevant information, if the polymer has been developed to be environmentally degradable.

C.2 **POLYMERS FOR WHICH A REDUCED TEST PACKAGE (RTP POLYMERS) IS ACCEPTABLE**

Under certain conditions the base-set test package for polymers can be reduced.

CRITERIA FOR POLYMERS FOR WHICH A REDUCED TEST PACKAGE IS ACCEPTABLE

Substances with a high number-average molecular weight, a low content of low molecular weight species and low solubility/extractivity will be regarded as being non-bioavailable. Consequently the following criteria shall be used to determine the polymers for which a reduced test package is acceptable:

(*a*) for non-readily degradable polymers placed on the European Communities' market in quantities of $\geq$ 1 t/a (or total quantities of $\geq$ 5 t), the following criteria define those polymers for which a reduced test package is acceptable:

     I. High number-average molecular weight (M_n). The competent authority shall decide whether or not a polymer satisfies this criterion;

     II. Extractivity in water (3.6.1) $<$ 10 mg/l excluding any contribution from additives and impurities;

     III. Less than 1% with MW $<$ 1000; the percentage refers only to molecules (components) directly derived from and including monomer(s), excluding other components e.g. additives or impurities.

If all the criteria are fulfilled, the polymer is regarded as a polymer for which a reduced test package is acceptable;

(*b*) in the case of non-readily degradable polymers placed on the European Communities' market in quantities $<$ 1 t/a (or total quantities of $<$ 5 t), it is sufficient that criteria I and II are fulfilled.

If it is not possible to prove the criteria with the assigned tests, the notifier has to demonstrate compliance with the criteria by other means.

Under certain circumstances toxicological and ecotoxicological tests may be required.

C.2.1   **RTP POLYMERS PLACED ON THE EUROPEAN COMMUNITIES' MARKET IN QUANTITIES OF $\geq$ 1 TONNE PER ANNUM (OR TOTAL QUANTITIES OF $\geq$ 5 TONNES): FULL LIST OF INFORMATION AND TESTS REQUIRED**

0.   **IDENTITY OF MANUFACTURER AND THE IDENTITY OF THE NOTIFIER: LOCATION OF THE PRODUCTION SITE**

For substances manufactured outside the European Communities and for which, for the purpose of notification, the notifier has been designated as the manufacturer's sole representative, the identities and the addresses of the importers who will be bringing the substance into the European Communities.

1.   **IDENTITY OF THE SUBSTANCE**

1.1   **Name**

1.1.1   Names in the IUPAC nomenclature

1.1.2   Other names (usual name, trade name, abbreviation)

1.1.3   CAS number and CAS name (if available)

1.2	**Molecular and structural formula**
1.2.1	Number-average molecular weight
1.2.2	Molecular weight distribution (MWD)
1.2.3	Identity and concentration of starting monomers and starting substances which will be bound in the polymer
1.2.4	Indication of end groups and identity and frequency of reactive functional groups

1.3	**Composition of the substance**
1.3.1	Degree of purity (%)
1.3.2	Nature of impurities, including by-products
1.3.2.1	Identity of non-reacted monomers
1.3.3	Percentage of (significant) main impurities
1.3.3.1	Percentage of non-reacted monomers
1.3.4	If the substance contains a stabilizing agent or an inhibitor or other additives, specify: nature, order of magnitude: ... ppm, ...%
1.3.5	Spectral data (UV, IR, NMR or mass spectrum)
1.3.6.1	GPC

1.4	**Methods of detection and determination**

A full description of the methods used or the appropriate bibliograhical references.

Apart from methods of detection and determination, information shall be given on analytical methods which are known to the notifier and allow detection of a substance and its transformation products after discharge into the environment as well as determination of the direct exposure of humans.

2.	**INFORMATION ON THE SUBSTANCE**

2.0	**Production**

Information given in this section should be sufficient to allow an approximate but realistic estimation of human and environmental exposure associated with the production process. Precise details of the production process, particularly those of a commercially sensitive nature, are not required.

2.0.1	Technological process used in production
2.0.2	Exposure estimates related to production:

— working environment,
— environment

2.1	**Proposed uses**

Information given in this section should be sufficient to allow an approximate but realistic estimation of human and environmental exposure to the substances as associated with the proposed/expected uses.

2.1.1	Types of use: description of the function and the desired effects

2.1.1.1   Technological process(es) related to the use of the substance (where known)

2.1.1.2   Exposure estimate(s) related to the use (where known):
— working environment,
— environment

2.1.1.3   Form under which the substance is marketed: substance, preparation, product

2.1.1.4   Concentration of the substance in marketing preparations and products (where known)

2.1.2   Fields of application with approximate breakdown:
— industries,
— farmers and skilled trades,
— use by the public at large

2.1.3   Where known and where appropriate, the identity of the recipients of the substance

2.1.4   Waste quantities and composition of waste resulting from the proposed uses (where known)

2.2   **Estimated production and/or imports for each of the anticipated uses or fields of application**

2.2.1   Overall production and/or imports in tonnes per year:
— the first calendar year,
— the following calendar years

For the substances manufactured outside the European Communities and for which, for the purpose of notification, the notifier has been designated as the manufacturer's sole representative, this information must be given for each of the importers identified under section 0 above.

2.2.2   Production and/or imports, broken down in accordance with 2.1.1. and 2.1.2 expressed as a percentage:
— the first calendar year,
— the following calendar years

2.3   **Recommended methods and precautions concerning:**

2.3.1   Handling

2.3.2   Storage

2.3.3   Transport

2.3.4   Fire (nature of combustion gases or pyrolysis, where proposed uses justify this)

2.3.5   Other dangers, particularly chemical reaction with water

2.3.6   If relevant, information concerning the susceptibility of the substance to explode when presented in the form of a dust

2.4   **Emergency measures in the case of accidental spillage**

2.5   **Emergency measures in the case of injury to persons (e.g. poisoning)**

2.6   **Packaging**

3.   PHYSICO-CHEMICAL PROPERTIES OF THE SUBSTANCE

3.0   **State of the substance at 20°C and 101.3 kPa**

3.1   **Melting range (e.g. from the thermal stability test)**

3.3   **Relative density**

3.6.1   Water extractivity

3.10   **Flammability**

3.11   **Explosive properties**

3.12   **Auto-flammability**

3.15   **Particle size**

For those substances which may be marketed in a form which gives rise to the danger of exposure by the inhalatory route, a test should be conducted to determine the particle distribution of the substance as it will be marketed.

3.16   **Thermal stability**

3.17   **Extractivity with:**
— water at pH 2 and 9 at 37°C
— cyclohexane

4.   TOXICOLOGICAL STUDIES

On a case by case basis and without delaying acceptance of the notification the competent authority may on the basis of the presence of reactive groups or structural physical characteristics or knowledge about the properties of low molecular weight components of the polymer or exposure potential require certain tests to be carried out. In particular tests for inhalation toxicity (e.g. 4.1.2, 4.2.1) may be required if exposure by the inhalatory route is considered possible.

5.   ECOTOXICOLOGICAL STUDIES

On a case by case basis and without delaying acceptance of the notification, the competent authority may on the basis of the presence of reactive groups, structural/physical characteristics or knowledge of the properties of low molecular weight components of the polymer or exposure potential, require certain tests to be carried out.

In particular, the following additional tests may be required:
— Light-stability, if the polymer is not specifically light-stabilized
— Long-term extractivity (leachate test)

Depending on the results of this test, any appropriate test on the leachate may be requested on a case by case basis.

6.   **Possibility of rendering the substance harmless**

6.1   **For industry/skilled trades**

6.1.1   Possibility of recycling

6.1.2   Possibility of neutralization of unfavourable effects

6.1.3   Possibility of destruction

— controlled discharge,
— incineration,
— water purification station,
— others

6.2   **For the public at large**

6.2.1   Possibility of recycling

6.2.2   Possibility of neutralization of unfavourable effects

6.2.3   Possibility of destruction:

— controlled discharge,
— incineration,
— water purification station,
— others

C.2.2   **RTP POLYMERS PLACED ON THE EUROPEAN COMMUNITIES' MARKET IN QUANTITIES OF < 1 TONNE PER ANNUM (OR TOTAL QUANTITIES OF < 5 TONNES): FULL LIST OF INFORMATION AND TESTS REQUIRED**

0.   **IDENTITY OF MANUFACTURER AND THE IDENTITY OF THE NOTIFIER: LOCATION OF THE PRODUCTION SITE**

For substances manufactured outside the European Communities and for which, for the purpose of notification, the notifier has been designated as the manufacturer's sole representative, the identities and the addresses of the importers who will be bringing the substance into the European Communities.

1.   **IDENTITY OF THE SUBSTANCE**

1.1   **Name**

1.1.1   Names in the IUPAC nomenclature

1.1.2   Other names (usual name, trade name, abbreviation)

1.1.3   CAS number and CAS name (if available)

1.2   **Molecular and structural formula**

1.2.1   Number-average molecular weight

1.2.2   Molecular weight distribution (MWD)

1.2.3   Identity and concentration of starting monomers and starting substances which will be bound in the polymer

1.2.4   Indication of end groups and identity and frequency of reactive functional groups

1.3   **Composition of the substance**

1.3.1   Degree of purity (%)

1.3.2   Nature of impurities, including by-products

1.3.2.1   Identity of non-reacted monomers

1.3.3	Percentage of (significant) main impurities
1.3.3.1	Percentage of non-reacted monomers
1.3.4	If the substance contains a stabilizing agent or an inhibitor or other additives, specify: nature, order of magnitude: … ppm, …%
1.3.5	Spectral data (UV, IR, NMR or mass spectrum)
1.3.6.1	GPC

1.4   **Methods of detection and determination**

A full description of the methods used or the appropriate bibliographical references.

Apart from methods of detection and determination, information shall be given on analytical methods which are known to the notifier and allow detection of a substance and its transformation products after discharge into the environment as well as determination of the direct exposure of humans.

2.   **INFORMATION ON THE SUBSTANCE**

2.0   **Production**

Information given in this section should be sufficient to allow an approximate but realistic estimation of human and environmental exposure associated with the production process. Precise details of the production process, particularly those of a commercially sensitive nature, are not required.

2.0.1   Technological process used in production

2.0.2   Exposure estimates related to production:
— working environment,
— environment

2.1   **Proposed uses**

Information given in this section should be sufficient to allow an approximate but realistic estimation of human and environmental exposure to the substances as associated with the proposed/expected uses

2.1.1   Types of use: description of the function and the desired effects

2.1.1.1   Technological process(es) related to the use of the substance (where known)

2.1.1.2   Exposure estimate(s) related to the use (where known):
— working environment,
— environment

2.1.1.3   Form under which the substance is marketed: substance, preparation, product

2.1.1.4   Concentration of the substance in marketing preparations and products (where known)

2.1.2   Fields of application with approximate breakdown:
— industries,
— farmers and skilled trades,
— use by the public at large

2.1.3   Where known and where appropriate, the identity of the recipients of the substance

2.1.4   Waste quantities and composition of waste resulting from the proposed uses (where known)

2.2   **Estimated production and/or imports for each of the anticipated uses or fields of application**

2.2.1   Overall production and/or imports in tonnes per year:

— the first calendar year,
— the following calendar years

For the substances manufactured outside the European Communities and for which, for the purpose of notification, the notifier has been designated as the manufacturer's sole representative, this information must be given for each of the importers identified under section 0 above.

2.2.2   Production and/or imports, broken down in accordance with 2.1.1. and 2.1.2 expressed as a percentage:

— the first calendar year,
— the following calendar years

2.3   **Recommended methods and precautions concerning:**

2.3.1   Handling

2.3.2   Storage

2.3.3   Transport

2.3.4   Fire (nature of combustion gases or pyrolysis, where proposed uses justify this)

2.3.5   Other dangers, particularly chemical reaction with water

2.3.6   If relevant, information concerning the susceptibility of the substance to explode when presented in the form of a dust

2.4   **Emergency measures in the case of accidental spillage**

2.5   **Emergency measures in the case of injury to persons (e.g. poisoning)**

2.6   **Packaging**

3.   **PHYSICO-CHEMICAL PROPERTIES OF THE SUBSTANCE**

3.0   **State of the substance at 20°C and 101.3 kPa**

3.1   **Melting range (e.g. from the thermal stability test)**

3.6.1   Water extractivity

3.10   **Flammability**

SCHEDULE 3   Regulation 5

(This Schedule sets out the provisions of Annex VIII to the Directive)

Additional Information and Tests required Under Regulation 5

Tests under this Part shall be according to methods recognised and recommended by the competent international bodies where such recommendations exist.

If it is not technically possible or if it does not appear scientifically necessary to give information, the reasons shall be clearly stated and subject to acceptance by the competent authority.

The name of the body or bodies responsible for carrying out the studies shall be indicated.

LEVEL 1

Physico-chemical studies

Further studies on physico-chemical properties dependent upon the results of the studies laid down in Annex VII to the Directive. Such further studies could include for example the development of analytical methods which make it possible to observe and detect a substance or its transformation products and studies on thermal decomposition products.

Toxicological studies

Fertility studies (one species, one generation, male and female, most appropriate route of administration)

If there are equivocal findings in the first generation, study of a second generation is required.

Depending upon the dosing schedule it may be possible in this study to obtain an indication of teratogenicity. A positive indication should be examined in a formal teratology study.

— Teratology study (one species, most appropriate route of administration)

This study is required if teratogenicity has not been examined in the fertility study.

— Sub-chronic and/or chronic toxicity study, including special studies (one species, male and female, most appropriate route of administration) shall be required if the results of the repeated-dose study in Annex VII to the Directive or other relevant information demonstrate the need for further appropriate investigation.

The effects which would indicate the need for such a study could include for example:

  (*a*) serious or irreversible lesions;

  (*b*) a very low or absence of a ''no effect'' level;

  (*c*) a clear relationship in chemical structure between the substance being studied and other substances which have been proved dangerous.

— Additional mutagenesis studies and/or screening study(ies) for carcinogenesis as prescribed in the testing strategy described in Annex V to the Directive

When both tests in the base set are negative, further tests shall be conducted according to the specific properties and the proposed use of the substance.

When a test or both tests were positive in the base set, a supplementary study should include the same or different end points in other *in vivo* test methods.

— Basic toxicokinetic information.

Ecotoxicity studies

— Prolonged toxicity study with Daphnia magna (21 days).
— Tests on higher plants.
— Tests on earthworms.
— Further toxicity studies with fish.
— Tests for species accumulation: one species, preferably fish.
— Supplementary degradation study(ies), if sufficient degradation has not been proved by the studies laid down in Annex VII to the Directive.
— Further studies on absorption/desorption dependent upon the results of the investigations laid down in Annex VII to the Directive.

LEVEL 2

Toxicological studies

This test programme shall cover the following aspects unless there are strong reasons to the contrary, supported by evidence, that it should not be followed:

— Chronic toxicity study.
— Carcinogenicity study.
— Fertility study (e.g. three-generation study): only if an effect on fertility has been established at level 1.
— Developmental toxicity study on perinatal and postnatal effects.
— Teratology study (species not employed in the respective level 1).
— Additional toxicokinetic studies which cover biotransformation, pharmokinetics.
— Additional tests to investigate organ or system toxicity.

Ecotoxicological studies

— Additional tests for accumulation, degradation, mobility and absorption/desorption.
— Further toxicity studies with fish.
— Toxicity studies with birds.
— Additional toxicity studies with other organisms.

SCHEDULE 4   Regulation 24

Fees for Notifications etc.

Column 1 *Subject matter*	Column 2 *Fee payable* £
For the evaluation of a notification under regulation 4 (''base set'') (See Note 1)	5,500 (+350 VAT)
For the evaluation of a notification under regulation 5(1)(*a*)	2,000
For the evaluation of a notification under regulation 5(1)(*b*)	4,200
For the evaluation of a notification under regulation 5(1)(*c*)	3,500
For a notification under regulation 6 (see Note 2)—	
(*a*) quantity of the new substance equal to or more than 100 kg (regulation 6(1))	950 (+ 87·50 VAT)
(*b*) quantity of the new substance up to 100 kg (regulation 6(2))	800 (+ 87·50 VAT)
For an application made by a notifier for an exemption relating to him under regulation 23	2,000

	£
Note 1. Rebate where an adequate draft risk assessment is included	2,000 (and 350 VAT)
Note 2. Rebate where an adequate draft risk assessment is included	500 (and 87·50 VAT)

EXPLANATORY NOTE
(This note is not part of the Regulations.)

These Regulations implement as respects Northern Ireland the provisions of Council Directive 92/32/EEC (O.J. No. L154, 5.6.92, p. 1) ("the Directive") amending for the 7th time Council Directive 67/548/EEC (O.J. No. L196, 16.8.67, p. 1 (O.J./SE1967, p. 234)) relating to the classification, packaging and labelling of dangerous substances insofar as those provisions relate to the placing on the market of new substances together with the Commission Directive 93/105/EEC (O.J. No. L294, 30.11.93, p. 21) setting out Annex VII D of the Directive (relating to polymers). The Regulations supersede the Notification of New Substances Regulations (Northern Ireland) 1985 which they revoke.

Part I   Miscellaneous and general — Regulations 1 to 3

Regulation 2 defines the expressions used in the Regulations, in particular "new substance" means a substance which does not appear in the European Inventory of Existing Commercial Chemical Substances ("EINECS") and the competent authority for Northern Ireland is the Department of the Environment and the Department of Economic Development acting jointly.

With certain specified exceptions the Regulations are applied by regulation 3 to new substances which are placed on the market either alone or in preparations.

Part II   Notifications — Regulations 4 to 15

By regulation 4, a person responsible for placing a new substance on the market in a quantity of one tonne or more per year is required to send a notification to the competent authority which shall include the particulars about the substance specified in Part A of Schedule 2. Further testing is required when the quantity of the substance placed on the market reaches 10 tonnes per manufacturer per annum or a total of 50 tonnes (regulation 5).

By regulation 6, reduced notification requirements for new substances placed on the market in quantities of less than one tonne per year are imposed and, with certain specified exceptions, new substances are deemed to have been notified if placed on the market in quantities of less than 10 kg per year. Special notification requirements relate to new substances which are polymers as defined in regulation 2(1) (regulation 7).

By regulation 8, new substances which have been duly notified may be placed on the market no sooner than 60 days after the notification was received by the competent authority, or in cases where the substance is subject to reduced notification requirements under regulation 6, no sooner than 30 days after the receipt of the notification. Where further tests are required to evaluate the risks created by the substance, the competent authority may require the notifier to carry out those tests (regulation 9).

By regulation 10, the notifier of a new substance already notified by him is required to inform the competent authority of any changes to the particulars previously notified and of changes in the quantity of the substance placed on the market. In the case of a substance that had previously been notified at least 10 years previously only limited information need be provided (regulation 11).

By regulation 12, in the case of substances manufactured outside the European Communities for which more than one notification has been made the duty to notify additional information under regulation 5 is imposed on each notifier established in Northern Ireland unless the manufacturer has appointed a sole representative when that duty is only imposed on that sole representative if established in Northern Ireland.

By regulation 13, where a substance has already been notified under the Directive, the competent authority may agree that a subsequent notifier may make use of the particulars previously notified with the consent of the previous notifier. For the purpose of avoiding the duplication of animal testing, a prospective notifier of a new substance is required to enquire from the competent authority whether the substance which he intends to notify has already been notified to the competent authority of any member State. If this is the case the prospective notifier is required to try to reach agreement with the previous notifier to share information with a view to reducing the amount of animal testing.

By regulation 14, the notifier is required to ensure that any tests carried out for the purpose of these Regulations conform to the principles of good laboratory practice. By regulation 15 notifications and reports submitted to the competent authority for Northern Ireland are required to be in English.

Part III Rights and duties of the competent authority — Regulations 16 and 17

By regulation 16, in the case of notifications received, the competent authority is required to carry out and keep up to date an assessment of the risks to human health and the environment created by the substance.

By regulation 17, the competent authority is required to send information about notifications and reports received to the European Commission in relation to the substance concerned.

Part IV Disclosure of information — Regulations 18 to 20

By regulation 18, a notifier may ask that information that is commercially sensitive is kept confidential, but certain information specified in the regulation cannot be kept confidential. Regulation 19 sets out the way in which confidential information is to be treated and by regulation 20, in certain circumstances, a new substance which has been notified may appear in the European List of Notified Chemical Substances ("ELINCS") in the form of its trade name.

Part V   Miscellaneous and General — Regulations 21 to 25

Regulation 21 makes provision for enforcement and provides for the Department of Economic Development to be the enforcing authority for the Regulations. By regulation 22 the placing on the market of substances that have not been duly notified is prohibited. Regulation 23 provides for exemption from the requirements of the Regulations in certain circumstances, and regulation 24 specifies fees to be charged for specified purposes.

Regulation 25 revokes the Notification of New Substances Regulations (Northern Ireland) 1985 (as amended) and provides for consequential amendments to the Chemicals (Hazard Information and Packaging) Regulations (Northern Ireland) 1993. This regulation also contains transitional provisions. In addition regulation 25 amends regulation 19(3) of the Chemicals (Hazard Information and Packaging) Regulations (Northern Ireland) 1993 to conform with the enabling power contained in section 2(2) of the European Communities Act 1972.

A person who contravenes the Regulations is guilty of an offence under Article 31 of the Health and Safety at Work (Northern Ireland) Order 1978.

1994 No. 7

ROAD TRAFFIC AND VEHICLES

Control of Traffic (Belfast) (No. 2) Order (Amendment) Order (Northern Ireland) 1994

Made	*11th January 1994*
Coming into operation . .	*22nd February 1994*

WHEREAS the Department of the Environment has published a notice in compliance with Article 23(1) and (2) of the Road Traffic (Northern Ireland) Order 1981(**a**);

AND WHEREAS no objection or representation has been received;

NOW THEREFORE the Department, in exercise of the powers conferred on it by Article 21(1) of the Road Traffic (Northern Ireland) Order 1981 and of every other power enabling it in that behalf, makes the following Order:

Citation and commencement

1. This Order may be cited as the Control of Traffic (Belfast) (No. 2) Order (Amendment) Order (Northern Ireland) 1994 and shall come into operation on 22nd February 1994.

Amendment

2. The Control of Traffic (Belfast) (No. 2) Order (Northern Ireland) 1987(**b**) shall be amended as follows—

(1) After Article 4 add the following new Articles—

"*Compulsory left-hand turn*

5. Every person causing or permitting a vehicle to proceed in a north-westerly direction along Little Patrick Street, Belfast, on reaching its junction with Nelson Street shall, except upon the direction or with the permission of a constable in uniform or of a traffic warden, cause or permit that vehicle to make a left-hand turn into Nelson Street.

(**a**) S.I. 1981/154 (N.I. 1); *see* Article 2(2) for the definition of "Department"
(**b**) S.R. 1987 No. 159 to which there are amendments not relevant to this Order

Compulsory right-hand turn

6. Every person causing or permitting a vehicle to proceed in a south-easterly direction along Little Patrick Street, Belfast, on reaching its junction with Nelson Street shall, except upon the direction or with the permission of a constable in uniform or of a traffic warden, cause or permit that vehicle to make a right-hand turn into Nelson Street.''.

(2) In Schedules 2 and 3 delete the items relating to Little Patrick Street.

Sealed with the Official Seal of the Department of the Environment on 11th January 1994.

(L.S.)   *E. J. Galway*

                               Assistant Secretary

EXPLANATORY NOTE

(This note is not part of the Order.)

This Order amends the Control of Traffic (Belfast) (No. 2) Order (Northern Ireland) 1987 (S.R. 1987 No. 159).

The effect of the amendment is to provide for a compulsory left-hand turn into Nelson Street, Belfast, for vehicles travelling in a north-westerly direction along Little Patrick Street, and for a compulsory right-hand turn into Nelson Street for vehicles travelling in a south-easterly direction along Little Patrick Street.

Any person who acts in contravention of the Order shall be guilty of an offence and shall be liable on summary conviction to a fine not exceeding level 3 on the standard scale (£400).

Traffic signs indicating the effect of the Order will in due course be erected on the roads.

1994 No. 8

CONTRACTS OF EMPLOYMENT AND REDUNDANCY PAYMENTS

Redundancy Payments (Health and Personal Social Services) (Modification) Order (Northern Ireland) 1994

Made	*14th January 1994*
Coming into operation . .	*11th February 1994*

The Department of Economic Development(**a**), in exercise of the powers conferred on it by sections 58A(*a*) and 59(3) of the Contracts of Employment and Redundancy Payments Act (Northern Ireland) 1965(**b**) and of every other power enabling it in that behalf, hereby makes the following Order:

Citation and commencement

1.—(1) This Order may be cited as the Redundancy Payments (Health and Personal Social Services) (Modification) Order (Northern Ireland) 1994 and shall come into operation on 11th February 1994.

(2) In this Order—

"relevant event" means any event occurring on or after the coming into operation of this Order on the happening of which an employee may become entitled to a redundancy payment in accordance with the provisions of the Act;

"the Act" means the Contracts of Employment and Redundancy Payments Act (Northern Ireland) 1965.

Application of Order

2. This Order applies to any person who, immediately before the occurrence of the relevant event, is employed by an employer referred to in Schedule 1, for the purposes of determining the entitlement of any such person to a redundancy payment under Part II of the Act and the amount of such payment.

(**a**) Functions of the Ministry of Health and Social Services under the Contracts of Employment and Redundancy Payments Act (Northern Ireland) 1965 (1965 c. 19 (N.I.)) were transferred to the Department of Manpower Services by S.R. & O. (N.I.) 1973 No. 504 Article 6 and Schedule 3. The Department of Manpower Services is now known as the Department of Economic Development; *see* S.I. 1982/846 (N.I. 11) Article 3

(**b**) 1965 c. 19 (N.I.). Articles 58A and 59(3) were inserted by Article 108(1) of and paragraph 5(8) and (9) of Schedule 5 to the Industrial Relations (Northern Ireland) Order 1992, S.I. 1992/807 (N.I. 5)

Application of certain redundancy payments provisions with modifications

3. In relation to any person to whom this Order applies, the provisions of Part II of the Act mentioned in Schedule 2 shall have effect subject to the modifications specified in that Schedule.

Transitional, supplementary and incidental provisions

4.—(1) Without prejudice to section 11(1) of the Interpretation Act (Northern Ireland) 1954(**a**), any reference in any enactment (including the Act) to any provision of Part II of the Act shall have effect, in relation to any person to whom this Order applies, as a reference to that provision as modified by this Order.

(2) Any document which refers, whether specifically or by means of a general description, to an enactment which is modified by any provision of this Order shall, except so far as the context otherwise requires, be construed as referring or as including a reference to that provision.

(3) Where a period of employment of a person to whom this Order applies falls to be computed in accordance with the provisions of the Act as modified by this Order, the provisions of this Order shall have effect in relation to any period whether falling wholly or partly before or after the coming into operation of this Order.

Sealed with the Official Seal of the Department of Economic Development on 14th January 1994.

(L.S.)   *D. Gibson*

                                         Under Secretary

(**a**)   1954 c. 33 (N.I.)

Employers for the purposes of Article 2

1. A Health and Social Services Board established under Article 16 of the Health and Personal Social Services (Northern Ireland) Order 1972(**a**).

2. The Northern Ireland Central Services Agency for the Health and Social Services established by Article 26 of the Health and Personal Social Services (Northern Ireland) Order 1972.

3. A Health and Social Services trust established under Article 10 of the Health and Personal Social Services (Northern Ireland) Order 1991(**b**).

4. A special health and social services agency established under Article 3 of the Health and Personal Social Services (Special Agencies) (Northern Ireland) Order 1990(**c**).

(**a**)   S.I. 1972/1265 (N.I. 14)
(**b**)   S.I. 1991/194 (N.I. 1)
(**c**)   S.I. 1990/247 (N.I. 3)

SCHEDULE 2   Article 3

Modifications to certain redundancy payments provisions of the Act

1. Section 11 of the Act(**a**) shall have effect as if—

(*a*) in subsection (1) for the words "has been continuously employed for the requisite period" there were substituted the words "has been employed in relevant health and personal social services service for the requisite period"; and

(*b*) after subsection (2) there were inserted the following subsection:—

"(3) In this section and Schedule 3—

(*a*) "relevant health and personal social services service" means—

(i) continuous employment by an employer referred to in Schedule 3A, or

(ii) where immediately before the relevant event a person has been successively employed by two or more employers referred to in Schedule 3A, such aggregate period of service with such employers as would be continuous employment if they were a single employer;

(*b*) "relevant event" means any event occurring on or after the coming into operation of the Redundancy Payments (Health and Personal Social Services) (Modification) Order (Northern Ireland) 1994 on the happening of which an employee may become entitled to a redundancy payment in accordance with this Act.".

2. Section 12 of the Act(**b**) shall have effect as if immediately after subsection (6) there were inserted—

"(7) Any reference in this section to re-engagement by the employer shall be construed as including a reference to re-engagement by any employer referred to in Schedule 3A and any reference in this section to an offer by the employer shall be construed as including a reference to an offer made by any such employer.".

3. Section 13 of the Act(**c**) shall have effect as if immediately after subsection (10) there were inserted the following subsection—

"(11) Any reference in this section to re-engagement by the employer shall be construed as including a reference to re-engagement by any employer referred to in Schedule 3A and any reference in this section to an offer by the employer shall be construed as including a reference to an offer made by any such employer.".

(**a**) Section 11 was amended by Article 82(1) of and Part II of Schedule 5 to the Industrial Relations (Northern Ireland) Order 1976, S.I. 1976/1043 (N.I. 16)

(**b**) Section 12 was amended by Article 82(1) of and Part II of Schedule 5 to the Industrial Relations (Northern Ireland) Order 1976, S.I. 1976/1043 (N.I. 16) and by Article 14(1) of the Employment (Miscellaneous Provisions) (Northern Ireland) Order 1990, S.I. 1990/246 (N.I. 2)

(**c**) Section 13 was substituted by Article 82(1) of and Part II of Schedule 5 to the Industrial Relations (Northern Ireland) Order 1976, S.I. 1976/1043 (N.I. 16)

4. Schedule 3 to the Act(**a**) shall have effect as if for paragraph 1 there were substituted the following paragraph—

"1. The amount of a redundancy payment to which an employee is entitled in any case to which the Redundancy Payments (Health and Personal Social Services) (Modification) Order (Northern Ireland) 1994 applies shall, subject to the following provisions of this Schedule, be calculated by reference to the period ending with the relevant date during which he has been employed in relevant health and personal social services service.".

5. The Act shall have effect as if after Schedule 3 there were inserted the following Schedule—

"SCHEDULE 3A

Employers with which employment may constitute relevant health and personal social services service

Any employer described in Schedule 1 to the Redundancy Payments (Health and Personal Social Services) (Modification) Order (Northern Ireland) 1994 whether or not in existence at the time of the relevant event.".

(**a**) Schedule 3 was amended by Article 82(1) and (3) of, and Part II of Schedule 5 and Schedule 7 to, the Industrial Relations (Northern Ireland) Order 1976, S.I. 1976/1043 (N.I. 16), Article 25(2) of and Schedule 4 to the Industrial Relations (Northern Ireland) Order 1987, S.I. 1987/936 (N.I. 9), Article 14(2) of the Employment (Miscellaneous Provisions) (Northern Ireland) Order 1990, S.I. 1990/246 (N.I. 2), S.R. 1992 No. 75, and Article 108(3) of and Schedule 6 to the Industrial Relations (Northern Ireland) Order 1992, S.I. 1992/807 (N.I. 5)

EXPLANATORY NOTE

(This note is not part of the Order.)

This Order modifies certain redundancy payments provisions of the Contracts of Employment and Redundancy Payments Act (Northern Ireland) 1965 ("the Act") in their application to persons employed in relevant health and personal social services service (service with the employers referred to in Schedule 3A to the Act as modified by this Order) so that a change of employer does not break continuity for the purposes of the redundancy payments provisions of the Act.

1994   No. 9

CONTRACTS OF EMPLOYMENT AND REDUNDANCY PAYMENTS

Redundancy Payments (Local Government etc.) (Modification) (Amendment) Order (Northern Ireland) 1994

Made	*14th January 1994*
Coming into operation . .	*11th February 1994*

The Department of Economic Development(**a**), in exercise of the powers conferred on it by sections 58A(*a*) and 59(3) of the Contracts of Employment and Redundancy Payments Act (Northern Ireland) 1965(**b**) and of every other power enabling it in that behalf, hereby makes the following Order:

Citation, commencement and interpretation

1.—(1) This Order may be cited as the Redundancy Payments (Local Government etc.) (Modification) (Amendment) Order (Northern Ireland) 1994 and shall come into operation on 11th February 1994.

(2) In this Order the "principal Order" means the Redundancy Payments (Local Government etc.) (Modification) Order (Northern Ireland) 1986(**c**).

Amendments to the principal Order

2. The principal Order shall be amended as follows—

(*a*) in Article 1(2) in the definition of "relevant event" after the second reference to "the Act" there shall be added

"or, in relation to any person to whom this Order applies by reason of an amendment contained in the Redundancy Payments (Local Government etc.) (Modification) (Amendment) Order (Northern Ireland) 1994, any event occurring on or after the coming into operation of that Order on the happening of which an employee may become entitled to a redundancy payment in accordance with the provisions of the Act.";

(*b*) in Article 4(3) for the words "subject to paragraph (4)" there shall be substituted the words "Subject to paragraphs (4) and (5),";

(*c*) after Article 4(4) there shall be added—

(**a**) Functions of the Ministry of Health and Social Services under the Contracts of Employment and Redundancy Payments Act (Northern Ireland) 1965 (1965 c. 19 (N.I.)) were transferred to the Department of Manpower Services by S.R. & O. (N.I.) 1973 No. 504 Article 6 and Schedule 3. The Department of Manpower Services is now known as the Department of Economic Development; *see* S.I. 1982/846 (N.I. 11) Article 3

(**b**) 1965 c. 19 (N.I.). Articles 58A and 59(3) were inserted by Article 108(1) of and paragraph 5(8) and (9) of Schedule 5 to the Industrial Relations (Northern Ireland) Order 1992, S.I. 1992/807 (N.I. 5)

(**c**) S.R. 1986 No. 206 as amended by S.R. 1987 No. 28

"(5) Where a period of employment of a person to whom this Order applies by reason of an amendment contained in the Redundancy Payments (Local Government etc.) (Modification) (Amendment) Order (Northern Ireland) 1994 falls to be computed in accordance with the provisions of the Act as modified by this Order, the provisions of this Order shall have effect in relation to any period whether falling wholly or partly before or after the coming into operation of that Order.";

(*d*) in Schedule 1 for entry 30 there shall be substituted—

"30. The Fair Employment Commission for Northern Ireland.";

(*e*) in Schedule 1 after entry 35 there shall be added—

"36. Governors of the Armagh Observatory as defined in section 8 of the University and Collegiate and Scientific Institutions Act (Northern Ireland) 1938(**a**).

37. The Independent Commission for Police Complaints for Northern Ireland.

38. The Northern Ireland Schools Examinations and Assessment Council.

39. The Northern Ireland Curriculum Council.

40. The Council for Catholic Maintained Schools.".

Sealed with the Official Seal of the Department of Economic Development on 14th January 1994.

(L.S.)

D. Gibson

Under Secretary

(**a**) 1938 c. 18 (N.I.)

EXPLANATORY NOTE

(This note is not part of the Order.)

This Order, which comes into operation on 11th February 1994, amends the Redundancy Payments (Local Government etc.) (Modification) Order (Northern Ireland) 1986 as amended ("the 1986 Order"). The 1986 Order modifies certain redundancy payments provisions of the Contracts of Employment and Redundancy Payments Act (Northern Ireland) 1965 ("the 1965 Act"). The 1986 Order applies to persons who, immediately before the event on the happening of which they might become entitled to a redundancy payment, were employed by one of the employers listed in Schedule 1 to that Order. Such persons who have been successively employed by 2 or more of the employers referred to in paragraph 5 of Schedule 2 to that Order, will, for the purposes of determining their entitlement to a redundancy payment under the 1965 Act and the amount of such payment, have their service aggregated so that it counts as continuous employment.

This Order adds to the list of employers to whose employees the 1986 Order applies.

1994 No. 10

FISHERIES

Fisheries Amendment Byelaws (Northern Ireland) 1994

Made	*10th January 1994*
Coming into operation . .	*14th February 1994*

The Fisheries Conservancy Board for Northern Ireland, in exercise of the powers conferred on it by sections 26(1)(a) and 37(b) of the Fisheries Act (Northern Ireland) 1966(c) and of every other power enabling it in that behalf, with the approval of the Department of Agriculture hereby makes the following Byelaws:

Citation and commencement

1. These Byelaws may be cited as the Fisheries Amendment Byelaws (Northern Ireland) 1994 and shall come into operation on 14th February 1994.

Amendment of the Fisheries Consolidated and Amendment Byelaws (Northern Ireland) 1989

2. The Fisheries Consolidated and Amendment Byelaws (Northern Ireland) 1989(d) shall be amended as provided in Byelaw 3.

3. In Part II after Byelaw 15 there shall be inserted:—

"*Issue of tidal draft net licences*

15A.—(1) The maximum number of tidal draft net licences issued in any calendar year shall not exceed 6.

(2) An application for such a licence shall be received on or before 1st March in the calendar year to which the licence is to relate.

(3) Where an application for such a licence is received from a person to whom a licence was issued at any time during the period of 3 years preceding 31st December 1993, such an application shall be deemed to have been received before an application received from any other person.

(4) Where the number of applications for such licences received on or before 1st March in any calendar year exceeds 6, the licences shall, subject to paragraph (3), be issued according to the order in which applications for those licences were received.".

(a) As amended by S.I. 1991/1446 (N.I. 13) Article 8(3)
(b) As amended by S.I. 1991/1446 (N.I. 13) Article 9
(c) 1966 c. 17 (N.I.)
(d) S.R. 1989 No. 483 to which there are amendments not relevant to the subject matter of these Byelaws

Sealed with the Common Seal of the Fisheries Conservancy Board for Northern Ireland on 10th January 1994.

(L.S.)   *Dr. J. Parsons*

                                  Chairman

(L.S.)   *W. F. Smith*

                                  Secretary

The Department of Agriculture hereby approves the foregoing Byelaws.

Sealed with the Official Seal of the Department of Agriculture on 14th January 1994.

(L.S.)   *P. T. Toal*

                               Assistant Secretary

EXPLANATORY NOTE

(This note is not part of the Byelaws.)

These Byelaws further amend the Fisheries Consolidated and Amendment Byelaws (Northern Ireland) 1989.

Byelaw 3 prescribes the maximum number of licences for fishing with tidal draft nets which the Fisheries Conservancy Board for Northern Ireland may issue in any calendar year, provides for a closing date for receipt of applications for licences and for the priority in which licences are to be issued.

1994 No. 11

ANIMALS

Diseases of Animals (Modification) Order (Northern Ireland) 1994

Made	*14th January 1994*
Coming into operation . .	*21st February 1994*

The Department of Agriculture, being satisfied that the modification of Schedule 2 to the Diseases of Animals (Northern Ireland) Order 1981(a) ("the principal Order") set out in Articles 3 and 4 is necessary or expedient both for the purposes of the principal Order and this Order, in exercise of the powers conferred on it by Articles 2(3) and 16(2) of the principal Order and of every other power enabling it in that behalf, hereby makes the following Order:

Citation, commencement and interpretation

1.—(1) This Order may be cited as the Diseases of Animals (Modification) Order (Northern Ireland) 1994 and shall come into operation on 21st February 1994.

(2) In this Order "the principal Order" means the Diseases of Animals (Northern Ireland) Order 1981.

Diseases of animals

2. Part III of Schedule 1 to the principal Order(b) shall be modified by adding to the list of diseases of animals specified in that Part the following:—

"45. Porcine respiratory corona virus.

46. Epizootic haemorrhagic disease.".

Power to slaughter

3.—(1) Part I of Schedule 2 to the principal Order shall be modified as provided in paragraphs (2) and (3).

(2) Paragraph 5 shall be renumbered paragraph 5(1) and thereafter there shall be added—

"(2) The Department may cause to be slaughtered—

(*a*) any animal (other than cattle) affected or suspected of being affected with brucellosis; or

---

(a) S.I. 1981/1115 (N.I. 22)
(b) As modified by S.R. 1985 No. 64, S.R. 1988 No. 287, S.R. 1990 No. 135, S.R. 1991 No. 250, S.R. 1991 No. 456, S.R. 1992 No. 552 and S.R. 1993 No. 43

(*b*) any animal (including cattle) which is or has been in contact with an animal affected with brucellosis, or which appears to the Department to have been in any way exposed to the infection of brucellosis.''.

(3) After ''infectious bovine rhinotracheitis'' in the list of diseases specified in paragraph 10 (**a**) the following shall be added, that is to say—

''*Aujeszky's disease, Porcine respiratory corona virus, Contagious agalactia, Peste des petits ruminants, Goat pox, Vesicular stomatitis, Rift valley fever, Epizootic haemorrhagic disease.*''.

Compensation in respect of the slaughter of animals

4.—(1) Part II of Schedule 2 to the principal Order(**b**) shall be modified as provided in paragraphs (2) to (4).

(2) For paragraph 5 there shall be substituted the following paragraph—

''5. *Brucellosis:* (1) The compensation shall, in all or any cases where cattle are slaughtered in pursuance of an order under paragraph 5(1) of Part I, be such as is provided in that Order.

(2) The compensation shall, in all or any cases where animals are slaughtered in pursuance of paragraph 5(2) of Part I, be—

(*a*) if the animal was affected with brucellosis, one half of its value immediately before it became so affected; and

(*b*) in every other case, the value of the animal immediately before it was slaughtered.''.

(3) After ''infectious bovine rhinotracheitis'' in the list of diseases specified in paragraph 12 there shall be added—

''*Aujeszky's disease, Porcine respiratory corona virus, Contagious agalactia, Goat pox.*''.

(4) After paragraph 12A there shall be added—

''12B. *Peste des petits ruminants, Vesicular stomatitis, Rift valley fever, Epizootic haemorrhagic disease:*

The compensation shall—

(*a*) where the animal slaughtered was affected with any of the above diseases, be the value of the animal immediately before it became so affected; and

(*b*) in every other case be the value of the animal immediately before it was slaughtered.''.

Sealed with the Official Seal of the Department of Agriculture on 14th January 1994.

(L.S.) *P. T. Toal*

Assistant Secretary

(**a**) As modified by S.R. 1986 No. 79 Article 2(1)
(**b**) Relevant modifying Orders are S.R. 1986 No. 79 and S.R. 1990 No. 135

EXPLANATORY NOTE
(This note is not part of the Order.)

Article 2 of this Order further modifies Schedule 1 to the Diseases of Animals (Northern Ireland) Order 1981 ("the principal Order") by adding porcine respiratory corona virus and epizootic haemorrhagic disease to the list of diseases of animals in Part III of that Schedule. Of the diseases being so added epizootic haemorrhagic disease is being added to implement the notifiability requirements relating to that disease in Council Directive 92/119/EEC of 17th December 1992 introducing Community measures for the control of certain animal diseases and specific measures relating to swine vesicular disease (O.J. No. L62, 15.3.93, p. 69).

Article 3 further modifies Part I of Schedule 2 to the principal Order by extending the powers of the Department of Agriculture for Northern Ireland ("the Department") to slaughter animals so that it includes—

(a) any animal affected or suspected of being affected with Aujeszky's disease, porcine respiratory corona virus, contagious agalactia, peste des petits ruminants, goat pox, vesicular stomatitis, rift valley fever and epizootic haemorrhagic disease and, in the case of animals other than cattle, brucellosis; and

(b) any animal in contact with an animal affected by those diseases or in any way exposed to the infection of them.

The powers of the Department are being so extended in relation to peste des petits ruminants, goat pox, vesicular stomatitis, rift valley fever and epizootic haemorrhagic disease to implement the slaughter requirements relating to those diseases in Council Directive 92/119/EEC.

Article 4 further modifies Part II of Schedule 2 to the principal Order by extending the powers of the Department of Agriculture to pay compensation for any animals so slaughtered.

1994   No. 12

EDUCATION

**Colleges of Education (Grant Conditions) Regulations
(Northern Ireland) 1994**

Made	*17th January 1994*
Coming into operation . .	*7th February 1994*

The Department of Education, in exercise of the powers conferred on it by Articles 66(3), (4) and (5)(**a**) and 134(1)(**b**) of the Education and Libraries (Northern Ireland) Order 1986(**c**) and of every other power enabling it in that behalf, hereby makes the following Regulations:

Citation and commencement

1. These Regulations may be cited as the Colleges of Education (Grant Conditions) Regulations (Northern Ireland) 1994 and shall come into operation on 7th February 1994.

Revocations

2. The following Regulations are hereby revoked:

Training Colleges (Grant Conditions) Regulations (Northern Ireland) 1956(**d**);

Colleges of Education (Grant Conditions) Amending Regulations (Northern Ireland) 1968(**e**);

Colleges of Education (Grant Conditions) Amending Regulations (Northern Ireland) 1969(**f**);

Colleges of Education (Grant Conditions) Amending Regulations (Northern Ireland) 1970(**g**);

Colleges of Education (Grant Conditions) Amendment Regulations (Northern Ireland) 1976(**h**).

Interpretation

3. In these Regulations—

"agreement" means an agreement made between the trustees of a college and the Department conferring upon the Department the right to

---

(**a**) Article 66(4) to (11) was substituted by S.I. 1993/2810 (N.I. 12) Article 50(1) and Schedule 4 Part II
(**b**) As amended by S.I. 1993/2810 (N.I. 12) Article 50(1) and Schedule 4 Part II
(**c**) S.I. 1986/594 (N.I. 3)
(**d**) S.R. & O. (N.I.) 1956 No. 9 (p. 123)
(**e**) S.R. & O. (N.I.) 1968 No. 284
(**f**) S.R. & O. (N.I.) 1969 No. 160
(**g**) S.R. & O. (N.I.) 1970 No. 13
(**h**) S.R. 1976 No. 166

appoint, after consultation with the trustees, members to the Board of Governors of the college amounting to not more than one-third of the total number of members of the Board of Governors;

"college" means a college of education in respect of which grants are paid by the Department under Article 66(2) or (3) of the Order;

"premises" means premises in respect of which payment of grant has been or is to be made under these Regulations and includes land;

"replacement premises" in relation to a college means any premises which replace any existing premises of that or any other college;

"the Order" means the Education and Libraries (Northern Ireland) Order 1986.

Application for grant

4. An application for payment of grant in respect of approved expenditure incurred for the provision or alteration of the premises of a college or for the initial provision of equipment for such a college shall be made by the trustees in whom the ownership of the premises is, or is to be vested, and shall be in such form and contain such particulars and information as the Department may determine.

Amounts of grant

5.—(1) Where an agreement has been made the Department may, subject to these Regulations, pay grants to the trustees of a college in respect of approved expenditure incurred for—

(*a*) the provision of a new college; or

(*b*) the alteration of an existing college; or

(*c*) the initial provision of equipment for such new or existing college,

equal to eighty-five per cent of that expenditure.

(2) Where no agreement has been made, paragraph (1) shall have effect as if for the words "eighty-five per cent" there were substituted "sixty-five per cent".

(3) Without prejudice to the provisions of paragraphs (1) and (2) expenditure incurred for the replacement of equipment for a college shall be met in such manner as the Department may approve.

Grant conditions

6.—(1) No payments of grant shall be made to the trustees of a college under these Regulations unless—

(*a*) the premises are vested in approved trustees for an estate in fee simple or for such lesser estate as the Department shall deem sufficient upon trust irrevocable during the term of the said estate to maintain and carry on a college; and

(*b*) the trustees provide or undertake to provide such additional sum as will when added to the grant be sufficient in the opinion of the Department to meet the total amount of the approved expenditure.

(2) The Department may require that the trustees shall submit for its approval sketch plans, working drawings, specifications and tenders and furnish such other documents and information as the Department may specify with respect to any transactions or works in respect of which grant is sought.

(3) The trustees shall furnish or cause to be furnished to the Department all such receipts, architect's certificates or other documents as the Department may require for the purpose of vouching the approved expenditure in respect of which grant is to be paid.

(4) In accepting payment of a grant the trustees and each of them shall be deemed to have entered into a covenant with the Department binding upon the trustees and their successors in title for the due performance and observance of the following conditions so as to—

    (*a*) insure and keep insured the premises against loss or damage by fire or flood and against such other risks as the Department may direct, in some insurance office of repute for a sum equal to the replacement value thereof; and insure adequately against loss, damage and any accident caused by, or related to a boiler installed on the premises;

    (*b*) produce to the Department on request any policy of insurance for the time being in force and the receipt for the last premium due thereunder and, if any loss or damage by fire or flood or otherwise is caused to the premises or any part thereof, expend in re-building or reinstating such premises, all or so much of the money received under such policy of insurance as the Department may require.

(5) In the event of a breach of any of the conditions specified in this regulation the persons to whom grant was paid or their successors in title for the time being shall repay to the Department the full amount of grant or such lesser amount as the Department considers equitable.

Prohibition on use of the premises for political meetings etc

7. The trustees shall not cause or permit the premises to be used for political purposes, or for the transaction of any political business or for any purpose connected directly or indirectly with Parliamentary Northern Ireland Assembly or Local Government elections or a poll pursuant to section 1 of the Northern Ireland Constitution Act 1973(**a**) except as polling booths on the requisition of the officer responsible under the enactments governing such elections or poll as the case may be; provided that this regulation shall not prevent the holding on the premises of meetings of college societies in accordance with arrangements approved by the Board of Governors of the college.

Payment of grant

8.—(1) Except as provided for in paragraphs (2) and (3) no payment of grant shall be made in respect of expenditure incurred for the provision or alteration of the premises of a college without the prior approval of the Department or where works in relation to those premises have not been completed to the satisfaction of the Department.

(**a**) 1973 c. 36

(2) Where such expenditure has been incurred without the prior approval of the Department the payment of grant in respect of that expenditure may be reduced by such amount as the Department considers equitable in the circumstances.

(3) The Department may make payments of grant by instalments but the final instalment shall not be paid until all the work has been completed to the satisfaction of the Department and any defects liability period prescribed in any contract entered into by the trustees has expired.

Termination of an agreement

9.—(1) Subject to paragraphs (2) and (3) the trustees of a college or their successors in title for the time being may terminate an agreement by notice in writing given to the Department specifying the date (being a date not earlier than two years from the date on which such notice is given) on which the agreement is to terminate.

(2) On or before the date specified in accordance with paragraph (1) there shall be payable by the trustees or their successors in title for the time being to the Department an amount equal to the difference between the amount actually paid under Article 66(3) of the Order whilst the agreement is in force and the amount which would have been so paid if the agreement had not been in force.

(3) Where any amount has not been paid to the Department in accordance with paragraph (2) the agreement shall remain in force until that amount has been so paid.

Duty to pursue application for compensation under the Criminal Damage Compensation (Northern Ireland) Order 1977

10. Where the premises have been damaged in circumstances where compensation under the Criminal Damage Compensation (Northern Ireland) Order 1977(**a**) is likely to be payable the trustees shall take all reasonable steps to pursue an application under that Order and use any compensation paid (or such part thereof as the Department may require) for the purpose of reinstating the premises.

Amounts payable to the Department in respect of a college closure

11. Where any premises in respect of which the Department has paid grant under Article 66(3) of the Order cease to be used for approved purposes of a college there shall be payable to the Department by the persons to whom grant was paid or by their successors in title for the time being such sum as the Department considers equitable but not exceeding—

(*a*) in respect of grants paid prior to 2nd August 1984 and within a period of 50 years from the date of payment of grant (or where the grant is payable by instalments from the date of payment of the first instalment) either—

(**a**) S.I. 1977/1247 (N.I. 14)

    (i) the total amount of grant paid in respect of approved expenditure incurred for the provision or alteration of the premises; or

    (ii) such proportion of the value of the premises as the proportion that the amount of grant was of the approved cost of the provision or alteration of the premises,

    whichever is the lesser.

  (*b*) in respect of grant paid at any time after 1st August 1984—

    (i) such proportion of the value of the premises as the proportion that the amount of grant was of the approved costs of the provision or alteration of the premises; and

    (ii) if the Department so determines, interest on that sum from the date on which the premises ceased to be used for approved purposes of a college until the date of payment to the Department.

Amounts payable to the Department in respect of certain sites

12. Where any site in respect of which the Department has at any time after 1st August 1984 paid grant under Article 66(3) of the Order ceases in the opinion of the Department to be required for the purposes of a college there shall be payable to the Department by the persons to whom the grant was paid or by their successors in title for the time being such sum as the Department considers equitable but not exceeding—

  (*a*) such proportion of the value of the site as the proportion that the amount of grant was of the approved cost of the acquisition of the site; and

  (*b*) if the Department so determines, interest on that sum from the date on which the site ceased to be so required until the date of payment to the Department.

Amount of grant in respect of a replacement college

13.—(1) Where the Department proposes to pay grant under Article 66(3) of the Order in respect of expenditure incurred for the provision or alteration of the premises of a college and in the opinion of the Department the premises provided or altered are replacement premises the Department may—

  (*a*) where the proceeds resulting from the disposal of the replaced premises are realised before expenditure is incurred for the provision or alteration of the replacement premises, reduce the amount of grant so payable by such amount as the Department considers equitable;

  (*b*) where the replaced premises continue to be used for approved purposes of a college until such time as expenditure is incurred for the provision or alteration of the replacement premises, require that when the replaced premises cease to be so used the persons to whom the grant was paid or their successors in title for the time being shall pay to the Department such amount as it considers equitable.

  (2) The amount by which grant may be reduced under paragraph (1)(*a*) or the amount payable to the Department under paragraph (1)(*b*) shall consist of a sum not exceeding—

(*a*) such proportion of the value of the replaced premises as the proportion that the amount of grant is or was of the approved cost of the provision or alteration of the replacement premises; and

(*b*) if the Department so determines, interest on that sum from the date on which the replaced premises ceased to be used for approved purposes of a college until the date of the payment of a grant under paragraph (1)(*a*) or, as the case may be, the payment to the Department under paragraph (1)(*b*).

14. For the purposes of regulations 11, 12 and 13—

(*a*) the value of the premises or a site shall be the amount which the premises or site might be expected to realise if sold on the open market on the date on which the premises ceased to be used or the site ceased to be required for the purposes of a college and where the Department certifies that it is not possible to reach agreement as to such value, the dispute as to such value shall be referred to and determined by the Lands Tribunal for Northern Ireland;

(*b*) in the calculation of either the amount by which the grant may be reduced or the amount payable to the Department as appropriate there shall be taken into account such costs incurred by the persons to whom grant was paid or by their successors in title for the time being as the Department determines are reasonable;

(*c*) interest shall be at the rate of 8 per cent per annum.

Recovery of sums payable to the Department

15. Any sum payable to the Department under these Regulations may be recovered by it as a civil debt.

Sealed with the Official Seal of the Department of Education on 17th January 1994.

(L.S.)   *J. A. Mills (Miss)*
                                                  Assistant Secretary

EXPLANATORY NOTE
(This note is not part of the Regulations.)

These Regulations revoke the Training Colleges (Grant Conditions) Regulations (Northern Ireland) 1956, as amended. The Regulations relate to voluntary colleges of education and in particular—

(*a*) provide that where an agreement has been made between the trustees of a college and the Department in regard to the appointment of the Board of Governors then the Department may pay grant equal to eighty-five per cent of approved expenditure incurred for the provision of a new college, the alteration of an existing college or the initial provision of certain equipment; and where no agreement has been made between the trustees of the college and the Department in regard to the appointment of the Board of Governors, the Department may pay grant equal to sixty-five per cent of such approved expenditure (regulation 5);

(*b*) prescribe the conditions under which grants may be made by the Department of Education in respect of expenditure incurred for the provision or alteration of the premises of a voluntary college of education (regulation 6);

(*c*) prohibit, subject to an exception, the use of the premises for political meetings or the transaction of political business and restrict the use of the premises for any purpose connected with elections (regulation 7);

(*d*) provide that expenditure must, except under certain circumstances, be approved by the Department before it is incurred and that payments of grant may be made by instalments if certain conditions are satisfied (regulation 8);

(*e*) provide for repayment of grant where the trustees of a college or their successors in title terminate an agreement between them and the Department (regulation 9);

(*f*) require in certain circumstances that the trustees pursue an application for compensation under the Criminal Damage Compensation (Northern Ireland) Order 1977 and to use compensation received to reinstate the premises (regulation 10);

(*g*) provide that where premises cease to be used as a college, or where a site ceases to be so required, certain sums are payable to the Department by the persons to whom grant was paid or by their successors in title (regulations 11 and 12);

(*h*) provide for reduction or repayment of grant where grant is paid towards expenditure to replace existing premises (regulation 13);

(*i*) provide for the recovery of sums payable to the Department (regulation 15).

1994   No. 13

EDUCATION

Schools (Expulsion of Pupils) (Appeal Tribunals) Regulations (Northern Ireland) 1994

Made	*17th January 1994*
Coming into operation . .	*17th February 1994*

The Department of Education, in exercise of the powers conferred on it by Articles 49(10)(**a**) and 134(1)(**b**) of the Education and Libraries (Northern Ireland) Order 1986(**c**) and of every other power enabling it in that behalf, hereby makes the following Regulations:

Citation and commencement

1. These Regulations may be cited as the Schools (Expulsion of Pupils) (Appeal Tribunals) Regulations (Northern Ireland) 1994 and shall come into operation on 17th February 1994.

Interpretation

2. In these Regulations—

"appeal" means an appeal by virtue of Article 49(6) of the 1986 Order and "appellant" shall be construed accordingly;

"board" means the education and library board for the area in which the school from which the pupil was expelled is situated;

"school" means a grant-aided school.

Constitution of appeal tribunals

3. An appeal tribunal shall be constituted in accordance with Schedule 1.

Procedure of appeal tribunals

4. Schedule 2 shall have effect in relation to the procedure on appeals.

Sealed with the Official Seal of the Department of Education on 17th January 1994.

(L.S.)

J. S. Smith
Assistant Secretary

(**a**)   As substituted by S.I. 1993/2810 (N.I. 12) Article 39
(**b**)   As amended by S.I. 1993/2810 (N.I. 12) Article 50(1) and Schedule 4 Part II
(**c**)   S.I. 1986/594 (N.I. 3)

SCHEDULE 1

1. Subject to the provisions of this Schedule, an appeal tribunal shall consist of three or five members selected by the board or, on behalf of the board, by the Chief Executive of the board or his nominee from a panel of persons appointed by the board under paragraph 2; and sufficient persons may be appointed to enable two or more appeal tribunals to sit at the same time.

2. The panel of persons appointed by the board to act as members of appeal tribunals shall comprise—

(*a*) persons appearing to the board to represent the interests of controlled schools in the area of the board;

(*b*) persons appearing to the board, after consultation with the Council for Catholic Maintained Schools and such other bodies as the board considers appropriate, to represent the interests of voluntary schools in the area of the board and persons appearing to the board to represent the interests of grant-maintained integrated schools in the area of the board;

(*c*) persons who have experience in education, are acquainted with the educational arrangements in the area of the board or are parents of registered pupils at a school,

but shall not include any person employed by the board otherwise than as a full-time teacher.

3. The membership of an appeal tribunal shall comprise—

(*a*) at least one person falling within the category of persons mentioned in paragraph 2(*a*);

(*b*) at least one person falling within the category of persons mentioned in paragraph 2(*b*);

(*c*) at least one person falling within the category of persons mentioned in paragraph 2(*c*).

4. The members of an appeal tribunal shall elect one of their number to be chairman of the tribunal.

5. A person shall not be a member of an appeal tribunal for the consideration of an appeal against a decision if he was among those who made the decision or took part in discussions as to whether the decision should be made.

6. A person who is a teacher at a school shall not be a member of an appeal tribunal for the consideration of an appeal involving a question as to whether or not a pupil should be re-admitted to that school.

SCHEDULE 2   Regulation 4

1. An appeal shall be by notice in writing setting out the grounds on which it is made.

2. Two or more appeal tribunals may sit at the same time.

3. Where the issues raised by two or more appeals are substantially similar or connected the board may determine that those appeals be combined and dealt with in the same proceedings.

4. An appeal tribunal shall give to the appellant an opportunity to make written representations and an opportunity of appearing and making oral representations and may allow the appellant to be accompanied by a friend or to be represented.

5. An appeal tribunal shall give to the expelling authority an opportunity to make written representations and shall give a representative of the expelling authority an opportunity of appearing and of making oral representations.

6. An appeal tribunal may request the expelling authority to supply it with relevant information including information about the procedures followed in relation to the expulsion of pupils from the school.

7. In considering the appeal, the appeal tribunal shall have regard in particular to any representations made to it under paragraph 4 or 5 and to whether the procedures in relation to the expulsion of pupils from the school were properly followed.

8. The board shall set time limits for the hearing and determination of appeals and in setting those limits shall have regard to the need to secure that appeals are disposed of without delay.

9. An appeal shall be heard in private except where the board determines otherwise.

10. In the event of disagreement among the members of an appeal tribunal the appeal under consideration shall be decided by a simple majority of the votes cast.

11. The decision of an appeal tribunal and the grounds on which that decision was made shall be communicated by the tribunal in writing to the appellant and to the expelling authority.

12. Subject to paragraphs 1 to 11, all matters relating to the procedure on appeals, including the time within which they are to be brought, shall be determined by the board.

EXPLANATORY NOTE

(This note is not part of the Regulations.)

Under Article 49(6) of the Education and Libraries (Northern Ireland) Order 1986, as substituted by Article 39 of the Education and Libraries (Northern Ireland) Order 1993, the parent of a pupil or the pupil himself, if he has attained the age of eighteen, may appeal to an appeal tribunal against a decision to expel him from a grant-aided school. These Regulations provide for the constitution and procedure of such appeal tribunals.

Regulation 2 contains definitions.

Regulation 3 provides that an appeal tribunal shall be constituted in accordance with Schedule 1 and regulation 4 provides for the procedure on appeals to be in accordance with Schedule 2.

Paragraphs 1 to 3 of Schedule 1 relate to the selection, appointment, size and membership of appeal tribunals. Paragraph 4 provides for the election of a chairman of an appeal tribunal. Paragraphs 2, 5 and 6 disqualify certain persons or descriptions of persons from membership of an appeal tribunal.

Paragraph 1 of Schedule 2 deals with the initiation of appeals. Paragraph 2 provides for two or more appeal tribunals to sit at the same time. Paragraph 3 prescribes the circumstances in which two or more appeals may be combined. Paragraph 4 provides for the appellant to make written representations and to appear before an appeal tribunal to make oral representations, and to be accompanied at the hearing or to be represented. Paragraph 5 provides for the education and library board ("the board"), in the case of a pupil expelled from a controlled school in the area of that board, or the Board of Governors, in the case of a pupil expelled from any other grant-aided school, by or on whose behalf the decision under appeal was taken, to make written representations and to nominate a representative to appear before an appeal tribunal to make oral representations. Paragraph 6 allows the tribunal to request information from the board or from the Board of Governors by or on whose behalf the decision under appeal was taken. Paragraph 7 requires the tribunal, when considering the appeal, to take into account the representations made by or on behalf of the appellant and the board or the Board of Governors and to have regard to whether the correct procedures were followed when expelling the pupil from the school. Paragraph 8 provides for time limits to be set on the hearing and determination of appeals. Paragraph 9 provides for appeals to be heard in private except where the board determines otherwise. Paragraph 10 states how a decision is to be reached in the event of disagreement among the members of an appeal tribunal. Paragraph 11 prescribes how and to whom the decision of an appeal tribunal is to be communicated. Paragraph 12 provides for all other matters relating to the procedure on appeals, including the time within which they are to be brought, to be determined by the board.

1994   No. 14

Temporary Speed Limit (Motorway M1)
Order (Northern Ireland) 1994

This Order, being of a temporary character, is not printed at length in this volume.

1994   Nos. 15, 16

These Orders have been exempted from printing by the Statutory Rules (Northern Ireland) Order 1979. Summaries are given in the List of Statutory Rules of a Local Character under the heading ROADS.

1994 No. 17 (C. 1)

PENSIONS

The Pension Schemes (1993 Act) (Commencement No. 1) Order (Northern Ireland) 1994

| *Made* | . | . | . | . | . | *19th January 1994* |

The Department of Health and Social Services, in exercise of the powers conferred on it by section 186(2) and (3) of the Pension Schemes (Northern Ireland) Act 1993(**a**) and of all other powers enabling it in that behalf, hereby makes the following order:

Citation and interpretation

1.—(1) This order may be cited as the Pension Schemes (1993 Act) (Commencement No. 1) Order (Northern Ireland) 1994.

(2) In this order any reference to a numbered section or Schedule is a reference to the section of, or, as the case may be, the Schedule to, the Pension Schemes (Northern Ireland) Act 1993.

(3) The Interpretation Act (Northern Ireland) 1954(**b**) shall apply to this order as it applies to a Measure of the Northern Ireland Assembly.

Appointed day

2. The day appointed for the coming into operation of the Pension Schemes (Northern Ireland) Act 1993, with the exception of—

(*a*) Part II of Schedule 4 (provisions relating to equal access) and section 182(1) so far as it relates to it; and

(*b*) Schedule 6 (re-enactment or amendment of certain provisions not in force) and section 184 so far as it relates to it,

is 7th February 1994.

Sealed with the Official Seal of the Department of Health and Social Services on 19th January 1994.

(L.S.)   *R. McMurray*
                                                  Assistant Secretary

---

(**a**) 1993 c. 49
(**b**) 1954 c. 33 (N.I.)

EXPLANATORY NOTE

(This note is not part of the Order.)

This order brings into operation on 7th February 1994, subject to minor exceptions, the Pension Schemes (Northern Ireland) Act 1993 ("the Act"). The exceptions are Part II of Schedule 4 (repeal of equal access requirements) and Schedule 6 (re-enactment or amendment of certain provisions not in force).

The Act, which consolidates in relation to Northern Ireland certain enactments relating to pension schemes, includes some provisions which are not yet in operation or not fully in operation. Schedule 8 to the Act identifies those provisions and makes transitory modifications. In particular paragraph 3(1) of that Schedule provides that sections 98 to 103 relating to annual increases of pensions in payment (limited price indexation) shall have effect only for the purposes of section 104. Paragraphs 2 and 4 to 8, which deal with the rule against perpetuities, guaranteed minimum pensions for women paying reduced rate contributions, judicial pensions and friendly societies, omit, or in the case of paragraph 7, substitute, certain words in the Act until the day appointed for the coming into operation of those provisions.

1994 No. 18

ROAD TRAFFIC AND VEHICLES

Road Traffic (Third-Party Risks) Order (Northern Ireland) 1994

Made	*19th January 1994*
Coming into operation . .	*1st March 1994*

The Department of the Environment, in exercise of the powers conferred on it by Article 90(2)(*b*) of the Road Traffic (Northern Ireland) Order 1981(**a**) and of all other powers enabling it in that behalf, hereby makes the following Order:

Citation and commencement

1. This Order may be cited as the Road Traffic (Third-Party Risks) Order (Northern Ireland) 1994 and shall come into operation on 1st March 1994.

Amendment of the 1981 Order

2. In Article 90(2)(*b*) of the Road Traffic (Northern Ireland) Order 1981 (which removes the requirement for third-party insurance or security where £15,000 is kept deposited with the Accountant-General of the Supreme Court of Northern Ireland), for "£15,000" there shall be substituted "£500,000".

Sealed with the Official Seal of the Department of the Environment on 19th January 1994.

(L.S.)   *Trevor Pearson*
                                             Assistant Secretary

---

(**a**)   S.I. 1981/154 (N.I. 1); *see* Article 2(2) for the definition of "Department"

EXPLANATORY NOTE

(This note is not part of the Order.)

Article 90(2)(*b*) of the Road Traffic (Northern Ireland) Order 1981 removes the requirement of the user of a motor vehicle to have third-party insurance or security, provided £15,000 is kept deposited with the Accountant-General of the Supreme Court of Northern Ireland. This Order increases that amount to £500,000.

1994 No. 19

This Order has been exempted from printing by the Statutory Rules (Northern Ireland) Order 1979. A summary is given in the List of Statutory Rules of a Local Character under the heading ROADS.

1994   No. 20

WATER AND SEWERAGE

The Prevention of Pollution (Erne System) Regulations (Northern Ireland) 1994

Made	.	.	.	.	*20th January 1994*
Coming into operation		.	.		*1st April 1994*

Whereas it appears to the Department of the Environment expedient to make provision for prohibiting or restricting the keeping or use on waterways of vessels provided with sanitary appliances from which polluting matter passes or can pass into the waterway;

AND WHEREAS the Department has published a notice in compliance with paragraph 1 of Schedule 2 to the Water Act (Northern Ireland) 1972(**a**);

AND WHEREAS no objection has been received;

NOW THEREFORE the Department, in exercise of the powers conferred by section 12 of the Water Act (Northern Ireland) 1972 and now vested in it(**b**) and of every other power enabling it in that behalf, makes the following regulations:

Citation and commencement

1. These regulations may be cited as the Prevention of Pollution (Erne System) Regulations (Northern Ireland) 1994 and shall come into operation on 1st April 1994.

Interpretation

2. In these regulations—

"Erne System" means Upper and Lower Lough Erne and such portions of the River Erne and the tributaries of both of the Loughs as are in Northern Ireland and including all locks, quays, jetties, harbours and canals;

"hirer" means any person to whom a vessel shall be on hire or any person in charge thereof by the appointment or with the permission of the owner.

(**a**)   1972 c. 5 (N.I.); Sch. 2 was amended by para 13 of Sch. 3 to the Water and Sewerage Services (Northern Ireland) Order 1973 (S.I. 1973/70 (N.I. 2))

(**b**)   S.R. & O. (N.I.) 1973 No. 504 Art. 4

Application

3. These regulations shall apply to all vessels first licensed or registered on or after 1st April 1994 with the Department of Agriculture under the Lough Erne (Navigation) Bye-laws (Northern Ireland) 1978(**a**) and to all other vessels from 1st April 1996.

Prohibition on use of certain vessels

4. No person being the owner or the hirer shall keep or use or knowingly permit to be kept or used on the Erne System any vessel provided with a sanitary appliance of such a design that polluting matter passes or can pass into a waterway.

Penalties

5. Any person who contravenes regulation 4 shall be guilty of an offence and liable on summary conviction to a fine not exceeding £1,000.

Sealed with the Official Seal of the Department of the Environment on 20th January 1994.

(L.S.) *J. McConnell*

Assistant Secretary

(**a**) S.R. 1978 No. 43; relevant amending bye-laws are S.R. 1986 No. 1

EXPLANATORY NOTE

(This note is not part of the Regulations.)

These regulations shall apply to all vessels first licensed or registered on or after 1st April 1994 with the Department of Agriculture under the Lough Erne (Navigation) Bye-laws (Northern Ireland) 1978 and to all other vesssels from the 1st April 1996 (regulation 3).

The regulations prohibit the keeping or use on the Erne System of vessels that can discharge the contents of their sanitary appliances (toilets) directly into the water (regulation 4).

Any person who acts in contravention of the regulations shall be guilty of an offence and shall be liable on summary conviction to a fine not exceeding £1,000 (regulation 5).

1994   No. 21

SOCIAL SECURITY

The Social Security (Adjudication) (Amendment) Regulations (Northern Ireland) 1994

Made	*21st January 1994*
Coming into operation . .	*28th February 1994*

The Department of Health and Social Services for Northern Ireland, in exercise of the powers conferred on it by sections 25(1)(*b*), 30(8), 33(10) and 59(1) and (2) of the Social Security Administration (Northern Ireland) Act 1992(**a**) and of all other powers enabling it in that behalf, and after agreement by the Social Security Advisory Committee that the proposals to make these regulations need not be referred to it(**b**), hereby makes the following regulations:

Citation, commencement and interpretation

1.—(1) These regulations may be cited as the Social Security (Adjudication) (Amendment) Regulations (Northern Ireland) 1994 and shall come into operation on 28th February 1994.

(2) The Interpretation Act (Northern Ireland) 1954(**c**) shall apply to these regulations as it applies to a Measure of the Northern Ireland Assembly.

Amendment of the Social Security (Adjudication) Regulations

2.—(1) The Social Security (Adjudication) Regulations (Northern Ireland) 1987(**d**) shall be amended in accordance with paragraphs (2) and (3).

(2) In regulation 64A(**e**) (date from which revised decision has effect on a review in specified circumstances)—

(*a*) in paragraph (3) at the beginning there shall be inserted "Subject to paragraph (3A),"; and

(*b*) after paragraph (3) there shall be inserted the following paragraph—

"(3A) A determination on a claim or question shall not be revised on review, in consequence of a determination by a Commissioner in another case that a decision of an adjudicating authority was erroneous in point of law, under section 23(2) or 28(2)(*d*) of the Administration Act so as to make benefit payable or to increase the amount of benefit

---

(**a**) 1992 c. 8
(**b**) *See* section 150(1)(*b*) of the Social Security Administration (Northern Ireland) Act 1992
(**c**) 1954 c. 33 (N.I.)
(**d**) S.R. 1987 No. 82; relevant amending regulations are S.R. 1987 No. 466, S.R. 1988 No. 369, S.R. 1991 No. 406 and S.R. 1992 Nos. 36 and 83
(**e**) Regulation 64A was inserted by regulation 2(2) of S.R. 1991 No. 406 and amended by regulation 12(3) of S.R. 1992 No. 36

payable in respect of that claim or question for any period prior to the date of that Commissioner's determination.".

(3) In regulations 65(3), 66(1), 69(1) as continued in operation by regulation 10 of the Social Security (Adjudication) (Amendment No. 2) Regulations (Northern Ireland) 1987(a) and as amended by regulation 8 of those regulations, and 71 for "regulation 64A(2) or (3)" there shall be substituted "regulation 64A(2), (3) or (3A)".

Sealed with the Official Seal of the Department of Health and Social Services for Northern Ireland on 21st January 1994.

(L.S.)   *W. G. Purdy*
                                                          Assistant Secretary

---

(a)   S.R. 1987 No. 466

EXPLANATORY NOTE

(This note is not part of the Regulations.)

These regulations amend regulation 64A of the Social Security (Adjudication) Regulations (Northern Ireland) 1987 to ensure that a decision on a claim or question shall not be revised on review so as to make benefit payable or increase the amount of benefit payable in respect of that claim or question for any period before the date of the Commissioner's decision on which the review was based.

Some consequential amendments are also made.

1994 No. 22

ROAD AND RAILWAY TRANSPORT

Bus Permits (Designated Bodies) (Northern Ireland) Order 1994

Made	*24th January 1994*
Coming into operation . .	*1st March 1994*

The Department of the Environment, in exercise of the powers conferred on it by section 10B(6) of the Transport Act (Northern Ireland) 1967(**a**), and of all other powers enabling it in that behalf, and it appearing to the Department that the bodies designated under Article 2(1) are bodies concerned with education, religion, social welfare, recreation, or other activities to the benefit of the community, hereby makes the following Order:

Citation and commencement

1. This Order may be cited as the Bus Permits (Designated Bodies) (Northern Ireland) Order 1994 and shall come into operation on 1st March 1994.

Designated bodies

2.—(1) The bodies specified in column (2) of the Schedule are hereby designated for the purposes of section 10B(6) of the Transport Act (Northern Ireland) 1967 as entitled to grant permits in relation to the use of a small bus.

(2) A body designated in said column (2) may grant permits to the classes of body specified in relation thereto in column (3).

Returns

3. Every designated body which grants permits shall send to the Department—

(*a*) a copy of every such permit, and

(*b*) particulars of any variation or revocation of every such permit

within one month of the grant, variation or revocation as the case may be.

Sealed with the Official Seal of the Department of the Environment on 24th January 1994.

(L.S.)   *Trevor Pearson*
Assistant Secretary

(**a**) 1967 c. 37 (N.I.); Article 10B was inserted by Article 3 of S.I. 1990/994 (N.I. 7). The functions of the Ministry of Development under the Transport Act (Northern Ireland) 1967 transferred to the Department of the Environment under Article 4 of S.R. & O. (N.I.) 1973 No. 504

SCHEDULE   (see Article 2(1))

(1) *Item No.*	(2) *Designated Bodies*	(3) *Classes of Bodies to whom the Designated Body may grant permits*
1.	The Education and Library Boards established under Article 3 of the Education and Libraries (Northern Ireland) Order 1986(**a**)	Schools or other bodies which enable the designated body to carry out its functions under said Order.
2.	The Health and Social Services Boards established under Article 16 of the Health and Personal Social Services (Northern Ireland) Order 1972(**b**)	Voluntary organisations to whom the designated body may make grants under Article 71 of the said Order.
3.	District councils established under section 1 of the Local Government Act (Northern Ireland) 1972(**c**)	(*a*) Bodies which are established to provide an educational, recreational, religious, social or welfare facility within the area of the council. (*b*) Bodies which operate wholly or mainly within the area of the council and whose primary purpose is to promote social welfare.

(**a**)   S.I. 1986/594 (N.I. 3)
(**b**)   S.I. 1972/1265 (N.I. 14) as amended by S.I. 1991/194 (N.I. 1)
(**c**)   1972 c. 9

(1)	(2)	(b)	(3)
Item No.	*Designated Body* *(a)* *Name*	*Address of main or only administrative centre, or registered office*	*Classes of Bodies to whom the Designated Body may grant permits*
4.	Age Concern Northern Ireland	6 Lower Crescent BELFAST BT7 1NR	Bodies comprised in the designated body.
5.	Apostolic Church of Northern Ireland	113 Great Victoria Street BELFAST BT2 7AH	Bodies which are members of the designated body.
6.	Association of Local Authorities of Northern Ireland	123 York Street BELFAST BT15 1AB	Bodies which are members of or associated with the designated body.
7.	Baptist Union of Ireland	117 Lisburn Road BELFAST BT9 7AF	Bodies which are comprised in or members of the designated body.
8.	Barnardos	414 Antrim Road BELFAST BT15 5GA	Bodies comprised in the designated body.
9.	The Boys' Brigade in Northern Ireland	Boys' Brigade House 14 May Street BELFAST BT1 4NR	Bodies comprised in the designated body.
10.	British Red Cross Society	87 University Street BELFAST BT7 1HP	Bodies comprised in the designated body.
11.	Children's Project (Northern Ireland)	301 Antrim Road BELFAST BT15 2HF	Bodies comprised in the designated body.
12.	Church of Ireland (Diocese of Armagh)	Church House 46 Abbey Street Armagh	Bodies which are members of the designated body.
13.	Church of Ireland (Diocese of Clogher)	The rectory Rossfad Ballinamallard	Bodies which are members of the designated body.
14.	Church of Ireland (Diocesan Office for the Dioceses of Connor and Down and Dromore)	12 Talbot Street BELFAST BT1 2LE	Bodies which are members of the designated body.

(1)	(2)		(3)
Item No.	*Designated Body* *(a)* *Name*	*(b)* *Address of main or only administrative centre, or registered office*	*Classes of Bodies to whom the Designated Body may grant permits*
15.	Church of Ireland (Diocese of Derry and Raphoe)	Diocesan Office London Street Londonderry	Bodies which are members of the designated body.
16.	Community Relations in Schools	412 Newtownards Road BELFAST BT4 1HH	Bodies comprised in the designated body.
17.	The Corrymeela Community	BALLYCASTLE Co. Antrim BT54 6QU	Bodies comprised in the designated body.
18.	Department of Economic Development (Training and Employment Agency)	Clarendon House 9/21 Adelaide Street BELFAST BT2 8DJ	(*a*) Bodies comprised in the designated body. (*b*) Employment and Training bodies funded by the Agency.
19.	Disability Action	2 Annadale Avenue BELFAST BT7 3JR	Bodies which are comprised in or members of the designated body.
20.	The Extern Organisation	5-11 Verner Street BELFAST BT7 2AA	Bodies which are comprised in, members of, or affiliated to the designated body.
21.	Hunterhouse College (Private)	Finaghy BELFAST BT10 0LE	Bodies comprised in the designated body.
22.	The Methodist Church in Ireland	1 Fountainville Avenue BELFAST BT9 6AN	Bodies which are members of or associated with the designated body.
23.	National Federation of Gateway Clubs	4 Annadale Avenue BELFAST BT7 3JH	Bodies comprised in the designated body.

(1) Item No.	(2) Designated Body (a) Name	(b) Address of main or only administrative centre, or registered office	(3) Classes of Bodies to whom the Designated Body may grant permits
24.	Northern Ireland Association for the Care and Resettlement of Offenders	169 Ormeau Road BELFAST BT7 1SQ	Bodies comprised in the designated body.
25.	PHAB (Northern Ireland) Limited	25 Alexander Gardens BELFAST BT15 3LJ	Bodies affiliated to the designated body.
26.	Police Authority for Northern Ireland	River House High Street BELFAST BT1 2QB	Bodies which are comprised in or members of the designated body.
27.	The Presbyterian Church in Ireland	Church House Fisherwick Place BELFAST BT1 6DW	Bodies which are members of or associated with the designated body.
28.	The Free Presbyterian Church of Ulster	C/o Martyrs Memorial Free Presbyterian Church 356 Ravenhill Road BELFAST BT6	Bodies which are members of or associated with the designated body.
29.	Queen's University of Belfast	University Road BELFAST BT7 1NN	Bodies comprised in the designated body.
30.	The Royal Society for Mentally Handicapped Children and Adults (MENCAP)	Segal House 4 Annadale Avenue BELFAST BT7 3JH	Bodies comprised in the designated body.
31.	Royal Society for the Protection of Birds	The Lodge Sandy BEDFORDSHIRE SG19 2DL	Bodies consisting of members of the society established as branches of the society in accordance with the societies charter and statutes made thereunder.
32.	St. John Ambulance	Erne Purdysburn Hospital Saintfield Road BELFAST BT8 8RA	Bodies comprised in the designated body.

(1)	(2)		(3)
Item No.	*Designated Body* *(a)* *Name*	*(b)* *Address of main or only administrative centre, or registered office*	*Classes of Bodies to whom the Designated Body may grant permits*
33.	St. Mary's College	191 Falls Road BELFAST BT12 6FE	Bodies comprised in the designated body.
34.	The Salvation Army Ireland Division	4 Curtis Street BELFAST BT1 2ND	Bodies comprised in the designated body.
35.	Save the Children Fund Northern Ireland	Popper House 41 Wellington Park BELFAST BT9 6DN	Bodies which are comprised in, members of, or affiliated to the designated body.
36.	The Scout Association in Northern Ireland	38 Dublin Road BELFAST BT2 7HN	Bodies which are members of the designated body.
37.	The Sports Council for Northern Ireland	House of Sport Upper Malone Road BELFAST BT9 5LA	Bodies comprised in and associated with the designated body.
38.	Stranmillis College	Stranmillis Road BELFAST BT9 5DY	Bodies comprised in the designated body.
39.	Transport Training Services Ltd	15 Dundrod Road Nutts Corner CRUMLIN Co. Antrim BT29 4SS	Bodies comprised in the designated body.
40.	The Ulster Temple	276 Ravenhill Road BELFAST BT6 8GJ	Bodies comprised in and associated with the designated body.
41.	University of Ulster (at Coleraine)	Cromore Road COLERAINE BT52 1SA	Bodies comprised in the designated body.
42.	University of Ulster Students' Union (at Jordanstown)	Shore Road NEWTOWNABBEY BT37 0QB	Bodies comprised in the designated body.
43.	YMCA — Ireland	St. George's Building 37/41 High Street BELFAST BT1 2AB	Bodies comprised in the designated body.
44.	Youth Action Northern Ireland	Hampton Glenmachan Park BELFAST BT4 2PJ	Bodies affiliated to the designated body.

(1) *Item No.*	(2) *Designated Body* *(a) Name*	*(b)* *Address of main or only administrative centre, or registered office*	(3) *Classes of Bodies to whom the Designated Body may grant permits*
45.	Youth Hostel Association of Northern Ireland	56 Bradbury Place BELFAST BT7 1RU	Bodies comprised in the designated body.
46.	Youthnet	86 Lisburn Road BELFAST BT9 6AF	Bodies which are members of the designated body.

EXPLANATORY NOTE

(This note is not part of the Order.)

Section 10A of the Transport Act (Northern Ireland) 1967 (as inserted by Article 3 of S.I. 1990/994 (N.I. 7)) exempts motor vehicles from the provisions of section 4(2) of that Act (requirement of road service licence) and Articles 59 and 60 of the Road Traffic (Northern Ireland) Order 1981 (as amended by S.I. 1991/197 (N.I. 3)) (licensing of public service vehicles and drivers, etc) where those vehicles are being used by designated bodies in accordance with the requirements of section 10B(2) of that Act.

This Order designates bodies which may grant permits in relation to the use of small buses under section 10B(6) of that Act.

A designated body may grant a permit to the bodies specified in relation to it in the Schedule (Article 2(2)).

Article 3 requires every designated body within one month to send the Department a copy of every permit granted by it and within the same period particulars of any variation or revocation.

A designated body may grant a permit to itself under Article 10B(3) of the said Act.

1994 No. 23

ROAD AND RAILWAY TRANSPORT

Buses (Section 10B Permits) Regulations (Northern Ireland) 1994

Made . . . . . *24th January 1994*

Coming into operation . . *1st March 1994*

The Department of the Environment(**a**), in exercise of the powers conferred on it by sections 10D, 45 and 81 of the Transport Act (Northern Ireland) 1967(**b**), and of all other powers enabling it in that behalf, hereby makes the following Regulations:

Citation and commencement

1. These Regulations may be cited as the Buses (Section 10B Permits) Regulations (Northern Ireland) 1994 and shall come into operation on 1st March 1994.

Interpretation

2. In these Regulations—

"the 1967 Act" means the Transport Act (Northern Ireland) 1967;

"the 1981 Order" means the Road Traffic (Northern Ireland) Order 1981(**c**);

"Department" means the Department of the Environment;

"holder" means a body to which a permit has been granted.

Conditions to be fulfilled by driver

3. The driver of a vehicle used under a permit shall fulfil the following conditions—

(*a*) he shall hold a current full licence under Part II of the 1981 Order(**d**) which authorises him to drive a category B motor vehicle and shall have held that licence for at least two years; and

(*b*) he shall be 21 years of age or over.

(**a**) The functions of the Ministry of Development under the Transport Act (Northern Ireland) 1967 transferred to the Department of the Environment by S.R. & O. (N.I.) 1973 No. 504 Art. 4

(**b**) 1967 c. 37 (N.I.); *see* section 81 for the definition of "prescribed"; section 10D was inserted by Art. 3 of S.I. 1990/994 (N.I. 7); section 45 was amended by reg. 5(4) of S.R. & O. (N.I.) 1972/359 and Art. 10(2) of S.I. 1984/1986 (N.I. 15)

(**c**) S.I. 1981/154 (N.I. 1)

(**d**) As substituted by Art. 3 of and Sch. 1 to the Road Traffic (Amendment) (Northern Ireland) Order 1991 (S.I. 1991/197 (N.I. 3))

Form of permits

4.—(1) Every permit in relation to the use of a large bus or a small bus—

(*a*) shall specify—

    (i) the Department or other body by whom it was granted and the date on which it was granted;

    (ii) the body to whom it was granted;

    (iii) its number; and

    (iv) whether it authorises the use of a small or large bus; and

(*b*) shall describe—

    (i) the conditions to be complied with when a vehicle is used under the permit; and

    (ii) the classes of persons who may be carried in the vehicle as passengers when it is being used under the permit by means of the following letter code:

Class A   Members of the body holding the permit;

Class B   Persons whom the body exists to benefit, and persons assisting them;

Class C   Persons who are physically or mentally handicapped or seriously ill, and persons assisting them;

Class D   Pupils or students of any school, college, university or other educational establishment, and staff or other helpers accompanying them;

Class E   Other class of persons specified in the permit.

(2) The conditions mentioned in paragraph (1)(*b*)(i) shall include the requirements of regulation 3 (conditions to be fulfilled by the driver), and regulation 5(4) (display of the disc).

Disc

5.—(1) The Department or other body granting a permit under section 10B of the 1967 Act shall issue with it a disc which—

(*a*) shall specify—

    (i) the holder of the permit related to that disc;

    (ii) the number of that permit;

    (iii) the date that permit was granted; and

    (iv) the Department or other body which issued the disc; and

(*b*) shall contain—

    (i) the words "Transport Act (Northern Ireland) 1967 section 10B permit vehicle"; and

    (ii) an indication by way of the letter code contained in regulation 4(1)(*b*)(ii) of the classes of passengers who may be carried in any vehicle used under the related permit.

(2) Where a permit authorises the use of a large bus, the disc related to that permit shall be red and shall be headed with the words "large bus disc".

(3) Where a permit authorises the use of a small bus, the disc related to that permit shall be purple and shall be headed with the words "small bus disc".

(4) The holder shall during such time as the vehicle is being used under the permit cause the disc related to that permit to be affixed to the inside of the vehicle in such a position that the disc—

(*a*) does not interfere unduly with the driver's view, and

(*b*) can easily be read in daylight from the outside of the vehicle.

Duplicate permits and discs

6.—(1) If a permit or disc has been lost or destroyed, the holder shall forthwith notify the Department or other body by whom the permit or disc was granted or issued and the Department or body, if satisfied that the permit or disc has been lost or destroyed, shall issue a duplicate of the permit or disc marked as such.

(2) If a permit or disc referred to in paragraph (1) of which a duplicate has been issued is subsequently recovered by the holder he shall forthwith return it to the Department or other body.

(3) If a permit or disc becomes defaced or illegible the holder shall forthwith return it to the Department or body by whom it was granted or issued, and on such return the Department or body shall issue a duplicate of the permit or disc marked as such.

(4) A duplicate of a permit or disc issued in accordance with paragraph (1) or (3) shall have the same effect as the original.

Sealed with the Official Seal of the Department of the Environment on 24th January 1994.

(L.S.)   *Trevor Pearson*
                                                         Assistant Secretary

---

EXPLANATORY NOTE

(This note is not part of the Regulations.)

Sections 10A and 10B of the Transport Act (Northern Ireland) 1967, (as inserted by Article 3 of the Transport (Amendment) (Northern Ireland) Order 1990), make provision for the exemption of certain vehicles and their drivers from public service vehicle licensing requirements when those vehicles are used in accordance with a permit. These Regulations relate to vehicles used under such permits and make provision for—

(1) conditions to be fulfilled by the driver (regulation 3);

(2) the form of permits (regulation 4);

(3) the issue, form and display of discs (regulation 5); and

(4) the issue of duplicate permits and discs (regulation 6).

1994 No. 24

LANDLORD AND TENANT

The Registered Rents (Increase) Order (Northern Ireland) 1994

Made	*25th January 1994*
Coming into operation . .	*7th March 1994*

The Department of the Environment, in exercise of the powers conferred on it by Article 33(2) of the Rent (Northern Ireland) Order 1978(a) (hereinafter called "the Order") and of all other powers enabling it in that behalf, having complied with the requirements of Article 33(1) of the Order and determined that the rents hereinafter mentioned should be increased, hereby makes the following order:

Citation and commencement

1. This order may be cited as the Registered Rents (Increase) Order (Northern Ireland) 1994 and shall come into operation on 7th March 1994.

Increase of registered rents

2. The rents registered under Part V of the Order for dwelling-houses which are let under regulated tenancies shall be increased by 7·5 per cent.

Sealed with the Official Seal of the Department of the Environment on 25th January 1994.

(L.S.)

J. McCormick
Assistant Secretary

(a)   S.I. 1978/1050 (N.I. 20); *see* Article 2(2) for the definition of "the Department"

EXPLANATORY NOTE

(This note is not part of the Order.)

This order increases the rents of regulated tenancies registered with the Department of the Environment by 7·5 per cent from 7th March 1994. Under Article 22(4) of the Rent (Northern Ireland) Order 1978 a notice of increase of rent which gives effect to such increases shall not take effect earlier than 4 weeks after the commencement of this order, i.e., not earlier than 4th April 1994.

Before a landlord may recover an increased rent he must give a tenant at least 4 weeks' notice of the increase in accordance with Article 22(3)(*b*).

1994   No. 25

This Order has been exempted from printing by the Statutory Rules (Northern Ireland) Order 1979. A summary is given in the List of Statutory Rules of a Local Character under the heading ROADS.

1994 No. 26

INSOLVENCY

The Insolvency (Amendment) Rules (Northern Ireland) 1994

Made	*26th January 1994*
Coming into operation . .	*1st March 1994*

To be laid before Parliament

The Lord Chancellor, in exercise of the powers conferred on him by Article 359 of the Insolvency (Northern Ireland) Order 1989(**a**) and section 19(3) of the Registration of Deeds Act (Northern Ireland) 1970(**b**), with the concurrence of the Department of Economic Development and after consulting the committee existing for that purpose under Article 360 of the said Order, and with the concurrence of the Department of the Environment for Northern Ireland in the exercise of the powers conferred on him by section 19(3) of the said Act, hereby makes the following Rules:

Citation and commencement

1. These Rules may be cited as the Insolvency (Amendment) Rules (Northern Ireland) 1994 and shall come into operation on 1st March 1994.

Interpretation

2. In these Rules—

"the principal Rules" means the Insolvency Rules (Northern Ireland) 1991(**c**) and a rule referred to by number means the rule so numbered in the principal Rules.

Application

3. The principal Rules shall have effect subject to the amendments set out in the Schedule.

Dated 26th January 1994. *Mackay of Clashfern*, C.

The Department of Economic Development hereby concurs with the foregoing Rules.

(**a**) S.I. 1989/2405 (N.I. 19)
(**b**) 1970 c. 25 (N.I.) sub-section (3) was added to section 19 by S.I. 1989/2405 (N.I. 19) Article 381 and Schedule 9 paragraph 79
(**c**) S.R. 1991 No. 364

Sealed with the Official Seal of the Department of Economic Development on 27th January 1994.

(L.S.)   *A. L. Brown*

Assistant Secretary

The Department of the Environment for Northern Ireland hereby concurs with the foregoing Rules.

Sealed with the Official Seal of the Department of the Environment for Northern Ireland on 27th January 1994.

(L.S.)   *Trevor Pearson*

Assistant Secretary

Amendments to the principal Rules

Rule 1.24

1. There shall be substituted for paragraph (5) of Rule 1.24 the following paragraphs—

"(4A) The chairman shall also send notice of the result of the meetings to the Enforcement of Judgments Office and where each of the meetings has approved the proposal a list of the persons bound by the arrangement shall accompany such notice.

(5) The notice under paragraphs (4) and (4A) shall be sent immediately after a copy of the chairman's report is filed in court under paragraph (3).".

Rule 4.007

2. There shall be substituted for paragraphs (4) to (6) of Rule 4.007 the following paragraphs—

"(4) There shall in any case be delivered with the petition—

(*a*) one copy of the petition to be sent to the Enforcement of Judgments Office;

(*b*) if the company is in the course of being wound up voluntarily, and a liquidator has been appointed, one copy to be sent to him;

(*c*) if an administration order is in force in relation to the company, one copy to be sent to the administrator;

(*d*) if an administrative receiver has been appointed in relation to the company, one copy to be sent to him;

(*e*) if there is in force for the company a voluntary arrangement under Part II of the Order, one copy for the supervisor of the arrangement; and

(*f*) if the company is an authorised institution or former authorised institution within the meaning of the Banking Act 1987(**a**) and the petitioner is not the Bank of England, one copy to be sent to the Bank.

(5) Each of the copies delivered shall have applied to it the seal of the court, and, except the copy mentioned in paragraph (4)(*a*) shall be issued to the petitioner.

(6) The court shall fix a venue for the hearing of the petition; and this shall be endorsed on any copy issued to the petitioner under paragraph (5) and on the copy mentioned in paragraph (4)(*a*).".

Rule 4.011

3. There shall be substituted for paragraph (1) of Rule 4.011 the following paragraph—

"(1) When the petition is filed, the court shall forthwith give notice of its presentation to the Enforcement of Judgments Office by sending to that Office the copy petition mentioned in Rule 4.007(4)(*a*).".

Rule 4.015

4. There shall be substituted for paragraphs (2) and (3) of Rule 4.015 the following paragraphs—

(**a**) 1987 c. 22

"(2) If the petition is dismissed or withdrawn, the court shall give notice thereof to the Enforcement of Judgments Office by sending to that Office a sealed copy of the order made by the court in that behalf.

(3) Where an administration order is made whilst a winding-up petition is pending, the court shall give notice of the dismissal of the petition pursuant to Article 24(1) to the Enforcement of Judgments Office by sending to that Office a sealed copy of the order made by the court in that behalf.".

Rule 5.06

5. In sub-paragraph (*d*) of Rule 5.06(1), the word "and" shall be deleted.

6. There shall be substituted for sub-paragraph (*e*) of Rule 5.06(1) the following sub-paragraphs—

"(*e*) that the nominee under the proposal (naming him) is a person who is qualified to act as an insolvency practitioner in relation to the debtor, and is willing to act in relation to the proposal; and

(*f*) where the applicant has authorised his solicitor to accept service of documents on his behalf, the name and address for service on that solicitor.".

Rules 5.08 to 5.10

7. There shall be substituted for Rules 5.08 to 5.10 the following Rules—

"Action to follow making of order

5.08.—(1) Where an interim order is made, the court shall forthwith—

[FORM 5.2]

(*a*) send at least 2 sealed copies of the order to the person who applied for it; and that person shall serve one of the copies on the nominee under the debtor's proposal, and

(*b*) give to the Enforcement of Judgments Office notice of the making of the order and of the date the interim order ceases to have effect by sending to that Office a sealed copy of the order.

(2) The applicant shall also forthwith give notice of the making of the order to any person who was given notice of the hearing pursuant to Rule 5.06(4) and was not present or represented at it.

[*E.r. 5.7*]

Extension of operation of interim order

5.09. If an order is made extending the period for which an interim order has effect, the court shall give to the Enforcement of Judgments Office notice of the making of the order and of the date to which the operation of the interim order has been extended by sending to that Office a sealed copy of the order.

[FORM 5.3]

Discharge of interim order

5.10. If an order is made discharging an interim order, the court shall give notice of the making of the order to the Enforcement of Judgments Office by sending to that Office a sealed copy of the order.".

Rule 5.25

8. There shall be substituted for paragraph (3) of Rule 5.25 the following paragraph—

"(3) A copy of the chairman's report and, in the case of a proposal approved with modifications, a copy of the modified proposal approved by the meeting shall, within 4 days of the meeting being held, be filed in court; and the court shall cause those copies to be endorsed with the date of filing.".

9. In Rule 5.25, after paragraph (4), there shall be inserted the following paragraph—

"(4A) The chairman shall also send notice of the result of the meeting to the Enforcement of Judgments Office and where the meeting has approved the proposal a list of the persons bound by the arrangement shall accompany such notice.".

Rule 6.004

10. In Rule 6.004, after paragraph (4), there shall be added the following paragraph—

"(5) There shall be delivered with the application 4 copies thereof. Each of the copies delivered shall have applied to it the seal of the court and shall be issued to the debtor; and if the court shall fix a venue for the hearing of the application under Rule 6.005(2), this shall be endorsed on any copy so issued.".

Rule 6.005

11. There shall be substituted for paragraph (2) of Rule 6.005 the following paragraph—

"(2) If the application is not dismissed under paragraph (1), the court shall fix a venue for it to be heard, and the debtor shall give at least 7 days' notice of it by sending a sealed copy of the application endorsed in accordance with Rule 6.004(5) to—

    (*a*) the creditor, and

    (*b*) whoever is named in the statutory demand as the person with whom the debtor may enter into communication with reference to the demand (or, if more than one person is so named, the first of them).".

Rule 6.009

12. There shall be substituted for paragraphs (2) to (6) of Rule 6.009 the following paragraphs—

"(1A) With the petition there shall be delivered to the court 2 copies of the document referred to in regulation 3 of the Insolvency (Registration of Deeds) Regulations (Northern Ireland) 1991(**a**) one of which shall be prepared on paper having the specifications and characteristics prescribed for use for the purpose of a memorial of a deed or conveyance to be registered at the Registry of Deeds under the Registration of Deeds Act (Northern Ireland) 1970(**b**) and shall bear the name and address of the solicitor or party presenting it and both of which shall be endorsed with the following form of certificate:

"The High Court hereby certifies that the above information is correct.
Master (Bankruptcy)
Date: ".

(2) No petition shall be filed unless there is produced with it the receipt for the deposit payable on presentation.

(**a**) S.R. 1991 No. 382
(**b**) 1970 c. 25

(3) The following copies of the petition shall also be delivered to the court with the petition—

(*a*) one for service on the debtor,

(*b*) one to be exhibited to the affidavit verifying that service,

(*c*) one to be sent to the Enforcement of Judgments Office,

(*d*) if there is in force for the debtor a voluntary arrangement and the petitioner is not the supervisor of the arrangement, one copy for him, and

(*e*) where the petition is against a solicitor, one to be sent to the Law Society of Northern Ireland.

(4) Each copy delivered to the court under paragraph (3) shall have applied to it the seal of the court, and, except the copies mentioned in paragraph (3)(*c*) and (*e*), shall be issued to the petitioner.

(5) The date and time of filing the petition shall be endorsed on the petition and on each of the copies delivered to the court under paragraph (3).

(6) The court shall fix a venue for hearing the petition, and this also shall be endorsed on the petition and on any copy so delivered.''.

Rule 6.012

13. There shall be substituted for paragraph (1) of Rule 6.012 the following paragraph—

''(1) When the petition is filed, the court shall forthwith—

(*a*)give notice of its presentation to the Enforcement of Judgments Office by sending to that Office the copy petition mentioned in Rule 6.009(3)(*c*),

(*b*) register the petition in the Registry of Deeds in accordance with section 3A(1) of the Registration of Deeds Act (Northern Ireland) 1970(**a**), and

(*c*) where the petition is against a solicitor, give notice of its presentation to the Law Society of Northern Ireland by sending to the Society the copy petition mentioned in Rule 6.009(3)(*e*).''.

Rule 6.024

14. There shall be substituted for paragraph (2) of Rule 6.024 the following paragraph—

''(2) If the petition is dismissed or withdrawn, or if proceedings on it are stayed, the court shall give notice thereof to the Enforcement of Judgments Office by sending to that Office a sealed copy of the order made by the court in that behalf.''.

15. There shall be substituted for sub-paragraph (*c*) of Rule 6.024(3) the following sub-paragraph—

''(*c*) give notice of the dismissal of the petition to the Enforcement of Judgments Office by sending to that Office a sealed copy of the order.''.

Rule 6.038

16. There shall be substituted for Rule 6.038 the following Rule—

(**a**) 1970 c. 25 (N.I.), section 3A was inserted by S.I. 1989/2405 (N.I. 19) Article 381 and Schedule 9 paragraph 77

"*Procedure for presentation and filing*

6.038.—(1) The petition and the statement of affairs shall be filed in court, together with 2 copies of the statement.

(2) No petition shall be filed unless there is produced with it the receipt for the deposit payable on presentation.

(3) The following copies of the petition shall be delivered to the court with the petition—

(*a*) one to be returned to the petitioner;

(*b*) one to be sent to the Enforcement of Judgments Office;

(*c*) one to be sent to the official receiver;

(*d*) where the petition is against a solicitor, one to be sent to the Law Society of Northern Ireland; and

(*e*) the remaining copy to be retained by the court, to be sent to an insolvency practitioner if appointed under Article 247(2).

(4) Each copy of the petition delivered to the court under paragraph (3) shall have applied to it the seal of the court.

(5) Subject to paragraph (6), the court may hear the petition forthwith. If it does not do so, it shall fix a venue for the hearing.

(6) If the petition contains particulars of a voluntary arrangement in force for the debtor, the court shall fix a venue for the hearing and give at least 14 days' notice of it to the supervisor of the voluntary arrangement; the supervisor may appear and be heard on the petition.

(7) Any venue fixed shall be endorsed on each of the copies of the petition delivered to the court under paragraph (3), except the copy mentioned in paragraph (3)(*e*).

(8) Of the 2 copies of the statement of affairs—

(*a*) one shall be sent by the court to the official receiver; and

(*b*) the other shall be retained by the court to be sent to the insolvency practitioner (if appointed).

(9) The affidavit verifying the debtor's statement of affairs may be sworn before an officer of the court duly authorised in that behalf.

(10) Where the court hears a petition forthwith, or it will in the opinion of the court otherwise expedite the delivery of any document to the official receiver, the court may, instead of sending that document to the official receiver, direct the bankrupt forthwith to deliver it to him.

(11) Where a petition contains a request for the appointment of a person as trustee in accordance with Article 270(4) (appointment of former supervisor as trustee) the person whose appointment is sought shall, not less than 2 days before the day appointed for hearing the petition, file in court a report including particulars of—

(*a*) a date on which he gave written notification to creditors bound by the voluntary arrangement of the intention to seek his appointment as trustee, such date to be at least 10 days before the day on which the report under this paragraph is filed, and

(*b*) details of any response from creditors to that notice, including any objections to his appointment.

(12) With the petition there shall be delivered to the court 2 copies of the document referred to in regulation 3 of the Insolvency (Registration of Deeds)

Regulations (Northern Ireland) 1991 one of which shall be prepared on paper having the specifications and characteristics prescribed for use for the purpose of a memorial of a deed or conveyance to be registered at the Registry of Deeds under the Registration of Deeds Act (Northern Ireland) 1970 and shall bear the name and address of the solicitor or party presenting it and both of which shall be endorsed with the following form of certificate:

"The High Court hereby certifies that the above information is correct.
Master (Bankruptcy)
Date: ".

[*E.r. 6.42*]".

Rule 6.039

17. There shall be substituted for paragraph (1) of Rule 6.039 the following paragraph—

"(1) When the petition is filed, the court shall forthwith—

(*a*) send to the official receiver the copy petition mentioned in Rule 6.038 (3)(*c*), and

(*b*) give notice of the presentation of the petition to the Enforcement of Judgments Office by sending to that Office the copy petition mentioned in Rule 6.038 (3)(*b*), and

(*c*) register the petition in the Registry of Deeds in accordance with section 3A(1) of the Registration of Deeds Act (Northern Ireland) 1970, and

(*d*) where the petition is against a solicitor, give notice of its presentation to the Law Society of Northern Ireland by sending to the Society the copy petition mentioned in Rule 6.038 (3)(*d*).".

Rule 6.040

18. There shall be substituted for paragraph (2) of Rule 6.040 the following paragraph—

"(2) If the petition is dismissed or withdrawn, or if proceedings on it are stayed, the court shall give notice thereof to the Enforcement of Judgments Office by sending to that Office a sealed copy of the order made by the court in that behalf.".

19. There shall be substituted for sub-paragraph (*c*) of Rule 6.040(3) the following sub-paragraph—

"(*c*) give notice of the dismissal of the petition to the Enforcement of Judgments Office by sending to that Office a sealed copy of the order.".

Rule 6.200

20. In paragraph (4) of Rule 6.200, the words "not less than" shall be deleted.

Rule 7.03

21. In Rule 7.03, after paragraph (5), there shall be inserted the following paragraph—

"(5A) The Master may authorise any act of a formal or administrative character which is not by statute his responsibility to be carried out by the Principal Clerk or any other officer of the court acting on his behalf in accordance with directions given by the Chancery Judge.

[*E.r. 13.2(2)*]".

Rule 12.03

22. In sub-paragraph (*a*) of Rule 12.03(2) there shall be added after the word "proceedings" the words "or under a maintenance assessment made under the Child Support (Northern Ireland) Order 1991"(**a**).

(**a**) S.I. 1991/2628 (N.I. 23)

EXPLANATORY NOTE

(This note is not part of the Rules.)

These Rules amend the Insolvency Rules (Northern Ireland) 1991 [S.R. 1991 No. 364], which set out the detailed procedures for the conduct of all company and individual insolvency proceedings under the Insolvency (Northern Ireland) Order 1989; to—

(*a*) provide that the chairman of meetings of the company and of its creditors in company voluntary arrangement proceedings shall send notice of the result of the meeting to the Enforcement of Judgments Office and where each meeting has approved the proposal a list of the persons bound by the arrangement shall accompany such notice (Schedule, paragraph 1);

(*b*) make similar provisions for reporting the result of the meeting of creditors in an individual voluntary arrangement to the Enforcement of Judgments Office (Schedule, paragraph 9);

(*c*) alter the method by which the court gives notice of certain proceedings (Schedule, paragraphs 3, 4, 7, 13, 14, 15, 17, 18 and 19);

(*d*) transfer the obligation to prepare and supply certain documents from the court to the party having carriage of proceedings (Schedule, paragraphs 2, 12 and 16);

(*e*) require the debtor, instead of the court, to notify the other parties of the hearing to set aside a statutory demand. (Schedule, paragraphs 10 and 11);

(*f*) provide that the affidavit to accompany an application to the court for an interim order in individual voluntary arrangement proceedings shall give the name and address for service of documents on the applicant's solicitor, where the applicant has authorised the solicitor to accept service of documents on his behalf (Schedule, paragraph 6);

(*g*) provide that an up to date copy of the proposal for an individual voluntary arrangement, incorporating any modifications approved at the meeting of creditors, shall be placed on file with the chairman's report (Schedule, paragraph 8);

(*h*) provide for the Master to authorise the Principal Clerk, or other officer of the court acting on his behalf, to carry out acts of a formal or administrative character where those acts are not by statute the responsibility of the Master (Schedule, paragraph 21); and

(*i*) to include within those obligations which are not provable in bankruptcy proceedings a maintenance assessment made under the Child Support (Northern Ireland) Order 1991 [S.I. 1991/2628 (N.I. 23)] as a consequence of its amending Article 255 of the Insolvency (Northern Ireland) Order 1989 (Schedule, paragraph 22).

The Rules will come into operation on 1st March 1994.

1994　No. 27

ROAD TRAFFIC AND VEHICLES

Control of Traffic (Carrickfergus) Order (Northern Ireland) 1994

Made	.	.	.	.	*28th January 1994*
Coming into operation		.	.		*10th March 1994*

WHEREAS the Department of the Environment has published a notice in compliance with Article 23(1) and (2) of the Road Traffic (Northern Ireland) Order 1981(**a**);

AND WHEREAS no objection or representation has been received;

NOW THEREFORE the Department, in exercise of the powers conferred on it by Article 21(1) of the Road Traffic (Northern Ireland) Order 1981 and of every other power enabling it in that behalf, makes the following Order:

Citation and commencement

1. This Order may be cited as the Control of Traffic (Carrickfergus) Order (Northern Ireland) 1994 and shall come into operation on 10th March 1994.

Prohibition of left-hand turn

2. Subject to Article 3 a person shall not cause or permit a vehicle travelling in a southerly direction along Victoria Road, Carrickfergus, to make a left-hand turn into Windermere Road.

Exemptions

3. Article 2 shall not apply to—

(*a*) vehicles being used for fire brigade, ambulance, police or military purposes; or

(*b*) a vehicle, the driver of which is acting upon the direction or with the permission of a constable in uniform or of a traffic warden.

Sealed with the Official Seal of the Department of the Environment on 28th January 1994.

(L.S.)　　　　　　　　　　　　　　　　*E. J. Galway*

Assistant Secretary

(**a**)　S.I. 1981/154 (N.I. 1); *see* Article 2(2) for the definition of "Department"

EXPLANATORY NOTE

(This note is not part of the Order.)

This Order prohibits vehicles travelling in a southerly direction along Victoria Road, Carrickfergus, from making a left-hand turn into Windermere Road.

Any person who acts in contravention of the Order shall be guilty of an offence and shall be liable on summary conviction to a fine not exceeding level 3 on the standard scale (£400).

Traffic signs indicating the effect of the Order will in due course be erected on the road.

1994 No. 28

PLANT HEALTH

**Plant Health (Amendment) (Potatoes) Order
(Northern Ireland) 1994**

Made	*28th January 1994*
Coming into operation . .	*1st March 1994*

The Department of Agriculture, in exercise of the powers conferred on it by sections 2(**a**), 3(1)(**b**), 3A(**c**), 3B(1)(**d**) and 4(1)(**e**) of the Plant Health Act (Northern Ireland) 1967(**f**) and of all powers enabling it in that behalf, hereby makes the following Order:

Citation and commencement

1. This Order may be cited as the Plant Health (Amendment) (Potatoes) Order (Northern Ireland) 1994 and shall come into operation on 1st March 1994.

Amendment of the Plant Health Order (Northern Ireland) 1993

2. The Plant Health Order (Northern Ireland) 1993(**g**) shall be amended as provided in Articles 3 to 5.

3. In Article 3(1) (Interpretation) after the definition of "responsible person" there shall be inserted the following definition—

"the ring rot Directive" means Council Directive 93/85/EEC of 4th October 1993 on the control of potato ring rot(**h**);".

4. For Articles 38 to 42 (Potato ring rot) there shall be substituted—

"*Special measures for the control of potato ring rot*

38.—(1) The provisions of—

(*a*) the ring rot Directive specified in paragraph (2); and

(*b*) the second paragraph of article 11 of and the Annexes to the ring rot Directive,

---

(**a**) As amended by S.R. & O. (N.I.) 1972 No. 351 Art. 3 and Sch. 2; 1979 c. 2, s. 177(1) and Sch. 4 Pt. II; and S.I. 1984/702 (N.I. 2) Art. 15(2)
(**b**) As amended by S.R. & O. (N.I.) 1972 No. 351 Art. 3 and Sch. 2
(**c**) Inserted by S.I. 1975/1038 (N.I. 8) Art. 11(2)
(**d**) Inserted by S.I. 1984/702 (N.I. 2) Art. 15(2)
(**e**) As amended by S.I. 1984/702 (N.I. 2) Art. 15(2)
(**f**) 1967 c. 28 (N.I.)
(**g**) S.R. 1993 No. 256
(**h**) O.J. L.259, 18.10.93, p. 1

shall have effect as if they were incorporated in this Order and this Order shall be construed and have effect accordingly.

(2) It shall be the duty of the Department to give effect to the requirements of paragraphs 1 and 2 of article 2, paragraph 1 of article 4 and articles 5 and 6 of the ring rot Directive.

39. A person who suspects the occurrence or actual presence of potato ring rot in growing potatoes or harvested, stored or marketed tubers shall immediately notify the Department or an inspector who shall determine whether any further investigation is necessary.

40. Subject to Article 41(2), a person shall not—

(a) hold or handle any plant or tuber affected with potato ring rot or any other object or material affected with it otherwise than in compliance with the provisions of Articles 39 to 42;

(b) plant any tuber or plant designated to be contaminated with potato ring rot under article 5(1)(a) of the ring rot Directive and a notice under paragraph (1)(c) or (2)(i) of Article 22 may require any such tuber or plant to be—

(i) destroyed; or

(ii) otherwise disposed of for the purposes set out in point 1 of Annex IV to the ring rot Directive but only if there is no identifiable risk of potato ring rot spreading;

(c) plant any plant or tuber determined as probably contaminated with potato ring rot under article 5(1)(b) of the ring rot Directive and a notice under paragraph (1)(c) or (2)(i) of Article 22 may require any such tuber or plant to be put to an appropriate use or disposed of in accordance with point 2 of Annex IV to the ring rot Directive but only if there is no identifiable risk of potato ring rot spreading.

41.—(1) Subject to paragraph (2), a notice under paragraph (1)(c) or 2(i) of Article 22 may require any machinery, vehicle, vessel, store, or units thereof and any other objects including packaging material designated as contaminated under article 5(1)(a) of the ring rot Directive or determined as probably contaminated under paragraph (1)(b) of that article to be—

(a) destroyed; or

(b) cleansed and disinfected using appropriate methods as specified in point 3 of Annex IV to the ring rot Directive, whereupon they shall not be treated as contaminated.

(2) The Department or an inspector may by notice in writing given to the person having possession of the plants or tubers authorise exemptions from the requirements of article 6 of the ring rot Directive as applied by Article 38(2) and of Article 40 and paragraphs (1) and (3) for experimental or scientific purposes or for work on varietal selection if it or he as the case may be is satisfied that any such exemption would not prejudice the control of potato ring rot or create a risk of its spread.

(3) Subject to paragraph (2) and without prejudice to the provisions of Article 40(*b*) and (*c*) and paragraph (1), a notice under Article 22 may require a series of measures as specified in point 4 of Annex IV to the ring rot Directive to be implemented.

(4) A person shall not plant seed potatoes unless they—

(*a*) meet the requirements of Directive 77/93/EEC on the protective measures against the introduction into the Community of organisms harmful to plants or plant products and against their spread within the Community(**a**); and

(*b*) derive in a direct line from material obtained under an officially approved programme which has been found free from potato ring rot in official or officially supervised testing pursuant to article 8(1) of the ring rot Directive using the method set out in Annex I to that Directive.

(5) The testing referred to in paragraph (4)(*b*) shall be carried out—

(*a*) in a case where contamination affects seed potato production, on the plants in the initial clonal selection; and

(*b*) in any other case, either on the plants of the initial clonal selection or on representative samples of the basic seed potatoes or earlier propagations.

42. The Department may in accordance with article 11 of the ring rot Directive take such additional or stricter measures as it may consider necessary to combat potato ring rot or to prevent it from spreading.''.

5. In Schedule 14 (Instruments amending and supplementing Council Directive 77/93/EEC)—

(*a*) after the entry relating to the Act concerning the conditions of accession of the Hellenic Republic and the adjustment of the Treaties there shall be inserted the following entries:—

"Council Directive 69/464/EEC O.J. No. L.323, 24.12.69, p. 1.

Council Directive 69/465/EEC O.J. No. L.323, 24.12.69, p. 3.'';

(*b*) after the entry relating to Council Directive 93/19/EEC there shall be added the following entry—

"Council Directive 93/85/EEC O.J. No. L.259, 18.10.93, p. 1.''.

Sealed with the Official Seal of the Department of Agriculture on 28th January 1994.

(L.S.)   *I. C. Henderson*

Assistant Secretary

(**a**) O.J. No. L.26, 31.1.77, p. 20 as last amended by Commission Directive 93/110/EEC (O.J. No. L.303, 10.12.93, p. 19)

EXPLANATORY NOTE

(This note is not part of the Order.)

This Order which implements as respects Northern Ireland the requirements of Council Directive 93/85/EEC on the control of potato ring rot (O.J. No. L.259, 18.10.93, p. 1) substitutes for Articles 38 to 42 of the Plant Health Order (Northern Ireland) 1993 more extensive provisions for preventing the spread of potato ring rot following the creation of the single market. This Order also contains minor and consequential amendments.

1994   No. 29

ROAD AND RAILWAY TRANSPORT

Level Crossing (Eglinton) Order (Northern Ireland) 1994

Made	*28th January 1994*
Coming into operation . .	*28th March 1994*

WHEREAS the railway undertaking made an application to the Department in accordance with section 66(4) of the Transport Act (Northern Ireland) 1967(**a**);

AND WHEREAS before making the application the railway undertaking gave notice in accordance with section 66(5) and (6) of that Act to the council in whose district the crossing is situated;

AND WHEREAS the Department did not receive from that council any representation in respect of the said application;

NOW THEREFORE the Department of the Environment(**b**), in exercise of the powers conferred by section 66(1) and (2) of the Transport Act (Northern Ireland) 1967 and of all other powers enabling it in that behalf, makes the following Order:

Citation, commencement and interpretation

1.—(1) This Order may be cited as the Level Crossing (Eglinton) Order (Northern Ireland) 1994 and shall come into operation on 28th March 1994.

(2) In this Order "the crossing" means the Eglinton Level Crossing in the townland of Donnybrewer and County of Londonderry whereby the road known as Station Road is crossed by the railway between Castlerock and Londonderry Stations.

Suspension of statutory provisions

2. While this Order remains in force—

(*a*) section 47 of the Railways Clauses Consolidation Act 1845(**c**) (requirements as to gates);

(*b*) section 6 of the Railways Clauses Act 1863(**d**) (requirements as to lodges, etc.); and

---

(**a**) 1967 c. 37 (N.I.); section 66 was substituted by S.I. 1984/1986 (N.I. 15) Art. 15 and S.I. 1990/994 (N.I. 7) Sch. 2
(**b**) The functions of the Ministry of Development under the Transport Act (Northern Ireland) 1967 transferred to the Department of the Environment by S.R. & O. (N.I.) 1973 No. 504 Art. 4
(**c**) 1845 c. 20
(**d**) 1863 c. 92

(*c*) any other statutory provision imposing requirements to the same or similar effect as those contained in the enactments mentioned in paragraphs (*a*) and (*b*),

shall not apply in relation to the crossing.

Provision of automatic equipment

3. The railway undertaking shall at the crossing—

(*a*) provide, maintain and operate the barriers, lights, automatic and other devices, excluding traffic signs specified in Schedule 1, and shall give notice in writing to the Department of the Environment as soon as the provision thereof is complete;

(*b*) secure the provision, maintenance and operation by that Department of the traffic signs specified in Schedule 1; and

(*c*) comply with the conditions and requirements specified in Schedule 2.

Revocation

4. The Level Crossing (Eglinton) Order (Northern Ireland) 1983(**a**) is revoked.

Sealed with the Official Seal of the Department of the Environment on 28th January 1994.

(L.S.)   *Trevor Pearson*
Assistant Secretary

(**a**)   S.R. 1983 No. 195

SCHEDULE 1   Article 3(a) and (b)

PARTICULARS OF THE BARRIERS, LIGHTS, TRAFFIC SIGNS AND OTHER DEVICES

1. Cattle-cum-trespass guards of standard railway design shall be provided adjacent to the ground which is made up to the level of the carriageway. The guards shall extend the full distance between the fence on each side of the railway.

2. A barrier shall be pivoted as close to the railway as practicable on the left hand side of the road on each approach to the crossing.

3. It shall be possible to raise and lower the barriers. When lowered, the barrier shall be as nearly horizontal as possible, be as nearly as possible at right angles to the centre line of the carriageway and shall extend across the left hand side of the road. The tip of each barrier shall extend to a point within 800 mm of the centre of the carriageway and no closer than 150 mm and a clear exit of at least 3 metres of carriageway width shall be left to the right hand edge of the carriageway.

4. When the barriers are fully lowered their uppermost surfaces shall be not less than 900 mm above the road surface at the centre of the carriageway and the underclearance between the barriers and the road surface shall not exceed 1000 mm.

5. When in the fully raised position the barriers shall be inclined towards the carriageway at an angle of between 5 and 10 degrees from the vertical. No part of either barrier or of any attachment thereto which is less than 5 metres above the level of the carriageway shall be horizontally displaced from the nearer edge of the carriageway by less than 450 mm. No part of any barrier or any attachment thereto which in either case is less than 2 metres above the level of the footway shall normally be horizontally displaced from that edge of the footway further from the carriageway by less than 150 mm.

6. The barriers shall be as light as possible but shall also be strong enough to prevent distortion or fracture likely to be caused by wind pressure. It shall be possible to raise them by hand. The barriers shall be at least 125 mm deep at their mid-point and at least 75 mm deep at their tip.

7. Two electric lamps, each of not less than 5 watts nominal rating and with lenses of not less than 50 mm diameter, shall be fitted to each barrier, one within 150 mm of its tip and the other near its centre. When illuminated, the lamps shall show a red light in each direction along the carriageway.

8. The barriers shall display on both front and rear faces alternate red and white bands each approximately 600 mm long and to the full depth of the barriers. A band of red retro-reflecting material not less than 50 mm deep shall be provided along the full length of each red band.

9. Suitable screening shall be provided for each barrier machine to guard against danger to persons from the operating mechanism and moving parts of the machine.

10. A traffic light signal as prescribed by regulation 13(4) of the Regulations shall be provided on the left hand side of the road on each approach to the crossing and as close as practicable to the barrier. There shall be an additional traffic light signal of the same type on the right hand side of the road on each approach to the crossing so

located as to be either in line with or on the railway side of the stop line mentioned in paragraph 12. The traffic light signals on each side of the railway shall be positioned so as to face outwards from the crossing towards approaching road traffic. All the signals shall be capable of directional adjustment.

11. An audible warning device shall be provided on or adjacent to each left hand side traffic light signal post on each approach to the crossing. Facilities shall be provided to reduce the sound output of these devices and any reduced sound output shall operate between 23.30 hours and 07.00 hours approximately.

12. A reflectorised stop line of the size and type shown in diagram 1001 in the Regulations shall be provided across the left hand side of the carriageway on each approach to the crossing approximately 1 metre before the left hand side traffic light signal.

13. A reflectorised pedestrian stop line of the size and type shown in diagram 1003.2 in the Regulations shall be provided across the right hand side of the carriageway on each approach to the crossing and any made up ground on both sides of the carriageway on both sides of the railway. The line shall be not less than 1 metre before the right hand side traffic light signal and not nearer than 2 metres to the running edge of the nearest rail and shall be as nearly as possible at right angles to the centre line of the carriageway.

14. Where the road passes over the crossing, reflectorised edge of carriageway road markings of the size and type shown in diagram 1011 in the Regulations shall be provided along each edge of any made up ground along each edge of the carriageway.

15. The centre line of the carriageway shall be marked on the crossing between the stop lines mentioned in paragraph 12 and for a distance of at least 14 metres on each side of the railway measured along the centre of the carriageway from the stop lines with a reflectorised warning road marking of the size and type shown in diagram 1004 in the Regulations.

16. A traffic sign of the size, colour and type shown in diagram 863 in the Regulations shall be provided below or adjacent to each traffic light signal and shall face outwards from the crossing towards approaching road traffic.

17. A traffic sign of the size, colour and type shown in diagram 649.2 in the Regulations shall be provided on each road approach to the crossing facing traffic approaching the crossing.

18. A telephone mounted in a cabinet and connected to the monitoring signal box at Londonderry shall be provided on or adjacent to each right hand side traffic light signal post. In the event of the Londonderry signal box being closed the same monitoring equipment shall be provided at Coleraine signal box. A traffic sign of the size, colour and type shown in diagram 854 in the Regulations shall be provided on the door of the cabinet.

19. Two independent power supplies shall be provided at the crossing, one of which may consist of standby batteries of sufficient capacity to operate the whole installation for 12 hours.

20. In this Schedule—

"the Regulations" means the Traffic Signs Regulations (Northern Ireland)
    1979(**a**).

(**a**) S.R. 1979 No. 386; relevant amending Regulations are S.R. 1982 No. 389, S.R. 1984 No. 58 and
    S.R. 1986 No. 173

SCHEDULE 2

Article 3(c)

CONDITIONS AND REQUIREMENTS TO BE COMPLIED WITH BY THE RAILWAY UNDERTAKING

1. The carriageway shall be at least 5.0 metres wide at the crossing.

2. The ground at the two edges of the carriageway over the crossing shall be made up to the level of the carriageway for a distance of not less than 1 metre beyond each edge.

3. The surface of the carriageway over the crossing shall be maintained in good and even condition.

4. The barriers shall be kept in the fully raised position except during the time when engines, carriages or other vehicles passing along the railway have occasion to cross the road.

5. The electric lamps on each barrier mentioned in Schedule 1 shall be lit at all times except when the barriers are in the fully raised position.

6. If the road approaches to the crossing are lit the crossing shall be lit to at least the same standard.

7. Visual indicators and an audible alarm shall be provided in the monitoring signal box. The indicators shall show when the barriers are raised and when the main power supply is available, and the alarm shall sound if a period of approximately 3 minutes elapses and there is no indication that the barriers are raised.

8. The barriers, the audible warning devices and the traffic light signals mentioned in Schedule 1 shall be activated automatically, as described in paragraph 9, by the approach of a train but means shall also be provided at the crossing for their manual operation and control.

9. When the train either occupies a track circuit or operates a treadle the audible warning devices and the traffic light signals shall begin to operate and the barriers shall be lowered in accordance with the following sequence—

(*a*) the amber lights shall show and the audible warning shall begin. The lights shall show for approximately 3 seconds;

(*b*) immediately the amber lights are extinguished the intermittent red lights shall begin to show;

(*c*) 4 to 8 seconds later, the barriers shall begin to descend and shall take a further 6 to 8 seconds to reach the lowered position;

(*d*) not less than 27 seconds shall elapse between the time when the amber lights first show and the time when the train reaches the crossing;

(*e*) the intermittent red lights shall continue to show and the audible warning devices shall continue to sound until the barriers have begun to rise and all said lights and devices shall be switched off before the barriers have risen to an angle of 45 degrees above the horizontal. However, if the barriers have not fully raised within 7.5 seconds of having started to rise then the red road lights will be illuminated until both barriers are proved fully up.

10. Both barriers shall rise as soon as possible after the train has passed the crossing.

11. In the event of the failure of both intermittent red lights in any of the road traffic signals, when the intermittent red lights should be shown, both barriers shall descend immediately (if not already lowered) and shall remain lowered.

12. Should a total power failure occur both barriers shall descend under gravity or remain lowered as the case may be. If after the barriers have begun to lower one barrier fails to reach the fully lowered position, neither barrier shall rise until both have been fully lowered.

13. If either barrier fails to rise from the lowered position the intermittent red lights shall continue to show, provided a total power failure has not occurred.

EXPLANATORY NOTE

(This note is not part of the Order.)

This Order provides for the provision and maintenance of a system of automatic barriers in lieu of an automatic open crossing at the Eglinton railway level crossing. Section 47 of the Railways Clauses Consolidation Act 1845 (which requires the railway undertaking to provide gates and gate-keepers), section 6 of the Railways Clauses Act 1863 (requirements as to lodges, etc.) and any other statutory provision imposing requirements to the same or similar effect, shall not apply to the crossing whilst this Order remains in force.

Schedule 1 sets out the particulars of barriers, lights, traffic signs and other devices which are to be provided at the crossing. Schedule 2 states the conditions and requirements with which the railway undertaking must comply in relation to the crossing.

This Order revokes the Level Crossing (Eglinton) Order (Northern Ireland) 1983.

1994 No. 30

ROAD AND RAILWAY TRANSPORT

Level Crossing (Lock) Order (Northern Ireland) 1994

Made	.	.	.	.	*28th January 1994*
Coming into operation		.	.	*21st March 1994*

WHEREAS the railway undertaking made an application to the Department in accordance with section 66(4) of the Transport Act (Northern Ireland) 1967(**a**);

AND WHEREAS before making the application the railway undertaking gave notice in accordance with section 66(5) and (6) of that Act to the council in whose district the crossing is situated;

AND WHEREAS the Department did not receive from that council any representation in respect of the said application;

NOW THEREFORE the Department of the Environment(**b**), in exercise of the powers conferred by section 66(1) and (2) of the Transport Act (Northern Ireland) 1967 and of all other powers enabling it in that behalf, makes the following Order:

Citation, commencement and interpretation

1.—(1) This Order may be cited as the Level Crossing (Lock) Order (Northern Ireland) 1994 and shall come into operation on 21st March 1994.

(2) In this Order "the crossing" means the Lock Level Crossing in the townland of Lower Campsie and County of Londonderry whereby the road known as Donnybrewer Road is crossed by the railway between Castlerock and Londonderry Stations.

Suspension of statutory provisions

2. While this Order remains in force—

(*a*) section 47 of the Railways Clauses Consolidation Act 1845(**c**) (requirements as to gates);

(*b*) section 6 of the Railways Clauses Act 1863(**d**) (requirements as to lodges, etc.); and

---

(**a**) 1967 c. 37 (N.I.); section 66 was substituted by S.I. 1984/1986 (N.I. 15) Art. 15 and S.I. 1990/994 (N.I. 7) Sch. 2

(**b**) The functions of the Ministry of Development under the Transport Act (Northern Ireland) 1967 transferred to the Department of the Environment by S.R. & O. (N.I.) 1973 No. 504 Art. 4

(**c**) 1845 c. 20

(**d**) 1863 c. 92

(*c*) any other statutory provision imposing requirements to the same or similar effect as those contained in the enactments mentioned in paragraphs (*a*) and (*b*),

shall not apply in relation to the crossing.

Provision of automatic equipment

3. The railway undertaking shall at the crossing—

(*a*) provide, maintain and operate the barriers, lights, automatic and other devices, excluding traffic signs specified in Schedule 1, and shall give notice in writing to the Department of the Environment as soon as the provision thereof is complete;

(*b*) secure the provision, maintenance and operation by that Department of the traffic signs specified in Schedule 1; and

(*c*) comply with the conditions and requirements specified in Schedule 2.

Sealed with the Official Seal of the Department of the Environment on 28th January 1994.

(L.S.)

Trevor Pearson

Assistant Secretary

SCHEDULE 1   Article 3(a) and (b)

PARTICULARS OF THE BARRIERS, LIGHTS, TRAFFIC SIGNS AND OTHER DEVICES

1. Cattle-cum-trespass guards of standard railway design shall be provided adjacent to the ground which is made up to the level of the carriageway. The guards shall extend the full distance between the fence on each side of the railway.

2. A barrier shall be pivoted as close to the railway as practicable on the left hand side of the road on each approach to the crossing.

3. It shall be possible to raise and lower the barriers. When lowered, the barrier shall be as nearly horizontal as possible, be as nearly as possible at right angles to the centre line of the carriageway and shall extend across the left hand side of the road. The tip of each barrier shall extend to a point within 800 mm of the centre of the carriageway and no closer than 150 mm and a clear exit of at least 3 metres of carriageway width shall be left to the right hand edge of the carriageway.

4. When the barriers are fully lowered their uppermost surfaces shall be not less than 900 mm above the road surface at the centre of the carriageway and the underclearance between the barriers and the road surface shall not exceed 1000 mm.

5. When in the fully raised position the barriers shall be inclined towards the carriageway at an angle of between 5 and 10 degrees from the vertical. No part of either barrier or of any attachment thereto which is less than 5 metres above the level of the carriageway shall be horizontally displaced from the nearer edge of the carriageway by less than 450 mm. No part of any barrier or any attachment thereto which in either case is less than 2 metres above the level of the footway shall normally be horizontally displaced from that edge of the footway further from the carriageway by less than 150 mm.

6. The barriers shall be as light as possible but shall also be strong enough to prevent distortion or fracture likely to be caused by wind pressure. It shall be possible to raise them by hand. The barriers shall be at least 125 mm deep at their mid-point and at least 75 mm deep at their tip.

7. Two electric lamps, each of not less than 5 watts nominal rating and with lenses of not less than 50 mm diameter, shall be fitted to each barrier, one within 150 mm of its tip and the other near its centre. When illuminated, the lamps shall show a red light in each direction along the carriageway.

8. The barriers shall display on both front and rear faces alternate red and white bands each approximately 600 mm long and to the full depth of the barriers. A band of red retro-reflecting material not less than 50 mm deep shall be provided along the full length of each red band.

9. Suitable screening shall be provided for each barrier machine to guard against danger to persons from the operating mechanism and moving parts of the machine.

10. A traffic light signal as prescribed by regulation 13(4) of the Regulations shall be provided on the left hand side of the road on each approach to the crossing and as close as practicable to the barrier. There shall be an additional traffic light signal of the same type on the right hand side of the road on each approach to the crossing so

located as to be either in line with or on the railway side of the stop line mentioned in paragraph 12. The traffic light signals on each side of the railway shall be positioned so as to face outwards from the crossing towards approaching road traffic. All the signals shall be capable of directional adjustment.

11. An audible warning device shall be provided on or adjacent to each left hand side traffic light signal post on each approach to the crossing. Facilities shall be provided to reduce the sound output of these devices and any reduced sound output shall operate between 23.30 hours and 07.00 hours approximately.

12. A reflectorised stop line of the size and type shown in diagram 1001 in the Regulations shall be provided across the left hand side of the carriageway on each approach to the crossing approximately 1 metre before the left hand side traffic light signal.

13. A reflectorised pedestrian stop line of the size and type shown in diagram 1003.2 in the Regulations shall be provided across the right hand side of the carriageway on each approach to the crossing and any made up ground on both sides of the carriageway on both sides of the railway. The line shall be not less than 1 metre before the right hand side traffic light signal and not nearer than 2 metres to the running edge of the nearest rail and shall be as nearly as possible at right angles to the centre line of the carriageway.

14. Where the road passes over the crossing, reflectorised edge of carriageway road markings of the size and type shown in diagram 1011 in the Regulations shall be provided along each edge of any made up ground along each edge of the carriageway.

15. The centre line of the carriageway shall be marked on the crossing between the stop lines mentioned in paragraph 12 and for a distance of at least 14 metres on each side of the railway measured along the centre of the carriageway from the stop lines with a reflectorised warning road marking of the size and type shown in diagram 1004 in the Regulations.

16. A traffic sign of the size, colour and type shown in diagram 863 in the Regulations shall be provided below or adjacent to each traffic light signal and shall face outwards from the crossing towards approaching road traffic.

17. A traffic sign of the size, colour and type shown in diagram 649.2 in the Regulations shall be provided on each road approach to the crossing facing traffic approaching the crossing.

18. A telephone mounted in a cabinet and connected to the monitoring signal box at Londonderry shall be provided on or adjacent to each right hand side traffic light signal post. In the event of the Londonderry signal box being closed the same monitoring equipment shall be provided at Coleraine signal box. A traffic sign of the size, colour and type shown in diagram 854 in the Regulations shall be provided on the door of the cabinet.

19. Two independent power supplies shall be provided at the crossing, one of which may consist of standby batteries of sufficient capacity to operate the whole installation for 12 hours.

20. In this Schedule—

"the Regulations" means the Traffic Signs Regulations (Northern Ireland) 1979(**a**).

(**a**) S.R. 1979 No. 386; relevant amending Regulations are S.R. 1982 No. 389, S.R. 1984 No. 58 and S.R. 1986 No. 173

SCHEDULE 2

CONDITIONS AND REQUIREMENTS TO BE COMPLIED WITH BY THE RAILWAY UNDERTAKING

1. The carriageway shall be at least 5.0 metres wide at the crossing.

2. The ground at the two edges of the carriageway over the crossing shall be made up to the level of the carriageway for a distance of not less than 1 metre beyond each edge.

3. The surface of the carriageway over the crossing shall be maintained in good and even condition.

4. The barriers shall be kept in the fully raised position except during the time when engines, carriages or other vehicles passing along the railway have occasion to cross the road.

5. The electric lamps on each barrier mentioned in Schedule 1 shall be lit at all times except when the barriers are in the fully raised position.

6. If the road approaches to the crossing are lit the crossing shall be lit to at least the same standard.

7. Visual indicators and an audible alarm shall be provided in the monitoring signal box. The indicators shall show when the barriers are raised and when the main power supply is available, and the alarm shall sound if a period of approximately 3 minutes elapses and there is no indication that the barriers are raised.

8. The barriers, the audible warning devices and the traffic light signals mentioned in Schedule 1 shall be activated automatically, as described in paragraph 9, by the approach of a train but means shall also be provided at the crossing for their manual operation and control.

9. When the train either occupies a track circuit or operates a treadle the audible warning devices and the traffic light signals shall begin to operate and the barriers shall be lowered in accordance with the following sequence—

(a) the amber lights shall show and the audible warning shall begin. The lights shall show for approximately 3 seconds;

(b) immediately the amber lights are extinguished the intermittent red lights shall begin to show;

(c) 4 to 8 seconds later, the barriers shall begin to descend and shall take a further 6 to 8 seconds to reach the lowered position;

(d) not less than 27 seconds shall elapse between the time when the amber lights first show and the time when the train reaches the crossing;

(e) the intermittent red lights shall continue to show and the audible warning devices shall continue to sound until the barriers have begun to rise and all said lights and devices shall be switched off before the barriers have risen to an angle of 45 degrees above the horizontal. However, if the barriers have not fully raised within 7.5 seconds of having started to rise then the red road lights will be illuminated until both barriers are proved fully up.

10. Both barriers shall rise as soon as possible after the train has passed the crossing.

11. In the event of the failure of both intermittent red lights in any of the road traffic signals, when the intermittent red lights should be shown, both barriers shall descend immediately (if not already lowered) and shall remain lowered.

12. Should a total power failure occur both barriers shall descend under gravity or remain lowered as the case may be. If after the barriers have begun to lower one barrier fails to reach the fully lowered position, neither barrier shall rise until both have been fully lowered.

13. If either barrier fails to rise from the lowered position the intermittent red lights shall continue to show, provided a total power failure has not occurred.

EXPLANATORY NOTE

(This note is not part of the Order.)

This Order provides for the provision and maintenance of a system of automatic barriers in lieu of an automatic open crossing at the Lock railway level crossing. Section 47 of the Railways Clauses Consolidation Act 1845 (which requires the railway undertaking to provide gates and gate-keepers), section 6 of the Railways Clauses Act 1863 (requirements as to lodges, etc.) and any other statutory provision imposing requirements to the same or similar effect, shall not apply to the crossing whilst this Order remains in force.

Schedule 1 sets out the particulars of barriers, lights, traffic signs and other devices which are to be provided at the crossing. Schedule 2 states the conditions and requirements with which the railway undertaking must comply in relation to the crossing.

1994   No. 31

HEALTH AND PERSONAL SOCIAL SERVICES

Optical Charges and Payments (Amendment) Regulations (Northern Ireland) 1994

Made	*31st January 1994*
Coming into operation . .	*21st February 1994*

The Department of Health and Social Services, in exercise of the powers conferred on it by Articles 98 and 106 of, and Schedule 15 to, the Health and Personal Social Services (Northern Ireland) Order 1972(**a**) and of all other powers enabling it in that behalf, with the approval of the Department of Finance and Personnel, hereby makes the following regulations:

Citation, commencement and interpretation

1.—(1) These regulations may be cited as the Optical Charges and Payments (Amendment) Regulations (Northern Ireland) 1994 and shall come into operation on 21st February 1994.

(2) In these regulations, "the principal regulations" means the Optical Charges and Payments Regulations (Northern Ireland) 1989(**b**).

Amendment of regulation 1 of the principal regulations

2. In regulation 1(2) of the principal regulations (interpretation) in the definition of "health service sight test fee"—

(*a*) in sub-paragraph (*a*) for "£33·75" there shall be substituted "£34·22"; and

(*b*) in sub-paragraph (*b*) for "£12·75" there shall be substituted "£12·92".

Sealed with the Official Seal of the Department of Health and Social Services on 31st January 1994.

(L.S.)   *Joan Dixon*
                                         Assistant Secretary

(**a**) S.I. 1972/1265 (N.I. 14) as amended by S.I. 1984/1158 (N.I. 8) Article 3(2) and paragraph 3 of Schedule 1; S.I. 1988/2249 (N.I. 24) paragraphs 4 and 5 of Article 8, and S.I. 1991/194 (N.I. 1) Article 34 and Part II of Schedule 5; there are other amendments which are not relevant
(**b**) S.R. 1989 No. 114 as amended by S.R. 1991 No. 496, and S.R. 1992 No. 155

Sealed with the Official Seal of the Department of Finance and Personnel on 31st January 1994.

(L.S.) *Doreen Brown*
Assistant Secretary

EXPLANATORY NOTE

(This note is not part of the Regulations.)

These regulations further amend the Optical Charges and Payments Regulations (Northern Ireland) 1989 ("the principal regulations") which provide for payments to be made, by means of a voucher system, in respect of costs incurred by certain categories of persons in connection with the supply, replacement and repair of optical appliances.

Regulation 2 amends the definition of "health service sight test fee" in regulation 1(2) of the principal regulations by increasing by 1·33 per cent the amount by which entitlement to assistance with the cost of a private sight test, and the value of a voucher towards such cost or towards the supply of glasses or contact lenses, is calculated.

1994 No. 32

Medicines (Advisory Board on the Registration of Homeopathic Products) Order 1994

This Order has been made by the Secretary of State concerned with health in England, the Secretaries of State respectively concerned with health and with agriculture in Scotland and in Wales, the Minister of Agriculture, Fisheries and Food, the Department of Health and Social Services for Northern Ireland, and the Department of Agriculture for Northern Ireland, acting jointly, in exercise of the powers conferred by section 4 of the Medicines Act 1968.

In pursuance of paragraph 11 of Schedule 4 to that Act this Order has been registered as a Northern Ireland statutory rule under the Statutory Rules (Northern Ireland) Order 1979. It is printed in full in the volume of United Kingdom Statutory Instruments for 1994 and has been numbered 102 in that series.

1994 No. 33

Medicines (Standard Provisions for Licences and Certificates) Amendment Regulations 1994

These Regulations have been made by the Secretary of State concerned with health in England, the Secretaries of State respectively concerned with health and with agriculture in Scotland and in Wales, the Minister of Agriculture, Fisheries and Food, the Department of Health and Social Services for Northern Ireland, and the Department of Agriculture for Northern Ireland, acting jointly, in exercise of the powers conferred by sections 47(1) and 129(5) of the Medicines Act 1968.

In pursuance of paragraph 11 of Schedule 4 to that Act these Regulations have been registered as a Northern Ireland statutory rule under the Statutory Rules (Northern Ireland) Order 1979. They are printed in full in the volume of United Kingdom Statutory Instruments for 1994 and have been numbered 103 in that series.

1994 No. 34

Medicines (Labelling and Leaflets) Amendment Regulations 1994

These Regulations have been made by the Secretaries of State respectively concerned with health in England, in Wales and in Scotland and the Department of Health and Social Services for Northern Ireland, acting jointly as the Health Ministers in exercise of the powers conferred by sections 85(1), 86(1) and 91(3) of the Medicines Act 1968.

In pursuance of paragraph 11 of Schedule 4 to that Act these Regulations have been registered as a Northern Ireland statutory rule under the Statutory Rules (Northern Ireland) Order 1979. They are printed in full in the volume of United Kingdom Statutory Instruments for 1994 and have been numbered 104 in that series.

1994 No. 35

ANIMALS

Bovine Embryo Collection and Transplantation Regulations (Northern Ireland) 1994

Made		*31st January 1994*
Coming into operation	. .	*7th March 1994*

The Department of Agriculture, in exercise of the powers conferred on it by Article 5(1) and (2) of the Artificial Reproduction of Animals (Northern Ireland) Order 1975(**a**) and section 2(1) of the Welfare of Animals Act (Northern Ireland) 1972(**b**), and of every other power enabling it in that behalf and after consultation as to regulation 11 with such persons appearing to it to represent the interests concerned as it considers appropriate hereby makes the following Regulations:—

Citation and commencement

1. These Regulations may be cited as the Bovine Embryo Collection and Transplantation Regulations (Northern Ireland) 1994 and shall come into operation on 7th March 1994.

Interpretation

2.—(1) In these Regulations—

"bovine embryo collection team" means a group of technicians who collect, process and store embryos under the supervision of a team veterinarian;

"bovine embryo transplantation team" means a group of technicians who transplant embryos under the supervision of a team veterinarian;

"collection" in relation to any embryo means the collection of that embryo from a cow;

"the Directive" means Council Directive 89/556/EEC on animal health conditions governing intra-Community trade in and importation from third countries of embryos of domestic animals of the bovine species(**c**);

"embryo" has the same meaning as in the Directive;

"intra-Community trade" means export to any Member State of the Economic Community other than the United Kingdom;

(**a**) S.I. 1975/1834 (N.I. 17)
(**b**) 1972 c. 7 (N.I.)
(**c**) O.J. No. L302, 19.10.89, p. 1 as amended by Council Directive 90/425/EEC (O.J. No. L224, 18.8.90, p. 29)

"processing" in relation to any embryo means the examination, washing, treating and placing in identified and sterile containers of that embryo;

"team veterinarian" means a veterinary surgeon who is responsible for supervising the activities of a bovine embryo collection or a bovine embryo transplantation team, as the case may be;

"transplantation" means the transplantation into a cow of an embryo collected from another cow;

"veterinary prohibition or quarantine measures" means measures imposed by the Department of Agriculture for the purpose of controlling or eradicating an outbreak of disease in bovine animals; and

"veterinary surgeon" means a veterinary surgeon (or veterinary practitioner) registered or recognised under the Veterinary Surgeons Act 1966(**a**).

(2) In relation to any embryo "the donor cow" means the cow from which it is collected and "the recipient cow" means the cow into which it is transplanted.

Licences

3. Any licence granted under these Regulations—

(*a*) shall be in writing;

(*b*) may be granted subject to conditions; and

(*c*) may be modified or suspended by notice in writing given to the holder thereof at any time.

Application

4.—(1) Subject to paragraph (2) these Regulations apply to—

(*a*) the collection, processing, storage and transport of embryos produced by *in vivo* fertilisation; and

(*b*) the transplantation of embryos.

(2) These Regulations do not apply in relation to embryos produced for the purposes of research carried out in accordance with the conditions of a valid licence issued under the Animals (Scientific Procedures) Act 1986(**b**).

Licensing of bovine embryo collection teams and their facilities

5.—(1) Upon the Department being satisfied that a bovine embryo collection team complies with paragraph (*a*) of Chapter I of Annex A to the Directive, and has at its disposal—

(*a*) permanent laboratory facilities as specified in paragraphs (*c*) and (*d*) of that Chapter; or

---

(*b*) mobile laboratory facilities as specified in paragraphs (*c*) and (*e*) of that Chapter and which have contact with such permanent laboratory facilities,

it shall licence that team for the purposes of collecting and processing, and those permanent or mobile laboratory facilities for the purposes of processing, any embryos.

(2) Upon the Department being satisfied that a bovine embryo collection team complies with paragraph (*a*) of Chapter I of Annex A to the Directive and has at its disposal a mobile laboratory which—

(*a*) has separate parts so that there is no contact between used and unused equipment and materials;

(*b*) carries sufficient equipment to enable the examination and manipulation of embryos to be carried out without contaminating them; and

(*c*) has contact with a permanently sited laboratory to ensure the sterilisation of its equipment and the provision of fluids and other products necessary for the collection and manipulation of embryos,

it shall licence that team for the purposes of collecting and processing, and that mobile laboratory for the purposes of processing, embryos which are not intended for intra-Community trade.

(3) The Department shall issue to each bovine embryo collection team licensed under this regulation a distinguishing registration number.

Collection of bovine embryos

6.—(1) Subject to paragraphs (3) and (4), a person shall not collect any embryo unless—

(*a*) he is a member of a bovine embryo collection team licensed for the purpose under regulation 5(1) or (2);

(*b*) at the date of collection, the donor cow is not subject to any veterinary prohibition or quarantine measures and shows no clinical sign of infectious disease;

(*c*) if the embryo was conceived using raw semen, at the date the donor cow was inseminated with that semen the bovine animal from which the semen came was not subject to any veterinary prohibition or quarantine measures and showed no sign of infectious disease; and

(*d*) the embryo is collected and processed in accordance with Schedule 1 in laboratory facilities licensed for the purpose under regulation 5(1) or (2).

(2) A person shall not collect any embryo for the purpose of intra-Community trade unless—

(*a*) he is a member of a bovine embryo collection team licensed for the purpose under regulation 5(1);

(*b*) the embryo was conceived as a result of artificial insemination with semen from a bovine animal standing at a semen collection centre as defined in Article 2(*b*) of Council Directive 88/407/EEC laying down the animal health requirements applicable to intra-Community trade in, and imports of, deep-frozen semen of domestic animals of the bovine species(**a**) or as a result of natural service by bulls whose health status complies with Annex B to that Directive if authorised under Article 3(*a*), second indent, of Council Directive 89/556/EEC;

(*c*) the donor cow complies with the requirements of Annex B to the Directive; and

(*d*) the embryo is collected and processed in accordance with paragraph 1(*a*) to (*l*) of Chapter II of Annex A to the Directive in laboratory facilities licensed for the purpose under regulation 5(1).

(3) An embryo may be collected by a member of a bovine embryo collection team licensed under regulation 5(1) or (2), or a veterinary surgeon, for transplantation without being processed in accordance with Schedule 1 if—

(*a*) it is intended for use in the United Kingdom without being frozen or stored;

(*b*) the recipient cow is owned by the same person as the donor cow;

(*c*) at the date of collection, the donor cow is not subject to any veterinary prohibition or quarantine measures; and

(*d*) if the embryo was conceived using raw semen, at the date when the donor cow was inseminated with that semen the bovine animal from which the semen came was not subject to any veterinary prohibition or quarantine measures.

(4) Where the Department thinks fit, it may licence the collection, by a member of a bovine embryo collection team licensed under regulation 5(1) or (2) or a veterinary surgeon, of an embryo not intended for intra-Community trade where the conditions specified in this regulation are not satisfied in relation thereto.

Processing

7. A person shall not process any embryo under these Regulations unless he is a member of a bovine embryo collection team licensed for the purpose under regulation 5(1) or (2).

Storage and transport

8.—(1) A person shall not store any embryo except in premises which—

(*a*) comply with paragraph 2 of Chapter II of Annex A to the Directive;

(*b*) are licensed by the Department for the purpose; and

(*c*) subject to paragraph (4), are under the supervision of a veterinary surgeon approved in writing by the Department who, in the case of embryos intended for intra-Community trade, shall be a team veterinarian.

(**a**) O.J. No. L194, 22.7.1988, p. 10 as amended by Council Directive 90/120/EEC (O.J. No. L71, 17.3.90, p. 37) and Council Directive 90/425/EEC (O.J. No. L224, 18.8.90, p. 29)

(2) A person shall not transport any embryo except under satisfactory hygienic conditions.

(3) A person shall not transport any embryo for the purposes of intra-Community trade except in a sealed container marked in accordance with paragraph (3) of Chapter II of Annex A to the Directive.

(4) Notwithstanding paragraph (1) a person may store an embryo other than under the supervision of a veterinary surgeon approved under that paragraph if he is licensed for the purpose by the Department and the embryo is not intended for intra-Community trade.

Licensing of bovine embryo transplantation teams

9. Upon the Department being satisfied that a bovine embryo transplantation team—

(*a*) is supervised by a veterinary surgeon; and

(*b*) has at its disposal a room or area equipped for cleaning and sterilising instruments and equipment used in the transplantation of embryos;

it shall licence that team and those facilities for the purposes of the transplantation of embryos.

Transplantation of bovine embryos

10.—(1) A person shall not carry out any transplantation unless he is—

(*a*) a member of a bovine embryo transplantation team licensed for the purpose under regulation 9; or

(*b*) a veterinary surgeon.

(2) A person who is not a veterinary surgeon, shall only carry out a transplantation if—

(*a*) he is competent to do so;

(*b*) he has been trained by a team veterinarian in methods and techniques of hygiene; and

(*c*) the transplantation is carried out under the supervision of the team veterinarian.

(3) A veterinary surgeon shall only carry out a transplantation if he clinically examines the recipient cow before doing so and satisfies himself that—

(*a*) it is suitable to receive the embryo; and

(*b*) there is no reason at that time to believe that the cow would not be able to carry to term a normal calf of the breed and type of the embryo being transplanted and to calve naturally.

(4) A person who is not a veterinary surgeon shall only carry out the transplantation of an embryo if the team veterinarian, or a veterinary surgeon nominated for the purpose by him, has clinically examined the recipient cow within 30 days preceding the transplantation and has certified, in the form specified in Schedule 2, that—

(*a*) he has done so and that the cow is suitable to receive the embryo; and (*b*) he knows of no reason existing at the time of his examination which would cause him to believe that the cow would not be able to carry to term a normal calf of the breed and type specified in the certificate and to calve naturally.

(5) A person shall not transplant any embryo which has been collected, processed or stored in contravention of the provisions of these Regulations.

Requirements to use anaesthetics

11.—(1) A person shall not *per vaginam* collect any embryo from, or transplant any embryo into, a cow for the time being situate on agricultural land unless a general or an epidural anaesthetic has first been administered to the cow.

(2) A person who contravenes paragraph (1) shall be guilty of an offence under section 2 of the Welfare of Animals Act (Northern Ireland) 1972(**a**).

Record keeping

12.—(1) A team veterinarian responsible for supervising the activities of a bovine embryo collection team shall keep a record of those activities in accordance with paragraph 1(*o*) of Chapter II to Annex A of the Directive.

(2) A person (whether a veterinary surgeon or not) supervising any storage premises licensed under regulation 8(1) shall keep such records as may be necessary to comply with paragraph 2(iii) of Chapter II of Annex A to the Directive.

(3) A team veterinarian responsible for the supervision of the activities of a bovine embryo transplantation team shall keep a record, in relation to each transplantation carried out by a member of that team, of—

(*a*) the breed, age and identification of the recipient cow;

(*b*) the place where the transplantation was carried out; and

(*c*) the identification of the embryo together with details of its donor cow, if known.

Transitional provisions

13.—(1) Subject to paragraph (2), after 31st January 1999 a person shall not use any embryo collected before the date these Regulations come into operation, except in accordance with a licence issued by the Department.

(2) Notwithstanding the provisions of paragraph (1), a person may use any embryo collected in the period from 31st December 1990 until the date these Regulations come into operation if the embryo was collected in accordance with the provisions of the Directive.

(3) In the case of embryos collected before the coming into operation of these Regulations, it shall be a defence for any person charged with failing to keep any records required under regulation 12 to show that the information required thereunder to be recorded was not available.

(**a**) 1972 Ch. 7

Sealed with the Official Seal of the Department of Agriculture on 31st January 1994.

(L.S.) *D. A. J. Hirrell*

Assistant Secretary

Conditions relating to the collection and processing of bovine embryos

1. The embryo shall be processed in either a permanent laboratory facility or a mobile laboratory facility licensed under regulation 5(1) or (2), which is not situated in a zone subject to veterinary prohibition or quarantine measures.

2. All implements which come into contact with the embryo or donor cow during the collection and processing of the embryo shall not have been used previously or shall have been properly disinfected or sterilised prior to use.

3. Products of animal origin used during collection of an embryo and in the medium used to transport it shall be obtained from sources which present no animal health risk or shall have been so treated prior to such use so that such risk is prevented.

4. Storage and transportation flasks shall be properly disinfected or sterilised before the commencement of the initial filling operation.

5. The cryogenic agents used in the storage and transportation flasks shall not have been previously used for other products of animal origin.

6. Each embryo container and the containers in which they are stored and transported shall be clearly marked with—

   (*a*) the registration number issued to the relevant bovine embryo collection team under regulation 5(3);

   (*b*) the date of the collection of the embryo; and

   (*c*) either—

       (i) the breed and identification of the donor cow and the bovine animal from which the semen used to conceive the embryo was collected;

       or

       (ii) a code from which this information can be readily established.

7. Each embryo shall be washed at least 10 times in a special fluid for embryos which shall be changed each time. Each wash shall be a 100-fold dilution of the previous wash and a sterile micro-pipette shall be used to transfer the embryo between washes.

8. After the last wash carried out under paragraph 7, each embryo shall be subjected to microscopic examination over its entire surface to determine that the *zona pellucida* is intact and is free from any adherent material.

9. Each consignment of embryos (that is to say a quantity of embryos removed in one operation from a single donor cow) that has successfully undergone the examination provided for in paragraph 8 shall be placed in a sterile container marked in accordance with paragraph 6 and which shall be sealed immediately.

SCHEDULE 2   Regulation 10(4)

CERTIFICATE

Bovine Embryo Transplantation

Breed and type of embryo(s) ....

Registration number of collection team ....

1. I hereby certify that the animal(s) identified in the Schedule overleaf was/were clinically examined by me on (date) .... at (address of premises)

....

....

....

....

2. I found the animal(s) to be in good health.

3. I was unable to detect any significant abnormalities of the reproductive tract(s) or birth canal(s).

4. I found the animal(s) to be in appropriate bodily condition and of a suitable size and conformation to receive the intended embryo(s).

5. On the basis of the above examination, I am of the opinion that the animal(s) specified in the second column of the Annex to this certificate is/are suitable to receive the embryo(s) specified opposite thereto. I know of no reason existing at the time of my examination which would cause me to believe that the animal(s) would not be able to carry to term a normal calf of the breed and type so specified in relation to it/them and to calve naturally.

Signed .... RCVS

Name (Block Capitals) ....

Date ....

Name of Practice ....

Address of Practice ....

....

....

ANNEX

	Recipient Identification (Ear Tag No.)	Recipient Breed and Type	Breed and Type of Intended Embryo(s)
1			
2			
3			
4			
5			
6			
7			
8			
9			
10			
11			
12			

The examining Veterinary Surgeon is required to sign immediately beneath the last entry on the above Schedule.

EXPLANATORY NOTE

(This note is not part of the Regulations.)

These Regulations regulate the collection, processing, storage, transportation and transplantation of bovine embryos. They implement the parts of Council Directive 89/556/EEC on animal health conditions governing intra-Community trade in and importation from third countries of embryos of domestic animals of the bovine species (O.J. No. L302, 19.10.89, p. 1) which deal with these matters.

They enable the Department to licence teams of technicians which carry out the collection of bovine embryos from donor cows (regulation 5) and their transplantation into recipient cows (regulation 9) together with the laboratory and other facilities used for those purposes. They regulate the collection, processing, storage and transportation of bovine embryos (regulations 6 to 8 and Schedule 1). They also regulate their transplantation (regulation 10 and Schedule 2) and include a requirement to use anaesthetics during collection and transplantation (regulation 11). They also impose requirements for record keeping (regulation 12). Regulation 13 makes certain transitional provisions.

Any person who fails to comply with any condition subject to which a licence under these Regulations is granted, who contravenes any provision of these Regulations (other than regulation 11) or knowingly or recklessly makes a statement false in a material particular for the purposes of obtaining a licence under these Regulations shall be guilty of an offence and shall be liable on summary conviction to a fine not exceeding £2,000 and to imprisonment for a term not exceeding 3 months. Any person who contravenes regulation 11 shall be guilty of an offence under section 2 of the Welfare of Animals Act (Northern Ireland) 1972 and shall be liable on summary conviction to imprisonment for a term not exceeding 3 months or to a fine not exceeding level 4 on the standard scale (currently £1,000) or both.

1994   No. 36

This Order has been exempted from printing by the Statutory Rules (Northern Ireland) Order 1979. A summary is given in the List of Statutory Rules of a Local Character under the heading ROADS.

1994   No. 37

FAMILY LAW

CHILD SUPPORT

The Child Support (Miscellaneous Amendments and Transitional Provisions) Regulations (Northern Ireland) 1994

Made	*3rd February 1994*
Coming into operation . .	*7th February 1994*

The Department of Health and Social Services, in exercise of the powers conferred on it by Articles 18, 19(6), 32(1) and (2), 39(3) and (4), 44, 47 and 48(4) of, and paragraphs 1(3), 4(1), 6(6) and 8(*a*) of Schedule 1 to, the Child Support (Northern Ireland) Order 1991(**a**) and of all other powers enabling it in that behalf, hereby makes the following regulations:

PART I

GENERAL

Citation, commencement and interpretation

1.—(1) These regulations may be cited as the Child Support (Miscellaneous Amendments and Transitional Provisions) Regulations (Northern Ireland) 1994 and shall come into operation on 7th February 1994.

(2) In these regulations—

"Collection and Enforcement Regulations" means the Child Support (Collection and Enforcement) Regulations (Northern Ireland) 1992(**b**);

"Fees Regulations" means the Child Support Fees Regulations (Northern Ireland) 1993(**c**);

"Maintenance Assessment Procedure Regulations" means the Child Support (Maintenance Assessment Procedure) Regulations (Northern Ireland) 1992(**d**);

"Maintenance Assessments and Special Cases Regulations" means the Child Support (Maintenance Assessments and Special Cases) Regulations (Northern Ireland) 1992(**e**).

(**a**)   S.I. 1991/2628 (N.I. 23)
(**b**)   S.R. 1992 No. 390
(**c**)   S.R. 1993 No. 73
(**d**)   S.R. 1992 No. 340; relevant amending regulations are S.R. 1993 No. 164
(**e**)   S.R. 1992 No. 341; to which there are amendments not relevant to these regulations

PART II

AMENDMENT OF REGULATIONS

Amendment of the Collection and Enforcement Regulations

2. In regulation 9(*e*) of the Collection and Enforcement Regulations (deduction from earnings orders) at the beginning there shall be inserted "except in the case of a Category A or Category B interim maintenance assessment within the meaning of regulation 8(1A) and (1B) of the Child Support (Maintenance Assessment Procedure) Regulations (Northern Ireland) 1992,"(**a**).

Amendment of the Fees Regulations

3.—(1) The Fees Regulations shall be amended in accordance with paragraphs (2) to (4).

(2) In Regulation 1(2) (citation, commencement and interpretation) for the definition of "collection fee" there shall be substituted the following definition—

" "collection fee" means a fee in respect of services provided by the Department for the collection of child support maintenance or for enforcing payment of such maintenance or both such collection and such enforcement;".

(3) In regulation 3 (liability to pay fees) for paragraph (3) there shall be substituted the following paragraph—

"(3) In a case falling within paragraph (1)(*b*) the fee payable shall be the assessment fee and if, but only if, collection or enforcement services (or both) are provided by the Department, the collection fee.".

(4) In regulation 4 (fees) for paragraph (2) there shall be substituted the following paragraph—

"(2) Where a collection fee is payable under regulation 3(2) or (3) the first such fee shall become payable on the date the Department first takes action to collect or enforce payment of child support maintenance, and any subsequent fee which becomes so payable shall be payable on the date the assessment fee becomes payable.".

Amendment of the Maintenance Assessment Procedure Regulations

4.—(1) The Maintenance Assessment Procedure Regulations shall be amended in accordance with paragraphs (2) to (5).

(2) In regulation 10(4) (notification of a new or a fresh maintenance assessment) for sub-paragraph (*c*) there shall be substituted the following sub-paragraphs—

"(*c*) where a fresh maintenance assessment is made following a review under Article 20 of the Order, Articles 18, 19 and 22 of the Order;

(**a**) Regulation 8 (1A) and (1B) was inserted by regulation 4(3)(*a*) of S.R. 1993 No. 164

(*d*) where a fresh maintenance assessment is made following a review under Article 21 of the Order, Articles 18, 19 and 20 of the Order.''.

(3) In regulation 19(2) (fresh assessments following a review on a change of circumstances) for the words after ''the provisions of paragraph 6 of Schedule 1 to the Order would apply to that assessment,'' there shall be substituted—

''he shall not make a fresh assessment if—

(*a*) where the amount fixed by the original assessment is less than the amount that would be fixed by the fresh assessment, the difference between the two amounts is less than £5·00 a week, and

(*b*) where the amount fixed by the original assessment is more than the amount that would be fixed by the fresh assessment, the difference between the two amounts is less than £1·00 a week.''.

(4) In regulation 20(2) (fresh assessments following a review on a change of circumstances: special case) for ''that difference is less than £1·00 per week'' there shall be substituted—

''that difference is less than—

(*a*) where the aggregate amount fixed by the original assessments is less than the aggregate amount that would be fixed by the fresh assessments, £5·00 a week, and

(*b*) where the aggregate amount fixed by the original assessments is more than the aggregate amount that would be fixed by the fresh assessments, £1·00 a week''.

(5) In regulation 30(1) (effective dates of maintenance assessments following a review under Articles 18 to 21 of the Order) at the end there shall be added ''disregarding any previous assessment made following a review made under Article 20 or 21 of the Order''.

Amendment of the Maintenance Assessments and Special Cases Regulations

5.—(1) The Maintenance Assessments and Special Cases Regulations shall be amended in accordance with paragraphs (2) to (6).

(2) In regulation 3(1) (calculation of AG) for sub-paragraph (*b*) there shall be substituted the following sub-paragraph—

''(*b*) with respect to a person with care of one or more qualifying children—

(i) where one or more of those children is aged less than 11, an amount equal to the amount specified in column (2) of paragraph 1(1)(*e*) of the relevant Schedule (income support personal allowance for a single claimant aged not less than 25);

(ii) where none of those children are aged less than 11 but one or more of them is aged less than 14, an amount equal to 75 per centum of the amount specified in sub-paragraph (*b*)(i), and

(iii) where none of those children are aged less than 14 but one or more of them is aged less than 16, an amount equal to 50 per centum of the amount specified in sub-paragraph (*b*)(i);''.

(3) In regulation 6 (additional element) for paragraph (1) there shall be substituted the following paragraph—

''(1) For the purposes of the formula in paragraph 4(1) of Schedule 1 to the Order, the value of R is—

(*a*) where the maintenance assessment in question relates to one qualifying child, 0·15;

(*b*) where the maintenance assessment in question relates to two qualifying children, 0·20, and

(*c*) where the maintenance assessment in question relates to three or more qualifying children, 0·25.''.

(4) In regulation 11 (protected income)—

(*a*) in paragraph (1)(*k*) for ''£8·00'' there shall be substituted ''£30·00'';

(*b*) in paragraph 1(*l*) for ''10 per centum'' there shall be substituted ''15 per centum''.

(5) In regulation 23 (person caring for children of more than one absent parent)—

(*a*) in paragraph (2) at the beginning there shall be inserted ''Subject to paragraph (2A),'';

(*b*) after paragraph (2) there shall be inserted the following paragraph—

''(2A) In applying the provisions of paragraph (2) to the amount which is to be included in the maintenance requirements under regulation 3(1)(*b*)—

(*a*) first take the amount specified in regulation 3(1)(*b*)(i) and divide it by the relevant number;

(*b*) then apply the provisions of regulation 3(1)(*b*) as if the references to the amount specified in column (2) of paragraph 1(1)(*e*) of the relevant Schedule were references to the amount which is the product of the calculation required by sub-paragraph (*a*) above, and as if, in relation to an absent parent, the only qualifying children to be included in the assessment were those qualifying children in relation to whom he is the absent parent.'';

(*c*) in paragraph (3) for ''in paragraph (2)'' there shall be substituted ''In paragraphs (2) and (2A)''.

(6) In Schedule 3 (eligible housing costs) in paragraph 3 for sub-paragraph (5) there shall be substituted the following sub-paragraph—

''(5) Where a policy of insurance has been obtained and retained for the purpose of discharging a mortgage or charge on the home of the parent in question and also for the purpose of accruing profits on the maturity of the policy, there shall be eligible to be taken into account as a housing cost—

  (*a*) where the sum secured by the mortgage or charge does not exceed £60,000, the whole of the premiums paid under that policy, and

  (*b*) where the sum secured by the mortgage or charge exceeds £60,000, the part of the premiums paid under that policy which are necessarily incurred for the purpose of discharging the mortgage or charge or, where that part cannot be ascertained, 0.0277 per centum of the amount secured by the mortgage or charge.''.

PART III

TRANSITIONAL PROVISIONS

Interpretation

6.—(1) In this Part and Part IV—

"the Order" means the Child Support (Northern Ireland) Order 1991;

"excess" means the amount by which the formula amount exceeds the old amount;

"existing case" means a case in which before the date when these regulations come into operation, a maintenance assessment has been made which has an effective date which also falls before that date;

"formula amount" means the amount of child support maintenance that would, but for the provisions of this Part, be payable under the maintenance assessment in force on the date these regulations come into operation or, if there is no such assessment, under the first assessment to come into force on or after that date;

"new case" means a case in which the effective date of the maintenance assessment falls on or after the date when these regulations come into operation;

"old amount" means, subject to paragraph (2), the aggregate weekly amount which was payable under the orders, agreements or arrangements mentioned in regulation 7(1)(*a*);

"pending case" means a case in which an application for a maintenance assessment has been made before the date when these regulations come into operation but no maintenance assessment has been made before that date;

"transitional amount" means an amount determined in accordance with regulation 8, and

"transitional period" means a period of, where the formula amount does not exceed £60, 52 weeks, and in any other case 78 weeks, beginning with—

  (*a*) in relation to an existing case, the day that the maintenance assessment in that case is reviewed following an application under regulation 9(1) to (3);

(*b*) in relation to a new case, the effective date of the maintenance assessment in that case;

(*c*) in relation to a pending case, the effective date of the maintenance assessment in that case or the date when these regulations come into operation, whichever is the later.

(2) In determining the old amount the child support officer shall disregard any payments in kind and any payments made to a third party on behalf of or for the benefit of the qualifying child or qualifying children or the person with care.

Scope of this Part

7.—(1) Subject to paragraph (2), this Part applies to cases where—

(*a*) on 4th April 1993, and at all times thereafter until the date when a maintenance assessment was or is made under the Order, there was in force, in respect of one or more of the qualifying children in respect of whom an application for a maintenance assessment was or is made under the Order and the absent parent concerned, one or more—

(i) maintenance orders;

(ii) orders under section 151 of the Army Act 1955(**a**) (deductions from pay for maintenance of wife or child) or section 151 of the Air Force Act 1955(**b**) (deductions from pay for maintenance of wife or child) or arrangements corresponding to such an order and made under Article 1(*b*) or 3 of the Naval and Marine Pay and Pensions (Deductions for Maintenance) Order 1959(**c**), or

(iii) maintenance agreements (being agreements which are made or evidenced in writing), and

(*b*) the absent parent was on the relevant date and continues to be a member of a family, as defined in regulation 1(2) of the Maintenance Assessments and Special Cases Regulations, which includes one or more children;

(*c*) the formula amount exceeds the old amount.

(2) Nothing in this Part applies to—

(*a*) a Category A interim maintenance assessment within the meaning of regulation 8(1B) of the Maintenance Assessment Procedure Regulations(**d**) and made under Article 14 of the Order, or

(*b*) a case falling within the provisions of Part II of the Schedule to the Child Support (1991 Order) (Commencement No. 3 and Transitional Provisions) Order (Northern Ireland) 1992(**e**) (modification of maintenance assessment in certain cases).

(**a**) 1955 c. 18
(**b**) 1955 c. 19
(**c**) This Order in Council is not a statutory instrument but is published in the London Gazette 31 July 1959 page 4801
(**d**) Regulation 8(1B) was inserted by regulation 4(3)(*a*) of S.R. 1993 No. 164
(**e**) S.R. 1992 No. 467 (C. 20); relevant amending rules are S.R. 1993 No. 174 (C. 9)

(3) In paragraph 1(*b*) "the relevant date" means—

(*a*) in an existing case, the date these regulations come into operation;

(*b*) in a new case, the effective date of the maintenance assessment in that case, and

(*c*) in a pending case, the effective date of the maintenance assessment in that case or the date on which these regulations come into operation, whichever is the later.

Transitional amount of child support maintenance

8.—(1) In a case to which this Part applies the amount of child support maintenance payable under a maintenance assessment during the transitional period shall, instead of being the formula amount, be the transitional amount.

(2) The transitional amount is—

(*a*) where the formula amount is not more than £60, an amount which is £20 greater than the old amount;

(*b*) where the formula amount is more than £60—

    (i) during the first 26 weeks of the transitional period, the old amount plus either 25 per centum of the excess or £20·00, whichever is the greater;

    (ii) during the next 26 weeks of the transitional period, the old amount plus either 50 per centum of the excess or £40·00, whichever is the greater, and

    (iii) during the last 26 weeks of the transitional period, the old amount plus either 75 per centum of the excess or £60·00, whichever is the greater.

(3) If in any case the application of the provisions of this Part would result in an amount of child support maintenance becoming payable which is greater than the formula amount, then those provisions shall not apply or, as the case may be, shall cease to apply to that case and the amount of child support maintenance payable in that case shall be the formula amount.

PART IV

PROCEDURE ETC.

Procedure

9.—(1) The provisions of Part III shall not apply to a case in which there is a maintenance assessment in force on the date they come into operation unless the absent parent in relation to whom that assessment was made makes an application for a review of that assessment under Article 19 of the Order.

(2) Such an application must be made not later than 3 months after the date when these regulations come into operation, but if an application is made after that period it may be accepted if the Department is satisfied that there is good reason for its being made late.

(3) Where a maintenance assessment is reviewed solely because of the coming into operation of Part III the provisions of regulations 10(2) and 18 of the Maintenance Assessment Procedure Regulations shall not apply in relation to that review but instead the child support officer shall notify to the relevant persons (as defined in regulation 1(2) of those Regulations) details of how the provisions of Part III have been applied in that case.

Reviews on change of circumstances

10.—(1) The provisions of paragraphs (2) and (3) shall apply where there is a review of a previous assessment under Article 19 of the Order (reviews on change of circumstances) at any time when the amount payable under that assessment is the transitional amount.

(2) Where the child support officer determines that, were a fresh assessment to be made as a result of the review, the amount payable under it (disregarding the provisions of Part III) (in this regulation called "the reviewed formula amount") would be—

(*a*) more than the formula amount, the amount of child support maintenance payable shall be the transitional amount plus the difference between the formula amount and the reviewed formula amount;

(*b*) less than the formula amount but more than the transitional amount, the amount of child support maintenance payable shall be the transitional amount;

(*c*) less than the transitional amount, the amount of child support maintenance payable shall be the reviewed formula amount.

(3) The child support officer shall, in determining the reviewed formula amount, apply the provisions of regulations 19 to 21 of the Maintenance Assessment Procedure Regulations.

Reviews consequent on the amendments made by Part II

11.—(1) Where a child support officer reviews a maintenance assessment in consequence only of the amendments made by Part II he shall not make a fresh assessment if the difference between the amount of child support maintenance fixed by the assessment currently in force and the amount that would be fixed if a fresh assessment were to be made as a result of the review is less than £1·00 a week.

(2) For the purposes of regulations 16(2)(**a**) (intervals between periodical reviews and notice of a periodical review) and 30 (effective dates of maintenance assessments following a review under Articles 18 to 21 of the Order) of the Maintenance Assessment Procedure Regulations, a review such as is mentioned in paragraph (1) shall be disregarded.

(3) Except in relation to the amendment made by regulation 5(6), notwithstanding anything in regulation 30 of the Maintenance Assessment Procedure Regulations the effective date of a maintenance assessment such as is mentioned in paragraph (1) shall be the date when these regulations come into operation.

(**a**) Regulation 16(2) was substituted by regulation 4(6)(*a*) of S.R. 1993 No. 164

Reviews consequent on the provisions of Part III

12. For the purposes of regulations 16(1) and 30 of the Maintenance Assessment Procedure Regulations a review made following an application under regulation 9 shall be disregarded.

Notification

13. Regulations 16(4) to (7) and 18(1) and (2)(**a**) of the Maintenance Assessment Procedure Regulations shall not apply to a review such as is mentioned in regulations 11(1) and 12 above.

Sealed with the Official Seal of the Department of Health and Social Services on 3rd February 1994.

(L.S.) *W. G. Purdy*
Assistant Secretary

(**a**) Regulation 18(2) was amended by regulation 4(7)(*a*) of S.R. 1993 No. 164

EXPLANATORY NOTE

(This note is not part of the Regulations.)

Part I of these Regulations contains the normal citation, commencement and interpretation provisions.

Part II makes amendments to various regulations concerned with child support maintenance under the Child Support (Northern Ireland) Order 1991 (''the Order''). Part III makes transitional provisions and Part IV makes provision for the procedure to be followed in consequence of the other provisions of the regulations.

In Part II amendments are made to the Child Support (Collection and Enforcement) Regulations (Northern Ireland) 1992 to exclude interim maintenance assessments from the scope of regulation 9(*e*) of those regulations which requires a deduction from earnings order to state the level of protected earnings (regulation 2). The Child Support Fees Regulations (Northern Ireland) 1993 are amended to provide that a collection fee is payable in relation to an assessment made under the Order only where the Department of Health and Social Services is providing services for the collection or enforcement of payment of child support maintenance (regulation 3). The Child Support (Maintenance Assessment Procedure) Regulations (Northern Ireland) 1992 are amended to alter the amount by which a fresh assessment must differ from the original assessment before it has effect and to make drafting changes (regulation 4). The Child Support (Maintenance Assessments and Special Cases) Regulations (Northern Ireland) 1992 are amended so as to alter the amounts which are to be taken into account in assessing child support maintenance (regulation 5).

Part III makes further provision for those cases where on 4th April 1993 there was already in force a maintenance order or agreement. For cases fulfilling specified conditions transitional relief is provided for a period of up to 78 weeks.

Part IV makes provision about reviews of maintenance assessments to give effect to the other provisions of the regulations and for notification of such reviews.

1994 No. 38

HEALTH AND SAFETY

Notification of Cooling Towers and Evaporative Condensers Regulations (Northern Ireland) 1994

Made	*4th February 1994*
Coming into operation . .	*29th March 1994*

The Department of Economic Development being the Department concerned(**a**), in exercise of the powers conferred on it by Articles 17(1), (2) and (4) and 55(2) of, and paragraph 14(1) of Schedule 3 to, the Health and Safety at Work (Northern Ireland) Order 1978(**b**) and of every other power enabling it in that behalf, after consultation in accordance with Article 46(1) of that Order with the Health and Safety Agency for Northern Ireland and such other bodies as appeared to the Department to be appropriate, hereby makes the following Regulations:—

Citation and commencement

1. These Regulations may be cited as the Notification of Cooling Towers and Evaporative Condensers Regulations (Northern Ireland) 1994 and shall come into operation on 29th March 1994.

Interpretation

2. In these Regulations—

"cooling tower" means a device whose main purpose is to cool water by direct contact between that water and a stream of air;

"the Department" means the Department of Economic Development;

"evaporative condenser" means a device whose main purpose is to cool a fluid by passing that fluid through a heat exchanger which is itself cooled by contact with water passing through a stream of air;

"heat exchanger" means a device for transferring heat between fluids which are not in direct contact with one another;

"notifiable device" means a cooling tower or an evaporative condenser except where its water and electrical supplies are not connected and it contains no water that is exposed to air;

"premises" means all non-domestic premises used for or in connection with the carrying on of a trade, business or other undertaking (whether for profit or not) being premises where persons work.

(**a**) *See* Article 2(2) of S.I. 1978/1039 (N.I. 9)
(**b**) S.I. 1978/1039 (N.I. 9)

Notification of a notifiable device

3.—(1) Subject to this regulation and to regulation 4, it shall be the duty of each person who has, to any extent, control of premises to ensure that no notifiable device is situated on those premises unless the information set out in the Schedule has been notified in writing, on a form approved for the time being for the purposes of these Regulations by the Department, to the district council in whose district the premises are situated.

(2) Where the premises are to any extent under the control of the manufacturer of the device, it shall be sufficient compliance with paragraph (1) if the district council in whose district the premises are situated is notified of the address of the premises and the name and telephone number of a person who has, to any extent, control of those premises.

(3) Where a notification has been made in accordance with paragraph (1) or (2) and subsequently a change occurs which affects the particulars notified, a person upon whom the duty is imposed by either of those paragraphs shall ensure that the change is notified in writing to the district council concerned within one month after its occurrence.

(4) Where a notification has been made in accordance with paragraph (1), (2) or (3) and subsequently the device ceases to be, and is no longer intended to remain, a notifiable device, a person upon whom the duty is imposed by any of those paragraphs shall as soon as is reasonably practicable after the cessation ensure that the fact is notified in writing to the district council concerned.

(5) Paragraph (4) shall not apply in any case where the operation of a notifiable device is suspended for the purpose of maintenance or by reason of seasonal shutdown.

Transitional provision

4. Where a notifiable device is situated on premises before 30th September 1994 it shall be sufficient compliance with regulation 3 if the notification required by that regulation is made by that date.

Sealed with the Official Seal of the Department of Economic Development on 4th February 1994.

(L.S.)   *Philip B. Strong*
                                      Assistant Secretary

SCHEDULE   Regulation 3(1)

Information to be notified to the district council

1. The address of the premises where the notifiable device is to be situated.

2. The name, address and telephone number of a person who has, to any extent, control of the premises referred to in paragraph 1.

3. The number of notifiable devices at the premises referred to in paragraph 1.

4. The location on the premises of each notifiable device referred to in paragraph 3.

EXPLANATORY NOTE

(This note is not part of the Regulations.)

These Regulations require a person who has, to any extent, control of non-domestic premises used as a place of work to ensure that no notifiable device (as defined in regulation 2) is situated on the premises unless information specified in the Schedule has been notified in writing to the district council in whose district the premises are situated (regulation 3(1)). Where the premises on which the notifiable device is to be situated are under the control of the manufacturer of the device, regulation 3(2) provides that it shall be sufficient compliance with regulation 3(1) if the address of the premises and the name and telephone number of a person who has, to any extent, control of the premises is notified to the district council. Changes to the information required to be notified under regulation 3(1) or (2) must be notified within one month after their occurrence (regulation 3(3)). Where a device ceases to be, and is no longer intended to remain, a notifiable device that fact must be notified to the district council concerned as soon as reasonably practicable after the cessation (regulation 3(4)). The requirement in regulation 3(4) will not apply where the operation of a notifiable device is suspended for the purpose of maintenance or by reason of seasonal shutdown (regulation 3(5)).

The Regulations also contain a transitional provision (regulation 4).

Any person who contravenes the Regulations is guilty of an offence under Article 31 of the Health and Safety at Work (Northern Ireland) Order 1978.

1994   No. 39

This Order has been exempted from printing by the Statutory Rules (Northern Ireland) Order 1979. A summary is given in the List of Statutory Rules of a Local Character under the heading ROADS.

1994   No. 40

FISHERIES

Angling (Department of Agriculture Waters) Amendment Byelaws (Northern Ireland) 1994

Made . . . . . *4th February 1994*

Coming into operation . . *9th March 1994*

The Fisheries Conservancy Board for Northern Ireland, in exercise of the powers conferred on it by section 26(1)(**a**) of the Fisheries Act (Northern Ireland) 1966(**b**) and of every other power enabling it in that behalf, with the approval of the Department of Agriculture, hereby makes the following Byelaws:

Citation and commencement

1. These Byelaws may be cited as the Angling (Department of Agriculture Waters) Amendment Byelaws (Northern Ireland) 1994 and shall come into operation on 9th March 1994.

Amendment of the Angling (Department of Agriculture Waters) Byelaws (Northern Ireland) 1989

2. The Schedule to the Angling (Department of Agriculture Waters) Byelaws (Northern Ireland) 1989(**c**) shall be amended as follows:—

in the entries relating to the River Bush and tributaries in the second column ("Methods of Angling") in the entry opposite paragraphs (*h*) and (*c*) in the first column, after the words "fly fishing only from 1st March–30th June" there shall be added:—

"Worm fishing shall be permitted from 1st March until 30th June provided only that a single hook of size 2 or greater is used. Such a hook shall be one on which the barb is turned to face towards the shank and shall have minimum dimensions as follows:

(*a*) the gape (being the aperture from the out-turned shank to the tip of the out-turn before the barb is formed) shall be 8 mm;

(*b*) the barb (being the point of the hook from the tip of the out-turn to its own tip or extremity) shall be 4 mm".

(**a**)   As amended by S.I. 1991/1446 (N.I. 13) Article 8(3)
(**b**)   1966 c. 17 (N.I.)
(**c**)   S.R. 1989 No. 482 as amended by S.R. 1992 No. 357 Byelaw 6

Sealed with the Common Seal of the Fisheries Conservancy Board for Northern Ireland on 4th February 1994.

(L.S.)   *Dr. J. Parsons*

Chairman

(L.S.)   *W. F. Smith*

Secretary

The Department of Agriculture hereby approves the foregoing Byelaws.

Sealed with the Official Seal of the Department of Agriculture on 7th February 1994.

(L.S.)   *L. Sinclair*

Assistant Secretary

EXPLANATORY NOTE

(This note is not part of the Byelaws.)

These Byelaws further amend the Schedule to the Angling (Department of Agriculture Waters) Byelaws (Northern Ireland) 1989 to permit worm fishing on the River Bush and its tributaries from 1st March until 30th June provided only that a single hook of size 2 or greater is used. Such a hook shall be one on which the barb is turned to face towards the shank and shall have specified minimum dimensions.

1994   No. 41

GAS

Gas Undertaker (Premier Transco Limited) Order (Northern Ireland) 1994

Made	*7th February 1994*
Coming into operation . .	*1st April 1994*

To be laid before Parliament under paragraph 3(3) of Schedule 1 to the Northern Ireland Act 1974

The Department of Economic Development, in exercise of the powers conferred by Article 14(1) of the Gas (Northern Ireland) Order 1977(**a**) and now vested in it(**b**) and of every other power enabling it in that behalf, on the application of Premier Transco Limited, hereby makes the following Order:

Citation and commencement

1. This Order may be cited as the Gas Undertaker (Premier Transco Limited) Order (Northern Ireland) 1994, and shall come into operation on 1st April 1994.

Declaration of an undertaker for the supply of gas

2. Premier Transco Limited is hereby declared to be an undertaker for the supply of gas.

Sealed with the Official Seal of the Department of Economic Development on 7th February 1994.

(L.S.)

D. B. McIlldoon
Assistant Secretary

(**a**) S.I. 1977/596 (N.I. 7)
(**b**) By S.I. 1982/846 (N.I. 11) Article 4

EXPLANATORY NOTE

(This note is not part of the Order.)

This Order declares Premier Transco Limited to be an undertaker for the supply of gas. That Company will accordingly have the powers (including powers to acquire land compulsorily) and duties of a gas undertaker under the Gas (Northern Ireland) Order 1977.

1994   No. 42

HEALTH AND PERSONAL SOCIAL SERVICES

The Northern Ireland Regional Medical Physics Agency (Establishment and Constitution) Order (Northern Ireland) 1994

Made	*8th February 1994*
Coming into operation . .	*1st April 1994*

The Department of Health and Social Services, in exercise of the powers conferred on it by Article 3(1), (2), (4) and (6) of the Health and Personal Social Services (Special Agencies) (Northern Ireland) Order 1990(a) and of all other powers enabling it in that behalf, and after consultation, in accordance with Article 3(5) of that Order, with such bodies as it recognises as representing officers who in its opinion are likely to be transferred or affected by transfers in pursuance of this order, hereby makes the following order:

Citation, commencement and interpretation

1.—(1) This order may be cited as the Northern Ireland Regional Medical Physics Agency (Establishment and Constitution) Order (Northern Ireland) 1994 and shall come into operation on 1st April 1994.

(2) In this order—

"The Agency" means the Northern Ireland Regional Medical Physics Agency;

"member" includes chairman.

Establishment of the Northern Ireland Regional Medical Physics Agency

2. There is hereby established a special health and social services agency which shall be known as the Northern Ireland Regional Medical Physics Agency.

Constitution of the Agency

3. The Agency shall consist of such number of members as the Department may determine, all of whom shall be appointed by the Department.

Tenure of office

4. Subject to Article 5, the tenure of office of a member shall be four years or such other lesser period as may be determined by the Department at the time the appointment is made.

(a) S.I. 1990/247 (N.I. 3)

Termination of tenure of office

5.—(1) A member may resign his office at any time during the period for which he was appointed by giving notice in writing to the Department.

(2) Where the Department is satisfied that it is not in the interests of the Agency or the health and personal social services that a person whom it has appointed as a member should continue to hold that office, it may forthwith terminate that member's tenure of office.

(3) Where the place of a member becomes vacant before the expiration of his tenure of office whether by death, resignation or otherwise, the vacancy shall be filled by appointment by the Department and any person so appointed shall hold office for the remainder of the tenure of office of the former member.

Proceedings of the Agency

6. The proceedings of the Agency shall not be invalidated by any vacancy in the membership of the Agency or by any defect in the appointment of any of its members.

Transfer of staff

7. Any officer of the Eastern Health and Social Services Board who immediately before the date upon which this order comes into operation is employed by that Board in one of the divisions specified in the Schedule to the order shall be transferred to the Agency on the date of the coming into operation of this order and the contract of employment between each such officer and the Eastern Health and Social Services Board shall be modified so as to substitute the Agency as the employer.

Enforceability of rights and liabilities

8. Any right or liability which was enforceable by or against the Eastern Health and Social Services Board in respect of the employment by that Board of any officer who is transferred to the employment of the Agency by virtue of Article 7 shall be enforceable by or against the Agency.

Protection of officers

9. The scale of renumeration of any officer transferred to the employment of the Agency by virtue of Article 7 and, taken as a whole, the other terms and conditions of the employment of that officer shall be no less favourable than the scale of renumeration, terms and conditions enjoyed by him immediately before the transfer.

Sealed with the Official Seal of the Department of Health and Social Services on 8th February 1994.

(L.S.)

John McGrath
Assistant Secretary

SCHEDULE   Article 7

Northern Ireland Regional Medical Physics Service

SIX DIVISIONS

1. Radiation Protection and Dosimetry	— Forster Green Hospital Belfast BT8 4HD
	— Royal Victoria Hospital Belfast BT12 6BA
2. Radiotherapy Physics	— Belvoir Park Hospital Belfast BT8 8JR
3. Radioisotope	— Royal Victoria Hospital Belfast BT12 6BA
	— Belvoir Park Hospital Belfast BT8 8JR
4. Radiodiagnostic Physics	— Royal Victoria Hospital Belfast BT12 6BA
5. Ultrasound	— Royal Victoria Hospital Belfast BT12 6BA
6. Clinical Instrumentation and Patient Measurement	— Royal Victoria Hospital Belfast BT12 6BA
	— Belvoir Park Hospital Belfast BT8 8JR

EXPLANATORY NOTE

(This note is not part of the Order.)

This order provides for the establishment and constitution of a special health and social services agency, to be known as the Northern Ireland Regional Medical Physics Agency, for the purpose of carrying out such functions as the Department of Health and Social Services may direct in accordance with Article 4(1) of the Health and Personal Social Services (Special Agencies) (Northern Ireland) Order 1990.

1994 No. 43

ROAD TRAFFIC AND VEHICLES

Motor Vehicles (Driving Licences) (Designation of Relevant External Law) Order (Northern Ireland) 1994

Made	.	.	.	.	*8th February 1994*
Coming into operation		.	.	*14th March 1994*	

The Department of the Environment, in exercise of the powers conferred on it by Article 5(2)(*b*) and (*c*) of the Road Traffic (Northern Ireland) Order 1981(**a**) and of all other powers enabling it in that behalf, makes the following Order:

Citation and commencement

1. This Order may be cited as the Motor Vehicles (Driving Licences) (Designation of Relevant External Law) Order (Northern Ireland) 1994 and shall come into operation on 14th March 1994.

Designation of relevant external law

2. The law for the time being in force in the Isle of Man which corresponds to Part II of the Road Traffic (Northern Ireland) Order 1981(**b**) is hereby designated as one which makes satisfactory provision for—

(*a*) tests of competence to drive any class of goods vehicle or any class of passenger-carrying vehicle; and

(*b*) the granting of licences to drive any class of goods vehicle or any class of passenger-carrying vehicle.

Sealed with the Official Seal of the Department of the Environment on 8th February 1994.

(L.S.)   *Trevor Pearson*
                                                              Assistant Secretary

---

(**a**) S.I. 1981/154 (N.I. 1); Article 5 was substituted by Sch. 1 to S.I. 1991/197 (N.I. 3). *See* Art. 2(2) for the definition of "Department"
(**b**) Part II was substituted by Sch. 1 to S.I. 1991/197 (N.I. 3)

EXPLANATORY NOTE

(This note is not part of the Order.)

This Order designates the law of the Isle of Man as one which makes satisfactory provision for (*a*) tests of competence to drive goods and passenger-carrying vehicles for the purposes of Article 5(2)(*b*) of the Road Traffic (Northern Ireland) Order 1981 and (*b*) for the granting of licences to drive such vehicles for the purposes of Article 5(2)(*c*) of that Order.

1994 No. 44

HEALTH AND SAFETY

Control of Industrial Major Accident Hazards (Amendment) Regulations (Northern Ireland) 1994

Made	*10th February 1994*
Coming into operation . .	*21st March 1994*

The Department of Economic Development, being a Department designated by the European Communities (Designation) Order 1983(**a**) for the purposes of section 2(2) of the European Communities Act 1972(**b**) in relation to measures relating to the prevention and limitation of the effects of accidents arising from industrial activities involving dangerous substances, in exercise of the powers conferred on it by the said section 2(2) and being the Department concerned(**c**) in exercise of the powers conferred by Articles 17(1), (2), (3), (5) and (6), 40(2) and (4) and 55(2) of, and paragraphs 1(1) (2), 14(1) and 19 of Schedule 3 to, the Health and Safety at Work (Northern Ireland) Order 1978(**d**) and of every other power enabling it in that behalf, after consultation in accordance with Article 46(1) of that Order with the Health and Safety Agency for Northern Ireland and such other bodies as appeared to it to be appropriate, hereby makes the following Regulations:—

Citation and commencement

1. These Regulations may be cited as the Control of Industrial Major Accident Hazards (Amendment) Regulations (Northern Ireland) 1994, and shall come into operation on 21st March 1994.

Interpretation

2.—(1) In these Regulations "the principal Regulations" means the Control of Industrial Major Accident Hazards Regulations (Northern Ireland) 1985(**e**).

(2) The Interpretation Act (Northern Ireland) 1954(**f**) shall apply to these Regulations as it applies to a Measure of the Northern Ireland Assembly.

Revocation

3. Regulation 3(1)(*f*) of the principal Regulations is hereby revoked.

(**a**) S.I. 1983/603
(**b**) 1972 c. 68
(**c**) *See* Article 2(2) of S.I. 1978/1039 (N.I. 9)
(**d**) S.I. 1978/1039 (N.I. 9)
(**e**) S.R. 1985 No. 175, as amended by S.R. 1988 No. 388 and S.R. 1991 No. 141
(**f**) 1954 c. 33 (N.I.)

Application of the principal Regulations

4. Where an industrial activity becomes subject to regulations 7 to 12 of the principal Regulations in consequence of the revocation made by regulation 3 then, in relation to that activity, the principal Regulations shall have effect subject to the modifications specified in the Schedule.

Sealed with the Official Seal of the Department of Economic Development on 10th February 1994.

(L.S.)   *Philip B. Strong*
                                                  Assistant Secretary

Modification to the Principal Regulations in their Application to Additional Industrial Activities

1. In regulation 6(2)(*a*)(i), the reference to the coming into operation of this regulation shall be construed as a reference to the coming into operation of these Regulations.

2. In regulations 7(2) and 10(3)(*a*), references to the coming into operation of the principal Regulations shall be construed as references to the coming into operation of these Regulations.

3. In each regulation or Schedule specified in Column 1 of the following Table, the date specified opposite thereto in Column 3 shall apply in substitution for the existing date referred to in that regulation or Schedule and specified in the corresponding entry opposite thereto in Column 2.

TABLE

Column 1 *Regulation or Schedule*	Column 2 *Existing date*	Column 3 *Substituted date*
Regulation 7(3)	8th July 1989	1st January 1997
Regulation 7(3)	1st January 1986	21st March 1994
Regulation 10(3)(*b*)	1st January 1986	21st March 1994
Regulation 11(3)	1st July 1986	21st September 1994
Regulation 12(4)	4th April 1992	21st December 1994
Schedule 7, paragraph 4	30th September 1985	20th March 1994

EXPLANATORY NOTE

(This note is not part of the Regulations.)

These Regulations amend the Control of Industrial Major Accident Hazards Regulations (Northern Ireland) 1985 ("the principal Regulations") by applying those Regulations to the industrial activities referred to in the following paragraph for the purpose of implementing in full in respect of Northern Ireland, Council Directive 82/501/EEC (O.J. No. L230, 5.8.82, p. 1) on the major accident hazards of certain industrial activities.

Regulation 3 amends regulation 3(1) of the principal Regulations by revoking sub-paragraph (*f*) which exempted from the application of the principal Regulations those industrial activities carried on at any site operated by a district council in accordance with Article 13(2) of the Pollution Control and Local Government (Northern Ireland) Order 1978 (S.I. 1978/1049 (N.I. 19)) or for which a licence issued in pursuance of Article 7 of that Order is in force.

Regulation 4 provides that where the industrial activities referred to in the previous paragraph become subject to certain provisions of the principal Regulations as a consequence of the amendment made by regulation 3, the principal Regulations shall be modified in relation to those activities in accordance with the Schedule to these Regulations.

The Schedule introduces new compliance dates and transitional provisions for the relevant industrial activities.

1994 No. 45

SOCIAL SECURITY

The Social Security Benefit (Persons Abroad) (Amendment) Regulations (Northern Ireland) 1994

Made	*11th February 1994*
Coming into operation . .	*8th March 1994*

The Department of Health and Social Services for Northern Ireland, in exercise of the powers conferred on it by section 113(1)(*a*) of the Social Security Contributions and Benefits (Northern Ireland) Act 1992(**a**) and of all other powers enabling it in that behalf, hereby makes the following regulations:

Citation, commencement and interpretation

1.—(1) These regulations may be cited as the Social Security Benefit (Persons Abroad) (Amendment) Regulations (Northern Ireland) 1994 and shall come into operation on 8th March 1994.

(2) In these regulations "the principal regulations" means the Social Security Benefit (Persons Abroad) Regulations (Northern Ireland) 1978(**b**).

Amendment of the principal regulations

2.—(1) Regulation 2 of the principal regulations(**c**) (modification of the Act in relation to sickness benefit, invalidity benefit, severe disablement allowance, unemployability supplement and maternity allowance) shall be amended in accordance with paragraphs (2) to (4).

(2) In paragraph (1)—

(*a*) at the beginning there shall be inserted "Except as provided by paragraph (1A) or (1B) below,";

(*b*) for the words from "sickness benefit" to "maternity allowance" there shall be substituted "any benefit in respect of incapacity";

(*c*) after "any day" there shall be inserted "falling within the first 26 weeks beginning with the day following the day on which he left Northern Ireland";

(*d*) for ", (*c*) and (*d*)" there shall be substituted "and (*c*)";

(**a**) 1992 c. 7
(**b**) S.R. 1978 No. 114; relevant amending regulations are S.R. 1983 No. 36, S.R. 1984 No. 317, S.R. 1986 No. 303 and S.R. 1990 No. 22
(**c**) Regulation 2 was amended by regulation 11 of S.R. 1983 No. 36, regulation 15 of S.R. 1984 No. 317, regulation 2 of S.R. 1986 No. 303 and regulation 3 of S.R. 1990 No. 22

(*e*) in sub-paragraph (*c*) for "since the absence began; or" there shall be substituted "since the absence began.''; and

(*f*) sub-paragraph (*d*) shall be omitted.

(3) After paragraph (1) there shall be inserted the following paragraphs—

"(1A) Subject to paragraph (1B), a person who is in receipt of attendance allowance or disability living allowance shall not by reason of being temporarily absent from Northern Ireland be disqualified for receiving any benefit in respect of incapacity if—

(*a*) the absence is for the specific purpose of being treated for incapacity which commenced before he left Northern Ireland; or

(*b*) in the case of sickness benefit and invalidity benefit the incapacity for work is the result of a personal injury of a kind mentioned in section 94(1) of the Social Security Contributions and Benefits (Northern Ireland) Act 1992 and the absence is for the specific purpose of receiving treatment which is appropriate to that injury; or

(*c*) on the day on which the absence began he was, and had for the past 6 months continuously been, incapable of work and on the day for which benefit is claimed he has remained continuously so incapable since the absence began.

(1B) A person who is a member of the family of a serving member of the forces and temporarily absent from Northern Ireland by reason only of the fact that he is living with that member shall not by reason of being temporarily absent be disqualified—

(*a*) for receiving any benefit in respect of incapacity except severe disablement allowance if—

(i) the absence is for the specific purpose of being treated for incapacity which began before he left Northern Ireland; or

(ii) in the case of sickness benefit and invalidity benefit the incapacity for work is the result of a personal injury of a kind mentioned in section 94(1) of the Social Security Contributions and Benefits (Northern Ireland) Act 1992 and the absence is for the specific purpose of receiving treatment which is appropriate to that injury; or

(iii) on the day on which the absence began he was, and had for the past 6 months continuously been, incapable of work and on the day for which benefit is claimed he has remained continuously so incapable since the absence began, or

(*b*) for the receipt of severe disablement allowance.".

(4) After paragraph (4) there shall be added the following paragraph—

"(5) In this regulation—

(*a*) "benefit in respect of incapacity" means sickness benefit, invalidity benefit, severe disablement allowance, an unemployability supplement or a maternity allowance;

(*b*) "member of the family of a serving member of the forces" means the spouse, son, daughter, step-son, step-daughter, father, father-in-law, step-father, mother, mother-in-law or step-mother of such a member; and

(*c*) "week" means any period of 7 days.".

Transitional provision

3.—(1) In this regulation "the former regulation 2" means regulation 2 of the principal regulations as in operation immediately before the coming into operation of these regulations.

(2) Where, immediately before the coming into operation of these regulations, a person was absent from Northern Ireland but by virtue of the former regulation 2 was not disqualified for receiving any benefit, allowance or supplement referred to in paragraph (1) of the former regulation 2, that person shall continue not to be disqualified in respect of any day, if he—

(*a*) has been continuously absent from Northern Ireland since the coming into operation of these regulations; and

(*b*) would, had the former regulation 2 been in operation on that day, have satisfied the provisions of that regulation in respect of that benefit, allowance or supplement.

Revocation

4. Regulation 3 of the Social Security Benefit (Persons Abroad) (Amendment) Regulations (Northern Ireland) 1990(**a**) is hereby revoked.

Sealed with the Official Seal of the Department of Health and Social Services for Northern Ireland on 11th February 1994.

(L.S.) *C. P. Moore*

Assistant Secretary

(**a**) S.R. 1990 No. 22

EXPLANATORY NOTE

(This note is not part of the Regulations.)

These regulations amend regulation 2 of the Social Security Benefit (Persons Abroad) Regulations (Northern Ireland) 1978 ("the principal regulations") which sets out the circumstances in which the disqualification for the receipt of certain benefits during periods of absence from Northern Ireland does not apply.

The benefits concerned are sickness benefit, invalidity benefit, severe disablement allowance, unemployability supplement and maternity allowance. Unemployability supplement ceased to be payable from 6th April 1987 except in the case of beneficiaries in receipt of it immediately before that date: it is still payable in that case — see Part I (unemployability supplement) of Schedule 7 to the Social Security Contributions and Benefits (Northern Ireland) Act 1992.

The principal effect of the regulations is to restrict entitlement to these benefits to the first 26 weeks of a period of temporary absence from Northern Ireland unless the recipient is either a member of the family of a serving member of the forces who is abroad and with whom he is living, or is a person in receipt of attendance allowance or disability living allowance (regulation 2).

These regulations contain a transitional provision which protects the position in respect of any day for a person who—

(a) was absent from Northern Ireland immediately before the coming into operation of these regulations and was not subject to the disqualification for receipt of the relevant benefit, allowance or supplement imposed by section 113 of the Social Security Contributions and Benefits (Northern Ireland) Act 1992 by virtue of regulation 2 of the principal regulations as in operation immediately before the coming into operation of these regulations ("the former regulation 2");

(b) has been continuously absent from Northern Ireland since the coming into operation of these regulations; and

(c) would have satisfied the former regulation 2 on that day (regulation 3).

The regulations contain a consequential revocation (regulation 4).

These regulations correspond to provision contained in regulations made by the Secretary of State for Social Security in relation to Great Britain and accordingly, by virtue of section 149(3) of, and paragraph 10 of Schedule 5 to, the Social Security Administration (Northern Ireland) Act 1992 (c. 8), are not subject to the requirement of section 149(2) of that Act for prior reference to the Social Security Advisory Committee.

1994 No. 46

ROAD TRAFFIC AND VEHICLES

Motor Vehicles (Third-Party Risks) Regulations (Northern Ireland) 1994

Made		*10th February 1994*
Coming into operation	. .	*1st April 1994*

The Department of the Environment, in exercise of the powers conferred on it by Articles 103(1) and 218(1) of the Road Traffic (Northern Ireland) Order 1981(**a**) and of all other powers enabling it in that behalf, hereby makes the following Regulations:

Citation and commencement

1. These Regulations may be cited as the Motor Vehicles (Third-Party Risks) Regulations (Northern Ireland) 1994 and shall come into operation on 1st April 1994.

Interpretation

2.—(1) In these Regulations—

"company" means an authorised insurer within the meaning of Part VIII of the Order;

"motor vehicle" has the meaning assigned to it by Articles 2 and 212 of the Order;

"the Order" means the Road Traffic (Northern Ireland) Order 1981;

"policy" means a policy of insurance in respect of third-party risks arising out of the use of motor vehicles which complies with the requirements of Part VIII of the Order;

"security" means a security in respect of third-party risks arising out of the use of motor vehicles which complies with the requirements of Part VIII of the Order;

"specified body" means any of the bodies referred to in sub-paragraph (*a*) or (*aa*) of Article 90(2)(**b**) of the Order.

(2) Any reference in these Regulations to a certificate in Form A, B, C, D, E or F shall be construed as a reference to a certificate in the form so headed and set out in Part I of Schedule 1 which has been duly made and completed subject to and in accordance with the provisions set out in Part II.

(**a**) S.I. 1981/154 (N.I. 1); *see* Article 2(2) for the definition of "Department" and "prescribed"
(**b**) Article 90 was amended by S.I. 1984/1986 (N.I. 15), S.I. 1991/194 (N.I. 1) and S.R. 1994 No. 18

Issue of certificates of insurance or security

3.—(1) A company shall issue to every holder of a security or of a policy other than a covering note issued by the company—

(*a*) in the case of a policy or security relating to one or more specified vehicles a certificate of insurance in Form A or a certificate of security in Form D in respect of each such vehicle;

(*b*) in the case of a policy or security relating to vehicles other than specified vehicles such number of certificates in Form B or Form D as may be necessary for the purpose of complying with the requirements of Article 180(4) of the Order and of these Regulations as to the production of evidence that a motor vehicle is not being driven in contravention of Article 90 of the Order;

Provided that where a security is intended to cover the use of more than ten motor vehicles at one time the company by whom it was issued may, subject to the consent of the Department issue one certificate only, and where such consent has been given the holder of the security may issue duplicate copies of such certificate duly authenticated by him up to such number and subject to such conditions as the Department may determine.

(2) Notwithstanding the foregoing provisions, where as respects third-party risks a policy or security relating to a specified vehicle extends also to the driving by the holder of other motor vehicles, not being specified vehicles, the certificate may be in Form A or Form D, as the case may be, containing a statement in either case that the policy or security extends to such driving of other motor vehicles. Where such a certificate is issued by a company they may, and shall in accordance with a demand made to them by the holder, issue to him a further such certificate or a certificate in Form B.

(3) On every policy in the form of a covering note issued by a company there shall be printed on the front or on the back a certificate of insurance in Form C.

(4) Every certificate of insurance or certificate of security shall be issued not later than four days after the date on which the policy or security to which it relates is issued or renewed.

Avoidance of certain exceptions to policies or securities

4. There shall not be inserted in any policy or security issued or given for the purposes of the Order any condition, restriction or limitation, as the case may be, with regard to any of the following matters—

(*a*) the age or physical or mental condition of persons driving the vehicle;

(*b*) the race, nationality, religion or occupation of persons driving the vehicle;

(*c*) the period of driving experience of persons driving the vehicle;

(*d*) the existence of any endorsement on the licence of a person driving the vehicle;

(*e*) the condition of the vehicle;

(*f*) the number of persons that the vehicle carries;

(*g*) the weight or physical characteristics of the goods that the vehicle carries;

(*h*) the times at which or the areas within which the vehicle is used;

(*i*) the horse-power or cylinder capacity or value of the vehicle;

(*j*) the carrying on the vehicle of any particular apparatus; or

(*k*) the carrying on the vehicle of any particular means of identification other than any means of identification required to be carried by or under the Vehicles (Excise) Act 1971(**a**).

Production of evidence as alternatives to certificates

5. The following evidence that a motor vehicle is not or was not being driven in contravention of Article 90 of the Order may be produced as an alternative to the production of a certificate of insurance or a certificate of security—

(1) a duplicate copy of a certificate of security issued in accordance with the proviso to regulation 3(1)(*b*);

(2) in the case of a motor vehicle of which the owner has for the time being deposited with the Accountant-General of the Supreme Court the sum for the time being specified in Article 90(2)(*b*) of the Order(**b**), a certificate in Form E signed by the owner of the motor vehicle or by some person authorised by him in that behalf that such sum is on deposit;

Provided that where a deposit is intended to cover the use of more than 10 motor vehicles at one time then the certificate of deposit may be in such form as the Department may determine;

(3) in the case of a motor vehicle owned by a specified body, a certificate in Form F signed by some person authorised in that behalf by such specified body that the said motor vehicle is owned by the said specified body;

(4) in the case of a vehicle normally based in the territory, other than the United Kingdom and Gibraltar, of a member State of the European Community or of Austria, Czech Republic, Finland, Hungary, Norway, Slovakia, Sweden or Switzerland, a document issued by the insurer of the vehicle which indicates the name of the insurer, the number or other identifying particulars of the insurance policy issued in respect of the vehicle and the period of the insurance cover. In this paragraph the territory of the State in which a vehicle is normally based is—

(*a*) the territory of the State in which the vehicle is registered, or

(*b*) in cases where no registration is required for the type of vehicle, but the vehicle bears an insurance plate or distinguishing sign analogous to a registration plate, the territory of the State in which the insurance plate or the sign is issued, or

---

(**a**) 1971 c. 10; the Act was extended to Northern Ireland by section 10 of the Finance Act 1991 (c. 31)
(**b**) Article 90(2)(*b*) was amended by S.R. 1994 No. 18

    (*c*) in cases where neither registration plate nor insurance plate nor distinguishing sign is required for the type of vehicle, the territory of the State in which the keeper of the vehicle is permanently resident.

Certain certificates to be destroyed

    6. Any certificate issued in accordance with regulation 5(2) or (3) shall be destroyed by the owner of the vehicle to which it relates before the motor vehicle is sold or otherwise disposed of.

Production of evidence of insurance or security on application for excise licences

    7.—(1) Any person applying for a vehicle licence under the Vehicles (Excise) Act 1971 shall, except as hereinafter provided and subject to the provisions of regulation 8 of the Motor Vehicles (International Motor Insurance Card) (Northern Ireland) Regulations 1969(**a**) produce to the Department either—

    (*a*) a certificate of insurance, certificate of security or duplicate copy of a certificate of security issued in accordance with these Regulations indicating that on the date when the licence comes into operation there will be in force the necessary policy or the necessary security in relation to the user of the motor vehicle by the applicant or by other persons on his order or with his permission and such further evidence as may be necessary to establish that the certificate relates to such user; or

    (*b*) in the case where the motor vehicle is one of more than ten motor vehicles owned by the same person in respect of which a policy or policies of insurance have been obtained by him from the same authorised insurer, a statement duly authenticated by the authorised insurer to the effect that on the date when the licence becomes operative an insurance policy which complies with Part VIII of the Order will be in force in relation to the user of the motor vehicle; or

    (*c*) evidence that Article 90 of the Order does not apply to the motor vehicle at a time when it is being driven under the owner's control, in accordance with the following provisions—

      (i) in the case of a motor vehicle of which the owner has for the time being deposited with the Accountant-General of the Supreme Court the sum for the time being specified in Article 90(2)(*b*) of the Order, a certificate in Form E signed by the owner of the motor vehicle or by some person authorised by him in that behalf that such sum is on deposit;

      (ii) in the case of a motor vehicle owned by a specified body a certificate in Form F signed by some person authorised in that behalf by such specified body that the vehicle in respect of which the application for a licence is made is owned by the said specified body.

(**a**)   S.R. & O. (N.I.) 1969 No. 129; to which there are amendments not relevant to these Regulations

(2) A person engaged in the business of letting motor vehicles on hire shall not, when applying for a licence under the Vehicles (Excise) Act 1971, be required to comply with the provisions of paragraph (1) if the motor vehicle in respect of which the licence is applied for is intended to be used solely for the purpose of being let on hire and driven by the person by whom the motor vehicle is hired or by persons under his control.

Keeping of records by companies

8.—(1) Every company by whom a policy or a security is issued shall keep a record of the following particulars relative thereto and of any certificates issued in connection therewith—

(*a*) the full name and address of the person to whom the policy, security or certificate is issued;

(*b*) in the case of a policy relating to one or more specified motor vehicles the registration mark of each such motor vehicle;

(*c*) the date on which the policy or security comes into force and the date on which it expires;

(*d*) in the case of a policy the conditions subject to which the persons or classes of persons specified in the policy will be indemnified;

(*e*) in the case of a security the conditions subject to which the undertaking given by the company under the security will be implemented;

and every such record shall be preserved for one year from the date of expiry of the policy or security.

(2) Every specified body shall keep a record of the motor vehicles owned by them in respect of which a policy or a security has not been obtained, and of any certificates issued by them under these Regulations in respect of such motor vehicles, and of the withdrawal or destruction of any such certificates.

(3) Any person who has deposited and keeps deposited with the Accountant-General of the Supreme Court the sum for the time being specified in Article 90(2)(*b*) of the Order shall keep a record of the motor vehicles owned by him and of any certificates issued by him or on his behalf under these Regulations in respect of such motor vehicles and of the withdrawal or destruction of any such certificates.

(4) Any company, specified body or other person by whom records of documents are required by these Regulations to be kept shall without charge furnish the Department or to any superintendent of the Royal Ulster Constabulary on request any particulars thereof.

Notification to the Department of ineffective policies or securities

9. Where to the knowledge of a company a policy or security issued by them ceases to be effective without the consent of the person to whom it was issued, otherwise than by effluxion of time or by reason of his death, the company shall forthwith notify the Department of the date on which the policy or security ceased to be effective.

Provided that such notification need not be made if the certificate relating to the policy or security has been received by the company from the person to whom the certificate was issued on or before the date on which the policy or security ceases to be effective.

Return of certificates to issuing company

10. Where a certificate of insurance has been delivered to the person by whom a policy has been effected, or where a certificate of security has been issued to the person to whom a security has been given and such policy or security has been cancelled in pursuance of the provisions of Article 95 of the Order, a new policy or security shall not be issued to that person nor shall the said policy or security be transferred to any other person unless and until the certificate has been returned to the company or the company are satisfied that it has been lost or destroyed.

Issue of fresh certificates

11. Where any company by whom a certificate of insurance or a certificate of security has been issued are satisfied that the certificate has become defaced or has been lost or destroyed they shall, if they are requested to do so by the person to whom the certificate was issued, issue to him a fresh certificate. In the case of a defaced certificate the company shall not issue a fresh certificate unless the defaced certificate is returned to the company.

Temporary use of existing forms

12. Nothing in these Regulations shall effect the validity of any certificate which has been issued before these Regulations came into operation in a form prescribed by the Regulations mentioned in Schedule 2, as in force immediately before the coming into operation of these Regulations, and any certificate in such a form may continue to be issued until the expiration of three years from the coming into operation of these Regulations.

Revocation

13. The Regulations set out in Schedule 2 are hereby revoked.

Sealed with the Official Seal of the Department of the Environment on 10th February 1994.

(L.S.)   *Trevor Pearson*
     Assistant Secretary

SCHEDULE 1 (see regulation 2(2))

PART I

FORM OF CERTIFICATES

FORM A

Certificate of Motor Insurance

Certificate No. .... Policy No. .... (Optional)

1. Registration mark of vehicle.

2. Name of policy holder.

3. Effective date of the commencement of insurance for the purposes of the relevant law.

4. Date of expiry of insurance.

5. Persons or classes of persons entitled to drive.

6. Limitations as to use.

I/We hereby certify that the policy to which this certificate relates satisfies the requirements of the relevant law applicable in Northern Ireland.

....
Authorised Insurers

NOTE: For full details of the insurance cover
reference should be made to the policy.

FORM B

Certificate of Motor Insurance

Certificate No. .... Policy No. .... (Optional)

1. Description of vehicles.

2. Name of policy holder.

3. Effective date of the commencement of insurance for the purposes of the relevant law.

4. Date of expiry of insurance.

5. Persons or classes of persons entitled to drive.

6. Limitations as to use.

I/We hereby certify that the policy to which this certificate relates satisfies the requirements of the relevant law applicable in Northern Ireland.

....
Authorised Insurers

NOTE: For full details of the insurance cover
reference should be made to the policy.

FORM C

Certificate of Motor Insurance

I/We hereby certify that this covering note satisfies the requirements of the relevant law applicable in Northern Ireland.

....
Authorised Insurers

FORM D

Certificate of Security

Certificate No. .... Security No. .... (Optional)

1. Name of holder of security.

2. Effective date of the commencement of security for the purposes of the relevant law.

3. Date of expiry of security.

4. Conditions to which security is subject.

I/We hereby certify that the security to which this certificate relates satisfies the requirements of the relevant law applicable in Northern Ireland.

....
Persons giving security

NOTE: For full details of the cover reference should be made to the security.

FORM E

Certificate of Deposit

I/We hereby certify that I am/we are the owner(s) of the vehicle of which the registration mark is .... and that in pursuance of the relevant law applicable in Northern Ireland I/we have on deposit with the Accountant-General of the Supreme Court the sum for the time being specified in Article 90(2)(*b*) of the Road Traffic (Northern Ireland) Order 1981.

Signed ....

on behalf of ....

FORM F

Certificate of Ownership

We hereby certify that the vehicle of which the registration mark is

.... is owned by ....

Signed ....

on behalf of ....

PART II

PROVISIONS RELATING TO THE FORMS AND COMPLETION OF CERTIFICATES

1. Every certificate shall be printed and completed in black on a white background. This provision shall not prevent the reproduction of a seal or monogram or similar device referred to in paragraph 2, or the presence of a background pattern (of whatever form and whether coloured or not) on the face of the form which does not materially affect the legibility of the certificate.

2. No certificate shall contain any advertising matter, either on the face or on the back thereof:

Provided that the name and address of the company by whom the certificate is issued, or a reproduction of the seal of the company or any monogram or similar device of the company, or the name and address of an insurance broker, shall not be deemed to be advertising matter for the purposes of this paragraph if it is printed or stamped at the foot or on the back of such certificate, or if it forms, or forms part of, any such background pattern as is referred to in paragraph 1.

3. The whole of each form as set out in Part I shall in each case appear on the face of the form, the items being in the order so set out and the certification being set out at the end of the form.

4. The particulars to be inserted on the said forms shall so far as possible appear on the face of the form, but where in the case of any of the numbered headings in Forms A, B or D, this cannot conveniently be done, any part of such particulars may be inserted on the back of the form, provided that their presence on the back is clearly indicated under the relevant heading.

5. The particulars to be inserted on any of the said forms shall not include particulars relating to any exceptions purporting to restrict the insurance under the relevant policy or the operation of the relevant security which are by regulation 4 rendered of no effect as respects the third-party liabilities required by Articles 92(**a**) and 93 of the Order to be covered by a policy or security.

6.—(1) In any case where it is intended that a certificate of insurance, certificate of security or a covering note shall be effective not only in Northern Ireland, but also in any of the following territories, that is to say Great Britain, the Isle of Man, the Island of Guernsey, the Island of Jersey or the Island of Alderney, Forms A, B, C and D may be modified by the addition thereto, where necessary, of a reference to the relevant legal provisions of such of those territories as may be appropriate.

(2) A certificate of insurance or a certificate of security may contain either on the face or on the back of the certificate a statement as to whether or not the policy or security to which it relates satisfies the requirements of the relevant law in any of the territories referred to in this paragraph.

7. Every certificate of insurance or certificate of security shall be duly authenticated by or on behalf of the company by whom it is issued.

(**a**)   Article 92 was amended by S.R. 1989 No. 84 and S.R. 1993 No. 57

SCHEDULE 2 (see regulation 13)

Regulations revoked

Title	Year and Number
Motor Vehicles (Third Party Risks) Regulations (Northern Ireland) 1972	S.R. & O. 1972 No. 235
Motor Vehicles (Third Party Risks) (Amendment) Regulations (Northern Ireland) 1973	S.R. & O. 1973 No. 447
Motor Vehicles (Third Party Risks) (Amendment) Regulations (Northern Ireland) 1974	S.R. 1974 No. 207
Motor Vehicles (Third Party Risks) (Amendment) Regulations (Northern Ireland) 1981	S.R. 1981 No. 357

EXPLANATORY NOTE

(This note is not part of the Regulations.)

These Regulations revoke and re-enact, with amendments, the Motor Vehicles (Third Party Risks) Regulations (Northern Ireland) 1972, as amended.

The principal amendments are—

(1) references to the amount to be kept deposited with the Accountant-General of the Supreme Court of Northern Ireland in lieu of an insurance policy or security have been amended from the amount of fifteen thousand pounds to the amount for the time being specified in Article 90(2)(*b*) of the Road Traffic (Northern Ireland) Order 1981 (currently £500,000); and

(2) to allow certificates of insurance or security to be produced on material other than paper or similar material.

1994 No. 47 (C. 2)

COMPANIES

Companies (1990 Order) (Commencement No. 5) Order (Northern Ireland) 1994

Made . . . . . *10th February 1994*

The Department of Economic Development, in exercise of the powers conferred on it by Article 1 of the Companies (Northern Ireland) Order 1990(**a**) and paragraph 2(1) of Schedule 1 to the Northern Ireland Act 1974(**b**) and of every other power enabling it in that behalf, hereby makes the following Order:

Citation and interpretation

1.—(1) This Order may be cited as the Companies (1990 Order) (Commencement No. 5) Order (Northern Ireland) 1994.

(2) In this Order "the 1986 Order" means the Companies (Northern Ireland) Order 1986(**c**) and "the 1990 Order" means the Companies (Northern Ireland) Order 1990.

Provisions of the 1990 Order brought into operation

2. Subject to Article 3, Articles 3 and 13 of the 1990 Order shall come into operation on 7th April 1994 for the purpose of inserting the new provision Article 250A into Part VIII of the 1986 Order.

Transitional provision

3.—(1) This Article applies where—

(*a*) the requirements of Article 250 of the 1986 Order as to the delivering of accounts and reports before the end of the period allowed for so doing have not been complied with before 7th April 1994, and

(*b*) those requirements have still not been complied with on that date.

(2) In such a case, the period by reference to the length of which the amount of the penalty is determined under Article 250A(2) of the 1986 Order shall be deemed to commence on 7th April 1994.

Sealed with the Official Seal of the Department of Economic Development on 10th February 1994.

(L.S.) *Miss A. L. Browne*
Assistant Secretary

(**a**) S.I. 1990/593 (N.I. 5)
(**b**) 1974 c. 28
(**c**) S.I. 1986/1032 (N.I. 6)

EXPLANATORY NOTE

(This note is not part of the Order.)

This Order brings into operation on 7th April 1994 Articles 3 and 13 of the Companies (Northern Ireland) Order 1990 for the purpose of inserting a new Article 250A (liability to civil penalty for failure to deliver accounts and reports under Article 250) into Part VIII of the Companies (Northern Ireland) Order 1986 ("the 1986 Order").

Article 3 makes transitional provision in cases where the requirements of Article 250 of the 1986 Order as to the delivery of accounts and reports have not been complied with before 7th April 1994, and have still not been complied with on that date. In such cases the period by reference to which the amount of the civil penalty is calculated under Article 250A(2) is deemed to commence on 7th April 1994.

NOTE AS TO EARLIER COMMENCEMENT ORDERS
(This note is not part of the Order.)

The following provisions of the Companies (Northern Ireland) Order 1990 have been brought into operation by commencement order made before the date of this Order:—

Provision	Date of Commencement	S.R. No.
Arts. 1 and 2	1st August 1990	1990 No. 246 (C. 9)
Art. 3 (partially)	1st August 1990 or 1st September 1991	1990 No. 246 (C. 9) or 1991 No. 267 (C. 13)
Arts. 4 to 12 Schs. 1 to 5	1st August 1990 or 1st September 1991	1990 No. 246 (C. 9) or 1991 No. 267 (C. 13)
Art. 13 (partially)	1st August 1990	1990 No. 246 (C. 9)
Art. 14	1st September 1991	1991 No. 267 (C. 13)
Arts. 15 to 24, Schs. 6 to 9	1st August 1990	1990 No. 246 (C. 9)
Art. 25, Sch. 10	1st August 1990 or 1st October 1990 or 1st September 1991	1990 No. 246 (C. 9) or 1991 No. 267 (C. 13)
Art. 26 (partially)	1st August 1990 or 1st September 1991	1990 No. 246 (C. 9) or 1991 No. 267 (C. 13)
Art. 27 (partially)	1st August 1990 or 29th March 1993	1990 No. 246 (C. 9) or 1993 No. 63 (C. 4)
Arts. 28 to 32	29th March 1993	1993 No. 63 (C. 4)
Art. 33, Sch. 11	1st August 1990	1990 No. 246 (C. 9)
Art. 34	1st August 1990 or 29th March 1993	1990 No. 246 (C. 9) or 1993 No. 63 (C. 4)
Arts. 35 to 42, Sch. 12	1st August 1990 or 21st November 1991	1990 No. 246 (C. 9) 1991 No. 499 (C. 23)

Arts. 43 to 46	1st August 1990 or 29th March 1993	1990 No. 246 (C. 9) or 1993 No. 63 (C. 4)
Art. 47	1st August 1990	1990 No. 246 (C. 9)
Art. 49 (partially) Sch. 14	1st August 1990	1990 No. 246 (C. 9)
Art. 50 (partially)	1st August 1990	1990 No. 246 (C. 9)
Art. 51	1st August 1990 or 29th March 1993	1990 No. 246 (C. 9) or 1993 No. 63 (C. 4)
Arts. 52 and 53	1st August 1990	1990 No. 246 (C. 9)
Arts. 54 to 56	1st August 1990 or 29th March 1993	1990 No. 246 (C. 9) or 1993 No. 63 (C. 4)
Art. 57 (partially)	1st August 1990 or 29th March 1993	1990 No. 246 (C. 9) or 1993 No. 63 (C. 4)
Sch. 15 (partially)	1st August 1990 or 1st September 1991 or 29th March 1993	1990 No. 246 (C. 9) or 1991 No. 267 (C. 13) or 1993 No. 63 (C. 4)

1994 No. 48

POLICE

Royal Ulster Constabulary (Discipline and Disciplinary Appeals) (Amendment) Regulations 1994

Made		*11th February 1994*
Coming into operation . .		*31st March 1994*

To be laid before Parliament

The Secretary of State, in pursuance of sections 25 and 26 of the Police Act (Northern Ireland) 1970(**a**), and after consulting the Police Authority and the Police Association in accordance with section 34(2) of the said Act, hereby makes the following regulations:—

Citation and commencement

1. These regulations may be cited as the Royal Ulster Constabulary (Discipline and Disciplinary Appeals) (Amendment) Regulations 1994 and shall come into operation on 31st March 1994.

Interpretation

2. In these regulations any reference to the principal regulations is a reference to the Royal Ulster Constabulary (Discipline and Disciplinary Appeals) Regulations 1988(**b**).

Disciplinary Hearings: Ranks of and below Chief Superintendent

3. Schedule 4 to the principal regulations shall be amended as follows—

(*a*) in paragraph 2 there shall be added at the end the words "The member who is senior in rank shall be chairman but if the members are of equal rank the chief constable shall designate one of them chairman.";

(*b*) in paragraph 6 in the first column (Description of officer or disciplinary board conducting the hearing)—

(i) in sub-paragraph (*a*) for the words "a chairman of a rank not lower than senior assistant chief constable and one other member" there shall be substituted the words "2 members"; and

(ii) in sub-paragraph (*b*) the words from "disciplinary board" to the end shall be omitted.

(**a**) 1970 c. 9 (N.I.) as amended by S.I. 1977/53 (N.I. 2) and S.I. 1987/938 (N.I. 10) and modified by S.I. 1973/2163
(**b**) S.R. 1988 No. 10, amended by S.R. 1989 No. 471

P. B. B. Mayhew

Northern Ireland Office   One of Her Majesty's Principal
11th February 1994   Secretaries of State

EXPLANATORY NOTE

(This note is not part of the Regulations.)

These regulations further amend the Royal Ulster Constabulary (Discipline and Disciplinary Appeals) Regulations 1988 (the principal regulations).

Regulation 3 provides that the chairman of a disciplinary board appointed by the chief constable under paragraph 2 of Schedule 4 to the principal regulations shall be the member who is senior in rank or, if both members are of the same rank, shall be designated by the chief constable. The regulation also broadens the powers of a disciplinary board consisting of 2 members of a rank not lower than assistant chief constable to include dismissal and requirement to resign.

1994 No. 49

POLICE

Royal Ulster Constabulary Reserve (Part-time) (Discipline and Disciplinary Appeals) (Amendment) Regulations 1994

Made	*11th February 1994*
Coming into operation . .	*31st March 1994*

To be laid before Parliament

The Secretary of State, in pursuance of section 26 of the Police Act (Northern Ireland) 1970(**a**), and after consulting the Police Authority and the Police Association in accordance with section 34(2) of the said Act, hereby makes the following regulations:—

Citation and commencement

1. These regulations may be cited as the Royal Ulster Constabulary Reserve (Part-time) (Discipline and Disciplinary Appeals) (Amendment) Regulations 1994 and shall come into operation on 31st March 1994.

Interpretation

2. In these regulations any reference to the principal regulations is a reference to the Royal Ulster Constabulary Reserve (Part-time) (Discipline and Disciplinary Appeals) Regulations 1988(**b**).

Internal appeals

3. In regulation 22(4) of the principal regulations there shall be substituted for the words "senior assistant" the word "deputy".

P. B. B. Mayhew

Northern Ireland Office
11th February 1994

One of Her Majesty's Principal
Secretaries of State

(**a**) 1970 c. 9 (N.I.) as amended by S.I. 1977/53 (N.I. 2) and S.I. 1987/938 (N.I. 10) and modified by S.I. 1973/2163
(**b**) S.R. 1988 No. 8, amended by S.R. 1989 No. 472

EXPLANATORY NOTE
(This note is not part of the Regulations.)

These regulations amend the Royal Ulster Constabulary Reserve (Part-time) (Discipline and Disciplinary Appeals) Regulations 1988 (the principal regulations).

Regulation 3 amends regulation 22 of the principal regulations which granted the accused in disciplinary proceedings a right of appeal to the chief constable or to an officer not below the rank of senior assistant chief constable appointed by him by providing that the officer to be so appointed shall, with effect from 31st March 1994, be not below the rank of deputy chief constable.

1994 No. 50

FAIR EMPLOYMENT

Fair Employment (Increase of Compensation Limit) Order (Northern Ireland) 1994

Made	*15th February 1994*
Coming into operation . .	*15th March 1994*

Whereas it appears to the Department of Economic Development ("the Department")(**a**) that there has been a change in the value of money since the commencement of section 50(1) of the Fair Employment (Northern Ireland) Act 1989(**b**);

And whereas it appears to the Department that the sum substituted by Article 4 of this Order for the sum for the time being specified in section 26(4) of the Fair Employment (Northern Ireland) Act 1976 ("the 1976 Act")(**c**) is justified by that change;

Now therefore the Department in exercise of the powers conferred on it by section 26(9) of the 1976 Act and of every other power enabling it in that behalf, hereby makes the following Order:

Citation and commencement

1. This Order may be cited as the Fair Employment (Increase of Compensation Limit) Order (Northern Ireland) 1994 and shall come into operation on 15th March 1994.

Interpretation

2. The Interpretation Act (Northern Ireland) 1954(**d**) shall apply to this Order as it applies to a Measure of the Northern Ireland Assembly.

Application

3. Article 4 shall have effect in relation to any compensation awarded to a person under section 26(1)(b) of the 1976 Act after this Order comes into operation.

Increase of compensation limit

4. In section 26(4) of the 1976 Act, for the sum of £30,000 there shall be substituted the sum of £35,000.

(**a**) Formerly the Department of Manpower Services; *see* S.I. 1982/846 (N.I. 11) Article 3
(**b**) 1989 c. 32
(**c**) 1976 c. 25; section 26 was inserted by section 50 of the Fair Employment (Northern Ireland) Act 1989
(**d**) 1954 c. 33 (N.I.)

Sealed with the Official Seal of the Department of Economic Development on 15th February 1994.

(L.S.)   *W. D. A. Haire*
Assistant Secretary

EXPLANATORY NOTE

(This note is not part of the Order.)

This Order increases from £30,000 to £35,000 the limit on the amount of compensation which can be awarded by the Fair Employment Tribunal under section 26(1)(b) of the Fair Employment (Northern Ireland) Act 1976 in claims for unlawful discrimination presented to it under section 24 of that Act.

The increase applies in any case where the Tribunal awards such compensation after 15th March 1994, the date when this Order comes into operation.

1994 No. 51

PENSIONS

Superannuation (Museums Council) Order (Northern Ireland) 1994

Made	*7th February 1994*
Coming into operation . .	*18th March 1994*

The Department of Finance and Personnel in exercise of the powers conferred by Article 3(4) and (7) of the Superannuation (Northern Ireland) Order 1972(**a**) and now vested in it(**b**) and of every other power enabling it in that behalf, hereby makes the following Order:

1. This Order may be cited as the Superannuation (Museums Council) Order (Northern Ireland) 1994 and shall come into operation on 18th March 1994.

2. There shall be added to the employments and offices listed in Schedule 1 to the Superannuation (Northern Ireland) Order 1972 with effect from 1st December 1993 employment in the Northern Ireland Museums Council.

Sealed with the Official Seal of the Department of Finance and Personnel on 7th February 1994.

(L.S.) *F. P. Smyth*
Assistant Secretary

(**a**) S.I. 1972/1073 (N.I. 10)
(**b**) By S.R. 1976 No. 281 Art. 3 and Sch. 1 and S.I. 1982/338 (N.I. 6) Art. 4

EXPLANATORY NOTE

(This note is not part of the Order.)

This Order adds employment in the Northern Ireland Museums Council to the schedule of employments for whom the Department of Finance and Personnel may make pension schemes. It is retrospective by virtue of Article 3(7) of the Superannuation (Northern Ireland) Order 1972.

1994 No. 52

FOOD

The Quick-frozen Foodstuffs (Amendment) Regulations (Northern Ireland) 1994

Made	*17th February 1994*
Coming into operation . .	*1st September 1994*

The Department of Health and Social Services, in exercise of the powers conferred on it by Articles 15(1), 16(1), 25(1)(*a*), (2)(*a*) and (3), 26(3) and 47(2) of the Food Safety (Northern Ireland) Order 1991(**a**), and of all other powers enabling it in that behalf and after consultation in accordance with Article 47(3) of the said Order with such organisations as appear to it to be representative of interests likely to be substantially affected by these Regulations hereby makes the following Regulations:

Citation and commencement

1. These Regulations may be cited as the Quick-frozen Foodstuffs (Amendment) Regulations (Northern Ireland) 1994 and shall come into operation on 1st September 1994.

Amendment of the Quick-frozen Foodstuffs Regulations (Northern Ireland) 1990

2.—(1) The Quick-frozen Foodstuffs Regulations (Northern Ireland) 1990(**b**) shall be amended in accordance with paragraphs (2) to (5).

(2) In regulation 2(1) (interpretation)—

(*a*) after the definition of "catering establishment" there shall be inserted—

" "monitoring", in the context of the monitoring of air temperatures, is the action performed by an instrument for the measurement of air temperatures which instrument then records (either continuously, or at frequent and regular intervals) the measurements it has made;";

(*b*) after the definition of "quick-frozen foodstuff" there shall be inserted—

" "retail display cabinet" means any cabinet from which a quick-frozen foodstuff is offered either for retail sale or for sale in the course of a cash-and-carry business;";

(**a**)   S.I. 1991/762 (N.I. 7). *See* Article 2(2) for the definitions of "regulations" and "the Department concerned"

(**b**)   S.R. 1990 No. 455; the relevant amending Regulations are S.R. 1991 No. 203 and S.R. 1992 No. 464

(c) immediately following the definition of sell, "and" shall be deleted and there shall be inserted—

" "storage" includes keeping in a warehouse; and".

(3) For "the Schedule" in regulation 3 there shall be substituted "Schedule 1".

(4) After regulation 6 there shall be inserted—

"Air temperature recording instruments in means of storage and transport

6A.—(1) Each manufacturer, storer, transporter, local distributor and retailer of any quick-frozen foodstuff shall ensure that any means of storage or transport (other than rail transport) used by him in respect of that foodstuff shall, at each stage during which such foodstuff is within his care and control, be fitted with an instrument for the measuring or monitoring of air temperature and which meets the applicable requirements laid down in Schedule 2.

(2) Each manufacturer, storer and transporter (the latter not including any transporter when carrying out local distribution) of any quick frozen foodstuff shall—

(a) at frequent and regular intervals record or ensure the recording of, by means of the instrument referred to in paragraph (1), the air temperatures to which such foodstuff is being subjected during its storage or transport;

(b) date all records of air temperatures obtained further to sub-paragraph (a) and keep such records for one year thereafter or such longer period as shall be justified according to the nature of the foodstuff in question; and

(c) upon the request of an authorised officer make such records available to that or another authorised officer.

Sampling and method of measuring temperatures

6B. Where, further to an inspection, an authorised officer has reasonable doubts that the temperatures that are being or have been maintained in respect of any quick frozen foodstuff are not the temperatures prescribed for such foodstuff in paragraphs 1(e) and (f) (as read with paragraph 2(c)) in Schedule 1, he shall further inspect such quick-frozen foodstuff and such temperatures in accordance with the provisions of Commissison Directive 92/2/EEC(**a**).".

(5) After "Schedule" in the heading to the Schedule there shall be added "1" and after that Schedule there shall be inserted—

(**a**) O.J. No. L34, 11.2.92, p. 30

"SCHEDULE 2   Regulation 6A

Requirements for instruments for measuring or monitoring air temperature in any means or storage or transport of quick-frozen foodstuffs

The applicable requirements for instruments for the measuring or monitoring of air temperature that must be fitted in any means of storage or transport (other than rail transport) of any quick-frozen foodstuff are as follows—

(*a*) in respect of any means of storage or transport other than those specified in sub-paragraphs (*b*), (*c*), (*d*), (*e*), (*f*) or (*g*), the instrument shall be a system suitable for the monitoring, at frequent and regular intervals, of air temperatures within such means;

(*b*) in respect of storage in a cold chamber with a capacity of less than 10m³ on premises used for the retail sale of quick-frozen foodstuffs, the instrument shall be a thermometer so placed as to be easily visible;

(*c*) in respect of storage in a retail display cabinet (other than an open retail display cabinet), the instrument shall be one or more thermometers so placed as to be easily visible;

(*d*) in respect of storage in an open retail display cabinet, the instrument shall be one or more thermometers so placed as to be easily visible and indicating the temperature at the air return side at the level of the clearly marked maximum load line for that cabinet;

(*e*) in respect of means of transport other than—

    (i) in a vehicle registered outside the United Kingdom, or

    (ii) a means of transport when being used in the course of local distribution,

    the instrument shall be a system for monitoring air temperatures that—

    (*aa*) has an accuracy of ±1°C when its sensor is measuring a temperature within the range of −25°C to +30°C;

    (*bb*) has a measuring accuracy which does not change by more than ±0.5°C when it is operating in temperatures within the range of −20°C to +30°C;

    (*cc*) has a display resolution of not more than 1°C, and

    (*dd*) is robust and shockproof;

(*f*) in respect of a vehicle registered outside the United Kingdom, the instrument shall be an instrument which has been approved by the competent authorities in the country in which the vehicle is registered;

(*g*) in respect of means of transport in the course of local distribution, the instrument shall be one or more thermometers so placed as to be easily visible.".

Sealed with the Official Seal of the Department of Health and Social Services on 17th February 1994.

(L.S.)   *D. A. Baker*

Assistant Secretary

EXPLANATORY NOTE

(This note is not part of the Regulations.)

These Regulations implement Commission Directives 92/1/EEC (O.J. No. L34, 11.2.92, p. 28) on the monitoring of temperatures of quick-frozen foodstuffs during transport, warehousing and storage, and 92/2/EEC (O.J. No. L34, 11.2.92, p. 30) laying down the sampling procedures and the European Economic Community's official method of analysis for the official control of the temperatures of such foodstuffs. This is done by way of amendment to the Quick-frozen Foodstuffs Regulations (Northern Ireland) 1990 (S.R. 1990 No. 455) which implemented the provisions of Council Directive 89/108/EEC (O.J. No. L40, 11.2.89, p. 34) on the approximation of the laws of the member States relating to quick-frozen foodstuffs for human consumption, which the provisions of the two Commission Directives now supplement (regulation 2).

The Regulations provide—

(*a*) that manufacturers, storers, transporters, local distributors and retailers of quick-frozen food should fit their means of storage or transport (excluding rail transport) of such food with appropriate instruments for monitoring or measuring air temperature (new regulation 6A(1)); and

(*b*) that manufacturers, storers and transporters should, by means of such instruments, record air temperatures during the storage and transport of quick-frozen foods, and keep such records for at least one year thereafter (new regulation 6A(2)).

Further requirements as to which instruments must be fitted in particular cases are given in new Schedule 2.

1994   No. 53

HOUSING

**Homes Insulation Scheme and Grants (Amendment)
Order (Northern Ireland) 1994**

Made . . . . . *18th February 1994*

Coming into operation . . *24th February 1994*

The Department of Economic Development, in exercise of the powers conferred by Article 86(1), (2), (3), (4)(*a*), (5) and (7) of the Housing (Northern Ireland) Order 1981(**a**) and now vested in it(**b**) and of every other power enabling it in that behalf, with the approval of the Department of Finance and Personnel(**c**), hereby makes the following Order:

Citation, commencement and interpretation

1.—(1) This Order may be cited as the Homes Insulation Scheme and Grants (Amendment) Order (Northern Ireland) 1994 and shall come into operation on 24th February 1994.

(2) In this Order—

"grant" means a grant paid under Article 86(1) of the Housing (Northern Ireland) Order 1981;

"the principal Order" means the Homes Insulation Scheme and Grants Order (Northern Ireland) 1991(**d**).

Amendment to the principal Order

2. Subject to Article 3, for Article 3 of the principal Order substitute the following—

"**3.** The grant shall be 100 per cent. of the cost of the works qualifying for it or £198·70 whichever is the lesser amount.".

Transitional provisions

3. The principal Order shall continue to apply in relation to any applications for grant made on or after the 19th May 1992 but before the coming into operation of this Order as if this Order had not been made.

(**a**)   S.I. 1981/156 (N.I. 3); Article 86 has been amended by Article 4(1) of S.R. 1984 No. 204
(**b**)   *See* S.R. 1984 No. 204
(**c**)   Formerly Department of Finance; *see* S.I. 1982/338 (N.I. 6) Article 3
(**d**)   S.R. 1991 No. 29 as amended by S.R. 1992 No. 183

Sealed with the Official Seal of the Department of Economic Development on 18th February 1994.

(L.S.)   *Douglas B. McIldoon*
                                                          Assistant Secretary

The Department of Finance and Personnel hereby approves the foregoing Order.

Sealed with the Official Seal of the Department of Finance and Personnel on 18th February 1994.

(L.S.)   *D. Thomson*
                                                          Assistant Secretary

---

EXPLANATORY NOTE

(This note is not part of the Order.)

This Order which comes into operation on 24th February 1994 amends the Homes Insulation Scheme and Grants Order (Northern Ireland) 1991 by increasing the monetary ceiling from £188 to £198·70 and increasing the grant payable from 95 per cent. to 100 per cent. of the cost of the works qualifying for it thereby removing the applicant's contribution.

The amendment effected by this Order does not apply to applications for grant made before the respective changes come into operation.

1994 No. 54

ROAD TRAFFIC AND VEHICLES

**Goods Vehicles (Certification) (Amendment) Regulations
(Northern Ireland) 1994**

Made . . . . . *17th February 1994*

Coming into operation . . *1st April 1994*

The Department of the Environment, in exercise of the powers conferred on it by Articles 53(3) and 218(1) of the Road Traffic (Northern Ireland) Order 1981(**a**) and of all other powers enabling it in that behalf, hereby makes the following Regulations:

Citation and commencement

1. These Regulations may be cited as the Goods Vehicles (Certification) (Amendment) Regulations (Northern Ireland) 1994 and shall come into operation on 1st April 1994.

Amendment of the 1990 Regulations

2. The Goods Vehicles (Certification) Regulations (Northern Ireland) 1990(**b**) are amended as follows—

(1) In regulation 2(1) (interpretation) insert in the appropriate place the following definition—

" "sold or supplied by retail" means first sold or supplied otherwise than to a person acquiring solely for the purposes of resale or re-supply for a valuable consideration;".

(2) In regulation 18 (exemptions)—

(*a*) after exemption 7 insert—

"(7A) a trailer until the end of the twelfth month from the date on which it was first sold or supplied by retail;"; and

(*b*) in exemption 12 omit paragraph (*c*).

Sealed with the Official Seal of the Department of the Environment on 17th February 1994.

(L.S.) *Trevor Pearson*
Assistant Secretary

(**a**) S.I. 1981/154 (N.I. 1); *see* Article 2(2) for the definition of "Department" and "prescribed"
(**b**) S.R. 1990 No. 224; relevant amending Regulations are S.R. 1991 No. 355 and 1993 No. 78

EXPLANATORY NOTE
(This note is not part of the Regulations.)

These Regulations amend the Goods Vehicles (Certification) Regulations (Northern Ireland) 1990 by adding to the 'exemptions from the requirement to have a goods vehicle certificate' an exemption for trailers until the end of the twelfth month from the date the trailer was first sold or supplied by retail.

1994   No. 55

EDUCATION

Educational and Library Services Etc. Grants Regulations (Northern Ireland) 1994

Made	*18th February 1994*
Coming into operation . .	*1st April 1994*

The Department of Education, in exercise of the powers conferred on it by Articles 115(1)(**a**) and 134(1)(**b**) of the Education and Libraries (Northern Ireland) Order 1986(**c**) and of every other power enabling it in that behalf, and with the approval of the Department of Finance and Personnel hereby makes the following Regulations:

Citation and commencement

1. These Regulations may be cited as the Educational and Library Services Etc. Grants Regulations (Northern Ireland) 1994 and shall come into operation on 1st April 1994.

Revocation

2. The Educational and Library Services Etc. Grants Regulations (Northern Ireland) 1973(**d**) are hereby revoked.

Payment of grants

3. Subject to the provisions of these Regulations, the Department may pay grants to persons (other than boards or the trustees or managers of a voluntary school or a grant-maintained integrated school) in respect of expenditure incurred or to be incurred by them—

    (*a*) for the purposes of, or in connection with, the provision (or proposed provision) of—

        (i) educational or library services; or

        (ii) social or cultural activities or services ancillary to education;

    (*b*) for the purposes of research relevant to the functions of the Department or of boards under the Education Orders.

4.—(1) The Department shall not pay grant to a person under these Regulations unless that person—

(**a**) As substituted by S.I. 1989/2406 (N.I. 20) Article 159
(**b**) As amended by S.I. 1993/2810 (N.I. 12) Article 50(1) and Schedule 4 Part II
(**c**) S.I. 1986/594 (N.I. 3)
(**d**) S.R. & O. (N.I.) 1973 No. 439

(*a*) satisfies the Department as to the purpose for which the service, activity or research is or is to be provided or conducted; and

(*b*) keeps such records and furnishes such statements of accounts and such other information and returns as the Department may require.

(2) The Department may require that such statements of accounts be certified by an accountant holding such qualifications as the Department may consider appropriate.

Amount of grant

5.—(1) The amount of grant to be paid in respect of expenditure incurred or to be incurred for any service, activity or research shall be determined by the Department after consideration of its character and cost and the financial resources of the person by whom or on whose behalf or under whose management it is or is to be provided or conducted.

(2) A grant may be paid by instalments on such date or dates as may be determined by the Department.

Withholding or reducing grant

6. In assessing the amount of grant payable under these Regulations, the Department shall have regard to payments made by it otherwise than under these Regulations or by another government department or by a board and if, having regard to such other payments, the Department considers that payment of grant should not be made in full, it may withhold or reduce the grant.

7. Where any of the requirements of these Regulations are not complied with the Department may withhold or reduce the amount of grant which would otherwise be payable.

Inspection

8. Where the Department has paid or proposes to pay grant under these Regulations, any premises or other thing used for the purposes of any service, activity or research to which the grant relates shall be open at all reasonable times to inspection by any person authorised by the Department in that behalf and that person shall be afforded all the facilities he requires for the purposes of such inspection.

Sealed with the Official Seal of the Department of Education on 18th February 1994.

(L.S.)   *R. J. Jordan*
                                      Assistant Secretary

The Department of Finance and Personnel hereby approves the foregoing Regulations.

Sealed with the Official Seal of the Department of Finance and Personnel
on 18th February 1994.

(L.S.) *R. Miller*

Assistant Secretary

EXPLANATORY NOTE

(This note is not part of the Regulations.)

These Regulations revoke and replace the Educational and Library
Services Etc. Grants Regulations (Northern Ireland) 1973 ("the 1973
Regulations"). They make provision for the payment of grants to certain
persons (other than education and library boards or the trustees or managers of
voluntary schools or grant-maintained integrated schools) for the purposes of
educational or library services, social or cultural activities or services
ancillary to education. In addition to the matters which could be grant-aided
under the 1973 Regulations, social activities may be grant-aided under these
Regulations.

1994   No. 56

RATES

Rates (Regional Rate) Order (Northern Ireland) 1994

Made	*21st February 1994*
Coming into operation . .	*1st April 1994*

To be laid before Parliament under paragraph 3(3) of Schedule 1 to the Northern Ireland Act 1974

The Department of Finance and Personnel(a), in exercise of the powers conferred on it by Articles 2(2), 7(1) and 27(4) of the Rates (Northern Ireland) Order 1977(b) and of every other power enabling it in that behalf, hereby makes the following Order:—

Citation and commencement

1. This Order may be cited as the Rates (Regional Rate) Order (Northern Ireland) 1994 and shall come into operation on 1st April 1994.

Regional rate

2. The regional rate for the year ending 31st March 1995 shall be 148·68 pence in the pound.

Reduction of regional rate on dwellings

3. The amount by which the normal regional rate fixed for the year ending 31st March 1995 under Article 2 is to be reduced for the purposes of paragraphs (2) and (3) of Article 27 of the Rates (Northern Ireland) Order 1977 shall be 74 pence.

Sealed with the Official Seal of the Department of Finance and Personnel on 21st February 1994.

(L.S.)   *F. P. Smyth*
                                             Assistant Secretary

(a)   Formerly the Department of Finance. *See* S.I. 1982/338 (N.I. 6) Article 3
(b)   S.I. 1977/2157 (N.I. 28)

EXPLANATORY NOTE

(This note is not part of the Order.)

This Order fixes 148·68 pence in the pound as the amount of the regional rate for the year ending 31st March 1995. It also fixes 74 pence as the amount by which the normal regional rate is reduced in respect of dwelling-houses and hereditaments which, though not dwelling-houses, are used partly for the purposes of private dwellings.

1994 No. 57

HEALTH AND PERSONAL SOCIAL SERVICES

The Health and Social Services Trusts (Consultation on Dissolution) (Amendment) Regulations (Northern Ireland) 1994

Made	*21st February 1994*
Coming into operation . .	*1st April 1994*

The Department of Health and Social Services, in exercise of the powers conferred on it by paragraphs 23(3) and 24(3) of Schedule 3 to the Health and Personal Social Services (Northern Ireland) Order 1991(**a**) and of all other powers enabling it in that behalf, hereby makes the following Regulations:

Citation, commencement and interpretation

1. These Regulations may be cited as the Health and Social Services Trusts (Consultation on Dissolution) (Amendment) Regulations (Northern Ireland) 1994 and shall come into operation on 1st April 1994.

Amendment of the Health and Social Services Trusts (Consultation on Dissolution) Regulations (Northern Ireland) 1992

2. The Health and Social Services Trusts (Consultation on Dissolution) Regulations (Northern Ireland) 1992(**b**) shall be amended as follows—

(*a*) in regulation 1(2), the full stop after the definition of "relevant Health and Social Services Council" shall be deleted and the following shall be added after that definition—

"; and

"staff interests" means such persons or bodies as the HSS trust which is to be dissolved may recognise as representing persons who are employed by or for the purposes of that trust, and who are, in its opinion, likely to be affected by an order under paragraph 23 or 24 of Schedule 3 to the Order.";

(*b*) in regulation 2(1), the words ", except in cases of urgency," shall cease to have effect;

(*c*) in regulation 2(1)(*a*) and (*b*) and (3), after the word "Council", in each place where that word occurs, there shall be added the words "and staff interests"; and

---

(**a**) S.I. 1991/194 (N.I. 1)
(**b**) S.R. 1992 No. 255

(*d*) after paragraph (2) of regulation 2 there shall be added the following paragraphs—

"(2A) Subject to paragraph (3), for the purposes of sub-paragraph (3) of paragraph 24 of Schedule 3 to the Order, the prescribed consultation which must be completed before the Department may make an order under that paragraph transferring or providing for the transfer of property, rights or liabilities of an HSS trust shall be—

(*a*) where the dissolution order in respect of that trust is to be made pursuant to paragraph 23(2)(*a*) of Schedule 3 to the Order, consultation by that trust with the relevant Health and Social Services Council and staff interests, the results of which shall, within such a period, if any, as the Department may determine, be reported by that trust to the Department;

(*b*) where the dissolution order in respect of that trust is to be made pursuant to paragraph 23(2)(*b*) of Schedule 3 to the Order, consultation by the Department with the relevant Health and Social Services Council and staff interests.

(2B) Consultation required by paragraph (2A) may be combined with the consultation required by paragraph (1); and where orders under paragraph 24 of Schedule 3 to the Order are to be made in respect of two or more HSS trusts, the consultation required by paragraph (2A)(*a*) may be undertaken jointly by the HSS trusts concerned.".

Sealed with the Official Seal of the Department of Health and Social Services on 21st February 1994.

(L.S.)   *John McGrath*
                                    Assistant Secretary

EXPLANATORY NOTE

(This note is not part of the Regulations.)

These Regulations amend the Health and Social Services Trusts (Consultation on Dissolution) Regulations (Northern Ireland) 1992 (''the principal regulations'') to provide for the consultation required before the Department makes an order under paragraph 24 of Schedule 3 to the Health and Personal Social Services (Northern Ireland) Order 1991 in connection with the transfer of the property, rights and liabilities, including staff, of a Health and Social Services trust which is to be dissolved.

The principal regulations provide for consultation required before the Department makes an order dissolving an HSS trust. These Regulations amend the principal regulations to provide that staff interests will be among those persons or bodies which must be consulted on an order dissolving an HSS trust. A definition of ''staff interests'' is added to regulation 1 of the principal regulations. The Regulations also amend the principal regulations to provide that consultation on the transfer of property, rights and liabilities should be subject to the same requirements as consultation on dissolution, and may be combined with that consultation and must be with the same persons or bodies.

1994 No. 58

PLANNING

Planning (Fees) (Amendment) Regulations (Northern Ireland) 1994

Made	*25th February 1994*
Coming into operation . .	*1st April 1994*

The Department of the Environment, in exercise of the powers conferred by Articles 127 and 129(1) of the Planning (Northern Ireland) Order 1991(**a**) and of all other powers enabling it in that behalf, makes the following regulations:

Citation and commencement

1. These regulations may be cited as the Planning (Fees) (Amendment) Regulations (Northern Ireland) 1994 and shall come into operation on 1st April 1994.

Amendment of regulations

2.—(1) The Planning (Fees) Regulations (Northern Ireland) 1992(**b**) are amended in accordance with paragraphs (2) to (7).

(2) In regulations 10(1) (reduced fees and refunds), 12(3) (fee for certain deemed applications), 15 (fee for applications for listed building consent) and 18(2) (fee for certain statutory authorities) for "£20" substitute "£23".

(3) In regulation 16(1) (fee for appeals) for "£46" substitute "£53".

(4) In regulation 17 (fee for application for a determination) for "£17" substitute "£20".

(5) In Part I of Schedule 1—

(*a*) in paragraph 4(1) (fee for application or deemed application by certain non-profit making organisations) for "£120" substitute "£138";

(*b*) in paragraph 5(2) and (3) (fee for certain applications for approval of reserved matters) for "£120" substitute "£138".

(6) For Part II of Schedule 1 substitute Part II set out in the Schedule to these regulations.

(7) In Schedule 2 (fees for applications for consent to display advertisements)—

(*a*) for "£33" where it twice occurs substitute "£38";

(*b*) for "£120" substitute "£138".

(**a**) S.I. 1991/1220 (N.I. 11); Art. 2(2) contains definitions of "the Department" and "prescribed"
(**b**) S.R. 1992 No. 97 as amended by S.R. 1993 No. 81

Revocation

3. Regulations 2(4), (5), (6)(*b*), (8), (9) and (10) of the Planning (Fees) (Amendment) Regulations (Northern Ireland) 1993(**a**) are hereby revoked.

Sealed with the Official Seal of the Department of the Environment on 25th February 1994.

(L.S.)

J. McConnell
Assistant Secretary

(**a**)   S.R. 1993 No. 81

SCHEDULE

Substitution for Part II of Schedule 1

"PART II

SCALES OF FEES

Category of Development	Fee Payable

1. The erection of dwelling houses.	(*a*) Where the application is for outline planning permission—
	   (i) £69 if the development involves only one dwelling house;
	   (ii) £138 for each 0.1 hectare of the site area, subject to a maximum of £3,450 if more than one dwelling house is to be created by the development;
	 (*b*) in other cases £138 for each dwelling house subject to a maximum of £6,900.

2. The erection of buildings (other than dwelling houses, buildings coming within category 3, 4 or 7 or buildings in the nature of plant or machinery).	(*a*) Where the application is for outline planning permission, £138 for each 0.1 hectare of the site area, subject to a maximum of £3,450;
	 (*b*) in other cases—
	   (i) where no floor space is to be created by the development, £69;
	   (ii) where the area of gross floor space to be created by the development does not exceed 40 square metres, £69;
	   (iii) where the area of gross floor space to be created by the development exceeds 40 square metres but does not exceed 75 square metres, £138; and
	   (iv) where the area of gross floor space to be created by the development exceeds 75 square metres, £138 for each 75 square metres subject to a maximum of £6,900.

Category of Development	Fee Payable
3. The erection, on land used for the purposes of agriculture, of buildings (other than glasshouses) to be used for agricultural purposes.	(*a*) Where the application is for outline planning permission, £138 for each 0.1 hectare of the site area, subject to a maximum of £3,450; (*b*) in other cases— (i) where the area of gross floor space to be created by the development does not exceed 300 square metres, £23; (ii) where the area of gross floor space to be created by the development exceeds 300 square metres but does not exceed 375 square metres, £138; and (iii) where the area of gross floor space to be created by the development exceeds 375 square metres, £138 for the first 375 square metres and £138 for each 75 square metres in excess of that figure, subject to a maximum of £6,900.
4. The erection of glasshouses on land used for the purposes of agriculture.	(*a*) Where the application is for outline planning permission, £138; (*b*) in other cases— (i) where the area of gross floor space to be created by the development does not exceed 465 square metres, £23; (ii) where the area of gross floor space to be created by the development exceeds 465 square metres, £822.
5. The erection, alteration or replacement of plant or machinery.	£138 for each 0.1 hectare of the site area, subject to a maximum of £3,450.
6. The enlargement, improvement or other alteration of existing dwelling houses.	(*a*) Where the application relates to one dwelling house, £69; (*b*) where the application relates to 2 or more dwelling houses, £138.

Category of Development	Fee Payable
7. (*a*) The carrying out of operations (including the erection of a building) within the curtilage of an existing dwelling house, for purposes ancillary to the enjoyment of the dwelling house as such, or the erection or construction of gates, fences, walls or other means of enclosure along a boundary of the curtilage of an existing dwelling house; or	£69.
(*b*) the construction of car parks, service roads and other means of access on land used for the purposes of a single undertaking, where the development is required for a purpose incidental to the existing use of the land.	£69.
8. (*a*) The winning and working of minerals (other than peat);	£69 for each 0.1 hectare of the site area, subject to a maximum of £10,350.
(*b*) the winning and working of peat.	£69 for each hectare of the site area up to a maximum of £10,350.
9. The carrying out of any operations connected with exploratory drilling for oil or natural gas.	£138 for each 0.1 hectare of the site area subject to a maximum of £10,350.
10. The installation of an overhead electricity line.	£59.
11. The construction or extension of a non-nuclear electricity generating station.	£117 for each 0.1 hectare of the site area, subject to a maximum of £21,300.
12. The carrying out of any operations not coming within any of the above categories.	£69 for each 0.1 hectare of the site area, subject to a maximum of £690.
13. The change of use of a building to use as one or more separate dwelling houses.	(*a*) Where the change is from a previous use as a single dwelling house to use as 2 or more single dwelling houses, £138 for each additional dwelling house to be created by the development;
	(*b*) in other cases, £138 for each dwelling house to be created by the development;

Category of Development	Fee Payable
	subject, in each case to a maximum of £6,900.
14. (*a*) The use of land for the disposal of refuse or waste materials or for the deposit of material remaining after minerals have been extracted from land; or (*b*) the use of land for the storage of minerals in the open.	£69 for each 0.1 hectare of the site area, subject to a maximum of £10,350.
15. (*a*) The making of a material change in the use of a building or land (other than a material change of use coming within any of the above categories); or	£138.
(*b*) the continuance of a use of land or the retention of buildings or works on land, without compliance with a condition subject to which a previous planning permission has been granted (including a condition requiring the discontinuance of the use or the removal of the building or works at the end of a specified period).".	£69.

EXPLANATORY NOTE
(This note is not part of the Regulations.)

These Regulations amend the Planning (Fees) Regulations (Northern Ireland) 1992 (the 1992 Regulations) which prescribe—

(1) fees payable to the Department of the Environment in respect of applications made under the Planning (Northern Ireland) Order 1991—

    (*a*) for planning permission for development or for approval of matters reserved in an outline planning permission;

    (*b*) for consent for the display of advertisements;

    (*c*) for listed building consent.

(2) fees payable to the Planning Appeals Commission in respect of appeals and applications for planning permission deemed to have been made on an appeal against enforcement notices by virtue of Article 71(3) of the 1991 Order.

The fees for appeals are increased by 15% to cover the cost of advertising notice of appeals (regulation 2(3)).

The Regulations increase all other fees by approximately 15% except those payable under categories 10 and 11 of Part II, Schedule 1 (installation of an overhead electricity line and the construction or extension of a non-nuclear generating station) which are increased by 3·7%.

Apart from the said categories 10 and 11 the reason for the increase is to cover the cost of determining planning applications in addition to making provision for the effects of inflation. In categories 10 and 11 the fees were introduced on 1st April 1992 at a level calculated to cover those costs.

The increase of 3·7% therefore relates only to inflation.

The provisions of the Planning (Fees) (Amendment) Regulations (Northern Ireland) 1993 referred to in regulation 3 are revoked.

1994 No. 59

AGRICULTURE

Milk Marketing Scheme (Postponement of Date of Revocation) Order (Northern Ireland) 1994

Made	*28th February 1994*
Coming into operation . .	*30th March 1994*

The Department of Agriculture, in exercise of the powers conferred on it by Article 4(3) of the Agriculture (Northern Ireland) Order 1993(**a**) and of every other power enabling it in that behalf, hereby makes the following Order:

Citation and commencement

1. This Order may be cited as the Milk Marketing Scheme (Postponement of Date of Revocation) Order (Northern Ireland) 1994 and shall come into operation on 30th March 1994.

Postponement of revocation of the Milk Marketing Scheme

2. Article 4(2) of the Agriculture (Northern Ireland) Order 1993 shall have effect with the substitution for "1st April 1994" of "1st January 1995".

Sealed with the Official Seal of the Department of Agriculture on 28th February 1994.

(L.S.) *P. T. Toal*

Assistant Secretary

(**a**) S.I. 1993/2665 (N.I. 10)

EXPLANATORY NOTE

(This note is not part of the Order.)

Article 4(2) of the Agriculture (Northern Ireland) Order 1993 ("the 1993 Order") specifies 1st April 1994 as the date on which the Milk Marketing Scheme (Northern Ireland) 1989 ("the Scheme") will be revoked. This Order substitutes 1st January 1995 for that date. However, where property, rights or liabilities of the Milk Marketing Board for Northern Ireland are transferred under a scheme of reorganisation approved under the 1993 Order, then under Article 4(3) of that Order the Scheme will instead be revoked on the date when that transfer takes place.

1994 No. 60

AGRICULTURE

Milk Marketing (Period for Making Applications) (Extension) Order (Northern Ireland) 1994

Made	*28th February 1994*
Coming into operation . .	*30th March 1994*

The Department of Agriculture, in exercise of the powers conferred on it by Article 5(7) of the Agriculture (Northern Ireland) Order 1993(a) and of every other power enabling it in that behalf, hereby makes the following Order:

Citation and commencement

1. This Order may be cited as the Milk Marketing (Period for Making Applications) (Extension) Order (Northern Ireland) 1994 and shall come into operation on 30th March 1994.

Extension of period for making applications

2. The period for making applications under Article 5 of the Agriculture (Northern Ireland) Order 1993(b) is hereby extended until 30th September 1994.

Sealed with the Official Seal of the Department of Agriculture on 28th February 1994.

(L.S.)   *P. T. Toal*

Assistant Secretary

(a) S.I. 1993/2665 (N.I. 10)
(b) S.I. 1993/2665 (N.I. 10) as read with S.R. 1993 No. 489

EXPLANATORY NOTE

(This note is not part of the Order.)

Article 5(1) of the Agriculture (Northern Ireland) Order 1993 provides for the period within which the Milk Marketing Board for Northern Ireland may apply to the Department of Agriculture for approval of a scheme for the reorganisation of the arrangements relating to the marketing of milk in Northern Ireland. The Milk Marketing (Period for Making Applications) (Extension) Order (Northern Ireland) 1993 extended that period to 31st March 1994. This Order further extends the period to 30th September 1994.

_____

1994   No. 61

Temporary Speed Limit (Motorway M1) (No. 2) Order (Northern Ireland) 1994

This Order, being of a temporary character, is not printed at length in this volume.

1994 No. 62

HEALTH AND PERSONAL SOCIAL SERVICES

The Health and Social Services Trusts (Public Meetings) Regulations (Northern Ireland) 1994

Made	.	.	.	.	*1st March 1994*
Coming into operation			.	.	*1st April 1994*

The Department of Health and Social Services, in exercise of the powers conferred on it by paragraph 7(2) and (3) of Schedule 3 to the Health and Personal Social Services (Northern Ireland) Order 1991(**a**) and of all other powers enabling it in that behalf, hereby makes the following Regulations:

Citation, commencement and interpretation

1.—(1) These Regulations may be cited as the Health and Social Services Trusts (Public Meetings) Regulations (Northern Ireland) 1994 and shall come into operation on 1st April 1994.

(2) In these Regulations, "the Order" means the Health and Personal Social Services (Northern Ireland) Order 1991.

Timing of the public meeting for the presentation of the audited accounts and annual report

2. For the purposes of paragraph 7(2) of Schedule 3 to the Order, the prescribed time for holding a public meeting of an HSS trust shall be on or before 30th September in every year, other than that which includes the operational date of the trust.

Other public meetings

3. For the purposes of paragraph 7(3) of Schedule 3 to the Order—

(*a*) the circumstances in which an HSS trust shall hold a public meeting are those where it has received an auditor's report made under the provisions of Article 92A(4) of the Health and Personal Social Services (Northern Ireland) Order 1972(**b**);

(*b*) the time for holding the meeting is as soon as practicable, and in any event not later than three months, after the date on which the HSS trust received that report; and

(*c*) the document which shall be presented at the meeting is that report.

(**a**) S.I. 1991/194 (N.I. 1)
(**b**) S.I. 1972/1265 (N.I. 14), as amended; the relevant amendment is Article 5 of the Health and Personal Social Services (Northern Ireland) Order 1994 (S.I. 1994/429 (N.I. 2))

Concurrent meetings

4. Nothing in these Regulations shall prevent a public meeting held pursuant to paragraph 7(2) of Schedule 3 to the Order in accordance with regulation 2 from being held on the same date and at the same time as a public meeting held pursuant to paragraph 7(3) of that Schedule in accordance with regulation 3.

Sealed with the Official Seal of the Department of Health and Social Services on 1st March 1994.

(L.S.)   *John McGrath*
                                            Assistant Secretary

---

EXPLANATORY NOTE

(This note is not part of the Regulations.)

These Regulations make provision for the timing of the public meetings at which HSS trusts shall present audited accounts and annual reports. They also provide that an HSS trust shall hold a public meeting to consider an auditor's report other than a report on the audited accounts and specify the timing of that meeting.

1994   No. 63

HEALTH AND PERSONAL SOCIAL SERVICES

The Health and Social Services Trusts (Membership and Procedure) Regulations (Northern Ireland) 1994

Made	*1st March 1994*
Coming into operation . .	*1st April 1994*

ARRANGEMENT OF REGULATIONS

17. Committee for appointing chief officer.

18. Committee for appointing executive directors other than chief officer.

19. Meetings and proceedings.

20. Disability of directors in proceedings on account of pecuniary interest.

PART IV

REVOCATION

21. Revocation.

SCHEDULE

Rules as to meetings and proceedings of HSS trusts.

The Department of Health and Social Services, in exercise of the powers conferred on it by Article 10(6) of the Health and Personal Social Services (Northern Ireland) Order 1991(**a**) and of all other powers enabling it in that behalf, hereby makes the following regulations:

PART I

GENERAL

Citation, commencement and interpretation

1.—(1) These Regulations may be cited as the Health and Social Services Trusts (Membership and Procedure) Regulations (Northern Ireland) 1994 and shall come into operation on 1st April 1994.

(2) In these regulations—

"the Order" means the Health and Personal Social Services (Northern Ireland) Order 1991;

"director" in relation to an HSS trust includes its chairman;

"executive director" and "non-executive director" have the meaning assigned to them in Article 10(4)(*a*) of the Order;

"health service body" means—

(*a*) a health authority, a Family Health Services Authority, a special health authority or an NHS trust respectively constituted under sections 8, 10 and 11 of the National Health Service Act 1977(**b**) and section 5 of the National Health Service and Community Care Act 1990(**c**);

(**a**) S.I. 1991/194 (N.I. 1)
(**b**) 1977 c. 49; sections 8 and 10 were amended by sections 1 and 2 of the National Health Service and
           Community Care Act 1990 (c. 19)
(**c**) 1990 c. 19

(b) a Health Board, a Special Health Board, the Common Services Agency for the Scottish Health Service or an NHS trust respectively constituted under sections 2, 10 and 12A of the National Health Service (Scotland) Act 1978(**a**);

(c) a State Hospital Management Committee constituted under section 91 of the Mental Health (Scotland) Act 1984(**b**);

(d) the Dental Practice Board or Scottish Dental Practice Board;

(e) the Public Health Laboratory Service Board; and

(f) the National Radiological Protection Board established by section 1 of the Radiological Protection Act 1970(**c**);

"health and social services body" means—

(a) a Health and Social Services Board;

(b) an HSS trust;

(c) the Agency; or

(d) a special agency;

"general dental practitioner" means a dental practitioner who is providing general dental services in accordance with arrangements made under Article 61 of the Health and Personal Social Services (Northern Ireland) Order 1972(**d**);

"general medical practitioner" means a medical practitioner who is providing general medical services in accordance with arrangements made under Article 56 of the Health and Personal Social Services (Northern Ireland) Order 1972;

"operational date" has the meaning assigned to it in paragraph 3(1)(e) of Schedule 3 to the Order;

"recognised qualification in social work" means a qualification specified in any direction issued by the Department under paragraph 6(2) of Schedule 3 to the Order for employment as a social worker in an HSS trust;

"the relevant committee" means a committee of an HSS trust appointed under either regulation 17 or regulation 18 whichever is appropriate;

"trade union" has the meaning assigned to it in Article 2(2) of the Industrial Relations (Northern Ireland) (No. 1) Order 1976(**e**).

(**a**)   1978 c. 29; section 2 was amended by paragraph 1 of Schedule 7 to the Health and Social Services and Social Security Adjudications Act 1983 (c. 41) and by section 28 of the National Health Service and Community Care Act 1990; section 10 was amended by paragraph 2 of Schedule 6 to the Health Services Act 1980 (c. 53); section 12A was inserted by section 31 of the National Health Service and Community Care Act 1990

(**b**)   1984 c. 36

(**c**)   1970 c. 46

(**d**)   S.I. 1972/1265 (N.I. 14)

(**e**)   S.I. 1976/1043 (N.I. 16)

(3) In regulation 20—

"securities" means—

(*a*) shares or debentures, whether constituting a charge on the assets of the company or other body or not, or rights or interests in any shares or such debentures; or

(*b*) rights (whether actual or contingent) in respect of money lent to or deposited with any industrial and provident society or building society,

"shares" means shares in the share capital of a company or other body or the stock of a company or other body.

PART II

MEMBERSHIP

Maximum number of directors

2. The maximum number of directors of an HSS trust shall be eleven.

Appointment of directors

3.—(1) All of the non-executive directors of an HSS trust shall be appointed by the Department.

(2) The executive directors of an HSS trust shall be appointed by the relevant committee.

Qualifications for appointments

4.—(1) The executive directors of an HSS trust shall include—

(*a*) the chief officer of the trust;

(*b*) the chief finance officer of the trust;

(*c*) except in the case of a trust mentioned in paragraph (2), a medical or dental practitioner and a registered nurse or registered midwife as defined in section 10(7) of the Nurses, Midwives and Health Visitors Act 1979(**a**); and

(*d*) in the case of a trust which, by virtue of an authorisation for the time being in operation under Article 3(1) of the Health and Personal Social Services (Northern Ireland) Order 1994(**b**), provides a significant level of personal social services on behalf of a Health and Social Services Board, a person holding a recognised qualification in social work.

(2) Paragraph 1(*c*) shall not apply in the case of a trust—

(*a*) which does not provide services directly to patients or clients; or

(*b*) whose principal function is to provide ambulance or patient or client transport services.

(**a**)   1979 c. 36
(**b**)   S.I. 1994/429 (N.I. 2)

Persons to be regarded as executive directors

5. A person who is not an employee of an HSS trust but—

(*a*) holds a post in a university with a medical or dental school, and also works for the trust; or

(*b*) is seconded from his employers to work for the trust,

is nevertheless, on appointment as a director, to be regarded as an executive rather than a non-executive director of the trust.

Joint directors

6. Where more than one person is appointed jointly to a post in an HSS trust which qualifies the holder for executive directorship or in relation to which an executive director is to be appointed, those persons shall become or be appointed an executive director jointly, and shall count for the purposes of regulation 2 as one person.

Tenure of office of chairman and directors

7.—(1) Subject to regulation 9, the chairman and non-executive directors of an HSS trust shall be appointed for such period not exceeding four years as the Department may specify on making the appointment.

(2) Subject to regulation 8, the tenure of office of executive directors, other than the chief officer and chief finance officer, shall be for such period as the relevant committee may specify on making the appointment.

Tenure and suspension of tenure of office of executive directors

8.—(1) Subject to paragraphs (2) to (4), an executive director of an HSS trust shall hold office—

(*a*) if he is not the chief officer or the chief finance officer, for as long as he holds a post in the trust;

(*b*) if he is the chief officer or the chief finance officer, for as long as he holds that post in the trust.

(2) If the HSS trust is of the opinion that it is not in its interests that an executive director of the trust other than the chief officer or chief finance officer should continue to hold office as director the trust shall forthwith terminate his tenure of office.

(3) If an executive director of an HSS trust is suspended from his post in the trust he shall be suspended from performing his functions as director for the period of his suspension.

(4) An executive director other than the chief officer or chief finance officer of an HSS trust may resign his office at any time during the period for which he was appointed by giving notice in writing to the chairman of the trust.

Termination of tenure of office of chairman and non-executive directors

9.—(1) The chairman or a non-executive director of an HSS trust may resign his office at any time during the period for which he was appointed by giving notice in writing to the Department.

(2) Where during his period of directorship a non-executive director of a trust is appointed chairman of the trust, his tenure of office as non-executive director shall terminate when his appointment as chairman takes effect.

(3) If the Department is of the opinion that it is not in the interests of the health and personal social services that a person who is appointed as chairman or non-executive director of an HSS trust should continue to hold that office the Department may, forthwith, terminate his tenure of office.

(4) If a chairman or non-executive director of an HSS trust has not attended a meeting of the trust for a period of six months, the Department shall forthwith terminate his tenure of office unless the Department is satisfied that—

(*a*) the absence was due to a reasonable cause; and

(*b*) the chairman or non-executive director will be able to attend meetings of the trust within such period as the Department considers reasonable.

(5) Where a person has been appointed the chairman or non-executive director of an HSS trust—

(*a*) if he becomes disqualified for appointment under regulation 11 the Department shall forthwith notify him in writing of such disqualification; or

(*b*) if it comes to the notice of the Department that at the time of his appointment he was so disqualified it shall forthwith declare that he was not duly appointed and so notify him in writing,

and upon receipt of any such notification, his tenure of office, if any, shall be terminated and he shall cease to act as chairman or non-executive director.

(6) If it appears to the Department that the chairman or non-executive director of an HSS trust has failed to comply with regulation 20 (disclosure etc. on account of pecuniary interest) it may forthwith terminate that person's tenure of office.

(7) Where a person appointed as a non-executive director pursuant to paragraph 3(1)(*d*) of Schedule 3 to the Order ceases to hold a post in the university in question the Department shall terminate his appointment as a non-executive director.

Eligibility for re-appointment

10.—(1) Subject to regulation 11 the chairman or non-executive director of an HSS trust shall, on the termination of the period of his tenure of office, be eligible for re-appointment.

(2) An executive director of an HSS trust other than the chief officer and the chief finance officer shall on the termination of the period of his tenure of office be eligible for re-appointment.

Disqualification for appointment of chairman and non-executive directors

11.—(1) Subject to regulation 12 a person shall be disqualified for appointment as the chairman or non-executive director of an HSS trust if—

(*a*) he has within the preceding five years been convicted in the United Kingdom, the Channel Islands or the Isle of Man of any offence and has had passed on him a sentence of imprisonment (whether suspended or not) for a period of not less than three months without the option of a fine; or

(*b*) he has been adjudged bankrupt or has made a composition or arrangement with his creditors; or

(*c*) he has been dismissed, otherwise than by reason of redundancy, from any paid employment with a health service body or a health and social services body; or

(*d*) he is a person whose tenure of office as the chairman, member or director of a health and social services body has been terminated because his appointment is not in the interests of the health and personal social services, for non-attendance at meetings or for non-disclosure of a pecuniary interest;

(*e*) he is a chairman, member, director or employee of a health and social services body; or

(*f*) he is a general medical practitioner or general dental practitioner or an employee of either of those; or

(*g*) he holds a paid appointment or office with a trade union which represents the interests of members who are employed by a health and social services body; or

(*h*) he has had his name removed, by a direction under Schedule 11 of the Health and Personal Social Services (Northern Ireland) Order 1972, from any list prepared under Part VI of that Order and has not subsequently had his name included in such a list.

(2) For the purposes of paragraph (1)(*a*) the date of conviction shall be deemed to be the date on which the ordinary period allowed for making an appeal or application with respect to the conviction expires, or if such an appeal or application is made, the date on which the appeal or application is finally disposed of or abandoned or fails by reason of it not being prosecuted.

(3) For the purposes of paragraph (1)(*c*) a person shall not be treated as having been in paid employment by reason only of his chairmanship, membership or directorship of a health service body or a health and social services body.

(4) A person shall not be disqualified by paragraph (1)(*e*) from being the non-executive director of an HSS trust referred to in paragraph 3(1)(*d*) of Schedule 3 to the Order by reason of his employment with a health and social services body.

Cessation of disqualification

12.—(1) Where a person is disqualified under regulation 11(1)(*b*) by reason of having been adjudged bankrupt—

(*a*) if the bankruptcy is annulled on the ground that he ought not to have been adjudged bankrupt or on the ground that his debts have been paid in full, the disqualification shall cease on the date of the annulment;

(*b*) if he is discharged the disqualification shall cease on the date of his discharge.

(2) Where a person is disqualified under regulation 11(1)(*b*) by reason of his having made a composition or arrangement with his creditors, if he pays his debts in full the disqualification shall cease on the date on which the payment is completed and in any other case it shall cease on the expiry of five years from the date on which the terms of the deed of composition or arrangement are fulfilled.

(3) Subject to paragraph (4), where a person is disqualified under regulation 11(1)(*c*) (dismissed employees) he may, after the expiry of a period of not less than two years, apply in writing to the Department to remove the disqualification and the Department may direct that the disqualification shall cease.

(4) Where the Department refuses an application to remove a disqualification no further application may be made by that person until the expiration of two years from the date of the application.

(5) Where a person is disqualified under regulation 11(1)(*d*) (certain chairmen and directors whose appointments have been terminated), the disqualification shall cease on the expiry of a period of two years or such longer period as the Department specifies when terminating his period of office but the Department may on application being made to it by that person, reduce the period of disqualification.

PART III

CONSTITUTION AND PROCEEDINGS

Appointment of vice-chairman

13.—(1) For the purpose of enabling the proceedings of the trust to be conducted in the absence of the chairman, the directors of an HSS trust may appoint a non-executive director from amongst them to be vice-chairman for such a period, not exceeding the remainder of his term as non-executive director of the trust, as they may specify on appointing him.

(2) Any non-executive director so elected may at any time resign from the office of vice-chairman by giving notice in writing to the chairman and the directors of the trust may thereupon appoint another non-executive director as vice-chairman in accordance with paragraph (1).

Powers of vice-chairman

14. Where the chairman of an HSS trust has died or has otherwise ceased to hold office or where he has been unable to perform his duties as chairman owing to illness, absence from Northern Ireland or any other cause, references to the chairman in the Schedule shall, so long as there is no chairman able to perform his duties, be taken to include references to the vice-chairman.

Appointment of committees and sub-committees

15.—(1) Subject to regulations 17 and 18 an HSS trust may appoint committees of the trust consisting wholly or partly of directors of the trust or wholly of persons who are not directors of the trust.

(2) A committee appointed under this regulation may appoint sub-committees consisting wholly or partly of members of the committee (whether or not they include the directors of the trust) or wholly of persons who are not members of the committee (whether or not they include directors of the trust).

Arrangements for the exercise of functions

16. Subject to regulations 17 and 18 an HSS trust may make arrangements for the exercise, on behalf of the trust, of any of its functions by a committee or sub-committee appointed by virtue of regulation 15 subject to such restrictions and conditions as the trust thinks fit.

Committee for appointing chief officer

17. An HSS trust shall appoint a committee whose members shall be the chairman and non-executive directors of the trust whose function will be to appoint the chief officer who, in accordance with regulation 4, will be an executive director of the trust.

Committee for appointing executive directors other than chief officer

18. An HSS trust shall appoint a committee whose members shall be the chairman, the non-executive directors and the chief officer whose function will be to appoint the executive directors of the trust other than the chief officer.

Meetings and proceedings

19.—(1) The meetings and proceedings of an HSS trust shall be conducted in accordance with the rules set out in the Schedule and with Standing Orders made under paragraph (2).

(2) Subject to those rules and to regulation 20 an HSS trust shall make and may vary or revoke Standing Orders for the regulation of its proceedings and business and provision may be made in such Standing Orders for the suspension of them.

(3) An HSS trust may make, vary and revoke Standing Orders relating to the quorum, proceedings and place of meetings of a committee or sub-committee but, subject to regulation 20 and to any such Standing Orders, the quorum, proceedings and place of meeting shall be such as the committee or sub-committee may determine.

(4) The proceedings of an HSS trust shall not be invalidated by any vacancy in its membership or by any defect in a director's appointment.

Disability of directors in proceedings on account of pecuniary interest

20.—(1) Subject to the following provisions of this regulation, if a director of an HSS trust has any pecuniary interest, direct or indirect, in any contract, proposed contract or other matter and is present at a meeting of the trust at which the contract or other matter is the subject of consideration, he shall at the meeting and as soon as practicable after its commencement disclose the fact and shall not take part in the consideration and discussion of the contract or other matter or vote on any question with respect to it.

(2) The Department may, subject to such conditions as it may think fit to impose, remove any disability imposed by this regulation, in any case in which it appears to it in the interests of the health and personal social services that the disability shall be removed.

(3) An HSS trust may, by Standing Orders made under regulation 19, provide for the exclusion of a director from a meeting of the trust while any contract, proposed contract, or other matter in whch he has a pecuniary interest, direct or indirect, is under consideration.

(4) Any remuneration, compensation or allowances payable to a director by virtue of paragraph 9 of Schedule 3 to the Order shall not be treated as a pecuniary interest for the purposes of this regulation.

(5) Subject to paragraphs (2) and (6), a director shall be treated for the purposes of this regulation as having indirectly a pecuniary interest in a contract, proposed contract or other matter if—

(*a*) he, or a nominee of his, is a director of a company or other body, not being a public body, with which the contract was made or is proposed to be made or which has a direct pecuniary interest in the other matter under consideration; or

(*b*) he is a partner of, or is in the employment of, a person with whom the contract was made or is proposed to be made or who has a direct pecuniary interest in the other matter under consideration and, in the case of married persons living together, the interest of one spouse shall be deemed for the purpose of this regulation to be also an interest of the other.

(6) A director shall not be treated as having a pecuniary interest in any contract, proposed contract or other matter by reason only—

(*a*) of his membership of a company or other body if he has no beneficial interest in any securities of that company or other body;

(*b*) of an interest in any company, body or person with which he is connected as mentioned in paragraph (5) which is so remote or insignificant that it cannot reasonably be regarded as likely to influence a director in the consideration or discussion of or in voting on, any question with respect to that contract or matter.

(7) Where a director—

(*a*) has an indirect pecuniary interest in a contract or other matter by reason only of a beneficial interest in securities of a company or other body; and

(*b*) the total nominal value of those securities does not exceed £5,000 or one hundredth of the total nominal value of the issued share capital of the company or body, whichever is the less; and (*c*) if the share capital is of more than one class, the total nominal value of shares of any one class in which he has the beneficial interest does not exceed one hundredth of the total issued share capital of that class,

this regulation shall not prohibit him from taking part in consideration or discussion of the contract or other matter or from voting on any question in respect to it without prejudice however to his duty to disclose his interest.

(8) This regulation applies to a committee or sub-committee of an HSS trust as it applies to the trust and applies to any member of any such committee or sub-committee (whether or not he is also a director of the trust) as it applies to a director of the trust.

PART IV

REVOCATION

Revocation

21. The Health and Social Services Trusts (Membership and Procedure) Regulations (Northern Ireland) 1991(**a**) are hereby revoked.

Sealed with the Official Seal of the Department of Health and Social Services on 1st March 1994.

(L.S.)   *John McGrath*
                                                   Assistant Secretary

---

(a) S.R. 1991 No. 450

Rules as to meetings and proceedings of HSS trusts

1. The first meeting of an HSS trust shall be held on such day and at such place as may be fixed by the chairman and he shall be responsible for convening the meeting.

2.—(1) The chairman may call a meeting of the HSS trust at any time.

(2) If a requisition for a meeting, signed by at least one third of the directors, is presented to the chairman and the chairman either—

(*a*) refuses to call a meeting; or

(*b*) without so refusing, does not within seven days after the requisition has been presented to him call a meeting,

those one third or more of the directors may forthwith call a meeting.

(3) Before each meeting of an HSS trust, a notice of the meeting which—

(*a*) specifies the business proposed to be transacted at it; and

(*b*) is signed by the chairman or by an officer of the trust authorised by the chairman to sign on his behalf,

shall be delivered to each director, or sent by post to his usual place of residence or business, so as to be available to him at least three clear days before the meeting.

(4) Lack of service of the notice on any director shall not affect the validity of a meeting.

(5) In the case of a meeting called by directors in default of the chairman, the notice shall be signed by those directors and no business shall be transacted at the meeting other than that specified in the notice.

3.—(1) At any meeting of an HSS trust the chairman, if present, shall preside.

(2) If the chairman and vice-chairman (if any) are absent such non-executive director as the directors present shall choose shall preside.

(3) Every question at a meeting shall be determined by a majority of the votes of the directors present voting on the question and, in the case of any equality of votes, the person presiding shall have a second casting vote.

(4) The names of the directors present at the meeting shall be recorded.

(5) No business shall be transacted at a meeting of an HSS trust unless one third of the whole number of directors are present including on or after the operational date at least one executive director and one non-executive director.

(6) The minutes of the proceedings of a meeting shall be drawn up and submitted for agreement at the next ensuing meeting where they will be signed by the person presiding at it.

4. Where a post of executive director is shared by more than one person in pursuance of regulation 6—

(*a*) both persons shall be entitled to attend meetings of the HSS trust;

(*b*) either of those persons shall be eligible to vote in the case of agreement between them;

(*c*) in the case of disagreement between them no vote shall be cast;

(*d*) the presence of either or both of those persons shall count as one person for the purpose of paragraph 3(5) of this Schedule.

EXPLANATORY NOTE

(This note is not part of the Regulations.)

These Regulations revoke and consolidate with amendments the Health and Social Services Trusts (Membership and Procedure) Regulations (Northern Ireland) 1991 (S.R. 1991 No. 450). They make provision concerning the membership and procedure of HSS trusts established under the Health and Personal Social Services (Northern Ireland) Order 1991.

They include in Part II provisions relating to:—

(*a*) the number, appointment, qualifications and description of directors and joint directorships (regulations 2 to 6);

(*b*) tenure of office of chairman and non-executive directors and termination thereof, tenure and suspension of tenure of office of executive directors, and eligibility for re-appointment (regulations 7 to 10);

(*c*) disqualification for appointment of chairman and non-executive directors and cessation of disqualification (regulations 11 and 12).

In Part III provisions are included relating to the appointment and powers of vice-chairmen (regulations 13 and 14), the appointment of and the exercise of functions by committees and sub-committees (regulations 15 to 18) and meetings and proceedings of a trust including disability for taking part in proceedings of a trust on account of pecuniary interest (regulations 19 and 20 and the Schedule).

Regulation 21 revokes the Health and Social Services Trusts (Membership and Procedure) Regulations (Northern Ireland) 1991.

The main changes from the Regulations revoked are—

(*a*) regulation 4(1)(*d*) provides that the executive directors of an HSS trust which provides personal social services shall include a person holding a recognised qualification in social work. Regulation 2 now contains a definition of "recognised qualification in social work";

(*b*) regulations 7, 8 and 9 are amended to remove references to "appointing authority" and reference is now made to the specific authority making the appointment, ie, the Department or the relevant committee. As a consequence, the definition of "appointing authority" has been removed from regulation 1(2); and

(*c*) regulation 17 is amended to reflect the fact that the chief officer of an HSS trust shall be an executive director of the trust.

1994 No. 64

HEALTH AND PERSONAL SOCIAL SERVICES

The Health and Social Services Trusts (Exercise of Functions) Regulations (Northern Ireland) 1994

Made	*1st March 1994*
Coming into operation . .	*1st April 1994*

The Department of Health and Social Services, in exercise of the powers conferred on it by Article 3(2) of the Health and Personal Social Services (Northern Ireland) Order 1994(**a**), and of all other powers enabling it in that behalf, hereby makes the following Regulations:

Citation and commencement

1.—(1) These Regulations may be cited as the Health and Social Services Trusts (Exercise of Functions) Regulations (Northern Ireland) 1994 and shall come into operation on 1st April 1994.

(2) In these Regulations, "the Order" means the Health and Personal Social Services (Northern Ireland) Order 1994.

Relevant functions of Health and Social Services Boards

2. The relevant functions of a Health and Social Services Board under the statutory provisions specified in column 1 of the Schedule are those functions specified in column 2 of the Schedule for the purposes of Article 3 of the Order.

Sealed with the Official Seal of the Department of Health and Social Services on 1st March 1994.

(L.S.) *John McGrath*
Assistant Secretary

(**a**) S.I. 1994/429 (N.I. 2)

SCHEDULE   Regulation 2

Relevant functions of Health and Social Services Boards

Statutory Provision	*Relevant functions of a Health and Social Services Board*
Children and Young Persons Act (Northern Ireland) 1968(**a**)	All functions.
Health and Personal Social Services (Northern Ireland) Order 1972(**b**)	Functions under Articles 14A, 15, 36, 36A, 37, 38, 39, 71(2), 99, 101, 101A and Schedule 6.
Chronically Sick and Disabled Persons (Northern Ireland) Act 1978(**c**)	Functions under sections 1(2), 2 and 12(1).
Matrimonial Causes (Northern Ireland) Order 1978(**d**)	Functions under Article 47.
Domestic Proceedings (Northern Ireland) Order 1980(**e**)	Functions under Article 11.
Mental Health (Northern Ireland) Order 1986(**f**)	All functions except that of designating a hospital under Article 46(1) for the purposes of Article 46(2)(*a*), and those under Articles 28(3), 42(9)(*a*), 46(3)(*a*), 86(2), 90(2), 108(2), 112, 113, 114, 116, 118, 121(1), 123(1)(*a*), 129(7) and 133(4).
Adoption (Northern Ireland) Order 1987(**g**)	All functions.
Disabled Persons (Northern Ireland) Act 1989(**h**)	All functions.

(**a**)   1968 c. 34 (N.I.), as amended; the relevant amending statutory provisions are S.I. 1972/1265 (N.I. 14), 1973 (c. 38), 1973 (c. 53), S.I. 1973/2163, 1975 (c. 18), 1978 (c. 23), S.I. 1980/563 (N.I. 5), S.I. 1980/704 (N.I. 6), S.I. 1981/1675 (N.I. 26), 1981 (c. 19), S.I. 1986/595 (N.I. 4), S.I. 1986/1888 (N.I. 18), S.I. 1987/2203 (N.I. 22), S.I. 1991/194 (N.I. 1) and S.I. 1994/429 (N.I. 2)
(**b**)   S.I. 1972/1265 (N.I. 14), as amended; the relevant amending statutory provisions are 1973 (c. 38), 1975 (c. 18), S.I. 1981/1675 (N.I. 26), S.I. 1986/595 (N.I. 4), S.I. 1986/1888 (N.I. 18), S.I. 1986/2229 (N.I. 24), S.I. 1991/194 (N.I. 1), S.I. 1992/3204 (N.I. 20) and S.I. 1994/429 (N.I. 2)
(**c**)   1978 c. 53
(**d**)   S.I. 1978/1045 (N.I. 15)
(**e**)   S.I. 1980/563 (N.I. 5)
(**f**)   S.I. 1986/595 (N.I. 4), as amended; the relevant amending statutory provisions are S.I. 1989/1341 (N.I. 12), S.I. 1991/194 (N.I. 1), S.I. 1992/3204 (N.I. 20), S.I. 1994/429 (N.I. 2) and S.R. 1994 No. 66
(**g**)   S.I. 1987/2203 (N.I. 22), as amended by S.I. 1988/594 (N.I. 2), 1990 (c. 37) and S.I. 1994/429 (N.I. 2)
(**h**)   1989 (c. 10), as amended by S.I. 1991/194 (N.I. 1), S.I. 1992/3204 (N.I. 20) and S.I. 1994/429 (N.I. 2)

EXPLANATORY NOTE

(This note is not part of the Regulations.)

These Regulations prescribe functions of a Health and Social Services Board under certain statutory provisions as "relevant functions" for the purposes of Article 3 of the Health and Personal Social Services (Northern Ireland) Order 1994 (the Order). The functions specified include functions placed directly on a Board by the statutory provision and functions exercisable by a Board on behalf of the Department of Health and Social Services.

Article 3 of the Order enables a Board, with the Department's approval, to delegate the exercise of the prescribed functions to a Health and Social Services trust.

1994   No. 65

HEALTH AND PERSONAL SOCIAL SERVICES

The Health and Social Services Trusts (Consequential Amendments) Regulations (Northern Ireland) 1994

Made	*1st March 1994*
Coming into operation . .	*1st April 1994*

The Department of Health and Social Services, in exercise of the powers conferred on it by Article 3(11) of the Health and Personal Social Services (Northern Ireland) Order 1994(a) and of all other powers enabling it in that behalf, hereby makes the following Regulations:

Citation and commencement

1. These Regulations may be cited as the Health and Social Services Trusts (Consequential Amendments) Regulations (Northern Ireland) 1994 and shall come into operation on 1st April 1994.

Amendment of Statutory Rules

2. The Statutory Rules referred to in the Schedules shall be amended as set out in those Schedules.

Sealed with the Official Seal of the Department of Health and Social Services on 1st March 1994.

(L.S.)   *John McGrath*
                                    Assistant Secretary

(a)   S.I. 1994/429 (N.I. 2)

INDEX TO THE SCHEDULES

SCHEDULE 1

Amendment of the Nursing Homes Regulations (Northern Ireland) 1993

1. The Nursing Homes Regulations (Northern Ireland) 1993(**a**) shall be amended as follows—

   (*a*) in regulation 1(2), after the definition of "adequate" there shall be added the following definition—

   " "authorised HSS trust" has the meaning assigned to it by Article 2B of the Mental Health (Northern Ireland) Order 1986(**b**);'';

   (*b*) in regulation 12(1), after the word "Board", in the first place where that word occurs, there shall be added the words "or an HSS trust";

   (*c*) in regulation 15(2)(*b*), after the word "Board" there shall be added the words "or an HSS trust";

   (*d*) in regulation 17(1) and (2), after the word "Board", in each place where that word occurs, there shall be added the words "or an HSS trust";

   (*e*) in Schedule 4, paragraph 2(*c*), after the word "Board" there shall be added the words "or an HSS trust";

   (*f*) in Schedule 4, paragraph 2(*h*), after the word "Board", in each place where that word occurs, there shall be added the words "or an authorised HSS trust"; and

   (*g*) in Schedule 4, paragraph 2(*i*), after the word "Board," there shall be added the words "HSS trust,".

(**a**) S.R. 1993 No. 92
(**b**) S.I. 1986/595 (N.I. 4); as amended by Schedule 1 to S.I. 1994/429 (N.I. 2)

SCHEDULE 2

Amendment of the Residential Care Homes Regulations (Northern Ireland) 1993

1. The Residential Care Homes Regulations (Northern Ireland) 1993(**a**) shall be amended as follows—

(*a*) in regulation 1(2), after the definition of "adequate" there shall be added the following definition—

" "authorised HSS trust" has the meaning assigned to it by Article 2B of the Mental Health (Northern Ireland) Order 1986(**b**);";

(*b*) in regulation 10(1), after the word "Board", in the first place where that word occurs, there shall be added the words "or an HSS trust";

(*c*) in regulation 14, after the word "Board" there shall be added the words "or an HSS trust";

(*d*) in Schedule 4, paragraph 2(*c*), after the word "Board" there shall be added the words "or an HSS trust";

(*e*) in Schedule 4, paragraph 2(*h*), after the word "Board", in each place where that word occurs, there shall be added the words "or an authorised HSS trust"; and

(*f*) in Schedule 4, paragraph 2(*i*), after the word "Board," there shall be added the words "HSS trust,".

(**a**) S.R. 1993 No. 91
(**b**) S.I. 1986/595 (N.I. 4); as amended by Schedule 1 to S.I. 1994/429 (N.I. 2)

SCHEDULE 3

Amendment of the Mental Health (Nurses, Guardianship, Consent to Treatment and Prescribed Forms) Regulations (Northern Ireland) 1986

1. The Mental Health (Nurses, Guardianship, Consent to Treatment and Prescribed Forms) Regulations (Northern Ireland) 1986(**a**) shall be amended as follows—

(*a*) in regulation 2, after the definition of "the Order" there shall be added the following definition—

" "authorised HSS trust" has the meaning assigned to it by Article 2B;";

(*b*) in regulation 2, in the definition of "private guardian"after the word "Board" there shall be added the words "or an authorised HSS trust";

(*c*) in regulation 2, after the definition of "private guardian" there shall be added the following definition—

" "responsible authority" has the meaning assigned to it by Article 2(2);";

(*d*) in regulation 4, for the words "responsible Board", in each place where those words occur, there shall be substituted the words "responsible authority";

(*e*) in regulation 4(*b*), for the words "that Board" there shall be substituted the words "that authority";

(*f*) in regulation 5 (1st line) and 5(*b*), for the words "responsible Board" and "that Board" there shall be substituted the words "responsible authority" and "that authority" respectively;

(*g*) in the Schedule, Index of Prescribed Forms, there shall be inserted at the appropriate place the following entry—

"5A. Medical practitioner's report that an application for assessment ought to be made in respect of an in-patient in a hospital not managed by an authorised HSS trust.";

(*h*) in the Schedule, Form 5A set out in the Annex to this Schedule shall be inserted at the appropriate place;

(*i*) in the Schedule, in Forms 1, 2, 3, 5 to 14, 19, 20 and 24, for the words "responsible Board", in each place where those words occur, there shall be substituted "responsible authority"; and

(*j*) in the Schedule, in Forms 2, 14, 17 and 19, for the words "name of Board", in each place where those words occur, there shall be substituted "name of Board or HSS trust".

(**a**) S.R. 1986 No. 174, as amended by S.R. 1992 No. 44

ANNEX

FORM 5A

MENTAL HEALTH (NORTHERN IRELAND) ORDER 1986

Article 7A (2)

MEDICAL PRACTITIONER'S REPORT THAT AN APPLICATION FOR ASSESSMENT OUGHT TO BE MADE IN RESPECT OF AN IN-PATIENT IN A HOSPITAL NOT MANAGED BY AN AUTHORISED HSS TRUST

To [name and address of HSS trust]

I [full name] am a medical practitioner on the staff of [name of hospital]

[Full name of patient] is an in-patient in this hospital and I hereby report for the purposes of Article 7A(2) of the Mental Health (Northern Ireland) Order 1986 that it appears to me that an application for assessment ought to be made in respect of the patient for the following reasons:—

[Reasons should indicate why an application for assessment is considered necessary]

Signed ....

Date ....

Time ....

SCHEDULE 4

Amendment of the Mental Health Review Tribunal (Northern Ireland) Rules 1986

1. The Mental Health Review Tribunal (Northern Ireland) Rules 1986(**a**) shall be amended as follows—

(*a*) in rule 2, the definition of "the Board's statement" shall be deleted and the following definitions shall be inserted before the definition of "chairman"—

" "authorised HSS trust" has the meaning assigned to it by Article 2B of the Order;";

"the authority's statement" means the statement provided by the responsible authority pursuant to rule 6(1);";

(*b*) in rule 2, in the definition of "party", for the words "responsible Board" there shall be substituted the words "responsible authority";

(*c*) in rule 2, in the definition of "private guardian", after the words "Health and Social Services Board" there shall be added the words "or authorised HSS trust";

(*d*) in rule 2, the definition of "responsible Board" shall be deleted and the following definition shall be substituted—

" "responsible authority" has the meaning assigned to it by Article 2(2) of the Order;";

(*e*) in rules 3(3), 4(1)(*a*), 6(1), (1)(*a*) and (4)(*a*), 12(1), 16(3), 21(4), 22(4), 25(2), 29(*b*) and 30, 30(*b*) and 30(*d*) and in the heading of the Schedule and paragraphs 3 and 4 of Part B of the Schedule, for the words "responsible Board", in each place where those words occur, there shall be substituted the words "responsible authority";

(*f*) in rules 6(2), (4) and (4)(*a*), 7 and 7(*c*), for the words "responsible Board's", in each place where those words occur, there shall be substituted the words "responsible authority's";

(*g*) in rule 8(2), for sub-paragraph (*a*) there shall be substituted the following sub-paragraph—

"(*a*) he is a member, director or officer of the responsible authority; or"; and

(*h*) in rule 30(*b*) and (*c*), for the word "Board's" there shall be substituted the word "authority's".

(**a**)　S.R. 1986 No. 193

SCHEDULE 5

Amendment of the Health and Personal Social Services (Assessment of Resources) Regulations (Northern Ireland) 1993

1. The Health and Personal Social Services (Assessment of Resources) Regulations (Northern Ireland) 1993(**a**) shall be amended as follows—

(*a*) in regulation 2(1), after the definition of "the Fund" there shall be added the following definition—

" "HSS trust" means a Health and Social Services trust established under Article 10 of the Health and Personal Social Services (Northern Ireland) Order 1991(**b**), by which functions are exercisable by virtue of an authorisation for the time being in operation under Article 3(1) of the Health and Personal Social Services (Northern Ireland) Order 1994(**c**);";

(*b*) in regulation 2(1), in the definition of "less dependent resident", after the word "Board" there shall be added the words "or an HSS trust";

(*c*) in regulations 3, 5 and 26(1), after the word "Board" there shall be added the words "or an HSS trust";

(*d*) in regulations 16(1)(*b*) and (4) and 17(4) and (5)—

(i) after the words "a Board", wherever those words occur, there shall be added the words "or an HSS trust"; and

(ii) after the words "the Board", wherever those words occur, there shall be added the words "or the HSS trust";

(*e*) in regulations 22(8), 26(2), 36(1) and 37(1), after the words "the Board" there shall be added the words "or the HSS trust";

(*f*) in Schedule 1, paragraphs 1 (in the definition of "protected amount"), 3, 10 and 11, after the word "Board", in each place where that word occurs, there shall be added the words "or an HSS trust";

(*g*) in Schedule 3, paragraph 18, after the word "Boards' " there shall be added the words "or HSS trusts' ";

(*h*) in Schedule 3, paragraphs 27 and 28(*b*), after the word "Board", in each place where that word occurs, there shall be added the words "or the HSS trust"; and

(*i*) in Schedule 4—

(i) in paragraph 8, after the word "Board" there shall be added the words "or an HSS trust"; and

(ii) in paragraph 18, after the word "Board" there shall be added the words "or the HSS trust".

(**a**) S.R. 1993 No. 127, as amended by S.R. 1993 No. 234
(**b**) S.I. 1991/194 (N.I. 1)
(**c**) S.I. 1994/429 (N.I. 2)

SCHEDULE 6

Amendment of the Residential Accommodation (Other Premises, Persons Ordinarily Resident and Exemptions) Regulations (Northern Ireland) 1993

1. The Residential Accommodation (Other Premises, Persons Ordinarily Resident and Exemptions) Regulations (Northern Ireland) 1993(**a**) shall be amended as follows—

(*a*) in regulation 2(1), after the definition of "Board" there shall be added the following definition—

" "HSS trust" means a Health and Social Services trust established under Article 10 of the Health and Personal Social Services (Northern Ireland) Order 1991(**b**), by which functions are exercisable by virtue of an authorization for the time being in operation under Article 3(1) of the Health and Personal Social Services (Northern Ireland) Order 1994(**c**);";

(*b*) in regulation 7(1)(*b*), after the word "Board" there shall be added the words "or the HSS trust";

(*c*) in regulation 7(2)(*a*), after the word "Board" there shall be added the words "or an HSS trust"; and

(*d*) in regulation 9(1)(*a*)(i), (1)(*b*) and (2)(*a*), after the word "Board" there shall be added the words "or an HSS trust".

(**a**) S.R. 1993 No. 163
(**b**) S.I. 1991/194 (N.I. 1)
(**c**) S.I. 1994/429 (N.I. 2)

SCHEDULE 7

Amendment of the Children and Young Persons (Boarding-Out) Regulations (Northern Ireland) 1976

1. The Children and Young Persons (Boarding-Out) Regulations (Northern Ireland) 1976(**a**) shall be amended as follows—

(*a*) in regulation 2,—

> (i) for the definition of "area authority" there shall be substituted the following definition—
>
> " "area authority" in relation to a child means—
>
> (*a*) a Health and Social Services Board in whose area the home of the foster parents is; or
>
> (*b*) an HSS trust in whose operational area the home of the foster parents is;";
>
> (ii) in the definition of "care authority", after the words "Health and Social Services Board" there shall be added the words "or an HSS trust";
>
> (iii) after the definition of "Health and Social Services Board" there shall be added the following definition—
>
> " "HSS trust" means a Health and Social Services trust established under Article 10 of the Health and Personal Social Services (Northern Ireland) Order 1991(**b**), by which functions are exercisable by virtue of an authorisation for the time being in operation under Article 3(1) of the Health and Personal Social Services (Northern Ireland) Order 1994(**c**);";
>
> (iv) in the definition of "social worker", after the words "Health and Social Services Board" there shall be added the words ", HSS trust"; and
>
> (v) in the definition of "voluntary organisation", for the words "or a Health and Social Services Board" there shall be substituted the words ", a Health and Social Services Board or an HSS trust"; and

(*b*) regulation 2 shall be numbered as regulation 2(1), and a new paragraph (2) shall be added as follows—

> "(2) Any reference to a Health and Social Services Board in these Regulations (other than regulation 28) shall include a reference to an HSS trust.".

(**a**) S.R. 1976 No. 19
(**b**) S.I. 1991/194 (N.I. 1)
(**c**) S.I. 1994/429 (N.I. 2)

SCHEDULE 8

Amendment of the Child-Minding (Registration Requirements) Regulations (Northern Ireland) 1974

1. The Child-Minding (Registration Requirements) Regulations (Northern Ireland) 1974(**a**) shall be amended as follows—

(*a*) in regulation 2, after the definition of "Health and Social Services Board" there shall be added the following definition—

" "HSS trust" means a Health and Social Services trust established under Article 10 of the Health and Personal Social Services (Northern Ireland) Order 1991(**b**), by which functions are exercisable by virtue of an authorisation for the time being in operation under Article 3(1) of the Health and Personal Social Services (Northern Ireland) Order 1994(**c**);";

(*b*) in regulation 3, —

   (i) after the words "Health and Social Services Board" there shall be added the words "or an HSS trust"; and

   (ii) in paragraphs (*a*), (*b*) and (*c*), after the word "Board", in each place where that word occurs, there shall be added the words "or the HSS trust"; and

(*c*) in the Schedule, after the word "Board", in each place where that word occurs, there shall be added the words "or the HSS trust".

(**a**) S.R. 1974 No. 318
(**b**) S.I. 1991/194 (N.I. 1)
(**c**) S.I. 1994/429 (N.I. 2)

SCHEDULE 9

Amendment of the Children and Young Persons (Voluntary Homes) Regulations (Northern Ireland) 1975

1. The Children and Young Persons (Voluntary Homes) Regulations (Northern Ireland) 1975(**a**) shall be amended as follows—

(*a*) in regulation 2, after the definition of "Health and Social Services Board" there shall be added the following definition—

" "HSS trust" means a Health and Social Services trust established under Article 10 of the Health and Personal Social Services (Northern Ireland) Order 1991(**b**), by which functions are exercisable by virtue of an authorisation for the time being in operation under Article 3(1) of the Health and Personal Social Services (Northern Ireland) Order 1994(**c**);"; and

(*b*) in regulation 9(2)(*b*), after the words "Health and Social Services Board" there shall be added the words "or the HSS trust".

(**a**) S.R. 1975 No. 293
(**b**) S.I. 1991/194 (N.I. 1)
(**c**) S.I. 1994/429 (N.I. 2)

SCHEDULE 10

Amendment of the Social Security (Credits) Regulations (Northern Ireland) 1975

1. The Social Security (Credits) Regulations (Northern Ireland) 1975(**a**) shall be amended as follows—

(*a*) in regulation 2(1), after the definition of "Health and Social Services Board" there shall be added the following definition—

" "HSS trust" means a Health and Social Services trust established under Article 10 of the Health and Personal Social Services (Northern Ireland) Order 1991(**b**), by which functions are exercisable by virtue of an authorisation for the time being in operation under Article 3(1) of the Health and Personal Social Services (Northern Ireland) Order 1994(**c**);"; and

(*b*) in regulation 9(4)(*a*)(iv)(*bb*), for the words "or a Health and Social Services Board" there shall be substituted the words ", a Health and Social Services Board or an HSS trust".

(**a**) S.R. 1975 No. 113, as amended; the relevant amending Regulations are S.R. 1982 No. 42
(**b**) S.I. 1991/194 (N.I. 1)
(**c**) S.I. 1994/429 (N.I. 2)

SCHEDULE 11

Amendment of the Social Security (Unemployment, Sickness and Invalidity Benefit) Regulations (Northern Ireland) 1984

1. The Social Security (Unemployment, Sickness and Invalidity Benefit) Regulations (Northern Ireland) 1984(**a**) shall be amended as follows—

(*a*) in regulation 1(2), after the definition of "Health and Social Services Board" there shall be added the following definition—

" "HSS trust" means a Health and Social Services trust established under Article 10 of the Health and Personal Social Services (Northern Ireland) Order 1991(**b**), by which functions are exercisable by virtue of an authorisation for the time being in operation under Article 3(1) of the Health and Personal Social Services (Northern Ireland) Order 1994(**c**);";

(*b*) in regulation 7(1)(*g*)(iii), for the words "or a Health and Social Services Board" there shall be substituted the words ", a Health and Social Services Board or an HSS trust"; and

(*c*) in regulation 11(4), for the words "or a Health and Social Services Board" there shall be substituted the words ", a Health and Social Services Board or an HSS trust".

(**a**) S.R. 1984 No. 245
(**b**) S.I. 1991/194 (N.I. 1)
(**c**) S.I. 1994/429 (N.I. 2)

SCHEDULE 12

Amendment of the Income Support (General) Regulations (Northern Ireland) 1987

1. The Income Support (General) Regulations (Northern Ireland) 1987(**a**) shall be amended as follows—

(*a*) in regulation 2(1), after the definition of "Health and Social Services Board" there shall be added the following definition—

" "HSS trust" means a Health and Social Services trust established under Article 10 of the Health and Personal Social Services (Northern Ireland) Order 1991(**b**), by which functions are exercisable by virtue of an authorisation for the time being in operation under Article 3(1) of the Health and Personal Social Services (Northern Ireland) Order 1994(**c**);'';

(*b*) in regulation 3(2)(*c*), after the words "Health and Social Services Board" there shall be added the words "or an HSS trust";

(*c*) in regulation 13(2)(*dd*), after the words "Health and Social Services Board" there shall be added the words "or an HSS trust";

(*d*) in regulation 13A(4)(*d*), after the words "Health and Social Services Board" there shall be added the words "or an HSS trust";

(*e*) in regulation 19(2), in the definition of "residential care home", after the words "Health and Social Services Board" there shall be added the words "or an HSS trust";

(*f*) in regulation 21(3), in the definition of "residential accommodation", after the words "Health and Social Services Board" there shall be added the words "or an HSS trust";

(*g*) in regulation 21(3B), after the words "Health and Social Services Board" there shall be added the words "or an HSS trust";

(*h*) in regulation 41(3)—

(i) after the words "Health and Social Services Board" there shall be added the words "or an HSS trust"; and

(ii) after the words "Health and Social Services Boards' " there shall be added "or HSS trusts' ";

(*i*) in Schedule 1, paragraph 2, after the words "Health and Social Services Board" there shall be added the words "or an HSS trust";

(*j*) in Schedule 2, paragraph 2A(3)(*b*), after the words "Health and Social Services Board" there shall be added the words "or an HSS trust";

(*k*) in Schedule 4, paragraph 11(2)(*d*), after the words "Health and Social Services Board" there shall be added the words "or an HSS trust";

(*l*) in Schedule 9, paragraphs 26, 27 and 28, after the words "Health and Social Services Board", in each place where those words occur, there shall be added the words "or an HSS trust"; and

(*m*) in Schedule 10, paragraph 17, after the words "Health and Social Services Board" there shall be added the words "or an HSS trust".

(**a**) S.R. 1987 No. 459, as amended; the relevant amending Regulations are S.R. 1988 No. 274, S.R. 1989 No. 249, S.R. 1991 No. 474, S.R. 1992 No. 147, S.Rs. 1993 Nos. 149 and 165

(**b**) S.I. 1991/194 (N.I. 1)

(**c**) S.I. 1994/429 (N.I. 2)

SCHEDULE 13

Amendment of the Housing Benefit (General) Regulations (Northern Ireland) 1987

1. The Housing Benefit (General) Regulations (Northern Ireland) 1987(**a**) shall be amended as follows—

    (*a*) in regulation 2(1), after the definition of "Health and Social Services Board" there shall be added the following definition—

        " "HSS trust" means a Health and Social Services trust established under Article 10 of the Health and Personal Social Services (Northern Ireland) Order 1991(**b**), by which functions are exercisable by virtue of an authorisation for the time being in operation under Article 3(1) of the Health and Personal Social Services (Northern Ireland) Order 1994(**c**);";

    (*b*) in regulation 3(2)(*f*), after the words "Health and Social Services Board" there shall be added the words "or an HSS trust";

    (*c*) in regulation 5(9)(*a*)(ii), in the definition of "residential accommodation", after the words "Health and Social Services Board" there shall be added the words "or an HSS trust";

    (*d*) in regulation 48A(2)(*d*), after the words "Health and Social Services Board" there shall be added the words ", HSS trust";

    (*e*) in Schedule 4, paragraphs 26 and 27, after the words "Health and Social Services Board", in each place where those words occur, there shall be added the words ", HSS trust";

    (*f*) in Schedule 4, paragraph 28—

        (i) after the words "Health and Social Services Board" there shall be added the words "or an HSS trust"; and

        (ii) after the words "Health and Social Services Boards' " there shall be added the words "or HSS trusts' "; and

    (*g*) in Schedule 5, paragraph 18—

        (i) after the words "Health and Social Services Board" there shall be added the words "or an HSS trust"; and

        (ii) after the words "Health and Social Services Boards' " there shall be added the words "or HSS trusts' ".

(**a**) S.R. 1987 No. 461, as amended; the relevant amending Regulations are S.R. 1989 No. 260, S.R. 1990 No. 297, S.R. 1993 No. 149
(**b**) S.I. 1991/194 (N.I. 1)
(**c**) S.I. 1994/429 (N.I. 2)

SCHEDULE 14

Amendment of the Family Credit (General) Regulations (Northern Ireland) 1987

1. The Family Credit (General) Regulations (Northern Ireland) 1987(**a**) shall be amended as follows—

(*a*) in regulation 2(1), after the definition of "the Fund" there shall be added the following definition—

" "HSS trust" means a Health and Social Services trust established under Article 10 of the Health and Personal Social Services (Northern Ireland) Order 1991(**b**), by which functions are exercisable by virtue of an authorisation for the time being in operation under Article 3(1) of the Health and Personal Social Services (Northern Ireland) Order 1994(**c**);";

(*b*) in Schedule 2, paragraphs 23 and 24, after the words "Health and Social Services Board", in each place where those words occur, there shall be added the words ", HSS trust"; and

(*c*) in Schedule 2, paragraph 25 and Schedule 3, paragraph 18—

(i) after the words "Health and Social Services Board" there shall be added the words "or an HSS trust"; and

(ii) after the words "Health and Social Services Boards' " there shall be added the words "or HSS trusts' ".

(**a**) S.R. 1987 No. 463, as amended; the relevant amending Regulations are S.R. 1989 No. 249 and S.R. 1992 No. 201
(**b**) S.I. 1991/194 (N.I. 1)
(**c**) S.I. 1994/429 (N.I. 2)

SCHEDULE 15

Amendment of the Social Security (Claims and Payments) Regulations (Northern Ireland) 1987

1. Regulation 42 of the Social Security (Claims and Payments) Regulations (Northern Ireland) 1987(**a**) shall be amended as follows—

   (*a*) in paragraph (5), after the words "Health and Social Services Board" there shall be added the words "or an HSS trust";

   (*b*) in paragraph (7)—

      (i) after the words "Health and Social Services Board", in the first place where those words occur, there shall be added the words "or an HSS trust";

      (ii) after the words "said Board" there shall be added the words "or said HSS trust";

      (iii) after the words "such Board" there shall be added the words "or such HSS trust";

      (iv) after the words "that Board", in each place where those words occur, there shall be added the words "or that HSS trust"; and

      (v) after the words "Health and Social Services Board", in the second and third places where those words occur, there shall be added the words "or HSS trust";

   (*c*) in paragraph (8)—

      (i) after the words "Health and Social Services Board", in each place where those words occur, there shall be added the words "or the HSS trust"; and

      (ii) after the words "that Board", in each place where those words occur, there shall be added the words "or that HSS trust"; and

   (*d*) in paragraph (9), after the definition of "Health and Social Services Board", there shall be added the following definition—

      " "HSS trust" means a Health and Social Services trust established under Article 10 of the Health and Personal Social Services (Northern Ireland) Order 1991(**b**), by which functions are exercisable by virtue of an authorisation for the time being in operation under Article 3(1) of the Health and Personal Social Services (Northern Ireland) Order 1994(**c**);".

(**a**) S.R. 1987 No. 465, as amended; the relevant amending Regulations are S.R. 1992 No. 7
(**b**) S.I. 1991/194 (N.I. 1)
(**c**) S.I. 1994/429 (N.I. 2)

SCHEDULE 16

Amendment of the Social Security (Attendance Allowance) Regulations (Northern Ireland) 1992

1. The Social Security (Attendance Allowance) Regulations (Northern Ireland) 1992(**a**) shall be amended as follows—

(*a*) in regulation 1(2), after the definition of "the 1991 Order" there shall be added the following definition—

" "HSS trust" means a Health and Social Services trust established under Article 10 of the 1991 Order, by which functions are exercisable by virtue of an authorisation for the time being in operation under Article 3(1) of the Health and Personal Social Services (Northern Ireland) Order 1994(**b**);"; and

(*b*) in regulation 8(7), after the words "Health and Social Services Board" there shall be added the words "or an HSS trust".

(**a**) S.R. 1992 No. 20, as amended; the relevant amending Regulations are S.R. 1992 No. 481 and S.Rs. 1993 Nos. 149 and 165

(**b**) S.I. 1994/429 (N.I. 2)

SCHEDULE 17

Amendment of the Social Security (Disability Living Allowance) Regulations (Northern Ireland) 1992

1. The Social Security (Disability Living Allowance) Regulations (Northern Ireland) 1992(**a**) shall be amended as follows—

(*a*) in regulation 1(2), after the definition of "care component" there shall be added the following definition—

" "HSS trust" means a Health and Social Services trust established under Article 10 of the 1991 Order, by which functions are exercisable by virtue of an authorisation for the time being in operation under Article 3(1) of the Health and Personal Social Services (Northern Ireland) Order 1994(**b**);";

(*b*) in regulation 9(2), after the words "Health and Social Services Board", in each place where those words occur, there shall be added the words "or an HSS trust"; and

(*c*) in regulation 10(9), after the words "Health and Social Services Board" there shall be added the words "or an HSS trust".

(**a**) S.R. 1992 No. 32, as amended; the relevant amending Regulations are S.R. 1992 No. 481, S.Rs. 1993 Nos. 149 and 165

(**b**) S.I. 1994/429 (N.I. 2)

SCHEDULE 18

**Amendment of the Disability Working Allowance (General) Regulations
(Northern Ireland) 1992**

1. The Disability Working Allowance (General) Regulations (Northern Ireland)
1992(**a**) shall be amended as follows—

 (*a*) in regulation 2, after the definition of "the Fund" there shall be added the
  following definition—

  " "HSS trust" means a Health and Social Services trust established under
   Article 10 of the Health and Personal Social Services (Northern
   Ireland) Order 1991(**b**), by which functions are exercisable by virtue
   of an authorisation for the time being in operation under Article 3(1) of
   the Health and Personal Social Services (Northern Ireland) Order
   1994(**c**);";

 (*b*) in Schedule 3, paragraphs 23 and 24, after the words "Health and Social
  Services Board", in each place where those words occur, there shall be added
  the words ", HSS trust";

 (*c*) in Schedule 3, paragraph 25—

  (i) after the words "Health and Social Services Board" there shall be added
   the words "or an HSS trust"; and

  (ii) after the words "Health and Social Services Boards' " there shall be
   added the words "or HSS trusts' "; and

 (*d*) in Schedule 4, paragraph 18, after the words "Health and Social Services
  Board" there shall be added the words "or an HSS trust".

(**a**) S.R. 1992 No. 78, as amended; the relevant amending Regulations are S.R. 1992 No. 201
(**b**) S.I. 1991/194 (N.I. 1)
(**c**) S.I. 1994/429 (N.I. 2)

SCHEDULE 19

Amendment of the Child Support (Maintenance Assessments and Special Cases) Regulations (Northern Ireland) 1992

1. The Child Support (Maintenance Assessments and Special Cases) Regulations (Northern Ireland) 1992(**a**) shall be amended as follows—

(*a*) in regulation 1(2), in the definition of ''family''—

   (i) after the words ''Health and Social Services Board'' there shall be added the words ''or an HSS trust''; and

   (ii) after the words ''that Board'' there shall be added the words ''or that HSS trust'';

(*b*) in regulation 1(2), after the definition of ''Health and Social Services Board'' there shall be added the following definition—

   '' ''HSS trust'' means a Health and Social Services trust established under Article 10 of the Health and Personal Social Services (Northern Ireland) Order 1991(**b**), by which functions are exercisable by virtue of an authorisation for the time being in operation under Article 3(1) of the Health and Personal Social Services (Northern Ireland) Order 1994(**c**);'';

(*c*) in regulation 1(2), in the definition of ''person'', after the word ''Board'' there shall be added the words ''or an HSS trust'';

(*d*) in regulation 25, after the words ''Health and Social Services Board'', in each place where those words occur, there shall be added the words ''or an HSS trust'';

(*e*) in regulation 27A(1)—

   (i) after the words ''Health and Social Services Board'' there shall be added the words ''or an HSS trust''; and

   (ii) after the words ''the Board'' there shall be added the words ''or the HSS trust'';

(*f*) in regulation 27A(2), after the words ''the Board'' there shall be added the words ''or the HSS trust'';

(*g*) in Schedule 2, paragraph 28(*a*), after the words ''Health and Social Services Board'' there shall be added the words ''or an HSS trust'';

(*h*) in Schedule 2, paragraph 29, after the words ''Health and Social Services Board,'' there shall be added the words ''an HSS trust,''; and

(*i*) in Schedule 2, paragraph 30—

   (i) after the words ''Health and Social Services Board'' there shall be added the words ''or an HSS trust''; and

   (ii) after the words ''Health and Social Services Boards' '' there shall be added the words ''or HSS trusts' ''.

(**a**)   S.R. 1992 No. 341, as amended; the relevant amending Regulations are S.R. 1993 No. 164
(**b**)   S.I. 1991/194 (N.I. 1)
(**c**)   S.I. 1994/429 (N.I. 2)

SCHEDULE 20

Amendment of the Child Support (Information, Evidence and Disclosure) Regulations (Northern Ireland) 1992

1. The Child Support (Information, Evidence and Disclosure) Regulations (Northern Ireland) 1992(**a**) shall be amended as follows—

(*a*) in regulation 1(2), after the definition of "Health and Social Services Board" there shall be added the following definition—

" "HSS trust" means a Health and Social Services trust established under Article 10 of the Health and Personal Social Services (Northern Ireland) Order 1991(**b**), by which functions are exercisable by virtue of an authorisation for the time being in operation under Article 3(1) of the Health and Personal Social Services (Northern Ireland) Order 1994(**c**);"; and

(*b*) in regulation 2(2), after sub-paragraph (*d*) there shall be added the following sub-paragraph—

"(*dd*) the HSS trust in whose operational area a person falling within a category listed in sub-paragraphs (*a*) and (*b*) resides or has resided, with respect to the matter listed in sub-paragraph (*a*) of regulation 3(1);".

(**a**) S.R. 1992 No. 339
(**b**) S.I. 1991/194 (N.I. 1)
(**c**) S.I. 1994/429 (N.I. 2)

SCHEDULE 21

Amendment of the Child Support (Maintenance Assessment Procedure) Regulations (Northern Ireland) 1992

1. Regulation 49 of the Child Support (Maintenance Assessment Procedure) Regulations (Northern Ireland) 1992(**a**) shall be amended as follows—

(*a*) after paragraph (*a*) there shall be added the following paragraph—

"(*aa*) an HSS trust established under Article 10 of the Health and Personal Social Services (Northern Ireland) Order 1991(**b**), by which functions are exercisable by virtue of an authorisation for the time being in operation under Article 3(1) of the Health and Personal Social Services (Northern Ireland) Order 1994(**c**);"; and

(*b*) in paragraph (*b*), —

(i) after the words "Health and Social Services Board" there shall be added the words "or an HSS trust";

(ii) after the words "that Board" there shall be added the words "or that HSS trust"; and

(iii) after the words "the Board" there shall be added the words "or the HSS trust".

(**a**) S.R. 1992 No. 340, as amended; the relevant amending regulations are S.R. 1993 No. 164
(**b**) S.I. 1991/194 (N.I. 1)
(**c**) S.I. 1994/429 (N.I. 2)

SCHEDULE 22

Amendment of the Adoption Agencies Regulations (Northern Ireland) 1989

1. The Adoption Agencies Regulations (Northern Ireland) 1989(a) shall be amended as follows—

  (a) in regulation 1(2), after the definition of "adoption panel" there shall be added the following definition—

  " "authorised HSS trust" means an HSS trust which is an adoption agency;";

  (b) in regulation 5—

   (i) at the beginning of paragraph (1), for the word "An" there shall be substituted the words "Subject to regulation 5A, an";

   (ii) in paragraph (3)(b), for the words "is a Board, at least one member of that Board;" there shall be substituted the words—

   "is—

    (i) a Board, at least one member of that Board; or

    (ii) an HSS trust, at least one director of that HSS trust;"; and

   (iii) in paragraph (3)(d), after the word "member" there shall be added the word ", director";

  (c) after regulation 5 there shall be added the following regulation—

  "*Establishment of joint panels and appointment of members*

  5A.—(1) Two or more adoption agencies may jointly establish an adoption panel ("a joint panel") or panels to carry out the functions specified in regulation 10 in relation to those agencies and shall appoint the persons referred to in paragraphs (2) and (3) to be members of such a joint panel, so however that no more than 10 members shall be appointed to a joint panel and the persons appointed to a joint panel shall include at least one man and one woman.

  (2) The adoption agencies shall appoint as chairman of a joint panel a person who has had such experience in adoption work as the agencies consider appropriate.

  (3) In addition to the chairman, the persons to be appointed to a joint panel shall include—

   (a) one social worker in the employment of one of the adoption agencies which establish the joint panel;

   (b) at least one of the following—

    (i) where a registered adoption society is one of the adoption agencies which establish the joint panel, a member of that society's management committee;

    (ii) where a Board is one of the adoption agencies which establish the joint panel, a member of that Board;

    (iii) where an HSS trust is one of the adoption agencies which establish the joint panel, a director of that HSS trust;

(a) S.R. 1989 No. 253

(*c*) one person nominated under Regulation 6(4) as the medical adviser to one of the adoption agencies which establish the joint panel; and

(*d*) at least one other person not being a member, director or an employee of any of the adoption agencies which establish the joint panel.

(4) A person appointed to a joint panel shall hold office subject to such conditions as to the period of his membership and otherwise as may be determined by the adoption agencies which establish the joint panel.

(5) A joint adoption panel shall make the recommendations specified in regulation 10 only when at least three of its members meet as a panel and one of those is a social worker in the employment of one of the adoption agencies which establish the joint panel.

(6) A joint adoption panel shall keep a written record of any of the recommendations specified in regulation 10 which it makes.'';

(*d*) in regulation 8(2)(*f*), after the word ''Board'' there shall be added the words ''or HSS trust'';

(*e*) in regulation 9(2)(*b*), after the word ''Board'' there shall be added the words '', HSS trust'';

(*f*) in regulation 12(2)(*c*), for the words ''the Board in whose area the prospective adopter resides,'' there shall be substituted the words—

''(i) the Board in whose area; or

(ii) the HSS trust in whose operational area,

the prospective adopter resides,'';

(*g*) in regulation 16(2)(*a*), after the word ''area'' there shall be added the words '', or the authorised HSS trust in whose operational area,''; and

(*h*) in the Schedule, Part I, paragraph 10, after the word ''Board'' there shall be added the words '', HSS trust''.

SCHEDULE 23

Amendment of the Education (Special Educational Needs) Regulations (Northern Ireland) 1985

1. The Education (Special Educational Needs) Regulations (Northern Ireland) 1985(**a**) shall be amended as follows—

   (*a*) in regulation 2, for paragraph (2) there shall be substituted the following paragraph—

   "(2) In these Regulations—

   "health and social services board" has the same meaning as in the Health and Personal Social Services (Northern Ireland) Order 1972; and

   "HSS trust" has the same meaning as in the Health and Personal Social Services (Northern Ireland) Order 1991,

   and any reference to a health and social services board or an HSS trust is, in relation to a particular child, a reference to—

   (*a*) the health and social services board in whose area that child lives; or

   (*b*) the HSS trust in whose operational area that child lives.";

   (*b*) in regulation 3, after the words "health and social services board" there shall be added the words "or the HSS trust";

   (*c*) in regulations 6, 8(*d*) and 10(1)(*c*), after the words "health and social services board" there shall be added the words "or an HSS trust"; and

   (*d*) in the Schedule, Appendix G, after the words "Health and Social Services Board" there shall be added the words "or an HSS trust".

(**a**) S.R. 1985 No. 365

EXPLANATORY NOTE

(This note is not part of the Regulations.)

These Regulations provide for amendments to subordinate legislation required as a consequence of the delegation, by virtue of an authorisation under Article 3(1) of the Health and Personal Social Services (Northern Ireland) Order 1994 (S.I. 1994/429 (N.I. 2)), of certain Health and Social Services Board functions to Health and Social Services trusts.

1994 No. 66

HEALTH AND PERSONAL SOCIAL SERVICES

The Health and Social Services Trusts (Consequential Amendments No. 2) Regulations (Northern Ireland) 1994

Made . . . . . *1st March 1994*

Coming into operation . . *1st April 1994*

To be laid before Parliament under paragraph 3(3) of Schedule 1 to the Northern Ireland Act 1974

The Department of Health and Social Services, in exercise of the powers conferred on it by Article 3(11) of the Health and Personal Social Services (Northern Ireland) Order 1994(**a**) and of all other powers enabling it in that behalf, hereby makes the following Regulations:

Citation and commencement

1.—(1) These Regulations may be cited as the Health and Social Services Trusts (Consequential Amendments No. 2) Regulations (Northern Ireland) 1994.

(2) These Regulations shall come into operation on 1st April 1994, immediately after the commencement of the amendments to the Mental Health (Northern Ireland) Order 1986(**b**) contained in Schedule 1 to the Health and Personal Social Services (Northern Ireland) Order 1994.

Amendment of the Mental Health (Northern Ireland) Order 1986

2. The Mental Health (Northern Ireland) Order 1986 shall be amended as follows—

(*a*) in Article 2(2A), after the words "Articles 7A," there shall be added "29,";

(*b*) in Article 29(4), after the words "Article 7(2) or (3)" there shall be added ", Article 7A(2)"; and

(*c*) in Article 62(2)(*a*), after the words "Article 7(2) or (3)" there shall be added ", 7A(2)".

Sealed with the Official Seal of the Department of Health and Social Services on 1st March 1994.

(L.S.)   *John McGrath*
                    Assistant Secretary

(**a**) S.I. 1994/429 (N.I. 2)
(**b**) S.I. 1986/595 (N.I. 4); as amended by S.I. 1994/429 (N.I. 2)

EXPLANATORY NOTE
(This note is not part of the Regulations.)

These Regulations amend the Mental Health (Northern Ireland) Order 1986 as a consequence of the delegation, by virtue of an authorisation under Article 3(1) of the Health and Personal Social Services (Northern Ireland) Order 1994 (S.I. 1994/429 (N.I. 2) (the "1994 Order"), of certain Health and Social Services Board functions to Health and Social Services trusts.

The amendments will ensure that the provisions of the Mental Health (Northern Ireland) Order 1986 relating to—

(*a*) the taking into custody of patients who are absent without leave; and

(*b*) consent to treatment,

apply also to patients detained, pending application for assessment, in a hospital managed by an HSS trust which has not had functions delegated to it under the 1994 Order, in the same way as they apply to patients detained in a hospital managed by an authorised HSS trust.

1994 No. 67

HEALTH AND PERSONAL SOCIAL SERVICES

The Mater Infirmorum Hospital
Health and Social Services Trust (Establishment) Order
(Northern Ireland) 1994

Made	*1st March 1994*
Coming into operation . .	*1st March 1994*

The Department of Health and Social Services, in exercise of the powers conferred on it by Article 10(1) of, and paragraphs 1, 3, 4, 5 and 6(2)(*d*) of Schedule 3 to, the Health and Personal Social Services (Northern Ireland) Order 1991(**a**) and of all other powers enabling it in that behalf, having consulted the persons or bodies referred to in Article 10(2) of that Order, hereby makes the following order:

Citation, commencement and interpretation

1.—(1) This order may be cited as the Mater Infirmorum Hospital Health and Social Services Trust (Establishment) Order (Northern Ireland) 1994 and shall come into operation on 1st March 1994.

(2) In this order—

"the Order" means the Health and Personal Social Services (Northern Ireland) Order 1991;

"establishment date" means 1st March 1994;

"operational date" has the meaning assigned to it in paragraph 3(1)(*e*) of Schedule 3 to the Order;

"the trust" means the Mater Infirmorum Hospital Health and Social Services Trust established by Article 2 of this order.

Establishment of the trust

2. There is hereby established an HSS trust which shall be called the Mater Infirmorum Hospital Health and Social Services Trust.

Nature and functions of the trust

3.—(1) The trust is established for the purposes specified in Article 10(1) of the Order.

(**a**) S.I. 1991/194 (N.I. 1); paragraph 1 of Schedule 3 is cited for the definition of "an order"

(2) The trust's functions (which include functions which the Department considers appropriate in relation to the provision of services by the trust for one or more relevant bodies) shall be to own and manage hospital accommodation and services provided at the Mater Infirmorum Hospital, 45/51 Crumlin Road, Belfast BT14 6AB and any associated premises.

Directors of the trust

4. The trust shall have, in addition to the chairman, 5 non-executive directors and 5 executive directors.

Operational date of the trust

5. The operational date of the trust shall be 1st April 1994.

Limited functions before operational date

6. Between its establishment and operational date, the trust shall have the limited functions of—

(*a*) entering into HSS contracts;

(*b*) entering into other contracts including contracts of employment; and

(*c*) doing such other things as are reasonably necessary,

for the purpose of enabling it to begin to operate satisfactorily with effect from its operational date.

Assistance by a relevant body before operational date

7.—(1) The Eastern Health and Social Services Board shall—

(*a*) until the operational date make such staff and facilities available to the trust as are required to enable the trust to carry out its limited functions pending the transfer or appointment of staff to or by the trust and the transfer of facilities to the trust;

(*b*) make available such premises as are required to enable the trust to carry out its limited functions pending the transfer of those premises to the trust.

(2) The Eastern Health and Social Services Board shall discharge the liabilities of the trust, incurred between the establishment date and the operational date, that are of a description specified in paragraph (3).

(3) The liabilities referred to in paragraph (2) are—

(*a*) liability for the remuneration and travelling or other allowances of the chairman and non-executive directors of the trust;

(*b*) liability for the travelling or other allowances of the members of committees and sub-committees of the trust who are not also directors of the trust;

(*c*) liability for the remuneration of persons employed by the trust; and

(*d*) liability for the remuneration of persons employed by the trust for the purpose of enabling it to begin to operate satisfactorily with effect from the operational date.

(4) The relevant body specified for the purposes of paragraph 3(1)(*f*) of Schedule 3 to the Order (relevant body which is to make the scheme under Article 11 of the Order for the transfer of staff) in relation to the trust shall be the Eastern Health and Social Services Board.

Restriction on disposal of assets

8. The sum specified for the purposes of paragraph 6(2)(*d*) of Schedule 3 to the Order (maximum value of freely disposable assets) in relation to the trust shall be £500,000.

Sealed with the Official Seal of the Department of Health and Social Services on 1st March 1994.

(L.S.)   *John McGrath*
                              Assistant Secretary

EXPLANATORY NOTE

(This note is not part of the Order.)

This order establishes the Mater Infirmorum Hospital Health and Social Services Trust, an HSS trust provided for in Article 10 of the Health and Personal Social Services (Northern Ireland) Order 1991. It also provides for the functions of the trust both before (Article 6) and after (Article 3) its operational date (the date on which it assumes all its functions). It specifies the operational date of the trust (Article 5) and makes provision for assistance to the trust by the Eastern Health and Social Services Board before its operational date (Article 7). Article 8 specifies £500,000 as the maximum value of freely disposable assets.

1994 No. 68

SOCIAL SECURITY

The Social Fund (Maternity and Funeral Expenses) (General) (Amendment) Regulations (Northern Ireland) 1994

Made	*2nd March 1994*
Coming into operation . .	*1st April 1994*

The Department of Health and Social Services for Northern Ireland, in exercise of the powers conferred on it by section 134(1)(*a*) of the Social Security Contributions and Benefits (Northern Ireland) Act 1992(**a**) and of all other powers enabling it in that behalf, hereby makes the following regulations:

Citation, commencement and interpretation

1.—(1) These regulations may be cited as the Social Fund (Maternity and Funeral Expenses) (General) (Amendment) Regulations (Northern Ireland) 1994 and shall come into operation on 1st April 1994.

(2) In these regulations "the principal regulations" means the Social Fund (Maternity and Funeral Expenses) (General) Regulations (Northern Ireland) 1987(**b**).

(3) The Interpretation Act (Northern Ireland) 1954(**c**) shall apply to these regulations as it applies to a Measure of the Northern Ireland Assembly.

Amendment of regulation 2 of the principal regulations

2. In regulation 2 of the principal regulations (interpretation)—

(*a*) after the definition of "claimant" the following definition shall be inserted—

" "close relative" means a parent, parent-in-law, son, son-in-law, daughter, daughter-in-law, step-parent, step-son, step-daughter, brother, sister or partner of any of the preceding persons;";

(*b*) for the definition of "responsible member" the following definition shall be substituted—

" "responsible person" is to be construed in accordance with regulation 6(1)(*b*);".

(**a**) 1992 c. 7
(**b**) S.R. 1987 No. 150; relevant amending regulations are S.R. 1988 Nos. 6 and 22, S.R. 1989 No. 71, S.R. 1990 No. 132, S.R. 1992 Nos. 6 and 394 and S.R. 1993 No. 99
(**c**) 1954 c. 33 (N.I.)

Amendment of regulation 6 of the principal regulations

3. In regulation 6 of the principal regulations (entitlement to a funeral payment)—

(*a*) for paragraph (1)(*b*) there shall be substituted—

"(*b*) the claimant (in this Part referred to as "the responsible person") accepts responsibility for the costs of a funeral and—

(i) the responsible person was the partner of the deceased, or

(ii) where the responsible person or that person's partner was a close relative of the deceased, it is reasonable for the responsible person to accept responsibility for those costs and there is no other person who was equally or more closely related to the deceased whom, on comparing that other person's income and capital with that of the responsible person and taking account of the nature and extent of that other person's contact with the deceased, it is reasonable to expect to meet those costs, or

(iii) where neither head (i) or (ii) applies, it is reasonable in view of the extent of the responsible person's or partner's acquaintanceship with the deceased for that person to accept responsibility for those costs, and";

(*b*) in paragraph (2) for "responsible member" each time it appears there shall be substituted "responsible person".

Amendment of regulation 7 of the principal regulations

4. In regulation 7 of the principal regulations (deductions from an award of a funeral payment) for "responsible member" each time it appears there shall be substituted "responsible person".

Sealed with the Official Seal of the Department of Health and Social Services for Northern Ireland on 2nd March 1994.

(L.S.) *W. G. Purdy*

Assistant Secretary

EXPLANATORY NOTE

(This note is not part of the Regulations.)

These regulations amend regulations 2, 6 and 7 of the Social Fund (Maternity and Funeral Expenses) (General) Regulations (Northern Ireland) 1987 by amending the conditions which a person must satisfy to be entitled to a funeral payment from the Social Fund.

These regulations make in relation to Northern Ireland only provision corresponding to provision contained in regulations made by the Secretary of State for Social Security in relation to Great Britain and accordingly, by virtue of section 149(3) of, and paragraph 10 of Schedule 5 to, the Social Security Administration (Northern Ireland) Act 1992 (c. 8), are not subject to the requirement of section 149(2) of that Act for prior reference to the Social Security Advisory Committee.

1994   No. 69

PENSIONS

The Guaranteed Minimum Pensions Increase Order (Northern Ireland) 1994

Made	*3rd March 1994*
Coming into operation . .	*6th April 1994*

Whereas the Secretary of State for Social Security has made an order(**a**) under section 109 of the Pension Schemes Act 1993(**b**):

Now, therefore, the Department of Health and Social Services for Northern Ireland, in exercise of the powers conferred on it by section 105 of the Pension Schemes (Northern Ireland) Act 1993(**c**) and of all other powers enabling it in that behalf, hereby makes the following order:

Citation, commencement and interpretation

1.—(1) This order may be cited as the Guaranteed Minimum Pensions Increase Order (Northern Ireland) 1994 and shall come into operation on 6th April 1994.

(2) The Interpretation Act (Northern Ireland) 1954(**d**) shall apply to this order as it applies to a Measure of the Northern Ireland Assembly.

Increase of guaranteed minimum pensions

2. For the purposes of section 105(1) of the Pension Schemes (Northern Ireland) Act 1993 the percentage by which there is to be an increase in the rate of that part of any guaranteed minimum pension which is attributable to earnings factors for the tax year 1988-89 and subsequent tax years shall be 1·8 per cent.

Sealed with the Official Seal of the Department of Health and Social Services for Northern Ireland on 3rd March 1994.

(L.S.)   *W. G. Purdy*
                                           Assistant Secretary

---

(**a**) S.I. 1994/500
(**b**) 1993 c. 48
(**c**) 1993 c. 49
(**d**) 1954 c. 33 (N.I.)

EXPLANATORY NOTE

(This note is not part of the Order.)

This order, which corresponds to an order (S.I. 1994/500) made by the Secretary of State for Social Security under section 109 of the Pension Schemes Act 1993, specifies 1·8 per cent. as the percentage by which that part of guaranteed minimum pensions attributable to earnings factors for the tax year 1988-89 and subsequent years and payable by occupational pension schemes is to be increased.

1994 No. 70

Temporary Speed Limit (Motorways M2 and M22) Order (Northern Ireland) 1994

This Order, being of a temporary character, is not printed at length in this volume.

1994 No. 71

POLICE

Royal Ulster Constabulary (Amendment) Regulations 1994

Made	*7th February 1994*
Coming into operation . .	*31st March 1994*

To be laid before Parliament

The Secretary of State, in pursuance of section 25 of the Police Act (Northern Ireland) 1970(**a**), read with section 18 of the Administrative and Financial Provisions Act (Northern Ireland) 1962(**b**), and after consulting in accordance with section 34(2) of the said Act of 1970, the Police Authority and the Police Association, and after taking into account the recommendations made by the Police Negotiating Board for the United Kingdom and furnishing that Board with a draft of the regulations in accordance with section 2(1) of the Police Negotiating Board Act 1980(**c**), hereby with the concurrence of the Treasury makes the following regulations:—

Citation, operation and effect

1.—(1) These regulations may be cited as the Royal Ulster Constabulary (Amendment) Regulations 1994.

(2) These regulations shall come into operation on 31st March 1994 but shall have effect for the purposes of regulation 3 as from 31st March 1993, and for the purposes of regulations 4 and 5 as from 31st August 1993.

Interpretation

2. In these regulations any reference to the principal regulations is a reference to the Royal Ulster Constabulary Regulations 1984(**d**).

Removal allowance

3. In paragraph (7) of regulation 43 of the principal regulations for "£1,257" there shall be substituted "£1,290".

(**a**) 1970 c. 9 (N.I.) as modified by S.I. 1973/2163 and S.I. 1981/1670
(**b**) 1962 c. 7 (N.I.)
(**c**) 1980 c. 10
(**d**) S.R. 1984 No. 62; the relevant amending regulations are S.R. 1984 No. 380, S.R. 1985 No. 119, S.R. 1985 No. 292, S.R. 1985 No. 362, S.R. 1986 No. 314, S.R. 1987 No. 205, S.R. 1987 No. 441, S.R. 1989 No. 207, S.R. 1990 No. 74, S.R. 1990 No. 435, S.R. 1991 No. 459, S.R. 1992 No. 447 and S.R. 1993 No. 207

Pay

4. In Schedule 5 to the principal regulations for the Tables A, B and C there shall be substituted respectively the Tables set out in the Schedule.

Dog handler's allowance

5. In Schedule 11 to the principal regulations in sub-paragraph 1(1)(*a*) for "£915" there shall be substituted "£930" and in sub-paragraph 1(1)(*b*) for "£1,251" there shall be substituted "£1,269".

	P. B. B. Mayhew
Northern Ireland Office	One of Her Majesty's
7th February 1994	Principal Secretaries of State

	Tim Wood
	Nicholas Baker
We concur	Two of the Lords Commissioners
2nd March 1994	of Her Majesty's Treasury

SCHEDULE   Regulation 4

Tables substituted for Tables A, B and C in Schedule 5 to the principal regulations with effect as from 31st August 1993

''TABLE A

Rank	Service in Rank	Annual Pay
		£
Chief Constable		80,841
	After 3 years	82,860
Deputy Chief Constable		64,674
	After 3 years	66,288
Senior Assistant Chief Constable		51,966
	After 3 years	53,268
Assistant Chief Constable		47,241
	After 3 years	48,426

TABLE B

Rank	Service in Rank	Annual Pay
		£
Chief Superintendent	Less than 1 year	40,071
	After 1 year	40,644
	After 2 years	41,556
	After 3 years	42,549
Superintendent	Less than 1 year	36,042
	After 1 year	36,960
	After 2 years	37,875
	After 3 years	39,135
Chief Inspector	Less than 1 year	26,496
	After 1 year	27,237
	After 2 years	27,978
	After 3 years	28,722
	After 4 years	29,472
Inspector	Less than 1 year	23,337
	After 1 year	24,066
	After 2 years	25,005
	After 3 years	25,749
	After 4 years	26,496
Sergeant	Less than 1 year	20,343
	After 1 year	21,267
	After 2 years	22,014
	After 3 years	22,743
	After 4 years	23,337

TABLE C

Annual Pay of Constables

Rank	Service in Rank	Annual Pay
		£
Constable	Before completing 1 year of service	12,744
	After 1 year of service	13,626
	After 2 years of service	16,044
	After 3 years of service	16,422
	After 4 years of service	16,965
	After 5 years of service	17,547
	After 6 years of service	18,105
	After 7 years of service	18,666
	After 8 years of service	19,218
	After 12 years of service	20,343
	After 15 years of service	21,267''

EXPLANATORY NOTE

(This note is not part of the Regulations.)

These regulations further amend the Royal Ulster Constabulary Regulations 1984 (the principal regulations).

Regulation 3 amends regulation 43 (removal allowance) of the principal regulations to increase the maximum amount payable in respect of incidental expenditure and has effect on and after 1st April 1993.

Regulation 4 increases the rate of pay for members of the force and regulation 5 increases the dog handler's allowance. Both regulations have effect on and after 1st September 1993.

Retrospection is authorised by section 18 of the Administrative and Financial Provisions Act (Northern Ireland) 1962.

1994   No. 72

POLICE

Royal Ulster Constabulary Reserve (Full-Time) (Appointment and Conditions of Service) (Amendment) Regulations 1994

Made	*7th February 1994*
Coming into operation . .	*31st March 1994*
To be laid before Parliament	

The Secretary of State, in pursuance of section 26 of the Police Act (Northern Ireland) 1970(**a**), read with section 18 of the Administrative and Financial Provisions Act (Northern Ireland) 1962(**b**), after consulting in accordance with section 34(2) of the said Act of 1970, the Police Authority and the Police Association, hereby with the concurrence of the Treasury makes the following regulations:—

Citation, operation and effect

1.—(1) These regulations may be cited as the Royal Ulster Constabulary Reserve (Full-Time) (Appointment and Conditions of Service) (Amendment) Regulations 1994.

(2) These regulations shall come into operation on 31st March 1994 but shall have effect for the purposes of regulation 3 as from 31st March 1993, and for the purposes of regulations 4 and 5 as from 31st August 1993.

Interpretation

2. In these regulations any reference to the principal regulations is a reference to the Royal Ulster Constabulary Reserve (Full-Time) (Appointment and Conditions of Service) Regulations 1988(**c**).

Removal allowance

3. In paragraph (6) of regulation 38 of the principal regulations for "£1,257" there shall be substituted "£1,290".

Pay

4. There shall be substituted for the Table in Schedule 3 to the principal regulations the Table set out in the Schedule.

(**a**) 1970 c. 9 (N.I.) as modified by S.I. 1973/2163 and S.I. 1981/1670
(**b**) 1962 c. 9 (N.I.)
(**c**) S.R. 1988 No. 36; the relevant amending regulations are S.R. 1988 No. 341, S.R. 1989 No. 208, S.R. 1990 No. 436, S.R. 1991 No. 460, S.R. 1992 No. 446 and S.R. 1993 No. 208

Dog handler's allowance

5. In Schedule 9 to the principal regulations in paragraph 1(1) for "£915" there shall be substituted "£930".

P. B. B. Mayhew
Northern Ireland Office
7th February 1994

One of Her Majesty's
Principal Secretaries of State

Tim Wood
Nicholas Baker

We concur
2nd March 1994

Two of the Lords Commissioners
of Her Majesty's Treasury

SCHEDULE   Regulation 4

Table substituted for the Table in Schedule 3 to the principal regulations with effect as from 31st August 1993

"TABLE

Scales of pay

Reckonable Service	Annual Pay
	£
Before completing 1 year of service	12,744
After 1 year of service	13,626
After 2 years of service	16,044
After 3 years of service	16,422
After 6 years of service	16,965
After 9 years of service	17,547
After 12 years of service	18,105
After 15 years of service	18,666
After 18 years of service	19,218"

EXPLANATORY NOTE

(This note is not part of the Regulations.)

These Regulations amend the Royal Ulster Constabulary Reserve (Full-Time) (Appointment and Conditions of Service) Regulations 1988 (the principal regulations).

Regulation 3 amends regulation 38 (removal allowance) of the principal regulations to increase the maximum amount payable in respect of incidental expenditure and has effect on and after 1st April 1993.

Regulation 4 increases the rate of pay for members of the force and regulation 5 increases the dog handler's allowance. Both regulations have effect on and after 1st September 1993.

Retrospection is authorised by Section 18 of the Administrative and Financial Provisions Act (Northern Ireland) 1962.

1994 No. 73

POLICE

Royal Ulster Constabulary Reserve (Part-Time) (Appointment and Conditions of Service) (Amendment) Regulations 1994

Made	*7th February 1994*
Coming into operation . .	*31st March 1994*

To be laid before Parliament

The Secretary of State, in pursuance of section 26 of the Police Act (Northern Ireland) 1970(**a**), read with section 18 of the Administrative and Financial Provisions Act (Northern Ireland) 1962(**b**), and after consulting in accordance with section 34(2) of the said Act of 1970, the Police Authority and the Police Association, hereby with the concurrence of the Treasury makes the following regulations:—

Citation, operation and effect

1.—(1) These regulations may be cited as the Royal Ulster Constabulary Reserve (Part-Time) (Appointment and Conditions of Service) (Amendment) Regulations 1994.

(2) These regulations shall come into operation on 31st March 1994 but shall have effect for the purposes of regulation 3 as from 31st August 1993.

Interpretation

2. In these regulations any reference to the principal regulations is a reference to the Royal Ulster Constabulary Reserve (Part-Time) (Appointment and Conditions of Service) Regulations 1988(**c**).

Pay

3. In regulation 18 of the principal regulations for "£6·02" there shall be substituted "£6·11".

(**a**) 1970 c. 9 (N.I.) as modified by S.I. 1973/2163 and S.I. 1981/1670
(**b**) 1962 c. 7 (N.I.)
(**c**) S.R. 1988 No. 35; the relevant amending regulations are S.R. 1989 No. 209, S.R. 1990 No. 437, S.R. 1991 No. 461, S.R. 1992 No. 445 and S.R. 1993 No. 209

	P. B. B. Mayhew
Northern Ireland Office	One of Her Majesty's
7th February 1994	Principal Secretaries of State
	Tim Wood
	Nicholas Baker
We concur	Two of the Lords Commissioners
2nd March 1994	of Her Majesty's Treasury

EXPLANATORY NOTE

(This note is not part of the Regulations.)

These regulations amend the Royal Ulster Constabulary Reserve (Part-Time) (Appointment and Conditions of Service) Regulations 1988.

Regulation 3 increases the rates of pay for members of the force with effect on and after 1st September 1993.

Retrospection is authorised by section 18 of the Administrative and Financial Provisions Act (Northern Ireland) 1962.

1994 No. 74

SOCIAL SECURITY

STATUTORY MATERNITY PAY; STATUTORY SICK PAY; HOUSING

The Social Security Benefits Up-rating Order (Northern Ireland) 1994

Made . . . . . *7th March 1994*

Coming into operation in accordance with Article 1(1)

ARRANGEMENT OF ARTICLES

PART I

INTRODUCTION

PART II

SOCIAL SECURITY BENEFITS AND PENSIONS

PART III

FAMILY CREDIT, DISABILITY WORKING ALLOWANCE, INCOME SUPPORT AND
HOUSING BENEFIT

PART IV

TRANSITIONAL PROVISIONS AND REVOCATION

SCHEDULES

Whereas the Secretary of State for Social Security has made an order(**a**) under sections 150 and 189(1), (3) and (4) of the Social Security Administration Act 1992(**b**):

Now, therefore, the Department of Health and Social Services for Northern Ireland, in exercise of the powers conferred on it by section 132 of the Social Security Administration (Northern Ireland) Act 1992(**c**) and of all other powers enabling it in that behalf, hereby makes the following order:

(**a**) S.I. 1994/542
(**b**) 1992 c. 5
(**c**) 1992 c. 8

PART I

INTRODUCTION

Citation and commencement

1.—(1) This order may be cited as the Social Security Benefits Up-rating Order (Northern Ireland) 1994 and shall come into operation for the purposes of—

(*a*) Articles 1, 2 and 21 on 1st April 1994;

(*b*) Article 10 on 3rd April 1994;

(*c*) Article 9 on 6th April 1994;

(*d*) Articles 3 to 6, 8 and 11 to 13 on 11th April 1994;

(*e*) Articles 14, 15 and 20 on 12th April 1994;

(*f*) Article 7 on 13th April 1994;

(*g*) Articles 16, 17 and 18, in so far as they relate to a particular beneficiary, on the first day of the first benefit week to commence for that beneficiary on or after 11th April 1994, and for the purposes of this sub-paragraph and sub-paragraph (*h*) below "benefit week" has the same meaning as in the Income Support Regulations;

(*h*) Article 19(*c*)(ii), in so far as the sums specified are relevant for the purposes of paragraph 9(2)(*a*) of Schedule 3 to the Income Support Regulations, on the first day of the benefit week to commence for the beneficiary on or after 11th April 1994; and

(*i*) except in a case to which sub-paragraph (*h*) applies, Article 19 in relation to a case where rent is payable at intervals of a week or any multiple thereof, on 4th April 1994, and in relation to any other case, on 1st April 1994.

(2) The increases made by this order in the sums specified for rates or amounts of benefit under the Contributions and Benefits Act or the Pension Schemes Act shall take effect for each case on the date specified in relation to that case in Article 6 of this order.

Interpretation

2. In this order, unless the context otherwise requires—

"the Contributions and Benefits Act" means the Social Security Contributions and Benefits (Northern Ireland) Act 1992(**a**);

"the Pension Schemes Act" means the Pension Schemes (Northern Ireland) Act 1993(**b**);

"the Income Support Regulations" means the Income Support (General) Regulations (Northern Ireland) 1987(**c**).

(**a**) 1992 c. 7
(**b**) 1993 c. 49
(**c**) S.R. 1987 No. 459; relevant amending provisions are S.R. 1988 Nos. 146, 274, 318 and 431, S.R. 1989 Nos. 139 and 249, S.R. 1990 Nos. 131, 213 and 346, S.R. 1991 Nos. 46 and 338, S.R. 1992 Nos. 6, 18 and 85 and S.R. 1993 Nos. 149, 150 and 373

PART II

SOCIAL SECURITY BENEFITS AND PENSIONS

Increase in rates or amounts of certain benefits under the Contributions and Benefits Act

3.—(1) The sums specified in paragraph (2) below shall be increased from and including the respective dates specified in Article 6 below so as to have effect as set out in Schedule 1 to this order.

(2) The sums mentioned in paragraph (1) above are the sums specified in Parts I, III, IV and V of Schedule 4 to the Contributions and Benefits Act (contributory periodical benefits, non-contributory periodical benefits, increases for dependants and rate of industrial injuries benefit, respectively), except in Part III the sum specified for age addition.

Increase in rates or amounts of certain pensions or allowances under the Contributions and Benefits Act

4.—(1) The sums specified in paragraphs (2), (3) and (4) below shall be increased from and including the respective dates specified in Article 6 below.

(2) The sums falling to be calculated under paragraph 13(4) of Schedule 7 to the Contributions and Benefits Act (calculation of weekly rate of retirement allowance) shall be increased by 1·8 per cent. of their amount apart from this order.

(3) In section 44(4) of the Contributions and Benefits Act (basic pension of Category A retirement pension)—

(*a*) for "£53·80" there shall be substituted "£55·25"; and

(*b*) for "£56·10" there shall be substituted "£57·60".

(4) It is hereby directed that the sums which are—

(*a*) the additional pensions in the rates of long-term benefits calculated by reference to any final relevant year earlier than the tax year 1993/1994;

(*b*) the increases in the rates of retirement pensions under Schedule 5 to the Contributions and Benefits Act (increase of pension where entitlement deferred); and

(*c*) payable to a pensioner as part of his Category A or Category B retirement pension by virtue of an order made under section 120 of the Social Security (Northern Ireland) Act 1975(**a**) or Article 64 of the Social Security (Northern Ireland) Order 1986(**b**),

shall in each case be increased by 1·8 per cent. of their amount apart from this order.

(**a**) 1975 c. 15; section 120 was amended by the Schedule to the Social Security (Miscellaneous Provisions) (Northern Ireland) Order 1977 (S.I. 1977/610 (N.I. 11)), paragraph 9 of Schedule 3 to the Social Security (Northern Ireland) Order 1979 (S.I. 1979/396 (N.I. 5)), Article 9(5) of the Social Security (Northern Ireland) Order 1985 (S.I. 1985/1209 (N.I. 16)), Schedule 10 to the Social Security (Northern Ireland) Order 1986 (S.I. 1986/1888 (N.I. 18)) and Schedule 2 to the Redundancy Fund (Abolition) (Northern Ireland) Order 1991 (S.I. 1991/196 (N.I. 2))

(**b**) S.I. 1986/1888 (N.I. 18)

*Increase in rates or amounts of certain benefits under the Pension Schemes
Act*

5.—(1) The sums specified in paragraph (2) below shall be increased
from and including the respective dates specified in Article 6 below.

(2) Sums which are payable by virtue of section 11(1) of the Pension
Schemes Act (increase of guaranteed minimum where commencement of
guaranteed minimum pension is postponed) to a person who is also entitled to
a Category A or Category B retirement pension (including sums payable by
virtue of section 13(2) and (3) of that Act), shall be increased by 1·8 per cent.
of their amount apart from this order where the increase under section 11(1) is
attributable to earnings factors for the tax year 1987/1988 and earlier tax
years(**a**).

*Dates on which sums specified for rates or amounts of benefit under the
Contributions and Benefits Act or the Pension Schemes Act are increased
by this order*

6.—(1) Paragraphs (2) to (9) of this Article, which are subject to the
provisions of paragraph (10) below, specify the date on which the increases
made by this order in the sums specified for rates or amounts of benefit under
the Contributions and Benefits Act or the Pension Schemes Act shall take
effect for each case.

(2) Subject to paragraph (3) below, the increases in the sums specified in
Articles 3, 4 and 11 of this order for the rates of Category A or Category B
retirement pension and graduated retirement benefit together with, where
appropriate, increases for dependants, shall take effect on 11th April 1994.

(3) In the case of a person over pensionable age whose entitlement to a
Category A retirement pension is deferred and for whom the rate of
unemployment benefit, sickness benefit or invalidity pension falls to be
calculated in accordance with section 25(5), 31(6) or 33(4) of the
Contributions and Benefits Act, the increases in the sums mentioned in
Articles 3, 4 and 11 of this order for Category A and Category B retirement
pension and graduated retirement benefit together with, where appropriate,
increases for dependants, shall take effect on 14th April 1994.

(4) The increases in the sums mentioned in Articles 4(4)(*c*) and 5(2) of
this order shall take effect on 11th April 1994.

(5) The increases in the sums specified for the rate of maternity
allowance, widowed mother's allowance, widow's pension, Category C and
Category D retirement pension, child's special allowance(**b**), attendance
allowance, invalid care allowance (except in a case where the Department has
made arrangements for it to be paid on a Wednesday) together with, where
appropriate, increases for dependants, and guardian's allowance shall in all
cases take effect on 11th April 1994.

(**a**) *See* section 132(4) of the Social Security Administration (Northern Ireland) Act 1992. The percentage
increase for the tax year 1988/1989 and subsequent tax years shall be the amount that would have been
specified under this order but for subsection (4), less the increase in the retail price index or 3%,
whichever is less. The increase in the retail price index for the period under review is 1·8%

(**b**) Child's special allowance is abolished except for existing beneficiaries as from 6th April 1987. *See*
section 56(6) of the Social Security Contributions and Benefits (Northern Ireland) Act 1992

(6) The increases in the sums specified for the rate of invalid care allowance (in a case where the Department has made arrangements for it to be paid on a Wednesday) together with, where appropriate, increases for dependants, disablement benefit together with increases of disablement pension, maximum disablement gratuity under paragraph 9(2) of Schedule 7 to the Contributions and Benefits Act, industrial death benefit by way of widow's and widower's pension and allowance in respect of children together with, where appropriate, increases for dependants, and the maximum of the aggregate of weekly benefit payable for successive accidents, under section 107(1) of the Contributions and Benefits Act, shall in all cases take effect on 13th April 1994.

(7) Where a person's weekly rate of Category A or Category B retirement pension falls to be increased under the provisions of section 47(1) or 50(2) of the Contributions and Benefits Act, by reference to the weekly rate of invalidity allowance to which he was previously entitled, the increase in the sum specified for the appropriate rate of invalidity allowance shall take effect on 11th April 1994 and where it does not fall to be so increased the sum so specified shall take effect on 14th April 1994.

(8) The increases in the sums specified for the rate of unemployment and sickness benefit, invalidity pension and severe disablement allowance together with, where appropriate, increases for dependants, shall in all cases take effect on 14th April 1994.

(9) The increases in the sums falling to be calculated in accordance with paragraph 13(4) of Schedule 7 to the Contributions and Benefits Act (retirement allowance) shall take effect on 13th April 1994.

(10) In the case of a person who is subject to the provisions of regulations made under section 71(1)(*b*) of the Social Security Administration (Northern Ireland) Act 1992 (adjustment of benefit for persons undergoing medical or other treatment as an in-patient in a hospital) the increase in the sum mentioned in Article 4(3)(*b*) of this order shall take effect in that case on the day on which the increase in the benefit payable to him apart from those regulations takes effect.

Increase in rate of certain workmen's compensation in respect of employment before 5th July 1948

7. In paragraph 2(6)(*c*) of Schedule 8 to the Contributions and Benefits Act (maximum weekly rate of lesser incapacity allowance supplementing workmen's compensation) for "£33·70" there shall be substituted "£34·50".

Earnings limits

8. In section 80(4) of the Contributions and Benefits Act (earnings limits in respect of child dependency increases) the sum specified in paragraph (*a*) is £120 and the sums specified in paragraph (*b*) are £16 and £120 respectively.

Statutory sick pay

9. In section 153(1) of the Contributions and Benefits Act (rate of payment) the sums specified in paragraph (*a*) are £52·50 and £195·00 respectively and the sum specified in paragraph (*b*) is £46·95.

Statutory maternity pay

10. In regulation 6 of the Statutory Maternity Pay (General) Regulations (Northern Ireland) 1987(**a**) (lower rate of statutory maternity pay) for "£47·95" there shall be substituted "£48·80".

Increase in rate of graduated retirement benefit and increments thereof

11.—(1) The sum of 7·35 pence referred to in section 35(1) of the National Insurance Act (Northern Ireland) 1966(**b**) (graduated retirement benefit) shall be increased by 1·8 per cent. and accordingly the reference in that provision to that sum shall have effect as a reference to 7·48 pence.

(2) The sums which are the increases of graduated retirement benefit under Schedule 2 to the Social Security (Graduated Retirement Benefit) (No. 2) Regulations (Northern Ireland) 1978(**c**) (increases for deferred entitlement to a Category A or Category B retirement pension) shall be increased by 1·8 per cent. of their amount apart from this order.

Increase in rates of disability living allowance

12. In regulation 4 of the Social Security (Disability Living Allowance) Regulations (Northern Ireland) 1992(**d**) (rate of benefit)—

    (*a*) in paragraph (1)(*a*) for "£44·90" there shall be substituted "£45·70";

    (*b*) in paragraph (1)(*b*) for "£30·00" there shall be substituted "£30·55";

    (*c*) in paragraph (1)(*c*) for "£11·95" there shall be substituted "£12·15";

    (*d*) in paragraph (2)(*a*) for "£31·40" there shall be substituted "£31·95"; and

    (*e*) in paragraph (2)(*b*) for "£11·95" there shall be substituted "£12·15".

Sums specified for child benefit

13. In regulation 2 of the Child Benefit and Social Security (Fixing and Adjustment of Rates) Regulations (Northern Ireland) 1976(**e**) (weekly rates of child benefit)—

    (*a*) in paragraph (1)(*a*) for "£10·00" there shall be substituted "£10·20";

    (*b*) in paragraph (1)(*b*) for "£8·10" there shall be substituted "£8·25"; and

    (*c*) in paragraph (2) for "£6·05" there shall be substituted "£6·15".

(**a**) S.R. 1987 No. 30; relevant amending provision is S.R. 1993 No. 150

(**b**) 1966 c. 6 (N.I.); section 35 was repealed by the Social Security Act 1973 (c. 38) but is continued in force by regulation 2 of the Social Security (Graduated Retirement Benefit) (No. 2) Regulations (Northern Ireland) 1987 (S.R. 1987 No. 105)

(**c**) S.R. 1978 No. 105; relevant amending regulations are S.R. 1989 No. 373

(**d**) S.R. 1992 No. 32; relevant amending provisions are S.R. 1993 Nos. 150 and 340

(**e**) S.R. 1976 No. 223; relevant amending provisions are S.R. 1977 No. 248, S.R. 1980 No. 37, S.R. 1991 No. 82 and S.R. 1993 Nos. 150 and 169

PART III

FAMILY CREDIT, DISABILITY WORKING ALLOWANCE, INCOME SUPPORT AND HOUSING BENEFIT

Family credit

14. In the Family Credit (General) Regulations (Northern Ireland) 1987(**a**)—

(*a*) in regulation 46(4) (determination of appropriate maximum family credit) the capital sum prescribed is £3,000;

(*b*) in regulation 46(4), (5) and (6) the amount specified for the credit in respect of a child or young person is nil;

(*c*) in regulation 47(1) (applicable amount) for ''£69·00'' there shall be substituted ''£71·70''; and

(*d*) in Schedule 4 (determination of maximum family credit) the sums prescribed shall be increased so as to have effect as set out in Schedule 2 to this order.

Disability working allowance

15. In the Disability Working Allowance (General) Regulations (Northern Ireland) 1992(**b**)—

(*a*) in regulation 51(4) (determination of appropriate maximum disability working allowance) the capital sum prescribed is £3,000;

(*b*) in regulation 51(4), (5) and (6) the amount specified for the allowance in respect of a child or young person is nil;

(*c*) in regulation 52(1) (applicable amount)—

(i) in sub-paragraph (*a*) for ''£41·40'' there shall be substituted ''£43·00'', and

(ii) in sub-paragraph (*b*) for ''£69·00'' there shall be substituted ''£71·70''; and

(*d*) in Schedule 5 (determination of appropriate maximum disability working allowance) the sums prescribed shall be increased so as to have effect as set out in Schedule 3 to this order.

Applicable amounts for income support

16.—(1) The sums relevant to the calculation of an applicable amount as specified in the Income Support Regulations shall be the sums set out in paragraphs (2) to (12) of this Article and the Schedules thereto; and for this purpose references in this Article to numbered regulations or Schedules are, unless the context otherwise requires, references to the regulations of, or Schedules to, the Income Support Regulations bearing those numbers.

(**a**) S.R. 1987 No. 463; relevant amending provisions are S.R. 1992 No. 403 and S.R. 1993 Nos. 150 and 373

(**b**) S.R. 1992 No. 78; relevant amending provisions are S.R. 1993 Nos. 150 and 373

(2) In regulations 17(1)(*b*), 18(1)(*c*), 21(1) and 71(1)(*a*)(ii), (*b*)(ii) and (iii), (*c*)(ii) and (*d*)(i), in paragraph 14(*a*) of Part III of Schedule 2 and paragraph 1(2) of Part I of Schedule 4 the sum specified is in each case £3,000.

(3) The sums specified in Part I of Schedule 2 (applicable amounts: personal allowances) shall be increased and those paragraphs in that Part of Schedule 2 where such a sum is specified shall have effect as set out in Schedule 4 to this order.

(4) In paragraph 3 of Part II of Schedule 2 (applicable amounts: family premium) for "£9·65" there shall be substituted "£10·05".

(5) The sums specified in Part IV of Schedule 2 (applicable amounts: weekly amounts of premiums) shall be increased and that Part of Schedule 2 shall have effect as set out in Schedule 5 to this order.

(6) In paragraph 11(1) of Schedule 3 (housing costs: non-dependant deductions)—

(*a*) in head (*a*) for "£21·00" there shall be substituted "£25·00"; and

(*b*) in head (*b*) for "£4·00" there shall be substituted "£5·00".

(7) In paragraph 11(2) of Schedule 3—

(*a*) in head (*a*) for "£70·00" there shall be substituted "£72·00";

(*b*) in head (*b*) for "£70·00", "£105·00" and "£8·00" there shall be substituted "£72·00", "£108·00" and "£9·00" respectively; and

(*c*) in head (*c*) for "£105·00", "£135·00" and "£12·00" there shall be substituted "£108·00", "£139·00" and "£13·00" respectively.

(8) In paragraph 6(2) of Schedule 4 (applicable amounts of persons in homes for persons in need and nursing homes) for "£215·00" there shall be substituted "£224·00" and those sums relevant to the calculation of an applicable amount which are specified in Schedule 4 shall be increased and those paragraphs in that Schedule where such a sum is specified shall have effect as set out in Part I of Schedule 6 to this order.

(9) Except as provided in paragraphs (2) and (8) of this Article, the sums specified in Schedule 4 are those set out in Part II of Schedule 6 to this order.

(10) Those sums relevant to the calculation of an applicable amount which are specified in Schedule 7 (applicable amounts in special cases) shall be increased and those paragraphs in that Schedule where such a sum is specified shall have effect as set out in Part I of Schedule 7 to this order.

(11) Except as provided in paragraph (10) above, the sums specified in Schedule 7 are those set out in Part II of Schedule 7 to this order.

(12) The sums specified in any provision of the Income Support Regulations set out in column (1) of Schedule 8 to this order are the sums set out in column (2) of that Schedule.

Income support transitional protection

17. Sums which are special transitional additions to income support payable in accordance with regulation 15 of the Income Support

(Transitional) Regulations (Northern Ireland) 1987(**a**) shall be increased by 3·5 per cent. of their amount apart from this order.

The relevant sum for income support

18. In section 125(7) of the Contributions and Benefits Act (trade disputes) for "£23·50" there shall be substituted "£24·50".

Housing benefit

19. In the Housing Benefit (General) Regulations (Northern Ireland) 1987(**b**)—

(*a*) in regulations 16(*b*) and 17(*c*) and in paragraph 14(*a*) of Schedule 2, in so far as they relate to rent, the sum specified in each case is £3,000;

(*b*) in regulation 63 (non-dependant deductions)—

(i) in paragraph (1)(*a*)(i) for "£21·00" there shall be substituted "£25·00",

(ii) in paragraph (1)(*b*)(i) for "£4·00" there shall be substituted "£5·00",

(iii) in paragraph (2)(*a*) for "£70·00" there shall be substituted "£72·00",

(iv) in paragraph (2)(*b*) for "£70·00", "£105·00" and "£8·00" there shall be substituted "£72·00", "£108·00" and "£9·00" respectively, and

(v) in paragraph (2)(*c*) for "£105·00", "£135·00" and "£12·00" there shall be substituted "£108·00", "£139·00" and "£13·00" respectively; and

(*c*) in Schedule 1 (ineligible service charges)—

(i) in paragraph 1A for "£15·75", "£15·75", "£7·95", "£10·45", "£10·45", "£5·25" and "£1·90" there shall be substituted "£16·30", "£16·30", "£8·25", "£10·80", "£10·80", "£5·45" and "£1·95" respectively, and

(ii) in paragraph 5(2) the sums specified are £8·60, £1·05, £0·70 and £1·05 respectively.

PART IV

TRANSITIONAL PROVISIONS AND REVOCATION

Transitional provisions

20. Notwithstanding the increases of the sums payable in respect of family credit and disability working allowance made by Articles 14 and 15 of

---

(**a**) S.R. 1987 No. 460; relevant amending regulations are S.R. 1988 Nos. 132 and 153, S.R. 1989 No. 371 and S.R. 1991 No. 341
(**b**) S.R. 1987 No. 461; relevant amending provisions are S.R. 1988 No. 314, S.R. 1989 No. 125, S.R. 1990 No. 136, S.R. 1991 No. 79, S.R. 1992 No. 85 and S.R. 1993 Nos. 150 and 381

this order, where a period of entitlement to family credit or disability working allowance is running at 12th April 1994, the rate at which it is payable shall be the weekly rate in force for the period prior to 12th April 1994 until the end of the period of entitlement.

Revocation

21. The Social Security Benefits Up-rating Order (Northern Ireland) 1993(**a**) is hereby revoked.

Sealed with the Official Seal of the Department of Health and Social Services for Northern Ireland on 7th March 1994.

(L.S.)   *W. G. Purdy*
Assistant Secretary

(**a**) S.R. 1993 No. 150

SCHEDULE 1   Article 3(1)

Schedule 4 to the Contributions and Benefits Act as amended by this order

SCHEDULE 4

RATES OF BENEFITS, ETC.

PART I

CONTRIBUTORY PERIODICAL BENEFITS

Description of benefit	Weekly rate
1. Unemployment benefit.	£45·45.
2. Sickness benefit.	£43·45.
3. Invalidity allowance.	(a) higher rate .... £12·15 (b) middle rate .... £ 7·60 (c) lower rate .... £ 3·80 (the appropriate rate being determined in accordance with section 34(3)).
4. Maternity allowance.	£44·55.
5. Category B retirement pension where section 50(1)(a)(i) applies.	£34·50.
6. Child's special allowance.	£11·00.

PART II

WIDOW'S PAYMENT

Widow's Payment.	£1,000·00.

PART III

NON-CONTRIBUTORY PERIODICAL BENEFITS

Description of benefit	Weekly rate
1. Attendance allowance.	(a) higher rate .... £45·70 (b) lower rate .... £30·55 (the appropriate rate being determined in accordance with section 65(3)).
2. Severe disablement allowance.	£34·80.
3. Age related addition.	(a) higher rate .... £12·15 (b) middle rate .... £ 7·60 (c) lower rate .... £ 3·80 (the appropriate rate being determined in accordance with section 69(1)).
4. Invalid care allowance.	£34·50.
5. Guardian's allowance.	£11·00.
6. Category C retirement pension.	(a) lower rate .... £20·65 (b) higher rate .... £34·50 (the appropriate rate being determined in accordance with section 78(5)).
7. Category D retirement pension.	The higher rate for Category C retirement pensions under paragraph 6 above.
8. Age addition (to a pension of any category, and otherwise under section 79).	£0·25.

PART IV

INCREASES FOR DEPENDANTS

Benefit to which increase applies (1)	*Increase for qualifying child* (2) £	*Increase for adult dependant* (3) £
1. Unemployment or sickness benefit—		
(*a*) unemployment benefit, where the beneficiary is under pensionable age	—	28·05
(*b*) unemployment benefit, where the beneficiary is over pensionable age	11·00	34·50
(*c*) sickness benefit, where the beneficiary is under pensionable age	—	26·90
(*d*) sickness benefit, where the beneficiary is over pensionable age.	11·00	33·10
2. Invalidity pension.	11·00	34·50
3. Maternity allowance.	—	26·90
4. Widowed mother's allowance.	11·00	—
5. Category A or B retirement pension.	11·00	34·50
6. Category C retirement pension.	11·00	20·65
7. Child's special allowance.	11·00	—
8. Severe disablement allowance.	11·00	20·70
9. Invalid care allowance.	11·00	20·65

PART V

RATE OF INDUSTRIAL INJURIES BENEFIT

Description of benefit, etc.	*Rate*
1. Disablement pension (weekly rates).	For the several degrees of disablement set out in column (1) of the following Table, the respective amounts in that Table, using—

(a) column (2) for any period during which the beneficiary is over the age of 18 or is entitled to an increase of benefit in respect of a child or adult dependant;

(b) column (3) for any period during which the beneficiary is not over the age of 18 and not so entitled;

TABLE

Degree of Disablement	*Amount*	
(1)	(2)	(3)
Per cent.	£	£
100	93·20	57·10
90	83·88	51·39
80	74·56	45·68
70	65·24	39·97
60	55·92	34·26
50	46·60	28·55
40	37·28	22·84
30	27·96	17·13
20	18·64	11·42

2. Maximum increase of weekly rate of disablement pension where constant attendance needed.

(a) except in cases of exceptionally severe disablement .... £37·40

(b) in any case of exceptionally severe disablement .... £74·80

3. Increase of weekly rate of disablement pension (exceptionally severe disablement).

£37·40

4. Maximum of aggregate of weekly benefit payable for successive accidents.

(a) for any period during which the beneficiary is over the age of 18 or is entitled to an increase in benefit in respect of a child or adult dependant .... £93·20

(b) for any period during which the beneficiary is not over the age of 18 and not so entitled .... £57·10

5. Unemployability supplement under paragraph 2 of Schedule 7.

£57·60

Description of benefit, etc.	*Rate*

6. Increase under paragraph 3 of Schedule 7 of weekly rate of unemployability supplement.

(*a*) if on the qualifying date the beneficiary was under the age of 35 or if that date fell before 5th July 1948 .... £12·15

(*b*) if head (*a*) above does not apply and on the qualifying date the beneficiary was under the age of 40 and he had not attained pensionable age before 6th April 1979 .... £12·15

(*c*) if heads (*a*) and (*b*) above do not apply and on the qualifying date the beneficiary was under the age of 45 .... £ 7·60

(*d*) if heads (*a*), (*b*) and (*c*) above do not apply and on the qualifying date the beneficiary was under the age of 50 and had not attained pensionable age before 6th April 1979 .... £ 7·60

(*e*) in any other case .... £ 3·80

7. Increase under paragraph 4 of Schedule 7 of weekly rate of disablement pension.

£11·00

8. Increase under paragraph 6 of Schedule 7 of weekly rate of disablement pension.

£34·50

9. Maximum disablement gratuity under paragraph 9 of Schedule 7.

£6,190·00

10. Widow's pension (weekly rates).

(*a*) initial rate .... £57·65

(*b*) higher permanent rate ...... £57·60

(*c*) lower permanent rate .... 30 per cent. of the first sum specified in section 44(4) (Category A basic retirement pension) (the appropriate rate being determined in accordance with paragraph 16 of Schedule 7)

11. Widower's pension (weekly rate).

£57·60

12. Weekly rate of allowance in respect of children under paragraph 18 of Schedule 7.

In respect of each qualifying child .... £11·00.

Schedule 4 to the Family Credit Regulations as amended by this order

SCHEDULE 4

Determination of maximum family credit: adult, child and young person credits

Adult, child, young person (1)	*Amount of credit* (2)
1. Adult.	1. £44·30.
2. Child—	2.
(*a*) aged less than 11 years;	(*a*) £11·20;
(*b*) aged not less than 11 but less than 16 years.	(*b*) £18·55.
3. Young person—	3.
(*a*) aged not less than 16 but less than 18 years;	(*a*) £23·05;
(*b*) aged not less than 18 but less than 19 years.	(*b*) £32·20.

Schedule 5 to the Disability Working Allowance Regulations as amended by this order

SCHEDULE 5

Determination of appropriate maximum disability working allowance: claimant, child and young person allowance

Claimant, child or young person (1)	*Amount of allowance* (2)
1. Single claimant.	1. £46·05.
2. Claimant who is a member of a married or unmarried couple, or is a lone parent.	2. £63·75.
3. Child—	3.
(*a*) aged less than 11 years;	(*a*) £11·20;
(*b*) aged not less than 11 but less than 16 years.	(*b*) £18·55.
4. Young person—	4.
(*a*) aged not less than 16 but less than 18 years;	(*a*) £23·05;
(*b*) aged not less than 18 but less than 19 years.	(*b*) £32·20.

SCHEDULE 4 Article 16(3)

Part I of Schedule 2 to the Income Support Regulations as amended by this order

SCHEDULE 2

Applicable amounts

PART I

PERSONAL ALLOWANCES

1. The weekly amounts specified in column (2) in respect of each person or couple specified in column (1) shall be the weekly amounts specified for the purposes of regulations 17(1)(*a*) and 18(1)(*a*) and (*b*) (applicable amounts and polygamous marriages).

Column (1)	Column (2)
Person or Couple	*Amount*
(1) Single claimant aged—	
(*a*) except where head (*b*) or (*c*) applies, less than 18;	(1) (*a*) £27·50;
(*b*) less than 18 who falls within any of the circumstances specified in Part II of Schedule 1A (circumstances in which a person aged 16 or 17 is eligible for income support) or who, had he been a registered person, would fall within any of those circumstances, and who—	(*b*) £36·15;
(i) is eligible for income support under regulation 13A (persons under 18 years), or	
(ii) is the subject of a direction under section 124(1) of the Contributions and Benefits Act (income support to avoid severe hardship);	
(*c*) less than 18 who satisfies the condition in paragraph 11(*a*);	(*c*) £36·15;
(*d*) not less than 18 but less than 25;	(*d*) £36·15;
(*e*) not less than 25.	(*e*) £45·70.
(2) Lone parent aged—	
(*a*) except where head (*b*) or (*c*) applies, less than 18;	(2) (*a*) £27·50;

Column (1)	Column (2)
Person or Couple	*Amount*
(*b*) less than 18 who falls within any of the circumstances specified in Part II of Schedule 1A or who, had he been a registered person, would fall within any of those circumstances, and who—	(*b*) £36·15;
(i) is eligible for income support under regulation 13A, or	
(ii) is the subject of a direction under section 124(1) of the Contributions and Benefits Act;	
(*c*) less than 18 who satisfies the condition in paragraph 11(*a*);	(*c*) £36·15;
(*d*) not less than 18.	(*d*) £45·70.
(3) Couple—	
(*a*) where both members are persons aged less than 18 and—	(3) (*a*) £54·55;
(i) at least one of them is treated as responsible for a child,	
(ii) had they not been members of a couple, each would be eligible for income support under regulation 13A,	
(iii) they are married and each member is either a registered person or a person to whom Part I of Schedule 1A applies,	
(iv) there is a direction under section 124(1) of the Contributions and Benefits Act in respect of each member, or	
(v) there is a direction under section 124(1) of the Contributions and Benefits Act in respect of one of them and the other is eligible for income support under regulation 13A;	
(*aa*) where both members are aged less than 18 and sub-paragraph (3)(*a*) does not apply but one	(*aa*) £36·15;

Column (1)	Column (2)
Person or Couple	*Amount*

member of the couple falls within any of the circumstances specified in Part II of Schedule 1A or who, had he been a registered person, would fall within any of those circumstances and that member—

   (i) is eligible for income support under regulation 13A, or

   (ii) is the subject of a direction under section 124(1) of the Contributions and Benefits Act;

(*b*) where both members are aged less than 18 and sub-paragraph (3)(*a*) or (*aa*) does not apply but one member of the couple—　　　　　　　　　(*b*) £27·50;

   (i) is eligible for income support under regulation 13A, or

   (ii) is the subject of a direction under section 124(1) of the Contributions and Benefits Act;

(*c*) where both members are aged not less than 18;　　　　　　　　　(*c*) £71·70;

(*d*) where one member is aged not less than 18 and the other member is a person under 18 who—　　　　　　　　　(*d*) £71·70;

   (i) is eligible for income support under regulation 13A, or

   (ii) is the subject of a direction under section 124(1) of the Contributions and Benefits Act;

(*e*) where one member is aged not less than 18 but less than 25 and the other member is a person under 18 who—　　　　　　　　　(*e*) £36·15;

   (i) is not eligible for income support under regulation 13A, or

Column (1)	Column (2)
Person or Couple	*Amount*
(ii) is not the subject of a direction under section 124(1) of the Contributions and Benefits Act;	
(*f*) where one member is aged not less than 25 and the other member is a person under 18 who—	(*f*) £45·70.
(i) is not eligible for income support under regulation 13A, and	
(ii) is not the subject of a direction under section 124(1) of the Contributions and Benefits Act.	

2. The weekly amounts specified in column (2) in respect of each person specified in column (1) shall be the weekly amounts specified for the purposes of regulations 17(1)(*b*) and 18(1)(*c*).

Column (1)	Column (2)
Child or young person	*Amount*
Person aged—	
(*a*) less than 11;	(*a*) £15·65;
(*b*) not less than 11 but less than 16;	(*b*) £23·00;
(*c*) not less than 16 but less than 18;	(*c*) £27·50;
(*d*) not less than 18.	(*d*) £36·15.

2A.—(1) The weekly amount for the purposes of regulations 17(1)(*bb*) and 18(1)(*cc*) in respect of a person who satisfies the conditions specified in sub-paragraph (2) shall be £48·00.

SCHEDULE 5

Part IV of Schedule 2 to the Income Support Regulations as amended by this order

PART IV

WEEKLY AMOUNTS OF PREMIUMS SPECIFIED IN PART III

Premium		*Amount*
15.—(1) Lone Parent Premium.	(1)	£ 5·10.
(2) Pensioner Premium for persons aged under 75—		
(*a*) where the claimant satisfies the condition in paragraph 9(*a*);	(2)	(*a*) £18·25;
(*b*) where the claimant satisfies the condition in paragraph 9(*b*).		(*b*) £27·55.
(2A) Pensioner Premium for persons aged 75 and over—		
(*a*) where the claimant satisfies the condition in paragraph 9A(*a*);	(2A)	(*a*) £20·35;
(*b*) where the claimant satisfies the condition in paragraph 9A(*b*).		(*b*) £30·40.
(3) Higher Pensioner Premium—		
(*a*) where the claimant satisfies the condition in paragraph 10(1)(*a*) or (*b*);	(3)	(*a*) £24·70;
(*b*) where the claimant satisfies the condition in paragraph 10(2)(*a*) or (*b*).		(*b*) £35·30.
(4) Disability Premium—		
(*a*) where the claimant satisfies the condition in paragraph 11(*a*);	(4)	(*a*) £19·45;
(*b*) where the claimant satisfies the condition in paragraph 11(*b*).		(*b*) £27·80.
(5) Severe Disability Premium—		
(*a*) where the claimant satisfies the condition in paragraph 13(2)(*a*);	(5)	(*a*) £34·30;
(*b*) where the claimant satisfies the condition in paragraph 13(2)(*b*)—		
(i) if there is someone in receipt of an invalid care allowance or if he or any partner satisfies that condition only by virtue of paragraph 13(3A),		(*b*) (i) £34·30,
(ii) if no one is in receipt of such an allowance.		(ii) £68·60.

Premium	*Amount*
(6) Disabled Child Premium.	(6) £19·45 in respect of each child or young person in respect of whom the condition specified in paragraph 14 is satisfied.
(7) Carer Premium.	(7) £12·40 in respect of each person who satisfies the condition specified in paragraph 14ZA.

SCHEDULE 6   Article 16(8) and (9)

Applicable amounts of persons in Homes for Persons in Need and Nursing Homes

PART I

PROVISIONS IN SCHEDULE 4 TO THE INCOME SUPPORT REGULATIONS AS AMENDED BY THIS ORDER

Homes for persons in need

6.—(1) Subject to sub-paragraph (2) and paragraphs 8 to 10, where the accommodation provided for the claimant is a home for persons in need, for persons in need of personal care by virtue of—

(*a*) old age and infirmity, the appropriate amount shall be £194·00 per week;

(*b*) past or present mental disorder but excluding mental handicap, the appropriate amount shall be £202·00 per week;

(*c*) past or present drug or alcohol dependence, the appropriate amount shall be £202·00 per week;

(*d*) mental handicap, the appropriate amount shall be £232·00 per week;

(*e*) physical disablement, the appropriate amount shall be—

(i) in the case of a person to whom paragraph 8 applies, £262·00 per week, or

(ii) in any other case £194·00 per week.

Nursing homes

7. Subject to paragraphs 8 to 10, where the accommodation provided for the claimant is a nursing home for persons in need of personal care by virtue of—

(*a*) past or present mental disorder but excluding mental handicap, the appropriate amount shall be £290·00 per week;

(*b*) mental handicap, the appropriate amount shall be £295·00 per week;

(*c*) past or present drug or alcohol dependence, the appropriate amount shall be £290·00 per week;

(*d*) physical disablement, the appropriate amount shall be—

(i) in the case of a person to whom paragraph 8 applies, £325·00 per week, or

(ii) in any other case, £290·00 per week;

(*e*) terminal illness, the appropriate amount shall be £290·00 per week; or

(*f*) any condition not falling within sub-paragraphs (*a*) to (*e*), the appropriate amount shall be £290·00 per week.

Personal allowances

12. The allowance for personal expenses for the claimant and each member of his family referred to in paragraph 1(1)(*b*) shall be—

(*a*) for the claimant £13·10; and, if he has a partner, for his partner, £13·10;

(*b*) for a young person aged 18, £13·10;

(*c*) for a young person aged under 18 but over 16, £9·10;

(*d*) for a child aged under 16 but over 11, £7·85;

(*e*) for a child aged under 11, £5·40.

PART II

OTHER SUMS SPECIFIED IN SCHEDULE 4 TO THE INCOME SUPPORT REGULATIONS

Paragraph in Schedule 4		*Specified Sum*	
2(2)(*b*)(i)	⎫	daily	£1·10
2(2)(*b*)(ii)	⎬ increases for meals	daily	£1·55
2(2)(*b*)(iii)	⎭	daily	£1·55

a

SCHEDULE 7   Article 16(10) and (11)

Applicable amounts in special cases

PART I

PROVISIONS IN SCHEDULE 7 TO THE INCOME SUPPORT REGULATIONS AS AMENDED BY THIS ORDER

Column (1)	Column (2)
Patients	
1. Subject to paragraphs 2, 2A, 3 and 16, a person who has been a patient for a period of more than 6 weeks and who is—	
(*a*) a single claimant;	1. (*a*) £14·40 plus any amount applicable under regulation 17(1)(*e*), (*f*) or (*g*);
(*b*) a lone parent;	(*b*) £14·40 plus any amounts applicable to him under regulation 17(1)(*b*), (*c*), (*e*), (*f*) or (*g*) or under regulation 17(1)(*d*) because of paragraph 8 or 14 of Schedule 2 (applicable amounts);
(*c*) a member of a couple—	
(i) where only one of the couple is a patient or, where both members of the couple are patients but only one has been a patient for that period,	(*c*) (i) the amount applicable in respect of both of them under regulation 17(1) (applicable amounts) reduced by £11·50,
(ii) where both members of the couple have been a patient for that period;	(ii) £28·80 plus any amounts which may be applicable under regulation 17(1)(*b*), (*c*), (*e*), (*f*) or (*g*) or under regulation 17(1)(*d*) because of paragraph 14 of Schedule 2;
(*d*) a member of a polygamous marriage—	
(i) where at least one member of the polygamous marriage is not a patient or has not been a patient for more than that period,	(*d*) (i) the applicable amount under regulation 18 (polygamous márriages) shall be reduced by £11·50 in respect of each such member who is a patient,

Column (1)	Column (2)
(ii) where all the members of the polygamous marriage have been patients for more than that period.	(ii) the applicable amount shall be £14·40 in respect of each member plus any amounts applicable under regulation 18(1)(*c*), (*d*), (*f*), (*g*) or (*h*), or (*e*) because of his satisfying the condition specified in paragraph 14 of Schedule 2.

2. A single claimant who has been a patient for a continuous period of more than 52 weeks where—

(*a*) the following conditions are satisfied—

    (i) a person has been appointed to act for him under regulation 33 of the Social Security (Claims and Payments) Regulations (Northern Ireland) 1987(**a**) (persons unable to act),

    (ii) his income support is payable to an administrative officer of the hospital or other institution either as or at the request of the person so appointed, and

    (iii) a registered medical practitioner treating him certifies that all or part of his income support cannot be used by him or on his behalf; or

(*b*) those conditions are not satisfied.

2. (*a*) Such amount (if any) not exceeding £11·50 as is reasonable having regard to the views of the hospital staff and the patient's relatives if available as to the amount necessary for his personal use; or

(*b*) £11·50.

2A. A single claimant who is detained under the provisions of the Mental Health (Northern Ireland) Order 1986(**b**) and who immediately before his detention under that Order was a prisoner.

2A.   £11·50.

(**a**) S.R. 1987 No. 465; relevant amending regulations are S.R. 1992 No. 7
(**b**) S.I. 1986/595 (N.I. 4)

Column (1)	Column (2)

3. Subject to paragraph 16—

   (*a*) a claimant who is not a patient and who is a member of a family of which another member is a child or young person who has been a patient for a period of more than 12 weeks; or

   (*b*) where the person is a member of a family and paragraph 1 applies to him and another member of the family who is a child or young person has been a patient for a period of more than 12 weeks.

3. (*a*) The amount applicable to him under regulation 17(1) or 18 except that the amount applicable under regulation 17(1)(*b*) or 18(1)(*c*) in respect of the child or young person referred to in column (1) of this paragraph shall be £11·50 instead of an amount determined in accordance with paragraph 2 of Schedule 2; or

   (*b*) the amount applicable to him under paragraph 1 except that the amount applicable under regulation 17(1)(*b*) or 18(1)(*c*) in respect of the child or young person referred to in column (1) of this paragraph shall be £11·50 instead of an amount determined in accordance with paragraph 2 of Schedule 2.

Single claimants temporarily in accommodation provided by a Health and Social Services Board

10A. A single claimant who is temporarily in accommodation referred to in sub-paragraph (*a*) or (*b*) (excluding heads (i) and (ii) of those sub-paragraphs) of the definition of "residential accommodation" in regulation 21(3) (special cases).

10A. £57·60 of which £13·10 is for personal expenses plus any amounts applicable under regulation 17(1)(*e*), (*f*) or (*g*).

Couples and members of polygamous marriages where one member is or all are temporarily in accommodation provided by a Health and Social Services Board

10B.—(1) A claimant who is a member of a couple and temporarily separated from his partner where one of them is living in the home while the other is in accommodation referred to in sub-paragraph (*a*) or (*b*) (excluding heads (i) and (ii) of those sub-paragraphs) of the definition of "residential accommodation" in regulation 21(3).

10B.—(1) The aggregate of the amount applicable to the member who remains in the home calculated as if he were a single claimant under regulation 17(1), 19 or 21 and in respect of the other member, £57·60 of which £13·10 is for personal expenses.

Column (1)	Column (2)

(2) A claimant who is a member of a polygamous marriage and who is temporarily separated from a partner of his where one is, or some are, living in the home while one is, or some are, in accommodation referred to in sub-paragraph (1).

(2) The aggregate of the amount applicable for the members of the polygamous marriage who remain in the home under regulation 18 and in respect of each member not in the home £57·60 of which £13·10 is for personal expenses.

(3) A claimant who is a member of a couple or a member of a polygamous marriage where both members of that couple or all the members of that marriage are in accommodation referred to in sub-paragraph (1).

(3) For each member of that couple or marriage £57·60 of which £13·10 is for personal expenses plus, if appropriate, the amount applicable under regulation 17(1)(*e*), (*f*) or (*g*) or 18(1)(*f*), (*g*) or (*h*).

Lone parents who are in residential accommodation temporarily

10C. A claimant who is a lone parent who has entered residential accommodation temporarily.

10C. £57·60 of which £13·10 is for personal expenses plus—

(*a*) in respect of each child or young person who is a member of his family, the amount in respect of him prescribed in paragraph 2(*a*), (*b*), (*c*) or (*d*) of Schedule 2 or under this Schedule as appropriate; and

(*b*) any amount which would be applicable to the claimant if he were not temporarily living away from the dwelling occupied as his home, under regulation 17(1)(*c*), (*e*), (*f*) or (*g*), or (*d*) in so far as that amount relates to the lone parent premium under paragraph 8 of Schedule 2.

Persons in residential accommodation

13.—(1) Subject to sub-paragraph (2), a person in, or only temporarily absent from, residential accommodation who is—

13.—(1) Any amount applicable under regulation 17(1)(*f*) or (*g*) or 18(1)(*g*) or (*h*) plus—

(*a*) a single claimant;

(*a*) £57·60 of which £13·10 is for personal expenses;

(*b*) a lone parent;

(*b*) the amount specified in head (*a*) of this column;

(*c*) one of a couple;

(*c*) twice the amount specified in head (*a*) of this column;

(*d*) a child or young person;

(*d*) the appropriate amount in respect of him prescribed in paragraph 2 of Schedule 2;

Column (1)	Column (2)

(*e*) a member of a polygamous marriage.

(*e*) the amount specified in head (*a*) multiplied by the number of members of the polygamous marriage in, or only temporarily absent from, that accommodation.

(2) A single claimant who has become a patient and whose residential accommodation was provided by and managed by the Department.

(2) Any amount applicable under regulation 17(1)(*f*) or (*g*) plus £13·10.

Persons in homes for persons in need or nursing homes who become patients

16. A claimant to whom regulation 19 applies immediately before he or a member of his family became a patient where—

(*a*) he or any member of his family has been a patient for a period of 6 weeks or less and the claimant—

    (i) continues to be liable to meet the weekly charge for the accommodation without reduction in respect of himself or that member of his family who is a patient,

16.(*a*) (i) The amount which would be applicable under regulation 19 as if the claimant or the member of the family who is a patient were resident in the accommodation to which regulation 19 applies,

    (ii) continues to be liable to meet the weekly charge for the accommodation but at a reduced rate,

    (ii) the amount which would be applicable under regulation 19 having taken into account the reduced charge, as if the claimant or the member of the family who is a patient were resident in the accommodation to which regulation 19 applies,

    (iii) is a single claimant and is likely to return to the accommodation, but has ceased to be liable to meet the weekly charge for that accommodation, or

    (iii) the amount applicable to him (if any) under paragraph 2(2) of Schedule 4 plus the amount in respect of him as an allowance for personal expenses prescribed by paragraph 12 of Schedule 4 as if he

Column (1)	Column (2)
	were residing in the accommodation to which regulation 19 applies plus any amount applicable under regulation 17(1)(*f*), or
(iv) is a single claimant who ceases to be liable to meet the weekly charge for the accommodation and who is unlikely to return to that accommodation;	(iv) the amount which would be applicable to him under regulation 17(1);
(*b*) he or his partner has been a patient for a period of more than 6 weeks and the patient is—	
(i) a single claimant,	(*b*) (i) £14·40 plus any amount applicable under regulation 17(1)(*f*) plus either the amount prescribed in paragraph 14 in respect of any retaining fee he is liable to pay for the accommodation or the amount applicable under regulation 17(1)(*e*), but not both,
(ii) a lone parent,	(ii) where one or more children or young persons remain in the accommodation, the amount applicable to the family as if regulation 19, having taken into account any reduction in charge, continued to apply to all the members of the family except that where the lone parent is the patient no amount shall be applicable in respect of him under paragraph 2(2) of Schedule 4 and for the amount in respect of the allowance for personal expenses prescribed by paragraph 12 of Schedule 4 there shall be substituted £14·40,

Column (1)	Column (2)
	— where all the children or young persons are absent from the accommodation, £14·40 plus any amounts applicable to him under regulation 17(1)(*b*), (*c*), (*d*) or (*f*) plus (if appropriate) either the amount applicable under column (2) of paragraph 14(*a*) or the amount applicable under regulation 17(1)(*e*), but not both,
	— where one or more children or young persons are also patients and have been so for more than 12 weeks, in respect of those children and young persons remaining in the accommodation and the lone parent patient, the amount specified in case one of column (2) of this head save that the child or young person who has been a patient for more than 12 weeks shall be disregarded as a member of the family in assessing the amount applicable under regulation 19, and in respect of each such child or young person there shall be added £11·50,
(iii) one of a couple or polygamous marriage and one of that couple or marriage is not a patient or has been a patient for 6 weeks or less,	(iii) where the members of the family not patients remain in the accommodation, the amount applicable to the family as if regulation

Column (1)	Column (2)
	19, having taken into account any reduction in charge, continued to apply to all the members of the family except that in respect of the member of the couple or polygamous marriage who has been a patient for more than 6 weeks no amount shall be applicable in respect of him under paragraph 2(2) of Schedule 4 and for the amount in respect of the allowance for personal expenses prescribed by paragraph 12 of Schedule 4 there shall be substituted £14·40,
	— where one or more children or young persons are also patients and have been so for more than 12 weeks, in respect of those children and young persons and the member of the couple or polygamous marriage remaining in the accommodation, the amount specified in case one of column (2) of this head save that the child or young person who has been a patient for more than 12 weeks shall be disregarded as a member of the family in assessing the amount applicable under regulation 19 and in respect of each such child or young person there shall be added £11·50,

Column (1)	Column (2)
(iv) one of a couple or polygamous marriage where all the members of that couple or marriage are patients and have been so for more than 6 weeks;	(iv) where there is no child or young person in the family, £14·40 in respect of each member of the couple or polygamous marriage plus any amount applicable under regulation 17(1)(*f*) or 18(1)(*g*) plus either the amount prescribed in paragraph 14 in respect of any retaining fee for the accommodation he is liable to pay or the amount applicable under regulation 17(1)(*e*) or 18(1)(*f*), but not both,
	— where there is a child or young person remaining in the accommodation, the amount which would be applicable in respect of the family as if regulation 19, having taken into account any reduction in charge, continued to apply to all the members of the family except that in respect of each member of the couple or polygamous marriage no amount shall be applicable in respect of him under paragraph 2(2) of Schedule 4 and for the amount in respect of the allowance for personal expenses prescribed by paragraph 12 of Schedule 4 in respect of each member there shall be substituted £14·40,
	— where there is a child or young person in the family but no

Column (1)	Column (2)
	child or young person remains in the accommodation, the amount applicable under column (2) of paragraph 1(*c*) or (*d*), as the case may be, plus either the amount applicable under column (2) of paragraph 14(*a*) or the amount applicable under regulation 17(1)(*e*) or 18(1)(*f*), but not both,
	— where one or more children or young persons are also patients and have been so for more than 12 weeks, in respect of those children and young persons remaining in the accommodation and the members of the couple or polygamous marriage, the amount specified in case 2 of column (2) of sub-paragraph (*b*)(iv) save that the child or young person who has been a patient for more than 12 weeks shall be disregarded as a member of the family in assessing the amount applicable under regulation 19, and in respect of each such child or young person there shall be added £11·50;

Column (1)	Column (2)
(*c*) a child or young person who has been a patient for a period of more than 12 weeks.	(c) the amount applicable under regulation 19 as if that child or young person was not a member of the family plus an amount of £11·50 in respect of that child or young person.

PART II

OTHER SUMS SPECIFIED IN SCHEDULE 7 TO THE INCOME SUPPORT REGULATIONS

Paragraph in Column (2) of Schedule 7	*Specified Sum*
7. Members of religious orders	Nil.
8. Prisoners	Nil.
14. Persons temporarily absent from home for persons in need or nursing home	80 per cent.
15. Persons from abroad	Nil.

Other applicable amounts specified in the Income Support Regulations

Provisions in Income Support Regulations	*Specified Sum*
Regulation 22(1)	Weekly applicable amount to be reduced by a sum equivalent to 40 per cent. of the relevant amount.
Regulation 22(2)(*a*)	£200.
Regulation 22(2)	Weekly applicable amount to be reduced by a sum equivalent to 20 per cent. of the relevant amount.
Regulation 71(1)(*a*)(i)	90 per cent. of the amount applicable or, as the case may be, of the reduced amount.
Regulation 71(1)(*b*)(i)	90 per cent. of the amount of the allowance for personal expenses or, as the case may be, of the reduced amount.
Regulation 71(1)(*c*)(i)	98 per cent. of the applicable amount for persons in residential accommodation.
Regulation 71(1)(*d*)	90 per cent. of the applicable amount.
Schedule 3, paragraph 7(1)(*a*) and (*b*) (i) and (2)	100 per cent. of the eligible interest.
Schedule 3, paragraph 7(1)(*b*)(ii), (2)(*a*) and (6)	50 per cent. of the eligible interest.
Schedule 3, paragraph 7(4)	The weekly amount of the eligible interest is the amount calculated by the formula $\dfrac{A \times B}{52}$.

EXPLANATORY NOTE
(This note is not part of the Order.)

This order, which corresponds to an order (S.I. 1994/542) made by the Secretary of State for Social Security under section 150 of the Social Security Administration Act 1992 (c. 5), increases the rates and amounts of certain social security benefits and other sums.

Part I relates to the citation, commencement and interpretation.

Part II relates to non income-related benefits. Article 3 and Schedule 1 increase the rates of benefits and increases of benefit (except age addition) specified in Parts I, III, IV and V of Schedule 4 to the Social Security Contributions and Benefits (Northern Ireland) Act 1992 ("the Contributions and Benefits Act").

Article 4 increases the rates and amounts of certain pensions and allowances under the Contributions and Benefits Act.

Article 5 increases the sums payable as part of a Category A or Category B retirement pension under sections 11(1) and 13(2) and (3) of the Pension Schemes (Northern Ireland) Act 1993 ("the Pension Schemes Act") on account of increases in guaranteed minimum pensions.

Article 6 specifies the dates from which the sums specified for rates or amounts of benefit under the Contributions and Benefits Act or the Pension Schemes Act are increased.

Article 7 increases the rate of certain workmen's compensation in respect of employment before 5th July 1948.

Article 8 specifies earnings limits for child dependency increases.

Article 9 specifies the weekly rates of statutory sick pay.

Article 10 increases the lower rate of statutory maternity pay.

Article 11 increases the rate of graduated retirement benefit under the National Insurance Act (Northern Ireland) 1966.

Article 12 specifies the increases in the weekly rates of disability living allowance.

Article 13 specifies the increases in the weekly rate of child benefit and one-parent benefit.

Part III relates to income-related benefits. Article 14 and Schedule 2 specify the applicable amount for family credit and the amount of the credits for an adult, child or young person which determines a family's maximum family credit and other miscellaneous amounts.

Article 15 and Schedule 3 specify the applicable amount for disability working allowance and the amount of the allowance for a claimant, child or young person which determines the appropriate maximum disability working allowance and other miscellaneous amounts.

Article 16 sets out the amount of sums relevant to the applicable amount for the purposes of income support. Article 16(3) and Schedule 4 set out the personal allowances; Article 16(4) and (5) and Schedule 5 set out the premiums; Article 16(8) and (9) and Schedule 6 set out the amounts relevant to beneficiaries in homes for persons in need and nursing homes; Article 16(10) and (11) and Schedule 7 set out the amounts relevant to special cases; and Article 16(12) and Schedule 8 set out other miscellaneous amounts.

Article 17 provides for the percentage increase of sums payable by way of special transitional additions to income support.

Article 18 specifies the sum by which any income support of a person involved in a trade dispute is reduced.

Article 19 sets out various sums relevant to the calculation of housing benefit.

Article 20 contains transitional provisions for family credit and disability working allowance.

Article 21 contains a consequential revocation.

1994   No. 75

SOCIAL SECURITY

The Social Security Benefits Up-rating Regulations (Northern Ireland) 1994

Made	*7th March 1994*
Coming into operation . .	*11th April 1994*

The Department of Health and Social Services for Northern Ireland, in exercise of the powers conferred on it by sections 57(1)(*a*)(ii) and 113(1)(*a*) of, and paragraph 2(3) of Schedule 7 to, the Social Security Contributions and Benefits (Northern Ireland) Act 1992(**a**) and section 135(3) of the Social Security Administration (Northern Ireland) Act 1992(**b**) and of all other powers enabling it in that behalf, hereby makes the following regulations which contain only provisions in consequence of an order(**c**) under section 132 of the Social Security Administration (Northern Ireland) Act 1992:

Citation, commencement and interpretation

1.—(1) These regulations may be cited as the Social Security Benefits Up-rating Regulations (Northern Ireland) 1994 and shall come into operation on 11th April 1994.

(2) In these regulations, unless the context otherwise requires, "the up-rating order" means the Social Security Benefits Up-rating Order (Northern Ireland) 1994(**c**).

Exceptions relating to payment of additional benefit under awards made before the commencing date

2. Section 135(3) of the Social Security Administration (Northern Ireland) Act 1992 shall not apply if a question arises as to either—

(*a*) the weekly rate at which the benefit is payable by virtue of the up-rating order; or

(*b*) whether the conditions for the receipt of the benefit at the altered rate are satisfied,

until the question has been determined in accordance with the provisions of that Act.

(**a**) 1992 c. 7
(**b**) 1992 c. 8
(**c**) S.R. 1994 No. 74

Persons not ordinarily resident in Northern Ireland

3. Regulation 5 of the Social Security Benefit (Persons Abroad) Regulations (Northern Ireland) 1978(**a**) (application of disqualification in respect of up-rating of benefit) shall apply to any additional benefit payable by virtue of the up-rating order.

Amendment of the Social Security (General Benefit) Regulations

4. In regulation 14 of the Social Security (General Benefit) Regulations (Northern Ireland) 1984(**b**) (earnings level for the purpose of unemployability supplement) for "£2,184" there shall be substituted "£2,236".

Amendment of the Social Security (Unemployment, Sickness and Invalidity Benefit) Regulations

5. In regulation 3(3) of the Social Security (Unemployment, Sickness and Invalidity Benefit) Regulations (Northern Ireland) 1984(**c**) (persons deemed to be incapable of work) for "£42·00" there shall be substituted "£43·00".

Revocation

6. The Social Security Benefits Up-rating Regulations (Northern Ireland) 1993(**d**) are hereby revoked.

Sealed with the Official Seal of the Department of Health and Social Services for Northern Ireland on 7th March 1994.

(L.S.)   *W. G. Purdy*

                                    Assistant Secretary

(**a**)   S.R. 1978 No. 114; relevant amending regulations are S.R. 1979 No. 392, S.R. 1988 No. 77, S.R. 1989 No. 373, S.R. 1990 No. 123 and S.R. 1992 No. 330
(**b**)   S.R. 1984 No. 92; relevant amending regulations are S.R. 1993 No. 159
(**c**)   S.R. 1984 No. 245; relevant amending regulations are S.R. 1987 No. 221, S.R. 1992 No. 146 and S.R. 1993 No. 159
(**d**)   S.R. 1993 No. 159

EXPLANATORY NOTE

(This note is not part of the Regulations.)

These regulations contain only provisions in consequence of an order under section 132 of the Social Security Administration (Northern Ireland) Act 1992 (c. 8) and accordingly, by virtue of section 149(3) of, and paragraph 3 of Schedule 5 to, that Act are not subject to the requirement of section 149(2) of that Act for prior reference to the Social Security Advisory Committee.

Regulation 2 provides that where a question has arisen about the effect of the Social Security Benefits Up-rating Order (Northern Ireland) 1994 ("the up-rating order") on a benefit already in payment the altered rates will not apply until the question is determined by an adjudicating authority.

Regulation 3 applies the provisions of regulation 5 of the Social Security Benefit (Persons Abroad) Regulations (Northern Ireland) 1978 so as to restrict the application of the increases specified in the up-rating order in cases where the beneficiary lives abroad.

Regulation 4 raises from £2,184 to £2,236 a year the earnings limit which applies to unemployability supplement.

Regulation 5 raises from £42·00 to £43·00 the earnings limit which applies to those undertaking work in certain circumstances while receiving sickness or invalidity benefit.

Regulation 6 contains a consequential revocation.

1994   No. 76

STATUTORY SICK PAY

The Statutory Sick Pay (Small Employers' Relief) (Amendment) Regulations (Northern Ireland) 1994

Made	*7th March 1994*
Coming into operation . .	*6th April 1994*

The Department of Health and Social Services for Northern Ireland, in exercise of the powers conferred on it by section 154(2) and (3) of the Social Security Contributions and Benefits (Northern Ireland) Act 1992(**a**) and section 131 of the Social Security Administration (Northern Ireland) Act 1992(**b**) and of all other powers enabling it in that behalf, hereby makes the following regulations:

Citation, commencement and interpretation

1.—(1) These regulations may be cited as the Statutory Sick Pay (Small Employers' Relief) (Amendment) Regulations (Northern Ireland) 1994 and shall come into operation on 6th April 1994.

(2) The Interpretation Act (Northern Ireland) 1954(**c**) shall apply to these regulations as it applies to a Measure of the Northern Ireland Assembly.

Amendment of the Statutory Sick Pay (Small Employers' Relief) Regulations

2.—(1) The Statutory Sick Pay (Small Employers' Relief) Regulations (Northern Ireland) 1991(**d**) shall be amended in accordance with paragraphs (2) and (3).

(2) In regulation 2(1) (employer's contributions payments) for "£16,000" there shall be substituted "£20,000".

(3) In regulation 3 (number of weeks) for "6" there shall be substituted "4".

Revocation

3. Regulation 2(2) of the Statutory Sick Pay (Small Employers' Relief) (Amendment) Regulations (Northern Ireland) 1992(**e**) is hereby revoked.

(**a**) 1992 c. 7
(**b**) 1992 c. 8
(**c**) 1954 c. 33 (N.I.)
(**d**) S.R. 1991 No. 137; amended by S.R. 1992 No. 139
(**e**) S.R. 1992 No. 139

Sealed with the Official Seal of the Department of Health and Social Services for Northern Ireland on 7th March 1994.

(L.S.) *W. G. Purdy*

Assistant Secretary

EXPLANATORY NOTE

(This note is not part of the Regulations.)

These regulations further amend the Statutory Sick Pay (Small Employers' Relief) Regulations (Northern Ireland) 1991 ("the principal regulations") by:

(1) amending the meaning of "small employer" so that an employer is a small employer when his contributions payments for the qualifying tax year (defined in the principal regulations) do not exceed £20,000 rather than £16,000 as previously (regulation 2(2)), and

(2) reducing the number of weeks, from 6 to 4, whereby an employee needs to have been entitled to statutory sick pay in any one period of incapacity for work before the small employer qualifies for relief on payments of statutory sick pay to that employee (regulation 2(3)).

Regulation 3 contains a consequential revocation.

1994   No. 77

SOCIAL SECURITY

The Income-Related Benefits (Miscellaneous Amendments) Regulations (Northern Ireland) 1994

Made	*7th March 1994*

Coming into operation in accordance with regulation 1(1)

The Department of Health and Social Services for Northern Ireland, in exercise of the powers conferred on it by sections 122(1)(*a*), (*b*) and (*c*), 123(1)(*d*)(i), 131(1), 132(3) and (4)(*a*) and (*b*), 133(2)(*d*)(ii) and 171(5) of the Social Security Contributions and Benefits (Northern Ireland) Act 1992(**a**) and of all other powers enabling it in that behalf, hereby makes the following regulations:

Citation, commencement and interpretation

1.—(1) These regulations may be cited as the Income-Related Benefits (Miscellaneous Amendments) Regulations (Northern Ireland) 1994 and shall come into operation—

(*a*) for the purposes of this regulation and regulation 4(1), (7) and (8)(*a*), on 31st March 1994;

(*b*) for the purposes of regulation 4(2) to (6), (8)(*b*) and (*c*) and (9), on 11th April 1994;

(*c*) for the purposes of regulations 2 and 3, on 12th April 1994.

(2) Regulation 4(7) and (8)(*a*) shall have effect in relation to any particular claimant at the beginning of the first benefit week to commence for that claimant on or after 31st March 1994 which applies in his case.

(3) Regulation 4(2) to (6), (8)(*b*) and (*c*) and (9) shall have effect in relation to any particular claimant at the beginning of the first benefit week to commence for that claimant on or after 11th April 1994 which applies in his case.

(4) For the purposes of paragraphs (2) and (3), the expressions "claimant" and "benefit week" have the same meanings as in the Income Support Regulations.

(5) Regulations 2 and 3 shall have effect in relation to any particular claimant—

(*a*) except where sub-paragraph (*b*) applies, on 12th April 1994, or

(*b*) where a claimant has an award of family credit or disability working allowance which is current on 11th April 1994, on the day following the expiration of that award.

(**a**) 1992 c. 7

(6) In these regulations—

"the Disability Working Allowance Regulations" means the Disability Working Allowance (General) Regulations (Northern Ireland) 1992(**a**);

"the Family Credit Regulations" means the Family Credit (General) Regulations (Northern Ireland) 1987(**b**);

"the Income Support Regulations" means the Income Support (General) Regulations (Northern Ireland) 1987(**c**).

(7) The Interpretation Act (Northern Ireland) 1954(**d**) shall apply to these regulations as it applies to a Measure of the Northern Ireland Assembly.

Amendment of the Disability Working Allowance Regulations

2.—(1) The Disability Working Allowance Regulations shall be amended in accordance with paragraphs (2) to (7).

(2) In regulation 22(4) (calculation of net earnings of employed earners) for sub-paragraph (*b*) there shall be substituted the following sub-paragraph—

"(*b*) where the weekly amount of those earnings equals or exceeds the lower earnings limit, an amount representing primary Class 1 contributions under the Contributions and Benefits Act, calculated by applying to those earnings the initial and main primary percentages applicable at the date of claim in accordance with section 8(1)(*a*) and (*b*) of that Act, and".

(3) In regulation 23 (calculation of bonus or commission)(**e**) for paragraph (*b*) there shall be substituted the following paragraph—

"(*b*) an amount representing primary Class 1 contributions under the Contributions and Benefits Act, calculated by applying to that part of the earnings the main primary percentage applicable at the date of claim, and".

(4) In regulation 25 (calculation of net profit of self-employed earners)(**f**)—

(*a*) for "one half of any premium paid in respect of a retirement annuity contract or a personal pension scheme" in each place where those words occur there shall be substituted "one half of the amount in respect of any qualifying premium calculated in accordance with paragraph (14A)"(**g**);

(**a**) S.R. 1992 No. 78; relevant amending regulations are S.R. 1992 No. 403 and S.R. 1993 Nos. 120 and 373
(**b**) S.R. 1987 No. 463; relevant amending rules are S.R. 1988 Nos. 131, 303 and 423, S.R. 1990 No. 138, S.R. 1992 Nos. 18, 148 and 403 and S.R. 1993 Nos. 120 and 373
(**c**) S.R. 1987 No. 459; relevant amending rules are S.R. 1988 Nos. 146, 318 and 431, S.R. 1989 Nos. 139, 249 and 395, S.R. 1990 Nos. 33, 131 and 346, S.R. 1991 No. 204, S.R. 1992 Nos. 18 and 201 and S.R. 1993 Nos. 120, 149, 233 and 373
(**d**) 1954 c. 33 (N.I.)
(**e**) Relevant amending regulations are S.R. 1992 No. 403
(**f**) Relevant amending regulations are S.R. 1993 No. 373
(**g**) Paragraph (14A) is inserted by regulation 2(4)(*c*) of these regulations

(*b*) in paragraph (14) for "In this regulation" there shall be substituted—

"In this regulation—

(*a*) "qualifying premium" means any premium which at the date of claim is payable periodically in respect of a retirement annuity contract or a personal pension scheme;

(*b*) ";

(*c*) after paragraph (14) there shall be inserted the following paragraph—

"(14A) The amount in respect of any qualifying premium shall be calculated by multiplying the daily amount of the qualifying premium by the number equal to the number of days in the assessment period; and for the purposes of this regulation the daily amount of the qualifying premium shall be determined—

(*a*) where the qualifying premium is payable monthly, by multiplying the amount of the qualifying premium by 12 and dividing the product by 365;

(*b*) in any other case, by dividing the amount of the qualifying premium by the number equal to the number of days in the period to which the qualifying premium relates.".

(5) In regulation 29(6) (notional income) for sub-paragraph (*b*) there shall be substituted the following sub-paragraph—

"(*b*) where the weekly amount of those earnings equals or exceeds the lower earnings limit, an amount representing primary Class 1 contributions under the Contributions and Benefits Act, calculated by applying to those earnings the initial and main primary percentages applicable at the date of claim in accordance with section 8(1)(*a*) and (*b*) of that Act, and".

(6) In regulation 46 (other amounts to be disregarded)—

(*a*) for "other than grant income and covenant income" there shall be substituted "other than grant income, covenant income and loans treated as income in accordance with regulation 47";

(*b*) after "sums disregarded under regulations 42(2)" there shall be inserted "and (2A)"(**a**).

(7) In Schedule 3 (sums to be disregarded in the calculation of income other than earnings)(**b**)—

(*a*) for paragraph 19 there shall be substituted the following paragraph—

"19. Where the claimant occupies a dwelling as his home and the dwelling is also occupied by a person other than one to whom paragraph 18 or 39 refers, and there is a contractual liability to make payments to the claimant in respect of the occupation of the dwelling by that person or a member of his family—

(**a**)　Paragraph (2A) was inserted by regulation 2(10) of S.R. 1992 No. 403

(**b**)　Relevant amending regulations are S.R. 1993 No. 120

(a) £4 of the aggregate of any payments made in respect of any one week in respect of the occupation of the dwelling by that person or a member of his family, or by that person and a member of his family, and

(b) a further £8·60, where the aggregate of any such payments is inclusive of an amount for heating.'';

(b) for paragraph 39 there shall be substituted the following paragraph—

''39. Where the claimant occupies a dwelling as his home and he provides in that dwelling board and lodging accommodation, an amount, in respect of each person for whom such accommodation is provided for the whole or any part of a week, equal to—

(a) where the aggregate of any payments made in respect of any one week in respect of such accommodation provided to such person does not exceed £20·00, 100 per cent. of such payments, or

(b) where the aggregate of any such payments exceeds £20·00, £20·00 and 50 per cent. of the excess over £20·00.'';

(c) after paragraph 49 there shall be added the following paragraph—

''50. Where the claimant is in receipt of any benefit under Parts II, III or V of the Contributions and Benefits Act, any increase in the rate of that benefit arising under Part IV (increases for dependants) or section 106(a) (unemployability supplement) of that Act where the dependant in respect of whom the increase is paid is not a member of the claimant's family.''.

Amendment of the Family Credit Regulations

3.—(1) The Family Credit Regulations shall be amended in accordance with paragraphs (2) to (14).

(2) In regulation 2(1) (interpretation)—

(a) in the definition of ''assessment period''(a) for ''regulation 14'' there shall be substituted ''regulation 14 or, as the case may be, 14A''(b);

(b) after the definition of ''date of claim'' there shall be inserted the following definition—

'' ''director'' means a director of a company, and for this purpose ''company'' means a company within the meaning of Article 3(1) of the Companies (Northern Ireland) Order 1986(c) or a body corporate to which, by virtue of Article 667 of that Order, any provision of that Order applies;''.

(3) In regulation 14(1) (normal weekly earnings of employed earners)(d)—

(a) The definition of ''assessment period'' was inserted by regulation 2(a) of S.R. 1992 No. 148
(b) Regulation 14A is inserted by regulation 3(4) of these regulations
(c) S.I. 1986/1032 (N.I. 6)
(d) Relevant amending regulations are S.R. 1992 No. 148

(*a*) after "an employed earner," there shall be inserted "except where those earnings arise from employment as a director,";

(*b*) for "his weekly earnings from that employment over" there shall be substituted "his earnings from that employment received in".

(4) After regulation 14 there shall be inserted the following regulation—

"Normal weekly earnings of directors

14A.—(1) Subject to paragraph (2) and regulation 17 (periods to be disregarded), where a claimant's income includes earnings from employment as a director, his normal weekly earnings from that employment shall be determined by reference to his earnings from that employment received in the year immediately preceding the week of claim.

(2) Where at the date of claim the claimant has been in employment as a director for less than a year, his normal weekly earnings from that employment shall be determined by reference to any earnings received in the period that he has been in that employment and by reference to an estimate of the earnings likely to be received in the remainder of the first year of the employment.".

(5) In regulation 15 (normal weekly earnings of self-employed earners)(**a**)—

(*a*) in paragraph (1) for sub-paragraph (*a*) there shall be substituted the following sub-paragraphs—

"(*a*) except where sub-paragraph (*aa*) or (*b*) applies, over a period of 6 consecutive complete months up to and including the second last complete month immediately preceding the date of claim;

(*aa*) except where sub-paragraph (*b*) applies, where the claimant provides in respect of the employment a statement of his earnings and expenses for the 6 consecutive complete months up to and including the last complete month immediately preceding the date of claim, over that period of 6 months;";

(*b*) for paragraph (2) there shall be substituted the following paragraph—

"(2) Subject to regulation 17, in a case where the claimant has been in employment as a self-employed earner for less than 7 complete months, his normal weekly earnings shall be determined over a period of 6 consecutive complete months commencing with the first complete month after the claimant began that employment, and that determination shall be based on either—

(*a*) where the claimant provides in relation to that employment a statement of his earnings and expenses for the complete months up to and including the last complete month immediately preceding the date of claim, the earnings he received in those months, or

---

(**a**) Relevant amending regulations are S.R. 1988 No. 423 and S.R. 1992 No. 403

(*b*) where no such statement is provided, any earnings he received in the period up to and including the second last complete month immediately preceding the date of claim,

together with an estimate of the earnings likely to be received in the balance of the 6 month period.'';

(*c*) after paragraph (3) there shall be added the following paragraph—

''(4) In this regulation a ''complete month'' begins on the first day of the month and ends on the last day of the month.''.

(6) For regulation 17 (periods to be disregarded)(**a**) there shall be substituted the following regulation—

''**17.** For the purposes of ascertaining a claimant's normal weekly earnings there shall be disregarded—

(*a*) where the claimant is a self-employed earner, any week or period of weeks in his assessment period during which no activities have been carried out for the purposes of the business;

(*b*) where the claimant is a director, any week or period of weeks in his assessment period during which he has done no work and in respect of which he has received no earnings, and

his normal weekly earnings shall be determined by reference to his earnings in the remainder of that period (the reduced period) and in these regulations any reference to an assessment period shall in its application to such a case be construed as a reference to that reduced period.''.

(7) In regulation 18 (calculation of weekly amount of income)(**b**)—

(*a*) in paragraph (2) for sub-paragraph (*a*) there shall be substituted the following sub-paragraph—

''(*a*) except where sub-paragraph (*b*) applies, by multiplying by 7 his earnings—

(i) received in the assessment period;

(ii) estimated for the assessment period, or

(iii) both received in and estimated for that period,

as the case may be, and dividing the product by the number equal to the number of days in that period;'';

(*b*) after paragraph (2) there shall be added the following paragraph—

''(3) For the purposes of regulation 14A (normal weekly earnings of directors), the weekly amount of earnings of a claimant shall be determined by dividing his earnings—

(*a*) received in the assessment period;

(*b*) estimated for the assessment period, or

(*c*) both received in and estimated for that period,

as the case may be, by the number equal to the number of weeks in that period.''.

(8) In regulation 20(4) (calculation of net earnings of employed earners)(**a**) for sub-paragraph (*b*) there shall be substituted the following sub-paragraph—

    ''(*b*) where the weekly amount of those earnings equals or exceeds the lower earnings limit, an amount representing primary Class 1 contributions under the Contributions and Benefits Act, calculated by applying to those earnings the initial and main primary percentages applicable at the date of claim in accordance with section 8(1)(*a*) and (*b*) of that Act, and''.

(9) After regulation 20 there shall be inserted the following regulation—

"Calculation of net earnings of directors

20ZA.—(1) For the purposes of regulation 14A (normal weekly earnings of directors), the earnings of a claimant to be taken into account shall be his net earnings derived from, or likely to be derived from, his employment as a director during the assessment period relevant to his case, and those net earnings shall be determined in accordance with paragraphs (2) to (4).

(2) There shall be disregarded from a claimant's net earnings any sum, where applicable, specified in Schedule 1 (persons not required to be available for employment).

(3) A claimant's net earnings shall, except where paragraph (4) applies, be calculated by taking into account his gross earnings from that employment, less—

    (*a*) any amount deducted from those earnings by way of—

        (i) income tax;

        (ii) primary Class 1 contributions under the Contributions and Benefits Act, and

    (*b*) one half of any sum paid by the claimant by way of a contribution towards an occupational or personal pension scheme.

(4) Where some or all of the claimant's earnings are estimated under regulation 14A(2), those net earnings shall be calculated by taking into account the estimated gross earnings, less—

    (*a*) an amount representing income tax, calculated by applying to those earnings the lower rate or, as the case may be, the lower rate and the basic rate of income tax in the year of assessment in which the claim was made, taking into account the personal relief to which the claimant would be entitled under sections 257(1), 257A(1) and 259 of the Income and Corporation Taxes Act 1988(**b**) (personal relief); except that if the period in respect of

---

(**a**)   Relevant amending regulations are S.R. 1988 No. 131 and S.R. 1992 Nos. 148 and 403

(**b**)   1988 c. 1; sections 257 to 257F were substituted for section 257 by section 33 of the Finance Act 1988 (c. 39); the amounts in sections 257(1) and 257A(1) were substituted by the Income Tax (Indexation) Order 1993 (S.I. 1993/755). Section 259 was amended by section 30 of, and paragraph 5(1) of Schedule 3 to, the Finance Act 1988 and paragraph 5 of Schedule 5 to the Finance (No. 2) Act 1992 (c. 48)

which the estimate is made is less than a year, the lower rate and, if appropriate, the basic rate of tax and the amount of the personal relief allowable under this sub-paragraph shall be reduced pro-rata;

(*b*) where the weekly amount of those earnings equals or exceeds the lower earnings limit, an amount representing primary Class 1 contributions under the Contributions and Benefits Act, calculated by applying to those earnings the initial and main primary percentages applicable at the date of claim in accordance with section 8(1)(*a*) and (*b*) of that Act, and

(*c*) one half of any sum which would be payable by the claimant by way of a contribution towards an occupational or personal pension scheme.''.

(10) In regulation 20A (calculation of bonus or commission)(**a**) for paragraph (*b*) there shall be substituted the following paragraph—

''(*b*) an amount representing primary Class 1 contributions under the Contributions and Benefits Act, calculated by applying to that part of the earnings the main primary percentage applicable at the date of claim, and''.

(11) In regulation 22 (calculation of net profit of self-employed earners)(**b**)—

(*a*) for ''one half of any premium paid in respect of a retirement annuity contract or a personal pension scheme'' in each place where those words occur there shall be substituted ''one half of the amount in respect of any qualifying premium calculated in accordance with paragraph (12A)''(**c**);

(*b*) in paragraph (12) for ''In this regulation'' there shall be substituted— ''In this regulation—

(*a*) ''qualifying premium'' means any premium which at the date of claim is payable periodically in respect of a retirement annuity contract or a personal pension scheme;

(*b*) '';

(*c*) after paragraph (12) there shall be inserted the following paragraph—

''(12A) The amount in respect of any qualifying premium shall be calculated by multiplying the daily amount of the qualifying premium by the number equal to the number of days in the assessment period; and for the purposes of this regulation the daily amount of the qualifying premium shall be determined—

(*a*) where the qualifying premium is payable monthly, by multiplying the amount of the qualifying premium by 12 and dividing the product by 365;

(**a**) Regulation 20A was inserted by regulation 9 of S.R. 1990 No. 138; relevant amending regulations are S.R. 1992 Nos. 148 and 403
(**b**) Relevant amending regulations are S.R. 1988 No. 423 and S.R. 1993 No. 373
(**c**) Paragraph (12A) is inserted by regulation 3(11)(*c*) of these regulations

(*b*) in any other case, by dividing the amount of the qualifying premium by the number equal to the number of days in the period to which the qualifying premium relates.''.

(12) In regulation 26(6) (notional income)(**a**) for sub-paragraph (*b*) there shall be substituted the following sub-paragraph—

''(*b*) where the weekly amount of those earnings equals or exceeds the lower earnings limit, an amount representing primary Class 1 contributions under the Contributions and Benefits Act, calculated by applying to those earnings the initial and main primary percentages applicable at the date of claim in accordance with section 8(1)(*a*) and (*b*) of that Act, and''.

(13) In regulation 42 (other amounts to be disregarded)—

(*a*) for "other than grant income and covenant income" there shall be substituted "other than grant income, covenant income and loans treated as income in accordance with regulation 42A"(**b**);

(*b*) after "sums disregarded under regulations 38(2)" there shall be inserted "and (2A)"(**c**).

(14) In Schedule 2 (sums to be disregarded in the calculation of income other than earnings)(**d**)—

(*a*) for paragraph 19 there shall be substituted the following paragraph—

''19. Where the claimant occupies a dwelling as his home and the dwelling is also occupied by a person other than one to whom paragraph 18 or 41 refers, and there is a contractual liability to make payments to the claimant in respect of the occupation of the dwelling by that person or a member of his family—

(*a*) £4 of the aggregate of any payments made in respect of any one week in respect of the occupation of the dwelling by that person or a member of his family, or by that person and a member of his family, and

(*b*) a further £8·60, where the aggregate of any such payments is inclusive of an amount for heating.'';

(*b*) for paragraph 41 there shall be substituted the following paragraph—

''41. Where the claimant occupies a dwelling as his home and he provides in that dwelling board and lodging accommodation, an amount, in respect of each person for whom such accommodation is provided for the whole or any part of a week, equal to—

(*a*) where the aggregate of any payments made in respect of any one week in respect of such accommodation provided to such person does not exceed £20·00, 100 per cent. of such payments, or

(**a**) Relevant amending regulations are S.R. 1988 No. 131
(**b**) Regulation 42A was inserted by regulation 2(5) of S.R. 1990 No. 297; relevant amending regulations are S.R. 1991 No. 326
(**c**) Paragraph (2A) was inserted by regulation 10(*b*) of S.R. 1992 No. 148
(**d**) Relevant amending rules are S.R. 1990 No. 138, S.R. 1992 No. 18 and S.R. 1993 No. 120

(*b*) where the aggregate of any such payments exceeds £20·00, £20·00 and 50 per cent. of the excess over £20·00.'';

(*c*) after paragraph 51 there shall be added the following paragraph—

''52. Where the claimant is in receipt of any benefit under Parts II, III or V of the Contributions and Benefits Act, any increase in the rate of that benefit arising under Part IV (increases for dependants) or section 106(*a*) (unemployability supplement) of that Act where the dependant in respect of whom the increase is paid is not a member of the claimant's family.''.

Amendment of the Income Support Regulations

4.—(1) The Income Support Regulations shall be amended in accordance with paragraphs (2) to (9).

(2) In regulation 19 (persons in residential care homes and nursing homes)—

(*a*) in paragraph (1ZD)(**a**) for ''property'' there shall be substituted ''home'';

(*b*) after paragraph (1ZJ)(**b**) there shall be inserted the following paragraph—

''(1ZK) Where a person is treated in accordance with paragraph (1ZI) as having a preserved right, paragraph (1ZF) shall apply to that person as if he had acquired a preserved right under paragraph (1ZB).''.

(3) In regulation 21(1) (special cases) for ''except where otherwise provided'' there shall be substituted ''except as provided in regulation 44(1) (modifications in respect of children and young persons)''.

(4) In regulation 42 (notional income)(**c**)—

(*a*) in paragraph (4)(*a*)(ii) the words from ''or accommodation charge'' to ''nursing homes)'' shall be omitted;

(*b*) after paragraph (4) there shall be inserted the following paragraph—

''(4A) Where the claimant lives in a residential care home or a nursing home, or is temporarily absent from such a home, any payment made by a person other than the claimant or a member of his family in respect of some or all of the cost of maintaining the claimant or a member of his family in that home shall be treated as possessed by the claimant or by that member of his family.'';

(*c*) in paragraph (8) for sub-paragraph (*b*) there shall be substituted the following sub-paragraph—

''(*b*) where the weekly amount of those earnings equals or exceeds the lower earnings limit, an amount representing primary Class 1

(**a**) Paragraph (1ZD) was inserted by regulation 2(5)(*b*) of S.R. 1993 No. 149
(**b**) Paragraph (1ZJ) was inserted by regulation 4(9)(*c*) of S.R. 1993 No. 373
(**c**) Relevant amending regulations are S.R. 1988 No. 318, S.R. 1989 No. 139, S.R. 1990 No. 33, S.R. 1991 No. 204, S.R. 1992 No. 201 and S.R. 1993 Nos. 120, 149, 195 and 233

contributions under the Contributions and Benefits Act, calculated by applying to those earnings the initial and main primary percentages in accordance with section 8(1)(*a*) and (*b*) of that Act, and''.

(5) In regulation 66(1) (other amounts to be disregarded)—

(*a*) for ''other than grant income and covenant income'' there shall be substituted ''other than grant income, covenant income and loans treated as income in accordance with regulation 66A''(**a**);

(*b*) after ''sums disregarded under regulation 62(2)'' there shall be inserted ''and (2A)''(**b**).

(6) In regulation 71(1) (applicable amounts in urgent cases)(**c**) for ''except where otherwise provided'' in each place where those words occur there shall be substituted ''except as provided in regulation 44(1) (modifications in respect of children and young persons)''.

(7) In Schedule 1 (persons not required to be available for employment)(**d**) for paragraph 5 (persons incapable of work) there shall be substituted the following paragraph—

''5. A person who—

(*a*) is entitled to sickness benefit or invalidity pension under Part II of the Contributions and Benefits Act, or severe disablement allowance under Part III of that Act, or is in receipt of statutory sick pay within the meaning of Part XI of that Act, or

(*b*) would be entitled to—

(i) sickness benefit but for the provisions of section 31(4) of the Contributions and Benefits Act (no entitlement to sickness benefit for the first three days of interruption of employment), or but for a failure to satisfy the contribution conditions specified for that benefit in paragraph 2 of Schedule 3 to the Contributions and Benefits Act, or

(ii) sickness benefit or invalidity benefit but for the provisions of regulation 7(1)(*c*) of the Social Security (Unemployment, Sickness and Invalidity Benefit) Regulations (Northern Ireland) 1984(**e**) (days not to be treated as days of unemployment or incapacity for work).''.

(8) In Schedule 3 (housing costs)(**f**) in paragraph 7 (interest on loans to acquire an interest in the dwelling occupied as the home)—

(*a*) in sub-paragraph (4) for the words from ''the basic rate'' to ''1988'' there shall be substituted ''the applicable percentage of income tax

---

(**a**) Regulation 66A was inserted by regulation 4(7) of S.R. 1990 No. 297; relevant amending regulations are S.R. 1991 Nos. 46 and 338
(**b**) Paragraph (2A) was inserted by regulation 7(*a*) of S.R. 1992 No. 147
(**c**) Relevant amending regulations are S.R. 1988 Nos. 146 and 318, S.R. 1989 Nos. 139 and 249 and S.R. 1993 Nos. 149 and 373
(**d**) Relevant amending regulations are S.R. 1988 No. 431
(**e**) S.R. 1984 No. 245; relevant amending regulations are S.R. 1988 No. 355
(**f**) Relevant amending regulations are S.R. 1988 No. 431 and S.R. 1990 No. 346

within the meaning of section 369(1A) of the Income and Corporation Taxes Act 1988''(**a**);

(*b*) in sub-paragraph (7) for head (*b*) there shall be substituted the following head—

''(*b*) has left that dwelling and either cannot or will not pay the interest on the loan, or has died,'';

(*c*) sub-paragraph (8) shall be omitted.

(9) In Schedule 9 (sums to be disregarded in the calculation of income other than earnings)(**b**)—

(*a*) in paragraph 15(2) ''or by the Department under Article 36(3) of the 1972 Order'' shall be omitted;

(*b*) for paragraph 19 there shall be substituted the following paragraph—

''19. Where the claimant occupies a dwelling as his home and the dwelling is also occupied by a person other than one to whom paragraph 18 or 20 refers, and there is a contractual liability to make payments to the claimant in respect of the occupation of the dwelling by that person or a member of his family—

(*a*) £4 of the aggregate of any payments made in respect of any one week in respect of the occupation of the dwelling by that person or a member of his family, or by that person and a member of his family, and

(*b*) a further £8·60, where the aggregate of any such payments is inclusive of an amount for heating.'';

(*c*) for paragraph 20 there shall be substituted the following paragraph—

''20. Where the claimant occupies a dwelling as his home and he provides in that dwelling board and lodging accommodation, an amount, in respect of each person for whom such accommodation is provided for the whole or any part of a week, equal to—

(*a*) where the aggregate of any payments made in respect of any one week in respect of such accommodation provided to such person does not exceed £20·00, 100 per cent. of such payments, or

(*b*) where the aggregate of any such payments exceeds £20·00, £20·00 and 50 per cent. of the excess over £20·00.'';

(*d*) after paragraph 52 there shall be added the following paragraph—

''53. Where the claimant is in receipt of any benefit under Parts II, III or V of the Contributions and Benefits Act, any increase in the rate of that benefit arising under Part IV (increases for dependants) or section 106(*a*) (unemployability supplement) of that Act where the dependant in respect of whom the increase is paid is not a member of the claimant's family.''.

(**a**) 1988 c. 1; subsection (1A) of section 369 was inserted by paragraph 13 of resolution no. 20 passed by the House of Commons on 7 December 1993, that resolution having statutory effect under section 1 of the Provisional Collection of Taxes Act 1968 (c. 2) as amended by section 205 of the Finance Act 1993 (c. 34), until the Finance Bill receives Royal Assent
(**b**) Relevant amending rules are S.R. 1988 No. 318, S.R. 1990 No. 131, S.R. 1992 No. 18 and S.R. 1993 Nos. 120, 149, 165 and 373

Sealed with the Official Seal of the Department of Health and Social Services for Northern Ireland on 7th March 1994.

(L.S.) *W. G. Purdy*
Assistant Secretary

EXPLANATORY NOTE

(This note is not part of the Regulations.)

These regulations further amend the Disability Working Allowance (General) Regulations (Northern Ireland) 1992, the Family Credit (General) Regulations (Northern Ireland) 1987 and the Income Support (General) Regulations (Northern Ireland) 1987. In particular they—

(*a*) further define the amount to be disregarded in the calculation of a student's income (regulations 2(6), 3(13) and 4(5));

(*b*) in the calculation of income other than earnings, provide a disregard in certain circumstances where an increase of a specified benefit is payable in respect of a dependant, and further define the amount to be disregarded in respect of payments made to a claimant where other persons occupy the claimant's home (regulations 2(7), 3(14) and 4(9)(*b*), (*c*) and (*d*));

(*c*) in the calculation of earnings, further specify the amount to be deducted for national insurance contributions in certain circumstances (regulations 2(2), 2(3), 2(5), 3(8), 3(10), 3(12) and 4(4)(*c*)).

With respect to disability working allowance and family credit they further amend the provisions specifying the amount to be deducted in respect of any premium paid towards a personal pension scheme in the calculation of earnings of self-employed earners (regulations 2(4) and 3(11)).

With respect to family credit they—

(*a*) provide specific rules for the calculation of earnings of company directors and define ''director'' (regulation 3(2), (3)(*a*), (4), (6), (7) and (9));

(*b*) amend the provisions specifying the earnings to be taken into account in the calculation of earnings of employed earners (regulation 3(3)(*b*));

(*c*) amend the provisions specifying the period over which a self-employed earner's earnings should be calculated (regulation 3(5)).

.a

With respect to income support they—

(*a*) further amend the provisions specifying the circumstances in which people in residential care homes and nursing homes have preserved rights (regulation 4(2));

(*b*) make minor amendments with respect to the calculation of the income and capital of a child (regulation 4(3) and (6));

(*c*) specify the circumstances in which people in residential care homes and nursing homes will be treated as having notional income (regulation 4(4)(*a*) and (*b*));

(*d*) amend the provision specifying that a person who is incapable of work does not have to be available for work (regulation 4(7));

(*e*) in the calculation of housing costs, alter the rate of deductions in respect of mortgage interest tax relief, amend the provisions specifying the circumstances in which mortgage interest can be met where the claimant's former partner has left the home, and remove the rule which allowed the amount of housing costs in the applicable amount to remain constant notwithstanding a reduction in interest rates (regulation 4(8));

(*f*) in the calculation of income other than earnings, make a minor amendment to the disregard of charitable or voluntary payments (regulation 4(9)(*a*)).

These regulations make in relation to Northern Ireland only provision corresponding to provision contained in regulations made by the Secretary of State for Social Security in relation to Great Britain and accordingly, by virtue of section 149(3) of, and paragraph 10 of Schedule 5 to, the Social Security Administration (Northern Ireland) Act 1992 (c. 8), are not subject to the requirement of section 149(2) of that Act for prior reference to the Social Security Advisory Committee.

1994 No. 78

SOCIAL SECURITY

The Social Security (Contributions) (Amendment) Regulations (Northern Ireland) 1994

Made	*7th March 1994*
Coming into operation . .	*6th April 1994*

The Department of Health and Social Services for Northern Ireland, in exercise of the powers conferred on it by sections 5 and 119 of the Social Security Contributions and Benefits (Northern Ireland) Act 1992(**a**) and of all other powers enabling it in that behalf, hereby makes the following regulations:

Citation and commencement

1. These regulations may be cited as the Social Security (Contributions) (Amendment) Regulations (Northern Ireland) 1994 and shall come into operation on 6th April 1994.

Amendment of the Social Security (Contributions) Regulations

2.—(1) The Social Security (Contributions) Regulations (Northern Ireland) 1979(**b**) shall be amended in accordance with paragraphs (2) and (3) of this regulation.

(2) In regulation 7(**c**) (lower and upper earnings limits for Class 1 contributions)—

(*a*) for "6th April 1993" there shall be substituted "6th April 1994";

(*b*) for "£56" and "£420" there shall be substituted respectively "£57" and "£430".

(3) In regulation 115D(1)(*b*)(**d**) (special provisions as to residence, rate, annual maximum and method of payment in respect of volunteer development workers) for "6·6 per cent." there shall be substituted "5·6 per cent.".

(**a**) 1992 c. 7
(**b**) S.R. 1979 No. 186; relevant amending regulations are S.R. 1980 No. 463, S.R. 1986 No. 71, S.R. 1989 No. 70, S.R. 1990 No. 97, S.R. 1991 No. 80 and S.R. 1993 No. 61
(**c**) Regulation 7 was amended by S.R. 1980 No. 463 and S.R. 1993 No. 61
(**d**) Regulation 115D was inserted by S.R. 1986 No. 71 and amended by S.R. 1989 No. 70, S.R. 1990 No. 97 and S.R. 1991 No. 80

Revocations

3. The following regulations are hereby revoked—

(*a*) the Social Security (Contributions) (Amendment No. 2) Regulations (Northern Ireland) 1991(**a**);

(*b*) the Social Security (Contributions) (Amendment No. 2) Regulations (Northern Ireland) 1993(**b**).

Sealed with the Official Seal of the Department of Health and Social Services for Northern Ireland on 7th March 1994.

(L.S.)   *W. G. Purdy*

                                                          Assistant Secretary

---

(**a**) S.R. 1991 No. 80
(**b**) S.R. 1993 No. 61

EXPLANATORY NOTE

(This note is not part of the Regulations.)

These regulations further amend the Social Security (Contributions) Regulations (Northern Ireland) 1979 ("the principal regulations").

They amend regulation 7 of the principal regulations by increasing the weekly lower and upper earnings limits for Class 1 contributions for the tax year beginning on 6th April 1994. The lower earnings limit is increased from £56 to £57 and the upper earnings limit from £420 to £430.

They also amend regulation 115D of the principal regulations by decreasing the weekly rate of Class 2 contributions payable by volunteer development workers from 6·6 to 5·6 per cent. of the lower earnings limit. For the tax year beginning on 6th April 1994, the weekly contributions for those workers will decrease from £3·70 to £3·19.

They contain revocations.

Regulations 2(1) and 3(b) of these regulations are made under section 5 of the Social Security Contributions and Benefits (Northern Ireland) Act 1992 and accordingly, by virtue of section 149(3) of, and paragraph 4 of Schedule 5 to, the Social Security Administration (Northern Ireland) Act 1992 (c. 8) ("the Act"), are not subject to the requirement of section 149(2) of the Act for prior reference to the Social Security Advisory Committee. Otherwise these regulations correspond to provision contained in regulations made by the Secretary of State for Social Security in relation to Great Britain and accordingly, by virtue of section 149(3) of, and paragraph 10 of Schedule 5 to, the Act, are not subject to the requirement of section 149(2) of the Act for prior reference to the Social Security Advisory Committee.

1994   No. 79

SOCIAL SECURITY

The Social Security (Contributions) (Re-rating and Northern Ireland National Insurance Fund Payments) Order (Northern Ireland) 1994

Made	*7th March 1994*
Coming into operation . .	*6th April 1994*

Whereas the Secretary of State for Social Security has made an order(**a**) under sections 141(4) and (5), 142(2), 143(1), 145(2) and 189(1) and (3) of the Social Security Administration Act 1992(**b**) and section 2(2) and (8) of the Social Security Act 1993(**c**):

Now, therefore, the Department of Health and Social Services for Northern Ireland, in exercise of the powers conferred on it by section 129 of the Social Security Administration (Northern Ireland) Act 1992(**d**) and Article 4(3) of the Social Security (Northern Ireland) Order 1993(**e**) and of all other powers enabling it in that behalf, and with the consent of the Department of Finance and Personnel in so far as its consent is required, hereby makes the following order:

Citation, commencement and interpretation

1.—(1) This order may be cited as the Social Security (Contributions) (Re-rating and Northern Ireland National Insurance Fund Payments) Order (Northern Ireland) 1994 and shall come into operation on 6th April 1994.

(2) In this order "the Act" means the Social Security Contributions and Benefits (Northern Ireland) Act 1992(**f**).

(3) The Interpretation Act (Northern Ireland) 1954(**g**) shall apply to this order as it applies to a Measure of the Northern Ireland Assembly.

Weekly earnings and percentage rate figures for secondary earnings brackets

2. In section 9(3) of the Act(**h**) (secondary earnings brackets and appropriate percentage rates)—

(**a**) S.I. 1994/544
(**b**) 1992 c. 5
(**c**) 1993 c. 3
(**d**) 1992 c. 8
(**e**) S.I. 1993/592 (N.I. 2)
(**f**) 1992 c. 7; relevant amending provision is S.R. 1993 No. 60
(**g**) 1954 c. 33 (N.I.)
(**h**) Section 9(3) was amended by Article 2 of S.R. 1993 No. 60

(*a*) for the weekly earnings figure £94·99 and the percentage rate figure 4·6, specified in respect of Bracket 1, there shall be substituted respectively the figures £99·99 and 3·6;

(*b*) for the weekly earnings figures £95·00 and £139·99 and the percentage rate figure 6·6, specified in respect of Bracket 2, there shall be substituted respectively the figures £100·00, £144·99 and 5·6;

(*c*) for the weekly earnings figures £140·00 and £194·99 and the percentage rate figure 8·6, specified in respect of Bracket 3, there shall be substituted respectively the figures £145·00, £199·99 and 7·6;

(*d*) for the weekly earnings figure £195·00 and the percentage rate figure 10·4, specified in respect of Bracket 4, there shall be substituted respectively the figures £200·00 and 10·2.

Rate of, and small earnings exception from, Class 2 contributions

3. In section 11 of the Act(**a**) (Class 2 contributions)—

(*a*) in subsection (1) (weekly rate) for "£5·55" there shall be substituted "£5·65";

(*b*) in subsection (4) (small earnings exception) for "£3,140" there shall be substituted "£3,200".

Amount of Class 3 contributions

4. In section 13(1) of the Act(**b**) (amount of Class 3 contributions) for "£5·45" there shall be substituted "£5·55".

Amount of, and lower and upper limits for, Class 4 contributions

5. In sections 15(3) and 18(1) of the Act(**c**) (Class 4 contributions recoverable under the Income Tax Acts and under regulations)—

(*a*) for "6·3 per cent." (amount of contribution) there shall be substituted in each of those sections "7·3 per cent.";

(*b*) for "£6,340" (lower limit) wherever it appears there shall be substituted in each of those sections "£6,490";

(*c*) for "£21,840" (upper limit) there shall be substituted in each of those sections "£22,360".

Prescribed percentage of estimated benefit expenditure

6. Article 4(3) of the Social Security (Northern Ireland) Order 1993 shall have effect with respect to the tax year 1994-95 and the prescribed percentage of estimated benefit expenditure for the financial year ending in that tax year shall be 16 per cent.

(**a**) Section 11(1) and (4) was amended by Article 3 of S.R. 1993 No. 60
(**b**) Section 13(1) was amended by Article 4 of S.R. 1993 No. 60
(**c**) Sections 15(3) and 18(1) were amended by Article 5 of S.R. 1993 No. 60

Sealed with the Official Seal of the Department of Health and Social Services for Northern Ireland on 7th March 1994.

(L.S.)   *W. G. Purdy*

Assistant Secretary

The Department of Finance and Personnel hereby consents to Article 6 of the foregoing order.

Sealed with the Official Seal of the Department of Finance and Personnel on 7th March 1994.

(L.S.)   *R. Miller*

Assistant Secretary

EXPLANATORY NOTE

(This note is not part of the Order.)

This order corresponds to an order (S.I. 1994/544) made by the Secretary of State for Social Security under sections 141(4) and (5), 142(2), 143(1), 145(2) and 189(1) and (3) of the Social Security Administration Act 1992 and section 2(2) and (8) of the Social Security Act 1993.

The order increases the amounts of weekly earnings specified in, and reduces the percentage rates appropriate to, the secondary earnings brackets in section 9(3) of the Social Security Contributions and Benefits (Northern Ireland) Act 1992 ("the Act"), which determine the amount of secondary Class 1 contributions payable under the Act (Article 2). The amounts of weekly earnings are increased, in respect of Bracket 1 from £94·99 to £99·99, in respect of Bracket 2 from £95·00 and £139·99 to £100·00 and £144·99 respectively, in respect of Bracket 3 from £140·00 and £194·99 to £145·00 and £199·99 respectively and in respect of Bracket 4 from £195·00 to £200·00. The percentage rates are reduced, in respect of Bracket 1 from 4·6 to 3·6 per cent., in respect of Bracket 2 from 6·6 to 5·6 per cent., in respect of Bracket 3 from 8·6 to 7·6 per cent. and in respect of Bracket 4 from 10·4 to 10·2 per cent.

The order increases the rate of Class 2 and amount of Class 3 contributions specified in sections 11(1) and 13(1) of the Act from £5·55 to £5·65 and from £5·45 to £5·55 respectively (Articles 3(*a*) and 4). It also increases, from £3,140 to £3,200, the amount of earnings specified in section 11(4) of the Act below which an earner may be excepted from liability for Class 2 contributions (Article 3(*b*)).

The order increases the amount of Class 4 contributions payable by increasing the percentage rate specified in sections 15(3) and 18(1) of the Act at which those contributions are charged from 6·3 to 7·3 per cent. It also increases, from £6,340 to £6,490 and from £21,840 to £22,360 respectively, the lower and upper limits of profits or gains specified in those sections between which Class 4 contributions are payable (Article 5).

The order provides for Article 4(3) of the Social Security (Northern Ireland) Order 1993 to have effect for the tax year 1994-95. It also provides that the amount of appropriated money to be paid into the Northern Ireland National Insurance Fund in that year shall not exceed in aggregate 16 per cent. of the estimated benefit expenditure for the financial year ending in that tax year (Article 6).

1994   No. 80

HOUSING; RATES

The Housing Benefit (General) (Amendment) Regulations (Northern Ireland) 1994

Made . . . . . *7th March 1994*

Coming into operation in accordance with regulation 1(1)

The Department of Health and Social Services for Northern Ireland, in exercise of the powers conferred on it by sections 122(1)(*d*) and 133(2)(i) of the Social Security Contributions and Benefits (Northern Ireland) Act 1992(**a**) and of all other powers enabling it in that behalf, with the consent of the Department of the Environment for Northern Ireland(**b**) so far as relates to matters with regard to which such consent is required, and after agreement by the Social Security Advisory Committee that proposals to make these regulations should not be referred to it(**c**), hereby makes the following regulations:

Citation, commencement and interpretation

1.—(1) These regulations may be cited as the Housing Benefit (General) (Amendment) Regulations (Northern Ireland) 1994 and shall come into operation as follows—

(*a*) regulation 1 on 1st April 1994;

(*b*) regulation 2—

(i) in any case to which paragraph (2) applies, on 1st April 1994;

(ii) in any other case, on 4th April 1994.

(2) This paragraph applies in any case where—

(*a*) rent is payable at intervals of one month or any other interval which is not a week or a multiple thereof, or

(*b*) payments by way of rates are not made together with payments of rent at weekly intervals or multiples thereof.

(3) In these regulations "the principal regulations" means the Housing Benefit (General) Regulations (Northern Ireland) 1987(**d**).

(4) The Interpretation Act (Northern Ireland) 1954(**e**) shall apply to these regulations as it applies to a Measure of the Northern Ireland Assembly.

(**a**) 1992 c. 7
(**b**) *See* section 171(6A) of the Social Security Contributions and Benefits (Northern Ireland) Act 1992 inserted by Article 3(3) of the Social Security (Amendment) (Northern Ireland) Order 1993 (S.I. 1993/1579 (N.I. 8))
(**c**) *See* section 150(1)(*b*) of the Social Security Administration (Northern Ireland) Act 1992 (c. 8)
(**d**) S.R. 1987 No. 461 to which there are amendments not relevant to these regulations
(**e**) 1954 c. 33 (N.I.)

Amendment of regulation 7 of the principal regulations

2.—(1) After regulation 7 of the principal regulations (circumstances in which a person is to be treated as not liable to make payments in respect of a dwelling) there shall be inserted the following regulation—

"*Persons from abroad*

7A.—(1) A person from abroad who is liable to make payments in respect of a dwelling shall be treated as if he were not so liable.

(2) In paragraph (1) a "person from abroad" means a person, other than a person to whom paragraph (3) or (5) applies, who has limited leave (as defined in section 33(1) of the 1971 Act) to enter or remain in the United Kingdom which was given in accordance with any provision in the immigration rules (as defined in that section) relating to—

(*a*) there being, or to there needing to be, no recourse to public funds, or

(*b*) there being no charge on public funds,

during that limited leave.

(3) Subject to paragraph (6) this paragraph applies to a person who—

(*a*) is a national of a European Economic Area State, a state which is a signatory to the European Convention on Social and Medical Assistance (done in Paris on 11th December 1953)(**a**), a state which is a signatory to the Council of Europe Social Charter (signed in Turin on 18th October 1961)(**b**), the Channel Islands or the Isle of Man, or

(*b*) having, during any one period of limited leave (including any such period as extended), supported himself without recourse to public funds other than any such recourse by reason of the previous application of this sub-paragraph, is temporarily without funds during that period of leave because remittances to him from abroad have been disrupted, provided that there is a reasonable expectation that his supply of funds will be resumed.

(4) In paragraph (1) "person from abroad" also means any person other than a person to whom paragraph (5) applies who—

(*a*) having a limited leave (as defined in section 33(1) of the 1971 Act) to enter or remain in the United Kingdom, has remained without further leave under that Act beyond the time limited by the leave;

(*b*) is the subject of a deportation order being an order under section 5(1) of the 1971 Act (deportation) requiring him to leave and prohibiting him from entering the United Kingdom except where his removal from the United Kingdom has been deferred in writing by the Secretary of State, or

(*c*) is adjudged by the immigration authorities to be an illegal entrant (as defined in section 33(1) of the 1971 Act) who has not subsequently been given leave under that Act to enter or remain in

(**a**)   Cmd. 9512
(**b**)   Cmd. 2643

the United Kingdom except a person who has been allowed to remain in the United Kingdom with the consent in writing of the Secretary of State.

(5) This paragraph applies to a person who—

(*a*) is an asylum seeker, and for this purpose a person—

   (i) becomes an asylum seeker when he has submitted a claim for asylum to the Secretary of State that it would be contrary to the United Kingdom's obligations under the Convention relating to the Status of Refugees done at Geneva on 28th July 1951, and the protocol to that convention, for him to be removed from, or required to leave, the United Kingdom and that claim is recorded by the Secretary of State as having been made, and

   (ii) ceases to be an asylum seeker when his claim is recorded by the Secretary of State as having been finally determined or abandoned;

(*b*) is awaiting the outcome of an appeal under Part II of the 1971 Act (including any period for which the appeal is treated as pending under section 33(4) of that Act);

(*c*) has no or no further right of appeal under the 1971 Act but has been allowed to remain in the United Kingdom while an application to remain is, or representations on his behalf are, being considered by the Secretary of State;

(*d*) except where he is a person to whom paragraph (4)(*b*) applies, has been granted permission to remain in the United Kingdom pending the removal from the United Kingdom of a person who is the subject of a deportation order but whose deportation has been deferred in writing by the Secretary of State;

(*e*) is subject to a direction for his removal from the United Kingdom but whose removal has been deferred in writing by the Secretary of State, or

(*f*) is in receipt of income support.

(6) Paragraph (3)(*b*) shall not apply to a person who has been temporarily without funds for any period, or the aggregate of any periods, exceeding 42 days during any one period of limited leave (including any such period as extended).

(7) In this regulation—

"the 1971 Act" means the Immigration Act 1971(**a**);

a "European Economic Area State" means a Member State or Norway, Sweden, Iceland, Austria or Finland.".

(2) Regulation 49 of the principal regulations (circumstances in which certain students are to be treated as not liable to make payments in respect of a dwelling) is hereby revoked.

(**a**) 1971 c. 77, as amended by the British Nationality Act 1981 (c. 61), section 39 and Schedule 4

(3) In the case of a person who was entitled to housing benefit in respect of 31st March 1994 or in a case to which regulation 1(1)(*b*)(ii) applies, 3rd April 1994, the preceding provisions of this regulation shall only apply to him—

(*a*) on the day immediately following the day on which the person's benefit period, which includes 31st March 1994 or, as the case may be, 3rd April 1994, ends, and

(*b*) on any day thereafter.

Sealed with the Official Seal of the Department of Health and Social Services for Northern Ireland on 7th March 1994.

(L.S.)

W. G. Purdy
Assistant Secretary

The Department of the Environment for Northern Ireland hereby consents to the foregoing Regulations.

Sealed with the Official Seal of the Department of the Environment for Northern Ireland on 8th March 1994.

(L.S.)

R. E. Aiken
Assistant Secretary

EXPLANATORY NOTE

(This note is not part of the Regulations.)

These regulations further amend the Housing Benefit (General) Regulations (Northern Ireland) 1987 ("the principal regulations").

Regulation 2(1) and (3) removes entitlement to housing benefit from certain persons from abroad, in particular those persons (other than asylum seekers) who enter the United Kingdom on the basis that they will have no recourse to public funds.

Regulation 2(2) revokes regulation 49 of the principal regulations.

1994 No. 81

HOUSING; RATES

The Housing Benefit (General) (Amendment No. 2) Regulations (Northern Ireland) 1994

Made . . . . . *7th March 1994*

Coming into operation in accordance with regulation 1(1)

The Department of Health and Social Services for Northern Ireland, in exercise of the powers conferred on it by sections 122(1)(*d*), 129(4) and 131(1) of the Social Security Contributions and Benefits (Northern Ireland) Act 1992(**a**) and of all other powers enabling it in that behalf, with the consent of the Department of the Environment for Northern Ireland(**b**) so far as relates to matters with regard to which such consent is required, and after agreement by the Social Security Advisory Committee that proposals to make these regulations should not be referred to it(**c**), hereby makes the following regulations:

Citation, commencement and interpretation

1.—(1) These regulations may be cited as the Housing Benefit (General) (Amendment No. 2) Regulations (Northern Ireland) 1994 and shall come into operation as follows—

(*a*) regulation 1 on 1st April 1994;

(*b*) regulations 2 to 5 in any case to which paragraph (2) applies, on 1st April 1994 and in any other case, on 4th April 1994.

(2) This paragraph applies in any case where—

(*a*) rent is payable at intervals of one month or any other interval which is not a week or a multiple thereof, or

(*b*) payments by way of rates are not made together with payments of rent at weekly intervals or multiples thereof.

(3) In these regulations "the principal regulations" means the Housing Benefit (General) Regulations (Northern Ireland) 1987(**d**).

(4) The Interpretation Act (Northern Ireland) 1954(**e**) shall apply to these regulations as it applies to a Measure of the Northern Ireland Assembly.

(**a**) 1992 c. 7
(**b**) *See* section 171(6A) of the Social Security Contributions and Benefits (Northern Ireland) Act 1992 inserted by Article 3(3) of the Social Security (Amendment) (Northern Ireland) Order 1993 (S.I. 1993/1579 (N.I. 8))
(**c**) *See* section 150(1)(*b*) of the Social Security Administration (Northern Ireland) Act 1992 (c. 8)
(**d**) S.R. 1987 No. 461; relevant amending regulations are S.R. 1989 Nos. 125 and 260, S.R. 1990 Nos. 136 and 345, S.R. 1991 No. 47, S.R. 1992 Nos. 35, 85, 404 and 549 and S.R. 1993 Nos. 145 and 154
(**e**) 1954 c. 33 (N.I.)

Amendment of regulation 18 of the principal regulations

2. In regulation 18(1) of the principal regulations (patients)—

(*a*) in sub-paragraphs (*a*), (*b*) and (*d*)(ii) for "£14·05" there shall be substituted "£14·40";

(*b*) in sub-paragraphs (*c*)(i) and (*d*)(i) for "£11·20" there shall be substituted "£11·50";

(*c*) in sub-paragraph (*c*)(ii) for "£28·10" there shall be substituted "£28·80".

Amendment of regulation 63 of the principal regulations

3. In regulation 63 of the principal regulations (non-dependant deductions)—

(*a*) in paragraph (1)—

    (i) in sub-paragraph (*a*)(ii) for "£2·00" there shall be substituted "£2·30";

    (ii) in sub-paragraph (*b*)(ii) for "£1·00" there shall be substituted "£1·15";

(*b*) in paragraph 2(*d*) for "£105·00" there shall be substituted "£108·00".

Amendment of Schedule 2 to the principal regulations

4. In Schedule 2 to the principal regulations (applicable amounts)—

(*a*) for Part I (personal allowances) there shall be substituted the Part set out in Schedule 1 to these regulations;

(*b*) in Part II (family premium) in paragraph 3 for "£9·65" there shall be substituted "£10·05";

(*c*) for Part IV (amounts of premiums specified in Part III) there shall be substituted the Part set out in Schedule 2 to these regulations.

Revocation

5. The Housing Benefit (General) (Amendment No. 2) Regulations (Northern Ireland) 1993(**a**) are hereby revoked.

Sealed with the Official Seal of the Department of Health and Social Services for Northern Ireland on 7th March 1994.

(L.S.)

W. G. Purdy
Assistant Secretary

(**a**) S.R. 1993 No. 154

The Department of the Environment for Northern Ireland hereby consents to the foregoing Regulations.

Sealed with the Official Seal of the Department of the Environment for Northern Ireland on 8th March 1994.

(L.S.) *R. E. Aiken*

Assistant Secretary

SCHEDULE 1   Regulation 4(*a*)

Substitution of Part I of Schedule 2 to the principal regulations

SCHEDULE 2

Applicable Amounts

PART I   Regulations 16(*a*)
and (*b*) and 17(*a*),
(*b*) and (*c*)

PERSONAL ALLOWANCES

1. The amounts specified in column (2) in respect of each person or couple specified in column (1) shall be the amounts specified for the purposes of regulations 16(*a*) and 17(*a*) and (*b*)—

Column (1) *Person or Couple*	Column (2) *Amount*
(1) Single claimant aged—	
(*b*) less than 25;	(1) (*b*) £36·15;
(*c*) not less than 25.	(*c*) £45·70.
(2) Lone parent aged—	
(*a*) less than 18;	(2) (*a*) £36·15;
(*b*) not less than 18.	(*b*) £45·70.
(3) Couple—	
(*a*) where both members are aged less than 18;	(3) (*a*) £54·55;
(*b*) where at least one member is aged not less than 18.	(*b*) £71·70.

2. The amounts specified in column (2) in respect of each person specified in column (1) shall be the amounts specified for the purposes of regulations 16(*b*) and 17(*c*)—

Column (1) *Child or Young Person*	Column (2) *Amount*
Person aged—	
(*a*) less than 11;	(*a*) £15·65;
(*b*) not less than 11 but less than 16;	(*b*) £23·00;
(*c*) not less than 16 but less than 18;	(*c*) £27·50;
(*d*) not less than 18.	(*d*) £36·15.

SCHEDULE 2   Regulation 4(*c*)

Substitution of Part IV of Schedule 2 to the principal regulations

PART IV   Regulations 16(*d*)
and 17(*e*)

AMOUNTS OF PREMIUMS SPECIFIED IN PART III

Premium	Amount
15.—(1) Lone Parent Premium.	(1) £11·25.
(2) Pensioner Premium for persons aged under 75—	
(*a*) where the claimant satisfies the condition in paragraph 9(*a*);	(2) (*a*) £18·25;
(*b*) where the claimant satisfies the condition in paragraph 9(*b*).	(*b*) £27·55.
(3) Pensioner Premium for persons aged 75 and over—	
(*a*) where the claimant satisfies the condition in paragraph 9A(*a*);	(3) (*a*) £20·35;
(*b*) where the claimant satisfies the condition in paragraph 9A(*b*).	(*b*) £30·40.
(4) Higher Pensioner Premium—	
(*a*) where the claimant satisfies the condition in paragraph 10(1)(*a*) or (*b*);	(4) (*a*) £24·70;
(*b*) where the claimant satisfies the condition in paragraph 10(2)(*a*) or (*b*).	(*b*) £35·30.
(5) Disability Premium—	
(*a*) where the claimant satisfies the condition in paragraph 11(*a*);	(5) (*a*) £19·45;
(*b*) where the claimant satisfies the condition in paragraph 11(*b*).	(*b*) £27·80.
(6) Severe Disability Premium—	
(*a*) where the claimant satisfies the condition in paragraph 13(2)(*a*);	(6) (*a*) £34·30;
(*b*) where the claimant satisfies the condition in paragraph 13(2)(*b*)—	
(i) in a case where there is someone in receipt of an invalid care allowance,	(*b*) (i) £34·30,
(ii) in a case where there is no one in receipt of such an allowance.	(ii) £68·60.

Premium	Amount
(7) Disabled Child Premium.	(7) £19·45 in respect of each child or young person in respect of whom the condition specified in paragraph 14 is satisfied.
(8) Carer Premium.	(8) £12·40 in respect of each person who satisfies the condition specified in paragraph 14ZA.

EXPLANATORY NOTE

(This note is not part of the Regulations.)

These regulations further amend the Housing Benefit (General) Regulations (Northern Ireland) 1987.

Regulations 2 and 4 state the amount of the sums relevant to the applicable amount for the purposes of housing benefit. Regulation 4(*a*) and Schedule 1 set out the personal allowances and regulation 4(*c*) and Schedule 2 set out the premiums.

Regulation 3 increases the deductions to be made in respect of non-dependants when assessing the maximum housing benefit for rate rebate purposes.

Regulation 5 contains consequential revocations.

1994 No. 82

STATUTORY SICK PAY

The Statutory Sick Pay (Rate of Payment) Order (Northern Ireland) 1994

Made	*8th March 1994*
Coming into operation . .	*6th April 1994*

The Department of Health and Social Services for Northern Ireland, in exercise of the powers conferred on it by section 153(2)(*a*) of the Social Security Contributions and Benefits (Northern Ireland) Act 1992(**a**) and of all other powers enabling it in that behalf, hereby makes the following order which contains only provision in consequence of an order(**b**) under section 132 of the Social Security Administration (Northern Ireland) Act 1992(**c**):

Citation, commencement and interpretation

1.—(1) This order may be cited as the Statutory Sick Pay (Rate of Payment) Order (Northern Ireland) 1994 and shall come into operation on 6th April 1994, immediately after the coming into operation of Article 9 of the Social Security Benefits Up-rating Order (Northern Ireland) 1994(**d**).

(2) In this order "the 1992 Act" means the Social Security Contributions and Benefits (Northern Ireland) Act 1992.

Substitution of provisions in section 153(1) of the 1992 Act

2. In section 153(1) of the 1992 Act(**e**) (rate of payment) for paragraphs (*a*) and (*b*) there shall be substituted the following paragraphs—

"(*a*) £52·50, in a case where the employee's normal weekly earnings under his contract of service with that employer are not less than £200·00; or

(*b*) £47·80, in any other case.".

Transitional provisions

3. Where in relation to statutory sick pay a period of entitlement as between an employer and an employee is running at 6th April 1994 and the employee's normal weekly earnings under his contract of service with that employer are not less than, or are treated for the purposes of section 153(1) of the 1992 Act as not less than, £195·00 they shall be treated for the purposes of that section as not less than £200·00 for the remainder of that period.

(**a**) 1992 c. 7
(**b**) S.R. 1994 No. 74
(**c**) 1992 c. 8
(**d**) S.R. 1994 No. 74
(**e**) Section 153(1) was amended by Article 2 of S.R. 1993 No. 152

Revocations

4. The Statutory Sick Pay (Rate of Payment) Order (Northern Ireland) 1991(**a**) so far as previously unrevoked and Article 2 of the Statutory Sick Pay (Rate of Payment) Order (Northern Ireland) 1993(**b**) are hereby revoked.

Sealed with the Official Seal of the Department of Health and Social Services for Northern Ireland on 8th March 1994.

(L.S.)   *W. G. Purdy*
                                        Assistant Secretary

(**a**)   S.R. 1991 No. 87
(**b**)   S.R. 1993 No. 152

EXPLANATORY NOTE

(This note is not part of the Order.)

This order, which comes into operation on 6th April 1994, substitutes alternative provisions for the paragraphs of subsection (1) of section 153 of the Social Security Contributions and Benefits (Northern Ireland) Act 1992 (c. 7) (rate of payment). The new provisions increase the lower rate of statutory sick pay from £46·95 to £47·80 per week. The higher rate remains unchanged at £52·50 per week. In addition the earnings band is altered so that the higher rate becomes payable where the employee's earnings are normally £200·00 or more per week (increased from £195·00 or more per week) (Article 2).

Article 3 contains transitional provisions for those employees who are incapable of work at the time of the change and would otherwise move from the higher to the lower rate of statutory sick pay.

Article 4 contains consequential revocations.

1994 No. 83

SOCIAL SECURITY

The Workmen's Compensation (Supplementation) (Amendment) Regulations (Northern Ireland) 1994

Made	.	.	.	.	*8th March 1994*
Coming into operation		.	.		*13th April 1994*

The Department of Health and Social Services for Northern Ireland, in exercise of the powers conferred on it by section 171(4) of, and paragraph 2 of Schedule 8 to, the Social Security Contributions and Benefits (Northern Ireland) Act 1992(**a**) and of all other powers enabling it in that behalf and with the consent of the Department of Finance and Personnel, hereby makes the following regulations:

Citation, commencement and interpretation

1.—(1) These regulations may be cited as the Workmen's Compensation (Supplementation) (Amendment) Regulations (Northern Ireland) 1994 and shall come into operation on 13th April 1994.

(2) These regulations shall be read as one with the Workmen's Compensation (Supplementation) Regulations (Northern Ireland) 1983(**b**) hereinafter referred to as "the principal regulations".

(3) In these regulations "the operative date" means 13th April 1994.

(4) The Interpretation Act (Northern Ireland) 1954(**c**) shall apply to these regulations as it applies to a Measure of the Northern Ireland Assembly.

Amendment of regulation 5 of the principal regulations

2. In regulation 5(2) of the principal regulations (lesser incapacity allowances) for "14th April 1993" there shall be substituted "13th April 1994".

Substitution of Schedule 1 to the principal regulations

3. For Schedule 1 to the principal regulations (table of rates of lesser incapacity allowance for beneficiaries to whom regulation 5(2) applies and table of loss of earnings and corresponding rate of lesser incapacity allowance) there shall be substituted the Schedule set out in the Schedule to these regulations.

(**a**) 1992 c. 7; paragraph 2 of Schedule 8 was amended by Article 7 of S.R. 1994 No. 74
(**b**) S.R. 1983 No. 101; relevant amending regulations are S.R. 1990 No. 445 and S.R. 1993 No. 153
(**c**) 1954 c. 33 (N.I.)

Transitional provision relating to amount of allowance payable

4.—(1) Paragraph (2) shall apply to a beneficiary who was, before the operative date, in receipt of a lesser incapacity allowance but in respect of whom the final calculation of earnings required by regulation 7(2) of the principal regulations had not been made by that date.

(2) In such a case as is referred to in paragraph (1) the beneficiary shall be treated as entitled, from the operative date, to an allowance at the rate to which he would have been entitled had the final calculation been made before the operative date.

Transitional provision relating to claims not made before the operative date

5.—(1) Paragraph (2) shall apply to a person whose claim for lesser incapacity allowance was not made before the operative date and who is awarded such allowance for a period after the operative date at one of the rates shown in the second column of Part II of Schedule 1 to the principal regulations.

(2) Any lesser incapacity allowance which is found to be payable to a person mentioned in paragraph (1) in respect of a period before the operative date shall—

(*a*) insofar as it relates to the period from 14th April 1993 to 12th April 1994 inclusive, be paid at the rate shown in the first column of Part I of Schedule 1 to the principal regulations which corresponds to the rate awarded to him for the period after the operative date; and

(*b*) insofar as it relates to a period before 14th April 1993, be paid at the rate or rates then in force which corresponds or correspond to the rate awarded to him for the period after the operative date.

Transitional provision relating to claims made but not determined before the operative date

6.—(1) Paragraph (2) shall apply to a person whose claim for lesser incapacity allowance was made but not determined before the operative date.

(2) Any lesser incapacity allowance which is found to be payable to a person mentioned in paragraph (1) in respect of a period before the operative date shall be paid at the rate or rates in force for that period which corresponds or correspond with that person's loss of earnings.

Transitional provision relating to review and appeal

7. Where a lesser incapacity allowance has been awarded to a person under the principal regulations before the operative date and a question arises as to the weekly rate of allowance payable in consequence of these regulations, the case shall be reviewed by the adjudication officer in the light of amendments made by, and transitional provisions contained in, these regulations and the allowance shall continue to be payable at the weekly rate specified in the award until the question has been determined in accordance with the provisions of the principal regulations.

Revocation

8. The Workmen's Compensation (Supplementation) (Amendment) Regulations (Northern Ireland) 1993(**a**) are hereby revoked.

Sealed with the Official Seal of the Department of Health and Social Services for Northern Ireland on 8th March 1994.

(L.S.)   *W. G. Purdy*
                                                                  Assistant Secretary

The Department of Finance and Personnel hereby consents to the foregoing Regulations.

Sealed with the Official Seal of the Department of Finance and Personnel on 8th March 1994.

(L.S.)   *D. Thomson*
                                                                  Assistant Secretary

(**a**) S.R. 1993 No. 153

SCHEDULE   Regulation 3

Schedule to be substituted for Schedule 1 to the principal regulations

SCHEDULE 1   Regulation 5

PART I

TABLE OF RATES OF LESSER INCAPACITY ALLOWANCE FOR
BENEFICIARIES TO WHOM REGULATION 5(2) APPLIES

Rate of lesser incapacity allowance from 14th April 1993 to 12th April 1994 inclusive	Rate of lesser incapacity allowance from 13th April 1994
£	£
2·90	2·95
7·55	7·75
12·80	13·10
18·35	18·80
26·45	27·10
33·70	34·50

PART II

TABLE OF LOSS OF EARNINGS AND CORRESPONDING RATE
OF LESSER INCAPACITY ALLOWANCE

Loss of earnings	Rate of lesser incapacity allowance
£	£
9·40	2·95
20·50	7·75
31·70	13·10
37·40	18·80
45·70	27·10
Over 45·70	34·50

EXPLANATORY NOTE

(This note is not part of the Regulations.)

These regulations amend the Workmen's Compensation (Supplementation) Regulations (Northern Ireland) 1983 by making adjustments to the lower rates of lesser incapacity allowance consequential upon the increase in the maximum rate of that allowance. The regulations also include transitional provisions and revoke the Workmen's Compensation (Supplementation) (Amendment) Regulations (Northern Ireland) 1993.

1994   No. 84

STATUTORY MATERNITY PAY

The Statutory Maternity Pay (Compensation of Employers) (Amendment) Regulations (Northern Ireland) 1994

Made	.	.	.	.	*8th March 1994*
Coming into operation		.	.		*6th April 1994*

The Department of Health and Social Services for Northern Ireland, in exercise of the powers conferred on it by section 163(1)(*c*) of the Social Security Contributions and Benefits (Northern Ireland) Act 1992(**a**) and of all other powers enabling it in that behalf, hereby makes the following regulations:

Citation and commencement

1. These regulations may be cited as the Statutory Maternity Pay (Compensation of Employers) (Amendment) Regulations (Northern Ireland) 1994 and shall come into operation on 6th April 1994.

Amendment of regulation 3 of the Statutory Maternity Pay (Compensation of Employers) Regulations

2. In regulation 3 of the Statutory Maternity Pay (Compensation of Employers) Regulations (Northern Ireland) 1987(**b**) (determination of the amount an employer shall be entitled to)—

(*a*) for "6th April 1991" there shall be substituted "6th April 1994";

(*b*) for "4·5 per cent." there shall be substituted "4 per cent.".

Revocation

3. The Statutory Maternity Pay (Compensation of Employers) (Amendment) Regulations (Northern Ireland) 1991(**c**) are hereby revoked.

Sealed with the Official Seal of the Department of Health and Social Services for Northern Ireland on 8th March 1994.

(L.S.)

W. G. Purdy

Assistant Secretary

(**a**) 1992 c. 7
(**b**) S.R. 1987 No. 80; regulation 3 was amended by S.R. 1988 No. 95 and S.R. 1991 No. 94
(**c**) S.R. 1991 No. 94

EXPLANATORY NOTE

(This note is not part of the Regulations.)

These regulations further amend the Statutory Maternity Pay (Compensation of Employers) Regulations (Northern Ireland) 1987 (''the principal regulations'').

The principal regulations enable an employer to recover payments of statutory maternity pay and an additional amount in respect of such pay. Regulation 2 of these regulations reduces the additional amount from 4·5 to 4 per cent. of the payment of statutory maternity pay. The reduction takes effect from 6th April 1994.

Regulation 3 of these regulations contains a revocation.

These regulations are made under section 163 of the Social Security Contributions and Benefits (Northern Ireland) Act 1992 and accordingly, by virtue of section 149(3) of, and paragraph 8 of Schedule 5 to, the Social Security Administration (Northern Ireland) Act 1992 (c. 8) (''the Act''), are not subject to the requirement of section 149(2) of the Act for prior reference to the Social Security Advisory Committee.

1994   No. 85

HOUSING

Homes Insulation Scheme and Grants (Amendment No. 2) Order (Northern Ireland) 1994

Made	*9th March 1994*
Coming into operation . .	*1st April 1994*

The Department of Economic Development, in exercise of the powers conferred by Article 86(1), (2), (3), (4)(*a*), (5) and (7) of the Housing (Northern Ireland) Order 1981(**a**) and now vested in it(**b**) and of every other power enabling it in that behalf, with the approval of the Department of Finance and Personnel(**c**), hereby makes the following Order:

Citation, commencement and interpretation

1.—(1) This Order may be cited as the Homes Insulation Scheme and Grants (Amendment No. 2) Order (Northern Ireland) 1994 and shall come into operation on 1st April 1994.

(2) In this Order—

"grant" means a grant paid under Article 86(1) of the Housing (Northern Ireland) Order 1981;

"the principal Order" means the Homes Insulation Scheme and Grants Order (Northern Ireland) 1991(**d**);

"the 1992 Order" means the Homes Insulation Scheme and Grants (Amendment) Order (Northern Ireland) 1992(**e**);

"the 1994 Order" means the Homes Insulation Scheme and Grants (Amendment) Order (Northern Ireland) 1994(**f**).

Amendment to the principal Order

2. Subject to Article 4, for paragraph 3(2) of the Schedule to the principal Order there shall be substituted the following—

"(2) In this paragraph "application on the grounds of special need" means an application made by a person who, or whose spouse, is, at the time of application, aged 60 or over or in receipt of income support, family credit, housing benefit, disability working allowance or disability living allowance within the meaning of Parts III and VII of the Social Security Contributions and Benefits (Northern Ireland) Act 1992(**g**).".

(**a**) S.I. 1981/156 (N.I. 3); Article 86 has been amended by Article 4(1) of S.R. 1984 No. 204
(**b**) *See* S.R. 1984 No. 204
(**c**) Formerly Department of Finance; *see* S.I. 1982/338 (N.I. 6) Article 3
(**d**) S.R. 1991 No. 29 as amended by S.R. 1992 No. 183 and S.R. 1994 No. 53
(**e**) S.R. 1992 No. 183
(**f**) S.R. 1994 No. 53
(**g**) 1992 c. 7

Revocation

3. Subject to Article 4, the Homes Insulation Scheme and Grants (Amendment) Order (Northern Ireland) 1992 is hereby revoked.

Transitional provisions

4.—(1) The Homes Insulation Scheme and Grants Order (Northern Ireland) 1991 as first enacted shall continue to apply in relation to any applications for grants made on or after 18th March 1991 but before 19th May 1992 as if the 1992 Order had not been made.

(2) The Homes Insulation Scheme and Grants Order (Northern Ireland) 1991 as amended by the 1992 Order shall continue to apply in relation to any applications for grant made on or after 19th May 1992 but before 24th February 1994 as if the 1994 Order had not been made.

(3) The principal Order shall continue to apply in relation to any applications for grant made on or after 24th February 1994 but before the coming into operation of this Order as if this Order had not been made.

Sealed with the Official Seal of the Department of Economic Development on 9th March 1994.

(L.S.)   *D. Gibson*

Under Secretary

The Department of Finance and Personnel hereby approves the foregoing Order.

Sealed with the Official Seal of the Department of Finance and Personnel on 9th March 1994.

(L.S.)   *D. Thomson*

Assistant Secretary

EXPLANATORY NOTE

(This note is not part of the Order.)

This Order which comes into operation on 1st April 1994 amends the Homes Insulation Scheme and Grants Order (Northern Ireland) 1991 by extending the scope of the grant to include those persons aged 60 or over and those in receipt of disability living allowance.

The amendments effected by this Order do not apply to applications for grant made before this Order comes into operation.

1994 No. 86

ROAD TRAFFIC AND VEHICLES

**Traffic Weight Restriction (Manooney Road, Killylea)
Order (Northern Ireland) 1994**

Made	*10th March 1994*
Coming into operation . .	*25th April 1994*

WHEREAS the Department of the Environment has published a notice in compliance with Article 23(1) and (2) of the Road Traffic (Northern Ireland) Order 1981(**a**);

AND WHEREAS no objection or representation has been received;

NOW THEREFORE the Department, in exercise of the powers conferred on it by Article 22(1) of the Road Traffic (Northern Ireland) Order 1981 and of every other power enabling it in that behalf and being satisfied that the road specified in Article 2 is unsuitable for use by certain classes of vehicles, makes the following Order:

Citation, commencement and interpretation

1.—(1) This Order may be cited as the Traffic Weight Restriction (Manooney Road, Killylea) Order (Northern Ireland) 1994 and shall come into operation on 25th April 1994.

(2) In this Order "maximum gross weight" has the meaning assigned to that term by regulation 2(1) of the Motor Vehicles (Construction and Use) Regulations (Northern Ireland) 1989(**b**).

Prohibition

2. Subject to Article 3 the use by vehicles exceeding 7.5 tonnes maximum gross weight is prohibited in Manooney Road, Unclassified No. 8733, Killylea, County Armagh.

Exceptions

3. The prohibition in Article 2 shall not apply to vehicles being used—

(*a*) by the owners or occupiers of lands abutting on or convenient to the road to gain access to such land; or

(*b*) in connection with the delivery to or collection from such land of goods of any kind including livestock; or

---

(**a**)   S.I. 1981/154 (N.I. 1) as amended by S.I. 1984/1986 (N.I. 15), Schedule 1, paragraph 3; *see* Article 2(2) for the definition of "Department"
(**b**)   S.R. 1989 No. 299

(*c*) for police or military purposes, or in an emergency for ambulance or fire brigade purposes; or

(*d*) in connection with public utility services in or adjacent to the road.

Sealed with the Official Seal of the Department of the Environment on 10th March 1994.

(L.S.)   *E. J. Galway*
                                          Assistant Secretary

---

EXPLANATORY NOTE

(This note is not part of the Order.)

This Order prohibits vehicles exceeding 7.5 tonnes maximum gross weight from using Manooney Road, Unclassified No. 8733, Killylea, County Armagh.

Vehicles requiring access are excepted from the provisions of the Order.

Any person who acts in contravention of the Order shall be guilty of an offence and shall be liable on summary conviction to a fine not exceeding level 3 on the standard scale (£400).

Traffic signs indicating the effect of the Order will in due course be erected on the road.

1994   No. 87

ROAD TRAFFIC AND VEHICLES

One-Way Traffic (Belfast) (Amendment) Order (Northern Ireland) 1994

Made	*10th March 1994*
Coming into operation . .	*21st April 1994*

WHEREAS the Department of the Environment has published a notice in compliance with Article 23(1) and (2) of the Road Traffic (Northern Ireland) Order 1981(**a**);

AND WHEREAS no objection or representation has been received;

NOW THEREFORE the Department, in exercise of the powers conferred on it by Article 21(1) of the Road Traffic (Northern Ireland) Order 1981 and of every other power enabling it in that behalf, makes the following Order:

Citation and commencement

1. This Order may be cited as the One-Way Traffic (Belfast) (Amendment) Order (Northern Ireland) 1994 and shall come into operation on 21st April 1994.

Amendment

2. Schedule 2 to the One-Way Traffic (Belfast) Order (Northern Ireland) 1986(**b**) shall be amended by the deletion therefrom of the following items—

Column 1	*Column 2*
St. Andrew's Square North, from its junction with St. Andrew's Square West to its junction with St. Andrew's Square East	Easterly from St. Andrew's Square West
St. Andrew's Square East, from its junction with St. Andrew's Square North to its junction with Hope Street	Southerly from St. Andrew's Square North

---

(**a**) S.I. 1981/154 (N.I. 1); *see* Article 2(2) for the definition of "Department".
(**b**) S.R. 1986 No. 6 to which there are no relevant amendments.

Sealed with the Official Seal of the Department of the Environment on 10th March 1994.

(L.S.)　　　　　　　　　　　　　　　　　*E. J. Galway*
　　　　　　　　　　　　　　　　　　　　Assistant Secretary

EXPLANATORY NOTE

(This note is not part of the Order.)

This Order amends the provisions of the One-Way Traffic (Belfast) Order (Northern Ireland) 1986

The effect of the amendment is to re-introduce a two-way traffic system in St. Andrew's Square East and in part of St. Andrew's Square North, Belfast.

1994 No. 88

HOUSING; RATES

The Housing Benefit (General) (Amendment No. 3) Regulations (Northern Ireland) 1994

Made	*11th March 1994*

Coming into operation in accordance with regulation 1(1)

The Department of Health and Social Services for Northern Ireland, in exercise of the powers conferred on it by sections 122(1)(*d*) and 132(3) and (4)(*a*) and (*b*) of the Social Security Contributions and Benefits (Northern Ireland) Act 1992(**a**) and section 61(3) of the Social Security Administration (Northern Ireland) Act 1992(**b**), and of all other powers enabling it in that behalf, with the consent of the Department of the Environment for Northern Ireland(**c**) so far as relates to matters with regard to which such consent is required, and after agreement by the Social Security Advisory Committee that proposals in respect of these regulations should not be referred to it(**d**), hereby makes the following regulations:

Citation, commencement and interpretation

1.—(1) These regulations may be cited as the Housing Benefit (General) (Amendment No. 3) Regulations (Northern Ireland) 1994 and shall come into operation as follows—

(*a*) regulation 1 on 1st April 1994;

(*b*) regulations 2 to 11—

(i) in any case to which paragraph (2) applies, on 1st April 1994;

(ii) in any other case, on 4th April 1994.

(2) This paragraph applies in any case where—

(*a*) rent is payable at intervals of one month or any other interval which is not a week or a multiple thereof, or

(*b*) payments by way of rates are not made together with payments of rent at weekly intervals or multiples thereof.

(3) In these regulations "the principal regulations" means the Housing Benefit (General) Regulations (Northern Ireland) 1987(**e**).

(**a**) 1992 c. 7

(**b**) 1992 c. 8

(**c**) *See* section 171(6A) of the Social Security Contributions and Benefits (Northern Ireland) Act 1992 inserted by Article 3(3) of the Social Security (Amendment) (Northern Ireland) Order 1993 (S.I. 1993/1579 (N.I. 8))

(**d**) *See* section 150(1)(*b*) of the Social Security Administration (Northern Ireland) Act 1992

(**e**) S.R. 1987 No. 461; relevant amending regulations are S.R. 1990 Nos. 136 and 297, S.R. 1991 Nos. 47 and 337, S.R. 1992 Nos. 35, 141 and 404 and S.R. 1993 Nos. 145 and 414

(4) The Interpretation Act (Northern Ireland) 1954(**a**) shall apply to these regulations as it applies to a Measure of the Northern Ireland Assembly.

Amendment of regulation 2 of the principal regulations

2. In regulation 2(1) of the principal regulations (interpretation)—

(*a*) the definition of "boarder" shall be omitted;

(*b*) after the definition of "person on income support" there shall be inserted the following definition—

    " "personal pension scheme" has the same meaning as in section 167(1) of the Social Security Administration (Northern Ireland) Act 1992(**b**) and, in the case of a self-employed earner, includes a scheme approved by the Board of Inland Revenue under Chapter IV of Part XIV of the Income and Corporation Taxes Act 1988(**c**);".

Amendment of regulation 25 of the principal regulations

3. In regulation 25 of the principal regulations (calculation of weekly income)—

(*a*) for "For the purposes of regulations 22 to 24 (average weekly income)" there shall be substituted "—(1) For the purposes of regulations 22 and 24 (average weekly earnings of employed earners and average weekly income other than earnings)";

(*b*) after paragraph (1) there shall be added the following paragraph—

    "(2) For the purposes of regulation 23 (average weekly earnings of self-employed earners) the weekly amount of earnings of a claimant shall be determined by dividing his earnings over the assessment period by the number equal to the number of days in that period and multiplying the quotient by 7.".

Amendment of regulation 29 of the principal regulations

4. In regulation 29(4) of the principal regulations (calculation of net earnings of employed earners)(**d**) for sub-paragraph (*b*) there shall be substituted the following sub-paragraph—

    "(*b*) an amount equivalent to the amount of the primary Class 1 contributions that would be payable by him under the Contributions and Benefits Act in respect of those earnings if such contributions were payable, and".

(**a**) 1954 c. 33 (N.I.)
(**b**) 1992 c. 8; section 167(1) was amended by the Pension Schemes (Northern Ireland) Act 1993 (c. 49) section 184 and Schedule 7, para 42
(**c**) 1988 c. 1
(**d**) Regulation 29(4) was amended by regulation 5 of S.R. 1992 No. 404

Amendment of regulation 30 of the principal regulations

5. In regulation 30(1) of the principal regulations (earnings of self-employed earners)(**a**) at the end there shall be added "unless at the date of claim the allowance has been terminated".

Amendment of regulation 31 of the principal regulations

6. In regulation 31 of the principal regulations (calculation of net profit of self-employed earners)—

(*a*) for "one half of any qualifying premium payable" in each place where those words occur there shall be substituted "one half of the amount calculated in accordance with paragraph (11A) in respect of any qualifying premium";

(*b*) for paragraph (11) there shall be substituted the following paragraphs—

"(11) In this regulation—

"qualifying premium" means any premium which is payable periodically in respect of a retirement annuity contract or a personal pension scheme and is so payable on or after the date of claim;

"retirement annuity contract" means an annuity contract for the time being approved by the Board of Inland Revenue as having for its main object the provision of a life annuity in old age or the provision of an annuity for a partner or dependant and in respect of which relief from income tax may be given on any premium.

(11A) The amount in respect of any qualifying premium shall be calculated by multiplying the daily amount of the qualifying premium by the number equal to the number of days in the assessment period; and for the purposes of this regulation the daily amount of the qualifying premium shall be determined—

(*a*) where the qualifying premium is payably monthly, by multiplying the amount of the qualifying premium by 12 and dividing the product by 365;

(*b*) in any other case, by dividing the amount of the qualifying premium by the number equal to the number of days in the period to which the qualifying premium relates.".

Amendment of regulation 35 of the principal regulations

7. In regulation 35(7) of the principal regulations (notional income)(**b**) for sub-paragraph (*b*) there shall be substituted the following sub-paragraph—

"(*b*) an amount equivalent to the amount of the primary Class 1 contributions that would be payable by him under the Contributions and Benefits Act in respect of those earnings if such contributions were payable, and".

(**a**) Regulation 30(1) was amended by regulation 5 of S.R. 1993 No. 145 and regulation 3 of S.R. 1993 No. 414

(**b**) Regulation 35(7) was amended by regulation 7 of S.R. 1992 No. 404

Amendment of regulation 55 of the principal regulations

8. In regulation 55(2)(*b*) of the principal regulations (calculation of covenant income where no grant income or no contribution is assessed) at the end there shall be added ''and (2A)''**(a)**.

Amendment of regulation 57 of the principal regulations

9. In regulation 57 of the principal regulations (other amounts to be disregarded)—

(*a*) for ''other than grant income and covenant income'' there shall be substituted ''other than grant income, covenant income and loans treated as income in accordance with regulation 57A''**(b)**;

(*b*) after ''sums disregarded under regulation 53(2)'' there shall be inserted ''or (2A)''.

Amendment of regulation 68 of the principal regulations

10. In regulation 68 of the principal regulations (date on which change of circumstances is to take effect)**(c)**—

(*a*) in paragraph (1) for ''paragraphs (2) to (5)'' there shall be substituted ''paragraphs (2) to (6)'';

(*b*) after paragraph (5) there shall be added the following paragraph—

''(6) Where the change of circumstances is that income, or an increase in the amount of income, other than a benefit or an increase in the amount of a benefit under the Contributions and Benefits Act, is paid in respect of a past period and there was no entitlement to income of that amount during that period, the change of circumstances shall take effect from the first day on which such income, had it been paid in that period at intervals appropriate to that income, would have fallen to be taken into account for the purposes of these regulations.'';

(*c*) paragraph (*b*) shall only apply in the case of a change of circumstances which affects entitlement to housing benefit, or the amount of housing benefit, where entitlement to housing benefit arose pursuant to a claim for that benefit determined on or after 1st April 1994 or, in a case to which regulation 1(1)(*b*)(ii) applies, 4th April 1994.

Amendment of Schedule 4 to the principal regulations

11. In Schedule 4 to the principal regulations (sums to be disregarded in the calculation of income other than earnings)—

(*a*) for paragraph 22(**d**) there shall be substituted the following paragraph—

''22. Where the claimant occupies a dwelling as his home and the dwelling is also occupied by a person other than one to whom

---

(**a**)   Regulation 53(2A) was inserted by regulation 4(*b*) of S.R. 1992 No. 141
(**b**)   Regulation 57A was inserted by regulation 3(9) of S.R. 1990 No. 297
(**c**)   Regulation 68 was amended by regulation 7 of S.R. 1992 No. 141
(**d**)   Paragraph 22 was amended by regulation 4 of S.R. 1992 No. 35

paragraph 21 or 45 refers and there is a contractual liability to make payments to the claimant in respect of the occupation of the dwelling by that person or a member of his family—

   (*a*) £4 of the aggregate of any payments made in respect of any one week in respect of the occupation of the dwelling by that person or a member of his family, or by that person and a member of his family, and

   (*b*) a further £8·60, where the aggregate of any such payments is inclusive of an amount for heating.'';

(*b*) for paragraph 45(**a**) there shall be substituted the following paragraph—

   ''45.—(1) Where the claimant occupies a dwelling as his home and he provides in that dwelling board and lodging accommodation, an amount, in respect of each person for whom such accommodation is provided for the whole or any part of a week, equal to—

   (*a*) where the aggregate of any payments made in respect of any one week in respect of such accommodation provided to such person does not exceed £20·00, 100% of such payments, or

   (*b*) where the aggregate of any such payments exceeds £20·00, £20·00 and 50% of the excess over £20·00.

   (2) In this paragraph ''board and lodging accommodation'' means accommodation provided to a person or, if he is a member of a family, to him or any other member of his family, for a charge which is inclusive of the provision of that accommodation and at least some cooked or prepared meals which both are cooked or prepared (by a person other than the person to whom the accommodation is provided or a member of his family) and are consumed in that accommodation or associated premises.'';

(*c*) after paragraph 54(**b**) there shall be added the following paragraph—

   ''55. Where the claimant is in receipt of any benefit under Parts II, III or V of the Contributions and Benefits Act, any increase in the rate of that benefit arising under Part IV (increases for dependants) or section 106(*a*) (unemployability supplement) of that Act where the dependant in respect of whom the increase is paid is not a member of the claimant's family.''.

Sealed with the Official Seal of the Department of Health and Social Services for Northern Ireland on 11th March 1994.

(L.S.)   *W. G. Purdy*

                         Assistant Secretary

The Department of the Environment for Northern Ireland hereby consents to the foregoing Regulations.

(**a**) Paragraph 45 was added by regulation 12(*c*) of S.R. 1990 No. 136
(**b**) Paragraph 54 was added by regulation 12(*e*) of S.R. 1993 No. 145

Sealed with the Official Seal of the Department of the Environment for Northern Ireland on 11th March 1994.

(L.S.)   *R. E. Aiken*
                                    Assistant Secretary

EXPLANATORY NOTE

(This note is not part of the Regulations.)

These regulations further amend the Housing Benefit (General) Regulations (Northern Ireland) 1987 in the following respects—

(*a*) they provide a definition of "personal pension scheme" and omit the definition of "boarder" (regulation 2);

(*b*) they further specify the amount to be deducted in certain circumstances in respect of national insurance contributions when calculating a person's income (regulations 4 and 7);

(*c*) with respect to the calculation of the earnings of self-employed earners, they amend the provisions for calculating the weekly amount of earnings; they amend the definition of earnings in relation to certain allowances paid to assist a person in carrying on his business; and they provide that a proportion of any premium paid in respect of a personal pension scheme shall be disregarded (regulations 3, 5 and 6);

(*d*) they further define the amount to be disregarded in calculating a student's covenant income and a student's income other than grant income and covenant income (regulations 8 and 9);

(*e*) they make further provision as to the date on which a change of circumstances is to take effect, where the change is in respect of a person's income (regulation 10);

(*f*) with respect to the calculation of income other than earnings they provide a disregard where an increase of a specified benefit is payable in respect of a dependant who is not a member of the claimant's family, and further define the amount to be disregarded in respect of payments made to a claimant where other persons occupy the claimant's home (regulation 11).

1994 No. 89

SOCIAL SECURITY

The Social Security Pensions (Home Responsibilities) Regulations (Northern Ireland) 1994

Made	*11th March 1994*
Coming into operation . .	*6th April 1994*

The Department of Health and Social Services for Northern Ireland, in exercise of the powers conferred on it by sections 21(3) and 171(5) of, and paragraph 5(7)(*b*) of Schedule 3 to, the Social Security Contributions and Benefits (Northern Ireland) Act 1992(**a**) and of all other powers enabling it in that behalf, hereby makes the following regulations:

Citation, commencement and interpretation

1.—(1) These regulations may be cited as the Social Security Pensions (Home Responsibilities) Regulations (Northern Ireland) 1994 and shall come into operation on 6th April 1994.

(2) In these regulations—

"the Act" means the Social Security Contributions and Benefits (Northern Ireland) Act 1992;

"child benefit" means child benefit within the meaning of section 137 of the Act;

"Personal Injuries Scheme", "Pneumoconiosis and Byssinosis Benefit Scheme", "Service Pensions Instrument" and "1914-1918 War Injuries Scheme" have the same meaning as assigned to them in regulation 2 of the Social Security (Overlapping Benefits) Regulations (Northern Ireland) 1979(**b**).

Preclusion from regular employment for the purpose of paragraph 5(7)(b) of Schedule 3 to the Act

2.—(1) For the purpose of paragraph 5(7)(*b*) of Schedule 3 to the Act a person shall, subject to paragraph (5) of this regulation, be taken to be precluded from regular employment by responsibilities at home in any year—

(*a*) throughout which he satisfies any of the conditions specified in paragraph (2) of this regulation;

(*b*) throughout which he satisfies the conditions specified in paragraph (3) of this regulation, or

---

(**a**) 1992 c. 7
(**b**) S.R. 1979 No. 242; relevant amending regulations are S.R. 1980 No. 451

(c) in which he satisfies, for part of the year, any of the conditions specified in paragraph (2) of this regulation and for the remainder of the year, the condition specified in paragraph (3)(a) of this regulation.

(2) The conditions specified in this paragraph are—

(a) that child benefit awarded to him was payable in respect of a child under the age of 16;

(b) that—

    (i) as a person to whom paragraph 4 of Schedule 1 to the Income Support (General) Regulations (Northern Ireland) 1987(**a**) applies he is not required to be available for employment, and

    (ii) income support is payable to him.

(3) The conditions specified in this paragraph are—

(a) that he was regularly engaged, for at least 35 hours per week, in caring for a person in respect of whom there was payable any of the benefits specified in paragraph (4) of this regulation;

(b) that those benefits were payable to that person for at least 48 weeks in that year.

(4) The benefits referred to in paragraph (3) of this regulation are an attendance allowance under section 64 of the Act, the care component of disability living allowance at the highest or middle rate prescribed in accordance with section 72 of the Act, a constant attendance allowance under any Service Pensions Instrument, Personal Injuries Scheme or 1914-1918 War Injuries Scheme, an increase of disablement pension under section 104 of the Act in respect of constant attendance and any benefit corresponding to such an increase under a Pneumoconiosis and Byssinosis Benefit Scheme or under regulations under paragraph 4(2) of Schedule 8 to the Act.

(5) Except where paragraph (6) of this regulation applies, paragraph (1) of this regulation shall not apply in relation to any year—

(a) if the person in question is a woman who has made or is treated as having made an election in accordance with regulations having effect under section 19(4) of the Act and that election had effect at the beginning of that year, or

(b) if the person in question does not furnish such information as the Department may from time to time require which is relevant to the question of whether in that year he was, within the meaning of these regulations, precluded from regular employment by responsibilities at home.

(6) This paragraph applies to a woman who throughout the period beginning on 6th April 1975 and ending on 5th April 1980—

(a) had no earnings in respect of which primary Class 1 contributions were payable, and

(b) was not at any time a self-employed earner.

(**a**) S.R. 1987 No. 459; paragraph 4 of Schedule 1 was substituted by regulation 11 of S.R. 1991 No. 338 and amended by S.R. 1992 No. 6

Revocations

3. The provisions specified in Columns (1) and (2) of the Schedule to these regulations are hereby revoked to the extent specified in Column (3) of that Schedule.

Sealed with the Official Seal of the Department of Health and Social Services for Northern Ireland on 11th March 1994.

(L.S.) *W. G. Purdy*

Assistant Secretary

Column (1)	Column (2)	Column (3)
The Social Security Pensions (Home Responsibilities and Miscellaneous Amendments) Regulations (Northern Ireland) 1978	S.R. 1978 No. 102	Regulations 1(2) and 2
The Social Security Pensions (Home Responsibilities) (Amendment) Regulations (Northern Ireland) 1981	S.R. 1981 No. 71	The whole regulations
The Social Security Pensions (Home Responsibilities) (Amendment) Regulations (Northern Ireland) 1988	S.R. 1988 No. 125	The whole regulations
The Disability Living Allowance and Disability Working Allowance (Consequential Provisions) Regulations (Northern Ireland) 1992	S.R. 1992 No. 6	Regulation 3

EXPLANATORY NOTE

(This note is not part of the Regulations.)

These regulations consolidate, with amendments, provisions contained in the Social Security Pensions (Home Responsibilities and Miscellaneous Amendments) Regulations (Northern Ireland) 1978, ("the 1978 Regulations") relating to the contribution conditions for entitlement to retirement pension applicable to persons who have home responsibilities. The amendments are contained in:

— regulation 2(1)(*b*) and (*c*) which relax the conditions subject to which a person may qualify for home responsibilities protection;

— regulation 2(6) which makes new provision for protection to be afforded to certain married women and widows who, prior to 6th April 1975, had elected to pay Class 1 national insurance contributions at the reduced rate.

The regulations revoke regulations 1(2) and 2 of the 1978 Regulations, the Social Security Pensions (Home Responsibilities) (Amendment) Regulations (Northern Ireland) 1981, the Social Security Pensions (Home Responsibilities) (Amendment) Regulations (Northern Ireland) 1988 and regulation 3 of the Disability Living Allowance and Disability Working Allowance (Consequential Provisions) Regulations (Northern Ireland) 1992.

These regulations make in relation to Northern Ireland only provision corresponding to provision contained in regulations made by the Secretary of State for Social Security in relation to Great Britain and accordingly, by virtue of section 149(3) of, and paragraph 10 of Schedule 5 to, the Social Security Administration (Northern Ireland) Act 1992 (c. 8), are not subject to the requirement of section 149(2) of that Act for prior reference to the Social Security Advisory Committee.

1994   No. 90

PUBLIC HEALTH

Interest on Recoverable Sanitation Expenses Order (Northern Ireland) 1994

Made	*11th March 1994*
Coming into operation . .	*14th April 1994*

The Department of Finance and Personnel(**a**), in exercise of the powers conferred upon it by section 5 of the Public Health and Local Government (Miscellaneous Provisions) Act (Northern Ireland) 1962(**b**), hereby makes the following Order:

1. This Order may be cited as the Interest on Recoverable Sanitation Expenses Order (Northern Ireland) 1994 and shall come into operation on 14th April 1994.

2. The Interest on Recoverable Sanitation Expenses Order (Northern Ireland) 1992(**c**) is hereby revoked.

3. The rate of interest on expenses recoverable under section 255 of the Public Health (Ireland) Act 1878(**d**) shall be 6½ per centum per annum.

Sealed with the Official Seal of the Department of Finance and Personnel on 11th March 1994.

(L.S.)

J. Walker
Assistant Secretary

(**a**) Formerly Department of Finance. *See* S.I. 1982/338 (N.I. 6) Art. 3
(**b**) 1962 c. 12 (N.I.)
(**c**) S.R. 1992 No. 568
(**d**) 1878 c. 52

EXPLANATORY NOTE

(This note is not part of the Order.)

This Order decreases from 9 to 6½ per centum per annum the rate of interest on certain expenses recoverable from owners of premises under the Public Health (Ireland) Act 1878.

1994   No. 91

LAND

Compulsory Acquisition (Interest) Order (Northern Ireland) 1994

Made   .   .   .   .   .   *11th March 1994*

Coming into operation   .   .   *14th April 1994*

The Department of Finance and Personnel(**a**), in exercise of the powers conferred on it by section 12 of the Public Health and Local Government (Miscellaneous Provisions) Act (Northern Ireland) 1955(**b**) and by section 14 of the Administrative and Financial Provisions Act (Northern Ireland) 1956(**c**) and paragraph 18 of Schedule 6 to the Local Government Act (Northern Ireland) 1972(**d**) and of every other power enabling it in that behalf hereby makes the following Order.

1. This Order may be cited as the Compulsory Acquisition (Interest) Order (Northern Ireland) 1994 and shall come into operation on 14th April 1994.

2. The Compulsory Acquisition (Interest) Order (Northern Ireland) 1992(**e**) is hereby revoked.

3. The rate of interest payable by virtue of section 22 of the Local Government Act (Northern Ireland) 1934(**f**), paragraph 22 of Schedule 5 to the Roads Act (Northern Ireland) 1948(**g**) or paragraph 18 of Schedule 6 to the Local Government Act (Northern Ireland) 1972 on compensation money in respect of land compulsorily acquired shall, in respect of any period after the coming into operation of this Order, be $6\frac{1}{2}$ per centum per annum.

Sealed with the Official Seal of the Department of Finance and Personnel on 11th March 1994.

(L.S.)   *J. Walker*

                                Assistant Secretary

(**a**)   Formerly Department of Finance. *See* S.I. 1982/338 (N.I. 6) Art. 3

(**b**)   1955 c. 13 (N.I.) as saved by 1972 c. 9 (N.I.) s. 149(3)

(**c**)   1956 c. 17 (N.I.)

(**d**)   1972 c. 9 (N.I.)

(**e**)   S.R. 1992 No. 567

(**f**)   1934 c. 22 (N.I.) as saved by 1972 c. 9 (N.I.) s. 149(3)

(**g**)   1948 c. 28 (N.I.) as amended by 1956 c. 17 (N.I.) Sch. 1 and as saved by S.I. 1980/1085 (N.I. 11) Art. 64(1) and Sch. 7 para. 6

EXPLANATORY NOTE

(This note is not part of the Order.)

This Order decreases from 9 to 6½ per centum per annum the rate of interest on compensation money payable under the enactments mentioned in this Order in respect of land which has been compulsorily acquired.

1994 No. 92

SOCIAL SECURITY

The Social Security (Categorisation of Earners) (Amendment) Regulations (Northern Ireland) 1994

Made	*14th March 1994*
Coming into operation . .	*6th April 1994*

The Department of Health and Social Services for Northern Ireland, in exercise of the powers conferred on it by sections 2(2) and 7(2) of the Social Security Contributions and Benefits (Northern Ireland) Act 1992(**a**) and of all other powers enabling it in that behalf, hereby makes the following regulations:

Citation, commencement and interpretation

1.—(1) These regulations may be cited as the Social Security (Categorisation of Earners) (Amendment) Regulations (Northern Ireland) 1994 and shall come into operation on 6th April 1994.

(2) In these regulations "the principal regulations" means the Social Security (Categorisation of Earners) Regulations (Northern Ireland) 1978(**b**).

Amendment of regulation 1 of the principal regulations

2. In regulation 1(2) of the principal regulations (interpretation) after the definition of "educational establishment" there shall be inserted the following definitions—

" "foreign employer" in paragraph 7(**c**) of Schedule 3 to these regulations means a person—

(*a*) who does not fulfil the conditions as to residence or presence in Northern Ireland prescribed under section 1(6)(*a*) of the Social Security Contributions and Benefits (Northern Ireland) Act 1992(**d**); and

(*b*) who, if he did fulfil the conditions as to residence or presence in Northern Ireland referred to in paragraph (*a*) of this definition, would be the secondary contributor in relation to any payment of earnings to, or for the benefit of, the person employed;

(**a**) 1992 c. 7
(**b**) S.R. 1978 No. 401; relevant amending regulations are S.R. 1980 No. 405 and S.R. 1984 No. 81
(**c**) Paragraph 7 is added by regulation 4 of these regulations
(**d**) *See* regulation 111 of S.R. 1979 No. 186; relevant amending regulations are S.R. 1992 No. 41

"host employer" in paragraph 7 of Schedule 3 to these regulations means a person having a place of business in Northern Ireland;".

Amendment of Schedule 1 to the principal regulations

3. In Part III of Schedule 1 to the principal regulations (employments which are to be disregarded) after paragraph 12(**a**) there shall be added the following paragraphs—

(*a*) in column (A)—

"13. Employment (other than employment described in paragraph 12 of column (A) of this Schedule) as a Queen's Gurkha officer or as any other member of the Brigade of Gurkhas of a person who was recruited for that Brigade in Nepal.";

(*b*) in column (B)—

"13. None.".

Amendment of Schedule 3 to the principal regulations

4. In Schedule 3 to the principal regulations (employments in respect of which persons are treated as secondary Class 1 contributors) after paragraph 6 there shall be added the following paragraphs—

(*a*) in column (A)—

"7. Employment by a foreign employer where—

(*a*) in pursuance of that employment the personal service of the person employed is made available to a host employer; and

(*b*) the personal service is rendered for the purposes of the business of that host employer; and

(*c*) that personal service for the host employer begins on or after 6th April 1994.";

(*b*) in column (B)—

"7. The host employer to whom the personal service of the person employed is made available.".

Sealed with the Official Seal of the Department of Health and Social Services for Northern Ireland on 14th March 1994.

(L.S.) *W. G. Purdy*

Assistant Secretary

(a) Paragraph 12 was inserted by S.R. 1980 No. 405 and amended by S.R. 1984 No. 81

EXPLANATORY NOTE

(This note is not part of the Regulations.)

These regulations further amend the Social Security (Categorisation of Earners) Regulations (Northern Ireland) 1978 ("the principal regulations").

Regulation 2 amends regulation 1 of the principal regulations by inserting definitions of "foreign employer" and "host employer".

Regulation 3 amends Part III of Schedule 1 to the principal regulations by extending the description of employments to be disregarded in relation to liability for contributions to members of the Brigade of Gurkhas recruited in Nepal.

Regulation 4 amends Schedule 3 to the principal regulations by extending the description of employments in respect of which persons are treated as secondary Class 1 contributors to workers seconded, on or after 6th April 1994, by foreign employers to employers in Northern Ireland.

These regulations make in relation to Northern Ireland only provision corresponding to provision contained in regulations made by the Secretary of State for Social Security in relation to Great Britain and accordingly, by virtue of section 149(3) of, and paragraph 10 of Schedule 5 to, the Social Security Administration (Northern Ireland) Act 1992 (c. 8), are not subject to the requirement of section 149(2) of that Act for prior reference to the Social Security Advisory Committee.

1994 No. 93

Road Races (Circuit of Ireland Rally) Order (Northern Ireland) 1994

This Order, being of a temporary character, is not printed at length in this volume.

1994 No. 94

SOCIAL SECURITY

The Social Security (Contributions) (Miscellaneous Amendments) Regulations (Northern Ireland) 1994

Made	*11th March 1994*
Coming into operation . .	*6th April 1994*

The Department of Health and Social Services for Northern Ireland, in exercise of the powers conferred on it by section 10(7) and (9) of, and paragraph 6(1) of Schedule 1 to, the Social Security Contributions and Benefits (Northern Ireland) Act 1992(**a**) and of all other powers enabling it in that behalf, and with the concurrence of the Inland Revenue in so far as their concurrence is required, hereby makes the following regulations:

Citation, commencement and interpretation

1.—(1) These regulations may be cited as the Social Security (Contributions) (Miscellaneous Amendments) Regulations (Northern Ireland) 1994 and shall come into operation on 6th April 1994.

(2) In these regulations "the principal regulations" means the Social Security (Contributions) Regulations (Northern Ireland) 1979(**b**).

Amendment of regulations 22C, 22D and 22F of the principal regulations

2.—(1) Regulations 22C, 22D and 22F of the principal regulations(**c**) (Class 1A contributions in respect of certain cars and certain earners) shall be amended in accordance with paragraphs (2) and (3) of this regulation.

(2) In regulation 22C (Class 1A contributions payable where two or more cars are made available concurrently)—

(*a*) for paragraph (1) there shall be substituted the following paragraph—

"(1) This regulation applies where the amount of any Class 1A contribution payable for any year does not reflect a reduction in the cash equivalent of the benefit of the car as provided for by paragraph 2 of Schedule 6 to the 1988 Act(**d**), because of the application of paragraph 4 of that Schedule (modified reduction in cash equivalent where two or more cars are made available concurrently).";

(*b*) in paragraph (2) for the words from "shall be so reduced" to "paragraph 5(3)" there shall be substituted "shall be equal to the amount which would have been payable if paragraph 4".

(**a**) 1992 c. 7
(**b**) S.R. 1979 No. 186; relevant amending regulations are S.R. 1981 No. 30, S.R. 1983 No. 64, S.R. 1985 No. 59, S.R. 1987 No. 143, S.R. 1990 No. 110, S.R. 1992 Nos. 126 and 280.
(**c**) Regulations 22A to 22G were inserted by regulation 2 of S.R. 1992 No. 126.
(**d**) Schedule 6 was substituted by paragraph 5 of Schedule 3 to the Finance Act 1993 (c. 34)

(3) In regulations 22D(3) and 22F(3)—

(a) for "paragraph 2(2)" there shall be substituted "paragraph 9";

(b) for "paragraph 3(2) of Schedule 6" there shall be substituted "paragraph 3(*a*) of Schedule 6";

(c) for "the said paragraph 3(2))" there shall be substituted "the said paragraph 3(*a*) of Schedule 6)";

(d) for "paragraphs 5(2) and 3(2) of Schedule 6" there shall be substituted "paragraphs 3(*b*) and 3(*a*) of Schedule 6";

(e) for "the said paragraphs 5(2) and 3(2))" there shall be substituted "the said paragraphs 3(*b*) and 3(*a*) of Schedule 6)";

in each place where they occur.

Amendment of Regulation 30 of Schedule 1 to the principal regulations

3. In Regulation 30(1)(*i*) of Schedule 1 to the principal regulations(**a**) (return by employer at end of year) the words from "and separately from" to the end of the sub-paragraph shall be omitted.

Amendment of section 10 of the Social Security Contributions and Benefits Act

4.—(1) In section 10(6) of the Social Security Contributions and Benefits (Northern Ireland) Act 1992(**b**) (Class 1A contributions)—

(a) for paragraphs (a) and (b) there shall be substituted the following paragraphs—

"(a) the car shall not be treated as being unavailable on a day by virtue of paragraph 9(*c*) of Schedule 6 to the Income and Corporation Taxes Act 1988 for the purposes of section 158(5) of that Act(**c**) or paragraph 3 or 6 of that Schedule, unless the person liable to pay the contribution has information to show that the condition specified in paragraph 9(*c*) is satisfied as regards that day;

(b) the use of the car for the earner's business travel shall be taken—

(i) for the purposes of sub-paragraph (1) of paragraph 2 of that Schedule to have amounted to less than 18,000 miles (or such lower figure as is applicable by virtue of sub-paragraph (*a*) of paragraph 3 of that Schedule); and

(ii) for the purposes of sub-paragraph (2) of paragraph 2 of that Schedule to have amounted to less than 2,500 miles (or such lower figure as is applicable by virtue of sub-paragraph (*b*) of paragraph 3 of that Schedule),

unless in either case the person liable to pay the contribution has information to show to the contrary; and";

(**a**) Paragraph (1) was substituted by regulation 2(7)(*a*) of S.R. 1981 No. 30, and amended by S.R. 1983 No. 64, S.R. 1985 No. 59, S.R. 1987 No. 143, S.R. 1990 No. 110 and S.R. 1992 No. 280, regulation 3(11) of which substituted sub-paragraphs (*g*) to (*i*)
(**b**) Relevant amending regulations are S.R. 1993 No. 437
(**c**) Section 158(5) was amended by paragraph 6(2) of Schedule 3 to the Finance Act 1993.

(*b*) in paragraph (*c*) for "paragraph 5(3)" there shall be substituted "paragraph 4".

(2) This regulation shall have effect for 1994-95 and for subsequent tax years.

Sealed with the Official Seal of the Department of Health and Social Services for Northern Ireland on 11th March 1994.

(L.S.) *W. G. Purdy*

Assistant Secretary

The Commissioners of Inland Revenue hereby concur.

L. J. H. Beighton
C. W. Corlett
14th March 1994 Two of the Commissioners of
Inland Revenue

EXPLANATORY NOTE

(This note is not part of the Regulations.)

These regulations further amend section 10(6) of the Social Security Contributions and Benefits (Northern Ireland) Act 1992 ("the Act") and the Social Security (Contributions) Regulations (Northern Ireland) 1979 ("the principal regulations").

Regulation 4 amends section 10(6) of the Act to give effect to the changes made to Schedule 6 to the Income and Corporation Taxes Act 1988 (c. 1) by section 72 of, and Schedule 3 to, the Finance Act 1993. The amendments to section 10(6) of the Act reflect those amendments and relate to the calculation of the cash equivalent of a car or fuel for the purposes of Class 1A contributions where cars or fuel are provided for private motoring to directors and certain employees. The amendments concern availability of the car in question and the use of the car for business travel.

Regulation 2 makes amendments to regulations 22C, 22D and 22F of the principal regulations consequential upon the amendments made to section 10(6) of the Act.

Regulation 3 amends Regulation 30(1) of Schedule 1 to the principal regulations so that on succession to, or cessation of, a business an employer need not record Class 1A contributions separately from the previous year's Class 1A contributions when completing annual returns.

These regulations make in relation to Northern Ireland only provision corresponding to provision contained in regulations made by the Secretary of State for Social Security in relation to Great Britain and accordingly, by virtue of section 149(3) of, and paragraph 10 of Schedule 5 to, the Social Security Administration (Northern Ireland) Act 1992 (c. 8), are not subject to the requirement of section 149(2) of that Act for prior reference to the Social Security Advisory Committee.

1994   No. 95

HEALTH AND PERSONAL SOCIAL SERVICES

Dental Charges (Amendment) Regulations (Northern Ireland) 1994

Made	*16th March 1994*
Coming into operation . .	*1st April 1994*

The Department of Health and Social Services, in exercise of the powers conferred on it by Articles 98 and 106 of, and Schedule 15 to, the Health and Personal Social Services (Northern Ireland) Order 1972(**a**) and of all other powers enabling it in that behalf, with the approval of the Department of Finance and Personnel, hereby makes the following regulations:

Citation, commencement and interpretation

1.—(1) These regulations may be cited as the Dental Charges (Amendment) Regulations (Northern Ireland) 1994 and shall come into operation on 1st April 1994.

(2) In these regulations, "the principal regulations" means the Dental Charges Regulations (Northern Ireland) 1989(**b**).

Amendment of regulation 4 of the principal regulations

2. In regulation 4(5) of the principal regulations (calculation of charges) for "£250·00" there shall be substituted "£275·00".

Revocation

3. Regulation 2(*c*) of the Health and Personal Social Services Dental Charges (Amendment) Regulations (Northern Ireland) 1993(**c**) is hereby revoked.

Application of regulations

4. The amendment made by regulation 2 applies only in relation to a contract or arrangement for the provision of general dental services made on or after 1st April 1994.

(**a**) S.I. 1972/1265 (N.I. 14), as amended by S.I. 1986/2229 (N.I. 24) Article 14, S.I. 1988/2249 (N.I. 24) Article 7 and S.I. 1991/194 (N.I. 1) Article 34 and Part II of Schedule 5; there are other amendments which are not relevant
(**b**) S.R. 1989 No. 111, as amended by S.R. 1991 No. 130 and S.R. 1993 No. 139
(**c**) S.R. 1993 No. 139

Sealed with the Official Seal of the Department of Health and Social Services on 16th March 1994.

(L.S.)   *Joan Dixon*
                                          Assistant Secretary

The Department of Finance and Personnel hereby approves the foregoing Regulations.

Sealed with the Official Seal of the Department of Finance and Personnel on 16th March 1994.

(L.S.)   *David Thomson*
                                          Assistant Secretary

––––––––––

EXPLANATORY NOTE

(This note is not part of the Regulations.)

These Regulations further amend the Dental Charges Regulations (Northern Ireland) 1989 ("the principal regulations") which relate to charges for dental treatment provided and dental appliances supplied as part of health service general dental services.

Regulation 2 amends regulation 4(5) of the principal regulations to increase from £250 to £275 the maximum charge which a patient may be required to pay towards the cost of his treatment or appliance under general dental services.

Regulation 4 provides that these new charges shall apply only where the arrangement for treatment or supply of a dental appliance is made on or after 1st April 1994.

1994 No. 96

LEGAL AID AND ADVICE

Legal Advice and Assistance (Financial Conditions) Regulations (Northern Ireland) 1994

Made	*16th March 1994*
Coming into operation . .	*11th April 1994*
To be laid before Parliament	

The Lord Chancellor, in exercise of the powers conferred by Articles 3(2), 7(3), 22 and 27 of the Legal Aid, Advice and Assistance (Northern Ireland) Order 1981(**a**) and now vested in him(**b**), hereby makes the following Regulations:—

Citation, commencement and interpretation

1.—(1) These Regulations may be cited as the Legal Advice and Assistance (Financial Conditions) Regulations (Northern Ireland) 1994 and shall come into operation on 11th April 1994.

(2) In these Regulations, "the Order" means the Legal Aid, Advice and Assistance (Northern Ireland) Order 1981.

Revocation

2. The Legal Advice and Assistance (Financial Conditions) Regulations (Northern Ireland) 1993(**c**) are hereby revoked.

Persons eligible for advice and assistance

3. For the weekly sum of £147 specified in Article 3(1) of the Order(**d**) there shall be substituted the weekly sum of £153.

Contributions from persons receiving advice and assistance

4. For the weekly sum of £61 specified in Article 7(2) of the Order(**e**) there shall be substituted the weekly sum of £63.

Dated 16th March 1994   *Mackay of Clashfern*, C.

(**a**) S.I. 1981/228 (N.I. 8); Article 27 is an interpretation provision and is recited because of the meaning assigned to the words "prescribed" and "regulations"
(**b**) S.I. 1982/159
(**c**) S.R. 1993 No. 123
(**d**) Which figure was most recently substituted by S.R. 1993 No. 123
(**e**) Which figure was most recently substituted by S.R. 1993 No. 123

EXPLANATORY NOTE

(This note is not part of the Regulations.)

These Regulations amend the Legal Aid, Advice and Assistance (Northern Ireland) Order 1981 so as to:

(*a*) increase the upper income limit to make legal advice and assistance available to those with disposable income of not more than £153 a week (instead of £147) (Regulation 3);

(*b*) increase the lower income limit below which legal advice and assistance is available without payment of a contribution to £63 a week (instead of £61) (Regulation 4).

No changes are made to the capital limits.

1994   No.   97

LEGAL AID AND ADVICE

Legal Aid (Financial Conditions) Regulations (Northern Ireland) 1994

Made	*16th March 1994*
Coming into operation . .	*11th April 1994*

To be laid before Parliament

The Lord Chancellor, in exercise of the powers conferred by Articles 9(2), 12(2), 22 and 27 of the Legal Aid, Advice and Assistance (Northern Ireland) Order 1981(**a**) and now vested in him(**b**), hereby makes the following Regulations:—

Citation, commencement and interpretation

1.—(1) These Regulations may be cited as the Legal Aid (Financial Conditions) Regulations (Northern Ireland) 1994 and shall come into operation on 11th April 1994.

(2) In these Regulations—

(*a*) "the Order" means the Legal Aid, Advice and Assistance (Northern Ireland) Order 1981;

(*b*) "personal injuries" includes any death and any disease or other impairment of a person's physical or mental condition.

Saving and revocation

2.—(1) These Regulations shall apply to any application for legal aid where the period of computation, as defined in Regulation 1(2) of the Legal Aid (Assessment of Resources) Regulations (Northern Ireland) 1981(**c**), begins on or after 11th April 1994.

(2) Regulation 3(1) of the Legal Aid (Financial Conditions) Regulations (Northern Ireland) 1992(**d**) and Regulation 4(1) of the Legal Aid (Financial Conditions) Regulations (Northern Ireland) 1993(**e**) are hereby revoked save in their application to any case to which paragraph (1) does not apply.

(**a**) S.I. 1981/228 (N.I. 8); Article 27 is an interpretation provision and is recited because of the meaning assigned to the words "prescribed" and "regulations"
(**b**) S.I. 1982/159
(**c**) S.R. 1981 No. 189; to which there are amendments not relevant to these Regulations
(**d**) S.R. 1992 No. 107
(**e**) S.R. 1993 No. 121

Persons eligible for legal aid

3.—(1) For the yearly sums specified in Article 9(1) of the Order(**a**) there shall be substituted—

(*a*) where legal aid is sought in connection with taking, defending or being a party to proceedings which include a claim in respect of personal injuries, for the yearly sum of ''£7,500'', the yearly sum of ''£7,780''; and

(*b*) in any other case, for the yearly sum of ''£6,800'' the yearly sum of ''£7,060''.

Contributions from persons receiving legal aid

4. For the yearly sum of ''£2,294'' specified in Article 12(1)(*a*) of the Order(**b**) there shall be substituted the yearly sum of ''£2,382''.

Dated 16th March 1994   *Mackay of Clashfern*, C.

(**a**)   Which figure was most recently substituted by S.R. 1992 No. 107
(**b**)   Which figure was most recently substituted by S.R. 1993 No. 121

EXPLANATORY NOTE

(This note is not part of the Regulations.)

These Regulations amend the Legal Aid, Advice and Assistance (Northern Ireland) Order 1981 so as to:

(*a*) increase the upper income limit to make legal aid available to those with disposable incomes of not more than £7,060 (instead of £6,800), or in connection with proceedings involving a personal injury £7,780 (instead of £7,500);

(*b*) increase the lower income limit below which legal aid is available without payment of a contribution to £2,382 (instead of £2,294).

No changes are made to the capital limits.

1994 No. 98

LEGAL AID AND ADVICE

Legal Advice and Assistance (Amendment) Regulations (Northern Ireland) 1994

Made	*16th March 1994*
Coming into operation . .	*11th April 1994*
To be laid before Parliament	

The Lord Chancellor, in exercise of the powers conferred by Articles 7(2), 22 and 27 of the Legal Aid, Advice and Assistance (Northern Ireland) Order 1981(**a**) and now vested in him(**b**), hereby makes the following Regulations:—

Citation and commencement

1. These Regulations may be cited as the Legal Advice and Assistance (Amendment) Regulations (Northern Ireland) 1994 and shall come into operation on 11th April 1994.

Revocation

2. Regulation 5 of the Legal Advice and Assistance (Amendment) Regulations (Northern Ireland) 1993(**c**) is hereby revoked.

Amendment to Schedule 2

3. For the table set out in Schedule 2 to the Legal Advice and Assistance Regulations (Northern Ireland) 1981(**d**), there shall be substituted the following table—
"

Disposable Income Range	*Maximum Contribution*
Exceeding £63 but not exceeding £70 a week	£7
Exceeding £70 but not exceeding £77 a week	£14
Exceeding £77 but not exceeding £84 a week	£21
Exceeding £84 but not exceeding £91 a week	£28
Exceeding £91 but not exceeding £98 a week	£35

(**a**) S.I. 1981/228'(N.I. 8); Article 27 is an interpretation provision and is recited because of the meaning assigned to the words "prescribed" and "regulations"
(**b**) S.I. 1982/159
(**c**) S.R. 1993 No. 124
(**d**) S.R. 1981 No. 366; to which the most recent relevant amendment was made by S.R. 1993 No. 124

Exceeding £98 but not exceeding £105 a week	£42
Exceeding £105 but not exceeding £112 a week	£49
Exceeding £112 but not exceeding £119 a week	£56
Exceeding £119 but not exceeding £126 a week	£63
Exceeding £126 but not exceeding £133 a week	£70
Exceeding £133 but not exceeding £140 a week	£77
Exceeding £140 but not exceeding £153 a week	£90

,,

Dated 16th March 1994   *Mackay of Clashfern*, C.

EXPLANATORY NOTE

(This note is not part of the Regulations.)

These Regulations amend the Legal Advice and Assistance Regulations (Northern Ireland) 1981 so as to substitute a new scale of contributions payable for legal advice and assistance under Article 7(2) of the Legal Aid, Advice and Assistance (Northern Ireland) Order 1981.

1994 No. 99

PENSIONS

Pensions Increase (Review) Order (Northern Ireland) 1994

Made	.	.	.	.	*16th March 1994*
Coming into operation		.	.		*11th April 1994*

Whereas by virtue of section 132 of the Social Security Administration (Northern Ireland) Act 1992(**a**) a direction(**b**) has been given by the Department of Health and Social Services that the sums which are the additional pensions in the rate of long-term benefits are to be increased by a specified percentage;

Now, therefore the Department of Finance and Personnel, in exercise of the powers conferred by Article 69(1), (2), (5) and (5ZA) of the Social Security Pensions (Northern Ireland) Order 1975(**c**) (which has effect as if it were contained in Part I of the Pensions (Increase) Act (Northern Ireland) 1971(**d**) and now vested in it(**e**) and of every other power enabling it in that behalf, hereby makes the following Order:

Citation and commencement

1. This Order may be cited as the Pensions Increase (Review) Order (Northern Ireland) 1994 and shall come into operation on 11th April 1994.

Interpretation

2.—(1) In this Order—

"the Act of 1971" means the Pensions (Increase) Act (Northern Ireland) 1971;

"basic rate" and "derivative pension" have the meanings given by section 15(1)(**f**) of the Act of 1971;

(**a**) 1992 c. 8
(**b**) Contained in S.R. 1994 No. 74
(**c**) S.I. 1975/1503 (N.I. 15); Art. 69 of S.I. 1975/1503 (N.I. 15) amended the Pensions (Increase) Act (Northern Ireland) 1971 (1971 c. 35 (N.I.)). Art. 69(5) was modified in its effect by Art. 69A (inserted by Art. 10(3) of the Social Security (Northern Ireland) Order 1979 (S.I. 1979/396 (N.I. 5)). Art. 69 was further amended by S.I. 1979/396 (N.I. 5) Arts. 10(2), 16 and Sch. 3, S.I. 1985/1209 (N.I. 16) Art. 25(2) and Sch. 6, S.I. 1986/1888 (N.I. 18), Arts. 11(8), 19(1)(*b*), 83(1) and Sch. 9, para. 58, S.I. 1990/1509 (N.I. 13) Arts. 3(7) and 7, by section 4 of and paragraph 14(19) of Schedule 2 to the Social Security (Consequential Provisions) (Northern Ireland) Act 1992 (1992 c. 9) and by section 184 of and paragraph 15(1) of Schedule 7 to the Pension Schemes (Northern Ireland) Act 1993 (1993 c. 49). Article 69A was amended by S.I. 1986/1888 (N.I. 18) Art. 11(9) and by section 184 of and paragraph 15(2) of Schedule 7 to the Pension Schemes (Northern Ireland) Act 1993
(**d**) 1971 c. 35 (N.I.)
(**e**) By S.R. 1976 No. 281 Art. 3 and Sch. 1 and S.I. 1982/338 (N.I. 6) Art. 4
(**f**) As amended by S.I. 1974/1267 (N.I. 2) Arts. 3(3) and 5(3)(*b*) and S.I. 1990/1509 (N.I. 13) Art. 3(6)

"existing Orders" means the Orders referred to in the Schedule;

"official pension" has the meaning given by section 5(1) of the Act of 1971;

"the Order of 1975" means the Social Security Pensions (Northern Ireland) Order 1975;

"pension authority" has the meaning given by section 7(1) of the Act of 1971;

"qualifying condition" means one of the conditions laid down in section 3 of the Act of 1971(**a**);

"relevant injury pension", "substituted pension" and "widow's pension" have the meanings given by section 15(1) of the Act of 1971.

(2) For the purpose of this Order the time when a pension "begins" is that stated in section 8(2) of the Act of 1971(**b**).

(3) Where, for the purposes of this Order, it is necessary to calculate the number of complete months in any period an incomplete month shall be treated as a complete month if it consists of at least 16 days.

Increases in certain pensions

3.—(1) The annual rate of an official pension may, if a qualifying condition is satisfied or the pension is a derivative or substituted pension or a relevant injury pension, be increased as set out in paragraphs (2) and (3) by the pension authority in respect of any period beginning on or after 11th April 1994.

(2) A pension beginning before 12th April 1993 may be increased by 1·8 per cent of the basic rate as increased by the amount of any increase under section 1 of the Act of 1971 or the existing Orders.

(3) A pension beginning on or after 12th April 1993 and before 11th April 1994 may be increased by 1·8 per cent multiplied by $\dfrac{A}{B}$

where A is the number of complete months in the period between the beginning of the pension and 10th April 1994 and B is 12.

Increase in certain lump sums

4. In respect of any lump sum or instalment of a lump sum which became payable before 11th April 1994 but after 11th April 1993 there may be paid an increase of 1·8 per cent of the amount of the lump sum or instalment (as increased by the amount of any increase under section 1 of the Act of 1971 or under the existing Orders) multiplied by

$\dfrac{A}{B}$ where:

(**a**) As amended by S.R. & O. (N.I.) 1972 No. 264, S.I. 1974/1267 (N.I. 2) Art. 5(2) and (3), S.I. 1987/2203 (N.I. 22) Art. 72(3) and Sch. 5 Part I and S.I. 1990/1509 (N.I. 13) Art. 3
(**b**) As amended by S.I. 1990/1509 (N.I. 13) Art. 3(5)

(*a*) A is the number of complete months in the period between the beginning date for the lump sum (or, if later, 12th April 1993) and the date on which it became payable; and

(*b*) B is 12.

Reduction in respect of guaranteed minimum pensions

5. Where—

(i) a person is entitled to a guaranteed minimum pension on 11th April 1994; and

(ii) entitlement to that guaranteed minimum pension arises from an employment from which (either directly or by virtue of the payment of a transfer credit) entitlement to the official pension also arises;

the amount by reference to which any increase in the rate of an official pension provided for by this Order is to be calculated shall be reduced by an amount equal to the rate of the guaranteed minimum pension unless the Department of Finance and Personnel(**a**) in accordance with the provisions of Article 69A(**b**) of the Order of 1975, otherwise directs.

6. The amount by reference to which any increase in the rate of a widow's or widower's pension provided for by this Order is to be calculated shall, where the pensioner becomes entitled on the death of the deceased spouse to a guaranteed minimum pension, be reduced in accordance with Article 69(5ZA)(**c**) of the Order of 1975.

Sealed with the Official Seal of the Department of Finance and Personnel on 16th March 1994.

(L.S.) *J. Walker*

Assistant Secretary

(**a**) *See* S.I. 1982/338 (N.I. 6) Art. 4
(**b**) Inserted by S.I. 1979/396 (N.I. 5) Art. 10(3)
(**c**) Inserted by S.I. 1990/1509 (N.I. 13) Art. 7(1)

SCHEDULE

Existing Orders

The Pensions Increase (Annual Review) Order (Northern Ireland) 1972(**a**).
The Pensions Increase (Annual Review) Order (Northern Ireland) 1973(**b**).
The Pensions Increase (Annual Review) Order (Northern Ireland) 1974(**c**).
The Pensions Increase (Annual Review) Order (Northern Ireland) 1975(**d**).
The Pensions Increase (Annual Review) Order (Northern Ireland) 1976(**e**).
The Pensions Increase (Annual Review) Order (Northern Ireland) 1977(**f**).
The Pensions Increase (Annual Review) Order (Northern Ireland) 1978(**g**).
The Pensions Increase (Review) Order (Northern Ireland) 1979(**h**).
The Pensions Increase (Review) Order (Northern Ireland) 1980(**i**).
The Pensions Increase (Review) Order (Northern Ireland) 1981(**j**).
The Pensions Increase (Review) Order (Northern Ireland) 1982(**k**).
The Pensions Increase (Review) Order (Northern Ireland) 1983(**l**).
The Pensions Increase (Review) Order (Northern Ireland) 1984(**m**).
The Pensions Increase (Review) Order (Northern Ireland) 1985(**n**).
The Pensions Increase (Review) Order (Northern Ireland) 1986(**o**).
The Pensions Increase (Review) Order (Northern Ireland) 1987(**p**).
The Pensions Increase (Review) Order (Northern Ireland) 1988(**q**).
The Pensions Increase (Review) Order (Northern Ireland) 1989(**r**).
The Pensions Increase (Review) Order (Northern Ireland) 1990(**s**).
The Pensions Increase (Review) Order (Northern Ireland) 1991(**t**).
The Pensions Increase (Review) Order (Northern Ireland) 1992(**u**).
The Pensions Increase (Review) Order (Northern Ireland) 1993(**v**).

(**a**) S.R. & O. (N.I.) 1972 No. 263
(**b**) S.R. & O. (N.I.) 1973 No. 364
(**c**) S.R. 1974 No. 296
(**d**) S.R. 1975 No. 269
(**e**) S.R. 1976 No. 276
(**f**) S.R. 1977 No. 277
(**g**) S.R. 1978 No. 269
(**h**) S.R. 1979 No. 338
(**i**) S.R. 1980 No. 364
(**j**) S.R. 1981 No. 307
(**k**) S.R. 1982 No. 303
(**l**) S.R. 1983 No. 289
(**m**) S.R. 1984 No. 340
(**n**) S.R. 1985 No. 268
(**o**) S.R. 1986 No. 213
(**p**) S.R. 1987 No. 70
(**q**) S.R. 1988 No. 61
(**r**) S.R. 1989 No. 72
(**s**) S.R. 1990 No. 86
(**t**) S.R. 1991 No. 84
(**u**) S.R. 1992 No. 69
(**v**) S.R. 1993 No. 125

EXPLANATORY NOTE

(This note is not part of the Order.)

Under Article 69 of the Social Security Pensions (Northern Ireland) Order 1975 as amended, and as modified by Article 69A of the Order of 1975, the Department of Finance and Personnel is required to provide by Order for increases in the rates of public service pensions.

The increase to be made in the rates of such pensions is the percentage (or in some circumstances a fraction of the percentage) by which the Department of Health and Social Services has, by virtue of the provisions of section 132 of the Social Security Administration (Northern Ireland) Act 1992, increased the sums which are the additional pensions in long term benefits, namely the additional pension entitlements accruing to employees in respect of their earnings after 5th April 1978.

For pensions which began before 12th April 1993 the increase is 1·8%.

For pensions which began on or after 12th April 1993 the increases are computed under the formula set out in Article 69(1)(*b*) of the Order of 1975 and are as follows:

Pensions Beginning	*Percentage Increase*	*Pensions Beginning*	*Percentage Increase*
12th April 1993 to 26th April 1993	1·8%	27th November 1993 to 26th December 1993	0·6%
27th April 1993 to 26th June 1993	1·65%	27th December 1993 to 26th January 1994	0·45%
27th May 1993 to 26th June 1993	1·5%	27th January 1994 to 26th February 1994	0·3%
27th June 1993 to 26th July 1993	1·35%	27th February 1994 to 26th March 1994	0·15%
27th July 1993 to 26th August 1993	1·2%	27th March 1994 onwards	Nil
26th August 1993 to 26th September 1993	1·05%		
27th September 1993 to 26th October 1993	0·9%		
27th October 1993 to 26th November 1993	0·75%		

A deferred lump sum which begins on or before 26th March 1994 and which becomes payable after 10th April 1994 receives the same percentage increase as a pension which begins on the same date.

Article 4 of the Order provides for increases on certain deferred lump sums which became payable after 11th April 1993 and before 11th April 1994.

This Order also provides that the amount by reference to which any increase in the rate of an official pension is to be calculated shall be reduced by an amount equal to the rate of the guaranteed minimum pension entitlement deriving from the employment which gives rise to the official pension. This is required by Article 69(5) of the Social Security Pensions (Northern Ireland) Order 1975 but Article 69A of that Order empowers the Department of Finance and Personnel to direct that in respect of specified cases or classes of case either no such reduction shall be made or the reduction shall be less than the rate of the guaranteed minimum pension. Article 69(5ZA) was inserted into Article 69 by Article 7 of the Pensions (Miscellaneous Provisions) (Northern Ireland) Order 1990. This applies Article 69(5) to a widow's or widower's pension.

1994   No. 100

HEALTH AND PERSONAL SOCIAL SERVICES

Optical Charges and Payments (Amendment No. 2) Regulations (Northern Ireland) 1994

Made	*18th March 1994*
Coming into operation . .	*1st April 1994*

The Department of Health and Social Services, in exercise of the powers conferred on it by Articles 98 and 106 of, and Schedule 15 to, the Health and Personal Social Services (Northern Ireland) Order 1972(**a**) and of all other powers enabling it in that behalf, with the approval of the Department of Finance and Personnel, hereby makes the following regulations:

Citation, commencement and interpretation

1.—(1) These regulations may be cited as the Optical Charges and Payments (Amendment No. 2) Regulations (Northern Ireland) 1994 and shall come into operation on 1st April 1994.

(2) In these regulations, "the principal regulations" means the Optical Charges and Payments Regulations (Northern Ireland) 1989(**b**).

Amendment of regulation 2 of the principal regulations

2. In regulation 2 of the principal regulations (charges for optical appliances supplied by a Board)—

(*a*) in paragraph (3) for "£36·90" there shall be substituted "£37·80"; and

(*b*) in paragraph (5)(*b*) for "£44·60" and "£72·50" in both places where they occur there shall be substituted "£46·40" and "£75·40" respectively.

Amendment of regulation 20 of the principal regulations

3. In regulation 20 of the principal regulations (redemption value of voucher for replacement or repair)—

(*a*) in paragraph (1)(*b*) for "£36·90" there shall be substituted "£37·80"; and

(*b*) in paragraph (3) for "£9·20" there shall be substituted "£9·60".

(**a**)   S.I. 1972/1265 (N.I. 14) as amended by S.I. 1984/1158 (N.I. 8) Article 3(2) and paragraph 3 of Schedule 1; S.I. 1988/2249 (N.I. 24) paragraphs 4 and 5 of Article 8, and S.I. 1991/194 (N.I. 1) Article 34 and Part II of Schedule 5; there are other amendments which are not relevant

(**b**)   S.R. 1989 No. 114 as amended by S.R. 1990 No. 99, S.R. 1991 Nos. 115 and 332, S.R. 1992 Nos. 155 and 242 and S.R. 1993 No. 141

Amendment of Schedules to the principal regulations

4.—(1) In Schedule 1 to the principal regulations (voucher letter codes and face values — supply and replacement) in column 3 (face value of voucher) for each amount specified in column 1 of the Table below (old amount) there shall be substituted the amount specified in relation to it in column 2 of that Table (new amount).

TABLE

Column 1 *Old amount*	Column 2 *New amount*
£ 24·40	£ 25·50
£ 38·40	£ 39·30
£ 52·40	£ 53·60
£102·80	£105·20
£ 42·10	£ 44·00
£ 55·50	£ 56·80
£ 66·80	£ 68·40
£113·00 (in both places where it appears)	£115·70
£ 36·90	£ 37·80

(2) In Schedule 2 to the principal regulations (prisms, tints, photochromic lenses, small and special glasses and complex appliances)—

(*a*) in paragraph 1(1)(*a*) (prism — single vision lens) for "£4·70" there shall be substituted "£4·90";

(*b*) in paragraph 1(1)(*b*) (prism — other lens) for "£5·90" there shall be substituted "£6·10";

(*c*) in paragraph 1(1)(*c*) (single vision tinted lens) for "£2·40" there shall be substituted "£2·50";

(*d*) in paragraph 1(1)(*d*) (other tinted lens) for "£2·90" there shall be substituted "£3·00";

(*e*) in paragraph 1(1)(*e*) (small glasses)—

   (i) in sub-head (i) for "£40·50" there shall be substituted "£42·10",

   (ii) in sub-head (ii) for "£36·00" there shall be substituted "£37.40", and

   (iii) in sub-head (iii) for "£19·40" there shall be substituted "£20·20";

(*f*) in paragraph 1(1)(*f*) (photochromic lenses) for "£2·40" there shall be substituted "£2·50" and for "£2·90" there shall be substituted "£3·00";

(*g*) in paragraph 1(1)(*g*) (specially manufactured frames) for "£40·50" there shall be substituted "£42·10";

(*h*) in paragraph 2(*a*) (minimum complex appliance payment — single vision lenses) for "£4·10" there shall be substituted "£4·20"; and

(*i*) in paragraph 2(*b*) (minimum complex appliance payment — other cases) for "£22·20" there shall be substituted "£22·70".

(3) For Schedule 3 to the principal regulations (voucher values — repair)(**a**) there shall be substituted the Schedule 3 set out in the Schedule.

Application of regulations

5. The amendments made by regulations 2, 3 and 4 and the Schedule apply only in relation to a voucher—

(*a*) accepted or used on or after 1st April 1994 pursuant to regulation 12 or regulation 18 of the principal regulations; or

(*b*) sent to the Agency pursuant to regulation 14(2)(*c*) of the principal regulations in respect of cost incurred on or after that date.

Sealed with the Official Seal of the Department of Health and Social Services on 18th March 1994.

(L.S.)

Joan Dixon

Assistant Secretary

The Department of Finance and Personnel hereby approves the foregoing Regulations.

Sealed with the Official Seal of the Department of Finance and Personnel on 18th March 1994.

(L.S.)

R. Miller

Assistant Secretary

(**a**) Schedule 3 was last substituted by S.R. 1993 No. 141

**Schedule 3 to the Principal Regulations as
substituted by these Regulations**

SCHEDULE 3   Regulation 20(2)
and (3)

Voucher Value — Repair

	Letter Codes — Values							
Nature of repair to appliance	A £	B £	C £	D £	E £	F £	G £	H & I £
Repair or replacement of one lens	7·90	14·80	22·00	47·80	17·20	23·60	29·40	53·00
Repair or replacement of two lenses	15·90	29·70	44·00	95·60	34·40	47·20	58·80	106.10
Repair or replacement of:								
the front of a frame	8·20	8·20	8·20	8·20	8·20	8·20	8·20	8·20
a side of a frame	4·80	4·80	4·80	4·80	4·80	4·80	4·80	4·80
the whole frame	9·60	9·60	9·60	9·60	9·60	9·60	9·60	9·60

EXPLANATORY NOTE

(This note is not part of the Regulations.)

These regulations further amend the Optical Charges and Payments Regulations (Northern Ireland) 1989 ("the principal regulations") which provide for payments to be made, by means of a voucher system, in respect of costs incurred by certain categories of persons in connection with the supply, replacement and repair of optical appliances.

The regulations increase the value of vouchers issued in respect of the cost of:—

(*a*) the supply and replacement of glasses and contact lenses (regulation 4(1)); and

(*b*) the repair or replacement of appliances (regulation 4(3) and the Schedule).

The increases in voucher values range from approximately 1·3% to 5·3% (approximately 2·3% or 4·5% in the case of vouchers for the supply of optical appliances).

Regulation 2 provides for an increase in the charges for glasses and contact lenses supplied by a Board or an HSS trust.

Regulation 3 makes consequential amendments to regulation 20 of the principal regulations (redemption value of voucher for replacement or repair).

Regulation 4(2) increases the additional values for vouchers in respect of prisms, tints, photochromic lenses and special categories of appliances.

1994 No. 101

Medicines (Products Other Than Veterinary Drugs) (Prescription Only) Amendment Order 1994

This Order has been made by the Secretaries of State concerned with health in England, in Wales and in Scotland respectively and the Department of Health and Social Services for Northern Ireland, acting jointly in exercise of the powers conferred by sections 58(1), (4) and (5) and 129(4) of the Medicines Act 1968.

In pursuance of paragraph 11 of Schedule 4 to that Act this Order has been registered as a Northern Ireland statutory rule under the Statutory Rules (Northern Ireland) Order 1979. It is printed in full in the volume of United Kingdom Statutory Instruments for 1994 and has been numbered 558 in that series.

1994   No. 102

This Order has been exempted from printing by the Statutory Rules (Northern Ireland) Order 1979. A summary is given in the List of Statutory Rules of a Local Character under the heading ROADS.

1994   No.   103

STATUTORY SICK PAY

The Statutory Sick Pay (Northern Ireland) Order 1994 (Consequential) Regulations (Northern Ireland) 1994

Made	*23rd March 1994*
Coming into operation . .	*6th April 1994*

The Department of Health and Social Services for Northern Ireland, in exercise of the powers conferred on it by section 154(1)(*a*) of the Social Security Contributions and Benefits (Northern Ireland) Act 1992(**a**), section 77(1) of the Social Security Administration (Northern Ireland) Act 1992(**b**) and Article 4 of the Statutory Sick Pay (Northern Ireland) Order 1994(**c**) and of all other powers enabling it in that behalf, by this statutory rule, which contains only regulations made consequential upon the Statutory Sick Pay (Northern Ireland) Order 1994, hereby makes the following regulations:

Citation, commencement and interpretation

1.—(1) These regulations may be cited as the Statutory Sick Pay (Northern Ireland) Order 1994 (Consequential) Regulations (Northern Ireland) 1994 and shall come into operation on 6th April 1994.

(2) In these regulations—

"the Contributions and Benefits Act" means the Social Security Contributions and Benefits (Northern Ireland) Act 1992;

"the Order" means the Statutory Sick Pay (Northern Ireland) Order 1994;

"the Compensation of Employers Regulations" means the Statutory Sick Pay (Compensation of Employers) and Miscellaneous Provisions Regulations (Northern Ireland) 1983(**d**);

"the Recoupment Regulations" means the Social Security (Recoupment) Regulations (Northern Ireland) 1990(**e**).

(3) The Interpretation Act (Northern Ireland) 1954(**f**) shall apply to these regulations as it applies to a Measure of the Northern Ireland Assembly.

(**a**)   1992 c. 7; section 154(1) is amended by Article 3(1) of the Statutory Sick Pay (Northern Ireland) Order 1994 (S.I. 1994/766 (N.I. 5)) with effect from 6th April 1994
(**b**)   1992 c. 8
(**c**)   S.I. 1994/766 (N.I. 5)
(**d**)   S.R. 1983 No. 54; relevant amending regulations are S.R. 1991 No. 138
(**e**)   S.R. 1990 No. 85; relevant amending regulations are S.R. 1991 No. 138
(**f**)   1954 c. 33 (N.I.)

Amendment of the Compensation of Employers Regulations

2. In regulation 2(1) of the Compensation of Employers Regulations (deductions from contributions payments) '', and an amount equal to 80 per cent. of the aggregate of such of those payments as do not so qualify,'' shall be omitted.

Amendment of the Recoupment Regulations

3. In regulation 2 of the Recoupment Regulations (relevant benefits) paragraphs 1(*l*) and (2A) shall be omitted.

Transitional provisions relating to the Compensation of Employers Regulations

4. The Compensation of Employers Regulations shall continue to have effect for the purpose of entitling an employer to recover an amount equal to 80 per cent. of the aggregate of any payments of statutory sick pay paid, (whether before or after 6th April 1994) which does not qualify for small employers' relief, in respect of any day of incapacity for work before 6th April 1994 as if Article 3 of the Order had not been enacted and regulation 2 had not come into operation.

Transitional provisions relating to the Recoupment Regulations

5. The Recoupment Regulations shall continue to have effect for the purpose of entitling the Department to recover—

    (*a*) an amount equal to any payment of statutory sick pay paid between 1st January 1989 and 5th April 1991; and

    (*b*) an amount equal to 80 per cent. of any payment of statutory sick pay paid between 6th April 1991 and 5th April 1994,

from compensation payments, as if Article 3(2) of the Order had not been enacted and regulation 3 had not come into operation.

Transitional provisions relating to statutory sick pay for women over the age of 60

6.—(1) Subject to paragraph (2), where a woman over the age of 60 has a period of incapacity for work in relation to her contract of service and that period of incapacity for work began before 6th April 1994 and had not come to an end before that date, a period of entitlement to statutory sick pay shall be deemed to arise subject to the provisions of section 149(3) of, and Schedule 11 to, the Contributions and Benefits Act, on the first day of incapacity arising on or after 6th April 1994.

(2) Where a woman over the age of 60 receives remuneration under a contract of service and such remuneration is equal to, or more than the appropriate rate of statutory sick pay as specified in section 153(1) of the Contributions and Benefits Act(**a**), no period of entitlement to statutory sick pay will arise.

(**a**)   Section 153(1)(*a*) and (*b*) are substituted by Article 2 of S.R. 1994 No. 82 with effect from 6th April 1994

Revocation

7. Regulation 3 of the Statutory Sick Pay (Compensation of Employers) (Consequential) Regulations (Northern Ireland) 1991(**a**) is hereby revoked.

Sealed with the Official Seal of the Department of Health and Social Services for Northern Ireland on 23rd March 1994.

(L.S.)   *W. G. Purdy*
                                                Assistant Secretary

---

(**a**) S.R. 1991 No. 138

EXPLANATORY NOTE

(This note is not part of the Regulations.)

These regulations are consequential upon the Statutory Sick Pay (Northern Ireland) Order 1994 ("the Order").

The Order removes the right of employers, except where small employers' relief applies, to recover 80 per cent. of sums paid by them by way of statutory sick pay.

Regulation 2 amends regulation 2(1) of the Statutory Sick Pay (Compensation of Employers) and Miscellaneous Provisions Regulations (Northern Ireland) 1983 by removing reference to the recovery of 80 per cent. of statutory sick pay.

Regulation 3 amends regulation 2 of the Social Security (Recoupment) Regulations (Northern Ireland) 1990 so that the Department of Health and Social Services for Northern Ireland ("the Department") can no longer recover from compensation payments the sum equivalent to 80 per cent. of statutory sick pay which the employer was liable to make.

Regulation 4 enables an employer to recover or to be repaid (as the case may be) 80 per cent. of payments of statutory sick pay paid which do not qualify for small employers' relief, in respect of any day of incapacity for work before 6th April 1994.

Regulation 5 enables the Department to recover from compensation payments any statutory sick pay paid by the employer which is recoverable for days of incapacity for work before 6th April 1994.

Regulation 6 enables women over the age of 60 who have a period of incapacity for work running at 6th April 1994 to qualify for statutory sick pay, except where remuneration under their contract of service is payable at a rate equal to, or more than statutory sick pay.

Article 4 of the Order is one of the enabling provisions under which these regulations are made. It is brought into operation on 23rd March 1994 by virtue of Article 1(2) of the Order. Since these regulations are made before the end of a period of 6 months from the commencement of the said Article 4, they are accordingly exempt, by virtue of section 150(5)(*b*) of the Social Security Administration (Northern Ireland) Act 1992 (c. 8), from reference to the Social Security Advisory Committee.

1994   No. 104

CLEAN AIR

The Alkali, &c. Works (Amendment) Order (Northern Ireland) 1994

Made ` . . . . .*	*23rd March 1994*
Coming into operation *. .*	*6th May 1994*

To be laid before Parliament under paragraph 3(3) of Schedule 1 to the Northern Ireland Act 1974

The Department of the Environment, in exercise of the powers conferred on it by Article 25(9) of the Clean Air (Northern Ireland) Order 1981(**a**) and of every other power enabling it in that behalf, hereby makes the following Order:

Citation and commencement

1. This Order may be cited as the Alkali, &c. Works (Amendment) Order (Northern Ireland) 1994 and shall come into operation on 6th May 1994.

Interpretation

2. In this Order, "the Alkali Act" means the Alkali, &c. Works Regulation Act 1906(**b**).

3. For paragraphs (30), (50), and (61) of the list of works mentioned in the First Schedule to the Alkali Act there shall be substituted the paragraphs so numbered in the Schedule.

Sealed with the Official Seal of the Department of the Environment on 23rd March 1994.

(L.S.)   *R. W. Rogers*
                                          Assistant Secretary

---

(**a**) S.I. 1981/158 (N.I. 4)
(**b**) 1906 c. 14 as amended by S.R. 1991 No. 49

Substitution of certain paragraphs for those contained in the List of Works in the First Schedule to the Alkali Act

(30) Gas and coke works

Works (not being producer gas works as defined in paragraph (29)) in which—

(a) coal, oil or other carbonaceous materials (excluding wood) or products of petroleum refining or natural gas or methane from coal mines or gas derived from fermentation of carbonaceous materials are handled or prepared for carbonisation or gasification or reforming and in which these materials are subsequently carbonised or gasified or reformed or odorised; or

(b) water gas is produced or purified; or

(c) coke or semi-coke or other solid smokeless fuel is produced and quenched, cut, crushed or graded; or

(d) gases derived from any processes mentioned in sub-paragraph (a) are subjected to purification processes.

(50) Acrylates works

Works in which acrylates are—

(a) made or purified; or

(b) made and polymerised; or

(c) purified and polymerised; or

(d) used in the manufacture of any chemical.

(61) Incineration works

Works for—

(a) the destruction by incineration of waste chemicals or waste plastic arising from the manufacture of a chemical or the manufacture of a plastic; or

(b) the destruction by incineration, other than incidentally in the course of burning other waste, of waste chemicals being, or comprising in elemental or compound form, bromine, cadmium, chlorine, fluorine, iodine, lead, mercury, nitrogen, phosphorus, sulphur or zinc; or

(c) the destruction by incineration of clinical waste, municipal waste or any mixture thereof; or

(d) the destruction by incineration of radioactive waste in any facility which is authorised for that purpose under section 13 of the Radioactive Substances Act 1993(**a**); or

(e) the destruction by incineration of other waste, including animal remains, where the works are capable of incinerating 1 tonne or more of waste per hour; or

(f) the cleaning for re-use, by burning out their residual contents, of metal containers used for the transport or storage of chemicals.

(a) 1993 c. 12

In this paragraph—

"clinical waste" has the same meaning as in the Waste Collection and Disposal Regulations (Northern Ireland) 1992(**a**);

"incineration" includes incineration by oxidation including pretreatment as well as pyrolysis or other thermal treatment processes;

"municipal waste" means household waste or commercial waste within the meaning of Article 36(2) and (3) of the Pollution Control and Local Government (Northern Ireland) Order 1978(**b**); and

"waste" has the same meaning as in Article 36(1) of the Pollution Control and Local Government (Northern Ireland) Order 1978.

(**a**)   S.R. 1992 No. 254
(**b**)   S.I. 1978/1049 (N.I. 19)

EXPLANATORY NOTE

(This note is not part of the Order.)

The discharge of certain noxious or offensive gases from certain types of works is subject to control under the Alkali, &c. Works Regulation Act 1906 ("the Act of 1906"). Article 25(9) of the Clean Air (Northern Ireland) Order 1981 empowers the Department to make orders varying or adding to the list of works in the Act of 1906. The existing list of such works is set out in the First Schedule to the Act of 1906, as substituted by the Alkali, &c. Works Order (Northern Ireland) 1991.

This order amends that list of works by substituting new paragraphs (30), (50), and (61) which describe gas and coke works, acrylates works, and incineration works, respectively.

1994   No. 105

Medicines (Veterinary Drugs) (Pharmacy and Merchants' List) (Amendment) Order 1994

This Order has been made by the Secretary of State concerned with health in England, the Secretaries of State respectively concerned with health and with agriculture in Scotland and in Wales, the Minister of Agriculture, Fisheries and Food, the Department of Health and Social Services for Northern Ireland, and the Department of Agriculture for Northern Ireland, acting jointly, in exercise of the powers conferred by sections 57(1) and (2) and 129(4) of the Medicines Act 1968.

In pursuance of paragraph 11 of Schedule 4 to that Act this Order has been registered as a Northern Ireland statutory rule under the Statutory Rules (Northern Ireland) Order 1979. It is printed in full in the volume of United Kingdom Statutory Instruments for 1994 and has been numbered 599 in that series.

1994   No. 106

Medicines (Products for Human Use — Fees) Amendment Regulations 1994

These Regulations have been made by the Secretary of State concerned with health in England, the Secretaries of State respectively concerned with health and with agriculture in Scotland and in Wales, the Minister of Agriculture, Fisheries and Food, the Department of Health and Social Services for Northern Ireland, and the Department of Agriculture for Northern Ireland, acting jointly, in exercise of the powers conferred by section 1(1) and (2) of the Medicines Act 1971.

In pursuance of paragraph 11 of Schedule 4 to that Act these Regulations have been registered as a Northern Ireland statutory rule under the Statutory Rules (Northern Ireland) Order 1979. They are printed in full in the volume of United Kingdom Statutory Instruments for 1994 and have been numbered 696 in that series.

1994   No. 107

PENSIONS

The Occupational Pension Schemes (Deficiency on Winding Up, etc.) Regulations (Northern Ireland) 1994

Made	*25th March 1994*
Coming into operation . .	*19th April 1994*

The Department of Health and Social Services for Northern Ireland, in exercise of the powers conferred on it by sections 140(5), 149(5)(*a*) and (*b*) and 178(3) of the Pension Schemes (Northern Ireland) Act 1993(**a**) and of all other powers enabling it in that behalf, hereby makes the following regulations:

Citation, commencement and interpretation

1.—(1) These regulations may be cited as the Occupational Pension Schemes (Deficiency on Winding Up, etc.) Regulations (Northern Ireland) 1994 and shall come into operation on 19th April 1994.

(2) These regulations apply to every occupational pension scheme which is not a money purchase scheme.

(3) In these regulations—

"the Act" means the Pension Schemes (Northern Ireland) Act 1993;

"actuary" means—

(*a*) a Fellow of the Institute of Actuaries,

(*b*) a Fellow of the Faculty of Actuaries, or

(*c*) a person with other actuarial qualifications who is approved by the Department as being a proper person to act for the purposes of section 140 of the Act (deficiencies in the assets of a scheme on winding up).

(4) The Interpretation Act (Northern Ireland) 1954(**b**) shall apply to these regulations as it applies to a Measure of the Northern Ireland Assembly.

Calculation of the value of scheme liabilities and assets

2.—(1) For the purposes of section 140(1) of the Act, the value of a scheme's liabilities and assets are, subject to paragraphs (2) and (3), to be determined by being calculated and verified in accordance with the Guidance Note "Retirement Benefits Schemes — Deficiency on Winding Up (GN19)"(**c**).

(**a**) 1993 c. 49
(**b**) 1954 c. 33 (N.I.)
(**c**) Guidance Note GN 19 was jointly published on 1st April 1993, and revised with effect from 1st October 1993, by the Institute of Actuaries and the Faculty of Actuaries; copies may be obtained from the Institute of Actuaries, Staple Inn Hall, High Holborn, London WC1V 7QJ or from the Faculty of Actuaries, 23 St. Andrew Square, Edinburgh EH2 1AQ

(2) In calculating the value of the scheme's liabilities, any provision of the scheme which limits the amount of its liabilities by reference to the amount of its assets shall be disregarded.

(3) A determination under paragraph (1) must be certified by an actuary appointed by the trustees of the scheme in question as being in accordance with the guidance referred to in that paragraph.

Scheme which applies to more than one employer

3. In the application of section 140 of the Act to a scheme which applies to earners in employments under different employers and in respect of which there are members in pensionable service under the scheme—

(*a*) that section shall be modified by inserting after subsection (1), the following subsections—

> "(1A) The amount of the debt due from each employer shall be such amount as, in the opinion of the actuary referred to in regulation 2(3) of the Occupational Pension Schemes (Deficiency on Winding Up, etc.) Regulations (Northern Ireland) 1994, bears the same proportion to the deficiency under the scheme as the amount of the scheme's liabilities attributable to employment with that employer (including liabilities in respect of any transfer credits allowed under the scheme in connection with employment with that employer) bears to the total amount of the scheme's liabilities.

> (1B) Where a scheme which applies to earners in employments under different employers is divided into two or more sections and the provisions of the scheme are such that—

>> (*a*) different sections of the scheme apply to different employers;

>> (*b*) contributions payable to the scheme by an employer, or by an earner in employment under that employer, are allocated to that employer's section; and

>> (*c*) a specified part or proportion of the assets of the scheme is attributable to each section and cannot be used for the purposes of any other such section,

> each section of the scheme shall be treated as a separate scheme for the purposes of this section."; and

(*b*) section 140(3) shall be modified—

> (i) by substituting the following definition for the definition of "the applicable time"—

>> " "the applicable time" means—

>>> (*a*) in relation to a scheme which is being wound up, any time—

>>>> (i) after the commencement of the winding up, or, where on 1st July 1992 a scheme was being wound up on or after that date, and

>>>> (ii) before a relevant insolvency event occurs in relation to all of the employers to whom the scheme relates; and

(*b*) in relation to a scheme which is not being wound up, each of the times on or after 1st July 1992 at which a relevant insolvency event occurs in relation to any of the employers to whom the scheme relates;''; and

(ii) by substituting the following definition for the definition of ''the employer''—

'' ''the employer'' means every employer of persons in the description or category of employment to which the scheme relates and includes any person who was an employer of such persons immediately before the scheme—

(*a*) commenced winding up, or

(*b*) if earlier, ceased to admit new members.''.

Scheme in respect of which there are no members in pensionable service

4. In the application of section 140 of the Act to a scheme in respect of which there are no members who are in pensionable service under the scheme—

(*a*) that section shall be modified in the manner provided by regulation 3(*b*)(ii);

(*b*) that section shall be further modified by inserting at the beginning of subsection (1) the words ''Subject to the following provisions of this section,'' and by adding after the subsections (1A) and (1B) inserted by regulation 3(*a*), the following subsections—

''(1C) Where by virtue of subsection (1) a debt (''the debt'') is due from the employer to the trustees of a scheme (''the original scheme'') and—

(*a*) arrangements have been made by the employer and the trustees of the original scheme under which the employer will make contributions to another occupational pension scheme so as to enable that other scheme to pay benefits (''the replacement benefits'') to persons who have accrued rights under the original scheme in place of the benefits that would be payable under the original scheme;

(*b*) contributions are made by the employer in accordance with those arrangements; and

(*c*) the replacement benefits are broadly equivalent to the benefits payable under the original scheme which they replace,

then the debt shall not be recoverable.

(1D) Where the arrangements referred to in subsection (1C) relate to part of the deficiency under the scheme then a corresponding part of the debt (''the relevant part'') shall not be recoverable.

(1E) If the employer fails or ceases, in whole or in part, duly to make contributions in accordance with the arrangements referred to in subsection (1C), or a relevant insolvency event occurs in relation to that employer, the debt or, as the case may be, the relevant part of it, shall again be recoverable.

(1F) Any amounts paid by the employer under arrangements to fund the provision of replacement benefits in accordance with subsection (1C) shall be offset against the debt or, as the case may be, the relevant part of the debt.

(1G) Where arrangements have been made to which subsection (1C) relates, the trustees of the original scheme may assign all such rights and powers as they possess in relation to the debt, or, as the case may be, the relevant part of the debt, to the trustees or managers of the scheme providing the replacement benefits.''; and

(*c*) where there is more than one employer within the meaning of that term as modified by paragraph (*a*), that section shall be further modified in the manner provided by regulation 3(*a*) and (*b*)(i).

Revocation

5. The Occupational Pension Schemes (Deficiency on Winding Up etc.) Regulations (Northern Ireland) 1992(**a**) are hereby revoked.

Sealed with the Official Seal of the Department of Health and Social Services for Northern Ireland on 25th March 1994.

(L.S.)   *W. G. Purdy*
                                              Assistant Secretary

---

(**a**) S.R. 1992 No. 300

EXPLANATORY NOTE
(This note is not part of the Regulations.)

These regulations, which modify section 140 of the Pension Schemes (Northern Ireland) Act 1993 (deficiencies in the assets of a scheme on winding up), consolidate, with amendments, provisions contained in the Occupational Pension Schemes (Deficiency on Winding Up etc.) Regulations (Northern Ireland) 1992 (the ''1992 Regulations''). The amendments are contained in:

— regulation 2 which amends the method of calculating a scheme's assets and liabilities and provides that such calculations shall be made in accordance with the valuation method set out in Guidance Note GN 19 published by the Institute of Actuaries and the Faculty of Actuaries;

— regulation 3 which amends the provision in relation to schemes which apply to more than one employer so that in certain circumstances each section of such a scheme is to be treated as a separate scheme;

— regulation 4 which amends the provision in relation to schemes in respect of which there are no members in pensionable service so that alternative arrangements for the payment of benefits exist in certain circumstances.

The regulations revoke the 1992 regulations.

1994   No. 108

HEALTH AND PERSONAL SOCIAL SERVICES

The Belfast City Hospital Health and Social Services Trust (Establishment) (Amendment) Order (Northern Ireland) 1994

Made	*25th March 1994*
Coming into operation . .	*1st April 1994*

The Department of Health and Social Services, in exercise of the powers conferred on it by Article 10(1) of, and paragraphs 1, 3 and 3A of Schedule 3 to, the Health and Personal Social Services (Northern Ireland) Order 1991(**a**), and of all other powers enabling it in that behalf, hereby makes the following order:

Citation, commencement and interpretation

1.—(1) This order may be cited as the Belfast City Hospital Health and Social Services Trust (Establishment) (Amendment) Order (Northern Ireland) 1994 and shall come into operation on 1st April 1994.

(2) In this order "the establishment order" means the Belfast City Hospital Health and Social Services Trust (Establishment) Order (Northern Ireland) 1992(**b**).

Amendment of the establishment order

2. The establishment order shall be amended in accordance with Articles 3 to 6.

Interpretation

3. In Article 1(2)—

(*a*) after the definition of "establishment date" there shall be inserted the following definition—

" "operational area" has the meaning assigned to it by paragraph 3A of Schedule 3 to the Order;" and

(*b*) after the definition of "operational date" there shall be inserted the following definition—

" "relevant functions" has the meaning assigned to it by Article 3(2) of the Health and Personal Social Services (Northern Ireland) Order 1994(**c**);".

(**a**) S.I. 1991/194 (N.I. 1); Article 10(1) was amended, and paragraph 3A of Schedule 3 was inserted, by S.I. 1994/429 (N.I. 2); paragraph 1 of Schedule 3 is cited for the definition of "an order"
(**b**) S.R. 1992 No. 490
(**c**) S.I. 1994/429 (N.I. 2); the relevant functions are specified in S.R. 1994 No. 64

Additional functions

4. For Article 3(2) there shall be substituted—

"(2) The trust's functions (which include functions which the Department considers appropriate in relation to the provision of services by the trust for one or more relevant bodies) shall be—

> (*a*) to own and manage hospital accommodation and services at the Belfast City Hospital, 51 Lisburn Road, Belfast, BT9 7AB and associated hospitals including the management of the teaching and research facilities associated with these hospitals and the support services related thereto; and

> (*b*) to exercise, on behalf of Health and Social Services Boards, such relevant functions as are so exercisable by the trust by virtue of authorisations for the time being in operation under Article 3(1) of the Health and Personal Social Services (Northern Ireland) Order 1994.".

Operational area of the trust

5. Immediately after Article 3 there shall be inserted the following Article—

"*Operational area of the trust*

3A. The operational area of the Belfast City Hospital Health and Social Services Trust shall be—

> (*a*) for the purposes of the statutory provisions specified in Part I of the Schedule, the Belfast City Hospital, 51 Lisburn Road, Belfast BT9 7AB and associated hospitals;

> (*b*) for the purposes of the statutory provisions specified in Part II of the Schedule, Northern Ireland.".

Schedule

6. At the end of the establishment order there shall be added the following Schedule—

"SCHEDULE   Article 3A

Operational Area

PART I

Statutory Provision	*Relevant Function*
Chronically Sick and Disabled Persons (Northern Ireland) Act 1978(**a**)	Relevant functions under section 12(1)
Mental Health (Northern Ireland) Order 1986(**b**)	All relevant functions except those under Articles 18 to 26, 28(5)(*a*), 29(2), 44(1)(*b*) and 46(5)

PART II

Statutory Provision	*Relevant Function*
Mental Health (Northern Ireland) Order 1986	Relevant functions under Articles 8(1), 15(3), 28(1) and (5)(*b*), 29(1), 42(4), 43(3), 44(5), 45(3), 79(3), 129(1) and (2), 131 and 132

         ".

Sealed with the Official Seal of the Department of Health and Social Services on 25th March 1994.

(L.S.)   *John McGrath*
              Assistant Secretary

(**a**)   1978 c. 53
(**b**)   S.I. 1986/595 (N.I. 4)

EXPLANATORY NOTE
(This note is not part of the Order.)

This order amends the Belfast City Hospital Health and Social Services Trust (Establishment) Order (Northern Ireland) 1992 (S.R. 1992 No. 490) ("the establishment order") with effect from 1st April 1994.

The new Article 3(2) of the establishment order substituted by Article 4 extends the existing functions of the Belfast City Hospital Health and Social Services Trust ("the trust") to include the exercise of relevant statutory functions which may be delegated to that trust by Health and Social Services Boards by virtue of authorisations made under Article 3(1) of the Health and Personal Social Services (Northern Ireland) Order 1994 (S.I. 1994/429 (N.I. 2)).

The new Article 3A and the Schedule inserted in the establishment order by Articles 5 and 6 specify the operational areas within which the trust may exercise the delegated functions.

1994   No. 109

HEALTH AND PERSONAL SOCIAL SERVICES

The Ulster, North Down and Ards Hospitals Health and Social Services Trust (Establishment) (Amendment) Order (Northern Ireland) 1994

Made	*25th March 1994*
Coming into operation . .	*1st April 1994*

The Department of Health and Social Services, in exercise of the powers conferred on it by Article 10(1) of, and paragraphs 1, 3 and 3A of Schedule 3 to, the Health and Personal Social Services (Northern Ireland) Order 1991(**a**), and of all other powers enabling it in that behalf, hereby makes the following order:

Citation, commencement and interpretation

1.—(1) This order may be cited as the Ulster, North Down and Ards Hospitals Health and Social Services Trust (Establishment) (Amendment) Order (Northern Ireland) 1994 and shall come into operation on 1st April 1994.

(2) In this order "the establishment order" means the Ulster, North Down and Ards Hospitals Health and Social Services Trust (Establishment) Order (Northern Ireland) 1992(**b**).

Amendment of the establishment order

2. The establishment order shall be amended in accordance with Articles 3 to 6.

Interpretation

3. In Article 1(2)—

(*a*) after the definition of "establishment date" there shall be inserted the following definition—

" "operational area" has the meaning assigned to it by paragraph 3A of Schedule 3 to the Order;" and

(*b*) after the definition of "operational date" there shall be inserted the following definition—

" "relevant functions" has the meaning assigned to it by Article 3(2) of the Health and Personal Social Services (Northern Ireland) Order 1994(**c**);".

(**a**) S.I. 1991/194 (N.I. 1); Article 10(1) was amended, and paragraph 3A of Schedule 3 was inserted, by S.I. 1994/429 (N.I. 2); paragraph 1 of Schedule 3 is cited for the definition of "an order"
(**b**) S.R. 1992 No. 494
(**c**) S.I. 1994/429 (N.I. 2); the relevant functions are specified in S.R. 1994 No. 64

Additional functions

4. For Article 3(2) there shall be substituted—

"(2) The trust's functions (which include functions which the Department considers appropriate in relation to the provision of services by the trust for one or more relevant bodies) shall be—

   (*a*) to own and manage hospital accommodation and services at the Ulster Hospital, 700 Upper Newtownards Road, Dundonald, Belfast, BT16 0RH; Bangor Hospital, Bangor, Co. Down BT20 4TA; Ards Hospital, Newtownards, Co. Down BT23 4AS and associated premises; and

   (*b*) to exercise, on behalf of Health and Social Services Boards, such relevant functions as are so exercisable by the trust by virtue of authorisations for the time being in operation under Article 3(1) of the Health and Personal Social Services (Northern Ireland) Order 1994.".

Operational area of the trust

5. Immediately after Article 3 there shall be inserted the following Article—

"*Operational area of the trust*

   3A. The operational area of the Ulster, North Down and Ards Hospitals Health and Social Services Trust shall be—

   (*a*) for the purposes of the statutory provisions specified in Part I of the Schedule, Ards Hospital, Newtownards, Co. Down, BT23 4AS;

   (*b*) for the purposes of the statutory provisions specified in Part II of the Schedule, Northern Ireland.".

Schedule

6. At the end of the establishment order there shall be added the following Schedule—

''SCHEDULE   Article 3A

Operational Area

PART I

Statutory Provision	*Relevant Function*
Chronically Sick and Disabled Persons (Northern Ireland) Act 1978**(a)**	Relevant functions under section 12(1)
Mental Health (Northern Ireland) Order 1986**(b)**	All relevant functions except those under Articles 18 to 26, 28(5)(*a*), 29(2), 44(1)(*b*) and 46(5)

PART II

Statutory Provision	*Relevant Function*
Mental Health (Northern Ireland) Order 1986	Relevant functions under Articles 8(1), 15(3), 28(1) and (5)(*b*), 29(1), 42(4), 43(3), 44(5), 45(3), 79(3), 129(1) and (2), 131 and 132

''.

Sealed with the Official Seal of the Department of Health and Social Services on 25th March 1994.

(L.S.)   *John McGrath*
                                          Assistant Secretary

---

(a) 1978 c. 53
(b) S.I. 1986/595 (N.I. 4)

EXPLANATORY NOTE

(This note is not part of the Order.)

This order amends the Ulster, North Down and Ards Hospitals Health and Social Services Trust (Establishment) Order (Northern Ireland) 1992 (S.R. 1992 No. 494) ("the establishment order") with effect from 1st April 1994.

The new Article 3(2) of the establishment order substituted by Article 4 extends the existing functions of the Ulster, North Down and Ards Hospitals Health and Social Services Trust ("the trust") to include the exercise of relevant statutory functions which may be delegated to that trust by Health and Social Services Boards by virtue of authorisations made under Article 3(1) of the Health and Personal Social Services (Northern Ireland) Order 1994 (S.I. 1994/429 (N.I. 2)).

The new Article 3A and the Schedule inserted in the establishment order by Articles 5 and 6 specify the operational areas within which the trust may exercise the delegated functions.

1994   No. 110

HEALTH AND PERSONAL SOCIAL SERVICES

The Down Lisburn Health and Social Services Trust (Establishment) (Amendment) Order (Northern Ireland) 1994

Made	*25th March 1994*
Coming into operation . .	*1st April 1994*

The Department of Health and Social Services, in exercise of the powers conferred on it by Article 10(1) of, and paragraphs 1, 3 and 3A of Schedule 3 to, the Health and Personal Social Services (Northern Ireland) Order 1991(**a**), and of all other powers enabling it in that behalf, hereby makes the following order:

Citation, commencement and interpretation

1.—(1) This order may be cited as the Down Lisburn Health and Social Services Trust (Establishment) (Amendment) Order (Northern Ireland) 1994 and shall come into operation on 1st April 1994.

(2) In this order "the establishment order" means the Down Lisburn Health and Social Services Trust (Establishment) Order (Northern Ireland) 1993(**b**).

Amendment of the establishment order

2. The establishment order shall be amended in accordance with Articles 3 to 6.

Interpretation

3. In Article 1(2)—

(*a*) after the definition of "establishment date" there shall be inserted the following definition—

" "operational area" has the meaning assigned to it by paragraph 3A of Schedule 3 to the order;" and

(*b*) after the definition of "operational date" there shall be inserted the following definition—

" "relevant functions" has the meaning assigned to it by Article 3(2) of the Health and Personal Social Services (Northern Ireland) Order 1994(**c**);".

(**a**) S.I. 1991/194 (N.I. 1); Article 10(1) was amended, and paragraph 3A of Schedule 3 was inserted, by
       S.I. 1994/429 (N.I. 2); paragraph 1 of Schedule 3 is cited for the definition of "an order"
(**b**) S.R. 1993 No. 355
(**c**) S.I. 1994/429 (N.I. 2); the relevant functions are specified in S.R. 1994 No. 64

a

Additional functions

4. In Article 3(2), at the end there shall be added—

"; and

    (*c*) to exercise, on behalf of Health and Social Services Boards, such relevant functions as are so exercisable by the trust by virtue of authorisations for the time being in operation under Article 3(1) of the Health and Personal Social Services (Northern Ireland) Order 1994.''.

Operational area of the trust

5. Immediately after Article 3 there shall be inserted the following Article—

''*Operational area of the trust*

    3A. The operational area of the trust shall be—

    (*a*) for the purposes of the statutory provisions specified in Part I of the Schedule, the local government districts of Down and Lisburn;

    (*b*) for the purposes of the statutory provisions specified in Part II of the Schedule, Northern Ireland.''.

Schedule

6. At the end of the establishment order there shall be added the following Schedule—

"SCHEDULE   Article 3A

Operational Area

PART I

Statutory Provision	Relevant Function
Children and Young Persons Act (Northern Ireland) 1968(**a**)	All relevant functions
Health and Personal Social Services (Northern Ireland) Order 1972(**b**)	All relevant functions
Chronically Sick and Disabled Persons (Northern Ireland) Act 1978(**c**)	All relevant functions
Matrimonial Causes (Northern Ireland) Order 1978(**d**)	All relevant functions
Domestic Proceedings (Northern Ireland) Order 1980(**e**)	All relevant functions
Mental Health (Northern Ireland) Order 1986(**f**)	All relevant functions
Adoption (Northern Ireland) Order 1987(**g**)	All relevant functions
Disabled Persons (Northern Ireland) Act 1989(**h**)	All relevant functions

(**a**)   1968 c. 34 (N.I.)
(**b**)   S.I. 1972/1265 (N.I. 14)
(**c**)   1978 c. 53
(**d**)   S.I. 1978/1045 (N.I. 15)
(**e**)   S.I. 1980/563 (N.I. 5)
(**f**)   S.I. 1986/595 (N.I. 4)
(**g**)   S.I. 1987/2203 (N.I. 22)
(**h**)   1989 c. 10

PART II

Statutory Provision	*Relevant Function*
Children and Young Persons Act (Northern Ireland) 1968	Relevant functions under Part VII and sections 82, 94(2), 99, 105(3), 142, 144(1) and (2), 145, 152, 154 to 159, 163(2) and 164
Health and Personal Social Services (Northern Ireland) Order 1972	Relevant functions under Articles 14A, 15, 36, 36A, 38(3) and (4), 99, 101, 101A and paragraphs 8 and 9 of Schedule 6
Chronically Sick and Disabled Persons (Northern Ireland) Act 1978	Relevant functions under section 2(c), (d) and (f)
Mental Health (Northern Ireland) Order 1986	Relevant functions under Articles 8(1), 15(3), 22(1), 28(1) and (5), 29(1) and (2), 42(4), 43(3), 44(5), 45(3), 79(3), 129(1) and (2), 131 and 132
Adoption (Northern Ireland) Order 1987	Relevant functions under Articles 11(1), 13(3)(a), 24, 31, 32, 59(4) and 66

”.

Sealed with the Official Seal of the Department of Health and Social Services on 25th March 1994.

(L.S.)   *John McGrath*
                                             Assistant Secretary

EXPLANATORY NOTE

(This note is not part of the Order.)

This order amends the Down Lisburn Health and Social Services Trust (Establishment) Order (Northern Ireland) 1993 (S.R. 1993 No. 355) ("the establishment order") with effect from 1st April 1994.

The new Article 3(2)(*c*) of the establishment order added by Article 4 extends the existing functions of the Down Lisburn Health and Social Services Trust ("the trust") to include the exercise of relevant statutory functions which may be delegated to that trust by Health and Social Services Boards by virtue of authorisations made under Article 3(1) of the Health and Personal Social Services (Northern Ireland) Order 1994 (S.I. 1994/429 (N.I. 2)).

The new Article 3A and the Schedule inserted in the establishment order by Articles 5 and 6 specify the operational areas within which the trust may exercise the delegated functions.

1994 No. 111

HEALTH AND PERSONAL SOCIAL SERVICES

The North Down and Ards Community Health and Social Services Trust (Establishment) (Amendment) Order (Northern Ireland) 1994

Made	*25th March 1994*
Coming into operation . .	*1st April 1994*

The Department of Health and Social Services, in exercise of the powers conferred on it by Article 10(1) of, and paragraphs 1, 3 and 3A of Schedule 3 to, the Health and Personal Social Services (Northern Ireland) Order 1991(a), and all other powers enabling it in that behalf, hereby makes the following order:

Citation, commencement and interpretation

1.—(1) This order may be cited as the North Down and Ards Community Health and Social Services Trust (Establishment) (Amendment) Order (Northern Ireland) 1994 and shall come into operation on 1st April 1994.

(2) In this order, "the establishment order" means the North Down and Ards Community Health and Social Services Trust (Establishment) Order (Northern Ireland) 1993(b).

Amendment of the establishment order

2. The establishment order shall be amended in accordance with Articles 3 to 6.

Interpretation

3. In Article 1(2)—

(*a*) after the definition of "establishment date" there shall be inserted the following definition—

" "operational area" has the meaning assigned to it by paragraph 3A of Schedule 3 to the Order;" and

(*b*) after the definition of "operational date" there shall be inserted the following definition—

" "relevant functions" has the meaning assigned to it by Article 3(2) of the Health and Personal Social Services (Northern Ireland) Order 1994(c);".

(a) S.I. 1991/194 (N.I. 1); Article 10(1) was amended, and paragraph 3A of Schedule 3 was inserted, by
S.I. 1994/429 (N.I. 2); paragraph 1 of Schedule 3 is cited for the definition of "an order"
(b) S.R. 1993 No. 354
(c) S.I. 1994/429 (N.I. 2); the relevant functions are specified in S.R. 1994 No. 64

Additional functions

4. For Article 3(2) there shall be substituted—

"(2) The trust's functions (which include functions which the Department considers appropriate in relation to the provision of services by the trust for one or more relevant bodies) shall be—

(*a*) to manage community-based health and personal social services provided from 23-25 Regent Street, Newtownards BT23 4AD and to own those and any associated premises; and

(*b*) to exercise, on behalf of Health and Social Services Boards, such relevant functions as are so exercisable by the trust by virtue of authorisations for the time being in operation under Article 3(1) of the Health and Personal Social Services (Northern Ireland) Order 1994.".

Operational area of the trust

5. Immediately after Article 3 there shall be inserted the following Article—

"*Operational area of the trust*

3A. The operational area of the North Down and Ards Community Health and Social Services Trust shall be—

(*a*) for the purposes of the statutory provisions specified in Part I of the Schedule, the local government districts of North Down and Ards;

(*b*) for the purposes of the statutory provisions specified in Part II of the Schedule, Northern Ireland.".

Schedule

6. At the end of the establishment order there shall be added the following Schedule—

"SCHEDULE   Article 3A

Operational Area

PART I

Statutory Provision	Relevant Function
Children and Young Persons Act (Northern Ireland) 1968(**a**)	All relevant functions
Health and Personal Social Services (Northern Ireland) Order 1972(**b**)	All relevant functions
Chronically Sick and Disabled Persons (Northern Ireland) Act 1978(**c**)	All relevant functions except those under section 12(1)
Matrimonial Causes (Northern Ireland) Order 1978(**d**)	All relevant functions
Domestic Proceedings (Northern Ireland) Order 1980(**e**)	All relevant functions
Mental Health (Northern Ireland) Order 1986(**f**)	All relevant functions except those under Articles 4 to 9, 11 to 17, 26, 28(1) and (4)(*b*), 29(1), 42, 43, 44(1)(*a*) and (5), 45, 46(1) and 61(2)
Adoption (Northern Ireland) Order 1987(**g**)	All relevant functions
Disabled Persons (Northern Ireland) Act 1989(**h**)	All relevant functions

(**a**)   1968 c. 34 (N.I.)
(**b**)   S.I. 1972/1265 (N.I. 14)
(**c**)   1978 c. 53
(**d**)   S.I. 1978/1045 (N.I. 15)
(**e**)   S.I. 1980/563 (N.I. 5)
(**f**)   S.I. 1986/595 (N.I. 4)
(**g**)   S.I. 1987/2203 (N.I. 22)
(**h**)   1989 c. 10

PART II

Statutory Provision	*Relevant Function*
Children and Young Persons Act (Northern Ireland) 1968	Relevant functions under Part VII and sections 82, 94(2), 99, 105(3), 142, 144(1) and (2), 145, 152, 154 to 159, 163(2) and 164
Health and Personal Social Services (Northern Ireland) Order 1972	Relevant functions under Articles 14A, 15, 36, 36A, 38(3) and (4), 99, 101, 101A and paragraphs 8 and 9 of Schedule 6
Chronically Sick and Disabled Persons (Northern Ireland) Act 1978	Relevant functions under section 2(*c*), (*d*) and (*f*)
Mental Health (Northern Ireland) Order 1986	Relevant functions under Articles 22(1), 28(5), 29(2), 129(1) and (2), 131 and 132
Adoption (Northern Ireland) Order 1987	Relevant functions under Articles 11(1), 13(3)(*a*), 24, 31, 32, 59(4) and 66

”.

Sealed with the Official Seal of the Department of Health and Social Services on 25th March 1994.

(L.S.)   *John McGrath*
                                            Assistant Secretary

EXPLANATORY NOTE

(This note is not part of the Order.)

This order amends the North Down and Ards Community Health and Social Services Trust (Establishment) Order (Northern Ireland) 1993 (S.R. 1993 No. 354) ("the establishment order") with effect from 1st April 1994.

The new Article 3(2) of the establishment order substituted by Article 4 extends the existing functions of the North Down and Ards Community Health and Social Services Trust ("the trust") to include the exercise of relevant statutory functions which may be delegated to that trust by Health and Social Services Boards by virtue of authorisations made under Article 3(1) of the Health and Personal Social Services (Northern Ireland) Order 1994 (S.I. 1994/429 (N.I. 2)).

The new Article 3A and the Schedule inserted in the establishment order by Articles 5 and 6 specify the operational areas within which the trust may exercise the delegated functions.

1994　No. 112

HEALTH AND PERSONAL SOCIAL SERVICES

The North and West Belfast Health and Social Services Trust (Establishment) (Amendment) Order (Northern Ireland) 1994

Made	.	.	.	.	*25th March 1994*
Coming into operation		.	.		*1st April 1994*

The Department of Health and Social Services, in exercise of the powers conferred on it by Article 10(1) of, and paragraphs 1, 3 and 3A of Schedule 3 to, the Health and Personal Social Services (Northern Ireland) Order 1991(**a**), and of all other powers enabling it in that behalf, hereby makes the following order:

Citation, commencement and interpretation

1.—(1) This order may be cited as the North and West Belfast Health and Social Services Trust (Establishment) (Amendment) Order (Northern Ireland) 1994 and shall come into operation on 1st April 1994.

(2) In this order "the establishment order" means the North and West Belfast Health and Social Services Trust (Establishment) Order (Northern Ireland) 1993(**b**).

Amendment of the establishment order

2. The establishment order shall be amended in accordance with Articles 3 to 6.

Interpretation

3. In Article 1(2)—

(*a*) after the definition of "establishment date" there shall be inserted the following definition—

" "operational area" has the meaning assigned to it by paragraph 3A of Schedule 3 to the Order;" and

(*b*) after the definition of "operational date" there shall be inserted the following definition—

" "relevant functions" has the meaning assigned to it by Article 3(2) of the Health and Personal Social Services (Northern Ireland) Order 1994(**c**);".

(**a**) S.I. 1991/194 (N.I. 1); Article 10(1) was amended, and paragraph 3A of Schedule 3 was inserted, by S.I. 1994/429 (N.I. 2); paragraph 1 of Schedule 3 is cited for the definition of "an order"
(**b**) S.R. 1993 No. 352
(**c**) S.I. 1994/429 (N.I. 2); the relevant functions are specified in S.R. 1994 No. 64

Additional functions

4. In Article 3(2), at the end there shall be added—

``; and

(*c*) to exercise, on behalf of Health and Social Services Boards, such relevant functions as are so exercisable by the trust by virtue of authorisations for the time being in operation under Article 3(1) of the Health and Personal Social Services (Northern Ireland) Order 1994.''.

Operational area of the trust

5. Immediately after Article 3 there shall be inserted the following Article—

``*Operational area of the trust*

3A. The operational area of the trust shall be—

(*a*) for the purposes of the statutory provisions specified in Part I of the Schedule, the following wards in the local government district of Belfast, that is to say Andersonstown, Ardoyne, Ballysillan, Beechmount, Bellevue, Castleview, Cavehill, Chichester Park, Cliftonville, Clonard, Crumlin, Duncairn, Falls, Falls Park, Fortwilliam, Glen Road, Glencairn, Glencolin, Highfield, Ladybrook, Legoniel, New Lodge, Shankill, St. Anne's, Upper Springfield, Water Works, Whiterock and Woodvale;

(*b*) for the purposes of the statutory provisions specified in Part II of the Schedule, Northern Ireland;

(*c*) for the purposes of the statutory provisions specified in Part III of the Schedule, Muckamore Abbey Hospital, 1 Abbey Road, Muckamore, Antrim, BT41 4SH and associated premises.''.

Schedule

6. At the end of the establishment order there shall be added the following Schedule—

"SCHEDULE

Operational Area

PART I

Statutory Provision	*Relevant Function*
Children and Young Persons Act (Northern Ireland) 1968(**a**)	All relevant functions
Health and Personal Social Services (Northern Ireland) Order 1972(**b**)	All relevant functions
Chronically Sick and Disabled Persons (Northern Ireland) Act 1978(**c**)	All relevant functions except those under section 12(1)
Matrimonial Causes (Northern Ireland) Order 1978(**d**)	All relevant functions
Domestic Proceedings (Northern Ireland) Order 1980(**e**)	All relevant functions
Mental Health (Northern Ireland) Order 1986(**f**)	All relevant functions except those under Articles 4 to 9, 11 to 17, 26, 28(1) and (4)(*b*), 29(1), 42, 43, 44(1)(*a*) and (5), 45, 46(1) and 61(2)
Adoption (Northern Ireland) Order 1987(**g**)	All relevant functions
Disabled Persons (Northern Ireland) Act 1989(**h**)	All relevant functions

(**a**) 1968 c. 34 (N.I.)
(**b**) S.I. 1972/1265 (N.I. 14)
(**c**) 1978 c. 53
(**d**) S.I. 1978/1045 (N.I. 15)
(**e**) S.I. 1980/563 (N.I. 5)
(**f**) S.I. 1986/595 (N.I. 4)
(**g**) S.I. 1987/2203 (N.I. 22)
(**h**) 1989 c. 10

PART II

Statutory Provision	*Relevant Function*
Children and Young Persons Act (Northern Ireland) 1968	Relevant functions under Part VII and sections 82, 94(2), 99, 105(3), 142, 144(1) and (2), 145, 152, 154 to 159, 163(2) and 164
Health and Personal Social Services (Northern Ireland) Order 1972	Relevant functions under Articles 14A, 15, 36, 36A, 38(3) and (4), 99, 101, 101A and paragraphs 8 and 9 of Schedule 6
Chronically Sick and Disabled Persons (Northern Ireland) Act 1978	Relevant functions under section 2(*c*), (*d*) and (*f*)
Mental Health (Northern Ireland) Order 1986	Relevant functions under Articles 8(1), 15(3), 22(1), 28(1) and (5), 29(1) and (2), 42(4), 43(3), 44(5), 45(3), 79(3), 129(1) and (2), 131 and 132
Adoption (Northern Ireland) Order 1987	Relevant functions under Articles 11(1), 13(3)(*a*), 24, 31, 32, 59(4) and 66

PART III

Statutory Provision	*Relevant Function*
Chronically Sick and Disabled Persons (Northern Ireland) Act 1978	Relevant functions under section 12(1)
Mental Health (Northern Ireland) Order 1986	All relevant functions except those under Articles 18 to 26, 28(5)(*a*), 29(2), 44(1)(*b*) and 46(5)

”.

Sealed with the Official Seal of the Department of Health and Social Services on 25th March 1994.

(L.S.)

John McGrath
Assistant Secretary

EXPLANATORY NOTE

(This note is not part of the Order.)

This order amends the North and West Belfast Health and Social Services Trust (Establishment) Order (Northern Ireland) 1993 (S.R. 1993 No. 352) ("the establishment order") with effect from 1st April 1994.

The new Article 3(2)(*c*) of the establishment order added by Article 4 extends the existing functions of the North and West Belfast Health and Social Services Trust ("the trust") to include the exercise of relevant statutory functions which may be delegated to that trust by Health and Social Services Boards by virtue of authorisations made under Article 3(1) of the Health and Personal Social Services (Northern Ireland) Order 1994 (S.I. 1994/429 (N.I. 2)).

The new Article 3A and the Schedule inserted in the establishment order by Articles 5 and 6 specify the operational areas within which the trust may exercise the delegated functions.

1994　No. 113

HEALTH AND PERSONAL SOCIAL SERVICES

The South and East Belfast Health and Social Services Trust (Establishment) (Amendment) Order (Northern Ireland) 1994

Made	*25th March 1994*
Coming into operation . .	*1st April 1994*

The Department of Health and Social Services, in exercise of the powers conferred on it by Article 10(1) of, and paragraphs 1, 3 and 3A of Schedule 3 to, the Health and Personal Social Services (Northern Ireland) Order 1991(**a**), and of all other powers enabling it in that behalf, hereby makes the following order:

Citation, commencement and interpretation

1.—(1) This order may be cited as the South and East Belfast Health and Social Services Trust (Establishment) (Amendment) Order (Northern Ireland) 1994 and shall come into operation on 1st April 1994.

(2) In this order "the establishment order" means the South and East Belfast Health and Social Services Trust (Establishment) Order (Northern Ireland) 1993(**b**).

Amendment of the establishment order

2. The establishment order shall be amended in accordance with Articles 3 to 6.

Interpretation

3. In Article 1(2)—

(*a*) after the definition of "establishment date" there shall be inserted the following definition—

" "operational area" has the meaning assigned to it by paragraph 3A of Schedule 3 to the Order;" and

(*b*) after the definition of "operational date" there shall be inserted the following definition—

" "relevant functions" has the meaning assigned to it by Article 3(2) of the Health and Personal Social Services (Northern Ireland) Order 1994(**c**);".

(**a**)　S.I. 1991/194 (N.I. 1); Article 10(1) was amended, and paragraph 3A of Schedule 3 was inserted, by S.I. 1994/429 (N.I. 2); paragraph 1 of Schedule 3 is cited for the definition of "an order"
(**b**)　S.R. 1993 No. 353
(**c**)　S.I. 1994/429 (N.I. 2); the relevant functions are specified in S.R. 1994 No. 64

Additional functions

4. In Article 3(2) at the end there shall be added—

"; and

(c) to exercise, on behalf of Health and Social Services Boards, such relevant functions as are so exercisable by the trust by virtue of authorisations for the time being in operation under Article 3(1) of the Health and Personal Social Services (Northern Ireland) Order 1994.".

Operational area of the trust

5. Immediately after Article 3 there shall be inserted the following Article—

"*Operational area of the trust*

3A. The operational area of the trust shall be—

(a) for the purposes of the statutory provisions specified in Part I of the Schedule, the local government district of Castlereagh and the following wards in the local government district of Belfast, that is to say Rosetta, Ballynafeigh, Cherryvalley, Knock, Ravenhill, Orangefield, The Mount, Island, Ballymacarrett, Sydenham, Bloomfield, Woodstock, Belmont, Stormont, Ballyhackamore, Finaghy, Upper Malone, Stranmillis, Malone, Botanic, Shaftesbury, Windsor and Blackstaff;

(b) for the purposes of the statutory provisions specified in Part II of the Schedule, Northern Ireland.".

Schedule

6. At the end of the establishment order there shall be added the following Schedule—

"SCHEDULE   Article 3A

Operational Area

PART I

Statutory Provision	Relevant Function
Children and Young Persons Act (Northern Ireland) 1968(**a**)	All relevant functions
Health and Personal Social Services (Northern Ireland) Order 1972(**b**)	All relevant functions
Chronically Sick and Disabled Persons (Northern Ireland) Act 1978(**c**)	All relevant functions
Matrimonial Causes (Northern Ireland) Order 1978(**d**)	All relevant functions
Domestic Proceedings (Northern Ireland) Order 1980(**e**)	All relevant functions
Mental Health (Northern Ireland) Order 1986(**f**)	All relevant functions
Adoption (Northern Ireland) Order 1987(**g**)	All relevant functions
Disabled Persons (Northern Ireland) Act 1989(**h**)	All relevant functions

(**a**) 1968 c. 34 (N.I.)
(**b**) S.I. 1972/1265 (N.I. 14)
(**c**) 1978 c. 53
(**d**) S.I. 1978/1045 (N.I. 15)
(**e**) S.I. 1980/563 (N.I. 5)
(**f**) S.I. 1986/595 (N.I. 4)
(**g**) S.I. 1987/2203 (N.I. 22)
(**h**) 1989 c. 10

PART II

Statutory Provision	*Relevant Function*
Children and Young Persons Act (Northern Ireland) 1968	Relevant functions under Part VII and sections 82, 94(2), 99, 105(3), 142, 144(1) and (2), 145, 152, 154 to 159, 163(2) and 164
Health and Personal Social Services (Northern Ireland) Order 1972	Relevant functions under Articles 14A, 15, 36, 36A, 38(3) and (4), 99, 101, 101A and paragraphs 8 and 9 of Schedule 6
Chronically Sick and Disabled Persons (Northern Ireland) Act 1978	Relevant functions under section 2(*c*), (*d*) and (*f*)
Mental Health (Northern Ireland) Order 1986	Relevant functions under Articles 8(1), 15(3), 22(1), 28(1) and (5), 29(1) and (2), 42(4), 43(3), 44(5), 45(3), 79(3), 129(1) and (2), 131 and 132
Adoption (Northern Ireland) Order 1987	Relevant functions under Articles 11(1), 13(3)(*a*), 24, 31, 32, 59(4) and 66

' ''.

Sealed with the Official Seal of the Department of Health and Social Services on 25th March 1994.

(L.S.)   *John McGrath*
                                   Assistant Secretary

EXPLANATORY NOTE

(This note is not part of the Order.)

This order amends the South and East Belfast Health and Social Services Trust (Establishment) Order (Northern Ireland) 1993 (S.R. 1993 No. 353) (''the establishment order'') with effect from 1st April 1994.

The new Article 3(2)(*c*) of the establishment order added by Article 4 extends the existing functions of the South and East Belfast Health and Social Services Trust (''the trust'') to include the exercise of relevant statutory functions which may be delegated to that trust by Health and Social Services Boards by virtue of authorisations made under Article 3(1) of the Health and Personal Social Services (Northern Ireland) Order 1994 (S.I. 1994/429 (N.I. 2)).

The new Article 3A and the Schedule inserted in the establishment order by Articles 5 and 6 specify the operational areas within which the trust may exercise the delegated functions.

1994   No. 114

HEALTH AND PERSONAL SOCIAL SERVICES

The Craigavon and Banbridge Community Health and Social Services Trust (Establishment) (Amendment) Order (Northern Ireland) 1994

Made	*25th March 1994*
Coming into operation . .	*1st April 1994*

The Department of Health and Social Services, in exercise of the powers conferred on it by Article 10(1) of, and paragraphs 1, 3 and 3A of Schedule 3 to, the Health and Personal Social Services (Northern Ireland) Order 1991(**a**), and of all other powers enabling it in that behalf, hereby makes the following order:

Citation, commencement and interpretation

1.—(1) This order may be cited as the Craigavon and Banbridge Community Health and Social Services Trust (Establishment) (Amendment) Order (Northern Ireland) 1994 and shall come into operation on 1st April 1994.

(2) In this order "the establishment order" means the Craigavon and Banbridge Community Health and Social Services Trust (Establishment) Order (Northern Ireland) 1993(**b**).

Amendment of the establishment order

2. The establishment order shall be amended in accordance with Articles 3 to 6.

Interpretation

3. In Article 1(2)—

(*a*) after the definition of "establishment date" there shall be inserted the following definition—

" "operational area" has the meaning assigned to it by paragraph 3A of Schedule 3 to the Order;" and

(*b*) after the definition of "operational date" there shall be inserted the following definition—

" "relevant functions" has the meaning assigned to it by Article 3(2) of the Health and Personal Social Services (Northern Ireland) Order 1994(**c**);".

(**a**) S.I. 1991/194 (N.I. 1); Article 10(1) was amended, and paragraph 3A of Schedule 3 was inserted, by S.I. 1994/429 (N.I. 2); paragraph 1 of Schedule 3 is cited for the definition of "an order"
(**b**) S.R. 1993 No. 456
(**c**) S.I. 1994/429 (N.I. 2); the relevant functions are specified in S.R. 1994 No. 64

Additional functions

4. For Article 3(2) there shall be substituted—

"(2) The trust's functions (which include functions which the Department considers appropriate in relation to the provision of services by the trust for one or more relevant bodies) shall be—

(*a*) to manage community-based health and personal social services provided from the Craigavon and Banbridge Community Unit, Bannvale House, Moyallan Road, Gilford BT63 5JY and to own those and any associated premises; and

(*b*) to exercise, on behalf of Health and Social Services Boards, such relevant functions as are so exercisable by the trust by virtue of authorisations for the time being in operation under Article 3(1) of the Health and Personal Social Services (Northern Ireland) Order 1994.".

Operational area of the trust

5. Immediately after Article 3 there shall be inserted the following Article—

"*Operational area of the trust*

3A. The operational area of the Craigavon and Banbridge Community Health and Social Services Trust shall be—

(*a*) for the purposes of the statutory provisions specified in Part I of the Schedule, the local government districts of Craigavon and Banbridge;

(*b*) for the purposes of the statutory provisions specified in Part II of the Schedule, Northern Ireland.".

Schedule

6. At the end of the establishment order there shall be added the following Schedule—

"SCHEDULE   Article 3A

Operational Area

PART I

Statutory Provision	Relevant Function
Children and Young Persons Act (Northern Ireland) 1968(**a**)	All relevant functions
Health and Personal Social Services (Northern Ireland) Order 1972(**b**)	All relevant functions
Chronically Sick and Disabled Persons (Northern Ireland) Act 1978(**c**)	All relevant functions
Matrimonial Causes (Northern Ireland) Order 1978(**d**)	All relevant functions
Domestic Proceedings (Northern Ireland) Order 1980(**e**)	All relevant functions
Mental Health (Northern Ireland) Order 1986(**f**)	All relevant functions
Adoption (Northern Ireland) Order 1987(**g**)	All relevant functions
Disabled Persons (Northern Ireland) Act 1989(**h**)	All relevant functions

(**a**)   1968 c. 34 (N.I.)
(**b**)   S.I. 1972/1265 (N.I. 14)
(**c**)   1978 c. 53
(**d**)   S.I. 1978/1045 (N.I. 15)
(**e**)   S.I. 1980/563 (N.I. 5)
(**f**)   S.I. 1986/595 (N.I. 4)
(**g**)   S.I. 1987/2203 (N.I. 22)
(**h**)   1989 c. 10

PART II

Statutory Provision	*Relevant Function*
Children and Young Persons Act (Northern Ireland) 1968	Relevant functions under Part VII and sections 82, 94(2), 99, 105(3), 142, 144(1) and (2), 145, 152, 154 to 159, 163(2) and 164
Health and Personal Social Services (Northern Ireland) Order 1972	Relevant functions under Articles 14A, 15, 36, 36A, 38(3) and (4), 99, 101, 101A and paragraphs 8 and 9 of Schedule 6
Chronically Sick and Disabled Persons (Northern Ireland) Act 1978	Relevant functions under section 2(*c*), (*d*) and (*f*)
Mental Health (Northern Ireland) Order 1986	Relevant functions under Articles 8(1), 15(3), 22(1), 28(1) and (5), 29(1) and (2), 42(4), 43(3), 44(5), 45(3), 79(3), 129(1) and (2), 131 and 132
Adoption (Northern Ireland) Order 1987	Relevant functions under Articles 11(1), 13(3)(*a*), 24, 31, 32, 59(4) and 66

".

Sealed with the Official Seal of the Department of Health and Social Services on 25th March 1994.

(L.S.)

John McGrath
Assistant Secretary

EXPLANATORY NOTE

(This note is not part of the Order.)

This order amends the Craigavon and Banbridge Community Health and Social Services Trust (Establishment) Order (Northern Ireland) 1993 (S.R. 1993 No. 456) ("the establishment order") with effect from 1st April 1994.

The new Article 3(2) of the establishment order substituted by Article 4 extends the existing functions of the Craigavon and Banbridge Community Health and Social Services Trust ("the trust") to include the exercise of relevant statutory functions which may be delegated to that trust by Health and Social Services Boards by virtue of authorisations made under Article 3(1) of the Health and Personal Social Services (Northern Ireland) Order 1994 (S.I. 1994/429 (N.I. 2)).

The new Article 3A and the Schedule inserted in the establishment order by Articles 5 and 6 specify the operational areas within which the trust may exercise the delegated functions.

1994 No. 115

HEALTH AND PERSONAL SOCIAL SERVICES

The Newry and Mourne Health and Social Services Trust (Establishment) (Amendment) Order (Northern Ireland) 1994

Made	*25th March 1994*
Coming into operation . .	*1st April 1994*

The Department of Health and Social Services, in exercise of the powers conferred on it by Article 10(1) of, and paragraphs 1, 3 and 3A of Schedule 3 to, the Health and Personal Social Services (Northern Ireland) Order 1991(**a**), and of all other powers enabling it in that behalf, hereby makes the following order:

Citation, commencement and interpretation

1.—(1) This order may be cited as the Newry and Mourne Health and Social Services Trust (Establishment) (Amendment) Order (Northern Ireland) 1994 and shall come into operation on 1st April 1994.

(2) In this order "the establishment order" means the Newry and Mourne Health and Social Services Trust (Establishment) Order (Northern Ireland) 1993(**b**).

Amendment of the establishment order

2. The establishment order shall be amended in accordance with Articles 3 to 6.

Interpretation

3. In Article 1(2)—

(*a*) after the definition of "establishment date" there shall be inserted the following definition—

" "operational area" has the meaning assigned to it by paragraph 3A of Schedule 3 to the Order;" and

(*b*) after the definition of "operational date" there shall be inserted the following definition—

" "relevant functions" has the meaning assigned to it by Article 3(2) of the Health and Personal Social Services (Northern Ireland) Order 1994(**c**);".

(**a**)   S.I. 1991/194 (N.I. 1); Article 10(1) was amended, and paragraph 3A of Schedule 3 was inserted, by
     S.I. 1994/429 (N.I. 2); paragraph 1 of Schedule 3 is cited for the definition of "an order"
(**b**)   S.R. 1993 No. 455
(**c**)   S.I. 1994/429 (N.I. 2); the relevant functions are specified in S.R. 1994 No. 64

Additional functions

4. In Article 3(2) at the end there shall be added—

''; and

(*c*) to exercise, on behalf of Health and Social Services Boards, such relevant functions as are so exercisable by the trust by virtue of authorisations for the time being in operation under Article 3(1) of the Health and Personal Social Services (Northern Ireland) Order 1994.''.

Operational area of the trust

5. Immediately after Article 3 there shall be inserted the following Article—

''*Operational area of the trust*

3A. The operational area of the Newry and Mourne Health and Social Services Trust shall be—

(*a*) for the purposes of the statutory provisions specified in Part I of the Schedule, the local government districts of Newry and Mourne;

(*b*) for the purposes of the statutory provisions specified in Part II of the Schedule, Northern Ireland.''.

Schedule

6. At the end of the establishment order there shall be added the following Schedule—

"SCHEDULE

Operational Area

PART I

Statutory Provision	Relevant Function
Children and Young Persons Act (Northern Ireland) 1968(**a**)	All relevant functions
Health and Personal Social Services (Northern Ireland) Order 1972(**b**)	All relevant functions
Chronically Sick and Disabled Persons (Northern Ireland) Act 1978(**c**)	All relevant functions
Matrimonial Causes (Northern Ireland) Order 1978(**d**)	All relevant functions
Domestic Proceedings (Northern Ireland) Order 1980(**e**)	All relevant functions
Mental Health (Northern Ireland) Order 1986(**f**)	All relevant functions except those under Articles 4 to 9 and 11 to 17, 26, 28(1) and (4)(*b*), 29(1), 42, 43, 44(1)(*a*) and (5), 45, 46(1) and 61(2)
Adoption (Northern Ireland) Order 1987(**g**)	All relevant functions
Disabled Persons (Northern Ireland) Act 1989(**h**)	All relevant functions

(**a**)   1968 c. 34 (N.I.)
(**b**)   S.I. 1972/1265 (N.I. 14)
(**c**)   1978 c. 53
(**d**)   S.I. 1978/1045 (N.I. 15)
(**e**)   S.I. 1980/563 (N.I. 5)
(**f**)   S.I. 1986/595 (N.I. 4)
(**g**)   S.I. 1987/2203 (N.I. 22)
(**h**)   1989 c. 10

Statutory Provision	*Relevant Function*
Children and Young Persons Act (Northern Ireland) 1968	Relevant functions under Part VII and sections 82, 94(2), 99, 105(3), 142, 144(1) and (2), 145, 152, 154 to 159, 163(2) and 164
Health and Personal Social Services (Northern Ireland) Order 1972	Relevant functions under Articles 14A, 15, 36, 36A, 38(3) and (4), 99, 101, 101A and paragraphs 8 and 9 of Schedule 6
Chronically Sick and Disabled Persons (Northern Ireland) Act 1978	Relevant functions under section 2(*c*), (*d*) and (*f*)
Mental Health (Northern Ireland) Order 1986	Relevant functions under Articles 22(1), 28(5), 29(2), 129(1) and (2), 131 and 132
Adoption (Northern Ireland) Order 1987	Relevant functions under Articles 11(1), 13(3)(*a*), 24, 31, 32, 59(4) and 66

",.

Sealed with the Official Seal of the Department of Health and Social Services on 25th March 1994.

(L.S.)

John McGrath
Assistant Secretary

EXPLANATORY NOTE
(This note is not part of the Order.)

This order amends the Newry and Mourne Health and Social Services Trust (Establishment) Order (Northern Ireland) 1993 (S.R. 1993 No. 455) ("the establishment order") with effect from 1st April 1994.

The new Article 3(2)(c) of the establishment order added by Article 4 extends the existing functions of the Newry and Mourne Health and Social Services Trust ("the trust") to include the exercise of relevant statutory functions which may be delegated to that trust by Health and Social Services Boards by virtue of authorisations made under Article 3(1) of the Health and Personal Social Services (Northern Ireland) Order 1994 (S.I. 1994/429 (N.I. 2)).

The new Article 3A and the Schedule inserted in the establishment order by Articles 5 and 6 specify the operational areas within which the trust may exercise the delegated functions.

1994   No. 116

HEALTH AND PERSONAL SOCIAL SERVICES

The Mater Infirmorum Hospital Health and Social Services Trust (Establishment) (Amendment) Order (Northern Ireland) 1994

Made	.	.	.	.	*25th March 1994*
Coming into operation		.	.		*1st April 1994*

The Department of Health and Social Services, in exercise of the powers conferred on it by Article 10(1) of, and paragraphs 1, 3 and 3A of Schedule 3 to, the Health and Personal Social Services (Northern Ireland) Order 1991(**a**), and of all other powers enabling it in that behalf, hereby makes the following order:

Citation, commencement and interpretation

1.—(1) This order may be cited as the Mater Infirmorum Hospital Health and Social Services Trust (Establishment) (Amendment) Order (Northern Ireland) 1994 and shall come into operation on 1st April 1994.

(2) In this order "the establishment order" means the Mater Infirmorum Hospital Health and Social Services Trust (Establishment) Order (Northern Ireland) 1994(**b**).

Amendment of the establishment order

2. The establishment order shall be amended in accordance with Articles 3 to 6.

Interpretation

3. In Article 1(2)—

(*a*) after the definition of "establishment date" there shall be inserted the following definition—

" "operational area" has the meaning assigned to it by paragraph 3A of Schedule 3 to the Order;" and

(*b*) after the definition of "operational date" there shall be inserted the following definition—

" "relevant functions" has the meaning assigned to it by Article 3(2) of the Health and Personal Social Services (Northern Ireland) Order 1994(**c**);".

(**a**) S.I. 1991/194 (N.I. 1); Article 10(1) was amended, and paragraph 3A of Schedule 3 was inserted, by S.I. 1994/429 (N.I. 2); paragraph 1 of Schedule 3 is cited for the definition of "an order"
(**b**) S.R. 1994 No. 67
(**c**) S.I. 1994/429 (N.I. 2); the relevant functions are specified in S.R. 1994 No. 64

Additional functions

4. For Article 3(2) there shall be substituted—

"(2) The trust's functions (which include functions which the Department considers appropriate in relation to the provision of services by the trust for one or more relevant bodies) shall be—

    (*a*) to own and manage hospital accommodation and services provided at the Mater Infirmorum Hospital, 45/51 Crumlin Road, Belfast, BT14 6AB and any associated premises; and

    (*b*) to exercise, on behalf of Health and Social Services Boards, such relevant functions as are so exercisable by the trust by virtue of authorisations for the time being in operation under Article 3(1) of the Health and Personal Social Services (Northern Ireland) Order 1994.".

Operational area of the trust

5. Immediately after Article 3 there shall be inserted the following Article—

"*Operational area of the trust*

3A. The operational area of the Mater Infirmorum Hospital Health and Social Services Trust shall be—

    (*a*) for the purposes of the statutory provisions specified in Part I of the Schedule, the Mater Infirmorum Hospital, 45/51 Crumlin Road, Belfast BT14 6AB and any associated premises;

    (*b*) for the purposes of the statutory provisions specified in Part II of the Schedule, Northern Ireland.".

Schedule

6. At the end of the establishment order there shall be added the following Schedule—

"SCHEDULE　　　　　　　Article 3A

Operational Area

PART I

Statutory Provision	*Relevant Function*
Chronically Sick and Disabled Persons (Northern Ireland) Act 1978(**a**)	Relevant functions under section 12(1)
Mental Health (Northern Ireland) Order 1986(**b**)	All relevant functions except those under Articles 18 to 26, 28(5)(*a*), 29(2), 44(1)(*b*) and 46(5)

PART II

Statutory Provision	*Relevant Function*
Mental Health (Northern Ireland) Order 1986	Relevant functions under Articles 8(1), 15(3), 28(1) and (5)(*b*), 29(1), 42(4), 43(3), 44(5), 45(3), 79(3), 129(1) and (2), 131 and 132

".

Sealed with the Official Seal of the Department of Health and Social Services on 25th March 1994.

(L.S.)　　　　　　　　　　　*John McGrath*
　　　　　　　　　　　　　　Assistant Secretary

(**a**)　1978 c. 53
(**b**)　S.I. 1986/595 (N.I. 4)

EXPLANATORY NOTE

(This note is not part of the Order.)

This order amends the Mater Infirmorum Hospital Health and Social Services Trust (Establishment) Order (Northern Ireland) 1994 (S.R. 1994 No. 67) (''the establishment order'') with effect from 1st April 1994.

The new Article 3(2) of the establishment order substituted by Article 4 extends the existing functions of the Mater Infirmorum Hospital Health and Social Services Trust (''the trust'') to include the exercise of relevant statutory functions which may be delegated to that trust by Health and Social Services Boards by virtue of authorisations made under Article 3(1) of the Health and Personal Social Services (Northern Ireland) Order 1994 (S.I. 1994/429 (N.I. 2)).

The new Article 3A and the Schedule inserted in the establishment order by Articles 5 and 6 specify the operational areas within which the trust may exercise the delegated functions.

1994   No.   117

HEALTH AND PERSONAL SOCIAL SERVICES

General Medical and Pharmaceutical Services (Amendment) Regulations (Northern Ireland) 1994

Made	*28th March 1994*
Coming into operation . .	*1st April 1994*

The Department of Health and Social Services, in exercise of the powers conferred on it by Articles 56, 63, 106 and 107(6) of the Health and Personal Social Services (Northern Ireland) Order 1972(**a**) and of all other powers enabling it in that behalf, and in conjunction with the Department of Finance and Personnel and after consultation with such organisations as appeared to the Department to be representative of the Medical and Pharmaceutical professions, as required by Articles 56(5) and 63(3) of that Order, hereby makes the following regulations:

Citation, commencement and interpretation

1.—(1) These regulations may be cited as the General Medical and Pharmaceutical Services (Amendment) Regulations (Northern Ireland) 1994 and shall come into operation on 1st April 1994.

(2) In these regulations, "the principal regulations" means the Health and Personal Social Services (General Medical and Pharmaceutical Services) Regulations (Northern Ireland) 1973(**b**).

Amendment of regulation 20 of the principal regulations

2. In regulation 20 of the principal regulations (assignment of persons to a doctor), in paragraph (2) after "list" there shall be inserted "and, where the application relates only to a specified person who has previously been removed from the list of the doctor, the circumstances of that removal.".

Amendment of regulation 23 of the principal regulations

3.—(1) In paragraph (1) of regulation 23 of the principal regulations (application by a doctor for removal of persons from his list) after "Regulation 22(3)" there shall be inserted "and subject to paragraphs (3) to (6)".

(**a**) S.I. 1972/1265 (N.I. 14), as amended by S.I. 1978/1907 (N.I. 26), S.I. 1981/432, S.I. 1986/2023 (N.I. 20), S.I. 1986/2229 (N.I. 24), S.I. 1988/2249 (N.I. 24), and S.I. 1991/194 (N.I. 1)
(**b**) S.R. & O. (N.I.) 1973 No. 421, relevant amending regulations are S.R. 1975 No. 180, S.R. 1983 No. 182, S.R. 1988 No. 395, S.R. 1989 No. 454, S.R. 1991 No. 97 and S.R. 1992 No. 200

(2) After paragraph (2) there shall be added the following paragraphs:

"(3) Where—

(*a*) a person on a doctor's list has committed an act of violence against the doctor or has behaved in such a way that the doctor has feared for his safety; and

(*b*) the doctor has reported the incident to the police,

the doctor may notify the Agency that he wishes to have that person removed from his list with immediate effect.

(4) Notification under paragraph (3) may be given by any means including telephone or fax, but if not given in writing shall subsequently be confirmed in writing within 7 days (and for this purpose a faxed notification is not a written one).

(5) The time at which the doctor notifies the Agency shall be the time at which he makes the telephone call or sends or delivers the notification to the Agency.

(6) Where pursuant to paragraph (3) a doctor has notified the Agency that he wishes to have a person's name removed from his list with immediate effect, he shall take all reasonable steps to inform the person concerned.".

Amendment of regulation 26 of the principal regulations

4. In regulation 26 of the principal regulations (doctors' lists), after paragraph (7) there shall be added the following paragraphs—

"(7A) Where a doctor has requested the Agency to remove a person from his list in accordance with paragraphs (1) and (2) of regulation 23, the removal shall take effect from the date mentioned in paragraph (1) of that regulation.

(7B) Where a doctor has requested the Agency to remove a person from his list with immediate effect in accordance with paragraphs (3) to (6) of regulation 23—

(*a*) the removal shall take effect at the time mentioned in paragraph (5) of that regulation; and

(*b*) on receipt of the notification mentioned in paragraph (3) of regulation 23, the Agency shall—

(i) in writing, acknowledge it and also give notice of the removal to the person concerned, and

(ii) take all reasonable steps to assign the person to another doctor before the end of the next working day, or as soon as possible thereafter, and regulation 20 shall apply to such an assignment as if the person had applied for an assignment in accordance with that regulation.".

Insertion of new regulation 36A into the principal regulations

5. After regulation 36 of the principal regulations there shall be inserted the following regulation—

"Additional professional services

36A.—(1) A chemist may, in addition, undertake to provide additional professional services.

(2) In these regulations, ''additional professional services'' means—

(*a*) publishing a leaflet (''practice leaflet'') which shall include—

    (i) a list of the pharmaceutical services which the chemist has undertaken to provide and for which his name is included in the pharmaceutical list,

    (ii) the name, address and telephone number of the premises from which he provides those services and the hours in each day of the week during which he provides those services from those premises,

    (iii) the arrangements made by the chemist to provide, or such arrangements as the chemist has made with other chemists to provide, pharmaceutical services to any person who needs those services in an emergency or outside of the normal hours during which the chemist provides pharmaceutical services,

    (iv) the procedure by which any person may comment upon the provision of pharmaceutical services undertaken by the chemist; and

(*b*) displaying such health promotion leaflets, posters and publications as the Board may, in consultation with the Local Pharmaceutical Committee, approve.''.

Amendment of regulation 40 of the principal regulations

6. In regulation 40 (prices and standards of drugs and appliances) in paragraph (1)(*d*), after ''appliances'' there shall be added ''and additional professional services''.

Amendment of Schedule 1 to the principal regulations

7. In Schedule 1 to the principal regulations (terms of service for doctors)—

(*a*) in paragraph 3 (persons for whose treatment a doctor is responsible), for sub-paragraph (5) there shall be substituted the following sub-paragraph—

''(5) Where a doctor—

    (*a*) refuses to accept a person who applies in accordance with regulation 19 for acceptance as a patient for the purposes of receiving general medical services other than maternity medical services and who is not included in the list of any other doctor practising in that area; or

    (*b*) refuses to accept as a temporary resident a person to whom regulation 27 applies; or

    (*c*) has requested the removal with immediate effect of a person from his list in accordance with paragraphs (3) to (6) of regulation 23, he shall on request give that person any immediately necessary treatment until the expiry of the period of 14 days beginning with the date when that person was refused acceptance (or, as the case may be, with the date when he requested the immediate removal of that person from his list), or until that person has been accepted by or assigned to another doctor, whichever occurs first.'';

(b) in paragraph 14 (deputies, assistants and partners),

   (i) in sub-paragraph (10), the words from '', whether'' to ''assistant,'' shall be omitted, and

   (ii) in sub-paragraph (11) for the words from ''A doctor'' to ''shall be'' there shall be substituted ''Where a doctor, whose name is included in the medical list, is acting as deputy to another doctor whose name is also included in that list, the deputy alone is''.

Amendment of Schedule 4 to the principal regulations

8. In Schedule 4 (terms of service for chemists)—

(a) in paragraph 4 after sub-paragraph (4) there shall be inserted the following sub-paragraph—

''(4A) A chemist who has undertaken to provide additional professional services within the meaning of regulation 36A shall, on request, permit the Board or another person on its behalf at any reasonable time to inspect the premises from which those services are provided for the purpose of satisfying itself that those services are being provided in accordance with the undertaking.'';

(b) in paragraph 8 after sub-paragraph (4)(b) there shall be inserted the following sub-paragraph—

''(c) The Agency shall make such payments, if any, as are provided for by the Drug Tariff to chemists who provide additional professional services within the meaning of regulation 36A.''.

Sealed with the Official Seal of the Department of Health and Social Services on 25th March 1994.

(L.S.)

Joan Dixon

Assistant Secretary

Sealed with the Official Seal of the Department of Finance and Personnel on 28th March 1994.

(L.S.)

F. G. McConnell

Assistant Secretary

EXPLANATORY NOTE

(This note is not part of the Regulations.)

These regulations further amend the Health and Personal Social Services (General Medical and Pharmaceutical Services) Regulations (Northern Ireland) 1973, ("the principal regulations").

The regulations make provision for the Central Services Agency to remove a person from a doctor's list of patients with immediate effect where requested to do so by a doctor as a result of an act of actual or threatened violence. The doctor is to remain responsible for immediately necessary treatment for a period of 14 days or until the person is transferred to the list of another doctor, if that happens sooner (regulations 2, 3, 4, and 7(*a*)).

The regulations also provide that where a doctor engages as a deputy another doctor who is himself on the medical list, that deputy alone is responsible, under the terms of service contained in Schedule 1 to the principal regulations, for his acts and omissions and those of any person employed by him or acting on his behalf (regulation 7(*b*)(ii)). A consequential amendment is effected by regulation 7(*b*)(i).

Regulation 5 inserts a new regulation 36A to enable chemists who wish to do so to undertake to provide "additional professional services" (for which they would receive extra remuneration) consisting of publishing a practice leaflet and displaying health promotion material. Regulations 6 and 8 make minor consequential amendments enabling payment to be made for these services and empowering Boards to inspect premises for the purpose of monitoring the services provided.

1994   No. 118

ANIMALS

Poultry Breeding Flocks and Hatcheries Scheme
Order (Northern Ireland) 1994

Made	*28th March 1994*
Coming into operation . .	*18th April 1994*

The Department of Agriculture, in exercise of the powers conferred on it by Articles 8(1) and (2) of the Diseases of Animals (Northern Ireland) Order 1981(**a**) and of every other power enabling it in that behalf, having consulted with the bodies which appeared to it to be substantially representative of the interests concerned and with the approval of the Department of Finance and Personnel(**b**) hereby makes the following Order:

Citation and commencement

1. This Order may be cited as the Poultry Breeding Flocks and Hatcheries Scheme Order (Northern Ireland) 1994 and shall come into operation on 18th April 1994.

Breeding flocks and hatcheries scheme

2. For the purposes of keeping poultry, so far as practicable, free from Salmonella and controlling and, so far as practicable, reducing the incidence of Salmonella, the Department hereby makes the Scheme set out in the Schedule.

Sealed with the Official Seal of the Department of Agriculture on 28th March 1994.

(L.S.)   *P. T. Toal*

Assistant Secretary

The Department of Finance and Personnel hereby approves the foregoing Order.

Sealed with the Official Seal of the Department of Finance and Personnel on 28th March 1994.

(L.S.)   *D. Thomson*

Assistant Secretary

(**a**) S.I. 1981/1115 (N.I. 22) to which there are amendments not relevant to the subject matter of this Order
(**b**) Formerly the Department of Finance. *See* S.I. 1982/338 (N.I. 6) Art. 3

Poultry Breeding Flocks and Hatcheries Scheme (Northern Ireland) 1994

Citation

1. This Scheme may be cited as the Poultry Breeding Flocks and Hatcheries Scheme (Northern Ireland) 1994.

Interpretation and application

2.—(1) In this Scheme—

"breeding flock" means any flock of poultry consisting of at least 250 birds of a single species which are kept or are being reared on a single premises for the production of hatching eggs;

"the Breeding Flocks Register" means the register kept by the Department under paragraph 3(2);

"chicks" means poultry less than 72 hours old which have not been fed;

"chick box liner" means any material used to line a box or other container in which chicks are transported from a hatchery to any rearing premises;

"composite faeces sample" means a sample of faeces consisting of a number of individual samples of faeces calculated in accordance with the appropriate provisions of Part I of Annex 2 each of which weighs not less than 1 gram and is taken from a site selected at random to represent the building or group of buildings on the holding from which it is taken;

"the Hatcheries Register" means the register kept by the Department under paragraph 4(2);

"hatchery" means any premises, with a total incubator capacity of not less than 1,000 eggs, on which the eggs of poultry are incubated or hatched and from which chicks are sold or supplied;

"hatching eggs" means eggs intended for incubation;

"house" means—

(*a*) a building (including a shed); or

(*b*) a part of a building separated from other parts of that building by a solid partition and having its own ventilation system;

"inspector" includes a veterinary inspector;

"laboratory" means any laboratory authorised in writing by the Department for the purposes of this Scheme which has the necessary facilities and personnel for carrying out tests on samples mentioned in Parts I and II of Annex 2 in accordance with the provisions of Part III of that Annex;

"poultry" means domestic fowls, turkeys, geese or ducks;

"premises" includes land;

"registered" in relation to any person means the entry in respect of any premises of that person's name in a register kept under this Scheme.

(2) The provisions of this Scheme shall not apply in the case of a breeding flock or hatchery which is kept solely for the production of hatching eggs for use in the manufacture of vaccines or for research or other scientific purposes.

Registration of breeding flocks

3.—(1) Any person who owns a breeding flock kept on any premises shall ensure that his name is registered in respect of those premises in the Breeding Flocks Register.

(2) The Department shall, for the purpose of sub-paragraph (1), keep a register of persons as being persons who own a breeding flock kept on the premises in respect of which they are registered.

(3) Where a person makes an application in writing to the Department to be registered in the Breeding Flocks Register in respect of any premises the Department shall, subject to sub-paragraph (4), so register him and shall issue to him a certificate of such registration.

(4) The Department shall refuse to register any person in the Breeding Flocks Register in respect of any premises unless all the particulars specified in Part I of Annex 1 are notified to it in writing.

(5) A person registered in the Breeding Flocks Register shall, within 28 days after each anniversary of the date of such registration, notify the Department in writing of any change in the particulars previously notified to it under this paragraph.

(6) Where a person registered in the Breeding Flocks Register fails to notify the Department in accordance with sub-paragraph (5) of any change in the particulars previously notified to it, the Department may revoke that registration.

(7) Where a person registered in the Breeding Flocks Register has notified the Department in accordance with sub-paragraph (5) that he no longer owns a breeding flock on the premises in respect of which he is registered and does not intend to do so for the next twelve months the Department shall revoke that registration.

Registration of hatcheries

4.—(1) Any person using any premises as a hatchery shall ensure that his name is entered in respect of those premises in the Hatcheries Register.

(2) The Department shall, for the purpose of sub-paragraph (1) keep a register of persons as being persons using as a hatchery any premises in respect of which they are registered.

(3) Where a person makes an application in writing to the Department to be registered in the Hatcheries Register in respect of any premises, the Department shall, subject to sub-paragraph (4), so register him and shall issue to him a certificate of such registration.

(4) The Department shall refuse to register any person in the Hatcheries Register in respect of any premises where all the particulars specified in Part II of Annex 1 are not notified to it in writing.

(5) A person registered in the Hatcheries Register in respect of any premises shall, within 28 days after each anniversary of the date of such registration, notify the Department in writing of any change in the particulars previously notified to it under this paragraph.

(6) Where a person registered in the Hatcheries Register fails to notify the Department in accordance with sub-paragraph (5) of any change in the particulars previously notified to it, the Department may revoke that registration.

(7) Where a person registered in the Hatcheries Register has notified the Department in accordance with sub-paragraph (5) that he no longer uses the premises in respect of which he is registered as a hatchery and does not intend to do so for the next twelve months, the Department shall revoke that registration.

Taking of samples from breeding flocks for bacteriological testing for salmonella

5.—(1) A person who is registered in the Breeding Flocks Register in respect of any premises on which a breeding flock is kept shall ensure that—

(a) in respect of the flock the samples taken in Part I of Annex 2 are taken in such manner and at such times as are so specified;

(*b*) those samples are identified in such a manner as to enable the laboratory to which they are submitted, or the inspector to which they are given, to know what type of samples they are, the date on which they were taken, the name of the person registered in the Breeding Flocks Register in respect of the premises from which they were taken, the address of those premises and the house (if any) on those premises from which they were taken;

(*c*) those samples (other than those required to be taken under the supervision of an inspector) are submitted, within 48 hours of being taken, to a laboratory for testing for the presence of salmonella in accordance with an appropriate bacteriological method set out in Part III of Annex 2; and

(*d*) in the case of samples required to be taken under the supervision of an inspector, they are given to him after being so taken for testing by the Department for salmonella in accordance with such a bacteriological method.

(2) Where samples taken in accordance with sub-paragraph (1)(*a*) are required to be submitted to a laboratory for testing under sub-paragraph (1)(*c*), they shall be kept in a refrigerator at between 1°C and 4°C unless they are so submitted within 24 hours of being taken.

Taking of blood samples from domestic fowl in breeding flocks for serological testing for Salmonella pullorum

6. Without prejudice to paragraph 5, a person who is registered in the Breeding Flocks Register in respect of any premises on which a breeding flock comprising domestic fowl is kept by him shall ensure that—

(*a*) the samples specified in Part I of Annex 3 are taken from the fowl in such manner and at such times as are so specified; and

(*b*) those samples are submitted to the Department for testing in accordance with the serological method set out in Part II of Annex 3.

Taking of samples from hatcheries for bacteriological testing for salmonella

7.—(1) A person who is registered in the Hatcheries Register in respect of any premises used by him as a hatchery shall ensure that—

(*a*) the samples specified in Part II of Annex 2 are taken from the poultry in the hatchery in such manner and at such times as are so specified;

(*b*) those samples are identified in such a manner as to enable the laboratory to which they are submitted, or the inspector to which they are given, to know what type of samples they are, the date on which they were taken, the name of the person registered in the Hatcheries Register in respect of the premises from which they were taken, the address of that hatchery and the address of the premises which supplied the hatching eggs to that hatchery;

(*c*) those samples other than those required to be taken under the supervision of an inspector are submitted, within 48 hours of being taken, to a laboratory for testing for the presence of salmonella in accordance with an appropriate bacteriological method set out in Part III of Annex 2;

(*d*) in the case of samples required to be taken under the supervision of an inspector, they are given to him after being so taken, for testing by the Department for salmonella in accordance with such a bacteriological method.

(2) Where samples taken in accordance with sub-paragraph (1)(*a*) are required to be submitted to a laboratory for testing under sub-paragraph (1)(*c*), they shall be kept in a refrigerator at between 1°C and 4°C unless they are so submitted within 24 hours of being taken.

Bacteriological testing of samples from breeding flocks and hatcheries and reporting of results of tests

8.—(1) The person in charge of a laboratory which accepts for testing a sample which has been submitted under paragraph 5(1)(c) or 7(1)(c) shall ensure that—

(a) the sample is tested for the presence of salmonella in accordance with an appropriate bacteriological method set out in Part III of Annex 2;

(b) the result of such a test is reported in writing as soon as practicable to the person who submitted the sample; and

(c) where, as a result of any test carried out in accordance with such a bacteriological method, a culture of salmonella is isolated from the sample, that a sub-culture is sent to the Department's Laboratory at Stoney Road, Stormont, Belfast.

(2) Where a person to whom a report is made under sub-paragraph (1)(b) is not the person registered in the Breeding Flocks Register or the Hatcheries Register, as the case may be, in respect of the premises from which the sample was taken, he shall immediately pass that report to the person so registered.

Tampering with samples

9.—(1) Except as provided for in this Scheme, a person, shall not treat or otherwise tamper with any sample which has been taken for the purposes of this Scheme.

(2) For the purposes of this paragraph a person shall be deemed to have treated a sample if he does anything in relation to it which is likely to affect the result of the test which may be carried out in accordance with this Scheme.

Keeping of records

10.—(1) A person who is registered in the Breeding Flocks Register in respect of any premises shall—

(a) in respect of each sample taken under and in accordance with paragraph 5(1)(a), keep a record containing the information specified in Part I of Annex 4 in relation to that sample;

(b) keep a record of the result of any test carried out which has been reported or passed to him in accordance with paragraph 8(1)(b) or (2);

(c) keep a record containing the information specified in Part II of Annex 4 of the movement of any poultry, chicks or eggs onto and off the premises.

(2) A person who is registered in the Hatcheries Register in respect of any premises shall—

(a) in respect of each sample taken under and in accordance with paragraph 7(1)(a) keep a record containing the information specified in Part I of Annex 4 in relation to that sample;

(b) keep a record of the result of any test which has been reported or passed to him in accordance with paragraph 8(1)(b) or (2); and

(c) keep a record containing the information specified in Part III of Annex 4 of the movement of any eggs onto and off, and of the movement of any chicks off the premises.

(3) A person shall—

(a) retain any record he is required to keep under sub-paragraphs (1) and (2) for a period of one year from the date on which the sample was taken or from the date of the test or from the date on which the movement took place, as the case may be; and (*b*) produce any such record to an inspector on demand at any reasonable time during that period and allow him to take a copy of it or an extract from it.

Prohibition on vaccination

11. A person shall not vaccinate any poultry with any vaccine which is likely to affect the result of any test carried out under this Scheme on any sample taken from poultry, except under the authority of and in accordance with the conditions of a licence issued by a veterinary inspector.

Powers of the Department in cases of default

12. If any person fails to take any action required to be taken by him under any of the provisions of this Scheme, the Department may, without prejudice to any proceedings arising out of such default, take, or cause to be taken, such action.

Transitional arrangements

13.—(1) Where any person who keeps a breeding flock on any premises was, immediately before the coming into operation of this Scheme, registered under and in accordance with Article 3(1) of the Poultry Breeding Flocks and Hatcheries (Registration and Testing etc) Order (Northern Ireland) 1990(**a**), he shall be deemed to be registered in respect of those premises in the Breeding Flocks Register.

(2) Where any person is deemed to be registered in the Breeding Flocks Register pursuant to sub-paragraph (1), the date of the coming into operation of this Scheme shall, for the purposes of paragraph 3(5), be treated as the date of that registration.

14.—(1) Where any person who uses any premises as a hatchery was, immediately before the coming into operation of this Scheme, registered under and in accordance with Article 4(1) of the Poultry Breeding Flocks and Hatcheries (Registration and Testing etc) Order (Northern Ireland) 1990, he shall be deemed to be registered in respect of those premises in the Hatcheries Register.

(2) Where any person is deemed to be registered in the Hatcheries Register pursuant to sub-paragraph (1), the date of the coming into operation of this Scheme shall, for the purposes of paragraph 4(5), be treated as the date of that registration.

(**a**) S.R. 1990 No. 50

ANNEX 1

PART I

PARTICULARS TO BE NOTIFIED TO THE DEPARTMENT FOR THE PURPOSES OF
PARAGRAPH 3(4)

1. The name, address and telephone number (if any) of the applicant, including, if appropriate, the names of any partners or the registered number of the company.

2. The address and telephone number of the premises on which the breeding flock to which the application relates is to be kept.

3. The name of the person in charge of the premises on which that flock is to be kept (if not the applicant).

4. The species of birds in that flock.

5. The approximate number of birds in that flock.

PART II Paragraph 4(4)

PARTICULARS TO BE NOTIFIED TO THE DEPARTMENT FOR THE PURPOSES OF
PARAGRAPH 4(4)

1. The name, address and telephone number (if any) of the applicant, including, if appropriate, the names of any partners or the registered number of the company.

2. The address and telephone number of the premises which are to be used as a hatchery.

3. The name of the person in charge of the premises which are to be used as a hatchery (if not the applicant).

4. The incubator capacity of the premises which are to be used as a hatchery and the species of birds to be hatched there.

PART I

SAMPLES TO BE TAKEN FROM BREEDING FLOCKS FOR BACTERIOLOGICAL TESTING

1. The number of sites from which separate faeces samples are to be taken in order to make a composite sample shall be as follows:

Number of birds kept in a house, or on premises on which birds have free access to more than one house, number of birds in each group of houses on such holding	Number of faeces samples to be taken in the house or group of houses on the premises
1– 29	A number equal to the total number of birds up to a maximum of 20 birds
30– 39	25
40– 49	30
50– 59	35
60– 89	40
90–199	50
200–499	55
500 or more	60

2. The samples to be taken shall comprise—

(*a*) one chick box liner, up to a maximum of 10, for every 500 chicks delivered from each hatchery to any rearing premises on any day, such samples to be taken on the day of the arrival of the chicks there;

(*b*) the carcases of all chicks, up to a maximum of 60, from each hatchery, which are dead on arrival at any rearing premises, such samples to be taken on the day of the arrival of the chicks there;

(*c*) a composite faeces sample taken from birds at 4 weeks of age and either at 2 weeks prior to them entering the laying phase or 2 weeks before moving to laying accommodation, the number of separate samples being taken in accordance with the table in paragraph 1;

(*d*) in the case of birds whose eggs are hatched at a hatchery with a total incubator capacity of less than 1,000 eggs a composite faeces sample taken from birds at the time they enter the laying phase and at intervals of 2 weeks thereafter in accordance with the table in paragraph 1.

3. Samples referred to in sub-paragraph 2(*d*) shall be taken under the supervision of an inspector at 56 day intervals.

SAMPLES TO BE TAKEN FROM HATCHERIES FOR BACTERIOLOGICAL TESTING

1. The samples to be taken shall comprise—

(*a*) a composite sample of meconium taken from 250 chicks, one such sample being taken every 7 days in the case of grandparent flocks and every 14 days in the case of parent flocks, from those chicks hatched from eggs supplied to the hatchery from any particular breeding flock (including flocks of less than 250 birds); or

(*b*) (i) the carcases of all chicks which are dead in the shells of eggs supplied to the hatchery from any particular breeding flock; and

    (ii) the carcases of all chicks hatched from eggs supplied to the hatchery from any particular breeding flock and which have been culled,

such samples being taken from grandparent flocks every 7 days and from parent flocks every 14 days, up to a maximum of 50 in total.

2. Samples taken for the purposes of paragraph 1 shall be taken under the supervision of an inspector, every 28 days in the case of grandparent flocks and every 56 days in the case of parent flocks.

BACTERIOLOGICAL METHODS FOR TESTING FOR SALMONELLA

1. Bacteriological method (Rappaports) for the detection of salmonella in chick box liners, composite faeces samples, meconium samples and carcases.

Samples submitted for testing for the presence of salmonella shall be examined in the following prescribed manner on consecutive days and, where a laboratory at which samples have been received for testing on any day is unable to commence such an examination on that day, the samples shall be stored in a refrigerator at between 1°C and 4°C until required for examination.

Day 1

(*a*) Chick box liners: a one gram portion shall be taken from a soiled area on each liner and the portions from separate liners shall be bulked together and placed in Buffered Peptone Water (BPW)(**a**), at the rate of 1 gram of liner in 10 ml of BPW up to a maximum of 10 grams in 100 ml of BPW.

(*b*) Composite faeces and meconium samples: the samples shall be thoroughly mixed and a sub-sample weighing not more than 10 grams shall be placed in BPW at the rate of 1 gram sample to 10 ml BPW to a maximum of 10 grams in 100 ml BPW.

(*c*) Carcases of chicks: there shall be removed samples of the yolk sac, liver and terminal intestines (to include portions of small intestines, large intestine and caecal tonsil). The samples of organs taken from the carcases of chicks submitted shall then be bulked together and placed in BPW at the rate of 1 gram of bulked tissue in 10 ml BPW up to a maximum of 10 grams of tissue in 100 ml BPW.

The inoculated BPW shall then be incubated at 37°C for 18-24 hours.

Day 2

0.1 ml from the incubated BPW shall be inoculated into 10 ml of Rappaports Vassiliadis (RV) broth or Rappaports Vassiliadis Soya Peptone (RVS)(**b**) broth and incubated at 41.5°C ± 0.5°C for 18-24 hours.

Day 3

The RV or RVS broth shall be plated out on to 2 plates of Selective Salmonella Agar (SSA) using a 10 microlitres loop. The SSA plates shall be inoculated with a droplet taken from the edge of the surface of the fluid and drawing the loop over the whole of one plate in a zigzag pattern and continuing to the second plate without recharging the loop. The space between the loop streaks shall be 0.5-1.0 cm. The plates shall be incubated at 37°C for 18-24 hours, and the RV or RVS broth reincubated at 41.5°C ± 0.5°C for a further 18-24 hours.

Day 4

(i) The plates of SSA shall be examined and a minimum of 3 colonies from the plates showing suspicion of salmonella growth shall be sub-cultured on to a blood agar plate and a MacConkey agar plate and into biochemical composite media or equivalent. These media shall be incubated at 37°C for 18-24 hours.

(ii) The reincubated RV or RVS broth shall be plated out, and the plates incubated, as described in Day 3.

Day 5

(i) The incubated plates and composite media or equivalent shall be examined and the findings recorded, discarding cultures which are obviously not salmonella. Slide serological tests shall be performed using salmonella polyvalent "O" (Groups A-S) and polyvalent "H" (phase 1 and 2) agglutinating sera on selected suspect colonies collected from the blood agar or MacConkey plates. If reactions occur with one or both sera, the colonies shall be typed to Group level by slide serology.

(ii) The plates of SSA prepared at Day 4 (ii) shall be examined and further action taken as described in Day 4 (i) and Day 5(i).

2. Bacteriological method (Selenite) for the detection of salmonella in chick box liners, composite faeces samples, meconium samples and carcases.

Samples submitted for testing for the presence of salmonella shall be examined in the following prescribed manner on consecutive days and, where a laboratory at which samples have been received for testing on any day is unable to commence such an examination on that day, the samples shall be stored in a refrigerator at between 1°C and 4°C until required for examination.

Day 1

(*a*) Chick box liners: a one gram portion shall be taken from a soiled area on each liner and the portions from separate liners shall be bulked together and placed in Selenite F broth(**c**) at the rate of 1 gram of liner to 10 ml broth up to a maximum of 10 grams of liner in 100 ml broth.

(*b*) Composite faeces and meconium samples: the sample shall be thoroughly mixed and a sub-sample weighing not more than 10 grams shall be placed in Selenite F broth at the rate of 1 gram of faeces to 10 ml broth up to a maximum of 10 grams of faeces in 100 ml broth.

(*c*) Carcases of chicks: there shall be removed samples of the yolk sac, liver and terminal intestines (to include portions of small intestines, large intestine and caecal tonsil).

The samples of organs taken from the carcases of chicks submitted shall then be bulked together and placed in Selenite F broth at the rate of 1 gram of bulked tissue in 10 ml of broth up to a maximum of 10 grams of tissue in 100 ml broth.

The inoculated Selenite F broth shall then be incubated at 37°C for 18-24 hours.

Day 2

 (i) The Selenite F broth shall be plated out on to two plates of Selective Salmonella Agar (SSA) using a 10 microlitres loop. The SSA plates shall be inoculated with a droplet taken from the edge of the surface of the fluid and drawing the loop over the whole of one plate in a zigzag pattern and continuing to the second plate without recharging the loop. The space between the loopstreaks shall be 0.5 cm-1.0 cm. The plates shall be incubated at 37°C for 18-24 hours.

 (ii) The Selenite F broth shall then be reincubated at 37°C for a further 18-24 hours.

Day 3

 (i) The plates of SSA shall be examined and a minimum of 3 colonies from the plates showing suspicion of salmonella growth shall be sub-cultured on to a blood agar plate and a MacConkey agar plate and into biochemical composite media or equivalent. These media shall be incubated at 37°C for 18-24 hours.

 (ii) The reincubated Selenite F broth shall be plated out and incubated as described in Day 2(i).

Day 4

 (i) The incubated plates and composite media or equivalent shall be examined and the findings recorded, discarding cultures which are obviously not salmonella. Slide serological tests shall be performed using salmonella polyvalent "O" (Groups A-S) and polyvalent "H" (phase 1 and 2) agglutinating sera on selected suspect colonies collected from the blood agar or MacConkey plates. If reactions occur with one or both sera, the colonies shall be typed to Group level by slide serology.

 (ii) The plates of SSA prepared at Day 3(ii) shall be examined and further action taken as described in Day 3(i) and Day 4(i).

3. In this Part "Selective Salmonella Agar" means a selective agar approved by the Department for the isolation of salmonella organisims.

 (**a**) Buffered Peptone Water — Edel and Kampelmacher (1973) (commercially available as Oxoid CM 509, Lab M46 or equivalent).

 (**b**) Rappaports Vassiliadis (RV) Broth — vassiliadis et al (1976) (commercially available as Oxoid CM 669 or equivalent) or Rappaports Vassiliadis Soya Peptone (RVS) Broth (Oxoid CM 866).

 (**c**) Selenite F broth — Liefson (1936) (commercially available as Oxoid CM 395 and L121, Lab M44a and 44b or equivalent).

(*a*), (*b*), (*c*) and selective salmonella agars should be reconstituted according to the manufacturer's instructions and in the case of selective salmonella agars poured into 9 cm diameter plates.

REFERENCES

References for the above substances are found in:

Liefson, E. (1936) American Journal of Hygiene 24, 423-432.

Edel, W. & Kampelmacher, E. H. (1973) Bulletin of the World Health Organisation 48, 167-174.

Anon (1969) ISO 6579 International Organisation for Standardisation, Geneva, Vassiliadis, P., Pateraki, E., Papaiconomou, N., Papadakis, J. A., and Trichopoulos, D. (1976) Annales de Microbiologie (Institut Pasteur) 127B, 195-200.

ANNEX 3

PART I

BLOOD SAMPLES TO BE TAKEN FOR SEROLOGICAL TESTING FOR SALMONELLA PULLORUM

1. Blood samples to be taken, by or under the supervision of an inspector, from domestic fowls between 3 and 5 weeks before they are transferred to laying accommodation or when they are between 16 and 22 weeks of age, whichever occurs later.

2. The number of birds from which blood samples shall be taken shall be a number calculated in accordance with the following table:—

Number of birds required to be sampled for testing for Salmonella pullorum

Number of birds kept in a house or, on premises on which birds have free access to more than one house, number of birds in each group of houses on such premises	Number of birds to be sampled in that house or in that group of houses on those premises
1– 29	A number equal to the total number of birds up to a maximum of 20 birds.
30– 39	25
40– 49	30
50– 59	35
60– 89	40
90–199	50
200–499	55
500 or more	60

3. The samples shall each comprise 0.02 ml of blood taken from a wing vein of a bird by pricking with a suitable needle.

PART II

SEROLOGICAL METHOD FOR TESTING FOR SALMONELLA PULLORUM

1. The rapid plate whole blood test shall be used for the testing of blood samples for *Salmonella pullorum* and those tests shall be carried out as follows:—

  (1) 0.02 ml of blood taken from a wing vein of a bird, after pricking with a suitable needle, shall be placed on a white ceramic tile using a loop of the appropriate size.

  (2) 0.04 ml of polyvalent crystal violet stained *Salmonella pullorum* antigen(**a**) shall be added to the blood and mixed with it.

  (3) The tile shall be rocked gently for 2 minutes after which time the test shall be read.

(**a**) S pullorum antigen must contain standard and variant strains of S pullorum stained with crystal violet and standardised against international standard sera raised against the standard and variant strains (O.I.E. 1986)

(4) All bleeding needles and loops must be washed in a normal saline solution(**a**) after each bird has been sampled and tested and that solution must be renewed after every 200 birds have been sampled and tested.

REFERENCE

O.I.E. (1986) International Zoosanitary Code 5th Edition, 362-364 (updated May 1988 as International Animal Health Code, updated pages 45 to 47).

(**a**)   Normal saline solution is prepared by dissolving saline tablets in water according to the manufacturer's instructions

PART I

RECORDS OF SAMPLES TAKEN IN RESPECT OF A BREEDING FLOCK OR A HATCHERY

1. In respect of each sample taken under and in accordance with paragraphs 5(1)(*a*) and 7(1)(*a*) the following information shall be kept—

(*a*) the date on which the sample was taken;

(*b*) a description of the type of sample taken; and

(*c*) in the case of samples taken in respect of a breeding flock, the identity of the house or group of houses from which the samples were taken and, in the case of samples taken from a hatchery, the address of the premises which supplied the hatching eggs to the hatchery from which the samples were obtained.

PART II   Paragraph 10(1)(*c*)

RECORDS OF THE MOVEMENT OF POULTRY, CHICKS AND EGGS ONTO AND OFF ANY PREMISES ON WHICH A BREEDING FLOCK IS KEPT

2. In respect of the movement of any poultry, chicks or eggs onto or off the premises on which the breeding flock is kept, the following information shall be kept—

(*a*) the date of the movement;

(*b*) the number of poultry, chicks or eggs moved;

(*c*) the identity of the house or group of houses in which any poultry, chicks or eggs moved onto the premises were placed or from which any poultry, chicks or eggs were moved off the premises;

(*d*) in the case of any poultry, chicks or eggs moved onto the premises, the address from which they were brought there; and

(*e*) in the case of any poultry, chicks or eggs moved off the premises, the address of the premises to which they were moved.

PART III   Paragraph 10(2)(*c*)

RECORDS OF THE MOVEMENT OF EGGS ONTO AND OFF, AND OF THE MOVEMENT OF CHICKS OFF, ANY PREMISES WHICH ARE USED AS A HATCHERY

3. In respect of the movement of eggs onto or off and the movement of chicks off any premises which are used as a hatchery, the following information shall be kept—

(*a*) the date of the movement;

(*b*) in the case of the movement of any eggs onto the premises, the address of the premises from which they were moved and the number of eggs moved; and

(*c*) in the case of the movement of any eggs or chicks off the premises the address of the premises to which they were moved and the number of eggs or chicks moved.

EXPLANATORY NOTE

(This note is not part of the Order.)

The Scheme set out in the Schedule to this Order ("the Scheme") supersedes the Poultry Breeding Flocks and Hatcheries (Registration and Testing etc) Order (Northern Ireland) 1990 ("the 1990 Order") which is now revoked (see S.R. 1994 No. 120). It continues to require a person keeping a breeding flock on any premises or using any premises as a hatchery—

(*a*) to have his name entered in respect of those premises in a register kept by the Department of Agriculture ("the Department"); and

(*b*) to carry out regular sampling in respect of that flock or hatchery.

The main changes of substance from the 1990 Order are:—

1. A person is no longer prohibited from keeping a breeding flock on any premises or using any premises as a hatchery unless he is registered by the Department.

2. A breeding flock is now defined as meaning a breeding flock with at least 250 birds.

3. Annual registration of breeding flocks and hatcheries has been replaced by a once and for all registration. Those previously registered under the 1990 Order are deemed to be registered under the Scheme from its date of operation. Registered persons are required to report changes of particulars within 28 days after the anniversary of registration.

4. Registration is no longer dependent on compliance with certain requirements relating to the keeping of a breeding flock on any premises or the use of any premises as a hatchery.

5. There are changes to the requirements for sampling flocks and hatcheries.

Any person who without lawful authority or excuse, proof of which lies on him, contravenes any provisions of the Scheme shall be guilty of offence against the Diseases of Animals (Northern Ireland) Order 1981. The penalty, on summary conviction, is a fine at Level 5 on the standard scale (currently £2,000) or in the case of an offence committed with respect to more than 5 animals, a fine at Level 3 on the standard scale (currently £400) for each animal; or in the case of an offence committed in relation to carcases or other inanimate things a fine at Level 5 on the standard scale (currently £2,000) together with a fine at Level 3 on the standard scale (currently £400) in respect of every 508 kilograms in weight of the carcases or other things after the first 508 kilograms.

1994   No. 119

ANIMALS

Breeding Flocks, Hatcheries and Animal Protein (Fees) Order (Northern Ireland) 1994

Made	*28th March 1994*
Coming into operation . .	*18th April 1994*

The Department of Agriculture, in exercise of the powers conferred on it by Article 50(1) of the Diseases of Animals (Northern Ireland) Order 1981(**a**) and of every other power enabling it in that behalf, with the approval of the Department of Finance and Personnel(**b**) hereby makes the following Order:

Citation and commencement

1. This Order may be cited as the Breeding Flocks, Hatcheries and Animal Protein (Fees) Order (Northern Ireland) 1994 and shall come into operation on 18th April 1994.

Interpretation

2. In this Order—

"the Breeding Flocks Scheme" means the Poultry Breeding Flocks and Hatcheries Scheme (Northern Ireland) 1994(**c**); and

"the Order" means "the Diseases of Animals (Animal Protein) (No. 2) Order (Northern Ireland) 1989"(**d**).

Fees

3. There shall be paid to the Department in respect of the transactions specified in column (2) of the Schedule the fees specified opposite thereto in column (3), such fees being payable within 14 days of demand.

Revocation

4. The Poultry Flocks, Hatcheries and Animal Protein (Fees) Order (Northern Ireland) 1990(**e**) and the Poultry Flocks, Hatcheries and Animal Protein (Fees) (Amendment) Order (Northern Ireland) 1992(**f**) are hereby revoked.

(**a**) S.I. 1981/1115 (N.I. 22) to which there are amendments not relevant to the subject matter of this Order
(**b**) Formerly Department of Finance: *See* S.I. 1982/338 (N.I. 6) Art. 3
(**c**) Set out in the Schedule to S.R. 1994 No. 118
(**d**) S.R. 1989 No. 347 as amended by S.R. 1992 No. 62 and S.R. 1993 No. 193
(**e**) S.R. 1990 No. 175
(**f**) S.R. 1992 No. 251

Sealed with the Official Seal of the Department of Agriculture on 28th March 1994.

(L.S.)   *P. T. Toal*

                                           Assistant Secretary

The Department of Finance and Personnel hereby approves the foregoing Order.

Sealed with the Official Seal of the Department of Finance and Personnel on 28th March 1994.

(L.S.)   *D. Thomson*

                                           Assistant Secretary

SCHEDULE　　　　　　　　　　　　Article 3

Payment to the Department

*NOTE— the fees payable under the Poultry Flocks, Hatcheries and Animal Protein (Fees) Order (Northern Ireland) 1990(**a**) immediately before coming into operation of the Breeding Flocks, Hatcheries and Animal Protein (Fees) Order (Northern Ireland) 1994(**b**) are shown in brackets.*

Item (1)	Transaction (2)	Fee (3)	Old Fee (4)
1.	Supervision by an inspector of the taking of samples from breeding flocks under paragraph 5(1)(*a*) of, and paragraph 2(*d*) of Part I of Annex 2, and paragraph 6(*a*) of, and paragraph 1 of Part I of Annex 3 to, the Breeding Flocks Scheme.	£27·60 for the first ½ hour (or part thereof) of each visit plus £7·20 per ½ hour (or part thereof) thereafter.	(£26·00 for the first ½ hour (or part thereof) of each visit plus £7·00 per ½ hour (or part thereof) thereafter.)
2.	Supervision by an inspector of the taking of samples from poultry in hatcheries under paragraph 7(1)(*a*) of, and Part II of Annex 2 to, the Breeding Flocks Scheme.	£27·60 for the first ½ hour (or part thereof) of each visit plus £7·20 per ½ hour (or part thereof) thereafter.	(£26·00 for the first ½ hour (or part thereof) of each visit plus £7·00 per ½ hour (or part thereof) thereafter.)
3.	Testing by the Department of composite faeces samples taken from breeding flocks under paragraph 5(1)(*a*) of, and paragraph 2(*d*) of Part I of Annex 2 to, the Breeding Flocks Scheme.	£　5·80	
4.	Testing by the Department of samples taken from poultry in hatcheries under paragraph 7(1)(*a*) of, and Part II of Annex 2 to, the Breeding Flocks Scheme, in the case of—		
	(*a*) a composite meconium sample;	£　5·80	(£　5·60)
	(*b*) the carcases of chicks dead in shell (up to a maximum of 50);	£ 11·05	(£ 10·65)
	(*c*) the carcases of chicks hatched from eggs (up to a maximum of 50).	£ 11·05	(£ 10·65)

(**a**)　S.R. 1990 No. 175 as amended by S.R. 1992 No. 251
(**b**)　S.R. 1994 No. 119

Item (1)	Transaction (2)	Fee (3)	Old Fee (4)
5.	Inspection of a laboratory which has applied for authorisation for the purposes of the Breeding Flocks Scheme, or the Order, or both.	£196·00	(£196·00)
6.	(a) Distribution of 2 quality assurance samples to a laboratory which has applied for authorisation for the purposes of the Breeding Flocks Scheme, or the Order, or both, to enable the Department to assess the accuracy of its testing for those purposes.	£ 86·00	(£ 85·00)
	(b) Distribution of 4 quality assurance samples to a laboratory authorised for the purposes of the Breeding Flocks Scheme, or the Order, or both, to enable the Department to assess the accuracy of its testing for those purposes.	£162·00	(£159·00)

EXPLANATORY NOTE

(This note is not part of the Order.)

This Order prescribes fees to be paid to the Department of Agriculture ("the Department") for certain business transacted under the Diseases of Animals (Northern Ireland) Order 1981. It repeals and replaces the Poultry Flocks, Hatcheries and Animal Protein (Fees) Order (Northern Ireland) 1990 so as to reflect the repeal of the Poultry Breeding Flocks and Hatcheries (Registration and Testing etc) Order (Northern Ireland) 1990 (by S.R. 1994 No. 120) and the Poultry Laying Flocks (Registration and Testing etc) Order (Northern Ireland) 1990 ("the Laying Flocks Order") (by S.R. 1993 No. 251) and the replacement of the former by a new and changed Poultry Breeding Flocks and Hatcheries Scheme Order (Northern Ireland) 1994 ("the 1994 Scheme Order"). The main changes of substance to this Order are as follows:—

1. There is no longer a requirement for annual registration and inspection, under the 1994 Scheme Order, of premises used for breeding flocks or hatcheries. Therefore fees for these services have been removed.

2. Supervision of sampling of breeding flocks immediately before lay is no longer required under the 1994 Scheme Order. Therefore the fee for this service has been removed.

3. Supervision of the taking of samples from breeding flocks using hatcheries of less than 1,000 egg capacity has been introduced by the 1994 Scheme Order and a fee for this service has been included.

4. Laboratories are no longer authorised for the purposes of the Laying Flocks Order so fees for the inspection and monitoring of such laboratories have been removed.

5. Most of the other fees have been increased.

1994 No. 120

ANIMALS

Poultry Breeding Flocks and Hatcheries (Registration and Testing etc) (Revocation) Order (Northern Ireland) 1994

Made	*28th March 1994*
Coming into operation . .	*18th April 1994*

The Department of Agriculture, in exercise of the powers conferred on it by Articles 5(1), 19(*h*), 44 and 60(1) of the Diseases of Animals (Northern Ireland) Order 1981(**a**) and of every other power enabling it in that behalf, hereby makes the following Order:

Citation and commencement

1. This Order may be cited as the Poultry Breeding Flocks and Hatcheries (Registration and Testing etc) (Revocation) Order (Northern Ireland) 1994.

Revocation

2. The Poultry Breeding Flocks and Hatcheries (Registration and Testing etc) Order (Northern Ireland) 1990(**b**) is hereby revoked.

Sealed with the Official Seal of the Department of Agriculture on 28th March 1994.

(L.S.)

            P. T. Toal
            Assistant Secretary

(**a**) S.I. 1981/1115 (N.I. 22) as amended by S.I. 1984/702 (N.I. 2) Art. 17
(**b**) S.R. 1990/50

EXPLANATORY NOTE

(This note is not part of the Order.)

This Order revokes the Poultry Breeding Flocks and Hatcheries (Registration and Testing etc) Order (Northern Ireland) 1990 which is replaced by the Poultry Breeding Flocks and Hatcheries Scheme Order (Northern Ireland) 1994.

1994   No. 121

Temporary Speed Limit (Motorway M2) Order (Northern Ireland) 1994

This Order, being of a temporary character, is not printed at length in this volume.

1994 No. 122

EDUCATION

Education (Individual Pupils' Achievements) (Information) (Amendment) Regulations (Northern Ireland) 1994

Made	*28th March 1994*
Coming into operation . .	*28th April 1994*

The Department of Education, in exercise of the powers conferred on it by Article 17A of the Education and Libraries (Northern Ireland) Order 1986(**a**) and Article 31(2) and (3) of the Education Reform (Northern Ireland) Order 1989(**b**) (''the 1989 Order'') and of every other power enabling it in that behalf, and after consulting as required by Article 31(4) of the 1989 Order, hereby makes the following Regulations:

Citation and commencement

1. These Regulations may be cited as the Education (Individual Pupils' Achievements) (Information) (Amendment) Regulations (Northern Ireland) 1994 and shall come into operation on 28th April 1994.

Amendment of the Education (Individual Pupils' Achievements) (Information) Regulations (Northern Ireland) 1991

2. For regulation 8 (Time and manner of provision of information to parents) of the Education (Individual Pupils' Achievements) (Information) Regulations (Northern Ireland) 1991(**c**) there shall be substituted—

''**8.**—(1) Subject to paragraph (2) the principal shall send the information (whether by post or otherwise) to the pupil's parent not later than 30th June in the school year to which the information relates.

(2) Where the principal receives information after 30th June in any school year consisting of the results of public examinations taken by a pupil at the school during that school year, he shall send that information (whether by post or otherwise) as soon as reasonably practicable to the parent of that pupil.''.

Sealed with the Official Seal of the Department of Education on 28th March 1994.

(L.S.)   *C. Jendoubi*
                             Assistant Secretary

(**a**)   S.I. 1986/594 (N.I. 3) Article 17A was inserted by Article 5 of S.I. 1987/167 (N.I. 2) and amended by
     S.I. 1989/2406 (N.I. 20) Articles 32 and 166 and Schedule 9
(**b**)   S.I. 1989/2406 (N.I. 20)
(**c**)   S.R. 1991 No. 351

EXPLANATORY NOTE

(This note is not part of the Regulations.)

These Regulations amend the Education (Individual Pupils' Achievements) (Information) Regulations (Northern Ireland) 1991. They change from 30th April to 30th June, the date by which a school principal must supply the parents of each pupil in the final year of Key Stage 2 with information about the pupil's educational achievements. This makes the date for the supply of that information in the case of a pupil who is at the end of Key Stage 2 the same as that for all other Key Stages.

1994 No. 123

AGRICULTURE

Feeding Stuffs (Amendment) Regulations (Northern Ireland) 1994

Made . . . . . *29th March 1994*

Coming into operation . . *28th April 1994*

The Department of Agriculture, being a Department designated(**a**), for the purposes of section 2(2) of the European Communities Act 1972(**b**) in relation to the common agricultural policy of the European Economic Community, in exercise of the powers conferred on it by that section and sections 66(1), 68(1), (1A) and (3), 69(1), (3), (6) and (7), 70(1), 73(3), 74(1), 74A(**c**), 84 and 86 of the Agriculture Act 1970(**d**) and of every other power enabling it in that behalf, after consultation with such persons or organisations as appear to it to represent the interests concerned, hereby makes the following Regulations:—

Citation and commencement

1. These Regulations may be cited as the Feeding Stuffs (Amendment) Regulations (Northern Ireland) 1994 and shall come into operation on 28th April 1994.

Amendment of the Feeding Stuffs Regulations (Northern Ireland) 1992

2. The Feeding Stuffs Regulations (Northern Ireland) 1992(**e**) shall be further amended in accordance with regulation 3.

3.—(1) In Schedule 4—

(*a*) in Part III ("PERMITTED EMULSIFIERS, STABILISERS, THICKENERS AND GELLING AGENTS")—

(i) in Chapter A, after the provisions relating to Microcrystalline cellulose there shall be inserted the following provisions:

(**a**) *See* S.I. 1972/1811
(**b**) 1972 c. 68; section 2 is subject to Schedule 2 to that Act and is to be read with S.I. 1984/703 (N.I. 3) and S.R. 1984 No. 253
(**c**) Inserted by 1972 c. 68 s. 4(1) and Schedule 4, paragraph 6
(**d**) 1970 c. 40 as amended by S.I. 1982/980
(**e**) S.R. 1992 No. 270 as amended by S.R. 1993 No. 349

''E460(ii)	Cellulose powder''

(ii) In Chapter B, after the provisions relating to Partial polyglycerol esters of polycondensed fatty acids of castor oil (polyglycerol polyricinoleate) there shall be added the following provisions:

''E499	Cassia Gum	Dogs, Cats	17600	Canned feeding stuffs only''

(b) in Part VII (''AROMATIC AND APPETISING SUBSTANCES''), in Columns 4 and 6 opposite reference to the additive Neohesperidine dihydrochalcone, there shall be inserted the following provisions:

—	—	—	''Calves Ovines	— —	30 30''

(2) In Schedule 7—

(a) after the provisions relating to item 2.2.2 (''Ammonium acetate in aqueous solution'') there shall be inserted the following provisions:

"2.2.3 Ammonium sulphate in aqueous solution	—	$(NH_4)_2SO_4$	—	Ammonium sulphate: min. 35%	—	Ruminants, from the start of rumination	Declarations to be made on the label or packaging of the product:
							— the words "Ammonium sulphate";
							— nitrogen and moisture contents;
							— animal species;
							— in the case of young ruminants, the incorporation rate in the daily ration may not exceed 0.5%;
							Declarations to be made on the label or packaging of compound feeding stuffs:
							— the words "Ammonium sulphate";
							— the amount of the product contained in the feeding stuff;
							— percentage of the total protein provided by non-protein nitrogen;
							— indication in the instructions for use of the level of total non-protein nitrogen which should not

be exceeded in the daily ration of each animal species;

— in the case of young ruminants, the incorporation rate in the daily ration may not exceed 0.5%.''

(b) after the provisions relating to item 3.1.4 (''Concentrated liquid sodium DL-Methionine technically pure'') there shall be inserted the following provisions:

''3.1.5 DL-methionine, technically pure protected with copolymer vinyl-pyridine/styrene	$CH_3S(CH_2)_2$—$CH(NH_2)$—COOH	—	DL-methionine: minimum 65% copolymer vinylpyridine/styrene: maximum 3%	Dairy Cows	Declarations to be made on the label or packaging of the product: — ''Protected methionine with copolymer vinyl-pyridine/styrene''; — DL-methionine and moisture contents — animal species''

(c) after the provisions relating to item 3.2.6 ("L-Lysine phosphate and its by-products produced by fermentation with *Brevibacterium lactofermentum* NRRL B-11470") there shall be inserted the following provisions:

				Declarations to be made on the label or packaging of the product:
"3.2.7 Mixtures of:		—		— the name "mixture of L-lysine monohydrochloride and DL-methionine protected with copolymer vinyl-pyridine/styrene";
(a) L-lysine-mono-hydrochloride, technically pure and,	$NH_2-(CH_2)_4-CH(NH_2)-COOH\cdot HCl$	L-lysine + DL–methionine: minimum 50% (including DL-methionine: minimum 15%)	Dairy Cows	— L-lysine, DL-methionine and moisture contents;
(b) DL-methionine, technically pure protected with copolymer vinyl-pyridine/styrene	$CH_3S(CH_2)_2-CH(NH_2)-COOH$	Copolymer vinyl-pyridine/ styrene: maximum 3%		— animal species".

(d) for the provisions relating to item 4 ("Hydroxy-analogues of amino acids") and item 4.1 ("Hydroxy-analogue of methionine and its salts") there shall be substituted the following provisions:

"4. Analogues of amino acids 4.1 Analogues of methionine					
4.1.1 Hydroxy-analogue of methionine	$CH_3S(CH_2)_2$—CH(OH)—COOH	—	Total of acids: minimum 85% Monomer acid: minimum 65%	all animal species	Declarations to be made on the label or packaging of the product: — if appropriate, the name (column 2); — monomer acid and total acids contents in the case of product 4.1.1 and monomer acid content in the case of product 4.1.2; — moisture content; — animal species
4.1.2 Calcium salt of hydroxy-analogue of methionine	[CH_3—S—$(CH_2)_2$—CH(OH)—$COO]_2Ca$	—	Monomer acid: minimum 83% Calcium: minimum 12%		Declarations to be made on the label or packaging of compound feeding stuffs: — if appropriate, the name (column 2);

— monomer acid and total acids contents in the case of product 4.1.1 and monomer acid content in the case of product 4.1.2;

— amount of the product contained in the feeding stuff''.

Sealed with the Official Seal of the Department of Agriculture for Northern Ireland on 29th March 1994.

(L.S.)

I. C. Henderson

Assistant Secretary

EXPLANATORY NOTE

(This note is not part of the Regulations.)

These Regulations further amend the Feeding Stuffs Regulations (Northern Ireland) 1992 ("the principal Regulations") and implement as respects Northern Ireland the following Community legislation:

1. Commission Directive 93/26/EEC (OJ No. L179, 22.7.93, p. 2) amending the Annex to Council Directive 82/471/EEC concerning certain products used in animal nutrition, (regulation 3(2)(*b*), (*c*) and (*d*));

2. Commission Directive 93/27/EEC (OJ No. L179, 22.7.93, p. 5) amending the Annexes to Council Directive 70/524/EEC concerning additives in feeding stuffs, (regulation 3(1)(*a*)(i) and (*b*));

3. Commission Directive 93/55/EEC (OJ No. L206, 18.8.93, p. 11) amending Annex I to Council Directive 70/524/EEC (regulation 3(1)(*a*)(ii));

4. Commission Directive 93/56/EEC (OJ No. L206, 18.8.93, p. 13) amending the Annex to Council Directive 82/471/EEC (regulation 3(2)(*a*) and (*d*)).

Regulation 3(1) amends Schedule 4 to the principal Regulations, which relates to permitted additives in feeding stuffs. Regulation 3(2) amends Schedule 7 to those Regulations, which relates to the control of certain products used in animal nutrition.

1994   No.   124

HEALTH AND PERSONAL SOCIAL SERVICES

Charges for Drugs and Appliances (Amendment) Regulations (Northern Ireland) 1994

Made	*29th March 1994*
Coming into operation . .	*1st April 1994*

The Department of Health and Social Services, in exercise of the powers conferred on it by Articles 98 and 106 of, and Schedule 15 to, the Health and Personal Social Services (Northern Ireland) Order 1972(**a**) and of all other powers enabling it in that behalf, with the approval of the Department of Finance and Personnel, hereby makes the following regulations:

Citation, commencement and interpretation

1.—(1) These regulations may be cited as the Charges for Drugs and Appliances (Amendment) Regulations (Northern Ireland) 1994 and shall come into operation on 1st April 1994.

(2) In these regulations, "the principal regulations" means the Health and Personal Social Services (Charges for Drugs and Appliances) Regulations (Northern Ireland) 1973(**b**).

Amendment of regulation 3 of the principal regulations

2. In regulation 3 (supply of drugs and appliances by chemists) in paragraphs (1)(*b*) and (3) for "£4·25" there shall be substituted "£4·75".

Amendment of regulation 5 of the principal regulations

3. In regulation 5(1)(*b*) (supply of drugs and appliances by doctors) for "£4·25" there shall be substituted "£4·75".

Amendment of regulation 6 of the principal regulations

4. In regulation 6(4) (prepayment certificates) for "£22·00" there shall be substituted "£24·60", and for "£60·60" there shall be substituted "£67·70".

Amendment of regulation 7 of the principal regulations

5. In regulation 7 (supply of drugs and certain appliances to out-patients by hospitals)—

(**a**) S.I. 1972/1265 (N.I. 14); the relevant amending instruments are S.I. 1986/2229 (N.I. 24) Article 14, S.I. 1988/2249 (N.I. 24) Article 7 and S.I. 1991/194 (N.I. 1) Article 34 and Part II of Schedule 5
(**b**) S.R. & O. (N.I.) 1973 No. 419; the last amending regulations are S.R. 1993 No. 140

(*a*) in paragraph (1)(*b*) for "£4·25" there shall be substituted "£4·75";

(*b*) in paragraphs (2)(*b*) and (3) for "£4·25" there shall be substituted "£4·75".

Amendment of Schedules to the principal regulations

6.—(1) In Schedule 1 for "£4·25" there shall be substituted "£4·75" and for "£8·50" there shall be substituted "£9·50".

(2) In Schedule 1A for "£8·50" there shall be substituted "£9·50".

(3) For Schedule 2 there shall be substituted the following Schedule—

"SCHEDULE 2   Regulation 10

Charges for Wigs and Fabric Supports

(1) Description	(2) Charges
Surgical Brassiere	£ 18·50
Abdominal or Spinal Support	£ 24·50
Stock Modacrylic Wig	£ 40·00
Partial Human Hair Wig	£104·00
Full Bespoke Human Hair Wig	£151·00"

Transitional provisions

7. Where on or after 1st April 1994—

(*a*) any appliance specified in Schedule 2 to the principal regulations is supplied pursuant to an order given before that date; or

(*b*) any pre-payment certificate is granted under regulation 6 of the principal regulations pursuant to an application under that regulation which was received before that date, the principal regulations shall have effect in relation to that supply or, as the case may be, that grant as if regulations 2, 3, 4, 5 and 6 of these regulations had not come into force.

Sealed with the Official Seal of the Department of Health and Social Services on 29th March 1994.

(L.S.)   *Joan Dixon*
                                            Assistant Secretary

The Department of Finance and Personnel hereby approves the foregoing Regulations

Sealed with the Official Seal of the Department of Finance and Personnel on 29th March 1994.

(L.S.)   *F. G. McConnell*
                                            Assistant Secretary

EXPLANATORY NOTE

(This note is not part of the Regulations.)

These regulations further amend the Health and Personal Social Services (Charges for Drugs and Appliances) Regulations (Northern Ireland) 1973 ("the principal regulations") which provide for the making and recovery of charges for drugs and appliances supplied by doctors and chemists providing pharmaceutical services, and by hospitals and HSS trusts to out-patients.

The charge for each item on prescription is increased from £4·25 to £4·75. The sums prescribed for the grant of prepayment certificates of exemption from prescription charges are increased from £22·00 to £24·60 for a 4-month certificate and from £60·60 to £67·70 for a 12-month certificate.

The charge for elastic stockings is increased from £4·25 to £4·75 for each item (from £8·50 to £9·50 per pair) and for tights from £8·50 to £9·50.

The charge for a partial human hair wig is increased from £93·00 to £104·00, and for a stock modacrylic wig from £36·00 to £40·00. The charge for a full bespoke human hair wig is increased from £135·00 to £151·00. The charge for a surgical brassiere is increased from £18·00 to £18·50 and for an abdominal or spinal support from £24·00 to £24·50.

Transitional arrangements are made in respect of pre-payment certificates and appliances ordered, before the coming into force of these regulations (Regulation 7).

1994   No. 125

Medicines (Control of Substances for Manufacture and Exportation of Specified Products for Human Use) Amendment Order 1994

This Order has been made by the Secretaries of State concerned with health in England, in Wales and in Scotland respectively and the Department of Health and Social Services for Northern Ireland, acting jointly in exercise of powers conferred by sections 49 and 129(4) of the Medicines Act 1968 or, as the case may be, those conferred by the said provisions and now vested in them, and those Secretaries together with the Minister of Agriculture, Fisheries and Food, the Secretaries of State concerned with agriculture in Scotland and in Wales respectively and the Department of Agriculture for Northern Ireland, acting jointly in exercise of powers conferred by sections 105(1)(*a*) and 129(4) of the Medicines Act 1968 or, as the case may be, those conferred by the said provisions and now vested in them.

In pursuance of paragraph 11 of Schedule 4 to that Act this Order has been registered as a Northern Ireland statutory rule under the Statutory Rules (Northern Ireland) Order 1979. It is printed in full in the volume of United Kingdom Statutory Instruments for 1994 and has been numbered 787 in that series.

1994   No. 126

Road Races (Cookstown 100) Order (Northern Ireland) 1994

This Order, being of a temporary character, is not printed at length in this volume.

1994 No. 127 (C. 3)

EDUCATION

The Education and Libraries (1993 Order) (Commencement No. 1) Order (Northern Ireland) 1994

| *Made* | . | . | . | . | . | *28th March 1994* |

The Department of Education, in exercise of the powers conferred on it by Article 1(4) of the Education and Libraries (Northern Ireland) Order 1993(**a**) and of every other power enabling it in that behalf, hereby makes the following Order.

Citation

1. This Order may be cited as the Education and Libraries (1993 Order) (Commencement No. 1) Order (Northern Ireland) 1994.

Interpretation

2. In this Order "the 1993 Order" means the Education and Libraries (Northern Ireland) Order 1993.

Commencement

3. The following provisions of the 1993 Order shall come into operation on 1st April 1994—

(*a*) Articles 26 and 27.

(*b*) Article 34 and Part I of Schedule 4; and

(*c*) Article 50(2) and Schedule 5 so far as relating to Articles 18, 20, 23, 24, 27, 28, 163 and 164 of, and Schedules 2 and 3 to, the 1989 Order.

4. The following provisions of the 1993 Order shall come into operation on 1st September 1994—

(*a*) Article 41;

(*b*) Article 50(2) and Schedule 5 so far as relating to—

(i) Articles 2(2), 65, 69A, 70(4) and 72 of the 1986 Order;

(ii) Articles 59, 143, 151 and 153 of the 1989 Order; and

(iii) the amendment in Schedule 9 to the 1989 Order to the definition of "supply teacher" in Article 2(2) of the 1986 Order.

(**a**) S.I. 1993/2810 (N.I. 12)

Sealed with the Official Seal of the Department of Education on 28th March 1994.

(L.S.)

C. Jendoubi (Mrs)
Assistant Secretary

EXPLANATORY NOTE

(This note is not part of the Order.)

This Order brings into operation on 1st April 1994 the provisions of the Education and Libraries (Northern Ireland) Order 1993 ("the 1993 Order") under which the Department may determine that two or more institutions of further education under the management of a board should be amalgamated to form a single institution of further education.

It also brings into operation on 1st April 1994 provisions of the 1993 Order relating to the establishment of the Northern Ireland Council for the Curriculum, Examinations and Assessment, and the abolition of the existing Northern Ireland Curriculum Council and the Northern Ireland Schools Examinations and Assessment Council.

It also brings into operation on 1st September 1994 provisions of the 1993 Order which remove the power of education and library boards and the Council for Catholic Maintained Schools to employ supply teachers.

1994   No.   128

AGRICULTURE

Seed Potatoes (Crop Fees) Regulations (Northern Ireland) 1994

Made	*29th March 1994*
Coming into operation . .	*2nd May 1994*

The Department of Agriculture, in exercise of the powers conferred on it by section 1(**a**) of the Seeds Act (Northern Ireland) 1965(**b**) and of all powers enabling it in that behalf, after consultation with representatives of such interests as appear to it to be concerned, hereby makes the following Regulations:

Citation, commencement and interpretation

1.—(1) These Regulations may be cited as the Seed Potatoes (Crop Fees) Regulations (Northern Ireland) 1994 and shall come into operation on 2nd May 1994.

(2) In these Regulations, "the Department" means the Department of Agriculture.

Fees

2.—(1) Subject to paragraph (2) every person who makes application to the Department for the certification of seed potato crops under regulation 5(1) of the Seed Potatoes Regulations (Northern Ireland) 1981(**c**) shall forward with that application the appropriate fee in accordance with the Schedule.

(2) For the purposes of determining the fee payable under paragraph (1) an application received by the Department after 19th May in any calendar year shall be treated as if it had been received on or before that date, where, in the opinion of the Department general weather conditions in Northern Ireland were unfavourable for the planting of seed potato crops before that date.

Sealed with the Official Seal of the Department of Agriculture on 29th March 1994.

(L.S.)

I. C. Henderson
Assistant Secretary

(**a**)   As amended by S.R. & O. (N.I.) 1972 No. 351 Art. 3 and Sch. 3
(**b**)   1965 c. 22 (N.I.)
(**c**)   S.R. 1981 No. 243 as amended by S.R. 1983 No. 244, S.R. 1985 No. 2, S.R. 1991 No. 397 and S.R. 1993 No. 372

SCHEDULE   Regulation 2(1)

Fees for the certification of seed potato crops

Applications	Fee
1. In the case of an application received by the Department on or before 19th May in any calendar year—	
(*a*) where the total area of the crop does not exceed 1 hectare	. . . £28·00
(*b*) where the total area of the crop exceeds 1 hectare	£14·00 per half hectare or part of a half hectare
2. In the case of an application received by the Department after 19th May in any calendar year—	
(*a*) where the total area of the crop does not exceed 1 hectare	. . . £42·00
(*b*) where the total area of the crop exceeds 1 hectare	£21·00 per half hectare or part of a half hectare

EXPLANATORY NOTE

(This note is not part of the Regulations.)

These Regulations set out the fees payable to the Department of Agriculture in respect of the certification of seed potato crops arising under the Seed Potatoes Regulations (Northern Ireland) 1981 (regulation 2(1) and the Schedule).

In the case of an application received by the Department on or before 19th May in any calendar year:

    (*a*) where the total area of the crop does not exceed 1 hectare the fee is £28·00;

    (*b*) where the total area of the crop exceeds 1 hectare the fee is £14·00 per half hectare or part of a half hectare.

In the case of an application received by the Department after 19th May in any calendar year:

    (*a*) where the total area of the crop does not exceed 1 hectare the fee is £42·00;

    (*b*) where the total area of the crop exceeds 1 hectare the fee is £21·00 per half hectare or part of a half hectare.

The Regulations also provide that where in the opinion of the Department general weather conditions in Northern Ireland were unfavourable to the planting of seed potatoes before 19th May the fees payable will be the same as if the application had been received by the Department before that date (regulation 2(2)).

1994 No. 129 (C. 4)

CRIMINAL PROCEDURE

The Criminal Justice (Confiscation) (1993 Order) (Commencement) Order (Northern Ireland) 1994

Made . . . . . *28th March 1994*

In exercise of the powers conferred on me by Article 1(2) of the Criminal Justice (Confiscation) (Northern Ireland) Order 1993(**a**), I hereby make the following Order:—

Citation

1. This Order may be cited as the Criminal Justice (Confiscation) (1993 Order) (Commencement) Order (Northern Ireland) 1994.

Appointed day

2. The day appointed for the coming into operation of the Criminal Justice (Confiscation) (Northern Ireland) Order 1993 shall be 1st April 1994.

P. B. B. Mayhew
Northern Ireland Office   One of Her Majesty's Principal
28th March 1994   Secretaries of State

(**a**) S.I. 1993/3146 (N.I. 13)

EXPLANATORY NOTE

(This note is not part of the Order.)

This Order appoints 1st April 1994 for the coming into operation of the Criminal Justice (Confiscation) (Northern Ireland) Order 1993.

1994   No. 130

ANIMALS

Specified Diseases (Notification and Movement Restrictions) (Amendment) Order (Northern Ireland) 1994

Made	*29th March 1994*
Coming into operation . .	*30th March 1994*

The Department of Agriculture, in exercise of the powers conferred on it by Articles 5(1), 10(6), 19(*e*), (*f*) and (*k*) and 60(1) of the Diseases of Animals (Northern Ireland) Order 1981(**a**) and of every other power enabling it in that behalf, hereby makes the following Order:

Citation and commencement

1. This Order may be cited as the Specified Diseases (Notification and Movement Restrictions) (Amendment) Order (Northern Ireland) 1994 and shall come into operation on 30th March 1994.

Amendment of the Specified Diseases (Notification and Movement Restrictions) Order (Northern Ireland) 1991

2. In Schedule 1 to the Specified Diseases (Notification and Movement Restrictions) Order (Northern Ireland) 1991(**b**) there shall be added to the list of specified diseases the following—

"8.   Teschen disease   All animals".

Sealed with the Official Seal of the Department of Agriculture on 29th March 1994.

(L.S.)

P. T. Toal

Assistant Secretary

(**a**)   S.I. 1981/1115 (N.I. 22) as amended by S.I. 1984/702 (N.I. 2) Art. 17
(**b**)   S.R. 1991 No. 455

EXPLANATORY NOTE

(This note is not part of the Order.)

This Order amends Schedule 1 to the Specified Diseases (Notification and Movement Restrictions) Order (Northern Ireland) 1991 ("the 1991 Order") by adding Teschen disease affecting all animals to the list of specified diseases in that Schedule.

The effect is to make Teschen disease subject to the controls specified in the 1991 Order.

1994 No. 131

PRIVATE STREETS

The Private Streets (Construction) Regulations (Northern Ireland) 1994

Made	*30th March 1994*
Coming into operation . .	*11th May 1994*

To be laid before Parliament under paragraph 3(3) of Schedule 1 to the Northern Ireland Act 1974.

ARRANGEMENT OF REGULATIONS

PART I

INTRODUCTORY

PART II

STANDARDS OF CONSTRUCTION

Part III

Deposit and Approval of Plans and Notice of Commencement and Completion of Stages of Work

Part IV

Inspections, Investigations and Tests

Part V

General

16. Step irons
17. Water
18. Sub-base and roadbase
19. Concrete grade C30/20
20. Concrete grade C20/40
21. Concrete grade C20/20
22. Concrete grade C7.5/40
23. Grass seed
24. Mild steel reinforcing
25. Waterproof membrane
26. Steel fabric reinforcement
27. Ready-mixed concrete
28. Block paving
29. Blinding

SCHEDULE 3 Detailed requirements — Setting out of street, site clearance, earthworks, preparation of sub-grade

1. Setting out
2. Tolerances
3. Site clearance
4. Removal of unsuitable material
5. Cuttings
6. Embankments
7. Earthworks to be kept free of water
8. Soiling and sowing
9. Safety fences

SCHEDULE 4 Detailed requirements — Drainage

1. General
2. Excavation for pipelines and manholes
3. Type, laying, bedding and protection of pipes
4. Backfilling
5. Connections to existing drains
6. Manholes, inspection chambers and catchpits
7. Gullies and connections
8. Testing and cleaning
9. Intercepting ditches and existing land drains
10. Sub-soil drainage

SCHEDULE 5 Detailed requirements — Carriageways

1. Camber, crossfall and superelevation
2. Types of construction
3. Drains, etc., to be completed first
4. Preparation of formation
5. Materials for sub-base and roadbase
6. Protection
7. Sub-base
8. Crushed rock roadbase
9. Bituminous roadbase
10-15. Flexible surfacing
16. Concrete carriageways
17. Block paving

SCHEDULE 6 Detailed requirements — Shared surfaces

1. Camber and crossfall
2. Types of construction
3. Rumble strips
4. Mountable shoulders

SCHEDULE 7 Detailed requirements — Footways, footpaths, footway crossings, kerbs, steps and stepped ramps, cycle tracks, verges and service strips

1. Drains, etc., to be completed first
2. Footways and footpaths
3. Footway crossings
4. Kerbs
5. Steps and stepped ramps
6. Cycle tracks
7. Verges
8. Service strips

The Department of the Environment, in exercise of the powers conferred on it by Article 5(1) and (2) of the Private Streets (Northern Ireland) Order 1980(**a**) and of every other power enabling it in that behalf, hereby makes the following regulations:

(**a**) S.I. 1980/1086 (N.I. 12) as amended by S.I. 1992/3203 (N.I. 19) Article 6; see Article 2(2) for the definition of "the Department"

PART I

INTRODUCTORY

Citation and commencement

1. These regulations may be cited as the Private Streets (Construction) Regulations (Northern Ireland) 1994 and shall come into operation on 11th May 1994.

Interpretation

2.—(1) In these regulations—

"anchoring material" means material placed around the barrel of a pipe to locate it securely in position;

"basecourse" means a course forming part of the surfacing immediately below the wearing course;

"bedding" means a layer of material for providing continuous support;

"benching" means a series of stepped platforms excavated in sloping ground to prevent the ground from sliding or a sloping surface formed on either side of, and above, a channel;

"binder" means a material for the purpose of holding solid particles together as a coherent mass;

"camber" means the convexity given to the curved cross section of a carriageway;

"carriageway" means a way comprised in or constituting a road being a way over which the public have a right of way for the passage of vehicles;

"catchment area" means the total area from which the run-off of all surface water flows by gravity to a collecting point;

"catchpit" means a pit excavated or a chamber constructed in and below the normal level of a ditch or drain to trap silt and solid matter and facilitate its removal;

"channel" means a narrow strip specially constructed to carry and lead away surface water;

"compaction" means the process of producing a closer packing of particles by rolling or other mechanical means;

"construction of a street" includes provision for the drainage and sewerage thereof;

"the Construction Products Directive" means Council Directive 89/106/EEC on the approximation of laws, regulations and administrative provisions of the member States relating to construction products(**a**);

(**a**) O.J. No L40, 11.2.89, p 12

"crossfall" means the difference in level measured transversely between two specified points on a surface expressed as a ratio of one vertical linear unit to a specified number of horizontal linear units;

"cutting" means that portion of the site of a road where the formation has been excavated below ground level;

"cycle track" means a way or part of a road for use only by pedal cycles;

"datum" means a known or assumed point, line or plane to which others may be referred;

"dowel bar" means a steel bar used for load transfer in structures or at transverse joints in concrete road slabs;

"EEA Agreement" means the Agreement on the European Economic Area signed at Oporto on 2nd May 1992 as adjusted by the Protocol signed at Brussels on 17th March 1993;

"EEA State" means a State which is a Contracting Party to the EEA Agreement other than the United Kingdom;

"embankment" means a ridge of earth, stones or other material constructed to carry a road at a higher level than the surrounding ground;

"fixing bracket" in relation to a manhole ladder means a member designed to connect the ladder to the supporting wall;

"flight of steps" means that part of a set of steps which consists of a series of consecutive steps;

"footpath" means a way, not being a footway, comprising a street over which the public have a right of way on foot only;

"footway" means a way which together with a carriageway comprises a street, being a way over which the public have a right of way on foot only;

"formation" means the surface of the sub-grade in its final shape after the completion of the earthworks;

"formation level" means the surface of the sub-grade;

"formwork" means temporary structures of timber, metal or other material comprising of moulds in which concrete is formed to the desired shape;

"foul water" means any water contaminated by domestic sewage or trade effluent;

"going" means in relation to a step or stepped ramp the distance (measured on plan) between its nosing and the nosing of the step, ramp or landing next above it;

"haunch" means continuous material support to the sides of a pipe above the bedding;

"landing" means a platform situated between consecutive flights of steps or stepped ramps or at the top or bottom of a flight of steps or stepped ramp;

"mountable shoulder" means an area abutting the carriageway constructed to carry heavy wheel loads to accommodate the turning of large vehicles;

"nosing" means the front edge of a step and includes the front edge of the top surface of any landing or ramp which is situated at the top end of a ramp;

"the Order" means the Private Streets (Northern Ireland) Order 1980;

"pavement" means the part of the road structure above the sub-grade;

"pitch line" means a notional line which connects the nosing of all steps in a flight with the nosing of the landing or ramp at the top of the flight and extends down to the landing or ramp at the bottom and forms the greatest possible angle to the horizontal;

"retaining wall" means a wall constructed to resist lateral pressure from the adjoining ground or to maintain in position a mass of earth;

"rise" means the vertical distance between two consecutive treads or between a tread and the top surface of a landing or ramp immediately above or below that tread;

"roadbase" means one or more layers of material constituting the main structural element of the pavement;

"rumble strip" means an area of carriageway which is surfaced using block paving and positioned at the entrance to a shared surface to emphasise the boundary between the two types of road;

"safety fence" means a rail on posts intended to minimise damage from impact to vehicles leaving the carriageway;

"service strip" means a verge adjacent to a shared surface provided specifically to contain mains, drains, pipes, cables or other apparatus;

"setting out" in relation to a street means establishing on the ground the required line and level to which the street is to be constructed;

"shared surface" means a road or part of a road which is provided for the joint use of pedestrians and vehicles and which does not include a footway;

"standpipe" in relation to the water test for testing drains means a vertical pipe connected to the pipe under test;

"stepped ramp" means a route for pedestrians formed by a combination of steps and ramps;

"storm water" means rain water discharged from a catchment area as a result of storm;

"stringer" in relation to a manhole ladder means the side members of the ladder to which the rungs are fitted;

"sub-base" means a layer of material situated between the roadbase and the sub-grade;

"sub-grade" means the upper part of the soil, natural or constructed, which supports the load transmitted by the overlying pavement;

"sub-soil" means the undisturbed stratum lying immediately below the topsoil;

"sump" means that portion of a catchpit lying below the level of the invert of the outlet pipe in order to trap silt and solid matter;

"superelevation" means the inward tilt or transverse inclination given to the cross section of a carriageway throughout the length of a horizontal curve to reduce the effects of centrifugal force on a moving vehicle and expressed as a ratio of one vertical linear unit to a specified number of horizontal linear units;

"surface water" means the run off of natural water from a surface including paved areas, roofs and unpaved land;

"surround" means material completely encasing a pipe;

"tamping" means compaction of loose material by repeated blows from a heavy headed tool;

"toe" in relation to the landing on a flight of steps means an integral part of the landing projecting into the ground to form an anchorage for the flight of steps;

"tread" means the upper surface of a step;

"trimming" means the final shaping of earthworks;

"valley curve" means a sagging curve on the vertical alignment of a road over which there is a reversal of gradient;

"wearing course" means the part of a carriageway which directly supports the traffic.

(2) In these regulations a reference to a British Standard shall be construed as a reference to a British Standard published by the British Standards Institution, Linford Wood, Milton Keynes MK14 6LE (Telephone Number Milton Keynes (0908) 221166).

(3) Schedule 1 sets out in tabular form the publications referred to in these regulations.

(4) In these regulations a reference to a publication shall be construed as relating to—

(*a*) the edition of the publication of the date mentioned in the reference together with any amendments mentioned in Schedule 1; and

(*b*) so much only thereof as is relevant in the context in which the publication is mentioned.

(5) In these regulations any requirement for goods or materials to comply with a standard (whether a British Standard or other named standard) shall be satisfied by compliance with that standard or with any of the following standards, that is to say—

(*a*) a relevant standard or code of practice of a national standards institution or equivalent body of any EEA State; or

(*b*) a relevant international standard recognised in any EEA State; or

(*c*) a relevant specification acknowledged for use as a standard by a public authority of any EEA State; or (*d*) traditional procedures of manufacture of a EEA State where these are the subject of a written technical description sufficiently detailed to permit assessment of the goods or materials for the use specified; or

(*e*) for goods or materials of an innovative nature or subject to an innovative process of manufacture and which fulfil the purpose provided for by the named standard—

    (i) a European Technical Approval issued in accordance with the Construction Products Directive; or

    (ii) a specification sufficiently detailed to permit assessment.

(6) The standard, code of practice, specification, technical description or European Technical Approval as set out in paragraph (5) must provide in use levels of safety, suitability and fitness for purpose equivalent to those required by the named standard insofar as such levels are not inconsistent with the essential requirements set out in terms of objectives in Annex 1 to the Construction Products Directive.

(7) Paragraph (5) applies to works in the same manner as it does to goods or materials but only insofar as the means of carrying out such works are indivisibly associated with the goods or materials for which a standard, code of practice, specification, technical description or European Technical Approval, as set out in the said paragraph (5) is proposed.

(8) Where goods or materials are used on the basis of a standard, code of practice, specification, technical description or European Technical Approval as set out in paragraph (5) testing and sampling may be carried out as specified in or applicable to such standard, code of practice, specification, technical description or European Technical Approval.

(9) Where testing is carried out in another EEA State such tests shall be undertaken by—

(*a*) an organisation accredited in a EEA State in accordance with the relevant parts of the BS7500:1989 (equivalent European Standard EN 45000 series) series of standards for the tests carried out; or

(*b*) an organisation offering suitable and satisfactory evidence of technical and professional competence and independence to fulfil the minimum conditions as set out in Annex IV of the Construction Products Directive.

(10) In these regulations the abbreviations and symbols listed in the following table are used—

Abbreviation or Symbol	Definition
BS	British Standard
e.g.	for example
EN	European Standard
etc.	and the rest; and so on
HMSO	Her Majesty's Stationery Office
i.e.	that is
kg	kilogram
KN	Kilo Newton
l	litre
m	metre
mm	millimetre
m^2	square metre
m^3	cubic metre
N/A	not applicable
N/mm^2	Newtons per square millimetre
No.	number
Ref.	reference
UPVC	Unplasticized Polyvinylchloride
μm	micron
±	plus or minus

Application

3. These regulations apply to the construction of streets in respect of which the Department has exercised street planning functions under Article 3(1) of the Order after the coming into operation of these regulations.

PART II

STANDARDS OF CONSTRUCTION

Goods and materials

4. All goods and materials used in the construction of a street shall comply with the detailed requirements set out in Schedule 2.

Preliminary works

5. The setting out of a street, clearance of the site of a street, earthworks and preparation of the sub-grade shall be carried out in accordance with the detailed requirements set out in Schedule 3.

Level of street

6.—(1) A street shall be constructed at such level as, having regard to the intended use of the premises abutting the street, will afford the easiest practicable gradients for communicating with any other street or intended street with which it may be connected.

(2) The maximum gradient of a street shall not exceed 10 per cent except where the topography of a site would render this impracticable.

(3) The minimum gradient shall not be less than 0.8 per cent except in valley curves.

Surface water drainage

7.—(1) A street shall be provided with a proper and sufficient drainage system for carrying off the surface water from the street.

(2) The drainage system provided shall comply with the detailed requirements set out in Schedule 4.

Location of services

8.—(1) Where mains, drains, pipes, cables or other apparatus are to lie within a street they shall where practicable be located under footways or verges.

(2) Where a shared surface is provided any mains, drains, pipes, cables or other apparatus shall where practicable be located in a service strip adjacent to the shared surface.

(3) Subject to paragraph (4) a manhole shall where practicable be so positioned that its cover can be located off the carriageway on a verge, footway or service strip.

(4) If it is not practicable to position a manhole in accordance with paragraph (3) it may be located—

(*a*) where carriageway width exceeds 6.5m, at the centre line of the carriageway; or

(*b*) where carriageway width is 6.5m or less, on the carriageway but not more than one third of the carriageway width distant from the nearest edge of the carriageway.

Sub-soil drainage

9.—(1) The sub-soil of the site of a street shall be effectively drained—

(*a*) where the water table is within 600mm of the formation;

(*b*) where there is water run-off or seepage from adjacent ground;

(*c*) where the sub-soil is waterlogged; and

(*d*) where springs, watercourses or existing drains are encountered.

(2) The sub-soil drainage provided shall comply with the detailed requirements set out in paragraph 10 of Schedule 4.

(3) Drains for the conveyance of sub-soil water shall not be permitted to discharge to a drain conveying foul water.

(4) Discharge to the drainage system shall.be through a catchpit.

Drains

10.—(1) A drain provided in the construction of a street shall—

(*a*) be of sufficient strength having regard to the manner in which it is bedded or supported and the maximum loads and forces to which it may be subjected, and be protected against damage;

(*b*) have all joints formed in such a manner—

    (i) as is appropriate to the materials of which the drain is made; and

    (ii) that, except for a drain for the conveyance of sub-soil water only, it shall remain watertight under all working conditions;

(*c*) except where it is provided for the conveyance of sub-soil water only, be laid in a straight line between points where changes of direction or gradient occur; and

(*d*) be of such capacity and so designed and constructed as to ensure that it is self-cleansing and efficiently carries away the maximum volume of matter which may be discharged into it.

(2) A drain provided in the construction of a street shall have such manholes as may be necessary, and every manhole shall—

(*a*) be so designed and constructed of brickwork, concrete or other suitable and durable material as to sustain the loads which may be imposed upon it and be watertight;

(*b*) be of such size and form as to permit ready access to the drain for inspection and cleansing;

(*c*) where the depth of the manhole so requires, have such step-irons, ladder or other fittings as to provide safe access to the level of the drain; and

(*d*) have a removable cover of adequate strength, constructed of suitable and durable material, which shall be non-ventilating where the manhole is in a drain which is to carry foul water.

(3) A drain which is to carry foul water shall be capable of withstanding a suitable test for watertightness after the work of laying the drain has been carried out, including any necessary work of haunching or surrounding it with concrete and backfilling the trench.

(4) The construction of a drain and its testing and the construction of the means of access to it shall be carried out in accordance with the detailed requirements set out in Schedule 4.

Carriageways and shared surfaces

11.—(1) A carriageway or a shared surface shall be so constructed that it will carry away surface water to the surface drain in the street.

(2) A camber or crossfall shall be in accordance with the detailed requirements set out in paragraph 1 of Schedule 5 or paragraph 1 of Schedule 6 as the case may require.

(3) A carriageway, or a shared surface, shall be constructed, laid and compacted on the sub-grade to provide a durable and satisfactory surface in accordance with the detailed requirements set out in paragraphs 2 to 17 of Schedule 5 or paragraphs 2 to 4 of Schedule 6 as the case may require.

Retaining walls, pipelines and other structures

12.—(1) Where the construction of a street necessitates the provision of a retaining wall with greater than 1m retention or a single span structure or pipe with greater than 2m clear span, the wall, structure or pipe as the case may be shall be designed and checked in accordance with the design criteria procedures set out in the Department of the Environment for Northern Ireland Technical Approval Scheme (3rd revision 1989) for the Design and Checking of Highway Structures Retaining Walls and Pipelines.

(2) Where the construction of a street necessitates the provision of a retaining wall with greater than 500mm retention but not exceeding 1m retention or a single span structure or pipe greater than 900mm but not exceeding 2m, the wall, structure or pipe as the case may be shall be certified to the Department by a Chartered Civil or Structural Engineer as having been designed in accordance with the requirements set out in the Scheme mentioned in paragraph (1).

Footways and footpaths

13.—(1) A footway shall be constructed with a crossfall towards the carriageway and shall be provided with kerbing between the carriageway and footway.

(2) Crossings of footways to permit vehicular access shall be provided where necessary.

(3) A wheelchair access to carriageways shall be provided at all road junctions.

(4) A footpath shall be constructed with a crossfall.

(5) The maximum longitudinal gradient of a footpath shall not exceed 10 per cent except where the topography of a site would render this impracticable.

(6) The minimum longitudinal gradient of a footpath shall not be less than 0.8 per cent except in valley curves.

(7) Steps or stepped ramps shall only be permitted where there is no practicable alternative means of providing access along a footpath.

(8) Where steps or stepped ramps have been permitted an alternative footpath route with normal gradients shall be provided.

(9) The construction of footways, footpaths, steps, stepped ramps, crossings of footways and kerbing shall be in accordance with the detailed requirements set out in paragraphs 1 to 5 of Schedule 7.

Cycle tracks

14. A cycle track shall be constructed to the same standard as a footway and in accordance with the detailed requirements set out in paragraph 6 of Schedule 7.

Lay-bys, bus bays, parking bays, turning areas, verges and service strips

15.—(1) A lay-by, bus bay, parking bay or turning area shall be constructed to the same standard as the adjoining carriageway in accordance with the detailed requirements set out in paragraphs 2 to 17 of Schedule 5.

(2) The construction of verges and service strips shall be in accordance with the detailed requirements set out in paragraphs 7 and 8 of Schedule 7.

(3) In this regulation—

''bus'' has the same meaning as in Article 1(2) of the Roads (Restriction of Waiting) Order (Northern Ireland) 1982(**a**);

''bus bay'' means that part of a road adjacent to the carriageway intended for the waiting of buses;

''lay-by'' means that part of a road adjacent to the carriageway intended for the waiting of vehicles;

''parking bay'' means a part of a road set aside for the parking of vehicles; and

''turning area'' means a part of a road intended for the turning of vehicles.

Part III

Deposit and Approval of Plans and Notice of Commencement and Completion of Stages of Work

Deposit of plans

16.—(1) A person who intends to construct a street to which these regulations apply shall not commence work until he has—

(*a*) deposited with the Department six sets of the plans mentioned in paragraph (2); and

(*b*) received the Department's approval of those plans in writing.

(2) Those plans are—

(*a*) a plan to a scale of not less than 1 in 500 showing—

    (i) the name, if any, of the street;

    (ii) the direction of the north point of the compass;

    (iii) the width, position and arrangement of the street;

    (iv) the land to be regarded for the purposes of adoption under Part III of the Order as being comprised in the street; and

    (v) such particulars as are necessary to show that the street will comply with these regulations; and

(*b*) a plan showing a longitudinal section and cross section of the street but, where the crossfall or camber varies, a plan showing the cross section of the street at intervals of not more than 25m.

(3) The plan referred to in sub-paragraph (*a*) of paragraph (2) shall (without prejudice to head (v) of that sub-paragraph) also show in particular—

(*a*) the provision intended for carrying off of surface water from the street including the invert levels and position of manholes and the connections to existing drains;

(*b*) the position, levels and gradients of drains intended for the conveyance of foul water and the invert levels and position of manholes and the connections to existing drains;

(**a**)   S.R. 1982 No 44

(c) the general location of mains, drains, pipes, cables and other apparatus; and

(d) the position of all structures, pipelines and flanking retaining walls together with outline proposals, detailed drawings and supporting calculations as required in accordance with the Scheme mentioned in regulation 12;

(4) The scale of the plan referred to in paragraph (2)(b) shall not be less than 1 in 500 horizontally and 1 in 100 vertically and cross sections shall indicate all particulars necessary to show that the street complies with the provisions of these regulations which apply to it including provisions relating to—

(a) the levels of the present surface of the ground over or through which the street is to pass, such levels being expressed by reference to either ordnance datum, or to an assumed datum clearly defined on the drawings;

(b) the levels and gradients of the street;

(c) the levels of the ground immediately abutting on each side of the street and the intended levels of the building sites on each side of the street;

(d) the carrying off of surface water from the street and the conveyance of foul water;

(e) the invert levels and gradients of all drains; and

(f) the levels and gradients of any intended or existing streets with which it is intended that the street shall connect, so far as it is necessary to show the levels and gradients at which the new street will connect with such intended or existing streets.

(5) In paragraph (4) "ordnance datum" means the datum for the system of levels shown on ordnance maps.

Notice of commencement and completion of stages of work

17.—(1) Subject to paragraph (2) a person who intends to construct a street in respect of which the plans referred to in regulation 16 have been approved shall give to the Department not less than three days notice, exclusive of Saturdays, Sundays and public holidays, in writing of the date and time at which it is intended to commence—

(a) the construction of the street;

(b) the construction of any drain;

(c) the testing of any drain;

(d) the covering up of any drain;

(e) the making of a connection to an existing drain;

(f) the covering up of the formation;

(g) the covering up of the sub-base;

(h) the covering up of each layer of the base; and

(i) the laying of the basecourse and wearing course, the concreting, or laying of block paving.

(2) The setting out of the street shall be completed prior to the giving of the notice referred to in paragraph (1).

(3) The person shall within fourteen days after the completion of the construction of the street give to the Department notice in writing of the completion.

(4) Where a person constructs a street without giving the notice required in paragraph (1) the Department may by notice in writing require him within seven days to cut into or lay open so much of the street as is necessary to enable the Department to ascertain whether any of these regulations have been contravened.

(5) Where a person receives a notice in writing from the Department setting out the extent to which the regulations have been contravened and alters or adds to the street so as to secure compliance with these regulations, he shall within fourteen days after the completion of such work give to the Department notice in writing of its completion.

Manner of giving notice and submitting plans

18.—(1) A person who is required by these regulations to give notice in writing to or deposit a plan with the Department shall sign that notice or plan, or cause it to be signed by a duly authorised agent.

(2) If a notice or plan is signed by an agent the notice or plan shall state the name and address of the person on whose behalf it has been signed.

PART IV

INSPECTIONS, INVESTIGATIONS AND TESTS

Access and facilities for inspection of work and testing

19.—(1) A person constructing a street shall when so requested supply to the Department such evidence as is necessary to show that a material used in the construction complies with these regulations and shall take such samples as are specified for testing purposes.

(2) An officer authorised by the Department may at any time inspect work in progress, carry out investigations and tests and take such samples as are necessary to ensure compliance with these regulations.

Expenses of carrying out investigations and tests and taking of samples

20. The Department may recover from the person by whom or on whose behalf the plans were deposited any expenses reasonably incurred by it in carrying out investigations and tests and the taking of samples.

Removal or alteration of work not in conformity with the regulations

21.—(1) If any work does not comply with these regulations, the Department may by notice in writing require the person by whom or on whose behalf the plans were deposited, within such reasonable time as the Department may specify in the notice either to remove the work or to carry out such alterations to it as may be necessary to make it comply with the regulations.

(2) If a requirement under paragraph (1) is not complied with within the time specified in the notice the Department may execute the works specified in the notice and may recover the expenses reasonably incurred by it from the person by whom or on whose behalf the plans were deposited.

PART V

GENERAL

Determination of matters under the regulations

22. Where any question arises under these regulations between the Department and the person by whom or on whose behalf the plans were deposited it shall be referred to arbitration under and in accordance with the Arbitration Act (Northern Ireland) 1937(**a**).

Revocation and transitional provisions

23.—(1) The Private Streets (Construction) Regulations (Northern Ireland) 1966(**b**) shall continue to apply to the construction of streets in respect of which the Department has exercised street planning functions before the coming into operation of these regulations.

(2) Except as provided by paragraph (1) the Private Streets (Construction) Regulations (Northern Ireland) 1966 shall cease to have effect.

Sealed with the Official Seal of the Department of the Environment on 30th March 1994.

(L.S.)

E. J. Galway
Assistant Secretary

(**a**) 1937 C. 8 (N.I.)
(**b**) S.R. & O. (N.I.) 1966 No. 262

SCHEDULE 1   Regulation 2(3) and (4)

Publications to which reference is made in the Regulations

TABLE A   BRITISH STANDARDS CITED IN REGULATION 2

Publication	Amendment		Citation
	Serial No	*Reference No or date*	
BS 7500 Series 1989	—	—	Regulation 2(9)(*a*)

TABLE B   PUBLICATION CITED IN REGULATION 12

Publication	Citation
The Technical Approval Scheme for the Design and Checking of Highway Structures, Retaining Walls and Pipelines (3rd Revision 1989). Published by the Department of Environment for Northern Ireland, Roads Service HQ, Clarence Court, Adelaide Street, Belfast	regulation 12(1)

TABLE C   BRITISH STANDARDS CITED IN SCHEDULE 2

Publication	Amendment		Citation
	Serial No	*Reference No or date*	
BS 12: 1991	1	AMD 7122	paragraph 7
BS 65: 1991	—	—	paragraph 12(5)
BS187: 1978	1	AMD 5427	paragraph 3(3)
BS 497: Part 1: 1976	1 2	AMD 5034 AMD 6643	paragraphs 13(3), 15
BS 594: Part 1: 1992	—	—	paragraphs 6(1), 6(2), 6(3)

SCHEDULE 1 — *continued*

Table C   British Standards Cited in Schedule 2 — *continued*

Publication	Amendment		Citation
	Serial No	*Reference No or date*	
BS 882: 1992	—	—	paragraph 1(1)
BS 1200: 1976	1 2 3	AMD 4510 AMD 4834 AMD 5126	paragraph 2
BS 1247: Part 2: 1990	—	—	paragraph 16
BS 1521: 1972 (1980)	1	AMD 3519	paragraph 25
BS 3148: 1980	—	—	paragraph 17
BS 3656: 1981 (1990)	1	AMD 5531	paragraph 12(7)
BS 3921: 1985	—	—	paragraphs 3(1), 3(4)
BS 4482: 1985	—	—	paragraph 24
BS 4483: 1985	—	—	paragraph 26
BS 4660: 1989	—	—	paragraph 12(6)
BS 4987: Part 1: 1988	1	AMD 6148	paragraphs 1(2), 5(1), 5(2), 5(3), 5(4)
BS 5178: 1975	—	—	paragraph 12(2)
BS 5328: Part 1: 1991	1	AMD 7174	paragraphs 19, 20, 21, 22, 27
BS 5328: Part 2: 1991	1	AMD 7175	paragraphs 19, 20, 21, 22, 27
BS 5328: Part 3: 1990	1 2	AMD 6927 AMD 7176	paragraphs 19, 20, 21, 22, 27
BS 5328: Part 4: 1990	1	AMD 6928	paragraphs 19, 20, 21, 22, 27

SCHEDULE 1 — *continued*

Table C   British Standards Cited in Schedule 2 — *continued*

Publication	Amendment		Citation
	Serial No	*Reference No or date*	
BS 5481: 1977 (1989)	1 2	AMD 3631 AMD 4436	paragraph 12(6)
BS 5911: Part 2: 1982	1	AMD 5146	paragraphs 13(1)(*a*), 13(1)(*b*), 14
BS 5911: Part 3: 1982	—	—	paragraph 12(3)
BS 5911: Part 100: 1988	1	AMD 6269	paragraph 12(1)
BS 5911: Part 114: 1992	—	—	paragraph 12(4)
BS 6073: Part 1: 1981	1 2	AMD 3944 AMD 4462	paragraph 3(2)
BS 7263: Part 1: 1990	—	—	paragraphs 10(1), 10(2), 11

TABLE D   BRITISH STANDARDS CITED IN SCHEDULE 3

Publication	Amendment		Citation
	Serial No.	*Reference No or date*	
BS 1377: Part 2: 1990	—	—	paragraph 4(2)(*f*)
BS 5930: 1981	—	—	paragraph 4(2)(*h*)

SCHEDULE 1 — *continued*

TABLE E   OTHER PUBLICATIONS CITED IN SCHEDULE 3

Publication	Citation
The Department of the Environment for Northern Ireland Manual of Contract Documents, Volume 1, Specification for Highway Works, Series 400, Safety Fences, Safety Barriers and Pedestrian Guardrails published by HMSO	paragraph 9(2)(*a*)
The Department of the Environment for Northern Ireland Manual of Contract Documents, Volume 3, Highway Construction Details, Section 2, Safety Fences and Barriers published by HMSO	paragraph 9(2)(*b*)

TABLE F   BRITISH STANDARDS CITED IN SCHEDULE 4

Publication	Amendment		Citation
	Serial No	Reference No or date	
BS 65: 1991	—	—	paragraph 3(4)
BS 449: Part 2: 1969	1 2 3 4 5 6 7 8	AMD 416 AMD 523 AMD 661 AMD 1135 AMD 1787 AMD 4576 AMD 5698 AMD 6255	paragraph 6(11)(*b*)
BS 497: Part 1: 1976	1 2	AMD 5034 AMD 6643	Paragraphs 6(13), 6(16)
BS 812: Part 110: 1990	—	—	paragraph 4(8)
BS 882: 1992	—	—	paragraph 3(7)
BS 1247: Part 2: 1990	—	—	paragraph 6(10)(*a*)

SCHEDULE 1 — *continued*

Table F   British Standards Cited in Schedule 4 — *continued*

Publication	Amendment		Citation
	Serial No	*Reference No or date*	
BS 1377: Part 2: 1990	—	—	paragraph 4(9)
BS 4211: 1987	1	AMD 7064	paragraph 6(11)(*f*)
BS 4660: 1989	—	—	paragraph 3(4)
BS 5178: 1975	—	—	paragraph 3(4)
BS 5481: 1977 (1989)	1 2	AMD 3631 AMD 4436	paragraph 3(4)
BS 5911: Part 3: 1982	—	—	paragraph 3(4)
BS 5911: Part 100: 1988	1	AMD 6269	paragraph 3(4)
BS 5911: Part 114: 1992	—	—	paragraph 3(4)
BS 5911: Part 200: 1989	—	—	paragraphs 6(4), 7(3), 7(5)
BS 6073: Part 1: 1981	1 2	AMD 3944 AMD 4462	paragraph 6(2)
BS 8005: Part 0: 1987	—	—	paragraph 1(4)
BS 8005: Part 1: 1987	—	—	paragraph 1(4)

TABLE G   OTHER PUBLICATIONS CITED IN SCHEDULE 4

Publication	Citation
The Department of Transport, Transport and Road Research Laboratory publications ''Simplified tables of external loads on buried pipelines'' 1986 and ''A guide to design loadings for buried rigid pipes'' 1983 published by HMSO	paragraphs 1(1), 2(6)

SCHEDULE 1 — *continued*

TABLE H   BRITISH STANDARDS CITED IN SCHEDULE 5

Publication	Amendment		Citation
	Serial No	Reference No or date	
BS 594: Part 1: 1992	—	—	paragraphs 12(3), 13(3), 13(4)
BS 594: Part 2: 1992	—	—	paragraphs 12(3), 13(3)
BS 598: Part 100: 1987	1	AMD 6122	paragraph 10(6)
BS 598: Part 101: 1987	—	—	paragraph 10(3)
BS 598: Part 102: 1989	1 2	AMD 6585 AMD 7534	paragraph 10(3)
BS 598: Part 104: 1989	1	AMD 6738	paragraph 10(3)
BS 598: Part 105: 1990	1	AMD 7294	paragraph 10(3)
BS 598: Part 106: 1990	—	—	paragraph 10(3)
BS 598: Part 107: 1990	—	—	paragraph 10(3)
BS 598: Part 108: 1990	—	—	paragraph 10(3)
BS 598: Part 109: 1990	—	—	paragraph 10(3)
BS 812: Part 1: 1975	1 2 3 4	AMD 2069 AMD 4572 AMD 4875 AMD 6587	paragraph 10(3)
BS 812: Part 2: 1975	1	AMD 4615	paragraph 10(3)
BS 812: Part 101: 1984	—	—	paragraph 10(3)
BS 812: Part 103: 1985	1	AMD 6003	paragraph 10(3)
BS 812: Section 105.1: 1989	—	—	paragraph 10(3)
BS 812: Part 111: 1990	—	—	paragraphs 7(1), 8(1), 10(3)
BS 1377: Part 2: 1990	—	—	paragraphs 6(7), 7(5), 8(3)

SCHEDULE 1 — *continued*

Table H   British Standards Cited in Schedule 5 — *continued*

Publication	Amendment		Citation
	Serial No	*Reference No or date*	
BS 2000: Part 105: 1991	—	—.	paragraph 10(3)
BS 3690: Part 3: 1990	—	—	paragraph 10(3)
BS 4483: 1985	—	—	paragraph 2(4)
BS 4987: Part 1: 1988	1	AMD 6148	paragraphs 9(1), 12(2), 13(2), 13(5), 14(2), 15
BS 4987: Part 2: 1988	1	AMD 6586	paragraphs 9(1), 9(2), 11(3), 12(2), 12(4), 13(2), 13(5)
BS 6677: Part 1: 1986	—	—	paragraph 17(4)
BS 6677: Part 3: 1986	—	—	paragraph 17(4)
BS 6717: Part 1: 1986	—	—	paragraph 17(1)
BS 6717: Part 3: 1989	—	—	paragraphs 2(1), 17(2)

SCHEDULE 1 — *continued*

TABLE I   OTHER PUBLICATIONS CITED IN SCHEDULE 5

Publication	Citation
The Department of the Environment Transport and Road Research Laboratory, Report LR90: 1967, Published by the Road Research Laboratory, Crowthorne, Berkshire.	paragraphs 6(6), 7(4), 8(2)
The Department of the Environment for Northern Ireland Manual of Contract Documents, Volume 1, Specification for Highway Works, Series 1000, Road Pavements — Concrete and Cement Bound Materials published by HMSO	paragraphs 16(1), 16(4)

TABLE J   BRITISH STANDARDS CITED IN SCHEDULE 6

Publication	Amendment		Citation
	Serial No	Reference No or date	
BS 4987: Part 1: 1988	1	AMD 6148	paragraph 2(2)(*b*)(ii)
BS 4987: Part 2: 1988	1	AMD 6586	paragraph 2(2)(*b*)(ii)

TABLE K   BRITISH STANDARDS CITED IN SCHEDULE 7

Publication	Amendment		Citation
	Serial No	Reference No or date	
BS 594: Part 1:1992	—	—	paragraph 2(6)(*a*)
BS 882: 1992	—	—	paragraph 2(13)

SCHEDULE 1 — *continued*

Table K   British Standards Cited in Schedule 7 — *continued*

Publication	Amendment		Citation
	Serial No	*Reference No or date*	
BS 1881: Part 101: 1983	1 2	AMD 6091 AMD 6728	paragraph 2(28)
BS 1881: Part 102: 1983	1 2	AMD 6090 AMD 6727	paragraph 2(28)
BS 1881: Part 108: 1983	1	AMD 6105	paragraph 2(28)
BS 1881: Part 111: 1983	1	AMD 6102	paragraph 2(28)
BS 1881: Part 112: 1983	1	AMD 6100	paragraph 2(28)
BS 1881: Part 116: 1983	1 2	AMD 6097 AMD 6720	paragraph 2(28)
BS 4483: 1985	—	—	paragraph 5(21)
BS 4987: Part 1: 1988	1	AMD 6148	paragraphs 2(5), 2(7)
BS 4987: Part 2: 1988	1	AMD 6586	paragraphs 2(5), 2(7)
BS 7263: Part 1: 1990	—	—	paragraphs 2(10), 4(2), 4(8)(*b*), 4(9)(*b*)

TABLE L   OTHER PUBLICATIONS CITED IN SCHEDULE 7

Publication	*Citation*
The Department of the Environment for Northern Ireland Layout of Housing Roads Design Guide 1988 published by HMSO	paragraphs 4(6), 8

SCHEDULE 2 Regulation 4

**Detailed Requirements for Goods and Materials to be used
in Construction of Streets**

Goods and Materials	*Specification*

1. Aggregates
   (1) for concrete — To BS 882: 1992.
   (2) for bituminous materials — Sound clean hard crushed rock graded to BS 4987: Part 1: 1988.

2. Building sand — To BS 1200: 1976: Table 1.

3. Bricks
   (1) Clay — Well fired solid common brick or ordinary quality to BS 3921: 1985.
   (2) Concrete — To BS 6073: Part 1: 1981.
   (3) Sand Lime — To BS 187: 1978
   (4) Engineering — To BS 3921: 1985: Table 4 Class B.

4. Bitumen — Straight run or cut back petroleum bitumen in accordance with the requirements of Schedule 5 paragraph 15.

5. Bitumen macadam
   (1) Carriageway and shared surface basecourse — 20mm dense graded basecourse to BS 4987: Part 1: 1988 supplemented by the requirements of paragraph 12 of Schedule 5 and paragraph 2(2)(*b*) of Schedule 6 respectively.
   (2) Carriageway and shared surface wearing course — 10mm or 14mm size close graded wearing course macadam to BS 4987: Part 1: 1988 supplemented by the requirements of paragraph 13 of Schedule 5 and paragraph 2(2)(*b*) of Schedule 6 respectively.
   (3) Footway basecourse — 20mm size dense basecourse in accordance with BS 4987: Part 1: 1988 subject to the requirements of paragraph 2(5) of Schedule 7.
   (4) Footway wearing course — 6mm size medium graded wearing course in accordance with BS 4987: Part 1: 1988 subject to the requirements of paragraph 2(6) of Schedule 7.

6. Asphalt
   (1) Carriageway and shared surface basecourse — 60 per cent coarse aggregate hot rolled asphalt to BS 594: Part 1: 1992 Table 2; Column 2/4, Binder to Table 1, Binder Numbers 3 or 5; supplemented by the requirements of paragraph 12 of Schedule 5.

SCHEDULE 2 — *continued*

(2) Carriageway and shared surface wearing course	30 per cent coarse aggregate hot rolled asphalt to BS 594: Part 1: 1992 Table 6, Column 6/4, Schedule 1B; Binder to Table 1, Binder Numbers 3 or 5; supplemented by the requirements of paragraph 13 of Schedule 5 and paragraph 2(2)(*b*) of Schedule 6 respectively.
(3) Footway or footpath wearing course	15 per cent coarse aggregate hot rolled asphalt to BS 594: Part 1: 1992 Table 6, Column 6/2, Schedule 1B; Binder to Table 1, Binder Numbers 3 or 5; supplemented by the requirements of paragraph 2(6) of Schedule 7.
7. Cement	Ordinary or rapid hardening Portland to BS 12: 1991.
8. Cement mortar	
(1) general use	1 part by volume of cement to 5 of building sand.
(2) for jointing pipes	1 part by volume of cement to 1 of building sand.
(3) for jointing kerbs	1 part by volume of cement to 3 of building sand.
9. Lime mortar	1 part by volume of hydrated lime to 2½ parts of building sand.
10. Kerbs and edgings	
(1) Concrete kerbs	Hydraulically compressed to BS 7263: Part 1: 1990 Type HB 2 of figure 1 (150mm × 125mm Type BN of figure 1 in shared surfaces).
(2) Concrete edgings	Hydraulically compressed to BS 7263: Part 1: 1990 Type ER or EF of figure 1.
11. Concrete flags	Hydraulically compressed to BS 7263: Part 1: 1990 Type E70.
12. Pipes	
(1) Concrete	To BS 5911: Part 100: 1988
(2) Concrete prestressed	To BS 5178: 1975
(3) Concrete perforated	To BS 5911: Part 3: 1982. With holes not greater than 10mm or less than 3mm; the total area of holes shall be not less than 1,000mm^2 per m length of pipe.
(4) Concrete porous	To BS 5911: Part 114: 1992.
(5) Clay	To BS 65: 1991.

SCHEDULE 2 — *continued*

(6) UPVC	To BS 5481: 1977 (1989) or BS 4660: 1989.
(7) Asbestos cement	To BS 3656: 1981 (1990).

13. Gullies, gully gratings and frames

   (1) Concrete gullies

      (*a*) Shall have an internal diameter of 375mm, and conform to BS 5911: Part 2: 1982.

      (*b*) Rectangular gullies shall conform to BS 5911: Part 2: 1982 and shall have internal dimensions of 300mm × 385mm with all other dimensions as per Table 3 of BS 5911: Part 2: 1982 for a gully of 375mm internal diameter.

   (2) Cast iron gullies   To the requirements of paragraph 7 of Schedule 4.

   (3) Gully gratings and frames   Cast iron to BS 497: Part 1: 1976: Table 7 BS Ref GA2/325.
The metal used for the manufacture of castings to be ductile iron as described in Para 3.1 of BS 497: Part 1: 1976.

14. Precast concrete manholes   To BS 5911: Part 2: 1982.

15. Manhole covers and frames   Grade A Class 2 and test load 350 KN. To BS 497: Part 1: 1976.

16. Step irons   To BS 1247: Part 2: 1990 and the requirements of paragraph 6(10) of Schedule 4.

17. Water   Mains supply, otherwise to BS 3148: 1980.

18. Sub-base and roadbase   Shall be hard sound uniformly graded crushed rock, reasonably cubical in shape and free of soil, slate, vegetable or other injurious matter and graded in accordance with the requirements of paragraphs 7 and 8 of Schedule 5 respectively.

19. Concrete grade C30/20   To BS 5328: Part 1: 1991 and Parts 2, 3 and 4: 1990 20mm nominal size aggregate with 270kg per m^3 minimum cement content and medium workability.

20. Concrete grade C20/40   To BS 5328: Part 1: 1991 and Parts 2, 3 and 4: 1990 40mm nominal size aggregate with 220kg per m^3 minimum cement content and medium workability.

SCHEDULE 2 — *continued*

21. Concrete grade C20/20

To BS 5328: Part 1: 1991 and Parts 2, 3 and 4: 1990 20mm nominal size aggregate with 220kg per m^3 minimum cement content and medium workability.

22. Concrete grade C7.5/40

To BS 5328: Part 1: 1991 and Parts 2, 3 and 4: 1990 40mm nominal size aggregate with 200kg per m^3 minimum cement content and medium workability.

23. Grass seed

Each 100kg of grass seed shall consist of—
60kg of red fescue S59
20kg of smooth stalked meadow grass
15kg of crested dogstail
  5kg of white clover.

24. Mild steel reinforcing

To BS 4482: 1985

25. Waterproof membrane

To BS 1521: 1972 (1980) Class B.1F.

26. Steel fabric reinforcement

To BS 4483: 1985 and the requirements of paragraph 2(1) and (4) of Schedule 5.

27. Ready-mixed concrete

To BS 5328: Part 1: 1991 and Parts 2, 3 and 4: 1990.

28. Block paving

Shall be in accordance with the requirements of paragraph 17 of Schedule 5.

29. Blinding

Shall be crushed rock of 19mm maximum size which is capable of filling the intricacies of the top layer of roadbase stone and being compacted to form a dense surface.

SCHEDULE 3

Detailed requirements — Setting out of street, site clearance, earthworks, preparation of sub-grade

Setting out

1.—(1) Before construction of the street is commenced—

(*a*) there shall be established on the ground by marker pegs the kerb line or the centre line, tangent points and intersection points and any other points necessary to provide intervisibility;

(*b*) the position of each marker peg shall be preserved during construction;

(*c*) works bench marks to the datum shown in the plans approved under regulation 16 shall be established and preserved during the course of the works and the levels of these shall be made available to the Department;

and in sub-paragraph (*c*) "bench marks" means well defined marks established as a datum for levelling.

(2) The line and levels of formation, side slopes, drains, carriageways, kerbs and footways shall be set out so as to obtain everywhere in as far as is reasonable the gradients and cross sections shown in the approved construction drawings.

Tolerances

2.—(1) Horizontal alignments shall be constructed within the tolerance of ± 12mm from the horizontal alignments as set out.

(2) The surface level of kerbs, pavement courses and formation shall lie within the tolerances stated in the following table when checked against the setting out.

TABLE

TOLERANCES IN SURFACE LEVELS

Flexible wearing course	± 6mm
Flexible basecourse	± 6mm
Concrete wearing course	± 3mm
Concrete block paving	± 3mm
Concrete flags	± 2mm
Kerbs	± 5mm
Roadbase	+ 10mm − 15mm
Sub-base	+ 10mm − 30mm
Formation	+ 20mm − 30mm

Site clearance

3.—(1) Before the commencement of any street works, other than setting out, the site of the street shall be cleared of all encumbrances.

(2) Disused underground structures, chambers and drains shall be removed to depths as found necessary and the voids shall be filled with compacted suitable material.

SCHEDULE 3 — *continued*

Removal of unsuitable material

4.—(1) The site of a street shall be cleared of unsuitable material.

(2) In sub-paragraph (1) "unsuitable material" includes—

(*a*) all vegetable matter;

(*b*) material from swamps, marshes and bogs;

(*c*) peat, logs, stumps and perishable material;

(*d*) material susceptible to spontaneous combustion;

(*e*) material in a frozen condition;

(*f*) clay of liquid limit exceeding 90 and/or plasticity index exceeding 65; as determined by the liquid limit test BS 1377: Part 2: 1990;

(*g*) material damaged by weather or site traffic; and

(*h*) soft material which can be moulded by light finger pressure, in accordance with BS 5930: 1981.

(3) Wherever unsuitable material occurs in the site of a street, it shall be removed down to a gravel, clay, rock or other suitable foundation.

(4) The excavation shall be filled with broken rock or granular material placed in layers not exceeding a loose depth of 225mm levelled and compacted by rolling with a roller of not less than 8 tonnes in weight.

Cuttings

5.—(1) Materials shall be excavated from the site of road cuttings to the line and level as shown on the approved drawings.

(2) Where it is not proposed to construct the sub-base and roadbase immediately after excavation, or if it is proposed that site traffic shall use the cutting, the surface at the bottom shall be left at least 300mm above formation level.

(3) Where solid rock occurs it shall be cut down to 150mm minimum thickness under the surfacing level to allow for a regulating course of roadbase material as specified in the detailed requirements of paragraph 8 of Schedule 5 or if the carriageway is to be of concrete construction, to permit the laying of a 75mm (minimum) regulating course of concrete grade C20/40.

(4) Subject to sub-paragraph (5) the side slopes of cuttings shall not be steeper than 1 in 1.5.

(5) Where a cutting is in solid rock the side slopes of the cutting shall not be steeper than 1 in 0.5.

Embankments

6.—(1) Where formation levels are higher than natural ground levels, the ground levels, after unsuitable materials have been removed shall be raised by placing suitable imported or excavated material in layers not exceeding a loose depth of 225mm and compacting each layer by rolling with a roller of not less than 8 tonnes in weight as soon as practicable after deposition and each layer shall be finished parallel with the running surface of the road.

(2) In areas of shallow filling where after removal of topsoil the ground level is within 300mm of formation level, site traffic shall not use the surface unless it is brought up and maintained at least 300mm above formation level.

(3) Where an embankment is to be placed on steeply sloping ground the surface shall be benched in steps or trenched, and under-drainage shall be provided where necessary.

SCHEDULE 3 — *continued*

(4) The side slopes of embankments shall not be steeper than 1 in 2.

Earthworks to be kept free of water

7. Water shall be prevented from accumulating in excavations and cuttings, on embankments or on the sub-grade.

Soiling and sowing

8.—(1) All verges and side slopes after trimming shall be soiled to an even surface with topsoil to a settled depth of not less than 100mm.

(2) The soil shall be dressed with an appropriate fertiliser, cultivated and sown with grass seed at the rate of 1kg to 110m^2.

(3) The grass seed shall be a tested mixture and certificates of purity and germination shall be provided and the mixture shall comply with the requirements of paragraph 23 of Schedule 2.

(4) In case of failure the sowing shall be repeated until a strong permanent growth is obtained.

Safety fences

9.—(1) Safety fences shall be erected alongside a carriageway—

(*a*) on embankments which slope downwards from the carriageway to a depth of 6m or more;

(*b*) on other embankments where there is a road, railway, water hazard or other feature (eg subway entrance) at or near the foot of the slope of the embankment;

(*c*) at obstructions including bridge piers or abutments; and

(*d*) on the outside of curves less than 850m radius on embankments between 3m and 6m in depth.

(2) Safety fences shall be in accordance with the following—

(*a*) The Department of the Environment for Northern Ireland Manual of Contract Documents, Volume 1, Specification for Highway Works, Series 400, Safety Fences, Safety Barriers and Pedestrian Guardrails; and

(*b*) The Department of the Environment for Northern Ireland Manual of Contract Documents, Volume 3, Highway Construction Details, Section 2, Safety Fences and Barriers.

SCHEDULE 4   Regulations 7(2),
9(2) and 10(4)

Detailed requirements — Drainage

General

1.—(1) Pipes shall be designed to withstand the loading calculated in accordance with the Department of Transport and Road Research Laboratory publications "Simplified tables of external loads on buried pipelines" 1986 and "A guide to design loadings for buried rigid pipes" 1983.

(2) Only one type of pipe complying with the relevant BS shall be used within any individual drain length between manholes.

(3) The type of pipe to be used shall be as indicated in Table B.

(4) The design and construction of drains shall in as far as is reasonable be in accordance with BS 8005: Part 0: 1987 and BS 8005: Part 1: 1987 except where this Schedule specifies otherwise.

(5) Pipes greater than 900mm diameter shall be classified as highway structures (i.e. buried rigid structures) and their design shall be carried out in accordance with regulation 12.

Excavation for pipelines and manholes

2.—(1) Any excessive excavation arising from the method of working or the removal of soft spots shall be filled with grade C7.5/40 concrete.

(2) Water shall not be allowed to accumulate in the excavation and, where practicable, pipe trenches shall be started at the lower end.

(3) A trench shall be excavated to a sufficient depth and width, as detailed in Table A, to enable the pipe and any joint, bedding, haunching and surround to be accommodated.

(4) The width of a trench to accommodate a pipe having an internal diameter as set out in column 1 of Table A shall be within the limits set out in columns 2 and 3 of that table.

(5) The said width shall be maintained up to a minimum of 300mm above the top of the pipe.

(6) Battering of the sides of trenches shall only be permitted where the pipe has been designed to withstand the loadings applicable under wide trench conditions calculated in accordance with the Department of Transport and Road Research Laboratory publications "Simplified tables of external loads on buried pipelines" 1986 and "A guide to design loadings for buried rigid pipes" 1983.

SCHEDULE 4 — *continued*

TABLE A

Column 1	Column 2	Column 3
Internal diameter of pipe in mm	*Minimum trench width in mm*	*Maximum trench width in mm*
100	430	630
150	490	690
225	580	780
300	680	880
375	950	1,150
450	1,030	1,230
525	1,120	1,320
600	1,240	1,440

(7) Where the trench is in ground that does not afford proper support to the pipe—

(*a*) it shall be excavated down to solid ground and extra depth refilled with grade C7.5/40 concrete; or

(*b*) the pipe shall be supported by piles.

Type, laying, bedding and protection of pipes

3.—(1) Immediately following the excavation of the trench, pipes shall be laid and jointed on granular material or concrete in accordance with sub-paragraphs (2) to (4).

(2) After jointing and before any backfilling the pipes shall be tested in accordance with the detailed requirements in paragraph 8. Pipes shall be laid so that each one is in contact with the bedding material throughout the length of the pipe, provision being made to accommodate the joints.

(3) The perforations in perforated pipes shall not be blocked and all pipelines shall be laid true to line and level.

(4) Pipes shall be in accordance with paragraph 12 of Schedule 2 and shall be jointed as indicated in Table B.

TABLE B

Type of pipe (not exceeding 600mm diameter)	*Joint type*	*Bedding class*
Concrete to BS 5911: Part 100: 1988. Standard pipes for diameter not exceeding 300mm; Class M pipe or Class H pipe for diameter greater than 300mm	Flexible spigot and socket joints as described in BS 5911: Part 100: 1988	B
Prestressed concrete pipes to BS 5178: 1975 for pipes diameter 450mm or greater	Flexible spigot and socket or rebated joints as described in BS 5178: 1975	B

SCHEDULE 4 — *continued*

Table B — *continued*

Type of pipe (not exceeding 600mm diameter)	Joint type	Bedding class
British Standard clay pipes to BS 65: 1991. Extra strength pipes to be used in all cases	Type 1 sockets with flexible joints as described in BS 65: 1991	B
UPVC pipes to BS 5481: 1977 (1989) or BS 4660: 1989	As described in BS 5481: 1977 (1989) or BS 4660: 1989	E
Perforated concrete pipes to BS 5911: Part 3: 1982	Ogee or rebated joints as described in BS 5911: Part 3: 1982	A
Porous concrete pipes to BS 5911: Part 114: 1992	Ogee or rebated joints as described in BS 5911: Part 114: 1992	A

(5) UPVC pipes shall—

(*a*) be stored and handled carefully and shall not be subjected to stresses which would induce permanent set or ovality; and

(*b*) be protected from the effects of temperature in accordance with the manufacturer's recommendations and shall not be laid in freezing conditions.

(6) Sufficient of the infill material shall be placed around the barrel of the pipes to prevent movement and stones, bricks or similar materials shall not be used below or against the pipes to locate them in position in the trench or to level the pipes.

(7) Granular bedding Type A shall comprise material to BS 882: 1992; Clause 5.3 with 10mm nominal size for pipes of 375mm diameter or less or 20mm nominal size for pipes of more than 375mm diameter.

(8) Selected fill Type B shall comprise uniform readily compactable material free from tree roots, vegetable matter, building rubbish and frozen soil, excluding clay lumps retained on 75mm sieve and stones retained on 25mm sieve.

(9) Granular bedding Type C shall be as specified for granular bedding Type A but to pass a 10mm sieve.

(10) For Class A bedding concrete grade C20/20 shall be placed in the excavation over the full width of the trench to give a minimum thickness of 100mm below the pipe.

(11) For Class B bedding—

(*a*) Type A granular material shall be placed by hand in the excavation below the level of the pipe barrel and shall be tamped by hand in layers not exceeding 150mm thick before compaction, to provide a dense, well compacted bed;

(*b*) the minimum thickness of the bed below the pipe shall be the greater of ¼ of the outside diameter of the pipe or 100mm;

(*c*) after the pipes have been properly bedded and tested Type A granular material shall be carefully placed into the spaces between the pipe and the sides of the trench to the level of half the pipe;

SCHEDULE 4 — *continued*

(*d*) the Type A granular material shall be thoroughly packed by careful tamping in layers not exceeding 150mm thick before compaction;

(*e*) the placing and tamping of the material shall proceed equally on both sides of the pipe;

(*f*) thereafter Type B selected fill shall be placed into the space between the pipe and the sides of the trench to the level of the crown of the pipe;

(*g*) the Type B fill shall be thoroughly packed and rammed by careful hand tamping in layers not exceeding 150mm thick before compaction;

(*h*) the placing and tamping of the material shall proceed equally on both sides of the pipe; and

(*i*) the bedding shall be completed by placing Type B fill material at least 300mm deep after compaction along the full width of the trench in 2 equal layers over the crown of the pipe, each layer lightly tamped by hand.

(12) For Class E bedding—

(*a*) Type C granular material shall be placed by hand in the excavation below the pipe and shall be tamped by hand in layers not exceeding 150mm thick before compaction to provide a dense well compacted bed free from soft spots throughout the length of the pipeline;

(*b*) the minimum thickness of the bed below the pipe shall be the greater of ¼ of the outside diameter of the pipe or 100mm;

(*c*) after the pipes have been properly bedded and tested, Type C granular material shall be carefully placed into the spaces between the pipe and the sides of the trench to the level of the crown of the pipe;

(*d*) the Type C granular material shall be thoroughly packed by careful hand tamping in layers not exceeding 150mm thick before compaction;

(*e*) the placing and tamping of the material shall proceed equally on both sides of the pipe; and

(*f*) Class E bedding shall be completed by placing Type C granular material over the crown of the pipe to a minimum depth of 150mm and the material shall be thoroughly compacted by hand tamping.

(13) Drains for the conveyance of sub-soil water shall be haunched using concrete grade C20/20. Haunching shall be a minimum of 50mm thick and shall extend from the pipe to the edge of the trench. The surface of the concrete shall be trowelled smooth and shall slope towards the pipe at a minimum grade of 1 in 12.

(14) During the placing of bedding, haunching, surrounding or anchoring materials, temporary side supports shall be removed and the full width of the trench shall be infilled with bedding, haunching, surrounding or anchoring material.

(15) Concrete for the protection of pipes shall be grade C20/20 and of minimum thickness 150mm.

(16) Concrete surrounds shall be provided for all pipes with less than 1.2m depth of cover.

(17) In order to avoid penetration of the sub-base by the concrete protection the minimum depth of cover to any concrete surround shall not be less than 625mm.

Backfilling

4.—(1) Backfilling shall wherever practicable take place immediately after the operations described in paragraph 3 have been completed.

SCHEDULE 4 — *continued*

(2) Except for drains for the conveyance of sub-soil water all backfilling shall consist only of suitable material deposited in layers not exceeding 225mm thick and each layer compacted to the degree of compaction required for earthworks and embankments.

(3) Any material which when excavated had been suitable for re-use, shall be replaced with suitable material if it has subsequently become unsuitable for backfilling.

(4) Suitable compacting equipment power rammers or vibrating plate compactors shall be used to compact the backfilling from 1m above the crown level of the pipe up to the appropriate level as described in sub-paragraphs (5) and (6).

(5) Backfilled material shall be terminated 75mm below surface level in grass areas and topsoiled over.

(6) In carriageways, footways and footpaths the backfilled material shall be brought up to formation level.

(7) Backfilling of drains for the conveyance of sub-soil water shall be with Type D filter material of clean, hard, crushed rock or gravel having a grading within the limits of Table C.

(8) The aggregate crushing value of the material shall not exceed 30 per cent as determined by the tests in BS 812: Part 110: 1990.

(9) The material passing the 425µm BS sieve shall be non-plastic when tested in accordance with BS 1377: Part 2: 1990.

(10) Filter material shall be deposited in layers not exceeding 225mm loose depth and each layer lightly compacted.

TABLE C   RANGE OF GRADING OF FILTER MATERIAL

BS Sieve Size	*Percentage by weight passing*
37.5 mm	100
10 mm	45-100
3.35 mm	25-80
600 µm	8-45
150 µm	0-10
75 µm	0-5

Connections to existing drains

5.—(1) Where necessary, existing drains shall be properly extended, connected and jointed to the new drains.

(2) Where a drain for the conveyance of sub-soil water or a drain for the conveyance of surface water from the road is to connect into an existing drain for the conveyance of storm water a suitable catchpit shall be provided.

(3) All necessary precautions shall be taken to prevent the entry of debris or any other material into any existing drain and a free and uninterrupted flow shall always be preserved therein.

Manholes, inspection chambers and catchpits

6.—(1) Manholes, inspection chambers and catchpits are referred to as chambers in this paragraph.

SCHEDULE 4 — *continued*

(2) Bricks for construction of chambers and adjusting courses shall be Class B engineering bricks or concrete bricks to BS 6073: Part 1: 1981 of average compressive strength $30N/mm^2$.

(3) Brick adjusting courses shall be kept to the minimum consistent with satisfactory construction of adjacent features and shall not exceed 300mm in depth.

(4) Chambers shall be constructed of either—

(*a*) precast concrete in accordance with BS 5911: Part 200: 1989 and to the sizes detailed in Table D and where precast units of appropriate diameter are used for the lower chamber the height shall not be less than 2m; above 2m taper units may be used to reduce the diameter to 900mm; or

(*b*) brick in accordance with sub-paragraph (2) and to the sizes detailed in Table E.

TABLE D

Dimension for Precast Concrete Chambers

Diameter of Pipe in mm	Depth of Chamber in m	Internal Diameter of Chamber in mm
150	up to 1.4	900
150	1.4 to 3.1	1050
225	up to 2.4	1050
225	2.4 to 3.2	1200
300	up to 3.275	1200
375	up to 3.35	1200
450	up to 3.75	1350
525	up to 3.825	1350
600	up to 3.9	1350
675	up to 4.0	1350
750	up to 4.075	1500
825	up to 4.15	1500
900	up to 4.225	1800

TABLE E

Dimension for Brick Chambers

Diameter of Pipe in mm	Depth of Chamber in m	Length and Breadth of Chamber in mm
Up to 225	Up to 1.4	900 × 675
Up to 225	1.4 to 2.5	1125 × 900
Up to 225	Over 2.5	1350 × 900
Over 225 and up to 375	Up to 2.5	1125 × 1125
Over 225 and up to 375	Over 2.5	1350 × 1125
Over 375 and up to 750	All depths	1350 × 1500

SCHEDULE 4 — *continued*

(5) Foundations to chambers shall be concrete grade C20/40 of minimum thickness 225mm.

(6) Channels up to 300mm diameter may be either vitrified clay or precast concrete; channels above 300mm diameter may be either preformed or formed in granolithic concrete.

(7) Benching shall be formed in grade C20/40 concrete and be rendered in granolithic concrete 50mm thick trowelled smooth and shall slope at 1 in 12 towards the main channel.

(8) Cover slabs of a suitable design shall be reinforced concrete grade C30/20.

(9) Chambers or systems collecting road surface water or water from sub-soil drains shall have a sump of not less than 225 mm depth below the invert of the outlet pipe.

(10) Where the depth of invert or sump of chambers below the finished surface of the carriageway or adjacent ground exceeds 900mm either—

    (*a*) step irons to BS 1247: Part 2: 1990 shall be built in at vertical intervals of 300mm and at 300mm centre to centre horizontally; or

    (*b*) in the case of brick chambers in addition to the requirements specified in sub-paragraph (*a*) step irons shall have 230mm $\pm$ 10mm tails.

(11) Where the depth to invert or sump of chambers below the finished surface of the carriageway or adjacent ground exceeds 2.5m—

    (*a*) a manhole ladder shall be provided instead of step irons;

    (*b*) manhole ladders and fixing brackets shall be of mild steel complying with the requirements of BS 449: Part 2: 1969 galvanised after manufacture;

    (*c*) the stringers shall be 64mm by 19mm minimum section and the rungs 25mm minimum diameter;

    (*d*) the stringers shall be placed not less than 380mm apart and connected to the supporting structure with fixing brackets of material equal in section to the stringers located at centres not exceeding 2m (minimum of 2 pairs of fixing brackets per ladder);

    (*e*) the fixing brackets shall be of sufficient length to give a clearance of not less than 210mm behind the rungs; and

    (*f*) the rungs shall be equally spaced at centres of between 230mm and 250mm and fixed to the stringers in accordance with BS 4211: 1987.

(12) Backfilling around chambers shall normally be similar to backfilling of trenches; however, where the design of the chamber is such that it requires concrete backfilling this shall be provided.

(13) All chambers shall be watertight on completion and shall be fitted with heavy duty double triangular covers to BS 497: Part 1: 1976 type MA-60, in carriageways, including shared surfaces.

(14) Chambers shall be provided at the start of the run of pipe, at sharp changes of direction, at the junctions of pipes or changes of diameter of pipes, or where excessive gradients require the positioning of back-drop chambers.

(15) Chambers shall be spaced at distances not greater than 90m.

(16) In footways, verges or service strips covers to BS 497: Part 1: 1976 type MB2-60 may be provided.

(17) In sub-paragraph (10) "tails" means that part of the step iron which forms the legs of the 'U-shape' and is measured from the free end to the first bend.

SCHEDULE 4 — *continued*

Gullies and connections

7.—(1) Gullies shall be as detailed in sub-paragraphs (2) to (9) and be capable of being easily rodded.

(2) Footway gullies shall be of cast iron 300mm long, 230mm wide and 280mm deep with a rodding eye and the grating shall be hinged and channelled.

(3) Carriageway, including shared surface, gullies shall be circular 375mm internal diameter or rectangular having internal dimensions 300mm × 385mm in accordance with BS 5911: Part 200: 1989.

(4) Gullies shall be fully surrounded with concrete grade C20/20 to a minimum thickness of 150mm.

(5) Gullies shall have 150mm outlet and all other dimensions shall be as detailed for 375mm diameter in Table 3 of BS 5911: Part 200: 1989.

(6) Untrapped gullies shall only be used for storm water drains.

(7) Carriageway gully gratings and frames shall comply with the requirements of paragraph 13(3) of Schedule 2.

(8) A sufficient number of gullies shall be provided to drain adequately the surface water from the street and the normal spacing of gullies shall be at 40m centres on both sides of a cambered street and at 30m centres on the low side of a street with crossfall.

(9) Where gradients fall below 0.8 per cent in valley curves or at points of reversal of crossfall closer gully spacing or precast concrete drainage units slotted to allow continuous access of surface water to a drain shall be required.

(10) Junction pipes for gullies which are laid but not immediately connected to gullies shall be fitted with suitable temporary stoppers or seals and the position of all such junctions shall be clearly marked by means of stakes or tracing wires.

(11) In sub-paragraph (2) "rodding eye" means an inclined shaft constructed in the line of a drain connected to the main pipeline to facilitate the clearance of blockages by rodding.

Testing and cleaning

8.—(1) All drains with watertight joints shall be tested between manholes by means of the water test or the air test referred to in sub-paragraphs (2) and (3) respectively—

(2) In the case of the water test—

(*a*) the pipes shall be filled with water under a head of not less than 1.2m above the crown of the pipe at the high end and not more than 6m above the pipe at the low end;

(*b*) steeply graded pipes shall be tested in stages where the latter head would be exceeded if the whole section were tested at once;

(*c*) a period of one hour shall be allowed for absorption;

(*d*) the loss of water over a period of 30 minutes shall be measured by adding water from a measuring vessel at regular intervals of 10 minutes and noting the quantity required to maintain the original water level in the standpipe; and

(*e*) the sewer or drain shall have passed the test if the volume of water added to the standpipe does not exceed 0.06 litres per hour per 100 linear metre per millimetre of nominal internal diameter over 300mm nominal diameter.

SCHEDULE 4 — *continued*

(3) In the case of the air test—

(*a*) the length of pipe under test shall be effectively plugged and air pumped in by suitable means, until a pressure of 100mm head of water is indicated; and

(*b*) the sewer shall have passed the test if the air pressure does not fall below 75mm head of water during a period of five minutes without further pumping after a period for requisite stabilisation.

(4) The drains referred to in sub-paragraph (1) shall be tested—

(*a*) after laying, including the placing of concrete, if any is required under this Schedule, but before backfilling; and

(*b*) after backfilling has been completed.

(5) Drains constructed of steel, spun iron or other material designed for high pressure shall be tested in accordance with sub-paragraphs (6) to (8).

(6) Pipes shall be tested for infiltration after backfilling.

(7) All inlets to the system shall be effectively closed and the residual flow shall be deemed to be infiltration.

(8) The amount of infiltration shall not exceed 0.1 litre per hour per 100 linear metre per millimetre of nominal bore of the pipe and infiltration to manholes shall not exceed 5 litres per hour per manhole.

(9) Should any drain fail to pass any of the tests in this paragraph, the defects shall be made good and the pipes re-tested until they comply with the requirements of the test.

(10) On completion of the work—

(*a*) all pipes shall be thoroughly cleaned and pipes not exceeding 400mm diameter shall be flushed with clean water while being rodded from manhole to manhole with a rubber tipped plunger 12mm less than the bore of the pipe; and

(*b*) chambers and sumps shall be washed down, emptied and left to dry and the pipe and filter of drains for the conveyance of sub-soil water shall at all times be kept free of obstructions.

Intercepting ditches and existing land drains

9.—(1) Intercepting ditches, and drains having a similar function to intercepting ditches, shall if practicable be constructed in advance of the excavation of cuttings and forming of embankments.

(2) Existing land drains severed by the works shall be located and connected into the intercepting ditches or new pipes which are provided for the interception of surface and sub-soil water.

Sub-soil drainage (see also regulation 9)

10.—(1) Perforated or porous concrete pipes for the purpose of sub-soil drainage shall be laid on one or both sides of the carriageway.

(2) The depth of cover shall not be less than 1.2m and the pipes shall be backfilled in accordance with the requirements in paragraph 4.

Detailed requirements — Carriageways

Camber, crossfall and superelevation

1.—(1) Carriageways shall be constructed with camber or crossfall of 1 in 40.

(2) Where the cross-section of a carriageway changes from camber to crossfall the rate of change shall not exceed 1 in 100.

(3) Subject to sub-paragraph (4) superelevation shall be applied to the carriageway and shall be 1 in 40.

(4) Where it is satisfied in any particular case that the requirement of sub-paragraph (3) as to the ratio of superelevation is unreasonable the Department may relax that requirement to permit superelevation not exceeding 1 in 25.

Types of construction

2.—(1) Subject to sub-paragraph (5) carriageways shall be of flexible, block paving or rigid construction as specified in Tables A, B or C—

TABLE A   FLEXIBLE CONSTRUCTION

Layer	Material	Depth of Material		
		Carriageway width greater than 6m (excluding carriageways serving industrial premises)	Carriageway 6m or less in width (excluding carriageways serving industrial premises)	Carriageways serving industrial premises
Blinding	Stone dust	75mm	75mm	75mm
Sub-base	Crushed rock in accordance with the requirements in paragraph 7	250mm	225mm	N/A
	Crushed rock in accordance with the roadbase requirements in paragraph 8	N/A	N/A	225mm
Roadbase	Crushed rock in accordance with the requirements in paragraph 8	225mm	150mm	N/A

SCHEDULE 5 — *continued*

TABLE A — Flexible Construction — *continued*

Layer	Material	Depth of Material		
		Carriageway width greater than 6m (excluding carriageways serving industrial premises)	*Carriageway 6m or less in width (excluding carriageways serving industrial premises)*	*Carriageways serving industrial premises*
	Bituminous roadbase in accordance with the requirements in paragraph 9	N/A	N/A	180mm
Basecourse	Bitumen macadam or asphalt in accordance with the requirements in paragraph 12(1)	50mm	50mm	60mm
Wearing course	Bitumen macadam or asphalt with chippings in accordance with the requirements in paragraph 13(1)	40mm	40mm	N/A
	Asphalt with chippings in accordance with the requirements in paragraph 13(3)	N/A	N/A	40mm
Chippings	Precoated chippings in accordance with the requirements in paragraph 13(4)	20mm	20mm	20mm

SCHEDULE 5 — *continued*

TABLE B   BLOCK PAVING

Layer	Material	Depth of Material		
		Carriageway width greater than 6m (excluding carriageways serving industrial premises)	*Carriageway 6m or less in width (excluding carriageways serving industrial premises)*	*Carriageways serving industrial premises*
Blinding	Stone dust	75mm	75mm	75mm
Sub-base	Crushed rock in accordance with the requirements in paragraph 7	250mm	225mm	225mm
Roadbase	Crushed rock in accordance with the requirements in paragraph 8	225mm	150mm	N/A
	Concrete C7.5/40	N/A	N/A	200mm
Laying Course	Graded sharp sand in accordance with BS 6717: Part 3: 1989	50mm	50mm	50mm
Surface Course	Concrete or other approved paving blocks in accordance with the requirements in paragraph 17	80mm	80mm	80mm

SCHEDULE 5 — *continued*

TABLE C   RIGID CONSTRUCTION

	Depth of Stone Dust Blinding Layer	Depth of Crushed Rock Roadbase (in accordance with the requirements in paragraph 8)	Depth of Concrete Slab (in accordance with the requirements in paragraph 16)	Transverse Joint Reinforcement (minimum)	Longitudinal Joint Reinforcement (minimum)	Transverse Joint Spacing (maximum)
Carriageway width greater than 6m (excluding carriageways serving industrial premises)	75mm	180mm	200mm	0.75kg per m^2	2.61kg per m^2	15m
Carriageway width 6m or less (excluding carriageways serving industrial premises)	75mm	180mm	150mm	0.75kg per m^2	1.8kg per m^2	12m
Carriageways serving industrial premises	75mm	250mm	220mm	0.75kg per m^2	3.41kg per m^2	20m

SCHEDULE 5 — *continued*

(2) In the case of flexible construction and block paving the blinding layer sub-base and roadbase shall extend 450mm beyond the kerb face on each side of the carriageway.

(3) In the case of rigid construction the blinding layer sub-base and roadbase shall extend 300mm beyond the kerb face on each side of the carriageway.

(4) Rigid construction shall be of reinforced concrete and fabric reinforcement No. B283 to BS 4483: 1985 may be used or alternatively No. C283 to BS 4483; 1985 with the addition of at least 5mm bars at 400mm centres placed transversely across the main reinforcement.

(5) Where the formation consists of solid rock the requirements of sub-paragraph (1) for the blinding layer set out in Tables A, B and C shall not apply.

Drains, etc. to be completed first

3. Before any carriageway construction work has begun the installation of all drains, pipes, cables and other apparatus shall be completed.

Preparation of formation

4.—(1) The formation shall be well cleaned of mud and slurry, properly trimmed to the line and level as shown on the approved plans and maintained free of standing water.

(2) When the formation has been prepared, construction traffic, apart from compaction equipment, shall not be allowed to run on it.

Materials for sub-base and roadbase

5.—(1) Subject to sub-paragraph (2) materials for sub-base and roadbase shall consist of crushed rock.

(2) Where it is satisfied in any particular case that the requirement of sub-paragraph (1) is unreasonable the Department may relax that requirement to permit the use of materials consisting of gravel (crushed or screened), bituminous or cement bound granular material or lean mix concrete.

Protection

6.—(1) During construction the sub-base, roadbase and surfacing shall be kept clean and free from clay or other deleterious materials.

(2) Construction shall be so organised that only traffic directly engaged in laying and compacting shall traverse the surface of the roadbase.

(3) Traffic which would damage the partially constructed road shall not be permitted to use it.

(4) Any damage to any layer shall be made good before the application of the subsequent layer.

(5) Where site construction traffic is to use a partially constructed road there shall be a minimum of 300mm thickness of compacted material, blinded by the application of crushed rock of 19mm maximum size compacted to form a dense even surface, provided to protect the formation.

(6) The blinding material shall not be frost susceptible as described in the Department of the Environment Transport and Road Research Laboratory Report LR90: 1967.

(7) The portion of blinding material passing the 425μm BS sieve when tested in compliance with BS: 1377: Part 2: 1990 shall be non-plastic.

SCHEDULE 5 — *continued*

Sub-base

7.—(1) Crushed rock sub-base shall consist of sound clean approved rock with a 10 per cent fines value of not less than 160 KN when tested in accordance with the requirements of BS 812: Part 111: 1990.

(2) Other materials shall conform to the appropriate BS.

(3) With the exception of the mixed materials, sub-base materials shall be graded in accordance with Table D—

TABLE D

110mm Crushed Rock: Range of Grading for Sub-base Material	
BS Sieve Size	Percentage by Mass passing
125.00mm	100
100.00mm	90-100
90.00mm	83-100
37.50mm	25-52
28.00mm	10-30
14.00mm	0-10
6.30mm	0-6
3.35mm	0-2

(4) Sub-base material used shall not be frost susceptible as defined by the test described in the Department of the Environment Transport and Road Research Laboratory Report LR 90: 1967.

(5) The material passing the 425μm BS sieve when tested in compliance with BS 1377: Part 2: 1990 shall be non-plastic.

(6) Where the total depth of sub-base is 250mm or less this shall be spread in one layer so that when compacted the total depth shall be in accordance with the requirements in paragraph 2.

(7) Compaction shall be by not less than the required number of passes of a roller as shown in Table E for the required compacted layer depth.

SCHEDULE 5 — *continued*
TABLE E

Compaction Requirements for Granular Sub-base and Roadbase Material

Type of compaction plant	Category	No. of passes of compaction equipment for layers not exceeding the following compacted depths			
		110mm	*150mm*	*225mm*	*250mm*
Smooth-wheeled roller (or vibratory roller operating without vibration)	Mass per m width of roll: over 2700kg up to 5400kg over 5400kg	16 8	N/A 16	N/A N/A	N/A N/A
Pneumatic-tyred roller	Mass per wheel: over 4000kg up to 6000kg over 6000kg up to 8000kg over 8000kg up to 12000kg over 12000kg	12 12 10 8	N/A N/A 16 12	N/A N/A N/A N/A	N/A N/A N/A N/A
Vibratory roller	Mass per metre width of vibrating roll: over 700kg up to 1300kg over 1300kg up to 1800kg over 1800kg up to 2300kg over 2300kg up to 2900kg over 2900kg up to 3600kg over 3600kg up to 4300kg over 4300kg up to 5000kg over 5000kg	16 6 4 3 3 2 2 2	N/A 16 6 5 5 4 4 3	N/A N/A 10 9 8 7 6 5	N/A N/A N/A 10 9 8 7 6
Vibrating plate compactor	Mass per sq metre of base plate: over 1400kg/m^2 up to 1800kg/m^2 over 1800kg/m^2 up to 2100kg/m^2 over 2100kg/m^2	8 5 3	N/A 8 6	N/A N/A 10	N/A N/A N/A
Vibro-tamper	Mass: over 50kg up to 65kg over 65kg up to 75kg over 75kg	4 3 2	8 6 4	N/A 10 8	N/A N/A N/A
Power rammer	Mass: 100kg up to 500kg over 500kg	5 5	8 8	N/A 12	N/A N/A

SCHEDULE 5 — *continued*

(8) When compaction has been completed the surface of the sub-base shall be true to line and level within the tolerances given in paragraph 2 of Schedule 3.

Crushed rock roadbase

8.—(1) Crushed rock roadbase shall consist of sound clean approved rock with a 10 per cent fines value of not less than 160KN when tested in accordance with the requirements of BS 812: Part 111: 1990. That material shall be graded in accordance with Table F:

TABLE F

65mm Crushed Rock: Range of Grading for Roadbase Material	
BS Sieve Size	*Percentage by Mass Passing*
65.00mm	100
50.00mm	67-100
37.50mm	52-70
28.00mm	30-45
14.00mm	10-28
6.30mm	6-10
2.36mm	0-6
1.16mm	0-2

(2) The material described in sub-paragraph (1) shall not be frost susceptible as defined by the test described in the Department of the Environment Transport and Road Research Laboratory Report LR 90: 1967.

(3) The material passing the 425μm BS sieve when tested in compliance with BS 1377: Part 2: 1990 shall be non-plastic.

(4) The roadbase material shall be laid in layers so that when compacted the total thickness shall be in accordance with the detailed requirements in paragraph 2.

(5) The minimum compacted layer depth of material laid in one layer shall be 110mm and the maximum compacted layer thickness laid in one layer shall be 225mm.

(6) The final layer of material shall be spread using a paving machine.

(7) Compaction shall be by not less than the required number of passes of a roller as shown in Table E for the required compacted layer depth.

(8) When compaction has been completed the surface shall be true to line and level and within the tolerances given in paragraph 2 of Schedule 3.

Bituminous roadbase

9.—(1) Bitumen macadam roadbase shall be manufactured and tested in accordance with BS 4987: Part 1: 1988 28mm size dense roadbase and transported, laid and compacted in accordance with BS 4987: Part 2: 1988 to the depth shown in Table A and subject to the requirements in paragraphs 10 and 11.

(2) Where a bituminous roadbase is to carry traffic prior to the application of the basecourse a tack coat in accordance with BS 4987: Part 2: 1988 shall be applied prior to the laying of the basecourse.

SCHEDULE 5 — *continued*

Flexible surfacing

10.—(1) The testing of materials for flexible surfacing shall be in accordance with sub-paragraphs (2) to (6).

(2) In the case of bituminous materials a sample of the proposed mix shall be submitted for testing at least three working days before being laid on the road and continuous daily sampling and testing shall be carried out during the progress of the works.

(3) The testing of bituminous materials shall be carried out by an approved laboratory as laid down in BS 598: Part 101: 1987; Part 102: 1989; Part 104: 1989; Part 105: 1990; Part 106: 1990; Part 107: 1990; Part 108: 1990 and Part 109: 1990; BS 812: Part 1: 1975; Part 2: 1975; Part 101: 1984; Part 103: 1985; Part 111: 1990 and Section 105.1: 1989; BS 2000: Part 105: 1991; BS 3690: Part 3: 1990; and copies of the certified results of the tests shall be given to the Department.

(4) In the event of failure to supply such certified results samples shall be taken from the road for testing.

(5) Where a sample fails to conform to the specifications in the relevant requirements in Schedule 2 the Department may order the replacement of material supplied during that day, or the carrying out of appropriate remedial measures.

(6) Samples shall be taken in accordance with BS 598: Part 100: 1987 and the manufacturer's instructions and recommendations provided these do not conflict with the BS.

11.—(1) The preparation for flexible surfacing shall be in accordance with sub-paragraphs (2) to (4).

(2) Before the application of the surfacing layers the surface of the roadbase shall be well compacted, free from mud, loose material or other deleterious materials, true to line and level and any deficiencies shall be made good with a regulating course of bitumen macadam of appropriate nominal size.

(3) Subject to sub-paragraph (4) the laying and compacting of bitumen macadam shall be in accordance with the recommendations in BS 4987: Part 2: 1988 and shall be machine laid in accordance with the BS.

(4) Notwithstanding the provisions of sub-paragraph (3) hand laying of bituminous material shall be permitted in the following circumstances—

(*a*) for laying regulating courses of irregular shape and varying thickness;

(*b*) in confined spaces where it is impracticable for a paver to operate; and

(*c*) for footways and footpaths.

12.—(1) The basecourse for flexible surfacing shall be in accordance with sub-paragraphs (2) to (4).

(2) Bitumen macadam basecourse shall be manufactured and tested in accordance with BS 4987: Part 1: 1988 20mm size dense basecourse and transported, laid and compacted in accordance with BS 4987: Part 2: 1988 to the depth shown in Table A.

(3) Asphalt basecourse shall be 60 per cent coarse aggregate hot rolled asphalt of depth shown in Table A and shall be manufactured and tested in accordance with BS 594: Part 1: 1992 Table 2 Column 2/4; binder to Table 1, binder numbers 3 or 5 and transported, laid and compacted in accordance with BS 594: Part 2: 1992.

(4) Where a basecourse is to carry traffic prior to the application of the wearing course, the depth shall be increased to 70mm compacted thickness and a tack coat in

SCHEDULE 5 — *continued*

accordance with BS 4987: Part 2: 1988 shall be applied prior to the laying of the wearing course.

13.—(1) The wearing course for flexible surfacing shall be in accordance with sub-paragraphs (2) to (5).

(2) Subject to sub-paragraph (5) bitumen macadam wearing course shall be manufactured and tested in accordance with BS 4987: Part 1: 1988 14mm close graded wearing course for Category B traffic and transported, laid and compacted in accordance with BS 4987: Part 2: 1988 to the depth shown in Table A.

(3) Asphalt wearing course shall be 30 per cent coarse aggregate manufactured and tested to BS 594: Part 1: 1992 Table 6 Column 6/4 Schedule 1B of depth shown in Table A and shall be covered with a layer of pre-coated chippings of size in accordance with the requirements in Table A applied as specified in BS 594: Part 2: 1992 Clause 7 and shall be transported, laid and compacted in accordance with BS 594: Part 2: 1992.

(4) The chippings shall comply with BS 594: Part 1: 1992 Clause 4 with a maximum aggregate abrasion value of 12 and a minimum polished stone value of 55.

(5) Where the depth of the basecourse has been increased to 70mm compacted thickness to comply with paragraph 12(4) bitumen macadam wearing course manufactured and tested in accordance with BS 4987: Part 1: 1988 10mm size close graded wearing course for Category B traffic and transported, laid and compacted in accordance with BS 4987: Part 2: 1988 to a compacted depth of 30mm may be used as an alternative to the requirements of paragraph 13(2).

14.—(1) The aggregates for flexible surfacing shall be in accordance with sub-paragraphs (2) and (3).

(2) The aggregates used for bituminous surfacing materials shall be sound, clean, hard broken rock graded to BS 4987: Part 1: 1988.

(3) Where they are used in the wearing course they shall have a maximum aggregate abrasion value of 16 and a minimum polished stone value of 45.

15. The binder for bitumen macadam roadbase, basecourse and wearing course shall be in accordance with BS 4987: Part 1: 1988.

Concrete carriageways

16.—(1) Subject to paragraph 2(1) concrete carriageways shall be in accordance with the Department of the Environment for Northern Ireland Manual of Contract Documents, Volume 1, Specification for Highway Works, Series 1000, Road Pavements — Concrete and Cement Bound Materials, and the following provisions.

(2) The depth of concrete slab shall be in accordance with the requirements in Table C.

(3) The concrete slab shall be reinforced to an extent not less than that specified in Table C.

(4) Transverse joints for concrete carriageways shall be in accordance with the Department of the Environment for Northern Ireland Manual of Contract Documents, Volume 1, Specification for Highway Works, Series 1000, Road Pavements — Concrete and Cement Bound Materials, and the requirements of sub-paragraphs (5) to (7).

(5) The spacing for transverse joints along the entire length of the carriageway shall be as specified in Table C.

SCHEDULE 5 — *continued*

(6) Every third joint shall be an expansion joint.

(7) The remainder shall be contraction joints.

(8) In sub-paragraph (6) "expansion joint" means a permanent joint between two slabs or elements of a structure which allows a small relevant movement perpendicular to the joint.

(9) In sub-paragraph (7) "contraction joint" means a joint to reduce stresses due to shrinkage or temperature change and to control the possibility of cracks.

Block paving

17.—(1) Subject to sub-paragraphs (3) and (4) concrete paving blocks shall be used and shall comply and be tested in accordance with BS 6717: Part 1: 1986.

(2) Subject to sub-paragraph (3) concrete paving blocks shall be laid in accordance with BS 6717: Part 3: 1989.

(3) Where it is satisfied in any particular case that the requirements of sub-paragraphs (1) and (2) are unreasonable the Department may relax those requirements to permit the use of proprietory shaped concrete paving blocks not complying with the requirements referred to in sub-paragraph (1) and to permit laying techniques different from those contained in the BS referred to in sub-paragraph (2) if the blocks are laid in accordance with the manufacturer's specification in relation thereto.

(4) Where it is satisfied in any particular case that the requirements of sub-paragraph (1) are unreasonable the Department may relax those requirements to permit type PB clay paving blocks manufactured in accordance with BS 6677: Part 1: 1986 and laid in accordance with BS 6677: Part 3: 1986.

SCHEDULE 6   Regulation 11(2) and (3)

Detailed Requirements — Shared Surfaces

Camber and crossfall

1.—(1) Subject to sub-paragraph (3) shared surfaces shall be constructed with camber or crossfall of 1 in 40.

(2) Where the cross-section of a shared surface changes from camber to crossfall the rate of change shall not exceed 1 in 100.

(3) Where a centre line drainage system is provided construction shall be with a fall of 1 in 40 towards the centre line.

Types of construction

2.—(1) Shared surfaces shall be of flexible, block paving or rigid construction in accordance with sub-paragraphs (2) to (4) as appropriate.

(2) In the case of flexible construction—

(a) the blinding layer, sub-base and roadbase shall be in accordance with the requirements in Table A of Schedule 5; and

(b) the basecourse and wearing course shall be either—

(i) bitumen macadam basecourse and wearing course in accordance with the requirements in Table A of Schedule 5; or

(ii) bitumen macadam basecourse manufactured and tested in accordance with BS 4987: Part 1: 1988 20mm size dense basecourse and transported, laid and compacted in accordance with BS 4987: Part 2: 1988 to a compacted depth of 55mm; and

35mm compacted depth of hot rolled asphalt wearing course with precoated chippings in accordance with the requirements in paragraph 13(3) and (4) of Schedule 5.

(3) In the case of block paving, construction using block paving shall comprise blinding layer, sub-base, roadbase, laying course and surface course in accordance with the requirements in Table B of Schedule 5.

(4) In the case of rigid construction, the construction for a rigid surface shall comprise blinding layer, roadbase and reinforced concrete in accordance with the requirements in Table C and paragraph 16 of Schedule 5.

Rumble strips

3.—(1) Subject to sub-paragraph (6) at the entrance to a shared surface a rumble strip shall be constructed in accordance with sub-paragraphs (2) to (5).

(2) Kerbs in accordance with paragraph 4(9) of Schedule 7 shall be laid in two rows 1.5m apart across the carriageway and shall abut the carriageway edges.

(3) The rectangular area enclosed by the kerbs and the edges of the carriageway shall be infilled with block paving in accordance with Table B of Schedule 5.

(4) Where the carriageway or shared surface on the higher side of the rumble strip is constructed with camber, gullies in accordance with paragraph 7 of Schedule 4 shall be sited on each side of the carriageway or shared surface immediately adjacent to the rumble strip.

(5) Where the carriageway or shared surface on the higher side of the rumble strip is constructed with crossfall a gully in accordance with paragraph 7 of Schedule 4 shall be sited on the lower side of the carriageway or shared surface immediately adjacent to the rumble strip.

SCHEDULE 6 — *continued*

(6) Where a shared surface is constructed of block paving a single row of kerbs in accordance with paragraph 4(9) of Schedule 7 shall be laid across the carriageway at the entrance to the shared surface instead of a rumble strip.

Mountable shoulders

4.—(1) Kerbs in accordance with paragraph 4(9)(*b*) of Schedule 7 shall be laid where the mountable shoulder abuts the carriageway.

(2) Kerbs in accordance with paragraph 4 of Schedule 7 shall be laid at the back of the mountable shoulder to provide a 40mm kerb face.

(3) The area of the mountable shoulder bounded by the kerbs shall be constructed in accordance with Table C and paragraph 16 of Schedule 5.

(4) As an alternative the area of the mountable shoulder bounded by the kerbs may be constructed using block paving in accordance with Table B and paragraph 17 of Schedule 5.

(5) The surface of the mountable shoulder shall fall towards the carriageway at a rate of 1 in 25.

Detailed requirements — Footways, Footpaths, Footway Crossings, Kerbs, Steps and Stepped Ramps, Cycle Tracks, Verges and Service Strips

Drains etc. to be completed first

1. Before any construction work in relation to a footway, footpath, cycle track, steps or stepped ramps is commenced the installation of all drains, pipes, cables and other apparatus shall be completed.

Footways and footpaths

2.—(1) The formation of footways and footpaths shall be prepared in accordance with paragraph 4 of Schedule 5 with a crossfall not exceeding 1 in 24 maximum or 1 in 40 minimum.

(2) For footways the crossfall shall be at 1 in 40 towards the carriageway.

(3) The base of footways and footpaths shall consist of crushed rock as specified in paragraphs 8(1) to (3) and (8) of Schedule 5 compacted to a minimum thickness of 150mm with a roller of at least 2.5 tonnes weight and blinded with just enough stone dust or fine granular material to give a close textured surface.

(4) Subject to sub-paragraphs (9), (16) and (30) footways and footpaths shall be of flexible construction, in accordance with sub-paragraphs (5) to (8).

(5) Basecourse shall be bitumen macadam manufactured and tested in accordance with BS 4987: Part 1: 1988 20mm size dense basecourse and transported, laid and compacted in accordance with BS 4987: Part 2: 1988 to a compacted depth of 50mm.

(6) Subject to sub-paragraph (7) the wearing course shall be—

(a) 15 per cent course aggregate hot rolled asphalt to BS 594: Part 1: 1992 Table 6, Column 6/2, Schedule 1B, binder to Table 1, binder number 3 or 5, laid to give a compacted depth of 25mm; and

(b) clean dry 10mm chippings of light colour distributed to the asphalt wearing course after the first pass of the roller at a rate of $1kg/m^2$ and rolled in.

(7) In a development with access to a road with a speed limit greater than 30 miles per hour bitumen macadam wearing course manufactured and tested in accordance with BS 4987: Part 1: 1988 and transported, laid and compacted in accordance with BS 4987: Part 2: 1988 to a compacted depth of 25mm on footways may be used as an alternative to the requirement of sub-paragraph (6).

(8) Compaction shall be by means of a roller of at least 2.5 tonnes weight.

(9) Where it is satisfied in any particular case that the requirements of sub-paragraphs (4) to (8) are unreasonable the Department may relax those requirements to permit the use of pre-cast concrete flags complying with and laid in accordance with sub-paragraphs (10) to (15).

(10) Flags to BS 7263: Part 1: 1990 Type E70 shall be laid on a 25mm ± 5mm thick bed of clean sharp sand on a 150mm stone base so that the whole area of the flag is supported.

(11) Joints shall be at right angles to the kerb or outer edge between 3mm and 9mm wide.

(12) Where flags are laid on a curve of 12m radius or less both edges of the flag shall be radially cut to the required line.

SCHEDULE 7 — *continued*

(13) Sharp sand shall comply with BS 882: 1992 grading C or M.

(14) Joints shall be close jointed and filled with fine dry sand.

(15) Flags shall be neatly trimmed round all street furniture.

(16) Where it is satisfied in any particular case that the requirements of sub-paragraphs (4) to (8) are unreasonable the Department may relax those requirements to permit the use of in-situ construction complying with sub-paragraphs (17) to (29).

(17) Concrete shall be used on a base which complies with sub-paragraph (3).

(18) Grade C30/20 concrete shall be laid to a finished minimum thickness of 90mm well compacted and the surface shall be given a suitable non-slip texture by brushing, screeding or the application of an indented roller and protected from frost, drying wind, direct sunshine and traffic for at least 48 hours.

(19) The concrete shall be compacted against a firm rigid temporary or permanent formwork at least as deep as the concrete thickness and adequately supported.

(20) All formwork shall be free from warp twists and kinks and where they are in contact with concrete shall be cleaned and oiled immediately before each use.

(21) Formwork shall be set and supported so as not to be displaced in line or level during the placing and compacting of the concrete.

(22) Temporary formwork shall be removed but not earlier than 48 hours after the placing of the concrete.

(23) The maximum free water to cement ratio for concrete grade C30/20 shall be 0.5.

(24) The concrete shall contain an air entraining agent so that the total volume of the mix shall be 5 per cent $\pm$ 1½ per cent.

(25) The air content shall be determined at least six times per day by a pressure type air meter and at such times as test specimens are made.

(26) Where any such determination of air content gives a result outside the specified limits a further test shall be made immediately on the next available load of concrete before discharging. Where the air content is still outside the limit steps shall be taken to adjust the air content of the concrete or improve its uniformity.

(27) The air entraining agent shall be added at the mixer by an apparatus capable of dispensing the correct amount so as to ensure uniform distribution of the agent throughout the batch during mixing.

(28) During the process of concreting 150mm test cubes shall be made, cured and tested all in accordance with BS 1881: Parts 101, 102, 108, 111, 112 and 116: 1983.

(29) Curing of exposed concrete surfaces shall be carried out immediately following the application of the surface texture described in sub-paragraph (18) using a suitable aluminised curing compound which shall be mechanically sprayed on to the surface at the rate of 0.22-0.27 $1/m^2$ using a fine spray or by covering with polythene sheeting.

(30) Where it is satisfied in any particular case that the requirements of sub-paragraphs (4) to (8) are unreasonable the Department may relax those requirements to permit the use of block paving complying with sub-paragraphs (31) to (33).

(31) The base for block paving on footways and footpaths shall be in accordance with sub-paragraph (3).

SCHEDULE 7 — *continued*

(32) The laying course for block paving shall be in accordance with the requirements of paragraph 2(1) of Schedule 5.

(33) Block paving shall be in accordance with the requirements of paragraph 17 of Schedule 5, 60mm thick.

Footway crossings

3.—(1) Crossings of a footway to permit vehicular access to places or premises other than private dwellings shall be constructed to carriageway standards in accordance with Schedule 5, with kerbs in accordance with paragraph 4.

(2) Crossings of a footway to permit vehicular access to private dwellings shall be constructed with kerbs in accordance with paragraph 4 and in accordance with sub-paragraphs (3) to (5) as appropriate.

(3) On a base in accordance with paragraph 2(3) but to a minimum compacted thickness of 225mm; flexible surfacing in accordance with paragraphs 2(4) to (8); or

(4) on a base in accordance with paragraph 2(3) with concrete C30/20 laid to a minimum thickness of 125mm in accordance with paragraph 16 of Schedule 5; or

(5) in accordance with the standards of the adjacent carriageway.

Kerbs

4.—(1) Kerbs shall be laid to a smooth flowing alignment in advance of the laying of the carriageway surfacing.

(2) Subject to sub-paragraph (6) kerbs shall be laid to provide a 125mm (40mm in shared surfaces) kerb face and shall be 255mm by 155mm hydraulically compressed concrete to BS 7263: Part 1: 1990 Type HB2 of Figure 1 (150mm $\times$ 125mm Type BN of Figure 1 in shared surfaces) set on a grade C7.5/40 cast in-situ concrete bed 400mm wide by 150mm deep and backed with grade C7.5/40 concrete.

(3) For radii of between 5.5m and 12m straight kerbs cut to 300mm length shall be used.

(4) For radii of less than 5.5m kerbs cut to 300mm lengths shall be used and mitered at each end so that when laid they shall have a uniform joint width in accordance with sub-paragraph (5).

(5) Joints shall be between 3mm and 6mm wide and filled with cement mortar.

(6) On shared surface roads kerbs in accordance with the Department of the Environment for Northern Ireland publication "Layout of Housing Roads Design Guide" 1988 may be used as an alternative to the requirement of sub-paragraph (2).

(7) At footway crossings and wheelchair accesses to carriageways—

(*a*) kerbing shall be continued at the carriageway edge and dropped to give an upstand of 10mm for the full width of the footway crossings and wheelchair accesses;

(*b*) the drop shall be achieved over one kerb length at each side of the footway crossings and wheelchair accesses;

(*c*) kerbs shall be set on a grade C7.5/40 cast-in-situ concrete bed 400mm wide by 175mm deep and backed with grade C7.5/40 concrete;

(*d*) the access width for a wheelchair shall be a minimum of 1.8m; and

(*e*) at junctions the footway crossing shall be located on the minor road behind the tangent point of the entry radius and enable crossing of the carriageway at right angles.

SCHEDULE 7 — *continued*

(8) Edgings shall—

(*a*) be provided at the rear of footways and at the sides of footpaths of flexible construction which are not retained by boundary or other walls;

(*b*) be 150mm by 50mm hydraulically compressed concrete to BS 7263: Part 1: 1990 Type ER or Type EF of Figure 1 and shall be set on a grade C7.5/40 cast in-situ concrete bed 250mm wide by 100mm deep backed with grade C7.5/40 concrete; and

(*c*) have the tops of square edgings set at the finished level of the footway or footpath but an upstand of 50mm shall be accepted for half round edgings.

(9) Where a rumble strip is required under paragraph 3 of Schedule 6—

(*a*) kerbs shall be laid to a smooth flowing alignment in advance of the laying of the carriageway; and

(*b*) kerbs shall be laid on flat to provide a total rise of 40mm from the carriageway surface to the top of the kerbs and shall be 255mm by 125mm hydraulically compressed concrete to BS 7263: Part 1: 1990 Type HB2 of Figure 1 set on a grade C7.5/40 cast in-situ concrete bed 400mm wide by 200mm deep and backed with grade C7.5/40 concrete.

Steps and stepped ramps

5.—(1) Steps and stepped ramps shall comply with sub-paragraphs (2) to (14).

(2) There shall be a landing at the top and the bottom of any flight of steps or stepped ramps.

(3) The going of a landing shall be not less than the width of the flight of steps or stepped ramps which it serves.

(4) Where the total rise of any flight of steps or stepped ramp exceeds 600mm a handrail shall be provided on both sides in accordance with sub-paragraph (16).

(5) Any flight of steps shall have a minimum of three rises and a maximum of 16 rises.

(6) There shall be a maximum of 24 rises on consecutive flights of steps or on a stepped ramp and the total rise shall not exceed 4m.

(7) The rise of any step on a flight of steps or stepped ramp shall be—

(*a*) uniform throughout its length;

(*b*) the same as the rise of every other step in the flight; and

(*c*) between 75mm and 180mm.

(8) The going of any step shall be the same as the going on every other step in the flight and be not less than 280mm.

(9) On a flight of steps the aggregate of the going and twice the rises of a step shall be not less than 500mm and not more than 700mm.

(10) Each tread on a flight of steps shall be a parallel tread and shall be level.

(11) The going of any ramp on a stepped ramp shall be the same as the going on every other ramp in the flight and shall be greater than 1m and less than 2m.

(12) The ramp of a stepped ramp shall slope towards the nosing of the step at a gradient not exceeding 1 in 12 but greater than 1 in 40.

(13) The width of any flight of steps, stepped ramp or landing shall be greater than 1.8m.

(14) The nosing of the treads on any flight of steps shall be parallel.

SCHEDULE 7 — *continued*

(15) In sub-paragraph (3) "going" means the distance across the landing measured along the projection of the centre line of the flight of steps, stepped ramp or section thereof at the top or bottom of which the landing is situated.

(16) Any handrail provided in accordance with sub-paragraph (4) shall be—

(*a*) so designed as to afford adequate means of support to the person using the flight of steps or stepped ramp;

(*b*) continuous for the length of the flight of steps or stepped ramp;

(*c*) securely fixed at a height of not less than 840mm nor more than 1m (measured vertically above the pitch line); and

(*d*) be terminated by a scroll or other suitable means.

(17) A flight of steps or stepped ramp shall be constructed using in-situ construction in accordance with the requirements of paragraph 2(17) and (19) to (29) and sub-paragraphs (18) to (24).

(18) Grade C30/20 concrete shall be laid to form the flight of steps or stepped ramp and have a minimum depth of 100mm at any point measured perpendicular to the pitch line.

(19) The concrete shall be well compacted and the surface finish given a suitable non-slip texture by brushing, screeding or the application of an indented roller and protected from frost, drying wind, direct sunshine and pedestrian traffic for at least 48 hours.

(20) Steel reinforcement to a flight of steps shall be in accordance with sub-paragraphs (21) to (24).

(21) Steel fabric reinforcement shall comply with BS 4483: 1985 and shall be delivered in flat mats.

(22) Transverse reinforcement shall be not less than 0.7kg per m^2.

(23) Longitudinal reinforcement shall be not less than 1.8kg per m^2.

(24) The reinforcement shall be so placed that after compaction of the concrete there shall be a minimum of 50mm cover to the reinforcement at any point measured perpendicular to the pitch line and it shall terminate at least 50mm and not more than 75mm from the edges of the steps and at all joints in the concrete.

(25) Landings to a flight of steps or stepped ramp shall be constructed using in-situ construction in accordance with the requirements of paragraph 2(17) and (19) to (29) and sub-paragraphs (26) to (28).

(26) Grade C30/20 concrete shall be laid to form the landings and have a minimum depth of 150mm.

(27) The concrete shall be well compacted and the surface finish given a suitable non-slip texture by brushing, screeding or the application of an indented roller and protected from frost, drying wind, direct sunshine and pedestrian traffic for at least 48 hours.

(28) The lowest landing to a flight of steps shall include a cast-in-situ toe 300mm wide and 300mm deep. This toe shall be parallel to the treads on the steps and shall form part of the landing.

(29) Steel reinforcement to landings adjoining a flight of steps shall be in accordance with the requirements of sub-paragraphs (21) to (23) and (30) to (33).

(30) The reinforcement shall be so placed that after compaction of the concrete it is 50mm below the finished surface of the slab.

SCHEDULE 7 — *continued*

(31) The reinforcement in the landing shall be continuous with the reinforcement in the steps.

(32) Where the lowest landing to a flight of steps includes a toe the reinforcement shall be returned down the vertical face and terminated at least 50mm and not more than 75mm from the bottom edge.

(33) The reinforcement in the landing shall be terminated at least 50mm and not more than 75mm from the edges of the landing.

Cycle tracks

6. Cycle tracks shall be constructed in accordance with paragraph 2(5) to (8) except that those requirements may not be relaxed by the Department.

Verges

7. Verges shall slope towards the carriageway at a grade not exceeding 1 in 20 and shall be soiled and sown in accordance with paragraph 8 of Schedule 3.

Service strips

8. Service strips shall comply with paragraph 5.2.18 of Chapter 5, Chapter 8 and paragraph 15.1.6 of Chapter 15 of the Department of Environment for Northern Ireland publication "Layout of Housing Roads Design Guide" 1988.

EXPLANATORY NOTE

(This note is not part of the regulations.)

These regulations make provision in relation to matters connected with or affecting the construction of private streets.

Part II and Schedules 2 to 7 prescribe standards and detailed requirements for the construction of private streets.

Part III provides for the deposit and approval of plans and for the giving of notice of the commencement and completion of the various stages of work to the Department by the person by whom or on whose behalf the plans are deposited.

Part IV relates to the inspection of work, the carrying out of such investigations and tests and the taking of samples to ensure that the work is in conformity with the regulations. It also provides for the removal or alteration of work not in conformity with the regulations. The Department is empowered to recover any expenses reasonably incurred by it in carrying out such investigations and tests or in removing or altering work.

Part V provides for the determination by arbitration of any question arising under the regulations between the Department and the person by whom or on whose behalf the plans are deposited.

It is an offence by virtue of Article 5(3) of the Private Streets (Northern Ireland) Order 1980 to contravene the regulations.

Schedule 1 provides a detailed list of the various technical publications which are referred to in the regulations. Copies are obtainable from the publishers referred to in that Schedule. Copies of British Standards may be obtained from any of the sales outlets operated by the British Standards Institution or by post from the British Standards Institute at Linford Wood, Milton Keynes MK14 6LE.

Detailed information on ordnance datum (see regulation 17(4)) is available from Department of the Environment (NI), Ordnance Survey Division, Colby House, Stranmillis, Belfast BT9 5BJ (telephone 661244).

Copies of Council Directive (89/0106/EEC) are available from the Commission of the European Communities, Windsor House, 9-15 Bedford Street, Belfast BT2 7EG.

These Regulations replace the Private Streets (Construction) Regulations (Northern Ireland) 1966 which are revoked by regulation 23.

1994   No.   132

ELECTRICITY

Electricity (Non-Fossil Fuel Sources) Order (Northern Ireland) 1994

Made	*31st March 1994*
Coming into operation . .	*31st March 1994*

The Department of Economic Development, in exercise of the powers conferred on it by Article 35(1) of the Electricity (Northern Ireland) Order 1992(**a**) and of every other power enabling it in that behalf, after consultation in accordance with the requirements of that article, hereby makes the following Order:

Citation, commencement and interpretation

1.—(1) This Order may be cited as the Electricity (Non-Fossil Fuel Sources) Order (Northern Ireland) 1994 and shall come into operation on 31st March 1994.

(2) In this Order—

"the Company" means Northern Ireland Electricity plc;

"condition precedent" means a condition described in the terms set out in Schedule 2 or in terms to the like effect;

"specified period" in relation to the Company means each successive period commencing and ending on the dates specified in Schedule 1 but so that—

(*a*) the first such period shall commence on 31 March 1994 or, where all the relevant arrangements made by the Company make provision as is mentioned in Article 3(1)(*a*), on the date on which all applicable conditions precedent have been satisfied in respect of any such arrangements;

(*b*) on any such day as is mentioned in Article 3(1)(*b*) there shall be substituted, in place of any specified period that would otherwise have commenced on that day, a period commencing on such day and expiring (subject to sub-paragraphs (*d*) and (*e*)) on the day on which the applicable condition precedent is satisfed either wholly or in part;

(**a**) S.I. 1992/231 (N.I. 1)

(*c*) upon the expiry of any specified period ascertained in accordance with this sub-paragraph or with sub-paragraph (*b*) the next specified period shall commence on the following day and shall continue, subject to sub-paragraphs (*d*) and (*e*), until the day on which the applicable condition precedent is either wholly satisfied or further satisfied in part;

(*d*) on any such day as is mentioned in Article 3(2)(*b*) the then current specified period shall forthwith terminate and shall be followed by a new period commencing immediately upon such termination; and

(*e*) any specified period which is current on the date of the end of any of the periods specified in Schedule 1 shall expire on that date;

"termination event" means an event described in the terms set out in Schedule 3 or in terms to the like effect.

(3) Any reference in this Order to relevant arrangements shall be construed as a reference to any arrangements evidence of the making of which is produced to the Director General of Electricity Supply for Northern Ireland in accordance with Article 2.

Requirement to make arrangements in relation to generating capacity from non-fossil fuel generating stations

2. The Company shall before 31st March 1994 make (in so far as it has not already done so) and produce to the Director evidence showing that it has made such arrangements as will secure that for each period shown in Schedule 1 (specified aggregate amounts of generating capacity) the aggregate amount of generating capacity available to it from non-fossil fuel generating stations of the descriptions specified in that Schedule will be not less than the amount for that period shown opposite each such description.

3.—(1) Where any relevant arrangements—

(*a*) provide that the availability of some or all of the capacity of the non-fossil fuel generating station in question is conditional upon the satisfaction of any condition precedent; and

(*b*) result, on the first day of any specified period, in part or all of such condition precedent not being satisfied as was due to have been satisfied under those arrangements on or prior to that day,

then, in relation to any day during that specified period or any subsequent specified period ascertained in accordance with Article 1(2), this Order shall have effect as if the relevant aggregate amount specified in relation to that period were the amount specified for the period which includes that day in Schedule 1, less (subject to the following proviso) an amount equal to the sum of any capacity whose availability is at that time conditional upon the satisfaction of such condition precedent and any capacity which has ceased to be available at that time by reason of the occurrence of any termination event:

Provided that the amount so specified shall not be reduced so as to be less than the relevant aggregate amount actually available to the Company under the relevant arrangements during the period in question.

(2) Where any relevant arrangements—

(*a*) provide that some or all of the generating capacity in question may reduce or cease to be available following the occurrence of any termination event; and

(*b*) result in some or all of that capacity not being available to the Company, on any day during any specified period, by reason of the occurrence of any such event,

then the specified period then current shall forthwith terminate and, in relation to any day during any subsequent specified period ascertained in accordance with Article 1(2), this Order shall have effect as if the relevant aggregate amount specified in relation to that period were the amount specified for the period which includes that day in Schedule 1, less an amount equal to the sum of any capacity which has ceased to be available at that time by reason of the occurrence of any such event and any capacity whose availability is at that time conditional upon the satisfaction of any condition precedent, but subject to the proviso contained in paragraph (1).

Sealed with the Official Seal of the Department of Economic Development on 31st March 1994.

(L.S.)

Douglas B. McIldoon
Assistant Secretary

SCHEDULE 1   Articles 1(2),
2 and 3(1) and (2)

Specified aggregate amounts of generating capacity

Description— *Generating Stations Driven or Fuelled by*	*Period*					
	1	*2*	*3*	*4*	*5*	*6-17*
Wind	—	6.426	12.664	12.664	12.664	12.664
Sewage Gas	—	0.100	0.560	0.560	0.560	0.560
Water	0.030	0.030	1.890	2.374	2.374	2.374

(*a*) Period 1 means 31st March 1994 to 30th September 1994.

Period 2 means 30th September 1994 to 31st March 1995.

Period 3 means 31st March 1995 to 30 September 1995.

Period 4 means 30th September 1995 to 31st March 1996.

Period 5 means 31st March 1996 to 31st March 1997.

Period 6 to Period 17 means each succeeding period of 12 months commencing on 31st March of one year and ending on 31st March of the following year, so that Period 17 commences on 31st March 2008 and ends on 31st March 2009.

(*b*) Amounts of generating capacity are expressed in megawatts (MW).

SCHEDULE 2

Conditions precedent

The conditions precedent are—

(1) that planning permission and all necessary consents (including any necessary wayleave consents), easements and rights to enable any relevant non-fossil fuel generating station to be constructed and operated in accordance with and as contemplated by the terms of the relevant arrangements have been granted;

(2) that planning permission and all necessary consents (including any necessary wayleave consents), easements and rights to enable the Company to comply with its obligations as contemplated by the terms of the relevant arrangements have been granted;

(3) that the operator of any relevant non-fossil fuel generating station has entered into, and there has come into force, an agreement providing for the connection of such station to a system of electric lines and electrical plant operated by the Company;

(4) that the operator of any relevant non-fossil fuel generating station is authorised by exemption or licence granted under Part II of the Electricity (Northern Ireland) Order 1992 to generate electricity and to convey electricity from the place at which it is generated to the point of delivery for the purposes of the relevant arrangements;

(5) that there have been satisfactorily completed such procedures and tests as from time to time constitute usual industry standards and practices for commissioning a relevant non-fossil fuel generating station in order to:—

(*a*) demonstrate that the relevant non-fossil fuel generating station is capable of commercial operation for the purposes of the relevant arrangements;

(*b*) establish the external physical conditions outside the control of the operator which are necessary for the operation of such station or which control the amount of electricity produced by the station; and

(*c*) establish the operating parameters within which such station can be operated in accordance with practices, methods and procedures which are or should be adopted by a person exercising that degree of judgement, skill, diligence and foresight which would ordinarily and reasonably be expected from a skilled and experienced operator engaged in the business of operating such a station lawfully.

SCHEDULE 3

Termination events

The termination events are:—

(1) the operator of any relevant non-fossil fuel generating station ceasing for any reason to be authorised by exemption or licence granted under Part II of the Electricity (Northern Ireland) Order 1992 to generate electricity for the purposes of giving a supply to any premises or enabling a supply to be given;

(2) the operator of any relevant non-fossil fuel generating station defaulting in the performance of any of his material obligations under the relevant arrangements and in the case of a default which is, in the opinion of the Company (acting reasonably), capable of remedy continuing to be unremedied at the expiry of 60 days following the date on which the Company shall have given notice thereof to the operator;

(3) a binding order being made or an effective resolution being passed for the winding up of the operator of any relevant non-fossil fuel generating station (otherwise than for the purposes of reconstruction or amalgamation on terms previously approved in writing by the Company (whose approval shall not unreasonably be withheld) and within 28 days of his appointment the liquidator of the operator not having provided to the Company a guarantee of performance of the obligations of the operator under the relevant arrangements in such form and amount as the Company (acting reasonably) may require.

EXPLANATORY NOTE

(This note is not part of the Order.)

This Order imposes on Northern Ireland Electricity plc ("NIE") an obligation to make arrangements to secure the availability, during specified periods, of specified amounts of generating capacity from certain non-fossil fuel generating stations. The arrangements must be made, and evidence of their making must be produced to the Director General of Electricity Supply for Northern Ireland, before 31stMarch 1994.

Article 2, read with Schedule 1, imposes on NIE an obligation to make arrangements to secure the availability, during specified periods, of specified amounts of generating capacity from non-fossil fuel generating stations of the descriptions specified in Schedule 1. The amounts of generating capacity are specified in megawatts (one megawatt equals one million watts).

Article 3 makes provision whereby, if certain conditions precedent described in Schedule 2 are not satisfied or if certain termination events described in Schedule 3 occur, the Order is to have effect as if the relevant period specified in Schedule 1 were replaced by a different period and, as a consequence, as if the relevant amount of capacity specified in that Schedule were a reduced amount. The amount of that reduction will be the amount of capacity which has ceased to be available by reason of the condition precedent not having been satisfied or the termination event having occurred.

1994   No. 133

COMPANIES

PARTNERSHIPS

Partnerships and Unlimited Companies (Accounts) Regulations (Northern Ireland) 1994

Made	*30th March 1994*
Coming into operation . .	*12th May 1994*

The Department of Economic Development, being a Department designated(**a**) for the purposes of section 2(2) of the European Communities Act 1972(**b**) in relation to measures relating to the drawing up, auditing and publication of accounts by partnerships, limited partnerships and unlimited companies, in exercise of the powers conferred on it by the said section 2(2) and of every power enabling it in that behalf, hereby makes the following Regulations:

Citation and commencement

1. These Regulations may be cited as the Partnerships and Unlimited Companies (Accounts) Regulations (Northern Ireland) 1994 and shall come into operation on 12th May 1994.

Interpretation

2.—(1) The Interpretation Act (Northern Ireland) 1954(**c**) shall apply to these Regulations as it applies to a Measure of the Northern Ireland Assembly.

(2) In these Regulations—

"the 1986 Order" means the Companies (Northern Ireland) Order 1986(**d**);

"the accounts", in relation to a qualifying partnership, means the annual accounts, the annual report and the auditors' report required by regulation 4;

"dealt with on a consolidated basis" means dealt with by the method of full consolidation, the method of proportional consolidation or the equity method of accounting;

(**a**)   S.I. 1991 755.
(**b**)   1972 c. 68; section 2 is subject to Schedule 2 to that Act and is to be read with S.I. 1984/703 (N.I. 3) and S.R. 1984 No. 253.
(**c**)   1954 c. 33 (N.I.)
(**d**)   S.I. 1986/1032 (N.I. 6); Part VIII of that Order dealing with accounts and audit has been substantially amended by the Companies (Northern Ireland) Order 1990 (S.I. 1990/593 (N.I. 5))

"financial year", in relation to a qualifying partnership, means any period of not more than 18 months in respect of which a profit and loss account of the partnership is required to be made up by or in accordance with its constitution or, failing any such requirement, each period of 12 months beginning on 31st March;

"the Fourth Directive" means the Fourth Council Directive (78/660/EEC) of 25th July 1978 on the annual accounts of certain types of companies(**a**), as amended;

"general partner" has the same meaning as in the Limited Partnerships Act 1907(**b**);

"limited company" means a company limited by shares or limited by guarantee;

"limited partnership" means a partnership formed in accordance with the Limited Partnerships Act 1907;

"qualifying company" has the meaning given by regulation 9;

"qualifying partnership" has the meaning given by regulation 3;

"the Seventh Directive" means the Seventh Council Directive (83/349/EEC) of 13th June 1983 on consolidated accounts(**c**), as amended;

and other expressions shall have the meanings ascribed to them by the 1986 Order.

(3) Any reference in these Regulations to the members of a qualifying partnership shall be construed, in relation to a limited partnership, as a reference to its general partner or partners.

Qualifying partnerships

3.—(1) A partnership which is governed by the laws of Northern Ireland is a qualifying partnership for the purposes of these Regulations if each of its members is—

(*a*) a limited company, or

(*b*) an unlimited company, or a Scottish firm, each of whose members is a limited company.

(2) Where the members of a qualifying partnership include—

(*a*) an unlimited company, or a Scottish firm, each of whose members is a limited company, or

(*b*) a member of another partnership each of whose members is—

(i) a limited company, or

(**a**) O.J. No. L222 of 14.8.1978, pages 11 to 31. Relevant amendments to the Fourth Directive have been made by — (i) the Seventh Council Directive (83/349/EEC) of 13th June 1983 on consolidated accounts (O.J. No. L193 of 18.7.1983, pages 1 to 17); and (ii) Council Directive (90/604/EEC) of 8th November 1990 on small and medium-sized companies (O.J. No. L317 of 16.11.90, pages 57 to 59)

(**b**) 1907 c. 24 (7 Edw 7)

(**c**) O.J. No. L193 of 18.7.1983, pages 1 to 17. Relevant amendments to the Seventh Directive have been made by Council Directive (90/604/EEC) of 8th November 1990 on small and medium-sized companies (O.J. No. L317 of 16.11.1990, pages 57 to 59)

    (ii) an unlimited company, or a Scottish firm, each of whose members is a limited company,

any reference in regulations 4 to 8 to the members of the qualifying partnership includes a reference to the members of that company, firm or other partnership.

(3) The requirements of regulations 4 to 8 shall apply without regard to any change in the members of a qualifying partnership which does not result in it ceasing to be such a partnership.

(4) Any reference in paragraph (1) or (2) to .a limited company, an unlimited company, or another partnership includes a reference to any comparable undertaking incorporated in or formed under the law of any country or territory outside Northern Ireland and any reference in those paragraphs to a Scottish firm includes a reference to any comparable undertaking formed under the law of any country or territory outside the United Kingdom.

Preparation of accounts of qualifying partnerships

4.—(1) Subject to regulation 7, the persons who are members of a qualifying partnership at the end of any financial year of the partnership shall, in respect of that year—

    (*a*) prepare the like annual accounts and annual report, and

    (*b*) cause to be prepared such an auditors' report,

as would be required under Part VIII of the 1986 Order (accounts and audit) if the partnership were a company formed and registered under that Order.

(2) The accounts required by this regulation—

    (*a*) shall be prepared within a period of 10 months beginning immediately after the end of the financial year, and

    (*b*) shall state that they are prepared under this regulation.

(3) The Schedule (which makes certain modifications and adaptations for the purposes of this regulation) shall have effect.

Delivery of accounts of qualifying partnerships to registrar etc.

5.—(1) Subject to regulation 7, each limited company which is a member of a qualifying partnership at the end of any financial year of the partnership shall append to the copy of its annual accounts which is next delivered to the registrar in accordance with Article 250 of the 1986 Order(**a**) a copy of the accounts of the partnership prepared for that year under regulation 4.

(2) Subject to regulation 7, a limited company which is a member of a qualifying partnership shall supply to any person upon request—

    (*a*) the name of each member which is to deliver, or has delivered, a copy of the latest accounts of the partnership to the registrar under paragraph (1), and

---

(**a**)   Article 250 was substituted by Article 13 of the Companies (Northern Ireland) Order 1990

(*b*) the name of each member incorporated in a member State other than the United Kingdom which is to publish, or has published, the latest accounts of the partnership in accordance with the provisions of the Fourth or Seventh Directive.

Publication of accounts of qualifying partnerships at head office

6.—(1) Subject to paragraph (2) and regulation 7, this regulation applies where a qualifying partnership's head office is in Northern Ireland and each of its members is—

(*a*) an undertaking comparable to a limited company which is incorporated in a country or territory outside the United Kingdom, or

(*b*) an undertaking comparable to an unlimited company or partnership—

   (i) which is incorporated in or formed under the law of such a country or territory, and

   (ii) each of whose members is such an undertaking as is mentioned in sub-paragraph (*a*).

(2) Paragraph (1) does not apply where any member of a qualifying partnership is—

(*a*) an undertaking comparable to a limited company which is incorporated in a member State other than the United Kingdom, or

(*b*) an undertaking comparable to an unlimited company or partnership—

   (i) which is incorporated in or formed under the law of such a State, and

   (ii) each of whose members is such an undertaking as is mentioned in sub-paragraph (*a*),

and (in either case) the latest accounts of the qualifying partnership have been or are to be appended to the accounts of any member of the partnership and published under the law of that State and in accordance with the provisions of the Fourth or Seventh Directive.

(3) The members of the qualifying partnership—

(*a*) shall make the latest accounts of the partnership available for inspection by any person, without charge and during business hours, at the head office of the partnership, and

(*b*) if any document comprised in those accounts is in a language other than English, shall annex to that document a translation of it into English, certified in accordance with regulation 5 of the Companies (Forms) (Amendment) Regulations (Northern Ireland) 1990(**a**) to be a correct translation.

(4) A member of the qualifying partnership shall supply to any person upon request—

(*a*) a copy of the accounts required by paragraph (3)(*a*) to be made available for inspection, and

---

(**a**) S.R. 1990 No. 383

(*b*) a copy of any translation required by paragraph 3(*b*) to be annexed to any document comprised in those accounts,

at a price not exceeding the administrative cost of making the copy.

Exemption from regulations 4 to 6 where accounts consolidated

7.—(1) The members of a qualifying partnership are exempt from the requirements of regulations 4 to 6 if the partnership is dealt with on a consolidated basis in group accounts prepared by—

(*a*) a member of the partnership which is established under the law of a member State, or

(*b*) a parent undertaking of such a member which is so established,

and (in either case) the conditions mentioned in paragraph (2) are complied with.

(2) The conditions are—

(*a*) that the group accounts are prepared and audited under the law of the member State concerned in accordance with the provisions of the Seventh Directive, and

(*b*) the notes to those accounts disclose that advantage has been taken of the exemption conferred by this regulation.

(3) Where advantage is taken of the exemption conferred by this regulation, any member of the qualifying partnership which is a limited company must disclose on request the name of at least one member or parent undertaking in whose group accounts the partnership has been or is to be dealt with on a consolidated basis.

Penalties for non-compliance with regulations 4 to 6

8.—(1) If, in respect of a financial year of a qualifying partnership, the requirements of paragraph (1) of regulation 4 are not complied with within the period referred to in paragraph (2) of that regulation, every person who was a member of the partnership at the end of that year is guilty of an offence and liable on summary conviction to a fine not exceeding £2,000.

(2) If the accounts of a qualifying partnership—

(*a*) a copy of which is delivered to the registrar under regulation 5, or

(*b*) which are made available for inspection under regulation 6,

do not comply with the requirements of regulation 4(1), every person who, at the time when the copy was so delivered or (as the case may be) the accounts were first made available for inspection, was a member of the partnership is guilty of an offence and liable on summary conviction to a fine not exceeding £2,000.

(3) If a member of a qualifying partnersnip fails to comply with regulation 5, 6 or 7(3), that member is guilty of an offence and liable on summary conviction to a fine not exceeding £2,000.

(4) It is a defence for a person charged with an offence under this regulation to show that he took all reasonable steps for securing that the requirements in question would be complied with.

(5) The following provisions of the 1986 Order(**a**), namely

(*a*) Article 679 (summary proceedings),

(*b*) Article 680A (offences by bodies corporate), and

(*c*) Article 680B (criminal proceedings against unincorporated bodies), shall apply to an offence under this regulation.

Qualifying companies

9.—(1) An unlimited company incorporated in Northern Ireland is a qualifying company for the purposes of these Regulations if each of its members is—

(*a*) a limited company, or

(*b*) another unlimited company, or a Scottish firm, each of whose members is a limited company.

(2) Any reference in paragraph (1) to a limited company or another unlimited company includes a reference to any comparable undertaking incorporated in or formed under the law of any country or territory outside Northern Ireland and any reference in that paragraph to a Scottish firm includes a reference to any comparable undertaking formed under the law of any country or territory outside the United Kingdom.

Delivery of accounts of qualifying companies to registrar

10. In Article 262(3) of the 1986 Order(**b**) (exemption from requirement to deliver accounts and reports for certain unlimited companies), for the words "if the company is a banking company or the parent company of a banking group or if" there shall be substituted the words "if—

(*a*) the company is a banking company or the parent company of a banking group, or

(*b*) the company is a qualifying company within the meaning of the Partnerships and Unlimited Companies (Accounts) Regulations (Northern Ireland) 1994, or

(*c*) ".

Notes to company accounts of membership of qualifying partnerships or companies

11.—(1) In Article 239(3) of the 1986 Order(**c**) (disclosure required in notes to accounts) for the words "paragraph 5(2), 6 or 20" there shall be substituted the words "paragraph 5(2), 6, 9A, 20 or 28A".

(2) After paragraph 9 of Schedule 5 to that Order(**d**) (disclosure of information related undertakings) there shall be inserted the following paragraph—

(**a**) Articles 680A and 680B were inserted by Article 20(1) of the Companies (No. 2) (Northern Ireland) Order 1990. S.I. 1990/1504 (N.I. 10)

(**b**) Article 262(3) was substituted by Article 19 of the Companies (Northern Ireland) Order 1990 and was amended by regulation 6 of, and paragraph 1 of Schedule 2 to the Companies (1986 Order) (Bank Accounts) Regulations (Northern Ireland) 1992 (S.R. 1992 No. 258)

(**c**) Article 239 was substituted by Article 8 of the Companies (Northern Ireland) Order 1990

(**d**) Schedule 5 was substituted by Article 8(2) of, and Schedule 3 to, the Companies (Northern Ireland) Order 1990

"Membership of certain undertakings

9A.—(1) The information required by this paragraph shall be given where at the end of the financial year the company is a member of a qualifying undertaking.

(2) There shall be stated—

(*a*) the name and legal form of the undertaking, and

(*b*) the address of the undertaking's registered office (whether in or outside Northern Ireland) or, if it does not have such an office, its head office (whether in or outside Northern Ireland).

(3) Information otherwise required by sub-paragraph (2) need not be given if it is not material.

(4) In this paragraph—

"member", "qualifying company" and "qualifying partnership" have the same meanings as in the Partnerships and Unlimited Companies (Accounts) Regulations (Northern Ireland) 1994.

"qualifying undertaking" means a qualifying partnership or a qualifying company.".

(3) After paragraph 28 of that Schedule there shall be inserted the following paragraph—

"Parent company's or group's membership of certain undertakings

28A.—(1) The information required by this paragraph shall be given where at the end of the financial year the parent company or group is a member of a qualifying undertaking.

(2) There shall be stated—

(*a*) the name and legal form of the undertaking, and

(*b*) the address of the undertaking's registered office (whether in or outside Northern Ireland) or, if it does not have such an office, its head office (whether in or outside Northern Ireland).

(3) Information otherwise required by sub-paragraph (2) need not be given if it is not material.

(4) In this paragraph—

"member", "qualifying company" and "qualifying partnership" have the same meanings as in the Partnerships and Unlimited Companies (Accounts) Regulations (Northern Ireland) 1994.

"qualifying undertaking" means a qualifying partnership or a qualifying company.".

Transitional provisions

12.—(1) The members of a qualifying partnership need not prepare accounts in accordance with regulation 4 for a financial year commencing before 23rd December 1994.

(2) Where advantage is taken of the exemption conferred by paragraph (1), regulations 5 and 6 shall not apply, and the amendments to the 1986 Order effected by regulation 11 shall be treated as not having been made.

Sealed with the Official Seal of the Department of Economic Development on 30th March 1994.

(L.S.)   *A. L. Brown*
                                              Assistant Secretary

SCHEDULE

Modifications and Adaptations for purposes of Regulation 4

1.—(1) Accounts prepared under regulation 4 shall comply with the requirements of Part VIII of the 1986 Order as to the content of accounts subject to the following, namely—

(*a*) the provisions of Article 267(2) and (3) of that Order(**a**) (meaning of "undertaking" and related expressions).

(*b*) the omission of the provisions mentioned in paragraph 2(1), and

(*c*) any necessary modifications to take account of the fact that partnerships are unincorporated.

(2) For the purposes of the provisions of Part VIII of the 1986 Order as applied to accounts so prepared, these Regulations shall be regarded as part of the requirements of that Order.

2.—(1) The provisions referred to in paragraph 1(1)(*b*) are—

(*a*) in Part I of Schedule 4 to the 1986 Order, paragraph 3(6) and, in paragraph 3(2), the words from "adopted" to the end;

(*b*) in Part II of that Schedule, paragraph 20;

(*c*) in Part III of that Schedule, paragraphs 36A(**b**), 41, 43, 44, 45(**c**), 50(3)(*b*), 51(2)(**d**), 53(**e**) and 54;

(*d*) in Schedule 4A to that Order(**f**), paragraphs 13(3) to (5), 14 and 15;

(*e*) in Schedule 5 to that Order(**g**), paragraphs 4, 5, 10, 12, 18, 19 and 29.

(*f*) in Schedule 6 to that Order(**h**), paragraphs 2 to 6, 8 and 9; and

(*g*) Schedule 7 to that Order(**i**), except paragraph 6.

(2) Sub-paragraph (1) shall not be construed as affecting the requirement to give a true and fair view under Articles 234 and 235 of the 1986 Order(**j**).

3. Part III of the Companies (Northern Ireland) Order 1990 (eligibility for appointment as auditors) shall apply to auditors appointed for the purposes of regulation 4 as if qualifying partnerships were companies formed and registered under the 1986 Order, subject to any necessary modifications to take account of the fact that partnerships are unincorporated.

(**a**) Article 267 was substituted by Article 24 of the Companies (Northern Ireland) Order 1990

(**b**) Paragraph 36A was inserted by Article 6(2) of, and paragraph 7 of Schedule 1 to, the Companies (Northern Ireland) Order 1990

(**c**) Paragraph 45 was amended by section 212(2) of, and paragraph 38 of Schedule 16 to, the Financial Services Act 1986 (c. 60)

(**d**) Paragraph 51(2) was amended by Article 6(2) of, and paragraph 9 of Schedule 1 to, the Companies (Northern Ireland) Order 1990

(**e**) Paragraph 53 was amended by Article 113 of, and Schedule 6 to, the Companies (No. 2) (Northern Ireland) Order 1990

(**f**) Schedule 4A was inserted by Article 7(2) of, and Schedule 2 to, the Companies (Northern Ireland) Order 1990

(**g**) Schedule 5 was substituted by Article 8(2) of, and Schedule 3 to, the Companies (Northern Ireland) Order 1990

(**h**) Schedule 6 was amended by Article 8(4) of, and Schedule 4 to, the Companies (Northern Ireland) Order 1990

(**i**) Schedule 7 was amended by Article 10(2) of, and Schedule 5 to, the Companies (Northern Ireland) Order 1990

(**j**) Articles 234 and 235 were substituted by Articles 6 and 7 of the Companies (Northern Ireland) Order 1990

EXPLANATORY NOTE

(This note is not part of the Regulations.)

1. These Regulations implemement Council Directive 90/605/EEC (Official Journal No. L317 of 16.11.1990, pages 60 to 62) which amends Directive 78/660/EEC on annual accounts (O.J. No. L222 of 14.8.1978, pages 11 to 31) (the Fourth EC Company Law Directive) and Directive 83/349/EEC on consolidated accounts (O.J. No. L193 of 18.7.1983, pages 1 to 17) (the Seventh EC Company Law Directive) as regards the scope of those Directives.

2. The scope of application of the Regulations is set out in regulations 3 (qualifying partnerships) and 9 (qualifying companies). They apply, in effect, to partnerships, limited partnerships and unlimited companies all of whose members having unlimited liability are limited companies.

3. Members of a qualifying partnership (general partners in the case of limited partnerships) are required by regulation 4 to prepare accounts and a directors' report, and to obtain an auditors' report on such accounts, in accordance with the provisions of Part VIII of the Companies (Northern Ireland) Order 1986 (the 1986 Order), subject to certain modifications set out in the Schedule to the Regulations. The Schedule disapplies requirements of Part VIII which do not derive from the European Community Directives on accounts.

4. Regulations 5 and 6 contain requirements about the publication of accounts prepared under the Regulations by members of qualifying partnerships.

5. Regulation 7 provides an exemption from the Regulations where the partnership has been dealt with in consolidated group accounts prepared by a member of the partnership established under the law of a member State of the EEC (or a parent of such a member), by the method of full or proportional consolidation or by the equity method of accounting.

6. Regulation 8 imposes criminal penalties for failure to comply with the Regulations.

7. Regulation 10 requires that unlimited companies which are qualifying companies deliver their accounts to the registrar of companies (they are already required to prepare accounts under Part VIII of the 1986 Order).

8. Regulation 11 imposes additional disclosure requirements in the notes to the accounts of companies which are members of qualifying partnerships or qualifying companies.

9. Regulation 12 permits the members of a qualifying partnership not to prepare accounts and a directors' report (and obtain an auditor's report on the accounts) under the Regulations for financial years commencing on a date prior to 23rd December 1994.

1994   No. 134

ROAD TRAFFIC AND VEHICLES

Off-Street Parking Bye-Laws (Northern Ireland) 1994

Made	*31st March 1994*
Coming into operation . .	*· 4th April 1994*

The Department of the Environment in exercise of the powers conferred on it by Article 105(1) of the Road Traffic (Northern Ireland) Order 1981(**a**) and of all other powers enabling it in that behalf, makes the following bye-laws:

Citation, commencement and interpretation

1.—(1) These bye-laws may be cited as the Off-Street Parking Bye-Laws (Northern Ireland) 1994 and shall come into operation on 4th April 1994.

(2) In these bye-laws—

"designated car park" means any car park specified in Part III of Schedule 1;

"disabled person's vehicle" means a vehicle lawfully displaying a badge of a form prescribed under Section 14 of the Chronically Sick and Disabled Persons (Northern Ireland) Act 1978(**b**);

"driver" means the person who whether as owner or otherwise has the charge or control of a vehicle or being present is entitled to give orders to the person having charge or control thereof;

"intoxicating liquor" means spirits, wine, beer, cider and any fermented, distilled or spirituous liquor with an alcohol content exceeding 1.2 per cent by volume;

"light goods vehicle" means a motor vehicle, constructed or adapted for use for the carriage of goods, the permissible maximum weight of which does not exceed 3.5 tonnes;

"motor car" means a mechanically propelled vehicle constructed solely for the carriage of passengers and their effects, seating not more than 6 persons in addition to the driver;

"motor cycle" means a mechanically propelled vehicle not being an invalid carriage or motor car having fewer than 4 wheels and the weight of which unladen does not exceed 410kgs;

"parking bay" means a space which is marked out in a parking place for the leaving of a vehicle;

(**a**)   S.I. 1981/154 (N.I. 1); *see* Article 2(2) for the definition of "Department"
(**b**)   1978 c. 53

"pay and display machine" means an apparatus approved by the Department for the purposes of these bye-laws being an apparatus designed to issue a ticket indicating the day and time at which it was issued and the number of hours for which it is valid.

Use of parking places

2. Each area of land specified by name in column 1 of Part I of Schedule 1 may be used subject to the provisions of these bye-laws as a parking place for such classes of vehicles, in such positions and on such days and during such hours and on payment of such charges as are specified in relation to that area in Part II of Schedule 1.

3. Where in Part I of Schedule 1 a parking place is described as available for vehicles of a specified class or in a specified position, the driver of a vehicle shall not permit it to wait in that parking place—

(*a*) unless it is of the specified class; or

(*b*) in a position other than that specified.

4. The driver of a vehicle, other than a disabled person's vehicle, shall not permit it to wait in a parking bay indicated by a sign as being reserved for a disabled person's vehicle.

5. The driver of a vehicle shall not permit it to wait in a parking place for longer than the maximum period permitted for waiting specified in Part I of Schedule 1 in relation to that parking place.

6. The driver of a vehicle using a parking place shall pay the appropriate charge in accordance with the scale of charges specified in Part II of Schedule 1.

7.—(1) Save as provided for in bye-law 10, in a parking place where charges are collected by means of a pay and display machine payment shall be made on parking the vehicle, by inserting into the machine a coin or combination of coins of appropriate denominations in payment of the charge relative to the period of time then chosen for which the machine will issue a ticket indicating the date and time of payment and the number of hours for which it is valid or the date and time at which the vehicle ought to leave the parking place.

(2) The driver of a vehicle shall not permit it to wait in a parking place longer than the period of time for which payment has been made in accordance with paragraph (1) unless a further payment is made in accordance with that paragraph.

8. The driver shall place the ticket issued in accordance with bye-law 7 on the vehicle in the following manner—

(*a*) in the case of a motor car or a light goods vehicle on the inside surface of the windscreen or on the dashboard area immediately below the windscreen on the inside of the vehicle so that the particulars recorded on the front of the ticket are clearly visible to a person standing at the front of the vehicle; and

(*b*) in the case of any other vehicle in a conspicuous position in front of the driving seat.

9. Where a vehicle is left parked in a parking place where charges are collected by means of a pay and display machine and the particulars on the ticket displayed on the vehicle in accordance with the provisions of bye-law 8 indicate that the period in respect of which payment was made has expired, for the purposes of any proceedings for an offence under bye-law 27 it shall be presumed, unless the contrary is proved, that said particulars are accurate.

10.—(1) The Department may on application from the driver or owner of a vehicle sell to him a season ticket on payment of the appropriate charge referred to in bye-law 6.

(2) A season ticket shall be valid only in respect of such parking places as are specified thereon for the period for which it is issued and for the vehicle in respect of which it is issued.

(3) The Department may by notice in writing served on the season ticket holder by recorded delivery post to the address stated on the season ticket holder's application, cancel a season ticket where:

(i) the season ticket holder has not complied with the current off-street parking bye-laws; or

(ii) a season ticket has been issued upon receipt of a cheque and the cheque is subsequently dishonoured; or

(iii) the season ticket holder has ceased to have an interest in the vehicle in respect of which the season ticket was issued.

(4) The issue of a season ticket shall not guarantee that any parking place will be available for the use of the season ticket holder.

(5) A season ticket shall include the following particulars:

(i) the registration mark of the vehicle in respect of which the season ticket has been issued;

(ii) the period during which the season ticket shall remain valid; and

(iii) the names of the parking places for which the season ticket is valid.

(6) Where a vehicle in respect of which a season ticket has been issued is left parked in a parking place the driver shall display the ticket in a conspicuous position behind the windscreen of that vehicle so as to be clearly visible to the Department's representative.

11. The driver of a vehicle using a parking place shall stop the engine as soon as the vehicle is in position in the parking place and shall not start the engine except when about to change the position of the vehicle in or to depart from the parking place.

12. A person shall not use a parking place in connection with the sale of anything to persons in or near the parking place or in connection with the selling or offering for hire of his skill or services.

13. Where a vehicle is left in a parking place in contravention of any of the provisions of bye-laws 3, 4, 5, 6, 12 or 21 a person authorised in that behalf by the Department may remove the vehicle or arrange for it to be removed from that parking place.

14. Any person removing or altering the position of a vehicle by virtue of bye-law 13 may do so by towing or driving the vehicle or in such other manner as he may think necessary and may take such measures in relation to the vehicle as he may think necessary to enable him to remove it or alter its position, as the case may be.

15. When a person authorised by the Department removes or makes arrangements for the removal of a vehicle from a parking place by virtue of bye-law 13 he shall make such arrangements as may be reasonably necessary for the safe custody of the vehicle.

16. If a vehicle is waiting in a parking place in contravention of the provision of bye-law 3(*b*) a person authorised in that behalf by the Department may alter or cause to be altered the position of the vehicle in order that its position shall comply with that provision.

17. The driver of a vehicle using a parking place shall not sound any horn or other similar instrument except when about to change the position of the vehicle in or to depart from the parking place.

18. A person shall not, except with the permission of any person duly authorised by the Department, drive any vehicle in a parking place other than for the purpose of leaving that vehicle in the parking place in accordance with the provision of these bye-laws or for the purpose of departing from the parking place.

19. A person shall not in a parking place play any ball game or wantonly shout or otherwise make any loud noise to the disturbance or annoyance of users of the parking place or residents of premises in the neighbourhood.

20. A person shall not in a parking place use any threatening, abusive or insulting language, gesture or conduct with intent to put any person in fear or so as to occasion a breach of the peace or whereby a breach of the peace is likely to be occasioned.

21. A person shall not use any part of a parking place or any vehicle left in a parking place—

(*a*) for sleeping or camping purposes;

(*b*) for eating or cooking purposes; or

(*c*) for the purposes of servicing or washing any vehicle or part thereof other than is reasonably necessary to enable that vehicle to depart from the parking place.

22. A person shall not use a parking place as a means of passage from one road to another road.

23. A person shall not use a parking place or any vehicle in a parking place in a designated car park for the purpose of consuming intoxicating liquor.

24. Where in a parking place signs are erected or surface markings are laid for the purpose of—

(*a*) indicating the entrance to or exit from the parking place; or

(*b*) indicating that a vehicle using the parking place shall proceed in a specified direction within the parking place;

a person shall not drive or cause or permit to be driven any vehicle—

(i) so that it enters the parking place otherwise than by an entrance, or leaves the parking place otherwise than by an exit, so indicated; or

(ii) in a direction other than that specified, as the case may be.

25. In a parking place a person shall not—

(*a*) erect or cause or permit to be erected any tent, booth, stand, building or other structure without the written consent of the Department;

(*b*) light or cause to be lit any fire.

26.—(1) A person shall not cause or permit a supermarket trolley to enter a parking place in or under a building and any trolley so left may be removed by a person authorised by the Department.

(2) A person authorised by the Department may remove a supermarket trolley from any other parking place if he considers that it is in such a position as to cause or to be likely to cause any obstruction or danger.

27. Any person who contravenes a bye-law shall be guilty of an offence and shall be liable on summary conviction to a fine not exceeding £100 for each offence.

Revocation

28. The Bye-Laws specified in Schedule 2 are hereby revoked.

Sealed with the Official Seal of the Department of the Environment on 31st March 1994.

(L.S.)

E. J. Galway
Assistant Secretary

SCHEDULE 1

PART I

(bye-laws 1(2), 2, 3, 5)

Name of Parking Place 1	Position in which vehicle may wait 2	Classes of Vehicle 3	Days of operation of parking place 4	Hours of operation of parking place 5	Maximum period for which vehicles may wait 6	Scale of Charges 7
1. Village, Ahoghill	Wholly within a parking bay where such has been marked out	All motor vehicles	All days	All hours	12 consecutive hours	No charge
2. Castle Street, Antrim	Wholly within a parking bay where such has been marked out	Motor car, motor cycle, invalid carriage and light goods vehicle	All days	All hours	12 consecutive hours	No charge
3. Central Car Park, Antrim	Wholly within a parking bay where such has been marked out	Motor car, motor cycle, invalid carriage and light goods vehicle	Monday Tuesday Wednesday Saturday	8.30 a.m. to 6.30 p.m.	10 hours	Tariff R as set out in Part II
				6.30 p.m. to 8.30 a.m.	12 consecutive hours	No charge

Location	Condition	Class of vehicle	Days	Hours	Maximum period	Charge
4. Dublin Road, Antrim	Wholly within a parking bay where such has been marked out	Motor car, motor cycle, invalid carriage and light goods vehicle	Thursday Friday	8.30 a.m. to 9.30 p.m.	12 hours	Tariff R as set out in Part II
				9.30 p.m. to 8.30 a.m.	11 consecutive hours	No charge
			Sunday	All hours	12 consecutive hours	No charge
			All days	All hours	12 consecutive hours	No charge
5. Railway Street, Antrim	Wholly within a parking bay where such has been marked out	Motor car, motor cycle, invalid carriage and light goods vehicle	Monday Tuesday Wednesday Saturday	8.30 a.m. to 6.30 p.m.	10 hours	Tariff O as set out in Part II
				6.30 p.m. to 8.30 a.m.	12 consecutive hours	No charge
			Thursday Friday	8.30 a.m. to 9.30 p.m.	12 hours	Tariff O as set out in Part II
				9.30 p.m. to 8.30 a.m.	11 consecutive hours	No charge

Name of Parking Place 1	*Position in which vehicle may wait* 2	*Classes of Vehicle* 3	*Days of operation of parking place* 4	*Hours of operation of parking place* 5	*Maximum period for which vehicles may wait* 6	*Scale of Charges* 7
6. Quay Street, Ardglass	Wholly within a parking bay where such has been marked out	Motor car, motor cycle, invalid carriage and light goods vehicle	Sunday	All hours	12 consecutive hours	No charge
			All days	All hours	12 consecutive hours	No charge
7. Dobbin Street Lane, Armagh (Excepting St. Malachy's part)	Wholly within a parking bay where such has been marked out	Motor car, motor cycle, invalid carriage and light goods vehicle	Monday Tuesday Thursday Friday Saturday	8.30 a.m. to 6.30 p.m.	10 hours	Tariff R as set out in Part II
				6.30 p.m. to 8.30 a.m.	14 consecutive hours	No charge
			Wednesday Sunday	All hours	14 consecutive hours	No charge

8. Dobbin Street Lane, Armagh (St. Malachy's Part)	Wholly within a parking bay where such has been marked out	Motor car, motor cycle, invalid carriage and light goods vehicle	This car park is not open for public use at any time during any Sunday in the year or on any of the following days before 1.00 p.m. – 6th January, 17th March, Ascension Day, Corpus Christi, 15th August, 1st November, 8th December 25th December	All hours except as specified in Column 4	14 consecutive hours	No charge
9. Friary Road, Armagh (West Side)	Wholly within a parking bay where such has been marked out	Motor car, motor cycle, invalid carriage and light goods vehicle	All days	All hours	14 consecutive hours	No charge

Name of Parking Place	Position in which vehicle may wait	Classes of Vehicle	Days of operation of parking place	Hours of operation of parking place	Maximum period for which vehicles may wait	Scale of Charges
1	2	3	4	5	6	7
10. Friary Road, Armagh	Wholly within a parking bay where such has been marked out	Motor car, motor cycle, invalid carriage and light goods vehicle	Monday Tuesday Thursday Friday Saturday	8.30 a.m. to 6.30 p.m.	10 hours	Tariff R as set out in Part II
				6.30 p.m. to 8.30 a.m.	14 consecutive hours	No charge
			Wednesday Sunday	All hours	14 consecutive hours	No charge
11. Linenhall Street, Armagh	Wholly within a parking bay where such has been marked out	Motor car, motor cycle, invalid carriage and light goods vehicle	Monday Tuesday Thursday Friday Saturday	8.30 a.m. to 6.30 p.m.	10 hours	Tariff R as set out in Part II
				6.30 p.m. to 8.30 a.m.	14 consecutive hours	No charge
			Wednesday Sunday	All hours	14 consecutive hours	No charge

12. Lonsdale Street, Armagh	Wholly within a parking bay where such has been marked out	Motor car, motor cycle, invalid carriage and light goods vehicle	All days	All hours	14 consecutive hours	No charge
13. Mall West, Armagh	Wholly within a parking bay where such has been marked out	Motor car, motor cycle, invalid carriage and light goods vehicle	Monday Tuesday Thursday Friday Saturday	8.30 a.m. to 6.30 p.m.	10 hours	Tariff R as set out in Part II
			Wednesday Sunday	6.30 p.m. to 8.30 a.m.	14 consecutive hours	No charge
				All hours	14 consecutive hours	No charge
14. Main Street, Ballinamallard	Wholly within a parking bay where such has been marked out	All motor vehicles	All days	All hours	24 consecutive hours	No charge
15. Ann Street, Ballycastle	Wholly within a parking bay where such has been marked out	Motor car, motor cycle, invalid carriage and light goods vehicle	All days	All hours	12 consecutive hours	No charge

Name of Parking Place	Position in which vehicle may wait	Classes of Vehicle	Days of operation of parking place	Hours of operation of parking place	Maximum period for which vehicles may wait	Scale of Charges
1	2	3	4	5	6	7
16. Castle Street, Ballycastle	Wholly within a parking bay where such has been marked out	Motor car, motor cycle, invalid carriage and light goods vehicle	All days	All hours	12 consecutive hours	No charge
17. Fairhill Street, Ballycastle	Wholly within a parking bay where such has been marked out	Motor car, motor cycle, invalid carriage and light goods vehicle	All days except when required for market purposes on the occasion of the annual fair known as "The Oul Lammas Fair"	All hours	12 consecutive hours	No charge
18. Harrier Way, (off Avondale Drive), Ballyclare	Wholly within a parking bay where such has been marked out	Motor car, motor cycle, invalid carriage and light goods vehicle	All days	All hours	12 consecutive hours	No charge

19. The Market Square, Ballyclare	Wholly within a parking bay where such has been marked out	Motor car, motor cycle, invalid carriage and light goods vehicle	All or part of this car park is not open for public use on those days requested by the Newtownabbey Borough Council on the occasion of any public procession, meeting, rejoicing illumination, fair or other civic occasion	All hours except on those days specified in Column 4	12 consecutive hours	No charge
20. Harbour Road, Ballyhalbert	Wholly within a parking bay where such has been marked out	Motor car, motor cycle, invalid carriage and light goods vehicle	All days	All hours	12 consecutive hours	No charge

Name of Parking Place 1	Position in which vehicle may wait 2	Classes of Vehicle 3	Days of operation of parking place 4	Hours of operation of parking place 5	Maximum period for which vehicles may wait 6	Scale of Charges 7
21. Portavogie Road, Ballyhalbert	Wholly within a parking bay where such has been marked out	Motor car, motor cycle, invalid carriage and light goods vehicle	All days	All hours	12 consecutive hours	No charge
22. Glenhead Road, Ballykelly	Wholly within a parking bay where such has been marked out	Motor car, motor cycle, invalid carriage and light goods vehicle	All days	All hours	12 consecutive hours	No charge
23. Ballymoney Road Car Park, Ballymena	Wholly within a parking bay where such has been marked out	Motor car, motor cycle, invalid carriage and light goods vehicle	Monday to Saturday	8.30 a.m. to 6.30 p.m.	10 hours	Tariff O is set out in Part II
				6.30 p.m. to 8.30 a.m.	12 consecutive hours	No charge
			Sunday	All hours	12 consecutive hours	No charge

Location	Position	Vehicle	Days	Hours	Period	Charge
24. Church Street, Ballymena	Wholly within a parking bay where such has been marked out	Motor car, motor cycle, invalid carriage and light goods vehicle	Monday Tuesday Wednesday Saturday	8.30 a.m. to 6.30 p.m.	10 hours	Tariff R as set out in Part II
				6.30 p.m. to 8.30 a.m.	12 consecutive hours	No charge
			Thursday Friday	8.30 a.m. to 9.45 p.m.	12 hours	Tariff R as set out in Part II
				9.45 p.m. to 8.30 a.m.	10 consecutive hours	No charge
			Sunday	All hours	12 consecutive hours	No charge
25. Coach Entry, Ballymena	Wholly within a parking bay where such has been marked out	Motor car, motor cycle, invalid carriage and light goods vehicle	Monday to Saturday	8.30 a.m. to 6.30 p.m.	10 hours	Tariff R as set out in Part II
				6.30 p.m. to 8.30 a.m.	12 consecutive hours	No charge
			Sunday	All hours	12 consecutive hours	No charge

Name of Parking Place	Position in which vehicle may wait	Classes of Vehicle	Days of operation of parking place	Hours of operation of parking place	Maximum period for which vehicles may wait	Scale of Charges
1	2	3	4	5	6	7
26. Garfield Place, Ballymena	Wholly within a parking bay where such has been marked out	Motor car, motor cycle, invalid carriage and light goods vehicle	Monday to Saturday	8.30 a.m. to 6.30 p.m.	10 hours	Tariff R as set out in Part II
				6.30 p.m. to 8.30 a.m.	12 consecutive hours	No charge
			Sunday	All hours	12 consecutive hours	No charge
27. Henry Street, Ballymena	Wholly within a parking bay where such has been marked out	All motor vehicles	All days	All hours	12 consecutive hours	No charge
28. Meeting-House Lane, Ballymena	Wholly within a parking bay where such has been marked out	Motor car, motor cycle, invalid carriage and light goods vehicle	Monday to Saturday	8.30 a.m. to 6.30 p.m.	10 hours	Tariff R as set out in Part II

Location	Condition	Vehicle	Days	Hours	Duration	Charge
29. Mount Street, Ballymena	Wholly within a parking bay where such has been marked out	Motor car, motor cycle, invalid carriage and light goods vehicle		6.30 p.m. to 8.30 a.m.	12 consecutive hours	No charge
			Sunday	All hours	12 consecutive hours	No charge
			All days	All hours	12 consecutive hours	No charge
30. Springwell Street, Ballymena	Wholly within a parking bay where such has been marked out	Motor car, motor cycle, invalid carriage and light goods vehicle	Monday Tuesday Wednesday Saturday	8.30 a.m. to 6.30 p.m.	10 hours	Tariff R as set out in Part II
				6.30 p.m. to 8.30 a.m. (at grade portion only)	12 consecutive hours	No charge
			Thursday Friday	8.30 a.m. to 9.45 p.m.	12 hours	Tariff R as set out in Part II
				9.45 p.m. to 8.30 a.m. (at grade portion only)	10 consecutive hours	No charge

Name of Parking Place	Position in which vehicle may wait	Classes of Vehicle	Days of operation of parking place	Hours of operation of parking place	Maximum period for which vehicles may wait	Scale of Charges
1	2	3	4	5	6	7
			Sunday	All hours (at grade portion only)	12 consecutive hours	No charge
31. Summerfield, Ballymena	Wholly within a parking bay where such has been marked out	Motor car, motor cycle, invalid carriage and light goods vehicle	Monday to Saturday	8.30 a.m. to 6.30 p.m.	10 hours	Tariff O as set out in Part II
			Sunday	6.30 p.m. to 8.30 a.m.	12 consecutive hours	No charge
32. Castle Street, Ballymoney	Wholly within a parking bay where such has been marked out	Motor car, motor cycle, invalid carriage and light goods vehicle	All days	All hours	12 consecutive hours	No charge

Location		Class of vehicle	Days	Hours	Period	Tariff R as set out in Part II
33. Church Street/ Main Street, Ballymoney	Wholly within a parking bay where such has been marked out	Motor car, motor cycle, invalid carriage and light goods vehicle	Tuesday Wednesday Thursday Friday Saturday	8.30 a.m. to 6.30 p.m.	10 hours	No charge
			Sunday Monday	6.30 p.m. to 8.30 a.m.	12 consecutive hours	No charge
34. Cockpit Brae (East Side), Ballymoney	Wholly within a parking bay where such has been marked out	Motor car, motor cycle, invalid carriage and light goods vehicle	All days	All hours	12 consecutive hours	No charge
35. Cockpit Brae, (West Side), Ballymoney	Wholly within a parking bay where such has been marked out	Motor car, motor cycle, invalid carriage and light goods vehicle	All days	All hours	12 consecutive hours	No charge
36. Dervock Road, Ballymoney	Wholly within a parking bay where such has been marked out	All motor vehicles	All days	All hours	12 consecutive hours	No charge
37. Gate End, Ballymoney	Wholly within a parking bay where such has been marked out	Motor car, motor cycle, invalid carriage and light goods vehicle	All days	All hours	12 consecutive hours	No charge

Name of Parking Place 1	Position in which vehicle may wait 2	Classes of Vehicle 3	Days of operation of parking place 4	Hours of operation of parking place 5	Maximum period for which vehicles may wait 6	Scale of Charges 7
38. Seymour Street, Ballymoney	Wholly within a parking bay where such has been marked out	Motor car, motor cycle, invalid carriage and light goods vehicle	All days	All hours	12 consecutive hours	No charge
39. Townhead Street, Ballymoney North	Wholly within a parking bay where such has been marked out	Motor car, motor cycle, invalid carriage and light goods vehicle	Tuesday Wednesday Thursday Friday Saturday	8.30 a.m. to 6.30 p.m.	10 hours	Tariff R as set out in Part II
			Sunday Monday	6.30 p.m. to 8.30 a.m.	12 consecutive hours	No charge
				All hours	12 consecutive hours	No charge
40. Townhead Street, Ballymoney South	Wholly within a parking bay where such has been marked out	Motor car, motor cycle, invalid carriage and light goods vehicle	All days	All hours	12 consecutive hours	No charge

41. Antrim Road, Ballynahinch	Wholly within a parking bay where such has been marked out	Motor car, motor cycle, invalid carriage and light goods vehicle	All days	All hours	12 consecutive hours	No charge
42. Lisburn Street, (North Side) Ballynahinch	Wholly within a parking bay where such has been marked out	Motor car, motor cycle, invalid carriage and light goods vehicle	All days	All hours	12 consecutive hours	No charge
43. Lisburn Street, (South Side) Ballynahinch	Wholly within a parking bay where such has been marked out	Motor car, motor cycle, invalid carriage and light goods vehicle	Monday to Saturday	8.00 a.m. to 10.00 p.m.	14 hours	Tariff Q as set out in Part II
				10.00 p.m. to 8.00 a.m.	10 consecutive hours	No charge
			Sunday	All hours	12 consecutive hours	No charge
44. Windmill Street, Ballynahinch	Wholly within a parking bay where such has been marked out	Motor car, motor cycle, invalid carriage and light goods vehicle	Monday to Saturday	8.00 a.m. to 10.00 p.m.	14 hours	Tariff Q as set out in Part II
				10.00 p.m. to 8.00 a.m.	10 consecutive hours	No charge
			Sunday	All hours	12 consecutive hours	No charge

Name of Parking Place 1	*Position in which vehicle may wait* 2	*Classes of Vehicle* 3	*Days of operation of parking place* 4	*Hours of operation of parking place* 5	*Maximum period for which vehicles may wait* 6	*Scale of Charges* 7
45. Springvale Road, Bally-walter	Wholly within a parking bay where such has been marked out	Motor car, motor cycle, invalid carriage and light goods vehicle	All days	All hours	12 consecutive hours	No charge
46. Bridge Street East, Banbridge	Wholly within a parking bay where such has been marked out	Motor car, motor cycle, invalid carriage and light goods vehicle	All days	All hours	14 consecutive hours	No charge
47. Church Square, Banbridge	Wholly within a parking bay where such has been marked out	Motor car, motor cycle, invalid carriage and light goods vehicle	All days	All hours	14 consecutive hours	No charge
48. Commercial Road, Banbridge	Wholly within a parking bay where such has been marked out	Motor car, motor cycle, invalid carriage and light goods vehicle	Monday Tuesday Wednesday Friday Saturday	8.30 a.m. to 6.30 p.m.	10 hours	Tariff R as set out in Part II
				6.30 p.m. to 8.30 a.m.	14 consecutive hours	No charge

			Days	Hours		Charge
49. Downshire Place, Banbridge	Wholly within a parking bay where such has been marked out	Motor car, motor cycle, invalid carriage and light goods vehicle	Thursday Sunday	All hours	14 consecutive hours	No charge
			Monday Tuesday Wednesday Friday Saturday	8.30 a.m. to 6.30 p.m.	10 hours	Tariff R as set out in Part II
			Thursday Sunday	6.30 p.m. to 8.30 a.m.	14 consecutive hours	No charge
50. Downshire Road, Banbridge	Wholly within a parking bay where such has been marked out	Motor car, motor cycle, invalid carriage and light goods vehicle	All days	All hours	14 consecutive hours	No charge
51. Kenlis Street, Banbridge	Wholly within a parking bay where such has been marked out	Motor car, motor cycle, invalid carriage and light goods vehicle	All days	All hours	14 consecutive hours	No charge
52. Townsend Street, Banbridge	Wholly within a parking bay where such has been marked out	Motor car, motor cycle, invalid carriage and light goods vehicle	All days	All hours	14 consecutive hours	No charge

Name of Parking Place	Position in which vehicle may wait	Classes of Vehicle	Days of operation of parking place	Hours of operation of parking place	Maximum period for which vehicles may wait	Scale of Charges
1	2	3	4	5	6	7
53. Abbey Street East, Bangor	Wholly within a parking bay where such has been marked out	Motor car, motor cycle, invalid carriage and light goods vehicle	Monday to Saturday	8.00 a.m. to 10.00 p.m.	14 hours	Tariff Q as set out in Part II
				10.00 p.m. to 8.00 a.m.	10 consecutive hours	No charge
			Sunday	All hours	12 consecutive hours	No charge
54. Abbey Street West, Bangor	Wholly within a parking bay where such has been marked out	Motor car, motor cycle, invalid carriage and light goods vehicle	All days	All hours	12 consecutive hours	No charge
55. Bingham Lane, Bangor	Wholly within a parking bay where such has been marked out	Motor car, motor cycle, invalid carriage and light goods vehicle	Monday to Saturday	8.00 a.m. to 10.00 p.m.	14 hours	Tariff Q as set out in Part II

	Position of vehicle	Class of vehicle	Days	Hours	Maximum period	Charge
56. Mills Road, Bangor	Wholly within a parking bay where such has been marked out	Motor car, motor cycle, invalid carriage and light goods vehicle	Sunday	10.00 p.m. to 8.00 a.m.	10 consecutive hours	No charge
				All hours	12 consecutive hours	No charge
57. Castle Square (North side of Market Street and part owned by North Down Borough Council), Bangor	Wholly within a parking bay where such has been marked out	Motor car, motor cycle, invalid carriage and light goods vehicle	Monday to Saturday	8.00 a.m. to 10.00 p.m.	14 hours	Tariff Q as set out in Part II
			Sunday	10.00 p.m. to 8.00 a.m.	10 consecutive hours	No charge
				All hours	12 consecutive hours	No charge
			Monday Tuesday Thursday Friday Saturday Sunday	All hours	12 consecutive hours	No charge
58. Castle Square (South side of Market Street), Bangor	Wholly within a parking bay where such has been marked out	Motor car, motor cycle, invalid carriage and light goods vehicle	All days	All hours	12 consecutive hours	No charge

Name of Parking Place	Position in which vehicle may wait	Classes of Vehicle	Days of operation of parking place	Hours of operation of parking place	Maximum period for which vehicles may wait	Scale of Charges
1	2	3	4	5	6	7
59. Castle Street, Bangor	Wholly within a parking bay where such has been marked out	Motor car, motor cycle, invalid carriage and light goods vehicle	All days	All hours	12 consecutive hours	No charge
60. Central Avenue, Bangor	Wholly within a parking bay where such has been marked out	Motor car, motor cycle, invalid carriage and light goods vehicle	All days	All hours	12 consecutive hours	No charge
61. Clifton Road, Bangor	Wholly within a parking bay where such has been marked out	Motor car, motor cycle, invalid carriage and light goods vehicle	All days	All hours	12 consecutive hours	No charge
62. Dufferin Avenue, Bangor	Wholly within a parking bay where such has been marked out	Motor car, motor cycle, invalid carriage and light goods vehicle	All days	All hours	12 consecutive hours	No charge

63. Holborn Avenue, Bangor	Wholly within a parking bay where such has been marked out	Motor car, motor cycle, invalid carriage and light goods vehicle	Monday to Saturday	8.00 a.m. to 10.00 p.m.	14 hours	Tariff Q as set out in Part II
				10.00 p.m. to 8.00 a.m.	10 consecutive hours	No charge
			Sunday	All hours	12 consecutive hours	No charge
64. Newtownards Road/Church Street, Bangor	Wholly within a parking bay where such has been marked out	Motor car, motor cycle, invalid carriage and light goods vehicle	All days	All hours	12 consecutive hours	No charge
65. The Vennel, Bangor	Wholly within a parking bay where such has been marked out	Motor car, motor cycle, invalid carriage and light goods vehicle	Monday to Saturday	8.00 a.m. to 10.00 p.m.	14 hours	Tariff Q as set out in Part II
				10.00 p.m. to 8.00 a.m.	10 consecutive hours	No charge
			Sunday	All hours	12 consecutive hours	No charge

Name of Parking Place	Position in which vehicle may wait	Classes of Vehicle	Days of operation of parking place	Hours of operation of parking place	Maximum period for which vehicles may wait	Scale of Charges
1	2	3	4	5	6	7
66. Ashdale Street, Belfast	Wholly within a parking bay where such has been marked out	Motor car, motor cycle, invalid carriage and light goods vehicle	All days	All hours	12 consecutive hours	No charge
67. Bridge End, Belfast	Wholly within a parking bay where such has been marked out	Motor car, motor cycle, invalid carriage and light goods vehicle	Monday to Saturday	8.00 a.m. to 11.00 p.m.	15 hours	Tariff D as set out in Part II
				11.00 p.m. to 8.00 a.m.	9 consecutive hours	No charge
			Sunday	All hours	12 consecutive hours	No charge
68. Charlotte Street, Belfast	Wholly within a parking bay where such has been marked out	Motor car, motor cycle, invalid carriage and light goods vehicle	Monday to Saturday	8.00 a.m. to 11.00 p.m.	15 hours	Tariff C1 as set out in Part II

No. and place	Position	Vehicle	Days	Hours	Period	Charge
				11.00 p.m. to 8.00 a.m.	9 consecutive hours	No charge
			Sunday	All hours	12 consecutive hours	No charge
69. 44-96 Cromac Street, Belfast	Wholly within a parking bay where such has been marked out	Motor car, motor cycle, invalid carriage and light goods vehicle	Monday to Saturday	8.00 a.m. to 6.30 p.m.	10½ hours	Tariff D as set out in Part II
				6.30 p.m. to 8.00 a.m.	12 consecutive hours	No charge
			Sunday	All hours	12 consecutive hours	No charge
70. 11-19 Dunbar Street, Belfast	Wholly within a parking bay where such has been marked out	Motor car, motor cycle, invalid carriage and light goods vehicle	Monday to Saturday	8.00 a.m. to 11.00 p.m.	15 hours	Tariff C1 as set out in Part II
				11.00 p.m. to 8.00 a.m.	9 consecutive hours	No charge
			Sunday	All hours	12 consecutive hours	No charge

Name of Parking Place	Position in which vehicle may wait	Classes of Vehicle	Days of operation of parking place	Hours of operation of parking place	Maximum period for which vehicles may wait	Scale of Charges
1	2	3	4	5	6	7
71. Dundela Crescent, Belfast	Wholly within a parking bay where such has been marked out	Motor car, motor cycle, invalid carriage and light goods vehicle	All days	All hours	12 consecutive hours	No charge
72. 31-35 Exchange Street, Belfast	Wholly within a parking bay where such has been marked out	Motor car, motor cycle, invalid carriage and light goods vehicle	Monday to Saturday	8.00 a.m. to 11.00 p.m.	15 hours	Tariff C1 as set out in Part II
				11.00 p.m. to 8.00 a.m.	9 consecutive hours	No charge
			Sunday	All hours	12 consecutive hours	No charge
73. Francis Street, Belfast	Wholly within a parking bay where such has been marked out	Motor car, motor cycle, invalid carriage and light goods vehicle	Monday to Saturday	8.00 a.m. to 11.00 p.m.	15 hours	Tariff B1 as set out in Part II

			Days	Hours		Charge
74. 7-43 Frederick Street, Belfast	Wholly within a parking bay where such has been marked out	Motor car, motor cycle, invalid carriage and light goods vehicle	Monday to Saturday	11.00 p.m. to 8.00 a.m.	9 consecutive hours	No charge
			Sunday	All hours	12 consecutive hours	No charge
			Monday to Saturday	8.00 a.m. to 11.00 p.m.	15 hours	Tariff C1 as set out in Part II
75. Grampian Avenue, Belfast	Wholly within a parking bay where such has been marked out	Motor car, motor cycle, invalid carriage and light goods vehicle	All days	All hours	12 consecutive hours	No charge
76. Hope Street (North Side), Belfast	Wholly within a parking bay where such has been marked out	Motor car, motor cycle, invalid carriage and light goods vehicle	Sunday	11.00 p.m. to 8.00 a.m.	9 consecutive hours	No charge
			Sunday	All hours	12 consecutive hours	No charge
			Monday to Saturday	8.00 a.m. to 11.00 p.m.	15 hours	Tariff B1 as set out in Part II

Name of Parking Place 1	Position in which vehicle may wait 2	Classes of Vehicle 3	Days of operation of parking place 4	Hours of operation of parking place 5	Maximum period for which vehicles may wait 6	Scale of Charges 7
				11.00 p.m. to 8.00 a.m.	9 consecutive hours	No charge
			Sunday	All hours	12 consecutive hours	No charge
77. Hope Street (South Side), Belfast	Wholly within a parking bay where such has been marked out	Motor car, motor cycle, invalid carriage and light goods vehicle	Monday to Saturday	8.00 a.m. to 11.00 p.m.	15 hours	Tariff B1 as set out in Part II
				11.00 p.m. to 8.00 a.m.	9 consecutive hours	No charge
			Sunday	All hours	12 consecutive hours	No charge

78. 165 Kent Street, Belfast	Wholly within a parking bay where such has been marked out	Motor car, motor cycle, invalid carriage and light goods vehicle	Monday to Saturday	8.00 a.m. to 11.00 p.m	15 hours	Tariff C1 as set out in Part II
				11.00 p.m. to 8.00 a.m.	9 consecutive hours	No charge
			Sunday	All hours	12 consecutive hours	No charge
79. 61-67 King Street, Belfast	Wholly within a parking bay where such has been marked out	Motor car, motor cycle, invalid carriage and light goods vehicle	Monday to Saturday	8.00 a.m. to 11.00 p.m.	15 hours	Tariff B1 as set out in Part II
				11.00 p.m. to 8.00 a.m.	9 consecutive hours	No charge
			Sunday	All hours	12 consecutive hours	No charge
80. Little Donegall Street, Belfast	Wholly within a parking bay where such has been marked out	Motor car, motor cycle, invalid carriage and light goods vehicle	Monday to Saturday	8.00 a.m. to 11.00 p.m.	15 hours	Tariff C1 as set out in Part II

Name of Parking Place 1	Position in which vehicle may wait 2	Classes of Vehicle 3	Days of operation of parking place 4	Hours of operation of parking place 5	Maximum period for which vehicles may wait 6	Scale of Charges 7
				11.00 p.m. to 8.00 a.m.	9 consecutive hours	No charge
81. Little Victoria Street, Belfast	Wholly within a parking bay where such has been marked out	Motor car, motor cycle, invalid carriage and light goods vehicle	Sunday	All hours	12 consecutive hours	No charge
			Monday to Saturday	8.00 a.m. to 11.00 p.m.	15 hours	Tariff B1 as set out in Part II
				11.00 p.m. to 8.00 a.m.	9 consecutive hours	No charge
			Sunday	All hours	12 consecutive hours	No charge
82. Madison Avenue, Belfast	Wholly within a parking bay where such has been marked out	Motor car, motor cycle, invalid carriage and light goods vehicle	All days	All hours	12 consecutive hours	No charge

83. Middlepath Street, Belfast	Wholly within a parking bay where such has been marked out	Motor car, motor cycle, invalid carriage and light goods vehicle	Monday to Saturday	8.00 a.m. to 6.30 p.m.	10½ hours	Tariff D as set out in Part II
				6.30 p.m. to 8.00 a.m.	12 consecutive hours	No charge
			Sunday	All hours	12 consecutive hours	No charge
84. Nile Street, Belfast (Park and Ride)	Wholly within a parking bay where such has been marked out	Motor car, motor cycle, invalid carriage and light goods vehicle	Monday to Saturday	8.00 a.m. to 6.30 p.m.	10½ hours	Tariff E as set out in Part II
				6.30 p.m. to 8.00 a.m.	12 consecutive hours	No charge
			Sunday	All hours	12 consecutive hours	No charge
85. Northumberland Street, Belfast	Wholly within a parking bay where such has been marked out	Motor car, motor cycle, invalid carriage and light goods vehicle	All days	All hours	12 consecutive hours	No charge

Name of Parking Place	Position in which vehicle may wait	Classes of Vehicle	Days of operation of parking place	Hours of operation of parking place	Maximum period for which vehicles may wait	Scale of Charges
1	2	3	4	5	6	7
86. 24-30 Ormeau Avenue, Belfast	Wholly within a parking bay where such has been marked out	Motor car, motor cycle, invalid carriage and light goods vehicle	Monday to Saturday	8.00 a.m to 11.00 p.m.	15 hours	Tariff B1 as set out in Part II
				11.00 p.m. to 8.00 a.m.	9 consecutive hours	No charge
			Sunday	All hours	12 consecutive hours	No charge
87. 20-32 Ormeau Road, Belfast	Wholly within a parking bay where such has been marked out	Motor car, motor cycle, invalid carriage and light goods vehicle	Monday to Saturday	8.00 a.m. to 6.30 p.m.	10½ hours	Tariff D as set out in Part II
				6.30 p.m. to 8.00 a.m.	12 consecutive hours	No charge
			Sunday	All hours	12 consecutive hours	No charge

88. Parkgate Avenue, Belfast	Wholly within a parking bay where such has been marked out	Motor car, motor cycle, invalid carriage and light goods vehicle	All days	All hours	12 consecutive hours	No charge
89. Ravenscroft Avenue, Belfast	Wholly within a parking bay where such has been marked out	Motor car, motor cycle, invalid carriage and light goods vehicle	All days	All hours	12 consecutive hours	No charge
90. Sandown Road, Ballyhackamore, Belfast	Wholly within a parking bay where such has been marked out	Motor car, motor cycle, invalid carriage and light goods vehicle	All days	All hours	12 consecutive hours	No charge
91. Station Street, Belfast	Wholly within a parking bay where such has been marked out	Motor car, motor cycle, invalid carriage and light goods vehicle	Monday to Saturday	8.00 a.m. to 11.00 p.m.	15 hours	Tariff C1 as set out in Part II
				11.00 p.m. to 8.00 a.m.	9 consecutive hours	No charge
			Sunday	All hours	12 consecutive hours	No charge

Name of Parking Place	Position in which vehicle may wait	Classes of Vehicle	Days of operation of parking place	Hours of operation of parking place	Maximum period for which vehicles may wait	Scale of Charges
1	2	3	4	5	6	7
92. Stroud Street, Belfast	Wholly within a parking bay where such has been marked out	Motor car, motor cycle, invalid carriage and light goods vehicle	Monday to Saturday	8.00 a.m. to 11.00 p.m.	15 hours	Tariff D as set out in Part II
				11.00 p.m. to 8.00 a.m.	9 consecutive hours	No charge
			Sunday	All hours	12 consecutive hours	No charge
93. Talbot Street, Belfast	Wholly within a parking bay where such has been marked out	Motor car, motor cycle, invalid carriage and light goods vehicle	Monday to Saturday	8.00 a.m. to 11.00 p.m.	15 hours	Tariff C1 as set out in Part II
				11.00 p.m. to 8.00 a.m.	9 consecutive hours	No charge
			Sunday	All hours	12 consecutive hours	No charge

94. Wandsworth Road, Belfast	Wholly within a parking bay where such has been marked out	Motor car, motor cycle, invalid carriage and light goods vehicle	All days	All hours	12 consecutive hours	No charge
95. Westminster Avenue East, Belfast	Wholly within a parking bay where such has been marked out	Motor car, motor cycle, invalid carriage and light goods vehicle	All days	All hours	12 consecutive hours	No charge
96. Westminster Avenue North, Belfast	Wholly within a parking bay where such has been marked out	Motor car, motor cycle, invalid carriage and light goods vehicle	All days	All hours	12 consecutive hours	No charge
97. Westminster Avenue West, Belfast	Wholly within a parking bay where such has been marked out	Motor car, motor cycle, invalid carriage and light goods vehicle	All days	All hours	12 consecutive hours	No charge
98. Windsor Street, Belfast	Wholly within a parking bay where such has been marked out	Motor car, motor cycle, invalid carriage and light goods vehicle	Monday to Saturday	8.00 a.m. to 11.00 p.m.	15 hours	Tariff C1 as set out in Part II
				11.00 p.m. to 8.00 a.m.	9 consecutive hours	No charge
			Sunday	All hours	12 consecutive hours	No charge

Name of Parking Place	Position in which vehicle may wait	Classes of Vehicle	Days of operation of parking place	Hours of operation of parking place	Maximum period for which vehicles may wait	Scale of Charges
1	2	3	4	5	6	7
99. York Street (at Lancaster Street) Belfast	Wholly within a parking bay where such has been marked out	Motor car, motor cycle, invalid carriage and light goods vehicle	Monday to Saturday	8.00 a.m. to 11.00 p.m.	15 hours	Tariff C1 as set out in Part II
				11.00 p.m. to 8.00 a.m.	9 consecutive hours	No charge
			Sunday	All hours	12 consecutive hours	No charge
100. York Street (at Westlink), Belfast	Wholly within a parking bay where such has been marked out	Motor car, motor cycle, invalid carriage and light goods vehicle	Monday to Saturday	8.00 a.m. to 6.30 p.m.	10½ hours	Tariff D as set out in Part II
				6.30 p.m. to 8.00 a.m.	12 consecutive hours	No charge
			Sunday	All hours	12 consecutive hours	No charge

101. Main Street, Bushmills	Wholly within a parking bay where such has been marked out	Motor car, motor cycle, invalid carriage and light goods vehicle	All days	All hours	12 consecutive hours	No charge
102. Beverley Road, Carnmoney	Wholly within a parking bay where such has been marked out	Motor car, motor cycle, invalid carriage and light goods vehicle	All days	All hours	12 consecutive hours	No charge
103. High Street, Carrickfergus	Wholly within a parking bay where such has been marked out	Motor car, motor cycle, invalid carriage and light goods vehicle	Monday to Saturday	8.30 a.m. to 6.30 p.m.	10 hours	Tariff R as set out in Part II
				6.30 p.m. to 8.30 a.m.	12 consecutive hours	No charge
			Sunday	All hours	12 consecutive hours	No charge
104. Joymount, Carrickfergus	Wholly within a parking bay where such has been marked out	Motor car, motor cycle, invalid carriage and light goods vehicle	Monday to Saturday	8.30 a.m. to 6.30 p.m.	10 hours	Tariff R as set out in Part II
				6.30 p.m. to 8.30 a.m.	12 consecutive hours	No charge
			Sunday	All hours	12 consecutive hours	No charge

Name of Parking Place	Position in which vehicle may wait	Classes of Vehicle	Days of operation of parking place	Hours of operation of parking place	Maximum period for which vehicles may wait	Scale of Charges
1	2	3	4	5	6	7
105. Lancasterian Street, Carrickfergus	Wholly within a parking bay where such has been marked out	Motor car, motor cycle, invalid carriage and light goods vehicle	Monday to Saturday	8.30 a.m. to 6.30 p.m.	10 hours	Tariff R as set out in Part II
				6.30 p.m. to 8.30 a.m.	12 consecutive hours	No charge
			Sunday	All hours	12 consecutive hours	No charge
106. St. Brides Street, Carrickfergus	Wholly within a parking bay where such has been marked out	Motor car, motor cycle, invalid carriage and light goods vehicle	Monday to Saturday	8.30 a.m. to 6.30 p.m.	10 hours	Tariff R as set out in Part II
				6.30 p.m. to 8.30 a.m.	12 consecutive hours	No charge
			Sunday	All hours	12 consecutive hours	No charge

Location	Position	Class of vehicle	Days	Hours	Duration	Tariff
107. West Street, Carrickfergus	Wholly within a parking bay where such has been marked out	Motor car, motor cycle, invalid carriage and light goods vehicle	Monday to Saturday	8.30 a.m. to 6.30 p.m.	10 hours	Tariff R as set out in Part II
				6.30 p.m. to 8.30 a.m.	12 consecutive hours	No charge
			Sunday	All hours	12 consecutive hours	No charge
108. Albert Street, Castlederg	Wholly within a parking bay where such has been marked out	All motor vehicles	All days	All hours	24 consecutive hours	No charge
109. Meetinghouse Lane, Castlederg	Wholly within a parking bay where such has been marked out	Motor car, motor cycle, invalid carriage and light goods vehicle	All days	All hours	24 consecutive hours	No charge
110. William Street, Castlederg	Wholly within a parking bay where such has been marked out	All motor vehicles	All days	All hours	24 consecutive hours	No charge
111. Market Yard, Claudy	Wholly within a parking bay where such has been marked out	Motor car, motor cycle, invalid carriage and light goods vehicle	All days	All hours	12 consecutive hours	No charge

Name of Parking Place 1	Position in which vehicle may wait 2	Classes of Vehicle 3	Days of operation of parking place 4	Hours of operation of parking place 5	Maximum period for which vehicles may wait 6	Scale of Charges 7
112. Main Street, Clogher	Wholly within a parking bay where such has been marked out	All motor vehicles	All days	All hours	24 consecutive hours	No charge
113. Main Road, Cloghy	Wholly within a parking bay where such has been marked out	Motor car, motor cycle, invalid carriage and light goods vehicle	All days	All hours	12 consecutive hours	No charge
114. Clough Roundabout, Clough	Wholly within a parking bay where such has been marked out	Motor car, motor cycle, invalid carriage and light goods vehicle	All days	All hours	12 consecutive hours	No charge
115. Lineside, Coalisland	Wholly within a parking bay where such has been marked out	Motor car, motor cycle, invalid carriage and light goods vehicle	All days	All hours	24 consecutive hours	No charge

Location	Position	Class of vehicle	Days	Hours	Period	Charge
116. Abbey Street, Coleraine	Wholly within a parking bay where such has been marked out	Motor car, motor cycle, invalid carriage and light goods vehicle	Monday to Saturday	8.30 a.m. to 6.30 p.m.	10 hours	Tariff R as set out in Part II
				6.30 p.m. to 8.30 a.m.	12 consecutive hours	No charge
			Sunday	All hours	12 consecutive hours	No charge
117. Long Commons, Coleraine	Wholly within a parking bay where such has been marked out	Motor car, motor cycle, invalid carriage and light goods vehicle	Monday to Saturday	8.30 a.m. to 6.30 p.m.	10 hours	Tariff R as set out in Part II
				6.30 p.m. to 8.30 a.m.	12 consecutive hours	No charge
			Sunday	All hours	12 consecutive hours	No charge
118. Mall, Coleraine	Wholly within a parking bay where such has been marked out	Motor car, motor cycle, invalid carriage and light goods vehicle	Monday to Saturday	8.30 a.m. to 6.30 p.m.	10 hours	Tariff R as set out in Part II

Name of Parking Place	Position in which vehicle may wait	Classes of Vehicle	Days of operation of parking place	Hours of operation of parking place	Maximum period for which vehicles may wait	Scale of Charges
1	2	3	4	5	6	7
119. Millburn Road, Coleraine	Wholly within a parking bay where such has been marked out			6.30 p.m. to 8.30 a.m.	12 consecutive hours	No charge
			Sunday	All hours	12 consecutive hours	No charge
120. Railway Place, Coleraine	Wholly within a parking bay where such has been marked out	Motor car, motor cycle, invalid carriage and light goods vehicle	All days	All hours	12 consecutive hours	No charge
121. Railway Road, Coleraine	Wholly within a parking bay where such has been marked out	Motor car, motor cycle, invalid carriage and light goods vehicle	Monday to Saturday	8.30 a.m. to 6.30 p.m.	10 hours	Tariff R as set out in Part II

122. Terrace Row, Coleraine	Wholly within a parking bay where such has been marked out		Sunday	6.30 p.m. to 8.30 a.m.	12 consecutive hours	No charge
123. Waterside, Coleraine	Wholly within a parking bay where such has been marked out	Motor car, motor cycle, invalid carriage and light goods vehicle	All days	All hours	12 consecutive hours	No charge
124. Castle Street/ Bridge Street, Comber	Wholly within a parking bay where such has been marked out	Motor car, motor cycle, invalid carriage and light goods vehicle	All days	All hours	12 consecutive hours	No charge
125. Glen Link, Comber	Wholly within a parking bay where such has been marked out	Motor car, motor cycle, invalid carriage and light goods vehicle	All days	All hours	12 consecutive hours	No charge
126. Killinchy Street, Comber	Wholly within a parking bay where such has been marked out	Motor car, motor cycle, invalid carriage and light goods vehicle	All days	All hours	12 consecutive hours	No charge

Name of Parking Place 1	Position in which vehicle may wait 2	Classes of Vehicle 3	Days of operation of parking place 4	Hours of operation of parking place 5	Maximum period for which vehicles may wait 6	Scale of Charges 7
127. Newtownards Road, Comber	Wholly within a parking bay where such has been marked out	Motor car, motor cycle, invalid carriage and light goods vehicle	All days	All hours	12 consecutive hours	No charge
128. Burn Road East, Cookstown	Wholly within a parking bay where such has been marked out	Motor car, motor cycle, invalid carriage and light goods vehicle	All days	All hours	24 consecutive hours	No charge
129. Burn Road West, Cookstown	Wholly within a parking bay where such has been marked out	Motor car, motor cycle, invalid carriage and light goods vehicle	All days	All hours	24 consecutive hours	No charge
130. Loy Street, Cookstown	Wholly within a parking bay where such has been marked out	Motor car, motor cycle, invalid carriage and light goods vehicle	All days	All hours	24 consecutive hours	No charge
131. Orritor Road, Cookstown	Wholly within a parking bay where such has been marked out	All motor vehicles	All days	All hours	24 consecutive hours	No charge

132. Union Place, Cookstown	Wholly within a parking bay where such has been marked out	Motor car, motor cycle, invalid carriage and light goods vehicle	All days	All hours	24 consecutive hours	No charge
133. Courthouse, Craigavon	Wholly within a parking bay where such has been marked out	Motor car, motor cycle, invalid carriage and light goods vehicle	All days	All hours	14 consecutive hours	No charge
134. Marlborough House, Craigavon	Wholly within a parking bay where such has been marked out	Motor car, motor cycle, invalid carriage and light goods vehicle	All days	All hours	14 consecutive hours	No charge
135. The Square, Crossgar	Wholly within a parking bay where such has been marked out	Motor car, motor cycle, invalid carriage and light goods vehicle	All days	All hours	12 consecutive hours	No charge
136. Railway Street, Donaghadee	Wholly within a parking bay where such has been marked out	Motor car, motor cycle, invalid carriage and light goods vehicle	All days	All hours	12 consecutive hours	No charge
137. Templepatrick Car Park, Donaghadee	Wholly within a parking bay where such has been marked out	Motor car, motor cycle, invalid carriage and light goods vehicle	All days	All hours	12 consecutive hours	No charge
138. Church Street, Downpatrick	Wholly within a parking bay where such has been marked out	Motor car, motor cycle, invalid carriage and light goods vehicle	All days	All hours	12 consecutive hours	No charge

Name of Parking Place	Position in which vehicle may wait	Classes of Vehicle	Days of operation of parking place	Hours of operation of parking place	Maximum period for which vehicles may wait	Scale of Charges
1	2	3	4	5	6	7
139. Irish Street, Downpatrick	Wholly within a parking bay where such has been marked out	Motor car, motor cycle, invalid carriage and light goods vehicle	Monday to Saturday	8.00 a.m. to 10.00 p.m.	14 hours	Tariff Q as set out in Part II
			Sunday	10.00 p.m. to 8.00 a.m.	10 consecutive hours	No charge
				All hours	12 consecutive hours	No charge
140. John Street, Downpatrick	Wholly within a parking bay where such has been marked out	Motor car, motor cycle, invalid carriage and light goods vehicle	All days	All hours	12 consecutive hours	No charge
141. Market Street, Downpatrick	Wholly within a parking bay where such has been marked out	Motor car, motor cycle, invalid carriage and light goods vehicle	All days	All hours	12 consecutive hours	No charge

142. Mount Crescent, Downpatrick	Wholly within a parking bay where such has been marked out	Motor car, motor cycle, invalid carriage and light goods vehicle	All days	All hours	12 consecutive hours	No charge
143. Scotch Street, Downpatrick	Wholly within a parking bay where such has been marked out	Motor car, motor cycle, invalid carriage and light goods vehicle	All days	All hours	12 consecutive hours	No charge
144. Cross Lane, Dromore, Co. Down	Wholly within a parking bay where such has been marked out	Motor car, motor cycle, invalid carriage and light goods vehicle	All days	All hours	14 consecutive hours	No charge
145. Gallows Street, Dromore, Co. Down	Wholly within a parking bay where such has been marked out	Motor car, motor cycle, invalid carriage and light goods vehicle	Monday to Saturday	8.30 a.m. to 6.30 p.m.	4 hours	No charge
				6.30 p.m. to 8.30 a.m.	14 consecutive hours	No charge
			Sunday	All hours	14 consecutive hours	No charge
146. Meeting Street, Dromore, Co. Down	Wholly within a parking bay where such has been marked out	Motor car, motor cycle, invalid carriage and light goods vehicle	All days	All hours	14 consecutive hours	No charge

Name of Parking Place	Position in which vehicle may wait	Classes of Vehicle	Days of operation of parking place	Hours of operation of parking place	Maximum period for which vehicles may wait	Scale of Charges
1	2	3	4	5	6	7
147. Drumquin Road, Dromore, Co. Tyrone	Wholly within a parking bay where such has been marked out	All motor vehicles	All days	All hours	24 consecutive hours	No charge
148. Main Street, Dromore, Co. Tyrone	Wholly within a parking bay where such has been marked out	All motor vehicles	All days	All hours	24 consecutive hours	No charge
149. Anne Street, Dungannon	Wholly within a parking bay where such has been marked out	Motor car, motor cycle, invalid carriage and light goods vehicle	All days	All hours	24 consecutive hours	No charge
150. Castle Hill, Dungannon	Wholly within a parking bay where such has been marked out	Motor car, motor cycle, invalid carriage and light goods vehicle	Monday to Saturday	8.30 a.m. to 6.30 p.m.	10 hours	Tariff R as set out in Part II
				6.30 p.m. to 8.30 a.m.	14 consecutive hours	No charge
			Sunday	All hours	24 consecutive hours	No charge

151. John Street, Dungannon	Wholly within a parking bay where such has been marked out	All motor vehicles	All days	All hours	24 consecutive hours	No charge
152. Scotch Street, North, Dungannon	Wholly within a parking bay where such has been marked out	Motor car, motor cycle, invalid carriage and light goods vehicle	Monday to Saturday	8.30 a.m. to 6.30 p.m.	10 hours	Tariff O as set out in Part II
			Sunday	6.30 p.m. to 8.30 a.m.	14 consecutive hours	No charge
153. Scotch Street South, Dungannon	Wholly within a parking bay where such has been marked out	Motor car, motor cycle, invalid carriage and light goods vehicle	All days	All hours	24 consecutive hours	No charge
154. Glenburn Road, Dunmurry	Wholly within a parking bay where such has been marked out	Motor car, motor cycle, invalid carriage and light goods vehicle	All days	All hours	12 consecutive hours	No charge
155. Berry Hill Road, Dunnamanagh	Wholly within a parking bay where such has been marked out	All motor vehicles	All days	All hours	24 consecutive hours	No charge

Name of Parking Place 1	Position in which vehicle may wait 2	Classes of Vehicle 3	Days of operation of parking place 4	Hours of operation of parking place 5	Maximum period for which vehicles may wait 6	Scale of Charges 7
156. Castle Park, Enniskillen	Wholly within a parking bay where such has been marked out	All motor vehicles	All days	All hours	24 consecutive hours	No charge
157. Derrychara Road, Enniskillen	Wholly within a parking bay where such has been marked out	Motor car, motor cycle, invalid carriage and light goods vehicle	All days	All hours	24 consecutive hours	No charge
158. Down Street/ Market Street/ Cross Street, Enniskillen	Wholly within a parking bay where such has been marked out	Motor car, motor cycle, invalid carriage and light goods vehicle	Monday to Saturday	8.30 a.m. to 6.30 p.m.	10 hours	Tariff R as set out in Part II
				6.30 p.m. to 8.30 a.m.	14 consecutive hours	No charge
			Sunday	All hours	24 consecutive hours	No charge

159. Eden Street, Enniskillen	Wholly within a parking bay where such has been marked out	Motor car, motor cycle, invalid carriage and light goods vehicle	Monday to Saturday	8.30 a.m. to 6.30 p.m.	10 hours	Tariff R as set out in Part II
				6.30 p.m. to 8.30 a.m.	14 consecutive hours	No charge
			Sunday	All hours	24 consecutive hours	No charge
160. Head Street, Enniskillen	Wholly within a parking bay where such has been marked out	Motor car, motor cycle, invalid carriage and light goods vehicle	Monday to Saturday	8.30 a.m. to 6.30 p.m.	10 hours	Tariff O as set out in Part II
				6.30 p.m. to 8.30 a.m.	14 consecutive hours	No charge
			Sunday	All hours	24 consecutive hours	No charge
161. Hollyhill Link, Enniskillen	Wholly within a parking bay where such has been marked out	All motor vehicles	All days	All hours	24 consecutive hours	No charge

Name of Parking Place	Position in which vehicle may wait	Classes of Vehicle	Days of operation of parking place	Hours of operation of parking place	Maximum period for which vehicles may wait	Scale of Charges
1	2	3	4	5	6	7
162. Quay Lane North, Enniskillen	Wholly within a parking bay where such has been marked out	Motor car, motor cycle, invalid carriage and light goods vehicle	Monday to Saturday	8.30 a.m. to 6.30 p.m.	10 hours	Tariff O as set out in Part II
				6.30 p.m. to 8.30 a.m.	14 consecutive hours	No charge
			Sunday	All hours	24 consecutive hours	No charge
163. Quay Lane South, Enniskillen	Wholly within a parking bay where such has been marked out	Motor car, motor cycle, invalid carriage and light goods vehicle	All days	All hours	24 consecutive hours	No charge
164. Queen Street, Enniskillen	Wholly within a parking bay where such has been marked out	Motor car, motor cycle, invalid carriage and light goods vehicle	All days	All hours	24 consecutive hours	No charge

						Tariff O as set out in Part II
165. Shore Road, Enniskillen	Wholly within a parking bay where such has been marked out	Motor car, motor cycle, invalid carriage and light goods vehicle	Monday to Saturday	8.30 a.m. to 6.30 p.m.	10 hours	Tariff O as set out in Part II
				6.30 p.m. to 8.30 a.m.	14 consecutive hours	No charge
			Sunday	All hours	24 consecutive hours	No charge
166. Wellington Place, Enniskillen	Wholly within a parking bay where such has been marked out	All motor vehicles	All days	All hours	24 consecutive hours	No charge
167. Main Street, Fintona	Wholly within a parking bay where such has been marked out	All motor vehicles	All days	All hours	24 consecutive hours	No charge
168. Edfield Road, Fivemiletown	Wholly within a parking bay where such has been marked out	All motor vehicles	All days	All hours	24 consecutive hours	No charge
169. The Commons, Fivemiletown	Wholly within a parking bay where such has been marked out	All motor vehicles	All days	All hours	24 consecutive hours	No charge

Name of Parking Place	Position in which vehicle may wait	Classes of Vehicle	Days of operation of parking place	Hours of operation of parking place	Maximum period for which vehicles may wait	Scale of Charges
1	2	3	4	5	6	7
170. Bridge Street, Garvagh	Wholly within a parking bay where such has been marked out	Motor car, motor cycle, invalid carriage and light goods vehicle	All days	All hours	12 consecutive hours	No charge
171. Castle Hill, Gilford	Wholly within a parking bay where such has been marked out	Motor car, motor cycle, invalid carriage and light goods vehicle	All days	All hours	14 consecutive hours	No charge
172. off Farmley Road, Glengormley	Wholly within a parking bay where such has been marked out	Motor car, motor cycle, invalid carriage and light goods vehicle	All days	All hours	12 consecutive hours	No charge
173. Fort Road, Helen's Bay	Wholly within a parking bay where such has been marked out	Motor car, motor cycle, invalid carriage and light goods vehicle	All days	All hours	12 consecutive hours	No charge
174. Ballynahinch Street, Hillsborough	Wholly within a parking bay where such has been marked out	Motor car, motor cycle, invalid carriage and light goods vehicle	All days	All hours	12 consecutive hours	No charge

175. Church Road, Holywood	Wholly within a parking bay where such has been marked out	Motor car, motor cycle, invalid carriage and light goods vehicle	Monday to Saturday	8.00 a.m. to 10.00 p.m.	14 hours	Tariff Q as set out in Part II
				10.00 p.m. to 8.00 a.m.	10 consecutive hours	No charge
			Sunday	All hours	12 consecutive hours	No charge
176. Hibernia Street, Holywood	Wholly within a parking bay where such has been marked out	Motor car, motor cycle, invalid carriage and light goods vehicle	Monday to Saturday	8.00 a.m. to 10.00 p.m.	14 hours	Tariff Q as set out in Part II
				10.00 p.m. to 8.00 a.m.	10 consecutive hours	No charge
			Sunday	All hours	12 consecutive hours	No charge
177. Hibernia Street South, Holywood	Wholly within a parking bay where such has been marked out	Motor car, motor cycle, invalid carriage and light goods vehicle	Monday to Saturday	8.00 a.m. to 10.00 p.m.	14 hours	Tariff Q as set out in Part II

Name of Parking Place	Position in which vehicle may wait	Classes of Vehicle	Days of operation of parking place	Hours of operation of parking place	Maximum period for which vehicles may wait	Scale of Charges
1	2	3	4	5	6	7
				10.00 p.m. to 8.00 a.m.	10 consecutive hours	No charge
178. Marine Parade, Holywood	Wholly within a parking bay where such has been marked out	Motor car, motor cycle, invalid carriage and light goods vehicle	Sunday	All hours	12 consecutive hours	No charge
179. Brownhill, Irvinestown	Wholly within a parking bay where such has been marked out	Motor car, motor cycle, invalid carriage and light goods vehicle	All days	All hours	12 consecutive hours	No charge
			All days	All hours	24 consecutive hours	No charge
180. Cow Fair, Keady	Wholly within a parking bay where such has been marked out	Motor car, motor cycle, invalid carriage and light goods vehicle	All days	All hours	14 consecutive hours	No charge

181. Glen Road, Keady	Wholly within a parking bay where such has been marked out	Motor car, motor cycle, invalid carriage and light goods vehicle	All days	All hours	14 consecutive hours	No charge
182. Kinelowen Street, Keady	Wholly within a parking bay where such has been marked out	Motor car, motor cycle, invalid carriage and light goods vehicle	All days	All hours	14 consecutive hours	No charge
183. Railway Street, Kesh	Wholly within a parking bay where such has been marked out	Motor car, motor cycle, invalid carriage and light goods vehicle	All days	All hours	24 consecutive hours	No charge
184. Bridge Street, Kilkeel	Wholly within a parking bay where such has been marked out	Motor car, motor cycle, invalid carriage and light goods vehicle	All days	All hours	14 consecutive hours	No charge
185. Ben Crom Place, Kilkeel	Wholly within a parking bay where such has been marked out	Motor car, motor cycle, invalid carriage and light goods vehicle	All days	All hours	14 consecutive hours	No charge
186. Newry Street, Kilkeel	Wholly within a parking bay where such has been marked out	Motor car, motor cycle, invalid carriage and light goods vehicle	All days	All hours	12 consecutive hours	No charge

Name of Parking Place	Position in which vehicle may wait	Classes of Vehicle	Days of operation of parking place	Hours of operation of parking place	Maximum period for which vehicles may wait	Scale of Charges
1	2	3	4	5	6	7
187. Greencastle Street, Kilkeel	Wholly within a parking bay where such has been marked out	Motor car, motor cycle, invalid carriage and light goods vehicle	All days	All hours	14 consecutive hours	No charge
188. Harbour Road, Kilkeel	Wholly within a parking bay where such has been marked out	Motor car, motor cycle, invalid carriage and light goods vehicle	All days	All hours	14 consecutive hours	No charge
189. Bridge Street, Kilrea	Wholly within a parking bay where such has been marked out	Motor car, motor cycle, invalid carriage and light goods vehicle	All days	All hours	12 consecutive hours	No charge
190. Shore Road, Kircubbin	Wholly within a parking bay where such has been marked out	Motor car, motor cycle, invalid carriage and light goods vehicle	All days	All hours	12 consecutive hours	No charge
191. The Green, Kircubbin	Wholly within a parking bay where such has been marked out	Motor car, motor cycle, invalid carriage and light goods vehicle	All days	All hours	12 consecutive hours	No charge

						Tariff R as set out in Part II
192. Agnew Street, Larne	Wholly within a parking bay where such has been marked out	Motor car, motor cycle, invalid carriage and light goods vehicle	Monday to Saturday	8.30 a.m. to 6.30 p.m.	10 hours	No charge
				6.30 p.m. to 8.30 a.m.	12 consecutive hours	No charge
			Sunday	All hours	12 consecutive hours	No charge
193. Bridge Street, Larne	Wholly within a parking bay where such has been marked out	Motor car, motor cycle, invalid carriage and light goods vehicle	All days	All hours	12 consecutive hours	No charge
194. Broadway, Larne	Wholly within a parking bay where such has been marked out	Motor car, motor cycle, invalid carriage and light goods vehicle	All days	All hours	12 consecutive hours	No charge
195. Circular Road East, Larne	Wholly within a parking bay where such has been marked out	Motor car, motor cycle, invalid carriage and light goods vehicle	All days	All hours	12 consecutive hours	No charge

Name of Parking Place	Position in which vehicle may wait	Classes of Vehicle	Days of operation of parking place	Hours of operation of parking place	Maximum period for which vehicles may wait	Scale of Charges
1	2	3	4	5	6	7
196. Circular Road West, Larne	Wholly within a parking bay where such has been marked out	Motor car, motor cycle, invalid carriage and light goods vehicle	Monday to Saturday	8.30 a.m. to 6.30 p.m.	10 hours	Tariff R as set out in Part II
				6.30 p.m. to 8.30 a.m.	12 consecutive hours	No charge
			Sunday	All hours	12 consecutive hours	No charge
197. Exchange Road, Larne	Wholly within a parking bay where such has been marked out	Motor car, motor cycle, invalid carriage and light goods vehicle	Monday to Saturday	8.30 a.m. to 6.30 p.m.	10 hours	Tariff O as set out in Part II
				6.30 p.m. to 8.30 a.m.	12 consecutive hours	No charge
			Sunday	All hours	12 consecutive hours	No charge

198. Fairhill, Larne	Wholly within a parking bay where such has been marked out	Motor car, motor cycle, invalid carriage and light goods vehicle	Monday to Saturday	8.30 a.m. to 6.30 p.m.	10 hours	Tariff R as set out in Part II
				6.30 p.m. to 8.30 a.m.	12 consecutive hours	No charge
			Sunday	All hours	12 consecutive hours	No charge
199. High Street, Larne	Wholly within a parking bay where such has been marked out	Motor car, motor cycle, invalid carriage and light goods vehicle	All days	All hours	12 consecutive hours	No charge
200. Inver, Larne	Wholly within a parking bay where such has been marked out	Motor car, motor cycle, invalid carriage and light goods vehicle	All days	All hours	12 consecutive hours	No charge
201. Narrow Gauge Road, Larne	Wholly within a parking bay where such has been marked out	Motor car, motor cycle, invalid carriage and light goods vehicle	Monday to Saturday	8.30 a.m. to 6.30 p.m.	10 hours	Tariff R as set out in Part II
				6.30 p.m. to 8.30 a.m.	12 consecutive hours	No charge
			Sunday	All hours	12 consecutive hours	No charge

Name of Parking Place	Position in which vehicle may wait	Classes of Vehicle	Days of operation of parking place	Hours of operation of parking place	Maximum period for which vehicles may wait	Scale of Charges
1	2	3	4	5	6	7
202. Ramp, Larne	Wholly within a parking bay where such has been marked out	All motor vehicles	All days	All hours	12 consecutive hours	No charge
203. Riverdale, Larne	Wholly within a parking bay where such has been marked out	Motor car, motor cycle, invalid carriage and light goods vehicle	All days	All hours	12 consecutive hours	No charge
204. Central Car Park, Limavady	Wholly within a parking bay where such has been marked out	Motor car, motor cycle, invalid carriage and light goods vehicle	Monday to Saturday	8.30 a.m. to 6.30 p.m.	10 hours	Tariff R as set out in Part II
				6.30 p.m. to 8.30 a.m.	12 consecutive hours	No charge
			Sunday	All hours	12 consecutive hours	No charge

					Tariff R as set out in Part II
205. Connell Street, Limavady	Wholly within a parking bay where such has been marked out	Motor car, motor cycle, invalid carriage and light goods vehicle	Monday to Saturday	8.30 a.m. to 6.30 p.m.	10 hours	No charge
			Sunday	6.30 p.m. to 8.30 a.m.	12 consecutive hours	No charge
				All hours	12 consecutive hours	No charge
206. Main Street, Limavady	Wholly within a parking bay where such has been marked out	Motor car, motor cycle, invalid carriage and light goods vehicle	All days	All hours	12 consecutive hours	No charge
207. Protestant Street, Limavady	Wholly within a parking bay where such has been marked out	Motor car, motor cycle, invalid carriage and light goods vehicle	All days	All hours	12 consecutive hours	No charge
208. Railway Station, Limavady	Wholly within a parking bay where such has been marked out	Motor car, motor cycle, invalid carriage and light goods vehicle	All days	All hours	12 consecutive hours	No charge

Name of Parking Place 1	*Position in which vehicle may wait* 2	*Classes of Vehicle* 3	*Days of operation of parking place* 4	*Hours of operation of parking place* 5	*Maximum period for which vehicles may wait* 6	*Scale of Charges* 7
209. Antrim Street, Lisburn	Wholly within a parking bay where such has been marked out	Motor car, motor cycle, invalid carriage and light goods vehicle	Monday to Saturday	8.00 a.m. to 10.00 p.m.	14 hours	Tariff Q as set out in Part II
				10.00 p.m. to 8.00 a.m.	10 consecutive hours	No charge
			Sunday	All hours	12 consecutive hours	No charge
210. Barrack Street, Lisburn	Wholly within a parking bay where such has been marked out	Motor car, motor cycle, invalid carriage and light goods vehicle	Monday to Saturday	8.00 a.m. to 10.00 p.m.	14 hours	Tariff Q as set out in Part II
				10.00 p.m. to 8.00 a.m.	10 consecutive hours	No charge
			Sunday	All hours	12 consecutive hours	No charge

211. Benson Street, Lisburn	Wholly within a parking bay where such has been marked out	Motor car, motor cycle, invalid carriage and light goods vehicle	All days	All hours	12 consecutive hours	No charge
212. Governor's Road, Lisburn	Wholly within a parking bay where such has been marked out	Motor car, motor cycle, invalid carriage and light goods vehicle	Monday to Saturday	8.00 a.m. to 10.00 p.m.	14 hours	Tariff Q as set out in Part II
				10.00 p.m. to 8.00 a.m.	10 consecutive hours	No charge
			Sunday	All hours	12 consecutive hours	No charge
213. Hillsborough Road Car Park, Lisburn	Wholly within a parking bay where such has been marked out	Motor car, motor cycle, invalid carriage and light goods vehicle	Monday to Saturday	8.00 a.m. to 10.00 p.m.	14 hours	Tariff Q as set out in Part II
				10.00 p.m. to 8.00 a.m.	10 consecutive hours	No charge
			Sunday	All hours	12 consecutive hours	No charge

Name of Parking Place	Position in which vehicle may wait	Classes of Vehicle	Days of operation of parking place	Hours of operation of parking place	Maximum period for which vehicles may wait	Scale of Charges
1	2	3	4	5	6	7
214. Laganbank Road, Lisburn	Wholly within a parking bay where such has been marked out	Motor car, motor cycle, invalid carriage and light goods vehicle	Monday to Saturday	8.00 a.m. to 10.00 p.m.	14 hours	Tariff Q as set out in Part II
				10.00 p.m. to 8.00 a.m.	10 consecutive hours	No charge
			Sunday	All hours	12 consecutive hours	No charge
215. Linenhall Street, Lisburn	Wholly within a parking bay where such has been marked out	Motor car, motor cycle, invalid carriage and light goods vehicle	Monday to Saturday	8.00 a.m. to 10.00 p.m.	14 hours	Tariff Q as set out in Part II
				10.00 p.m. to 8.00 a.m.	10 consecutive hours	No charge
			Sunday	All hours	12 consecutive hours	No charge

						Tariff Q as set out in Part II
216. Longstone Street Roundabout, Lisburn	Wholly within a parking bay where such has been marked out	Motor car, motor cycle, invalid carriage and light goods vehicle	Monday to Saturday	8.00 a.m. to 10.00 p.m.	14 hours	No charge
				10.00 p.m. to 8.00 a.m.	10 consecutive hours	No charge
			Sunday	All hours	12 consecutive hours	No charge
217. Quay Street, Lisburn	Wholly within a parking bay where such has been marked out	Motor car, motor cycle, invalid carriage and light goods vehicle	All days	All hours	12 consecutive hours	No charge
218. Queen's Road, Lisburn	Wholly within a parking bay where such has been marked out	Motor car, motor cycle, invalid carriage and light goods vehicle	All days	All hours	12 consecutive hours	No charge
219. Saintfield Road Roundabout, Lisburn	Wholly within a parking bay where such has been marked out	Motor car, motor cycle, invalid carriage and light goods vehicle	All days	All hours	12 consecutive hours	No charge

Name of Parking Place	Position in which vehicle may wait	Classes of Vehicle	Days of operation of parking place	Hours of operation of parking place	Maximum period for which vehicles may wait	Scale of Charges
1	2	3	4	5	6	7
220. Smithfield Square East, Lisburn	Wholly within a parking bay where such has been marked out	Motor car, motor cycle, invalid carriage and light goods vehicle	Monday to Saturday	8.00 a.m. to 10.00 p.m.	14 hours	Tariff Q as set out in Part II
				10.00 p.m. to 8.00 a.m.	10 consecutive hours	No charge
			Sunday	All hours	12 consecutive hours	No charge
221. Smithfield Square West, Lisburn	Wholly within a parking bay where such has been marked out	Motor car, motor cycle, invalid carriage and light goods vehicle	Monday to Saturday	8.00 a.m. to 10.00 p.m.	14 hours	Tariff Q as set out in Part II
				10.00 p.m. to 8.00 a.m.	10 consecutive hours	No charge
			Sunday	All hours	12 consecutive hours	No charge

222. New Bridge Road, Lisnaskea	Wholly within a parking bay where such has been marked out	All motor vehicles	All days	All hours	24 consecutive hours	No charge
223. Fair Green, Lisnaskea	Wholly within a parking bay where such has been marked out	Motor car, motor cycle, invalid carriage and light goods vehicle	All days	All hours	12 consecutive hours	No charge
224. Old Quarry, Lisnaskea	Wholly within a parking bay where such has been marked out	Motor car, motor cycle, invalid carriage and light goods vehicle	All days	All hours	12 consecutive hours	No charge
225. Altnagelvin, Londonderry	Wholly within a parking bay where such has been marked out	Motor car, motor cycle, invalid carriage and light goods vehicle	All days	All hours	12 consecutive hours	No charge
226. Bishop's Gate, Londonderry	Wholly within a parking bay where such has been marked out	Motor car, motor cycle, invalid carriage and light goods vehicle	All days	All hours	12 consecutive hours	No charge
227. Carlisle Road, Londonderry	Wholly within a parking bay where such has been marked out	Motor car, motor cycle, invalid carriage and light goods vehicle	Monday to Saturday	8.30 a.m. to 6.30 p.m.	10 hours	Tariff R as set out in Part II
				6.30 p.m. to 8.30 a.m.	12 consecutive hours	No charge

Name of Parking Place	Position in which vehicle may wait	Classes of Vehicle	Days of operation of parking place	Hours of operation of parking place	Maximum period for which vehicles may wait	Scale of Charges
1	2	3	4	5	6	7
			Sunday	All hours	12 consecutive hours	No charge
228. Courthouse, (formerly Masonic) Londonderry	Wholly within a parking bay where such has been marked out	Motor car, motor cycle, invalid carriage and light goods vehicle	Monday to Saturday	8.30 a.m. to 6.30 p.m.	10 hours	Tariff R as set out in Part II
			Sunday	6.30 p.m. to 8.30 a.m.	12 consecutive hours	No charge
229. Distillery Brae, Londonderry	Wholly within a parking bay where such has been marked out	Motor car, motor cycle, invalid carriage and light goods vehicle	All days	All hours	12 consecutive hours	No charge
230. Duke Street, Londonderry	Wholly within a parking bay where such has been marked out	Motor car, motor cycle, invalid carriage and light goods vehicle	All days	All hours	12 consecutive hours	No charge

231. East Wall, Londonderry	Wholly within a parking bay where such has been marked out	Motor car, motor cycle, invalid carriage and light goods vehicle	Monday to Saturday	8.30 a.m. to 6.30 p.m.	10 hours	Tariff R as set out in Part II
				6.30 p.m. to 8.30 a.m.	12 consecutive hours	No charge
			Sunday	All hours	12 consecutive hours	No charge
232. Foyle Road (GNR Site), Londonderry	Wholly within a parking bay where such has been marked out	Motor car, motor cycle, invalid carriage and light goods vehicle	All days	All hours	12 consecutive hours	No charge
233. Guildhall, Londonderry	Wholly within a parking bay where such has been marked out	Motor car, motor cycle, invalid carriage and light goods vehicle	Monday to Saturday	8.30 a.m. to 6.30 p.m.	10 hours	Tariff R as set out in Part II
				6.30 p.m. to 8.30 a.m.	12 consecutive hours	No charge
			Sunday	All hours	12 consecutive hours	No charge

Name of Parking Place	Position in which vehicle may wait	Classes of Vehicle	Days of operation of parking place	Hours of operation of parking place	Maximum period for which vehicles may wait	Scale of Charges
1	2	3	4	5	6	7
234. Lawrence Hill, Londonderry	Wholly within a parking bay where such has been marked out	Motor car, motor cycle, invalid carriage and light goods vehicle	All days	All hours	12 consecutive hours	No charge
235. Lorne, Londonderry	Wholly within a parking bay where such has been marked out	Motor car, motor cycle, invalid carriage and light goods vehicle	Monday to Saturday	8.30 a.m. to 6.30 p.m.	10 hours	Tariff R as set out in Part II
				6.30 p.m. to 8.30 a.m.	12 consecutive hours	No charge
			Sunday	All hours	12 consecutive hours	No charge
236. Queen's Quay, Londonderry	Wholly within a parking bay where such has been marked out	Motor car, motor cycle, invalid carriage and light goods vehicle	Monday to Saturday	8.30 a.m. to 6.30 p.m.	10 hours	Tariff R as set out in Part II
				6.30 p.m. to 8.30 a.m.	12 consecutive hours	No charge

No. & Location	Position	Class of vehicle	Days	Hours	Period	Charge
237. Shantallow, Londonderry	Wholly within a parking bay where such has been marked out	Motor car, motor cycle, invalid carriage and light goods vehicle	Sunday	All hours	12 consecutive hours	No charge
238. Simpson's Brae, Londonderry	Wholly within a parking bay where such has been marked out	Motor car, motor cycle, invalid carriage and light goods vehicle	All days	All hours	12 consecutive hours	No charge
239. Society Street, Londonderry	Wholly within a parking bay where such has been marked out	Motor car, motor cycle, invalid carriage and light goods vehicle	All days	All hours	12 consecutive hours	No charge
			Monday to Saturday	8.30 a.m. to 6.30 p.m.	10 hours	Tariff R as set out in Part II
				6.30 p.m. to 8.30 a.m.	12 consecutive hours	No charge
			Sunday	All hours	12 consecutive hours	No charge
240. Spencer Road/ Hill's Site, Londonderry	Wholly within a parking bay where such has been marked out	Motor car, motor cycle, invalid carriage and light goods vehicle	Monday to Saturday	8.30 a.m. to 6.30 p.m.	10 hours	Tariff R as set out in Part II

Name of Parking Place 1	Position in which vehicle may wait 2	Classes of Vehicle 3	Days of operation of parking place 4	Hours of operation of parking place 5	Maximum period for which vehicles may wait 6	Scale of Charges 7
241. Spencer Road/ Victoria Road, Londonderry	Wholly within a parking bay where such has been marked out	Motor car, motor cycle, invalid carriage and light goods vehicle		6.30 p.m. to 8.30 a.m.	12 consecutive hours	No charge
			Sunday	All hours	12 consecutive hours	No charge
			Monday to Saturday	8.30 a.m. to 6.30 p.m.	10 hours	Tariff R as set out in Part II
				6.30 p.m. to 8.30 a.m.	12 consecutive hours	No charge
			Sunday	All hours	12 consecutive hours	No charge

			Days	Hours	Duration	Charge
242.	Strand Road, Londonderry	Wholly within a parking bay where such has been marked out	Motor car, motor cycle, invalid carriage and light goods vehicle	All days	All hours	12 consecutive hours	No charge
243.	Union Street, Londonderry	Wholly within a parking bay where such has been marked out	Motor car, motor cycle, invalid carriage and light goods vehicle	All days	All hours	12 consecutive hours	No charge
244.	Victoria Market, Londonderry	Wholly within a parking bay where such has been marked out	Motor car, motor cycle, invalid carriage and light goods vehicle	Monday to Saturday	8.30 a.m. to 6.30 p.m.	10 hours	Tariff R as set out in Part II
				Sunday	6.30 p.m. to 8.30 a.m.	12 consecutive hours	No charge
245.	Waterside, Londonderry	Wholly within a parking bay where such has been marked out	Motor car, motor cycle, invalid carriage and light goods vehicle	All days	All hours	12 consecutive hours	No charge
246.	William Street, Londonderry	Wholly within a parking bay where such has been marked out	Motor car, motor cycle, invalid carriage and light goods vehicle	All days	All hours	12 consecutive hours	No charge

Name of Parking Place	Position in which vehicle may wait	Classes of Vehicle	Days of operation of parking place	Hours of operation of parking place	Maximum period for which vehicles may wait	Scale of Charges
1	2	3	4	5	6	7
247. Alexander Square I, Lurgan	Wholly within a parking bay where such has been marked out	Motor car, motor cycle, invalid carriage and light goods vehicle	Monday Tuesday Thursday Friday Saturday	8.30 a.m. to 6.30 p.m.	10 hours	Tariff R as set out in Part II
			Wednesday Sunday	6.30 p.m. to 8.30 a.m.	14 consecutive hours	No charge
				All hours	14 consecutive hours	No charge
248. Alexander Square II, Lurgan	Wholly within a parking bay where such has been marked out	Motor car, motor cycle, invalid carriage and light goods vehicle	All days	All hours	14 consecutive hours	No charge
249. Black's Court, Lurgan	Wholly within a parking bay where such has been marked out	Motor car, motor cycle, invalid carriage and light goods vehicle	All days	All hours	14 consecutive hours	No charge

			Days	Hours	Duration	Charge
250. Castle Lane, Lurgan	Wholly within a parking bay where such has been marked out	Motor car, motor cycle, invalid carriage and light goods vehicle	Monday Tuesday Thursday Friday Saturday	8.30 a.m. to 6.30 p.m.	10 hours	Tariff R as set out in Part II
				6.30 p.m. to 8.30 a.m.	14 consecutive hours	No charge
			Wednesday Sunday	All hours	14 consecutive hours	No charge
251. Foster Place, Lurgan	Wholly within a parking bay where such has been marked out	Motor car, motor cycle, invalid carriage and light goods vehicle	All days	All hours	12 consecutive hours	No charge
252. High Street, Lurgan	Wholly within a parking bay where such has been marked out	Motor car, motor cycle, invalid carriage and light goods vehicle	All days	All hours	12 consecutive hours	No charge
253. Moore's Lane, Lurgan	Wholly within a parking bay where such has been marked out	Motor car, motor cycle, invalid carriage and light goods vehicle	Monday Tuesday Thursday Friday Saturday	8.30 a.m. to 6.30 p.m.	10 hours	Tariff R as set out in Part II
				6.30 p.m. to 8.30 a.m.	14 consecutive hours	No charge

Name of Parking Place 1	Position in which vehicle may wait 2	Classes of Vehicle 3	Days of operation of parking place 4	Hours of operation of parking place 5	Maximum period for which vehicles may wait 6	Scale of Charges 7
			Wednesday Sunday	All hours	14 consecutive hours	No charge
254. Robert Street, Lurgan	Wholly within a parking bay where such has been marked out	Motor car, motor cycle, invalid carriage and light goods vehicle	All days	All hours	14 consecutive hours	No charge
255. Waring Street, Lurgan	Wholly within a parking bay where such has been marked out	Motor car, motor cycle, invalid carriage and light goods vehicle	All days	All hours	14 consecutive hours	No charge
256. Wesley Place, Lurgan	Wholly within a parking bay where such has been marked out	Motor car, motor cycle, invalid carriage and light goods vehicle	All days	All hours	14 consecutive hours	No charge
257. St. Lurach's Road, Maghera	Wholly within a parking bay where such has been marked out	Motor car, motor cycle, invalid carriage and light goods vehicle	All days	All hours	12 consecutive hours	No charge

258. King Street, Magherafelt	Wholly within a parking bay where such has been marked out	Motor car, motor cycle, invalid carriage and light goods vehicle	All days	All hours	12 consecutive hours	No charge
259. Rainey Street, Magherafelt	Wholly within a parking bay where such has been marked out	All motor vehicles	All days	All hours	12 consecutive hours	No charge
260. Union Road, Magherafelt	Wholly within a parking bay where such has been marked out	Motor car, motor cycle, invalid carriage and light goods vehicle	All days	All hours	12 consecutive hours	No charge
261. Tattinderry Road, Maguires-bridge	Wholly within a parking bay where such has been marked out	All motor vehicles	All days	All hours	24 consecutive hours	No charge
262. Ballywalter Road, Millisle	Wholly within a parking bay where such has been marked out	Motor car, motor cycle, invalid carriage and light goods vehicle	All days	All hours	12 consecutive hours	No charge
263. Ballywhiskin, Millisle	Wholly within a parking bay where such has been marked out	Motor car, motor cycle, invalid carriage and light goods vehicle	All days	All hours	12 consecutive hours	No charge

Name of Parking Place	Position in which vehicle may wait	Classes of Vehicle	Days of operation of parking place	Hours of operation of parking place	Maximum period for which vehicles may wait	Scale of Charges
1	2	3	4	5	6	7
264. Moss Road, Millisle	Wholly within a parking bay where such has been marked out	Motor car, motor cycle, invalid carriage and light goods vehicle	All days	All hours	12 consecutive hours	No charge
265. Main Street, Moira	Wholly within a parking bay where such has been marked out	Motor car, motor cycle, invalid carriage and light goods vehicle	All days	All hours	12 consecutive hours	No charge
266. Causeway Road, Newcastle	Wholly within a parking bay where such has been marked out	Motor car, motor cycle, invalid carriage and light goods vehicle	All days	All hours	12 consecutive hours	No charge
267. Shimna Road, Newcastle	Wholly within a parking bay where such has been marked out	Motor car, motor cycle, invalid carriage and light goods vehicle	All days	All hours	12 consecutive hours	No charge
268. Basin Walk, Newry	Wholly within a parking bay where such has been marked out	Motor car, motor cycle, invalid carriage and light goods vehicle	All days	All hours	14 consecutive hours	No charge

269. Bridge Street, Newry	Wholly within a parking bay where such has been marked out	Motor car, motor cycle, invalid carriage and light goods vehicle	All days	All hours	14 consecutive hours	No charge
270. Canal Bank I, Newry	Wholly within a parking bay where such has been marked out	Motor car, motor cycle, invalid carriage and light goods vehicle	All days	All hours	14 consecutive hours	No charge
271. Canal Bank II, Newry	Wholly within a parking bay where such has been marked out	Motor car, motor cycle, invalid carriage and light goods vehicle	Monday Tuesday Thursday Friday Saturday	8.30 a.m. to 6.30 p.m.	10 hours	Tariff R as set out in Part II
			Wednesday Sunday	6.30 p.m. to 8.30 a.m.	14 consecutive hours	No charge
272. Downshire Road, Newry	Wholly within a parking bay where such has been marked out	Motor car, motor cycle, invalid carriage and light goods vehicle	All days	All hours	14 consecutive hours	No charge
273. Edward Street, Newry	Wholly within a parking bay where such has been marked out	Motor car, motor cycle, invalid carriage and light goods vehicle	All days	All hours	14 consecutive hours	No charge

Name of Parking Place	Position in which vehicle may wait	Classes of Vehicle	Days of operation of parking place	Hours of operation of parking place	Maximum period for which vehicles may wait	Scale of Charges
1	2	3	4	5	6	7
274. Kilmorey Street East, Newry	Wholly within a parking bay where such has been marked out	Motor car, motor cycle, invalid carriage and light goods vehicle	All days	All hours	14 consecutive hours	No charge
275. Mill Street, Newry	Wholly within a parking bay where such has been marked out	Motor car, motor cycle, invalid carriage and light goods vehicle	Monday Tuesday Thursday Friday Saturday	8.30 a.m. to 6.30 p.m.	10 hours	Tariff R as set out in Part II
				6.30 p.m. to 8.30 a.m.	14 consecutive hours	No charge
			Wednesday Sunday	All hours	14 consecutive hours	No charge
276. Monaghan Street, Newry	Wholly within a parking bay where such has been marked out	Motor car, motor cycle, invalid carriage and light goods vehicle	Monday Tuesday Thursday Friday Saturday	8.30 a.m. to 6.30 p.m.	10 hours	Tariff R as set out in Part II

277. New Street, Newry	Wholly within a parking bay where such has been marked out	Motor car, motor cycle, invalid carriage and light goods vehicle	Wednesday Sunday	6.30 p.m. to 8.30 a.m.	14 consecutive hours	No charge
278. Railway Avenue, Newry	Wholly within a parking bay where such has been marked out	Motor car, motor cycle, invalid carriage and light goods vehicle	All days	All hours	14 consecutive hours	No charge
279. River Street, Newry	Wholly within a parking bay where such has been marked out	Motor car, motor cycle, invalid carriage and light goods vehicle	All days	All hours	14 consecutive hours	No charge
280. Ann Street, Newtownards	Wholly within a parking bay where such has been marked out	Motor car, motor cycle, invalid carriage and light goods vehicle	Monday to Saturday	8.00 a.m. to 10.00 p.m.	14 hours	Tariff O as set out in Part II
				10.00 p.m. to 8.00 a.m.	10 consecutive hours	No charge

Name of Parking Place 1	Position in which vehicle may wait 2	Classes of Vehicle 3	Days of operation of parking place 4	Hours of operation of parking place 5	Maximum period for which vehicles may wait 6	Scale of Charges 7
			Sunday	All hours	12 consecutive hours	No charge
281. Kennel Lane, Newtownards	Wholly within a parking bay where such has been marked out	Motor car, motor cycle, invalid carriage and light goods vehicle	Monday to Saturday	8.00 a.m. to 10.00 p.m.	14 hours	Tariff O as set out in Part II
				10.00 p.m. to 8.00 a.m.	10 consecutive hours	No charge
			Sunday	All hours	12 consecutive hours	No charge
282. Gas Works Site, Mill Street, Newtownards	Wholly within a parking bay where such has been marked out	Motor car, motor cycle, invalid carriage and light goods vehicle	Monday to Saturday	8.00 a.m. to 10.00 p.m.	14 hours	Tariff Q as set out in Part II
				10.00 p.m. to 8.00 a.m.	10 consecutive hours	No charge

283. Mill Street, Newtownards	Wholly within a parking bay where such has been marked out	Motor car, motor cycle, invalid carriage and light goods vehicle	Sunday	All hours	12 consecutive hours	No charge
			Monday to Saturday	8.00 a.m. to 10.00 p.m.	14 hours	Tariff Q as set out in Part II
				10.00 p.m. to 8.00 a.m.	10 consecutive hours	No charge
			Sunday	All hours	12 consecutive hours	No charge
284. Movilla Street, Newtownards	Wholly within a parking bay where such has been marked out	Motor car, motor cycle, invalid carriage and light goods vehicle	Monday to Saturday	8.00 a.m. to 10.00 p.m.	14 hours	Tariff Q as set out in Part II
				10.00 p.m. to 8.00 a.m.	10 consecutive hours	No charge
			Sunday	All hours	12 consecutive hours	No charge

Name of Parking Place	Position in which vehicle may wait	Classes of Vehicle	Days of operation of parking place	Hours of operation of parking place	Maximum period for which vehicles may wait	Scale of Charges
1	2	3	4	5	6	7
285. Old Cross Street East, Newtownards	Wholly within a parking bay where such has been marked out	Motor car, motor cycle, invalid carriage and light goods vehicle	Monday to Saturday	8.00 a.m. to 10.00 p.m.	14 hours	Tariff Q as set out in Part II
				10.00 p.m. to 8.00 a.m.	10 consecutive hours	No charge
			Sunday	All hours	12 consecutive hours	No charge
286. Old Cross Street West, Newtownards	Wholly within a parking bay where such has been marked out	Motor car, motor cycle, invalid carriage and light goods vehicle	Monday to Saturday	8.00 a.m. to 10.00 p.m.	14 hours	Tariff Q as set out in Part II
				10.00 p.m. to 8.00 a.m.	10 consecutive hours	No charge
			Sunday	All hours	12 consecutive hours	No charge

287. South Street/ Court Street, Newtownards	Wholly within a parking bay where such has been marked out	Motor car, motor cycle, invalid carriage and light goods vehicle	Monday to Saturday	8.00 a.m. to 10.00 p.m.	14 hours	Tariff Q as set out in Part II
				10.00 p.m. to 8.00 a.m.	10 consecutive hours	No charge
			Sunday	All hours	12 consecutive hours	No charge
288. South Street, Newtownards	Wholly within a parking bay where such has been marked out	Motor car, motor cycle, invalid carriage and light goods vehicle	Monday to Saturday	8.00 a.m. to 10.00 p.m.	14 hours	Tariff Q as set out in Part II
				10.00 p.m. to 8.00 a.m.	10 consecutive hours	No charge
			Sunday	All hours	12 consecutive hours	No charge
289. Talbot Street, Newtownards	Wholly within a parking bay where such has been marked out	Motor car, motor cycle, invalid carriage and light goods vehicle	All days	All hours	12 consecutive hours	No charge

Name of Parking Place	Position in which vehicle may wait	Classes of Vehicle	Days of operation of parking place	Hours of operation of parking place	Maximum period for which vehicles may wait	Scale of Charges
1	2	3	4	5	6	7
290. Upper Court Street, Newtownards	Wholly within a parking bay where such has been marked out	Motor car, motor cycle, invalid carriage and light goods vehicle	All days	All hours	12 consecutive hours	No charge
291. West Street, Newtownards	Wholly within a parking bay where such has been marked out	Motor car, motor cycle, invalid carriage and light goods vehicle	All days	All hours	12 consecutive hours	No charge
292. Townhall Street East, Newtown-stewart	Wholly within a parking bay where such has been marked out	All motor vehicles	All days	All hours	24 consecutive hours	No charge
293. Townhall Street West, Newtown-stewart	Wholly within a parking bay where such has been marked out	All motor vehicles	All days	All hours	24 consecutive hours	No charge
294. Castle Street, Omagh	Wholly within a parking bay where such has been marked out	Motor car, motor cycle, invalid carriage and light goods vehicle	All days	All hours	14 consecutive hours	No charge

295. Church Street, (North), Omagh	Wholly within a parking bay where such has been marked out	Motor car, motor cycle, invalid carriage and light goods vehicle	All days	All hours	24 consecutive hours	No charge
296. Church Street (South), Omagh	Wholly within a parking bay where such has been marked out	Motor car, motor cycle, invalid carriage and light goods vehicle	All days	All hours	24 consecutive hours	No charge
297. Cunningham Terrace, Omagh	Wholly within a parking bay where such has been marked out	All motor vehicles	All days	All hours	24 consecutive hours	No charge
298. Drumragh Avenue, Omagh	Wholly within a parking bay where such has been marked out	All motor vehicles	Monday to Saturday	8.30 a.m. to 6.30 p.m.	10 hours	Tariff R as set out in Part II
				6.30 p.m. to 8.30 a.m.	14 consecutive hours	No charge
			Sunday	All hours	14 consecutive hours	No charge

Name of Parking Place	*Position in which vehicle may wait*	*Classes of Vehicle*	*Days of operation of parking place*	*Hours of operation of parking place*	*Maximum period for which vehicles may wait*	*Scale of Charges*
1	2	3	4	5	6	7
299. Foundry Lane, Omagh	Wholly within a parking bay where such has been marked out	Motor car, motor cycle, invalid carriage and light goods vehicle	Monday to Saturday	8.30 a.m. to 6.30 p.m.	10 hours	Tariff R as set out in Part II
				6.30 p.m. to 8.30 a.m.	10 consecutive hours	No charge
			Sunday	All hours	24 consecutive hours	No charge
300. Johnston Park, Omagh	Wholly within a parking bay where such has been marked out	Motor car, motor cycle, invalid carriage and light goods vehicle	Monday to Saturday	8.30 a.m. to 6.30 p.m.	10 hours	Tariff R as set out in Part II
				6.30 p.m. to 8.30 a.m.	14 consecutive hours	No charge
			Sunday	All hours	24 consecutive hours	No charge

	Position	Class of vehicle	Days	Hours	Maximum period	Charge
301. Market Place, Omagh	Wholly within a parking bay where such has been marked out	All motor vehicles	All days	All hours	24 consecutive hours	No charge
302. Market Street, Omagh	Wholly within a parking bay where such has been marked out	Motor car, motor cycle, invalid carriage and light goods vehicle	Monday to Saturday	8.30 a.m. to 6.30 p.m.	10 hours	Tariff R as set out in Part II
				6.30 p.m. to 8.30 a.m.	14 consecutive hours	No charge
			Sunday	All hours	14 consecutive hours	No charge
303. New Brighton Terrace, Omagh	Wholly within a parking bay where such has been marked out	All motor vehicles	All days	All hours	24 consecutive hours	No charge
304. Old Mountfield Road, Omagh	Wholly within a parking bay where such has been marked out	All motor vehicles	All days	All hours	24 consecutive hours	No charge
305. Showgrounds, Omagh	Wholly within a parking bay where such has been marked out	All motor vehicles	Tuesday to Saturday	8.00 a.m. to 6.30 p.m.	10½ consecutive hours	No charge

Name of Parking Place 1	Position in which vehicle may wait 2	Classes of Vehicle 3	Days of operation of parking place 4	Hours of operation of parking place 5	Maximum period for which vehicles may wait 6	Scale of Charges 7
306. Bachelors Walk, Portadown	Wholly within a parking bay where such has been marked out	Motor car, motor cycle, invalid carriage and light goods vehicle	All days	All hours	14 consecutive hours	No charge
307. Castle Street, Portadown	Wholly within a parking bay where such has been marked out	All motor vehicles	All days	All hours	14 consecutive hours	No charge
308. Fair Green, Portadown	Wholly within a parking bay where such has been marked out	Motor car, motor cycle, invalid carriage and light goods vehicle	All days	All hours	12 consecutive hours	No charge
309. Foundry Street, Portadown	Wholly within a parking bay where such has been marked out	Motor car, motor cycle, invalid carriage and light goods vehicle	All days	All hours	14 consecutive hours	No charge
310. Marley Street, Portadown	Wholly within a parking bay where such has been marked out	Motor car, motor cycle, invalid carriage and light goods vehicle	All days	All hours	14 consecutive hours	No charge

311. Meadow Lane East, Portadown	Wholly within a parking bay where such has been marked out	Motor car, motor cycle, invalid carriage and light goods vehicle	Monday Tuesday Wednesday Friday Saturday	8.30 a.m. to 6.30 p.m.	10 hours	Tariff R as set out in Part II
				6.30 p.m. to 8.30 a.m.	14 consecutive hours	No charge
			Thursday Sunday	All hours	14 consecutive hours	No charge
312. Meadow Lane West, Portadown	Wholly within a parking bay where such has been marked out	Motor car, motor cycle, invalid carriage and light goods vehicle	Monday Tuesday Wednesday Friday Saturday	8.30 a.m. to 6.30 p.m.	10 hours	Tariff R as set out in Part II
				6.30 p.m. to 8.30 a.m.	14 consecutive hours	No charge
			Thursday Sunday	All hours	14 consecutive hours	No charge
313. River Bank, Portadown	Wholly within a parking bay where such has been marked out	Motor car, motor cycle, invalid carriage and light goods vehicle	All days	All hours	14 consecutive hours	No charge

Name of Parking Place	Position in which vehicle may wait	Classes of Vehicle	Days of operation of parking place	Hours of operation of parking place	Maximum period for which vehicles may wait	Scale of Charges
1	2	3	4	5	6	7
314. West Street, Portadown	Wholly within a parking bay where such has been marked out	Motor car, motor cycle, invalid carriage and light goods vehicle	All days	All hours	14 consecutive hours	No charge
315. Magowan Buildings I, Portadown	Wholly within a parking bay where such has been marked out	Motor car, motor cycle, invalid carriage and light goods vehicle	All days	All hours	12 consecutive hours	No charge
316. Magowan Buildings II, Portadown	Wholly within a parking bay where such has been marked out	Motor car, motor cycle, invalid carriage and light goods vehicle	Monday Tuesday Wednesday Friday Saturday	8.30 a.m. to 6.30 p.m.	10 hours	Tariff R as set out in Part II
				6.30 p.m. to 8.30 a.m.	14 consecutive hours	No charge
			Thursday Sunday	All hours	14 consecutive hours	No charge

317. William Street, Portadown	Wholly within a parking bay where such has been marked out	Motor car, motor cycle, invalid carriage and light goods vehicle	All days	All hours	14 consecutive hours	No charge
318. Wilson Street, Portadown	Wholly within a parking bay where such has been marked out	Motor car, motor cycle, invalid carriage and light goods vehicle	All days	All hours	14 consecutive hours	No charge
319. Woodhouse Street, Portadown	Wholly within a parking bay where such has been marked out	Motor car, motor cycle, invalid carriage and light goods vehicle	All days	All hours	14 consecutive hours	No charge
320. Meeting House Street, Portaferry	Wholly within a parking bay where such has been marked out	Motor car, motor cycle, invalid carriage and light goods vehicle	All days	All hours	12 consecutive hours	No charge
321. Knockinelder, Portaferry	Wholly within a parking bay where such has been marked out	Motor car, motor cycle, invalid carriage and light goods vehicle	All days	All hours	12 consecutive hours	No charge
322. The Square, Portaferry	Wholly within a parking bay where such has been marked out	Motor car, motor cycle, invalid carriage and light goods vehicle	All days	All hours	12 consecutive hours	No charge

Name of Parking Place 1	*Position in which vehicle may wait* 2	*Classes of Vehicle* 3	*Days of operation of parking place* 4	*Hours of operation of parking place* 5	*Maximum period for which vehicles may wait* 6	*Scale of Charges* 7
323. Dunluce Avenue, Portrush	Wholly within a parking bay where such has been marked out	Motor car, motor cycle, invalid carriage and light goods vehicle	All days	All hours	12 consecutive hours	No charge
324. Lansdowne Road, Portrush	Wholly within a parking bay where such has been marked out	Motor car, motor cycle, invalid carriage and light goods vehicle	All days	All hours	12 consecutive hours	No charge
325. Convention Avenue, Portstewart	Wholly within a parking bay where such has been marked out	Motor car, motor cycle, invalid carriage and light goods vehicle	All days	All hours	12 consecutive hours	No charge
326. The Diamond, Portstewart	Wholly within a parking bay where such has been marked out	Motor car, motor cycle, invalid carriage and light goods vehicle	All days	All hours	12 consecutive hours	No charge
327. John Street, Randalstown	Wholly within a parking bay where such has been marked out	Motor car, motor cycle, invalid carriage and light goods vehicle	All days	All hours	12 consecutive hours	No charge

328. Portglenone Road, Randalstown	Wholly within a parking bay where such has been marked out	Motor car, motor cycle, invalid carriage and light goods vehicle	All days	All hours	12 consecutive hours	No charge
329. Castle Street, Rathfriland	Wholly within a parking bay where such has been marked out	Motor car, motor cycle, invalid carriage and light goods vehicle	All days	All hours	14 consecutive hours	No charge
330. Downpatrick Street, Rathfriland	Wholly within a parking bay where such has been marked out	Motor car, motor cycle, invalid carriage and light goods vehicle	All days	All hours	14 consecutive hours	No charge
331. The Square I, Rostrevor	Wholly within a parking bay where such has been marked out	Motor car, motor cycle, invalid carriage and light goods vehicle	All days	All hours	14 consecutive hours	No charge
332. The Square II, Rostrevor	Wholly within a parking bay where such has been marked out	Motor car, motor cycle, invalid carriage and light goods vehicle	All days	All hours	14 consecutive hours	No charge
333. Downpatrick Street, Saintfield	Wholly within a parking bay where such has been marked out	Motor car, motor cycle, invalid carriage and light goods vehicle	All days	All hours	12 consecutive hours	No charge
334. Bowling Green, Strabane	Wholly within a parking bay where such has been marked out	All motor vehicles	All days	All hours	24 consecutive hours	No charge

Name of Parking Place	Position in which vehicle may wait	Classes of Vehicle	Days of operation of parking place	Hours of operation of parking place	Maximum period for which vehicles may wait	Scale of Charges
1	2	3	4	5	6	7
335. Branch Road, Strabane	Wholly within a parking bay where such has been marked out	Motor car, motor cycle, invalid carriage and light goods vehicle	All days	All hours	24 consecutive hours	No charge
336. Butcher Street, Strabane	Wholly within a parking bay where such has been marked out	Motor car, motor cycle, invalid carriage and light goods vehicle	Monday to Saturday	8.30 a.m. to 6.30 p.m.	10 hours	Tariff R as set out in Part II
				6.30 p.m. to 8.30 a.m.	14 consecutive hours	No charge
			Sunday	All hours	24 consecutive hours	No charge
337. Canal Basin, Strabane	Wholly within a parking bay where such has been marked out	All motor vehicles	All days	All hours	24 consecutive hours	No charge

338. Lower Main Street North, Strabane	Wholly within a parking bay where such has been marked out	Motor car, motor cycle, invalid carriage and light goods vehicle	Monday to Saturday	8.30 a.m. to 6.30 p.m.	10 hours	Tariff R as set out in Part II
				6.30 p.m. to 8.30 a.m.	14 consecutive hours	No charge
			Sunday	All hours	24 consecutive hours	No charge
339. Lower Main Street South, Strabane	Wholly within a parking bay where such has been marked out	Motor car, motor cycle, invalid carriage and light goods vehicle	Monday to Saturday	8.30 a.m. to 6.30 p.m.	10 hours	Tariff R as set out in Part II
				6.30 p.m. to 8.30 a.m.	14 consecutive hours	No charge
			Sunday	All hours	24 consecutive hours	No charge
340. Railway Street, Strabane	Wholly within a parking bay where such has been marked out	Motor car, motor cycle, invalid carriage and light goods vehicle	Monday to Saturday	8.30 a.m. to 6.30 p.m.	10 hours	Tariff R as set out in Part Ii

Name of Parking Place 1	Position in which vehicle may wait 2	Classes of Vehicle 3	Days of operation of parking place 4	Hours of operation of parking place 5	Maximum period for which vehicles may wait 6	Scale of Charges 7
				6.30 p.m. to 8.30 a.m.	14 consecutive hours	No charge
			Sunday	All hours	24 consecutive hours	No charge
341. Upper Main Street, Strabane	Wholly within a parking bay where such has been marked out	All motor vehicles	All days	All hours	24 consecutive hours	No charge
342. Sinton Park, Tandragee	Wholly within a parking bay where such has been marked out	Motor car, motor cycle, invalid carriage and light goods vehicle	All days	All hours	14 consecutive hours	No charge
343. Main Street, Tempo	Wholly within a parking bay where such has been marked out	Motor car, motor cycle, invalid carriage and light goods vehicle	All days	All hours	24 consecutive hours	No charge

344. The Diamond, Tempo	Wholly within a parking bay where such has been marked out	Motor car, motor cycle, invalid carriage and light goods vehicle	All days	All hours	24 consecutive hours	No charge
345. Main Street, Toome	Wholly within a parking bay where such has been marked out	Motor car, motor cycle, invalid carriage and light goods vehicle	All days	All hours	12 consecutive hours	No charge
346. King's Lane, Warrenpoint	Wholly within a parking bay where such has been marked out	Motor car, motor cycle, invalid carriage and light goods vehicle	All days	All hours	14 consecutive hours	No charge
347. Mary Street, Warrenpoint	Wholly within a parking bay where such has been marked out	Motor car, motor cycle, invalid carriage and light goods vehicle	All days	All hours	14 consecutive hours	No charge
348. Newry Street, Warrenpoint	Wholly within a parking bay where such has been marked out	Motor car, motor cycle, invalid carriage and light goods vehicle	All days	All hours	14 consecutive hours	No charge
349. The Square, Warrenpoint	Wholly within a parking bay where such has been marked out	Motor car, motor cycle, invalid carriage and light goods vehicle	All days	All hours	14 consecutive hours	No charge

Name of Parking Place	Position in which vehicle may wait	Classes of Vehicle	Days of operation of parking place	Hours of operation of parking place	Maximum period for which vehicles may wait	Scale of Charges
1	2	3	4	5	6	7
350. 487-489 Shore Road, Whiteabbey	Wholly within a parking bay where such has been marked out	Motor car, motor cycle, invalid carriage and light goods vehicle	All days	All hours	12 consecutive hours	No charge
351. 606-612 Shore Road, Whiteabbey	Wholly within a parking bay where such has been marked out	Motor car, motor cycle, invalid carriage and light goods vehicle	All days	All hours	12 consecutive hours	No charge
352. Old Cinema, Whitehead	Wholly within a parking bay where such has been marked out	Motor car, motor cycle, invalid carriage and light goods vehicle	All days	All hours	12 consecutive hours	No charge

PART II

Tariff B1.

Motor Cars, Invalid Carriages and Light Goods Vehicles:

Up to 1 hour	60p
Over 1 hour and not exceeding 2 hours	90p
Over 2 hours and not exceeding 3 hours	£1·40
Over 3 hours and not exceeding 4 hours	£2·00
Over 4 hours and not exceeding 5 hours	£2·80
Over 5 hours and not exceeding 6 hours	£3·60
Over 6 hours and not exceeding 7 hours	£4·50
Over 7 hours and not exceeding 8 hours	£5·50
Over 8 hours	£6·50
After 5.00 p.m. until closing	70p

12 Week Season Ticket: £312·00
(Valid Monday-Friday)

Motor Cycles:

Up to 4 hours	30p
Over 4 hours	60p
After 5.00 p.m. until closing	25p

Tariff C1.

Motor Cars, Invalid Carriages and Light Goods Vehicles:

Up to 1 hour	50p
Over 1 hour and not exceeding 2 hours	70p
Over 2 hours and not exceeding 3 hours	£1·00
Over 3 hours and not exceeding 4 hours	£1·40
Over 4 hours and not exceeding 5 hours	£1·90
Over 5 hours and not exceeding 6 hours	£2·50
Over 6 hours and not exceeding 7 hours	£3·10
Over 7 hours and not exceeding 8 hours	£3·70
Over 8 hours	£4·30
After 5.00 p.m. until closing	60p

12 Week Season Ticket: £206·40
(Valid Monday-Friday)

Motor Cycles:

Up to 4 hours	30p
Over 4 hours	60p
After 5.00 p.m. until closing	25p

Tariff D.

Motor Cars, Invalid Carriages and Light Goods Vehicles:

Up to 1 hour	40p
Over 1 hour and not exceeding 2 hours	50p
Over 2 hours and not exceeding 3 hours	70p
Over 3 hours and not exceeding 4 hours	90p
Over 4 hours and not exceeding 5 hours	£1·10
Over 5 hours and not exceeding 6 hours	£1·30
Over 6 hours and not exceeding 7 hours	£1·50
Over 7 hours and not exceeding 8 hours	£1·70
Over 8 hours	£2·00

12 Week Season Ticket: £96·00
(Valid Monday-Friday)

Motor Cycles: No charge

Tariff E.   **Motor Cars, Invalid Carriages and Light Goods Vehicles:**
Park and Ride

	A	B
Up to 2 hours	£ 1·05	40p
Over 2 hours and not exceeding 4 hours	£ 1·15	60p
Over 4 hours and not exceeding 6 hours	£ 1·40	80p
Over 6 hours and not exceeding 8 hours	£ 1·60	£ 1·00
Over 8 hours	£ 1·80	£ 1·30

A.   Includes Park and Ride bus fare
B.   Parking charge only

12 Week Season Ticket: £86·40   £62·40
(Valid Monday-Friday)

Tariff O.   **Motor Cars, Invalid Carriages and Light Goods Vehicles:**

Up to 3 hours	25p
Over 3 hours and not exceeding 6 hours	50p
Over 6 hours	60p

12 Week Season Ticket: £28·80
(Valid Monday-Friday)

Tariff Q.   **Motor Cars, Invalid Carriages and Light Goods Vehicles:**

Up to 1 hour	25p
Over 1 hour and not exceeding 2 hours	40p
Over 2 hours and not exceeding 3 hours	60p
Over 3 hours and not exceeding 4 hours	70p
Over 4 hours and not exceeding 5 hours	90p
Over 5 hours and not exceeding 6 hours	£ 1·20
Over 6 hours and not exceeding 7 hours	£ 1·50
Over 7 hours and not exceeding 8 hours	£ 1·90
Over 8 hours	£ 2·30
After 6.30 p.m. until closing	30p

12 Week Season Ticket: £110·40
(Valid Monday-Friday)

Tariff R.   **Motor Cars, Invalid Carriages and Light Goods Vehicles:**

Up to 2 hours	25p
Over 2 hours and not exceeding 3 hours	50p
Over 3 hours and not exceeding 4 hours	75p
Over 4 hours	£ 1·70
After 6.30 p.m. until closing	30p

12 Week Season Ticket: £ 81·60
(Valid Monday-Friday)

PART III

The following are designated car parks.

Village, Ahoghill
Castle Street, Antrim
Central Car Park, Antrim
Dublin Road, Antrim
Railway Street, Antrim
Cinema Car Park, Armagh
Dobbin Street Lane, Armagh (excepting St. Malachy's part)
Dobbin Street Lane, Armagh (St. Malachy's part)
Friary Road, Armagh (West Side)
Friary Road, Armagh
Linenhall Street, Armagh
Lonsdale Street, Armagh
Mall West, Armagh
Harrier Way, (off Avondale Drive), Ballyclare
The Market Square, Ballyclare
Ballymoney Road Car Park, Ballymena
Church Street, Ballymena
Coach Entry, Ballymena
Garfield Place, Ballymena
Henry Street, Ballymena
Meeting House Lane, Ballymena
Springwell Street, Ballymena
Summerfield, Ballymena
Bridge Street East, Banbridge
Church Square, Banbridge
Commercial Road, Banbridge
Downshire Place, Banbridge
Downshire Road, Banbridge
Kenlis Street, Banbridge
Abbey Street East, Bangor
Bingham Lane, Bangor
Castle Street, Bangor
Dufferin Avenue, Bangor
Holborne Avenue, Bangor
Castle Square, (North Side of Market Street and part owned by North Down
            Borough Council), Bangor
Castle Square, (South Side of Market Street), Bangor
Mills Road, Bangor
The Vennel, Bangor
Ashdale Street, Belfast
Bridge End, Belfast
Charlotte Street, Belfast
44-96 Cromac Street, Belfast
11-19 Dunbar Street, Belfast
Dundela Crescent, Belfast
31-35 Exchange Street, Belfast
Francis Street, Belfast
7-43 Frederick Street, Belfast
Hope Street, (North Side), Belfast
Hope Street, (South Side), Belfast
165 Kent Street, Belfast

61-67 King Street, Belfast
Little Donegall Street, Belfast
Little Victoria Street, Belfast
Madison Avenue, Belfast
Middlepath Street, Belfast
Nile Street, Belfast (Park and Ride)
Northumberland Street, Belfast
24-30 Ormeau Avenue, Belfast
Parkgate Avenue, Belfast
Ravenscroft Avenue, Belfast
Sandown Road, Ballyhackamore, Belfast
Station Street, Belfast
Stroud Street, Belfast
Talbot Street, Belfast
Wandsworth Road, Belfast
Westminster Avenue East, Belfast
Westminster Avenue North, Belfast
Westminster Avenue West, Belfast
Windsor Street, Belfast
York Street, (at Lancaster Street), Belfast
York Street, (at Westlink), Belfast
Beverley Road, Carnmoney
High Street, Carrickfergus
Joymount, Carrickfergus
St. Brides Street, Carrickfergus
Albert Street, Castlederg
Meetinghouse Lane, Castlederg
William Street, Castlederg
Clough Roundabout, Clough
Abbey Street, Coleraine
Long Commons, Coleraine
Mall, Coleraine
Millburn Road, Coleraine
Railway Place, Coleraine
Railway Road, Coleraine
Waterside, Coleraine
Castle Street/Bridge Street, Comber
Killinchy Street, Comber
Courthouse, Craigavon
Marlborough House, Craigavon
Church Street, Downpatrick
Irish Street, Downpatrick
Market Street, Downpatrick
Mount Crescent, Downpatrick
Scotch Street, Downpatrick
Cross Lane, Dromore, Co. Down
Gallows Street, Dromore, Co. Down
Meeting Street, Dromore, Co. Down
Castle Hill, Dungannon
Scotch Street North, Dungannon
Scotch Street South, Dungannon
Castle Hill, Gilford
Off Farmley Road, Glengormley
Church Road, Holywood

Hibernia Street, Holywood
Marine Parade, Holywood
Cow Fair, Keady
Glen Road, Keady
Kinelowen Street, Keady
Bridge Street, Kilkeel
Ben Crom Place, Kilkeel
Newry Street, Kilkeel
Greencastle Street, Kilkeel
Harbour Road, Kilkeel
Agnew Street, Larne
Bridge Street, Larne
Broadway, Larne
Circular Road East, Larne
Circular Road West, Larne
Exchange Road, Larne
Fairhill, Larne
High Street, Larne
Inver, Larne
Narrow Gauge Road, Larne
Riverdale, Larne
Central Car Park, Limavady
Connell Street, Limavady
Main Street, Limavady
Protestant Street, Limavady
Railway Station, Limavady
Antrim Street, Lisburn
Barrack Street, Lisburn
Benson Street, Lisburn
Governor's Road, Lisburn
Hillsborough Road Car Park, Lisburn
Laganbank Road, Lisburn
Linenhall Street, Lisburn
Longstone Street Roundabout, Lisburn
Quay Street, Lisburn
Queen's Road, Lisburn
Saintfield Road Roundabout, Lisburn
Smithfield Square East, Lisburn
Smithfield Square West, Lisburn
East Wall, Londonderry
Victoria Market, Londonderry
Alexander Square I, Lurgan
Alexander Square II, Lurgan
Black's Court, Lurgan
Castle Lane, Lurgan
Foster Place, Lurgan
High Street, Lurgan
Moore's Lane, Lurgan
Robert Street, Lurgan
Waring Street, Lurgan
Wesley Place, Lurgan
Causeway Road, Newcastle
Shimna Road, Newcastle
Basin Walk, Newry

Bridge Street, Newry
Canal Bank I, Newry
Canal Bank II, Newry
Downshire Road, Newry
Edward Street, Newry
Kilmorey Street East, Newry
Mill Street, Newry
Monaghan Street, Newry
New Street, Newry
Railway Avenue, Newry
River Street, Newry
Ann Street, Newtownards
Kennel Lane, Newtownards
Gas Works Site, Mill Street, Newtownards
Mill Street, Newtownards
Movilla Street, Newtownards
Old Cross Street East, Newtownards
Old Cross Street West, Newtownards
South Street/Court Street, Newtownards
South Street, Newtownards
West Street, Newtownards
Townhall Street East, Newtownstewart
Townhall Street West, Newtownstewart
Bachelors Walk, Portadown
Castle Street, Portadown
Fair Green, Portadown
Foundry Street, Portadown
Marley Street, Portadown
Meadow Lane East, Portadown
Meadow Lane West, Portadown
River Bank, Portadown
West Street, Portadown
Magowan Buildings I, Portadown
Magowan Buildings II, Portadown
William Street, Portadown
Wilson Street, Portadown
Woodhouse Street, Portadown
Dunluce Avenue, Portrush
Lansdowne Road, Portrush
The Diamond, Portstewart
John Street, Randalstown
Portglenone Road, Randalstown
Castle Street, Rathfriland
Downpatrick Street, Rathfriland
The Square I, Rostrevor
The Square II, Rostrevor
Bowling Green, Strabane
Butcher Street, Strabane
Canal Basin, Strabane
Lower Main Street North, Strabane
Lower Main Street South, Strabane
Railway Street, Strabane
Upper Main Street, Strabane
Sinton Park, Tandragee

Main Street, Toome
King's Lane, Warrenpoint
Mary Street, Warrenpoint
Newry Street, Warrenpoint
The Square, Warrenpoint
487-489 Shore Road, Whiteabbey
606-612 Shore Road, Whiteabbey
Old Cinema, Whitehead

Title	Year and Number
Off-Street Parking Bye-Laws (Northern Ireland) 1983	S.R. 1983 No. 240
Off-Street Parking (Amendment) Bye-Laws (Northern Ireland) 1984	S.R. 1984 No. 35
Off-Street Parking (Amendment No. 2) Bye-Laws (Northern Ireland) 1984	S.R. 1984 No. 39
Off-Street Parking (Amendment No. 3) Bye-Laws (Northern Ireland) 1984	S.R. 1984 No. 183
Off-Street Parking (Amendment No. 4) Bye-Laws (Northern Ireland) 1984	S.R. 1984 No. 203
Off-Street Parking (Amendment No. 5) Bye-Laws (Northern Ireland) 1984	S.R. 1984 No. 330
Off-Street Parking (Amendment No. 6) Bye-Laws (Northern Ireland) 1984	S.R. 1984 No. 390
Off-Street Parking (Amendment) Bye-Laws (Northern Ireland) 1985	S.R. 1985 No. 132
Off-Street Parking (Amendment No. 2) Bye-Laws (Northern Ireland) 1985	S.R. 1985 No. 140
Off-Street Parking (Amendment No. 3) Bye-Laws (Northern Ireland) 1985	S.R. 1985 No. 303
Off-Street Parking (Amendment) Bye-Laws (Northern Ireland) 1986	S.R. 1986 No. 197
Off-Street Parking (Amendment No. 2) Bye-Laws (Northern Ireland) 1986	S.R. 1986 No. 271
Off-Street Parking (Amendment No. 3) Bye-Laws (Northern Ireland) 1986	S.R. 1986 No. 298
Off-Street Parking (Amendment No. 2) Bye-Laws (Northern Ireland) 1987	S.R. 1987 No. 45
Off-Street Parking (Amendment) Bye-Laws (Northern Ireland) 1987	S.R. 1987 No. 49
Off-Street Parking (Amendment No. 3) Bye-Laws (Northern Ireland) 1987	S.R. 1987 No. 62
Off-Street Parking (Amendment No. 4) Bye-Laws (Northern Ireland) 1987	S.R. 1987 No. 109
Off-Street Parking (Amendment No. 5) Bye-Laws (Northern Ireland) 1987	S.R. 1987 No. 133
Off-Street Parking (Amendment No. 6) Bye-Laws (Northern Ireland) 1987	S.R. 1987 No. 181
Off-Street Parking (Amendment No. 7) Bye-Laws (Northern Ireland) 1987	S.R. 1987 No. 241
Off-Street Parking (Amendment No. 8) Bye-Laws (Northern Ireland) 1987	S.R. 1987 No. 324
Off-Street Parking (Amendment No. 9) Bye-Laws (Northern Ireland) 1987	S.R. 1987 No. 426

Title	Year and Number
Off-Street Parking (Amendment) Bye-Laws (Northern Ireland) 1988	S.R. 1988 No. 38
Off-Street Parking (Amendment No. 2) Bye-Laws (Northern Ireland) 1988	S.R. 1988 No. 106
Off-Street Parking (Amendment No. 3) Bye-Laws (Northern Ireland) 1988	S.R. 1988 No. 228
Off-Street Parking (Amendment No. 4) Bye-Laws (Northern Ireland) 1988	S.R. 1988 No. 277
Off-Street Parking (Amendment No. 5) Bye-Laws (Northern Ireland) 1988	S.R. 1988 No. 324
Off-Street Parking (Amendment No. 6) Bye-Laws (Northern Ireland) 1988	S.R. 1988 No. 399
Off-Street Parking (Amendment) Bye-Laws (Northern Ireland) 1989	S.R. 1989 No. 161
Off-Street Parking (Amendment No. 2) Bye-Laws (Northern Ireland) 1989	S.R. 1989 No. 200
Off-Street Parking (Amendment No. 3) Bye-Laws (Northern Ireland) 1989	S.R. 1989 No. 220
Off-Street Parking (Amendment No. 4) Bye-Laws (Northern Ireland) 1989	S.R. 1989 No. 456
Off-Street Parking (Amendment) Bye-Laws (Northern Ireland) 1990	S.R. 1990 No. 139
Off-Street Parking (Amendment No. 2) Bye-Laws (Northern Ireland) 1990	S.R. 1990 No. 140
Off-Street Parking (Amendment No. 3) Bye-Laws (Northern Ireland) 1990	S.R. 1990 No. 281
Off-Street Parking (Amendment) Bye-Laws (Northern Ireland) 1991	S.R. 1991 No. 3
Off-Street Parking (Amendment No. 2) Bye-Laws (Northern Ireland) 1991	S.R. 1991 No. 59
Off-Street Parking (Amendment No. 3) Bye-Laws (Northern Ireland) 1991	S.R. 1991 No. 177
Off-Street Parking (Amendment No. 4) Bye-Laws (Northern Ireland) 1991	S.R. 1991 No. 209
Off-Street Parking (Amendment No. 5) Bye-Laws (Northern Ireland) 1991	S.R. 1991 No. 270
Off-Street Parking (Amendment No. 6) Bye-Laws (Northern Ireland) 1991	S.R. 1991 No. 273
Off-Street Parking (Amendment No. 7) Bye-Laws (Northern Ireland) 1991	S.R. 1991 No. 403
Off-Street Parking (Amendment No. 8) Bye-Laws (Northern Ireland) 1991	S.R. 1991 No. 545
Off-Street Parking (Amendment) Bye-Laws (Northern Ireland) 1992	S.R. 1992 No. 317

Title	Year and Number
Off-Street Parking (Amendment No. 2) Bye-Laws (Northern Ireland) 1992	S.R. 1992 No. 345
Off-Street Parking (Amendment No. 3) Bye-Laws (Northern Ireland) 1992	S.R. 1992 No. 389
Off-Street Parking (Amendment) Bye-Laws (Northern Ireland) 1993	S.R. 1993 No. 56
Off-Street Parking (Amendment No. 2) Bye-Laws (Northern Ireland) 1993	S.R. 1993 No. 214
Off-Street Parking (Amendment No. 3) Bye-Laws (Northern Ireland) 1993	S.R. 1993 No. 264

EXPLANATORY NOTE

(This note is not part of the Bye-Laws.)

These Bye-Laws revoke and re-enact with minor amendments the Off-Street Parking Bye-Laws (Northern Ireland) 1983 and all subsequent amending bye-laws.

The principal provisions are as follows:—

They prescribe the waiting in a parking place of such classes of vehicles, in such position and on such days and during such hours and on payment of such charges as are specified.

They prescribe that the driver of a vehicle shall not permit it to wait in a parking place for longer than the maximum period permitted for waiting.

They prescribe that the driver of a vehicle using a parking place shall pay the appropriate charge in accordance with the scale of charges specified.

They prohibit the use of parking bays reserved for disabled persons' vehicles by any other vehicle.

They prescribe the method of operation of pay and display systems of collecting charges in car parks.

They prohibit trading in a car park.

They prohibit supermarket trolleys from multi-storey car parks.

They prohibit the use of a designated car park for the purpose of consuming intoxicating liquor.

Any person who contravenes a Bye-Law shall be guilty of an offence and shall be liable on summary conviction to a fine not exceeding £100 for each offence.

1994 No. 135

ROAD TRAFFIC AND VEHICLES

Taxis (Downpatrick) (Revocation) Bye-Laws (Northern Ireland) 1994

Made	*31st March 1994*
Coming into operation . .	*16th May 1994*

The Department of the Environment, in exercise of the powers conferred on it by Article 65(1) of the Road Traffic (Northern Ireland) Order 1981(**a**), and of all other powers enabling it in that behalf, makes the following Bye-Laws:

Citation and commencement

1. These Bye-Laws may be cited as the Taxis (Downpatrick) (Revocation) Bye-Laws (Northern Ireland) 1994 and shall come into operation on 16th May 1994.

Revocation

2. The Taxis (Downpatrick) Bye-Laws (Northern Ireland) 1990(**b**) are hereby revoked.

Sealed with the Official Seal of the Department of the Environment on 31st March 1994.

(L.S.)

Trevor Pearson
Assistant Secretary

(**a**) S.I. 1981/154 (N.I. 1); *see* Article 2(2) for the definition of "Department"
(**b**) S.R. 1990 No. 225

EXPLANATORY NOTE

(This note is not part of the Bye-Laws.)

These Bye-Laws revoke the Taxis (Downpatrick) Bye-Laws (Northern Ireland) 1990. The effect of the revocation is to abolish the taxi stands at Market Street Car Park.

1994 No. 136

Road Races (North West 200) Order (Northern Ireland) 1994

This Order, being of a temporary character, is not printed at length in this volume.

1994   No. 137

HOUSING; RATES

The Housing Benefit (General) (Amendment No. 4) Regulations (Northern Ireland) 1994

Made	*8th April 1994*
Coming into operation . .	*1st May 1994*

The Department of Health and Social Services for Northern Ireland, in exercise of the powers conferred on it by sections 122(1)(*d*), 129(4) and 131(1) of the Social Security Contributions and Benefits (Northern Ireland) Act 1992(**a**) and of all other powers enabling it in that behalf, with the consent of the Department of the Environment for Northern Ireland(**b**) so far as relates to matters with regard to which such consent is required, and after agreement by the Social Security Advisory Committee that proposals to make these regulations should not be referred to it(**c**), hereby makes the following regulations:

Citation, commencement and interpretation

1.—(1) These regulations may be cited as the Housing Benefit (General) (Amendment No. 4) Regulations (Northern Ireland) 1994 and shall come into operation on 1st May 1994.

(2) The Interpretation Act (Northern Ireland) 1954(**d**) shall apply to these regulations as it applies to a measure of the Northern Ireland Assembly.

Amendment of the Housing Benefit (General) Regulations

2. In paragraph 1 of Schedule 1 to the Housing Benefit (General) Regulations (Northern Ireland) 1987(**e**) (ineligible service charges) for sub-paragraph (*f*) there shall be substituted the following sub-paragraph—

"(*f*) charges in respect of general counselling or of any other support services, whoever provides those services, except where those services—

   (i) relate to the provision of adequate accommodation, or

   (ii) are provided to tenants by either—

      (*aa*) their landlord in person, or

(**a**) 1992 c. 7
(**b**) *See* section 171(6A) of the Social Security Contributions and Benefits (Northern Ireland) Act 1992 inserted by Article 3(3) of the Social Security (Amendment) (Northern Ireland) Order 1993 (S.I. 1993/1579 (N.I. 8))
(**c**) *See* section 150(1)(*b*) of the Social Security Administration (Northern Ireland) Act 1992 (c. 8)
(**d**) 1954 c. 33 (N.I.)
(**e**) S.R. 1987 No. 461, to which there are amendments not relevant to these regulations

(*bb*) someone employed by their landlord ("the employee"),

and the landlord or, as the case may be, the employee spends the majority of the time, during which he provides any services, in providing services the charges for which are eligible under these regulations (other than any that are eligible only under the terms of this head).".

Sealed with the Official Seal of the Department of Health and Social Services for Northern Ireland on 8th April 1994.

(L.S.) *W. G. Purdy*

Assistant Secretary

The Department of the Environment for Northern Ireland hereby consents to the foregoing Regulations.

Sealed with the Official Seal of the Department of the Environment for Northern Ireland on 8th April 1994.

(L.S.) *R. E. Aiken*

Assistant Secretary

EXPLANATORY NOTE

(This note is not part of the Regulations.)

These regulations further amend the Housing Benefit (General) Regulations (Northern Ireland) 1987. They provide that service charges for general counselling and support are eligible payments for housing benefit only where either the services are related to the provision of adequate accommodation or where the claimant's landlord or the landlord's employee spends the majority of the time, during which he provides services, in the provision of eligible services.

1994   No. 138

SOCIAL SECURITY

The Income Support (General) (Amendment) Regulations (Northern Ireland) 1994

Made	*8th April 1994*
Coming into operation . .	*2nd May 1994*

The Department of Health and Social Services for Northern Ireland, in exercise of the powers conferred on it by sections 122(1)(*a*) and 131(1) of the Social Security Contributions and Benefits (Northern Ireland) Act 1992(**a**) and of all other powers enabling it in that behalf, hereby makes the following regulations:

Citation, commencement and interpretation

1.—(1) These regulations may be cited as the Income Support (General) (Amendment) Regulations (Northern Ireland) 1994 and shall come into operation on 2nd May 1994.

(2) The Interpretation Act (Northern Ireland) 1954(**b**) shall apply to these regulations as it applies to a Measure of the Northern Ireland Assembly.

Amendment of Schedule 3 to the Income Support (General) Regulations

2. In Schedule 3 to the Income Support (General) Regulations (Northern Ireland) 1987(**c**) (housing costs) after paragraph 5 (circumstances in which no amount of housing costs may be met) there shall be inserted the following paragraph—

"Other housing costs which are not met

5A.—(1) Subject to sub-paragraphs (2) to (12), the housing costs referred to in paragraph 1(*a*), (*aa*) and (*b*) (eligible housing costs) shall not be met during the relevant period where those costs were incurred—

(*a*) after 2nd May 1994, and

(*b*) during that same relevant period.

(2) The "relevant period" is any period during which the person who incurred the cost is either—

(*a*) entitled to income support, or

(*b*) living as a member of a family one of whom is entitled to income support,

---

(**a**) 1992 c. 7
(**b**) 1954 c. 33 (N.I.)
(**c**) S.R. 1987 No. 459; relevant amending regulations are S.R. 1988 Nos. 318 and 431, S.R. 1990 No. 131 and S.R. 1993 Nos. 28, 373 and 479

together with any linked period that is to say a period falling between two such periods of entitlement to income support separated by not more than 26 weeks; and for the purposes of this paragraph two or more periods of entitlement and any intervening linked periods form a single relevant period.

(3) Where in the relevant period, before the housing costs referred to in sub-paragraph (1) were incurred ("the new liability"), housing costs of a kind referred to in paragraph 1(*a*), (*aa*) or (*b*) were applicable in the case of the claimant or a member of his family ("the former liability") then, in sub-paragraph (1), the housing costs which are not to be met are such costs, except those costs mentioned in sub-paragraphs (4) and (5)—

> (*a*) except in a case to which head (*b*) applies, as are equal to an amount (if any) by which the new liability exceeds the former liability, and
>
> (*b*) where—
>
>> (i) the former liability has remained and the new liability was incurred in addition to the former liability, and
>>
>> (ii) paragraph 4(6) (circumstances in which a person is or is not to be treated as occupying a dwelling as his home) does not apply in respect of the former liability and the new liability,
>
> as are equal to the amount of the new liability.

(4) The housing costs mentioned in this sub-paragraph are any housing costs in excess of the former liability which are attributable solely to movements in interest rates, and not to an increase in the amount borrowed.

(5) The housing costs mentioned in this sub-paragraph are those met under paragraph 8 (interest on loans for repairs and improvements to the dwelling occupied as the home), but as if for head (*k*) in paragraph 8(3) there was substituted the following head—

> "(*k*) provision of separate sleeping accommodation for children of different sexes aged 10 or over who are part of the same family as the claimant.".

(6) Notwithstanding sub-paragraph (1), the housing costs shall be met in accordance with the provisions of this Schedule in the case of a claimant who satisfies the conditions specified in sub-paragraph (7), (8), (9) or (10), but—

> (*a*) subject to any additional limitations imposed by the sub-paragraph, and
>
> (*b*) where the claimant satisfies the conditions in more than one of those sub-paragraphs, only one sub-paragraph shall apply in his case and the one that applies shall be the one most favourable to him.

(7) The conditions specified in this sub-paragraph are that—

> (*a*) during the relevant period the claimant or a member of his family acquires an interest ("the relevant interest") in a dwelling which he then occupies as his home, and

(*b*) in the week preceding the week in which the relevant interest was acquired, housing benefit was payable to the claimant or a member of his family;

so however that the amount to be met in accordance with this Schedule shall initially not exceed the aggregate of—

(i) the housing benefit payable for that week, and

(ii) any amount included in the applicable amount of the claimant or a member of his family in accordance with regulation 17(1)(*e*) or 18(1)(*f*) in that week,

and shall be increased subsequently only to the extent that it is necessary to take account of any increase, arising after the date of the acquisition, in expenditure on housing costs.

(8) The conditions specified in this sub-paragraph are that the loan was taken out, or an existing loan increased, either—

(*a*) to make adaptations to an existing property to meet the special needs of a disabled person, or

(*b*) to acquire alternative accommodation more suited to the special needs of a disabled person than the accommodation which was occupied before the acquisition by the claimant;

and in this sub-paragraph a disabled person is a person in respect of whom a disability premium, disabled child premium, higher pensioner premium or pensioner premium for persons aged 75 or over is included in his applicable amount or would be so included but for his failure to satisfy other conditions of entitlement to income support.

(9) The conditions specified in this sub-paragraph are that—

(*a*) the loan commitment increased in consequence of the disposal of the dwelling occupied as the home and the acquisition of an alternative such dwelling, and

(*b*) the change of dwelling was made solely by reason of the need to provide separate sleeping accommodation for children of different sexes aged 10 or over who are part of the same family as the claimant.

(10) The conditions specified in this sub-paragraph are that—

(*a*) during the relevant period the claimant or a member of his family acquires an interest (''the relevant interest'') in a dwelling which he then occupies as his home, and

(*b*) in the week preceding the week in which the relevant interest was acquired, the applicable amount of the claimant or a member of his family included an amount determined in accordance with paragraph 1(*c*) to (*g*);

so however that the amount to be met in accordance with this Schedule shall initially not exceed the amount so determined, and shall be increased subsequently only to the extent that it is necessary to take account of any increase, arising after the date of the acquisition, in expenditure on housing costs.

(11) Sub-paragraph (1) shall not apply in relation to—

(a) any accumulated arrears of interest whenever accumulated, and

(b) any interest on a loan for service charges imposed to meet the cost of repairs and improvements to the dwelling occupied as the home.

(12) Paragraphs 6 to 12 shall have effect subject to the provisions of this paragraph.''.

Sealed with the Official Seal of the Department of Health and Social Services for Northern Ireland on 8th April 1994.

(L.S.)

W. G. Purdy

Assistant Secretary

EXPLANATORY NOTE

(This note is not part of the Regulations.)

These Regulations further amend provisions in Schedule 3 to the Income Support (General) Regulations (Northern Ireland) 1987 which relate to housing costs.

Regulation 2 inserts a new paragraph 5A in Schedule 3 to those regulations and provides that payments made on loans taken out whilst the claimant or a member of his family is entitled to income support will not be met. A number of exceptions are made to this provision. They include loans taken out to meet the special needs of a disabled person (paragraph 5A(8)).

These regulations make in relation to Northern Ireland only provision corresponding to provision contained in regulations made by the Secretary of State for Social Security in relation to Great Britain and accordingly, by virtue of section 149(3) of, and paragraph 10 of Schedule 5 to, the Social Security Administration (Northern Ireland) Act 1992 (c. 8), are not subject to the requirement of section 149(2) of that Act for prior reference to the Social Security Advisory Committee.

1994   No. 139

ROAD TRAFFIC AND VEHICLES

Control of Traffic (Lisburn) Order (Northern Ireland) 1994

Made	*11th April 1994*
Coming into operation . .	*23rd May 1994*

WHEREAS the Department of the Environment has published a notice in compliance with Article 23(1) and (2) of the Road Traffic (Northern Ireland) Order 1981(**a**);

AND WHEREAS no objection or representation has been received;

NOW THEREFORE the Department, in exercise of the powers conferred on it by Article 21(1) of the Road Traffic (Northern Ireland) Order 1981 and of every other power enabling it in that behalf, makes the following Order:

Citation and commencement

1. This Order may be cited as the Control of Traffic (Lisburn) Order (Northern Ireland) 1994 and shall come into operation on 23rd May 1994.

Prohibition of right-hand turn

2. A person shall not, except upon the direction or with the permission of a constable in uniform or of a traffic warden, cause or permit a vehicle travelling in a northerly direction along Antrim Road, Lisburn, to make a right-hand turn into Clonevin Park.

Sealed with the Official Seal of the Department of the Environment on 11th April 1994.

(L.S.)

E. J. Galway
Assistant Secretary

(**a**) S.I. 1981/154 (N.I. 1); *see* Article 2(2) for the definition of "Department"

EXPLANATORY NOTE

(This note is not part of the Order.)

This Order prohibits vehicles travelling in a northerly direction along Antrim Road, Lisburn, from making a right-hand turn into Clonevin Park.

Any person who acts in contravention of the Order shall be guilty of an offence and shall be liable on summary conviction to a fine not exceeding level 3 on the standard scale (£400).

Traffic signs indicating the effect of the Order will in due course be erected on the road.

1994   No. 140

HEALTH AND PERSONAL SOCIAL SERVICES

The HSS Trusts (Originating Capital Debt) Order (Northern Ireland) 1994

Made	*31st March 1994*
Coming into operation . .	*31st March 1994*

The Department of Health and Social Services, in exercise of the powers conferred on it by Article 14(1) and (4) of the Health and Personal Social Services (Northern Ireland) Order 1991(**a**), and all other powers enabling it in that behalf, and with the approval of the Department of Finance and Personnel(**b**), hereby makes the following order:

Citation and commencement

1. This Order may be cited as the Health and Social Services Trusts (Originating Capital Debt) Order 1994 and shall come into operation on 31st March 1994.

Originating capital debt of HSS Trusts

2.—(1) The originating capital debt of an HSS trust specifed in column 1 of the Schedule shall be of the amount specified opposite it in column 2.

(2) Each originating capital debt specified in column 2 of the Schedule shall be divided between an initial loan of an amount specified opposite it in column 3 and public dividend capital of an amount specified opposite it in column 4.

Sealed with the Official Seal of the Department of Health and Social Services on 31st March 1994.

(L.S.)

B. McGahan
Assistant Secretary

The Department of Finance and Personnel hereby consents to the foregoing order.

Sealed with the Official Seal of the Department of Finance and Personnel on 31st March 1994.

(L.S.)

F. G. McConnell
Assistant Secretary

(**a**) S.I. 1991/194 (N.I. 1)
(**b**) *See* S.I. 1991/194 Article 14(8)

SCHEDULE

Originating Capital Debts

Column 1 *HSS trust*	Column 2 *Originating Capital Debt* £	Column 3 *Initial Loan* £	Column 4 *Public Dividend Capital* £
Royal Group of Hospitals and Dental Hospital HSS trust	80,408,000	40,204,000	40,204,000
Belfast City Hospital HSS trust	106,216,000	53,108,000	53,108,000
Green Park HSS trust	43,348,000	21,674,000	21,674,000
Eastern Ambulance Service HSS trust	1,768,000	884,000	884,000
Ulster, North Down and Ards Hospitals HSS trust	40,886,000	20,443,000	20,443,000
Craigavon Area Hospitals Group HSS trust	34,717,000	17,358,500	17,358,500

EXPLANATORY NOTE

(This note is not part of the Order.)

This order determines the amount of the originating capital debt provided for in Article 14 of the Health and Personal Social Services Order 1991 of HSS trusts established under that Order with an operational date of 1st April 1993. It provides also for the splitting of the originating capital debts into interest bearing loan and public dividend capital.

1994 No. 141 (C. 5)

ENVIRONMENTAL PROTECTION

The Genetically Modified Organisms (1991 Order) (Commencement No. 1) Order (Northern Ireland) 1994

Made . . . . . *12th April 1994*

The Department of the Environment, in exercise of the powers conferred on it by Article 1(2) of the Genetically Modified Organisms (Northern Ireland) Order 1991(**a**) and paragraph 2(1) of Schedule 1 to the Northern Ireland Act 1974(**b**) and of every other power enabling it in that behalf, hereby makes the following order:

Citation

1. This order may be cited as The Genetically Modified Organisms (1991 Order) (Commencement No. 1) Order (Northern Ireland) 1994.

Appointed day

2. The following provisions of the Genetically Modified Organisms (Northern Ireland) Order 1991 shall come into operation on 1st June 1994:

Articles 1 to 4,

Article 5(1)(*a*) (in so far as it relates to the import or acquisition of genetically modified organisms), (1)(*b*), (3)(*b*), (5), (7), (9) and (10),

Article 7 (in so far as it relates to the import, acquisition, release or marketing of genetically modified organisms),

Article 8(1), (2), (4) to (6), (6A)(**c**), (7) to (11),

Article 9(1)(**d**), (2), (5)(**e**) to (7),

Articles 10 to 12,

Article 13 (in so far as it relates to the import, acquisition, release or marketing of genetically modified organisms),

Article 14,

Article 15(1)(*a*), (*c*), (*e*) to (*l*), (*m*) in so far as it relates to Article 8, (*n*) and (*o*) and (2) to (11),

---

(**a**) S.I. 1991/1714 (N.I. 19)
(**b**) 1974 c. 28
(**c**) Article 8(6A) was inserted by regulation 13 of The Genetically Modified Organisms (Deliberate Release) Regulations (Northern Ireland) 1994 S.R. 1994 No. 144
(**d**) Article 9(1) was amended by regulation 3 of The Genetically Modified Organisms (Modification of Article 9 of the 1991 Order) Regulations (Northern Ireland) 1994 S.R. 1994 No. 142
(**e**) Article 9(5) was amended by regulation 9 of The Genetically Modified Organisms (Deliberate Release) Regulations (Northern Ireland) 1994 S.R. 1994 No. 144

Articles 16 to 18,

Article 19(1)(*c*) to (*h*), and (2) to (4),

Articles 20 to 25.

Sealed with the Official Seal of the Department of the Environment on 12th April 1994.

(L.S.)   *R. W. Rogers*

Assistant Secretary

EXPLANATORY NOTE

(This note is not part of the order.)

This order brings into operation on 1st June 1994 certain provisions of the Genetically Modified Organisms (Northern Ireland) Order 1991 which makes provision for the purpose of preventing or minimising any damage to the environment which may arise from the escape or release from human control of genetically modified organisms.

1994   No. 142

EUROPEAN COMMUNITIES

ENVIRONMENTAL PROTECTION

The Genetically Modified Organisms (Modification of Article 9 of the 1991 Order) Regulations (Northern Ireland) 1994

Made	*12th April 1994*
Coming into operation . .	*1st June 1994*

The Department of the Environment, being a Department designated(**a**) for the purposes of section 2(2) of the European Communities Act 1972(**b**) in relation to measures relating to the control and regulation of genetically modified organisms and of all other powers enabling it in that behalf, hereby makes the following regulations:

Citation and commencement

1. These regulations may be cited as The Genetically Modified Organisms (Modification of Article 9 of the 1991 Order) Regulations (Northern Ireland) 1994 and shall come into operation on 1st June 1994.

Interpretation

2.—(1) In these regulations "the 1991 Order" means the Genetically Modified Organisms (Northern Ireland) Order 1991(**c**).

(2) The Interpretation Act (Northern Ireland) 1954(**d**) shall apply to these regulations as it applies to a Measure of the Northern Ireland Assembly.

Modification of Article 9 of the 1991 Order

3. In Article 9(1) of the 1991 Order (consents: limitations and conditions) the words after "as it may think fit" shall be omitted.

Sealed with the Official Seal of the Department of the Environment on 12th April 1994.

(L.S.)
                                  R. W. Rogers
                                  Assistant Secretary

(**a**)   S.I. 1991/755
(**b**)   1972 c. 68
(**c**)   S.I. 1991/1714 (N.I. 19)
(**d**)   1954 c. 33 (N.I.)

EXPLANATORY NOTE

(This note is not part of the regulations.)

These regulations amend paragraph (1) of Article 9 of the Genetically Modified Organisms (Northern Ireland) Order 1991 in so far as that paragraph offends against Article 4.1 of Council Directive 90/220/EEC (O.J. No. L117, 8.5.90, p. 15) on the deliberate release into the environment of genetically modified organisms.

The effect of the amendment is to provide that limitations and conditions on consents granted by the Department may inter alia be imposed solely for the purpose of securing the health of persons at work.

Copies of the Directive and extracts from the Official Journal of the European Communities may be obtained from Her Majesty's Stationery Office, 16 Arthur Street, Belfast BT1 4GD.

1994   No. 143

HEALTH AND SAFETY

Genetically Modified Organisms (Contained Use) Regulations (Northern Ireland) 1994

Made	*12th April 1994*
Coming into operation . .	*1st June 1994*

ARRANGEMENT OF REGULATIONS

PART I

INTERPRETATION AND GENERAL

PART II

NOTIFICATION OF AND CONSENT FOR ACTIVITIES INVOLVING GENETIC MODIFICATION

PART III

CONDUCT OF ACTIVITIES INVOLVING GENETIC MODIFICATION

PART IV

DISCLOSURE OF INFORMATION NOTIFIED AND PUBLICITY

15. Disclosure of information notified.
16. Register of notifications.

PART V

ADDITIONAL DUTIES PLACED ON THE DEPARTMENT

17. Duties on receiving notifications.
18. Information to be sent to the Department of the Environment.
19. Reports to the European Commission.

PART VI

MISCELLANEOUS AND GENERAL

20. Exemption certificates.
21. Enforcement and civil liability.
22. Fees for notifications.
23. Revocation.
24. Transitional provisions.

THE SCHEDULES

The Department of Economic Development, the Department of Agriculture and the Department of the Environment being Departments designated(**a**) for the purpose of section 2(2) of the European Communities Act 1972(**b**) in relation to the control and regulation of genetically modified organisms, acting jointly in the exercise of the powers conferred on them by the said section 2, and the Department of Economic Development, acting as the Department concerned(**c**), in exercise of the powers conferred by Articles

(**a**) S.I. 1991/775
(**b**) 1972 c. 68
(**c**) *See* Article 2(2) of S.I. 1978/1039 (N.I. 9)

2(5), 17(1) to (5), 40(2), (4) and (6) and 55(2) of, and paragraphs 1(1) and (5), 3(1), 5(1), 7, 8, 9, 10, 12(1), 13, 14(1), 15 and 19 of Schedule 3 to, the Health and Safety at Work (Northern Ireland) Order 1978(**a**) and of every other power enabling them in that behalf, after consultation in accordance with Article 46(1) of that Order with the Health and Safety Agency for Northern Ireland and such other bodies as appeared to them to be appropriate, hereby make the following Regulations:—

PART I

INTERPRETATION AND GENERAL

Citation and commencement

1. These Regulations may be cited as the Genetically Modified Organisms (Contained Use) Regulations (Northern Ireland) 1994 and shall come into operation on 1st June 1994.

Interpretation

2.—(1) In these Regulations—

"the 1991 Regulations" shall be construed in accordance with regulation 23;

"accident" means any incident involving a significant and unintended release of genetically modified organisms in the course of an activity involving genetic modification which presents an immediate or delayed hazard to human health or to the environment;

"approved" means approved in writing for the time being by the Department;

"activity involving genetic modification" means any operation involving the contained use of a genetically modified organism;

"contained use" means any operation in which organisms are genetically modified or in which such genetically modified organisms are cultured, stored, used, transported, destroyed or disposed of and for which physical barriers or a combination of physical barriers with chemical or biological barriers or both, are used to limit their contact with the general population and the environment;

"the Department" means the Department of Economic Development;

"genetic modification" in relation to an organism means the altering of the genetic material in that organism by a way that does not occur naturally by mating or natural recombination or both and within the terms of this definition—

    (*a*) genetic modification occurs at least through the use of the techniques examples of which are listed in Part I of Schedule 1; and

---

(**a**)   S.I. 1978/1039 (N.I. 9)

(b) the techniques listed in Part II of that Schedule are not considered to result in genetic modification,

"genetic modification safety committee" means the committee established in accordance with regulation 11;

"micro-organism" means a microbiological entity, cellular or non-cellular, capable of replication or of transferring genetic material including animal or plant cell cultures;

"the notifier" shall be construed in accordance with regulation 10(1);

"organism" means a biological entity capable of replication or of transferring genetic material and includes a micro-organism;

"self-cloning" means the removal of nucleic acid from a cell or organism, followed by the re-insertion of all or part of that nucleic acid — with or without further enzymic, chemical or mechanical steps — into the same cell type (or cell-line) or into a phylogenetically closely related species which can naturally exchange genetic material with the donor species;

"Type A operation" means any activity involving genetically modified micro-organisms for the purposes of teaching, research, development, or for non-industrial or non-commercial purposes on a scale at which the practices and conditions of the operations relative to the culture, volume and numbers of organisms involved are such that—

(a) the system used to keep the organisms under containment reflects good microbiological practice and good occupational safety and hygiene; and

(b) it is possible easily to render the organisms inactive by standard laboratory decontamination techniques;

"Type B operation" means any activity involving the genetic modification of micro-organisms other than a Type A operation.

(2) Genetically modified organisms shall be classified—

(a) in the case of micro-organisms—

(i) as Group I micro-organisms if they comply with such of the criteria set out in Part I of Schedule 2 as are applicable to the particular case, determined in accordance with the guidelines set out in Part II of that Schedule which gives effect to Commission Decision 91/448/EEC(a), or

(ii) as Group II micro-organisms if they do not comply with the said criteria; or

(b) in the case of genetically modified organisms other than micro-organisms, in accordance with the criteria set out in Part III of Schedule 2.

(3) The Interpretation Act (Northern Ireland) 1954(b) shall apply to these Regulations as it applies to a Measure of the Northern Ireland Assembly.

(a) O.J. No. L239, 28.8.91, p. 23
(b) 1954 c. 33 (N.I.)

Application

3.—(1) These Regulations shall have effect with a view to protecting persons against risks to their health, whether immediate or delayed, and for the protection of the environment, arising from activities involving genetically modified organisms.

(2) Regulations 8 to 12 shall not apply to the transport of genetically modified organisms by road, rail, inland waterway, sea or air.

(3) These Regulations shall not apply to the genetic modification of organisms solely by any of the techniques referred to in Part III of Schedule 1 or to any organisms so modified.

(4) In so far as these Regulations relate to the protection of the environment, they shall only apply to genetically modified micro-organisms.

(5) These Regulations shall have effect without prejudice to any requirement imposed by or under any statutory provision which relates to public health or the protection of the environment.

Meaning of "work" and "at work"

4. For the purpose of these Regulations and Parts I and II of the Health and Safety at Work (Northern Ireland) Order 1978(a) the meaning of the word "work" shall be extended to include any activity involving genetic modification and the meaning of "at work" shall be extended accordingly.

Modification of Article 5(2) of the Health and Safety at Work (Northern Ireland) Order 1978

5. Article 5(2) of the Health and Safety at Work (Northern Ireland) Order 1978 shall be modified in relation to an activity involving genetic modification so as to have effect as if the reference to a self-employed person were a reference to any person who is not an employer or an employee and the reference to his undertaking included a reference to such an activity.

PART II

NOTIFICATION OF AND CONSENT FOR ACTIVITIES INVOLVING GENETIC MODIFICATION

Prohibition of certain work with genetically modified organisms outside containment

6.—(1) Subject to paragraph (2), any operation in which organisms are genetically modified or in which such genetically modified organisms are cultured, stored, used, transported, destroyed or disposed of is prohibited unless it is undertaken in conditions of contained use in accordance with these Regulations.

(2) Paragraph (1) shall not apply to an operation in which—

(a)　S.I. 1978/1039 (N.I. 9); Article 5(2) was modified by S.R. 1982 No. 273

(*a*) genetically modified organisms are cultured, stored, used, transported, destroyed or disposed of, where such organisms are or are contained in a product marketed in pursuance of—

(i) a consent granted by the Department of the Environment for Northern Ireland under Article 8(1) of the Genetically Modified Organisms (Northern Ireland) Order 1991(**a**), or

(ii) a written consent given by another competent authority of a member State in accordance with Article 13(4) of Council Directive 90/220/EEC(**b**) on the deliberate release into the environment of genetically modified organisms, and

in either case, the operation is conducted in accordance with any conditions or limitations attached to that consent,

(*b*) genetically modified organisms are released or marketed in circumstances in which the consent of the Department of the Environment for Northern Ireland is required under Article 8(1) of the Genetically Modified Organisms (Northern Ireland) Order 1991.

(3) In this regulation, "product" means a product consisting of or containing a genetically modified organism or a combination of genetically modified organisms.

Risk assessment

7.—(1) A person shall not—

(*a*) use any premises for activities involving genetic modification for the first time; or

(*b*) undertake any activity involving genetic modification,

unless he has ensured that, before commencing that use or activity, as the case may be, a suitable and sufficient assessment of the risks created thereby to human health and the environment has been made.

(2) Without prejudice to the generality of paragraph (1), the purposes of the assessment made under that paragraph shall include—

(*a*) classifying any genetically modified organisms involved in the activity in accordance with the provisions of Schedule 2; and

(*b*) where appropriate, making decisions about the levels of containment required for the activity concerned.

(3) A person making the assessment required by paragraph (1) shall in doing so—

(*a*) in particular, take due account of the matters set out in Schedule 3 in as far as they are relevant; and

(*b*) in a case in which the Department has approved a method in relation to the activity involving genetic modification concerned or in relation to a particular element of that assessment, undertake the assessment in accordance with that method.

(**a**) S.I. 1991/1714 (N.I. 19)
(**b**) O.J. No. L117, 8.5.90, p. 15

(4) An assessment made under paragraph (1) shall be reviewed forthwith if—

(*a*) there is reason to suspect that the assessment is no longer valid; or

(*b*) there has been a significant change in the activity to which the assessment relates.

(5) The person making the assessment required by paragraph (1) shall make a record of it and of any subsequent review under paragraph (4) and shall keep that record for at least 10 years from the date on which use of the premises or the activity, as the case may be, to which the assessment related, ceased.

Notification of the intention to use premises for activities involving genetic modification for the first time

8.—(1) Subject to paragraphs (2) to (6) and to regulation 10, a person shall not undertake any activity involving genetic modification at any premises for the first time, unless he has notified the Department of his intention to do so at least 90 days in advance or before such shorter time as the Department may approve and with that notification has furnished the information specified in Schedule 4.

(2) In the case of activities involving the genetic modification of micro-organisms, separate notifications shall be made of an intention to use the premises for activities involving genetically modified micro-organisms classified as Group I or Group II.

(3) In the case of activities involving genetically modified micro-organisms classified as Group II, the premises shall be used for those activities only after the Department has given its consent.

(4) In any other case, the use of the premises for the activity may be commenced at or after the end of the period of 90 days or such shorter period as the Department may have approved in pursuance of paragraph (1) unless the Department objects in writing before the end of the relevant period.

(5) In any case in which a consent is required under paragraph (3), the Department shall communicate its decision on the application in writing within 90 days after the application was received.

(6) Nothing in this regulation shall prevent a person from notifying under regulation 9 an individual activity which he intends to undertake in the premises at the same time as making a notification under this regulation; in such a case he shall not commence the activity except in accordance with the time periods specified in this regulation.

Notification of individual activities involving genetic modification

9.—(1) Subject to paragraphs (2) to (7) and to regulation 10, a person shall not undertake any activity involving genetic modification unless he has notified the Department of his intention to do so at least 60 days in advance or before such shorter time as the Department may approve and has furnished the information specified in the following paragraphs and, except in the case of an activity to which paragraph (5) applies, the activity may be commenced after the expiry of the relevant period if by then the Department has not objected in writing.

(2) In the case of an activity which is—

(*a*) a Type A operation involving only micro-organisms classified as Group I; or

(*b*) an activity involving genetically modified organisms other than micro-organisms and which satisfy the criteria set out in Part III of Schedule 2,

it shall be a sufficient compliance with paragraph (1) if the person undertaking the activity keeps a record of such activities and at the end of each calendar year notifies the Department—

(i) of the total number of risk assessments under regulation 7 undertaken during that year;

(ii) where appropriate, that he is intending to continue to undertake such activities; and

(iii) that the information notified to the Department in accordance with regulation 8 remains correct.

(3) In the case of an activity which is a Type B operation involving only micro-organisms classified as Group I, the information to be furnished for the purposes of paragraph (1) shall be that specified in Part I of Schedule 5.

(4) In the case of an activity which is—

(*a*) a Type A operation involving genetically modified micro-organisms classified as Group II; or

(*b*) an activity involving genetically modified organisms other than micro-organisms and which do not satisfy the criteria set out in Part III of Schedule 2,

the information to be furnished for the purposes of paragraph (1) shall be that specified in Parts I and II of Schedule 5.

(5) In the case of an activity which is a Type B operation involving genetically modified micro-organisms classified as Group II, the information to be furnished for the purposes of paragraph (1) shall be that specified in Parts I, II and III of Schedule 5 and the activity shall be commenced only after the Department has given its consent.

(6) In any case in which a consent is required under paragraph (5), the Department shall communicate its decision on the application in writing within 90 days after the application was received.

(7) The Department may accept as a single notification a connected programme of work covering more than one activity involving genetic modifications at one site, or a single activity carried on by the same person at more than one site.

Additional provisions relating to notifications and consents

10.—(1) Where necessary for the purpose of evaluating a notification made under regulation 8 or 9, the Department may require in writing the person making that notification (''the notifier'') to give such additional information relating to such notification as it may specify and, in such a case, the notifier shall not proceed with the activity involving genetic modification until the Department gives its approval, and the period between the time when the Department requires the information to be given and the notifier responds to the satisfaction of the Department shall not be taken into account in calculating any period of time referred to in these Regulations.

(2) Any consent given by the Department under regulation 8 or 9 may be given subject to conditions or to a limit of time and may be revoked or varied at any time and in such a case the person undertaking the activity shall comply with those conditions.

(3) In so far as it relates to the protection of the environment, the Department shall not give, vary or revoke a consent under regulation 8 or 9, or give its approval under paragraph (1), without the agreement of the Department of the Environment for Northern Ireland.

(4) Where the notifier subsequently makes a significant change in the use of any premises or in any activity to which the notification relates or becomes aware of any new information which would affect the information previously furnished, he shall forthwith notify the Department thereof.

(5) If information subsequently becomes available to the Department which could have significant consequences for the risks to human health or the environment created by an activity involving genetic modification which has been notified to it, it may require the notifier to modify the conditions under which the activity is undertaken, or to suspend or terminate the activity.

(6) Notifications made in pursuance of regulations 8 and 9 shall be in a form approved by the Department.

Establishment of a genetic modification safety committee

11. A person who makes an assessment in accordance with regulation 7(1) shall establish a genetic modification safety committee to advise him in relation to the making of that assessment.

PART III

CONDUCT OF ACTIVITIES INVOLVING GENETIC MODIFICATION

Standards of occupational and environmental safety and containment

12.—(1) In relation to any activity involving genetically modified micro-organisms classified as Group I, the principles of good microbiological practice and the following principles of good occupational safety and hygiene shall apply—

(*a*) to keep workplace and environmental exposure to any physical, chemical and biological agent adequately controlled;

(*b*) to exercise engineering control methods at source and to supplement these with appropriate personal protective clothing and equipment where necessary;

(*c*) to test and maintain control measures and equipment;

(*d*) to test, when necessary, for the presence of viable process organisms outside the primary physical containment;

(*e*) to provide training of personnel; and

(*f*) to formulate and implement local rules for the safety of personnel.

(2) For the purpose of paragraph (1) "adequate" in relation to the control of an agent means adequate having regard only to the nature of the agent and the nature and degree of exposure to such an agent.

(3) In relation to any activities involving genetically modified micro-organisms classified as Group II in Type A operations, in addition to the principles set out in paragraph (1) the containment measures shall be determined by a method approved by the Department.

(4) In relation to any activities involving genetically modified micro-organisms classified as Group II in Type B operations, in addition to the principles set out in paragraph (1) the containment measures set out in Schedule 6 shall be applied at a level appropriate to ensure a high level of health and safety and environmental protection.

(5) In relation to any activities involving genetically modified organisms other than micro-organisms, the principles set out in paragraph (1) shall be applied in as far as they are appropriate.

Emergency plans

13.—(1) Where the assessment made in accordance with regulation 7(1) shows that as a result of any reasonably foreseeable accident the health or safety of persons outside the premises in which an activity involving genetic modification is carried on is liable to be affected or that there is a risk of damage to the environment, the person undertaking the activity shall ensure that a suitable emergency plan is prepared with a view to securing the health and safety of those persons and the protection of the environment.

(2) Subject to paragraph (3), the person preparing an emergency plan under paragraph (1) shall consult such persons, bodies and authorities as are appropriate and shall inform the emergency services in writing of the plan and of the hazards to which the plan relates.

(3) Where an emergency plan required by paragraph (1) relates to a reasonably foreseeable accident which is liable to affect another member State, the person preparing that emergency plan shall, in addition to consulting the persons, bodies and authorities described in paragraph (2), forthwith consult the Department.

In this paragraph "reasonably foreseeable accident" shall be construed in accordance with paragraph (1).

(4) Where the Department has been consulted in accordance with paragraph (3), it shall consult the other member State in the drawing up and implementation of the emergency plan referred to in paragraph (3).

In this paragraph "the other member State" shall be construed in accordance with paragraph (3).

(5) Where the Department is required to be consulted in accordance with paragraph (3) the person preparing the emergency plan under paragraph (1)

shall not conclude the preparation of that plan without the consent of the Department.

(6) Subject to paragraph (5), where an emergency plan has been prepared in accordance with paragraph (1) the person undertaking the activity involving genetic modification shall take appropriate measures to inform persons who are liable to be affected by an accident of the safety measures to be taken and the correct behaviour to be adopted in the event of an accident.

(7) The information required to be given in pursuance of paragraph (6) shall be repeated and brought up to date at appropriate intervals and shall be made publicly available.

Notification of accidents

14.—(1) Where an accident occurs, the person undertaking the activity involving genetically modified organisms shall forthwith notify the Department of it and shall provide the following information—

(a) the circumstances of the accident;

(b) the identity and quantity of genetically modified organisms released;

(c) any information necessary to assess the effects of the accident on the health of the general population and on the environment; and

(d) the emergency measures taken.

(2) Where the Department receives a notification in pursuance of paragraph (1), the Department shall—

(a) ensure that any emergency, medium and long term measures are taken;

(b) immediately inform any other member State that could be affected by the accident;

(c) collect, where possible, the information necessary for a full analysis of the accident and, where appropriate, make recommendations to avoid similar accidents in the future and to limit their effects; and

(d) send to the European Commission the information provided for under paragraph (1), together with an analysis of the accident and details of any recommendations made in accordance with sub-paragraph (c).

PART IV
DISCLOSURE OF INFORMATION NOTIFIED AND PUBLICITY

Disclosure of information notified

15.—(1) The information notified in pursuance of regulations 8 to 10 shall not be treated as relevant information for the purposes of Article 30 of the Health and Safety at Work (Northern Ireland) Order 1978.

(2) Where the notifier indicates that the disclosure of certain information might harm his competitive position and should therefore be kept confidential, full justification for that indication shall be given and in such a case after consulting the notifier the Department shall decide which information shall be kept confidential and shall inform the notifier of its decision.

(3) Nothing in paragraph (2) shall apply to the following information which shall not be kept confidential—

    (*a*) the name and address of the notifier;

    (*b*) the location of the activity involving genetic modification;

    (*c*) the purpose of the activity;

    (*d*) the description of the genetically modified organism involved;

    (*e*) methods and plans for monitoring the genetically modified organism and for emergency response; and

    (*f*) the evaluation of foreseeable effects and in particular pathogenic effects and ecologically disruptive effects.

(4) Notwithstanding paragraph (3), where the Department is satisfied on the basis of detailed evidence submitted to it by the notifier and where appropriate, after consultation with the notifier, that it is necessary to withhold, for the time being, certain of the information specified in paragraph (3) in order to protect his intellectual property rights, the Department shall withhold that information to the extent and for so long as it is necessary to protect those rights.

(5) Information which is kept confidential in accordance with paragraph (2) or withheld in accordance with paragraph (4) shall be disclosed only—

    (*a*) to the Department of the Environment for Northern Ireland;

    (*b*) to the Department of Agriculture for Northern Ireland;

    (*c*) to the Health and Safety Executive(**a**);

    (*d*) to the European Commission or the competent authority for another member State;

    (*e*) for the purpose of any legal proceedings;

    (*f*) with the consent of the notifier; or

    (*g*) to the extent necessary to evaluate the notification.

(6) A person who receives information in accordance with sub-paragraph (*g*) of paragraph (5) shall not use that information except for a purpose of the Department or the Department of the Environment for Northern Ireland.

(7) Where the notifier has requested that certain information in the notification shall be kept confidential in accordance with paragraph (2) or withheld in accordance with paragraph (4), the Department shall not disclose any of that information (except in accordance with paragraph (5)) until at least 14 days after it has reached a decision under the relevant paragraph.

(8) After consulting the notifier, the Department may review any decision made under paragraph (2) or (4) and shall inform the notifier of the result of that review.

(9) Where the notifier withdraws a notification to which regulations 8 to 10 relate, the Department shall not thereafter disclose any of the information furnished with such notification.

(**a**) Established under 1974 c. 37 section 10(1)

Register of notifications

16.—(1) The Department shall maintain a register of notifications to which regulation 8(3) or 9(5) relate (for which the consent of the Department is required) and that register shall be open to inspection by members of the public at any reasonable time.

(2) The register referred to in paragraph (1) shall contain in relation to each such notification—

(*a*) such of the information referred to in regulation 15(3) as has not been withheld in accordance with paragraph (4) of that regulation; and

(*b*) a statement as to whether or not the consent of the Department has been given.

(3) The information referred to in paragraph (2)(*a*) shall be entered in the register within 14 days of its receipt by the Department and the information referred to in paragraph 2(*b*) within 14 days of the decision whether to give the consent or not having been made, except that where the notifier has requested that certain information specified in regulation 15(3) be withheld in accordance with regulation 15(4), that information shall only be entered in the register not less than 14 days but not more than 28 days after the Department has made a decision not to withhold that information.

(4) Copies of the register referred to in paragraph (1) shall be maintained at the office of the Department at 83 Ladas Drive, Belfast, BT6 9FJ.

PART V

ADDITIONAL DUTIES PLACED ON THE DEPARTMENT

Duties on receiving notifications

17. The Department shall examine a notification under regulation 8 or 9 for—

(*a*) the conformity with the requirements of these Regulations;

(*b*) the accuracy and completeness of the information given;

(*c*) the correctness of the classification of the organisms to which the notification relates in accordance with Schedule 2; and

(*d*) where appropriate, the adequacy of the waste management, safety and emergency response measures.

Information to be sent to the Department of the Environment

18. Forthwith after receipt, the Department shall send to the Department of the Environment for Northern Ireland a copy in each case of—

(*a*) any notification received under regulation 8 or 9;

(*b*) any requirement for further information under regulation 10(1) and any response thereto; and

(*c*) any notification relating to an accident under regulation 14,

and if requested to do so by the Department of the Environment for Northern Ireland shall require the notifier to give additional information under regulation 10(1).

Reports to the European Commission

19. The Department shall send to the European Commission reports of notifications for which a consent is required under regulation 9(5) and summary reports of the application of these Regulations in accordance with Article 18 of Council Directive No. 90/219/EEC(**a**) on the contained use of genetically modified micro-organisms.

PART VI

MISCELLANEOUS AND GENERAL

Exemption certificates

20.—(1) Subject to paragraph (2) and to any provisions imposed by the European Communities in respect of the control and regulation of genetically modified organisms, the Department may, with the agreement of the Department of the Environment for Northern Ireland in so far as the exemption relates to the environment, by a certificate in writing, exempt any person or class of persons, genetically modified organism or class of genetically modified organisms from all or any of the requirements or prohibitions imposed by these Regulations and any such exemption may be granted subject to conditions and to a limit of time and may be revoked by a certificate in writing at any time.

(2) The Department shall not grant any such exemption unless, having regard to the circumstances of the case and in particular to—

(*a*) the conditions, if any, that it proposes to attach to the exemption; and

(*b*) any requirements imposed by or under any statutory provision which applies to the case,

it is satisfied that the health and safety of persons who are likely to be affected by the exemption or the protection of the environment will not be prejudiced in consequence of it.

Enforcement and civil liability

21.—(1) In so far as any provision of regulations 6 to 14 is made under section 2 of the European Communities Act 1972(**b**)—

(*a*) the provisions of the Health and Safety at Work (Northern Ireland) Order 1978 relating to enforcement and offences shall apply to that provision as if that provision had been made under Article 17 of that Order; and

(*b*) in the event of a breach of duty imposed by that provision, it shall confer a right of action in civil proceedings if that breach of duty causes damage.

(**a**) O.J. No. L117, 8.5.90, p. 1
(**b**) 1972 c. 68

(2) Notwithstanding regulation 4 of the Health and Safety (Enforcing Authority) Regulations (Northern Ireland) 1993(**a**) ("the 1993 Regulations") the enforcing authority for these Regulations shall be the Department, except that in so far as these Regulations relate to agricultural activities within the meaning of regulation 2(1) of the 1993 Regulations the enforcing authority shall be the Department of Agriculture for Northern Ireland.

Fees for notifications

22.—(1) Fees shall be payable in accordance with paragraph (2) by a notifier to the Department in relation to any matter referred to in that paragraph.

(2) The fees referred to in paragraph (1) shall be—

(*a*) subject to sub-paragraph (*b*), on each notification of the intention to use premises for activities involving genetic modification for the first time under regulation 8, £100;

(*b*) on each notification of the intention to use premises for activities involving genetic modification for the first time, where a consent is required under regulation 8(3), £130;

(*c*) subject to sub-paragraph (*d*), on each notification of individual activities involving genetic modification under regulation 9, £180;

(*d*) on each notification of individual activities involving genetic modification for which a consent is required under regulation 9(5), £270.

(3) This regulation shall not apply to any notification made for the purposes of regulation 24(1) or (3) (which relates to transitional provisions).

Revocation

23. Subject to regulation 24, the Genetic Manipulation Regulations (Northern Ireland) 1991(**b**) ("the 1991 Regulations") are hereby revoked.

Transitional provisions

24.—(1) Where before 1st June 1994 a person had notified the Department of his intention to undertake activities involving genetic modification which complied with regulation 5(1) and (2)(*a*) of the 1991 Regulations as then in operation, that notification shall be treated as satisfying the requirements of regulation 8 except that regulation 8(3) shall apply to that activity on or after 1st June 1995.

(2) Before 30th August 1994 it shall be a sufficient compliance with regulation 8 if the notifier commences the activity having notified his intention to do so 30 days in advance or such shorter time in advance as the Department may approve and regulation 8(3) shall not apply to activities commenced before 30th August 1994 until 1st June 1995.

(**a**)   S.R. 1993 No. 147
(**b**)   S.R. 1991 No. 238

(3) Where before 1st June 1994 a person had notified the Department of his intention to undertake activities involving genetic modification which complied with regulation 5(1) and (2)(*b*) of the 1991 Regulations as then in operation, that notification shall be treated as satisfying the requirements of regulation 9 except that regulation 9(5) shall apply to that activity on or after 1st June 1995.

(4) Before 31st July 1994 it shall be a sufficient compliance with regulation 9 if the notifier of an activity involving genetic modification had notified it in accordance with that regulation 30 days in advance or such shorter time in advance as the Department may approve and regulation 9(5) shall not apply to activities commenced before 31st July 1994 until 1st June 1995.

(5) Regulation 10 shall apply to any notification made on or after 1st June 1994.

Sealed with the Official Seal of the Department of Economic Development on 12th April 1994.

(L.S.) *Philip B. Strong*
Assistant Secretary

Sealed with the Official Seal of the Department of Agriculture on 12th April 1994.

(L.S.) *I. C. Henderson*
Assistant Secretary

Sealed with the Official Seal of the Department of the Environment on 12th April 1994.

(L.S.) *R. W. Rogers*
Assistant Secretary

Definition of genetic modification

PART I

EXAMPLES OF TECHNIQUES CONSTITUTING GENETIC MODIFICATION

1. Examples of the techniques which constitute genetic modification which are referred to in sub-paragraph (*a*) of the definition of genetic modification in regulation 2(1) are—

(*a*) recombinant DNA techniques consisting of the formation of new combinations of genetic material by the insertion of nucleic acid molecules, produced by whatever means outside the cell, into any virus, bacterial plasmid or other vector system so as to allow their incorporation into a host organism in which they do not occur naturally but in which they are capable of continued propagation;

(*b*) techniques involving the direct introduction into an organism of heritable material prepared outside the organism including micro-injection, macro-injection and micro-encapsulation; and

(*c*) cell fusion (including protoplast fusion) or hybridization techniques where live cells with new combinations of heritable genetic material are formed through the fusion of two or more cells by means of methods that do not occur naturally.

PART II

TECHNIQUES WHICH ARE NOT CONSIDERED TO RESULT IN GENETIC MODIFICATION

2. The following techniques are not considered to result in genetic modification if they do not involve the use of recombinant-DNA molecules or genetically modified organisms—

(*a*) in vitro fertilization;

(*b*) conjugation, transduction, transformation or any other natural process; and

(*c*) polyploidy induction.

PART III

TECHNIQUES TO WHICH THESE REGULATIONS DO NOT APPLY

3. These Regulations shall not apply to the following techniques of genetic modification if they do not involve the use of genetically modified organisms as recipient or parental organisms—

(*a*) mutagenesis;

(*b*) the construction and use of somatic hybridoma cells (for example for the production of monoclonal antibodies);

(*c*) cell fusion (including protoplast fusion) of plant cells where the resulting organisms can also be produced by traditional breeding methods;

(*d*) self-cloning of non-pathogenic naturally occurring micro-organisms which fulfil the criteria of Group I for recipient micro-organisms; and

(*e*) self-cloning of non-pathogenic naturally occurring organisms other than micro-organisms which fulfil the criteria of Part III of Schedule 2.

Criteria for the classification of genetically modified organisms

PART I

CRITERIA AS APPLICABLE FOR CLASSIFICATION OF GENETICALLY MODIFIED MICRO-ORGANISMS AS GROUP I MICRO-ORGANISM

1. *Recipient or parental organism*

(*a*) non-pathogenic;

(*b*) no adventitious agents;

(*c*) proven and extended history of safe use or built-in biological barriers, which, without interfering with optimal growth in the reactor or fermenter, confer limited survivability and replicability, without adverse consequences in the environment.

2. *Vectors/Insert*

(*a*) well characterised and free from known harmful sequences;

(*b*) limited in size as much as possible to the genetic sequences required to perform the intended function;

(*c*) should not increase the stability of the construct in the environment (unless that is a requirement of intended function);

(*d*) should be poorly mobilisable;

(*e*) should not transfer any resistance markers to micro-organisms not known to acquire them naturally (if such acquisition could compromise use of drugs to control disease agents).

3. *Genetically modified micro-organisms*

(*a*) non-pathogenic;

(*b*) as safe in the reactor or fermenter as recipient or parental organism, but with limited survivability and/or replicability without adverse consequences in the environment.

4. *Other genetically modified micro-organisms that could be included in Group I if they meet the conditions in paragraph 3*

(*a*) those constructed entirely from a single prokaryotic recipient (including its indigenous plasmids and viruses) or from a single eukaryotic recipient (including its chloroplasts, mitochondria, plasmids, but excluding viruses);

(*b*) those that consist entirely of genetic sequences from different species that exchange these sequences by known physiological processes.

PART II

GUIDELINES AS APPLICABLE FOR CLASSIFICATION OF GENETICALLY MODIFIED MICRO-ORGANISMS AS GROUP I MICRO-ORGANISMS

For classification into Group I the following guidelines should be used to further interpret Part I.

5. *Characteristics of the recipient or parental organism(s)*

(1) Non-pathogenic

The recipient or parental organisms can be classified as non-pathogenic if they satisfy the conditions of one of the following heads—

(a) the recipient or parental strain should have an established record of safety in the laboratory and/or industry, with no adverse effects on human health and the environment;

(b) the recipient or parental strain does not meet the conditions of head (a) but it belongs to a species for which there is a long record of biological work including safety in the laboratory and/or industry, showing no adverse effects on human health and the environment;

(c) if the recipient or parental organism is a strain which does not satisfy the conditions of head (a) and belongs to a species for which there is no record of biological work including safe use in the laboratory and/or industry, appropriate testing (including, if necessary, animals) must be carried out, in order to establish non-pathogenicity and safety in the environment;

(d) if a non-virulent strain of an acknowledged pathogenic species is used, the strain should be as deficient as possible in genetic material that determines virulence so as to ensure no reversion to pathogenicity. In the case of bacteria, special attention should be given to plasmid or phage-borne virulence determinants.

(2) No adventitious agents

The recipient or parental strain/cell line should be free of known biological contaminating agents (symbionts, mycoplasms, viruses, viroids, etc.), which are potentially harmful.

(3) The recipient or parental strain/cell line should have proven and extended history of safe use or built-in biological barriers, which, without interfering with optimal growth in the reactor or fermenter, confer limited survivability and replicability, without adverse consequences in the environment (applicable only for Type B operations).

6. *Characteristics of the vector*

(1) The vector should be well characterised

For this purpose the following characteristics should be taken into account.

(a) Information on composition and construction

(i) the type of the vector should be defined (virus, plasmid, cosmid, phasmid, transposable element, minichromosome, etc.);

(ii) the following information on the constituent fragments of the vector should be available—

(aa) the origin of each fragment (progenitor genetic element, strain of organism in which the progenitor genetic element naturally occurred),

(bb) if some fragments are synthetic, their functions should be known;

(iii) the methods used for construction should be known.

(b) Information on vector structure

(i) the size of the vector should be known and expressed in basepairs or D;

(ii) the function and relative positions of the following should be known—

(aa) structural genes,

(*bb*)   marker genes for selection (antibiotic resistance, heavy metal resistance, phage immunity, genes coding for degradation of xenobiotics, etc.),

(*cc*)   regulatory elements,

(*dd*)   target sites (nic-sites, restriction endonuclease sites, linkers, etc.),

(*ee*)   transposable elements (including provirus sequences),

(*ff*)   genes related to transfer and mobilisation function (for example with respect to conjugation, transduction or chromosomal integration),

(*gg*)   replicon(s).

(2) The vector should be free from harmful sequences

The vector should not contain genes coding for potentially harmful or pathogenic traits (for example virulence determinants, toxins, etc.) unless for Type A operations, such genes constitute an essential feature of the vector without, under any conditions or circumstances, resulting in a harmful or pathogenic phenotype of the genetically modified micro-organism.

(3) The vector should be limited in size as much as possible to the genetic sequences required to perform the intended function.

(4) The vector should not increase the stability of the genetically modified micro-organism in the environment (unless that is a requirement of the intended function).

(5) The vector should be poorly mobilisable

(*a*) If the vector is a plasmid—

   (i) it should have a restricted host-range;

  (ii) it should be defective in transfer-mobilisation factors for example Tra⁻, Mob⁺, for Type A operations or Tra⁻, Mob⁻, for Type B operations.

(*b*) If the vector is a virus, cosmid or phasmid—

   (i) it should have a restricted host-range;

  (ii) it should be rendered non-lysogenic when used as a cloning vector (for example defective on the cI-lambda repressor).

(6) It should not transfer any resistance markers to micro-organisms not known to acquire them naturally (if such acquisition could compromise use of drugs to control disease agents).

7. *Required characteristics of the insert*

(1) The insert should be well characterised

For this purpose, the following characteristics should be taken into account.

(*a*) The origin of the insert should be known (genus, species, strain).

(*b*) The following information on the library from which the insert originated, should be known—

   (i) the source and method for obtaining the nucleic acid of interest (cDNA, chromosomal, mitochondrial, etc.);

  (ii) the vector in which the library was constructed (for example lambda gt 11, pBR 322, etc.) and the site in which the DNA was inserted;

 (iii) the method used for identification (colony, hybridization, immuno-blot, etc.);

 (iv) the strain used for library construction.

(*c*) If the insert is synthetic, its intended function should be identified.

(*d*) The following information on the structure of the insert is required—

    (i) information on structural genes, regulatory elements;

    (ii) size of the insert;

    (iii) restriction endonuclease sites flanking the insert;

    (iv) information on transposable elements and provirus sequences.

(2) The insert should be free from harmful sequences—

(*a*) the function of each genetic unit in the insert should be defined (not applicable for Type A operations);

(*b*) the insert should not contain genes coding for potentially harmful or pathogenic traits (for example virulence determinants, toxins, etc.), (unless for Type A operations, such genes constitute an essential part of the insert without, under any circumstances, resulting in a harmful or pathogenic phenotype of the genetically modified micro-organism).

(3) The insert should be limited in size as much as possible to the genetic sequences required to perform the intended function.

(4) The insert should not increase the stability of the construct in the environment (unless that is a requirement of intended function).

(5) The insert should be poorly mobilisable.

For instance, it should not contain transposing or transferable provirus sequences and other functional transposing sequences.

8. *Required characteristics of the genetically modified micro-organism*

(1) The genetically modified micro-organism should be non-pathogenic.

This requirement is reasonably assured by compliance with all the requirements above.

(2) (*a*) The genetically modified micro-organism should be as safe (to man and the environment) as the recipient or parental strains (applicable only for Type A operations);

    (*b*) the genetically modified micro-organisms should be as safe in the reactor or fermenter as the recipient or parental strains, but with limited survivability and/or replicability outside the reactor or fermenter without adverse consequences in the environment (applicable only for Type B operations).

9. *Other genetically modified micro-organisms that could be included in Group 1 if they meet the conditions in paragraph 8*

(1) Those constructed entirely from a single prokaryotic recipient (including its indigenous plasmids and viruses) or from a single eukaryotic recipient (including its chloroplasts, mitochondria, plasmids, but excluding viruses).

(2) Those that consist entirely of genetic sequences from different species that exchange these sequences by known physiological processes.

PART III

CRITERIA FOR THE CLASSIFICATION OF ORGANISMS OTHER THAN MICRO-ORGANISMS

An organism which satisfies the criteria of this Part is a genetically modified organism—

(*a*) which is not a genetically modified micro-organism; and

(*b*) which is as safe in the containment facility as any recipient or parental organism.

Matters to be taken into account in making a risk assessment under Regulation 7

Characteristics of the donor, recipient or (where appropriate) parental organism

1. The following matters shall be investigated and assessed in relation to any organism which is or will be a donor, recipient or parental organism—

(*a*) the name, species, subspecies and strain of the organism;

(*b*) the degree of relatedness between the donor, recipient and (where appropriate) parental organism in relation to which the assessment is being carried out;

(*c*) the sources of the organism;

(*d*) the reproductive cycle of the organism;

(*e*) history of prior genetic modifications to the organism;

(*f*) the stability of the genetic traits of the organism;

(*g*) the nature of the pathogenicity, virulence, infectivity, toxicity, and vectors of disease transmission of the organism;

(*h*) the base sequence, frequency of mobilisation and specificity of the organism's indigenous vectors;

(*i*) the presence in the organism of genes which confer resistance;

(*j*) the host range of an organism which is a parasite or pathogen;

(*k*) the organism's other potentially significant physiological traits, and the stability of those traits;

(*l*) the organism's natural habitat and geographic distribution;

(*m*) the climactic characteristics of the organism's natural habitat;

(*n*) the significant involvement of the organism in environmental processes, including nitrogen fixation and pH regulation;

(*o*) the interaction of the organism with other organisms in the environment and its effect on those organisms, including its likely competitive or symbiotic properties;

(*p*) the ability of the organism to form survival structures, including seeds, spores or sclerotia.

Characteristics of the modified organism

2. The following matters shall be investigated and assessed in relation to an organism in relation to which a risk assessment under regulation 7 is carried out—

(*a*) the description of the modification, including the technique used or proposed to be used to introduce a vector or insert into the organism;

(*b*) the nature and source of the vector introduced into the organism;

(*c*) the function of the genetic modification and/or of the new nucleic acid;

(*d*) the structure and amount of any vector or donor nucleic acid remaining in the final construction of the modified organism;

(*e*) the stability of the genetic traits introduced into the organism;

(*f*) the frequency of mobilisation of inserted vector or genetic transfer capability;

(*g*) the rate and level of expression of the new genetic material in the organism, and the method and sensitivity of measurement of that rate and level;

(*h*) the activity of the expressed protein.

Health considerations

3. The following matters shall be investigated and assessed in relation to an organism in relation to which a risk assessment under regulation 7 is carried out—

(*a*) toxic or allergenic effects of non-viable organisms and/or their metabolic products;

(*b*) product hazards;

(*c*) comparison of the modified micro-organism to the donor, recipient or (where appropriate) parental organism regarding pathogenicity;

(*d*) capacity for colonization;

(*e*) if the organism is pathogenic to humans who are immunocompetent—

    (i) diseases caused and mechanism of pathogenicity including invasiveness and virulence,

    (ii) communicability,

    (iii) infective dose,

    (iv) host range, possibility of alteration,

    (v) possibility of survival outside of human host,

    (vi) presence of vectors or means of dissemination,

    (vii) biological stability,

    (viii) antibiotic-resistance patterns,

    (ix) allergenicity,

    (x) availability of appropriate therapies.

Environmental considerations

4. The following matters shall also be investigated and assessed in relation to an organism in relation to which a risk assessment under regulation 7 is carried out—

(*a*) the factors affecting survival, multiplication and dissemination of the modified organism in the environment;

(*b*) the available techniques for detection, identification, and monitoring of the modified organism in the environment;

(*c*) the available techniques for detecting transfer of the new genetic material to other organisms;

(*d*) the known and predicted habitats of the modified organism;

(*e*) the ecosystems to which the modified organism could be disseminated as a result of an escape;

(*f*) the anticipated mechanism and result of interaction between the modified organism and the organisms which might be exposed in case of the escape of the organism;

(*g*) the known or predicted effects of the organism on plants and animals, including pathogenicity, infectivity, toxicity, virulence, vector or pathogen allergenicity, colonisation, predation, parasitism, symbiosis and competition;

(*h*) the known or predicted involvement of the organism in biogeochemical processes, including nitrogen fixation and pH regulation;

(*i*) the availability of methods for decontamination of the area in case of release to the environment.

Information required for a notification under Regulation 8(1)

A notification required for the purposes of regulation 8(1) shall include the following information—

(a) the name and address of the person responsible for carrying out the activity and the names of persons responsible for supervision, monitoring and safety together with details of their training and qualifications;

(b) address of the premises where the activity is to be carried on and its grid reference and, where appropriate, a description of the sections of the installation;

(c) a description of the nature of the activity to be undertaken, the likely scale of the operation and in particular, in the case of genetically modified micro-organisms, their classification in accordance with regulation 2(2);

(d) a summary of the risk assessment undertaken in accordance with regulation 7;

(e) the names of the members of the genetic modification safety committee and the capacity in which each member serves;

(f) comments made by the genetic modification safety committee on the local arrangements for risk assessment;

(g) the names of the biological and deputy biological safety officers concerned with the intended activities (if any);

(h) the name of the supervisory medical officer (if any);

(i) the arrangements for health surveillance (if any); and

(j) any other information the Department may require for the purpose of maintaining the register referred to in regulation 16.

Information required for a notification under Regulation 9

PART I

INFORMATION REQUIRED UNDER REGULATION 9(3)

1. A notification required for the purposes of regulation 9(3) shall include the following information—

(*a*) the name and address of the person responsible for carrying out the activity;

(*b*) address of the premises where the activity is to be carried out;

(*c*) the date of the notification referred to in regulation 8(1);

(*d*) the parental organism used, or where applicable the host-vector system used;

(*e*) the source and the intended function of the genetic material involved in the modification;

(*f*) the identity and characteristics of the genetically modified organism;

(*g*) the purpose of the activity including the expected results;

(*h*) where appropriate the culture volumes to be used or the scale of the activity;

(*i*) details of waste treatment including levels of live genetically modified micro-organisms in the waste; and

(*j*) a summary of the risk assessment required in accordance with regulation 7 and of the comments of the genetic modification safety committee on that risk assessment.

PART II

INFORMATION REQUIRED UNDER REGULATION 9(4)

2. In addition to the information required under Part I a notification made for the purposes of regulation 9(4) shall contain the following information—

(*a*) a description of the sections of the installation involved and the methods for handling the organisms;

(*b*) a description of the predominant meteorological conditions and the potential sources of danger arising from the location of the installation;

(*c*) a description of the protective and supervisory methods to be applied throughout the duration of the activity; and

(*d*) in the case of micro-organisms, the containment level to which the micro-organism has been allocated in accordance with the risk assessment made in accordance with regulation 7(1) and in any case the safety precautions to be observed.

PART III

INFORMATION REQUIRED UNDER REGULATION 9(5)

3. In addition to the information required under Parts I and II a notification made for the purposes of regulation 9(5) shall, subject to paragraph 4, contain the information specified in paragraph 5.

4. If it is not technically possible, or if it does not appear necessary to give the information specified in paragraph 5, the reason shall be stated. The level of detail required in response to each subset of considerations is likely to vary according to the nature and scale of the proposed activity. In the case of information already submitted to the Department by the notifier under these Regulations (or the 1991 Regulations) reference may be made to that information by him.

5. The additional information required is—

(*a*) information about the genetically modified micro-organisms—

  (i) the identity and characteristics of the genetically modified micro-organisms,

  (ii) the purpose of the contained use or the nature of the product,

  (iii) the host-vector system to be used where applicable,

  (iv) the culture volume to be used,

  (v) behaviour and characteristics of the micro-organisms in the case of changes in the conditions of containment or release into the environment,

  (vi) overview of the potential hazards associated with the release of the micro-organisms into the environment, and

  (vii) substances which are or may be produced in the course of use of the micro-organisms other than the intended product;

(*b*) information about personnel—

  (i) the maximum number of persons working in the installation, and

  (ii) the number of persons who will work directly with the micro-organisms;

(*c*) information about the installation—

  (i) the activity in which the micro-organisms are to be used,

  (ii) the technological processes used,

  (iii) a description of the sections of the installation involved, and

  (iv) the predominant meteorological conditions and specific hazards arising from the location of the installation;

(*d*) information about waste management—

  (i) types, quantities and potential hazards of wastes arising from the use of the micro-organisms,

  (ii) waste management techniques used including recovery of liquid or solid wastes and the inactivation techniques used, and

  (iii) ultimate form and destination of inactivated wastes;

(*e*) information about accident prevention and emergency response plans—

  (i) the sources of hazards and conditions under which accidents might occur,

  (ii) the preventive measures applied such as safety equipment, alarm systems, containment methods and procedures and available resources,

  (iii) a description of information given to workers, and

  (iv) the information necessary for the Department to evaluate any emergency plan prepared in accordance with regulation 13;

(*f*) the full risk assessment referred to in regulation 7; and

(*g*) any other information the Department may require for the purpose of maintaining the register referred to in regulation 16.

Containment measures for micro-organisms classified as Group II

1. The containment measures for Type B operations using micro-organisms classified as Group II shall be chosen by the user from the levels in the Table as appropriate to the micro-organism and the operation in question in order to ensure the protection of health of the general population and the environment.

2. Type B operations shall be considered in the terms of their unit operations. The characteristics of each operation will dictate the physical containment to be used at that stage. This will allow the selection and design of process, plant and operating procedures best fitted to ensure adequate and safe containment. Two important factors to be considered when selecting the equipment needed to implement the containment are the risk of, and the effects consequent on, equipment failure. Engineering practice may require increasingly stringent standards to reduce the risks of failure as the consequence of that failure becomes less tolerable.

TABLE

	Containment Levels		
Specifications	*B2*	*B3*	*B4*
1. Viable micro-organisms should be contained in a system which physically separates the process from the environment (closed system)	Yes	Yes	Yes
2. Exhaust gases from the closed system should be treated so as to:	Minimise release	Prevent release	Prevent release
3. Sample collection, addition of materials to a closed system and transfer of viable micro-organisms to another closed system, should be performed so as to:	Minimise release	Prevent release	Prevent release
4. Bulk culture fluids should not be removed from the closed system unless the viable micro-organisms have been:	Inactivated by validated means	Inactivated by validated chemical or physical means	Inactivated by validated chemical or physical means
5. Seals should be designed so as to:	Minimise release	Prevent release	Prevent release

TABLE

Specifications	Containment Levels		
	B2	B3	B4
6. Closed systems should be located within a controlled area	Optional	Optional	Yes, and purpose-built
(a) Biohazard signs should be posted	Optional	Yes	Yes
(b) Access should be restricted to nominated personnel only	Optional	Yes	Yes, via airlock
(c) Personnel should wear protective clothing	Yes, work clothing	Yes	Yes, a complete change
(d) Decontamination and washing facilities should be provided for personnel	Yes	Yes	Yes
(e) Personnel should shower before leaving the controlled area	No	Optional	Yes
(f) Effluent from sinks and showers should be collected and inactivated before release	No	Optional	Yes
(g) The controlled area should be adequately ventilated to minimise air contamination	Optional	Optional	Yes
(h) The controlled area should be maintained at an air pressure negative to atmosphere	No	Optional	Yes
(i) Input air and extract air to the controlled area should be HEPA filtered	No	Optional	Yes

TABLE

	Containment Levels		
Specifications	B2	B3	B4
(*j*) The controlled area should be designed to contain spillage of the entire contents of the closed system	Optional	Yes	Yes
(*k*) The controlled area should be sealable to permit fumigation	No	Optional	Yes
7. Effluent treatment before final discharge	Inactivated by validated means	Inactivated by validated chemical or physical means	Inactivated by validated physical means

EXPLANATORY NOTE

(This note is not part of the Regulations.)

1. These Regulations implement as regards Northern Ireland Council Directive 90/219/EEC (O.J. No. L117, 8.5.90, p. 1) on the contained use of genetically modified micro-organisms. The Regulations also revoke the Genetic Manipulation Regulations (Northern Ireland) 1991 ("the 1991 Regulations").

2. These Regulations have effect with a view to protecting persons and the environment from risks arising from activities involving the contained use of genetically modified organisms.

3. These Regulations do not apply to certain techniques listed in Part III of Schedule 1. Regulations 8 to 12 do not apply to the transport of genetically modified organisms by road, rail, inland waterway, sea or air.

Part I (Interpretation and general — Regulations 1 to 5)

4. In addition to defining the terms used and the scope of the Regulations, this Part extends the meaning of "work" in Parts I and II of the Health and Safety at Work (Northern Ireland) Order 1978 to include any activity involving the contained use of genetically modified organisms.

Part II (Notification of and consent for activities involving genetic modification — Regulations 6 to 11)

5. Part II prohibits the use of premises for activities involving the contained use of genetically modified organisms for the first time and also individual activities involving the contained use of those organisms unless a suitable risk assessment has been made. Provision is also made for prior notification of such first use of premises or individual activities to the Department of Economic Development ("the Department") and in certain specified cases the first use of premises for the activity concerned can be commenced only with the Department's consent.

6. Regulation 11 provides for the establishment of a genetic modification safety committee to advise in relation to any risk assessment required under the Regulations.

Part III (Conduct of activities involving genetic modification — Regulations 12 to 14)

7. The regulations in Part III specify standards of occupational and environmental safety required for the conduct of activities involving the contained use of genetically modified organisms and make provision in connection with the preparation of emergency plans where, as a result of a reasonably foreseeable accident, there is a risk to the health of persons outside the premises in which the activity is carried on or to the environment. Where another member State is liable to be affected by the reasonably foreseeable accident, the Department is required to consult that member State in the drawing up and implementation of the emergency plan. Information in relation to emergency plans must be made publicly available and updated. Where an accident occurs certain information is required to be notified to the Department which is under a duty to inform any other member State that could be affected and to send certain information to the European Commission.

Part IV (Disclosure of information notified and publicity — Regulations 15 and 16)

8. Part IV specifies the circumstances in which information provided to the Department is to be disclosed and also provides for a public register of notifications requiring consent to be kept.

Part V (Additional duties placed on the Department — Regulations 17 to 19)

9. Part V imposes duties on the Department to examine notifications received and send particulars notified to the Department of the Environment for Northern Ireland. The Department is also required to send to the European Commission reports of notifications for which a consent is required.

Part VI (Miscellaneous and general — Regulations 20 to 24)

10. Part VI provides for, in certain circumstances, exemptions from the Regulations to be granted by the Department, for enforcement by the Department or, in specified circumstances, by the Department of Agriculture,

and for fees to be charged by the Department in relation to notifications. Regulation 24 contains transitional provisions relating to notifications made under the 1991 Regulations so that they continue to have effect in certain circumstances.

11. Schedule 1 sets out examples of techniques which constitute genetic modification and the techniques which are not considered to result in genetic modification.

Schedule 2 sets out the criteria for classification of organisms.

Schedule 3 sets out the matters to be investigated and assessed in making a risk assessment under regulation 7.

Schedule 4 sets out the information required in relation to a notification of intention to use premises for activities involving genetic modification for the first time.

Schedule 5 sets out the information to be furnished where a person intends to undertake certain activities involving genetic modification.

Schedule 6 sets out containment measures to be applied in relation to activities involving certain genetically modified micro-organisms.

12. A person who contravenes these Regulations is guilty of an offence under Article 31 of the Health and Safety at Work (Northern Ireland) Order 1978.

1994   No. 144

EUROPEAN COMMUNITIES

ENVIRONMENTAL PROTECTION

The Genetically Modified Organisms (Deliberate Release) Regulations (Northern Ireland) 1994

Made . . . . .   *12th April 1994*

Coming into operation . .   *1st June 1994*

ARRANGEMENT OF REGULATIONS

PART I

GENERAL

PART II

RELEASE OF GENETICALLY MODIFIED ORGANISMS

PART III

MARKETING GENETICALLY MODIFIED ORGANISMS

PART IV

The Department of the Environment, being a Department designated(**a**) for the purposes of section 2(2) of the European Communities Act 1972(**b**), in relation to measures relating to the control and regulation of genetically modified organisms, in exercise of the powers conferred by that section and Articles 3(4) and (5), 4(8), 8(1), (4), (5), (7) and (11), 19(1) and 20(7) of the Genetically Modified Organisms (Northern Ireland) Order 1991(**c**), and of all other powers enabling it in that behalf and being of the opinion that the techniques referred to in regulation 3(*c*) would produce organisms which should for the purposes of the said Order be treated as having been genetically modified, hereby makes the following regulations:

(**a**) S.I. 1991/755
(**b**) 1972 c. 68
(**c**) S.I. 1991/1714 (N.I. 19). *See* Article 2(2) for the definition of "the Department". *See* Article 8(11) for the definition of "prescribed" in that Article

PART I

GENERAL

Citation and commencement

1. These regulations may be cited as The Genetically Modified Organisms (Deliberate Release) Regulations (Northern Ireland) 1994 and shall come into operation on 1st June 1994.

Interpretation

2.—(1) In these regulations—

"the Commission" means the Commission of the Communities;

"the Deliberate Release Directive" means Council Directive 90/220/ EEC(**a**) on the deliberate release into the environment of genetically modified organisms;

"genetically modified organisms" includes a combination of genetically modified organisms;

"heritable genetic material" means genes or other genetic material, in any form, whether in cellular or sub-cellular entities, which are capable of being replicated or transferred by any means;

"the Order" means the Genetically Modified Organisms (Northern Ireland) Order 1991;

"product" means a product consisting of or including genetically modified organisms and "approved product" means a product marketed in pursuance of and in accordance with a consent or a consent given by another competent authority of a member State under Article 13(4) of the Deliberate Release Directive.

(2) The Interpretation Act (Northern Ireland) 1954(**b**) shall apply to these regulations as it applies to a Measure of the Northern Ireland Assembly.

Artificial techniques of genetic modification

3. The following techniques are prescribed as artificial techniques for the purposes of Article 3(4) of the Order—

(*a*) the insertion by any method into a virus, bacterial plasmid or other vector system of a nucleic acid molecule, which has been produced by any method outside that virus, bacterial plasmid or other vector system, so as to produce a new combination of genetic material which is capable of being inserted into an organism in which that combination does not occur naturally and within which it will be heritable genetic material;

(*b*) the insertion into an organism, by micro-injection, macro-injection, micro-encapsulation or other direct means, of heritable genetic material prepared outside that organism;

(**a**) O.J. No. L117, 8.5.90, p. 15
(**b**) 1954 c. 33 (N.I.)

(c) the fusion (including protoplast fusion) or hybridisation, by any method that does not occur naturally, of 2 or more cells to form cells which have new combinations of heritable genetic material, and which (if derived solely from plant cells) cannot be produced by traditional breeding methods;

(d) where they involve the use of recombinant DNA molecules—

(i) *in vitro* fertilisation,

(ii) conjugation, transduction, transformation or any other natural process,

(iii) polyploidy induction.

Requirement to disregard capacity of certain organisms for causing harm, etc.

4.—(1) For the purposes of Articles 7(1), 9(5)(**a**) and (7)(*a*) and 14(1) of the Order there shall be disregarded—

(*a*) the capacity of genetically modified organisms of the description specified in paragraph (2) for causing harm of the description specified in paragraph (3), and

(*b*) harm, caused by genetically modified organisms of the description specified in paragraph (2), which is of the description specified in paragraph (3).

(2) The genetically modified organisms specified in this paragraph are genetically modified organisms which control—

(*a*) the number or activity (or both) of any organisms, or

(*b*) toxic wastes.

(3) The harm specified in this paragraph is harm caused to any organisms by genetically modified organisms which have been released or marketed in pursuance of and in accordance with—

(*a*) a consent, or

(*b*) a consent given by another competent authority of a member State under Article 13.4 of the Deliberate Release Directive.

PART II

RELEASE OF GENETICALLY MODIFIED ORGANISMS

Consent to release genetically modified organisms

5.—(1) Subject to paragraphs (3) and (4), the cases and circumstances prescribed under Article 8(1)(*a*) of the Order in relation to the release of any genetically modified organisms are any cases and circumstances other than the release of an approved product in accordance with the conditions and limitations to which the use of the product is subject.

(**a**)   Article 9(5) is amended by regulation 9

(2) An application for consent to release genetically modified organisms must be made in writing to the Department, and must be made either—

(a) for one or more releases of one or more descriptions of genetically modified organisms on the same site for the same purpose within a limited period, or

(b) for one or more releases of one description of genetically modified organisms on one or more sites for the same purpose within a limited period.

(3) Paragraph (1) shall not apply to a person who—

(a) has, in accordance with regulation 5(1)(a) of the Genetic Manipulation Regulations (Northern Ireland) 1991(**a**), notified the Department of Economic Development of his intention to carry out an activity involving an intentional introduction into the environment, and

(b) carries out the activity in accordance with that notification before 29th August 1994.

(4) Paragraph (1) shall not apply to a person who releases a product which was marketed in the United Kingdom before 1st June 1994 and is not an approved product.

Information to be contained in application for consent to release

6.—(1) Subject to regulation 7 (exemptions from regulation 6), the following is the information which an application for a consent to release genetically modified organisms must contain—

(a) the information prescribed in Schedule 1, to the extent that such information is appropriate to the proposed release;

(b) information on data or results from any previous release of the same organisms, or of organisms of the same description, which has been carried out by the applicant, and information from any previous application for the release of the organisms, or of organisms of the same description, which the applicant has submitted to the Department under these regulations or to another competent authority of a member State under Article 5 of the Deliberate Release Directive;

(c) a statement evaluating the impacts and risks posed to human health and the environment by the release of the organisms;

(d) a statement whether the detailed description of the organisms and the details of the purpose for which the organisms will be released have been published, and the bibliographic reference for any information so published;

(e) a summary, in the format established by the Commission under Article 9.1 of the Deliberate Release Directive, of the information contained in the application.

(**a**) S.R. 1991 No. 238

(2) The information prescribed in Schedule 1 shall be included in the application at the level of detail which is appropriate to the nature and scale of the proposed release.

(3) Where the applicant considers, on the basis that it is not technically possible or it does not appear to the applicant to be necessary, that it is not appropriate for the application to contain the information prescribed in one or more of the paragraphs of Schedule 1, the application shall contain a statement of the reasons why the inclusion of the information is not appropriate.

(4) The application must contain the description of the methods used to obtain the information contained in the application in accordance with paragraph (1) and a bibliographic reference, or, where standardised or internationally recognised methods are used, a reference to which method was used to obtain the information and its bibliographic references, together with the name of the body responsible for carrying out the studies.

(5) The application may in addition contain data or results from an application for consent to release genetically modified organisms previously made by some other person, provided that a copy of that person's agreement in writing is contained in the application.

Exemptions from regulation 6

7. An application for a consent to release genetically modified organisms need not contain the information prescribed in regulation 6(1)(*a*) and (*b*) if—

(*a*) the information was contained either—

    (i) in an application which was made by the same person in relation to a previous release of those organisms or of the same description of organisms, or

    (ii) in an application which was made by some other person in relation to a previous release of those organisms or of the same description of organisms,

(*b*) the application refers to the previous application in which the information was contained, and

(*c*) where paragraph (*a*)(ii) applies, the application contains the agreement in writing of the person who made the previous application to a reference to that application being made.

Advertisement of application for consent to release

8.—(1) Subject to paragraph (2), a person who makes an application for a consent to release genetically modified organisms shall, not less than 14 days and not more than 28 days after the date of acknowledgement of receipt of that application by the Department, cause to be published in a newspaper or newspapers circulating in the areas likely to be affected by the proposed release a notice containing the following information—

(*a*) the name and address of the applicant,

(*b*) the general description of the organisms to be released, (*c*) the location and general purpose of the release, and

(*d*) the foreseen dates of the release.

(2) Where the information on the location of the release which has been placed on the register maintained by the Department under Article 19 of the Order differs in its level of detail from that contained in the application for consent, the notice shall contain the level of detail regarding the location of the release which appears on the register.

(3) A person who makes an application for a consent to release genetically modified organisms shall, not less than 14 days and not more than 28 days after the date of acknowledgement of receipt of that application is sent to him by the Department, send to the following persons notice that he has made the application and the information prescribed in paragraph (1)(*a*) to (*d*)—

(*a*) the owner of the site of the proposed release, if a person other than the applicant,

(*b*) the district council for the area in which the site of the proposed release is situated,

(*c*) the Department of Agriculture for Northern Ireland,

(*d*) each member of the genetic modification safety committee established by the applicant under regulation 11 of the Genetically Modified Organisms (Contained Use) Regulations (Northern Ireland) 1994(**a**).

General condition on consents to release genetically modified organisms

9. For Article 9(5)(*b*) of the Order there shall be substituted the following sub-paragraph—

"(*b*) notify the Department of—

(i) any new information which becomes available with regard to any risks there are of damage to the environment being so caused, and

(ii) the effects of any releases by him for the assessment of any risks there are of damage to the environment being so caused by such organisms being released or marketed;".

PART III

MARKETING GENETICALLY MODIFIED ORGANISMS

Consent to market products containing genetically modified organisms

10.—(1) The cases prescribed under Article 8(1)(*a*) of the Order in relation to the marketing of any genetically modified organisms are any cases other than the marketing of a product in accordance with a written consent given by another competent authority of a member State under Article 13.4 of the Deliberate Release Directive.

(**a**) S.R. 1994 No. 143

(2) An application for a consent to market genetically modified organisms must be made in writing to the Department, and must be made either—

(a) where the product has not previously been marketed in pursuance of and in accordance with a consent granted by the Department under Article 8(1) of the Order or a written consent given by another competent authority of a member State in accordance with Article 13.4 of the Deliberate Release Directive, or

(b) where the product is intended for a use for which it has not previously been marketed in pursuance of and in accordance with a consent granted by the Department under Article 8(1) of the Order or a written consent given by another competent authority of a member State in accordance with Article 13.4 of the Deliberate Release Directive.

Information to be contained in application for consent to market

11.—(1) The following is the information which an application for a consent to market genetically modified organisms must contain—

(a) the information prescribed in Schedule 1, to the extent that such information is appropriate to the nature and scale of the release which may result from the marketing,

(b) information on data or results from any previous release of the organisms, or of organisms of the same description, which have been carried out by the applicant and information from any previous application for consent to release the organisms, or organisms of the same description which the applicant has submitted to the Department under these regulations or to another competent authority of a member State under Article 5 of the Deliberate Release Directive,

(c) subject to paragraph (5), the information prescribed in Schedule 2,

(d) a summary, in the format established by the Commission under Article 12.3 of the Deliberate Release Directive, of the information contained in the application.

(2) The information prescribed in Schedule 1 shall be included in the application at the level of detail which is appropriate to the nature and scale of the release which may result from the marketing, and shall take into account the diversity of sites of use of the product, including—

(a) information on data and results obtained from research and developmental releases concerning the ecosystems which could be affected by the use of the product, and

(b) an assessment of any risks for human health or the environment related to the genetically modified organisms contained in the product, including information obtained from the research and development stage on the impact of the release on the environment.

(3) Where the applicant considers, on the basis that it is not technically possible or it does not appear to the applicant to be necessary, that it is not appropriate for the application to contain the information prescribed in one or more of the paragraphs of Schedule 1, the application shall contain a

statement of the reasons why the inclusion of the information is not appropriate.

(4) The application must contain the description of the methods used to obtain the information prescribed in Schedule 1 and a bibliographic reference or, where standardised or internationally recognised methods are used, a reference to which method was used to obtain the information and its bibliographic references, together with the name of the body responsible for carrying out the studies.

(5) Where the applicant considers, on the basis of the results of any release in pursuance of and in accordance with a consent or a consent given by another competent authority of a member State under Article 13.4 of the Deliberate Release Directive, or on substantive, reasoned scientific grounds, that the placing on the market and use of the product do not pose a risk to human health or the environment, he may propose not to supply the information prescribed in Part II of Schedule 2.

(6) An application may in addition contain data or results from an application for consent to market genetically modified organisms previously submitted by some other person, provided that a copy of that person's agreement in writing is contained in the application.

Transitional provision for marketing

12. Regulation 10(1) shall not apply to a person who markets a product which—

(*a*) was marketed by him in the United Kingdom before 1st June 1994, and

(*b*) is not an approved product,

until 1st June 1996.

PART IV

DUTIES OF APPLICANTS AND THE DEPARTMENT AFTER THE MAKING OF APPLICATIONS

Duty of the applicant after applying for consent

13.—(1) In Article 8 of the Order (consents required by certain persons), after paragraph (6) there shall be inserted the following paragraph—

"(6A) Where an applicant for consent for releasing or marketing genetically modified organisms becomes aware, before his application is either granted or rejected, of any new information with regard to any risks there are of damage to the environment being caused as a result of the organisms being released or marketed, he shall notify the Department of that new information forthwith.".

(2) In Article 15(1)(*e*) of the Order (offences), after the words "Article 5(5) or (6)" there shall be inserted the words "or Article 8(6A)".

Duties of the Department on receiving applications for consent to release

14.—(1) The Department shall within 30 days of receiving an application for a consent to release genetically modified organisms forward to the Commission a summary of that application in the format established by the Commission under Article 9.1 of the Deliberate Release Directive.

(2) The Department shall on receipt and after acknowledgement of such an application—

(*a*) examine it for compliance with the Order and these regulations,

(*b*) evaluate the risks posed by the proposed release,

(*c*) if necessary, carry out such tests or inspections as may be necessary for control purposes,

(*d*) where appropriate, take into account any comments made by the competent authority or authorities of member States following the circulation to them by the Commission of the summary referred to in paragraph (1), and

(*e*) record its conclusions in writing.

Decisions by the Department on applications for consent to release

15.—(1) The Department shall not grant a consent to release genetically modified organisms as it relates to the protection of human health without the agreement of the Department of Economic Development.

(2) The Department shall give its decision in writing on an application for a consent to release genetically modified organisms to the applicant within 90 days of receipt of the application.

(3) The period prescribed in paragraph (2) shall not include any period beginning with and including the day on which the Department gives notice in writing under Article 8(6) of the Order that further information in respect of the application is required and ending with and including the day on which that information is received by the Department.

(4) The Department shall inform the competent authority or authorities of each member State and the Commission of its decision on each such application.

(5) The Department shall not revoke or vary a consent to release genetically modified organisms as it relates to the protection of human health without the agreement of the Department of Economic Development.

Duties of the Department in relation to applications for consent to market

16.—(1) The Department shall examine an application for consent to market genetically modified organisms for its compliance with the Order and these regulations, giving particular attention to the environmental risk assessment and the recommended precautions related to the safe use of the product.

(2) Before the end of a period of 90 days beginning with the day on which it receives any such application for consent to market genetically modified organisms the Department shall either—

(*a*) forward to the Commission—

  (i) the application,

  (ii) a summary of the application in the format established by the Commission under Article 12.3 of the Deliberate Release Directive,

  (iii) a statement of the conditions under which it proposes to consent to the marketing of the product,

  (iv) where acceded to by the Department, details of any proposal by the applicant under regulation 11(5) not to comply with any of the requirements of regulation 11(1)(*c*), and

  (v) its favourable opinion on the application, or

(*b*) inform the applicant that the proposal does not fulfil the conditions of the Order and these regulations and is rejected.

(3) The Department shall not forward its favourable opinion on the application as it relates to the protection of human health where the Department of Economic Development has informed it that it does not fulfil the conditions of the Order and these regulations.

(4) The period prescribed in paragraph (2) shall not include any period beginning with and including the day on which the Department gave notice under Article 8(6) of the Order that further information in respect of the application is required and ending with and including the day on which that information is received by the Department.

(5) The Department shall immediately inform the competent authority or authorities of each member State and the Commission of any other information it receives from the applicant before or after the granting of the consent.

(6) Where no objection has been raised by a competent authority of a member State the Department shall, within a period of 60 days following the day on which the documents referred to in paragraph (2)(*a*) were forwarded to the competent authority or authorities of the member States by the Commission, grant consent to market the genetically modified organisms and inform the competent authority or authorities of the member States and the Commission that it has done so.

(7) Where an objection has been raised by a competent authority of a member State and the Commission has taken a favourable decision under Article 13.3 of the Deliberate Release Directive, the Department shall grant consent to market the genetically modified organisms and inform the competent authority or authorities of the member States and the Commission that it has done so.

(8) The Department shall not revoke or vary a consent to market genetically modified organisms as it relates to the protection of human health without the agreement of the Department of Economic Development, and shall immediately inform the competent authority or authorities of each member State and the Commission of any decision to revoke or vary a consent.

PART V

REGISTER OF INFORMATION

Information to be included in register

17.—(1) The register maintained by the Department under Article 19 of the Order shall contain the particulars set out in paragraphs (2) to (7).

(2) In relation to a prohibition notice served under Article 7 of the Order—

(*a*) the name and address of the person on whom the notice is served,

(*b*) the description of the genetically modified organisms in relation to which the notice is served,

(*c*) the location at which the genetically modified organisms are proposed to be released,

(*d*) the purpose for which the genetically modified organisms are proposed to be released or marketed,

(*e*) the reason for the service of the notice,

(*f*) the date specified in the notice as the date on which the prohibition is to take effect.

(3) Subject to paragraph (4), in relation to an application for a consent under Article 8 of the Order—

(*a*) the name and address of the applicant,

(*b*) the general description of the genetically modified organisms in relation to which the application is being made,

(*c*) the location at which the genetically modified organisms are proposed to be released,

(*d*) the general purpose for which the genetically modified organisms are proposed to be released or marketed,

(*e*) the foreseen dates of the release,

(*f*) the methods and plans for monitoring the genetically modified organisms and for emergency response,

(*g*) the evaluation of the environmental impact of the genetically modified organisms, in particular any pathogenic and/or ecologically disruptive effects, and

(*h*) either—

   (i) the conditions or limitations under which the consent is granted, or

   (ii) a summary of the reasons for not granting the consent.

(4) Where—

(*a*) the application is for a consent to market genetically modified organisms,

(*b*) an application for a consent to release genetically modified organisms contains a statement that a detailed description of the organisms and the details of the purpose for which the organisms will be released have been published, or

(c) the Department is notified, under the conditions of a consent to release genetically modified organisms which it granted in relation to an application, that a detailed description of the organisms and the details of the purpose for which the organisms will be released have been published,

the information prescribed under paragraph (3)(b) shall be the detailed description of the organisms in relation to which the application is made and the information prescribed under paragraph (3)(d) shall be the details of the purpose for which the organisms will be released.

(5) In relation to consents granted under Article 8 of the Order—

(a) the fact that the consent has been granted, and a reference to the application in respect of which it was granted,

(b) any conditions or limitations to which the consent is subject,

(c) any information supplied to the Department in accordance with those conditions or limitations,

(d) the fact that the consent has been revoked or varied, and the contents of the notice by which the consent was revoked or varied.

(6) In relation to information furnished under Article 8(6A)(a) or 9(5)(b)(i)(**b**) of the Order, any new information which becomes available with regard to any risks there are of damage to the environment, and in relation to information furnished under Article 9(5)(b)(ii) of the Order, the effects of any releases for the assessment of any risks there are of damage to the environment.

(7) In relation to convictions for any offence under Article 15 of the Order—

(a) the name and address of the person convicted,

(b) the description of any genetically modified organisms in relation to which the conviction was obtained,

(c) the offence which was committed,

(d) the penalty imposed and any order made by the court under Article 17 of the Order.

Keeping of the register

18.—(1) The particulars prescribed in regulation 17(2) shall be placed on the register within 14 days of the prohibition notice being served.

(2) Subject to paragraphs (3) and (4) the particulars prescribed in regulation 17(3) shall be placed on the register within 14 days of the receipt by the Department of the application for consent to release or market.

(3) Where regulation 17(4)(c) applies, the particulars prescribed in regulation 17(3)(b) and (d) shall be placed on the register within 28 days of the Department being notified, under the conditions of a consent to release genetically modified organisms which it granted in relation to an application,

---

(**a**)   Article 8(6A) is inserted by regulation 13
(**b**)   Article 9(5)(b) is amended by regulation 9

that a detailed description of the organisms and the details of the purpose for which those organisms will be released have been published.

(4) The particulars prescribed in regulation 17(3)(*h*) shall be placed on the register within 14 days of the consent being either granted or not granted.

(5) The particulars prescribed in regulation 17(5)(*a*), (*b*) and (*d*) shall be placed on the register within 14 days of the consent being granted, revoked or varied, as appropriate.

(6) The particulars prescribed in regulation 17(5)(*c*), (6) and (7) shall be placed on the register within 14 days of their receipt by the Department.

Sealed with the Official Seal of the Department of the Environment on 12th April 1994.

(L.S.)

R. W. Rogers

Assistant Secretary

No. 144   *Environmental Protection*   799
SCHEDULE 1   regulations 6
and 11

Information to be contained in consent to release or market genetically modified organisms

PART I

GENERAL INFORMATION

1. The name and address of the applicant, and the name, qualifications and training of the responsible scientist and of every other person who will be responsible for planning and carrying out the release of the organisms, and for the supervision, monitoring and safety of the release.

PART II

INFORMATION RELATING TO THE ORGANISMS

Characteristics of donor, parental and recipient organisms

2. Scientific name and taxonomy.

3. Usual strain, cultivar or other name.

4. Phenotypic and genetic markers.

5. The degree of relatedness between the donor and recipient organisms or between the parental organisms.

6. The description of identification and detection techniques.

7. The sensitivity, reliability (in quantitative terms) and specificity of detection and identification techniques.

8. The description of the geographic distribution and of the natural habitat of the organisms including information on natural predators, prey, parasites, competitors, symbionts and hosts.

9. The potential of the organisms for genetic transfer and exchange with other organisms.

10. Verification of the genetic stability of the organisms and factors affecting that stability.

11. The following pathological, ecological and physiological traits—

(*a*) the classification of hazard according to existing Community rules concerning the protection of human health and the environment;

(*b*) the generation time in natural ecosystems, and sexual and asexual reproductive cycle;

(*c*) survivability, including seasonability and the ability to form survival structures, including seeds, spores and sclerotia;

(*d*) pathogenicity, including infectivity, toxigenicity, virulence, allergenicity, carrier (vector) of pathogen, possible vectors, host range including non-target organisms and possible activation of latent viruses (proviruses), and ability to colonise other organisms;

(*e*) antibiotic resistance, and potential use of these antibiotics in humans and domestic organisms for prophylaxis and therapy; and

(*f*) involvement in environmental processes, including primary production, nutrient turnover, decomposition of organic matter and respiration.

12. The sequence, frequency of mobilisation and specificity of indigenous vectors, and the presence in those vectors of genes which confer resistance to environmental stresses.

13. The history of genetic modification and of any application of additional techniques to the organism.

Characteristics of the vector

14. The nature and source of the vector.

15. The sequence of transposons, vectors and other non-coding genetic segments used to construct the genetically modified organisms and to make the introduced vector and insert function in those organisms.

16. The frequency of mobilisation, genetic transfer capabilities and/or methods of determination of the inserted vector.

17. The degree to which the vector is limited to the DNA required to perform the intended function.

Characteristics of the modified organisms

18. The methods used for the modification.

19. The methods used—

(*a*) to construct inserts and to introduce them into the recipient organism;

(*b*) to delete a sequence.

20. The description of any insert and/or vector construction.

21. The purity of the insert from any unknown sequence and information on the degree to which the inserted sequence is limited to the DNA required to perform the intended function.

22. The sequence, functional identity and location of the altered, inserted or deleted nucleic acid segments in question, and in particular any known harmful sequence.

Characteristics of the genetically modified organisms

23. The description of the genetic traits or phenotypic characteristics and in particular any new traits and characteristics which may be expressed or no longer expressed.

24. The structure and amount of any vector or donor nucleic acid remaining in the final construction of the modified organisms.

25. The stability of the organisms in terms of genetic traits.

26. The rate and level of expression of the new genetic material in the organisms, and the method and sensitivity of measurement of that rate and level.

27. The activity of the gene product.

28. The description of identification and detection techniques, including techniques for the identification and detection of the inserted sequence and vector.

29. The sensitivity, reliability (in quantitative terms), and specificity of detection and identification techniques.

30. The history of previous releases or uses of the organisms.

31. In relation to human health—
(a) the toxic or allergenic effects of the non-viable organisms and/or their metabolic products;
(b) the product hazards;
(c) the comparison of the organisms to the donor, recipient or (where appropriate) parental organisms regarding pathogenicity;
(d) the capacity of the organisms for colonisation; and
(e) if the organisms are pathogenic to humans who are immunocompetent—
  (i) diseases caused and mechanisms of pathogenicity including invasiveness and virulence,
  (ii) communicability,
  (iii) infective dose,
  (iv) host range and possibility of alteration,
  (v) possibility of survival outside of human host,
  (vi) presence of vectors or means of dissemination,
  (vii) biological stability,
  (viii) antibiotic-resistance patterns,
  (ix) allergenicity, and
  (x) availability of appropriate therapies.

PART III

INFORMATION RELATING TO CONDITIONS OF RELEASE

The release
32. The description of the proposed deliberate release, including the purpose or purposes of the release and the foreseen products of the release.

33. The foreseen dates of the release and time planning of the experiment including frequency and duration of releases.

34. The preparation of the site before the release.

35. The size of the site.

36. The methods to be used for the release.

37. The quantity of organisms to be released.

38. The disturbance of the site, including the type and method of cultivation and mining, irrigation, or other activities.

39. The worker protection measures taken during the release.

40. The post-release treatment of the site.

41. The techniques foreseen for elimination or inactivation of the organisms at the end of the experiment or other purpose of the release.

42. Information on results of previous releases of those organisms, or of organisms of the same type as those which are to be released, and in particular releases on a different scale or into different ecosystems.

The environment (both on the site and in the wider environment)

43. The geographical location and national grid reference of the site onto which the release will be made, or the foreseen areas of use of the product.

44. The physical or biological proximity of the site of the organisms to humans and other significant biota.

45. The proximity to significant biotopes or protected areas.

46. The size of the local human population.

47. The local economic activities which are based on the natural resources of the area.

48. The distance to the nearest drinking water supply zone and/or areas protected for environmental purposes.

49. The climatic characteristics of the region or regions likely to be affected.

50. The geographical, geological and pedological characteristics.

51. The flora and fauna, including crops, livestock and migratory species.

52. The description of the target and non-target ecosystems likely to be affected.

53. The comparison of the natural habitat of the recipient organisms with the proposed site or sites of release.

54. Any known planned developments or changes in land use in the region which could influence the environmental impact of the release.

PART IV

INFORMATION RELATING TO THE ORGANISMS AND THE ENVIRONMENT

Characteristics affecting survival etc.

55. The biological features which affect survival, multiplication and dispersal.

56. The known or predicted environmental conditions which may affect survival, multiplication and dissemination, including wind, water, soil, temperature and pH.

57. The sensitivity to specific agents.

Interactions with the environment

58. The predicted habitat of the organisms.

59. The studies on the behaviour and characteristics of the organisms and their ecological impact carried out in simulated natural environments, such as microcosms, growth rooms and greenhouses.

60. The capability of post-release transfer of genetic material—

(*a*) from the genetically modified organisms into organisms in affected ecosystems; and

(*b*) from indigenous organisms to the genetically modified organisms.

61. The likelihood of post-release selection leading to the expression of unexpected or undesirable traits in the genetically modified organisms.

62. The measures employed to ensure and to verify genetic stability, the description of genetic traits which may prevent or minimise dispersal of genetic material, and methods to verify genetic stability.

63. The routes of biological dispersal, known or potential modes of interaction with the disseminating agent, including inhalation, ingestion, surface contact and burrowing.

64. The description of ecosystems to which the organisms could be disseminated.

Potential environmental impact

65. The potential for excessive population increase of the organisms in the environment.

66. The competitive advantage of the organisms in relation to the unmodified recipient or parental organisms.

67. The identification and description of the target organisms.

68. The anticipated mechanism and result of interaction between the released organisms and the target organisms.

69. The identification and description of non-target organisms which may be affected.

70. The likelihood of post-release shifts in biological interactions or in the host range.

71. The known or predicted effects on plants and animals and non-target organisms in the environment, impact on population levels of competitors, prey, hosts, symbionts, predators, parasites and pathogens.

72. The known or predicted involvement of the organisms in biogeochemical processes.

73. Any other potentially significant interactions of the organisms with the environment.

PART V

INFORMATION RELATING TO MONITORING, CONTROL, WASTE TREATMENT AND EMERGENCY PLANS

Monitoring techniques

74. Methods for tracing the organisms, and for monitoring their effects.

75. Specificity (to identify the organisms, and to distinguish them from the donor, recipient or the parental organisms), sensitivity and reliability of the monitoring techniques.

76. Techniques for detecting transfer of the donated genetic material to other organisms.

77. Duration and frequency of the monitoring.

Control of the release

78. Methods and procedures to avoid and/or minimise the spread of the organisms beyond the site of release or the designated area for use.

79. Methods and procedures to protect the site from intrusion by unauthorised individuals.

80. Methods and procedures to prevent other organisms from entering the site.

Waste treatment

81. Type of waste generated.

82. Expected amount of waste.

83. Possible risks.

84. Description of treatment envisaged.

Emergency response plans

85. Methods and procedures for controlling the organisms in case of unexpected spread.

86. Methods, such as eradication of the organisms, for decontamination of the areas affected.

87. Methods for disposal or sanitation of plants, animals, soils, and any other thing exposed during or after the spread.

88. Methods for the isolation of the area affected by the spread.

89. Plans for protecting human health and the environment in case of the occurrence of an undesirable effect.

Additional information to be contained in consent to market products containing genetically modified organisms

PART I

GENERAL INFORMATION

1. The name of the product and the name of the genetically modified organisms in the product.

2. The name and address in the Community of the manufacturer or distributor of the product.

3. The specificity of the product and the exact conditions of use including, where appropriate, the type of environment and/or the geographical areas within the Community for which the product is suited.

4. The type of expected use of the product and the description of the persons who are expected to use the product.

PART II

ADDITIONAL RELEVANT INFORMATION

5. The measures to be taken in the event of the escape of the organisms in the product or misuse of the product.

6. Scientific instructions or recommendations for storage and handling of the product.

7. The estimated level and amount of production of the product within the Community and the estimated level and amount of imports of the product into the Community.

8. Information regarding the proposed packaging for the product and its appropriateness in order to avoid the escape of genetically modified organisms during storage or at a later stage.

9. Information regarding proposed labelling including the proposals for stating, in full or summarised form, the information prescribed in paragraphs 1 to 3, 5 and 6.

EXPLANATORY NOTE
(This note is not part of the regulations.)

These regulations, together with the Genetically Modified Organisms (Northern Ireland) Order 1991 ("the Order"), give effect to Council Directive 90/220/EEC (O.J. No. L117, 8.5.90, p. 15) on the deliberate release into the environment of genetically modified organisms.

Part I of the regulations makes provision as to interpretation of the regulations and as to the application of the definitions of "artificial techniques" and "harm" in the Order.

Part II of the regulations makes provision as to the circumstances in which consents for the release of genetically modified organisms to the environment are required, and as to applications for consents and the conditions on which consents are held.

Part III of the regulations makes provision as to the circumstances in which consents for the marketing of genetically modified organisms are required, and as to applications for consents to market.

Part IV of the regulations places duties on applicants and the Department following the making of applications for consents.

Part V makes provision as to the register of information required to be kept by the Department under Article 19 of the Order.

Article 15 of the Order makes provision for offences.

Copies of the Directive and extracts from the Official Journal of the European Communities may be obtained from Her Majesty's Stationery Office, 16 Arthur Street, Belfast BT1 4GD.